W9-CUQ-520

MODERN CRIMINAL JUSTICE

MODERN CRIMINAL JUSTICE

JACK WRIGHT, JR.
Associate Professor of Criminal Justice
Loyola University, New Orleans

PETER W. LEWIS
Associate Professor of Criminal Justice
University of South Florida

McGraw-Hill Book Company

New York St. Louis San Francisco Auckland Bogotá Düsseldorf
Johannesburg London Madrid Mexico Montreal New Delhi
Panama Paris São Paulo Singapore Sydney Tokyo Toronto

MODERN CRIMINAL JUSTICE

1 2 3 4 5 6 7 8 9 0 D O D O 7 8 3 2 1 0 9 8 7

This book was set in Times Roman by National ShareGraphics, Inc. The editors were Lyle Linder and Phyllis T. Dulan; the cover was designed by Albert M. Cetta; the production supervisor was Charles Hess. The drawings were done by J & R Services, Inc.
R. R. Donnelley & Sons Company was printer and binder.

Library of Congress Cataloging in Publication Data

Wright, Jack, date
Modern criminal justice.

Includes index.
1. Criminal justice, Administration of—United States.
I. Lewis, Peter W., joint author. II. Title.
HV8138.W72 364'.973 77-7505
ISBN 0-07-072075-4

In Memoriam
Jack Wright, Sr.

To my parents
William and Joyce Lewis

Contents

PART TWO
PLEA BARGAINING, SENTENCING, APPEALS, POST CONVICTION REMEDIES, AND THE CORRECTIONAL PROCESS

Preface

This text is written for a single introductory course in the American administration of criminal justice. As such, the text is designed to present an overview of the subject in the American context. Every effort was made to include some discussion of those areas which contribute significantly to a critical understanding of issues important to the subject.

As a discipline, the study of the criminal justice system must deal not only with the nature of crime, but also with the criminal-judicial process. The judicial process tends to be ignored (or given sparse treatment) in most introductory texts. We have attempted to overcome this "deficiency" by providing a more in-depth treatment of certain critical issues central to the criminal process. In addition, certain topics, usually found only in separate texts, are given more than a casual treatment.

The text consists of two parts. Part One considers the problems of defining crime, the criminal, and the relationship of the law to the administration of criminal justice. We thought it important in Part One to include a discussion of the "known" extent of crime as well as of victimless and organized crime. The latter two topics tend to be superficially treated in introductory texts.

Chapters Five, Six, and Seven focus on three of the most important agencies involving the social control of the apprehended offender. Chapter 5 on the American police system is examined more from the point of view of the uniformed police officer in a large metropolitan area than as a critical treatise involving academic abstracts and polemics. This is intentional. Both authors were given special permission to "ride"—especially on weekend nights—in high-crime patrol areas in the city of New Orleans over an extended period of time. The information and insights gained proved to be invaluable. The chapters on the bail process and the grand jury were included because millions of persons charged with committing a crime are processed every year through these institutions. The chapter (5) on the grand jury systems is especially detailed as, we have found in our experience, few students of the criminal justice system have more than a superficial knowledge of this critical stage of the criminal process.

Chapters Eight, Nine, Ten, and Eleven discuss the courts, the criminal process, and the steps in the administration of criminal justice. The stages of the criminal trial and many of the legal problems associated with the prosecution and defense of a criminal charge are given thorough examination. This enables the reader to understand many of the complexities involved in a criminal trial and to gain an appreciation of how certain American constitutional guarantees are designed to make it difficult to convict a person charged with a crime.

Part Two concentrates on plea bargaining which disposes of most criminal cases following a decision by the prosecutor to seek a conviction. Sentencing is analyzed inasmuch as all convicted persons must go through this critical stage of the criminal process. An historical and contemporary analysis of criminal confinement and alternatives to it is reviewed. Both authors have had some insightful and invaluable experience working in the day-to-day operations of a prison. The text concludes with a rather expansive discussion of the constitutional rights of prisoners. This has become an increasingly controversial area in criminal law, sufficiently important to deserve an entire chapter.

Because of page limitations (a consequence of an inflation-stricken economy) we were unable to discuss at length (or at all in some cases) certain critical topics that, arguably, deserve attention in an introductory text. We sacrificed those topics so that we could include others usually treated only in specialized texts (for example, organized crime, grand jury, victimless crimes, criminal trials, plea bargaining, and the constitutional rights of prisoners). Instructors can easily include a discussion of those topics that deserve attention in an introductory course—even though such topics have been omitted from this text.

While this book is a joint effort, the author of individual chapters should be acknowledged. For this purpose, it should be noted that Chapter 1 was truly a coauthored work. Professor Wright was the principal writer of Chapters 2, 3, 5, 13, and 14. Professor Lewis was the principal writer of Chapters 6, 7, 8, 9, 10, 11, 12, and 15. Special thanks is given to Professor Mannle for his definitive chapter on organized crime. In our view, Professor Mannle's chapter is the most enlightening and comprehensive single chapter on organized crime available. We appreciate his contribution.

Finally, special thanks must be acknowledged to those who assisted us in the preparation of the manuscript. Professor Lewis wishes to express his appreciation to Jeannette Owen, Pamela Campbell, and Paulette Ford (of the University of Missouri: Kansas City); and Magdalene Deutsch and Jerome Vermette (of the University of South Florida) for their very valuable and capable research and secretarial assistance. Special thanks is also extended to Professor Kenneth Peoples who provided a valuable critical review of each of Professor Lewis's chapters.

Professor Wright wishes to acknowledge the help of a number of scholars and friends who assisted in the completion of his chapters. Dr. D. Wood Harper, Jr., who is single-handedly attempting to rehabilitate the "upper ninth ward" in New Orleans, made numerous suggestions from his unique perspective on the sociology of crime in general and the proper treatment for drug addicts in particular. Dr. David Knox, for whom the behavioral approach was invented, as always, gave greatly needed "pep talks" during moments of discouragement and made editorial comments on how to improve the readability of the manuscript. Professor Bob Teagarden served as a reviewer for the entire manuscript, and his suggestions resulted in a number of changes which improved the final product.

A special thanks goes to Nancy Wingate who researched and wrote the section on the "Development of the London Police." A young woman with the sensitivity of a poet and the inquisitiveness of a Sherlock Holmes, she is considered one of the foremost authorities in America on the mystery story. Finally, an old friend and colleague, Professor Harold Vetter, provided initial encouragement and direction for the text, even though it would directly compete with his own fine book. His unselfish actions are the hallmark and touchstone of a true friend and professional. Both authors are indebted to him intellectually, professionally, and personally.

Special appreciation is extended to the production staff of McGraw-Hill, and especially to our editor, Dr. Lyle Linder, who painstakingly and patiently guided us through the preparation of the manuscript.

Jack Wright, Jr.
Peter W. Lewis

Part One

The Nature of Crime in America

Chapter 1

The Nature of Crime

Taffy was a Welshman, Taffy was a thief;
Taffy came to my house and stole a piece of beef;
I went to Taffy's house, Taffy was in bed,
I took a marrow-bone and beat him on the head.

I went to Taffy's house, Taffy wasn't in;
Taffy came to my house and stole a silver pin;
I went to Taffy's house, Taffy was in bed;
I took up the marrow-bone and flung it at his head,[1]

A headstrong six-year-old boy struggles up an escalator clearly marked "down." A bored twelve-year-old Huckelberry Finn skips school and spends the day hanging around a pool hall. An impatient motorist runs a red light. Four suburban couples with a yen for excitement and a flair for organization make arrangement to swap wives for a weekend. A male transvestite spends the afternoon shopping for a garter belt and matching panties in his size. In the back room of a ghetto grocery store, a man is shot to death in an argument over a poker hand.

What do all these acts have in common? They are all acts of deviance. To deviate is to wander, however slightly, from the societal norms regulating conduct. All criminal acts are deviant, but not all deviant behavior is criminal. Before we address ourselves to the specifics of criminal acts, we will discuss the general problem of deviant acts and the societal responses.

1.01 SOCIAL ORDER AND DEVIANCE

Criminologists and sociologists often ask the question: Why do we have deviant labels anyway? Since language is an attempt to convey meanings and make sense out of reality (or *construct* reality), what do the deviant labels we use tell us about the society in which we live?

The problem of deviance and reactive behaviors—both linguistic and physical—is as old as humanity and as inevitable as death and taxes. Whenever there are rules, there are deviants: people who are unable or unwilling to act according to the normative standards demanded by a given socity. In the story of Eden, God told Adam and Eve not to eat from the tree of knowledge of good and evil, and they promptly ate themselves out of Paradise!

A society without deviants is utterly impossible. This is because, to ensure perfect conformity, all members of the society would have to be biological mirrors of each other, pass through the same socialization experiences, internalize the same values, and subordinate individuality and egoism to the good of the group. It would be a brave new world composed of mindless robots.

Given that deviance is ubiquitously characteristic of humanity in groups, how does society go about obtaining a reasonable amount of conformity from so recalcitrant a creature as the human being? In all societies, being labeled deviant is a way of assigning moral inferiority. The deviant is tagged with an "essentializing label."[2] It is as though the person had no other identity. To be labeled deviant means to become a person whose entire personality can be reduced to one word, one label. It is a sociological shorthand which dehumanizes the person and separates him or her from the rest of the group. Rather than describing a person with a number of characteristics, such as "He is young, born in a large city, college educated, attends the Catholic church," we forego that and get to the essentializing label: "He's a fag (homosexual)."

This label creates a revulsion, a reaction, a feeling that something ought to be done about him. So, whether it be a sympathetic feeling of "You ought to see a psychiatrist," or a vengeful "They ought to lock you up," the reaction is one which attempts to isolate deviants from the community in such a way that they become invisible. Whether it is a maximum security penitentiary which doubles as a cotton plantation 200 miles south of Memphis or a mental institution 40 miles from a large northern industrial city, the deviant is punished, rehabilitated, treated, or warehoused—and frequently is put out of sight by the host society.

Labeling people as odd, peculiar, no good, hellraisers, immoral, fat, or criminal serves a positive function in society. When we see a deviant labeled as a criminal, it heartens us that we are honest. It indicates the boundaries of the societal control system. "They" are the bad guys; "we" are the good guys. Similarly, the label "fat" encourages the rest of us to believe that we are in the trim category. The label "homosexual" reassures us that we are straight. Prostitutes remind us that our wives have their sexual virtue, juvenile delinquents of what nice kids we have, atheists of the rightness of our religious beliefs, communists of the soundness of our democratic and political system, alcoholics of the moderation with which we drink, and hippies of our commitment to the work ethic. There are psychological overtones in social norms. We need labeled deviants as markers to show us where we stand in the social system. How would you ever know you were good if no one were ever designated as bad? Getting labeled as bad and deviant may be the result of being a member of a minority group whose values are in conflict with those groups powerful enough to enforce their concept of what is appropriate, moral, or legal.[3]

All societies are characterized by social conflict as various groups within them compete for positions of power and decision making. In a democratic society, one chief method of conflict resolution between groups is through the rule of law. The struggle of groups for dominance and promotion of their special interests is seen most visibly in the competition for legislative majorities and the resulting hold over, the regulatory police power of the state.

Those individuals who maintain minority-group orientations and find themselves out of step with the required behavior patterns are simply outlawed. Whether it be the conscientious objector who marches to the beat of a different drummer, the rural bootlegger to whom moonshining is a way of life, or the college student who prefers marijuana to martinis, each finds his or her behavior criminalized by a dominant power group.

The labeling of conscientious objectors, moonshiners, and dope smokers may perhaps be best explained by the conflict in society of groups with differing values, but this approach does not account for all deviant or illegal behaviors. Some conduct, such as that of burglars and muggers, would be disruptive to the smooth functioning of society if left uncontrolled. It is therefore branded as criminal. The group-conflict approach lends itself better to the explanation of the former situation—that of social, ideological, and political nonconformists. Violent criminals, on the other hand, are labeled as such because of the danger they represent.

Central questions are: What conduct should be considered criminal? How should we restrict the sphere of human action? To what extent should citizens be allowed to engage in antisocial behavior or to harm themselves through the use of alcohol, tobacco, or drugs? In short, what are or should be our tolerance limits?

If we allowed citizens large amounts of individual freedom, we would arguably increase the likelihood of deviance and/or criminality. If we increased the police powers of the state, we would correspondingly decrease crime, but individual freedom would suffer. Reporters who accompanied President Nixon on his 1972 trip to China were astonished that one could leave a wallet on a bed in an unlocked hotel room, that cars were not stolen, and the streets of Peking were relatively safe. By eliminating many of the constitutional guarantees we now have, we could reduce crime, but the result would approach the totalitarian society envisioned by George Orwell when he wrote *1984*. We cannot have it both ways.

Indeed, Packer argues that two competing systems of values underlie our system of criminal justice.[4] The *crime-control model* stresses the law-and-order approach. Here the central idea is to repress crime, that is, to separate the guilty from the innocent speedily and at a low cost, without being overly concerned about the constitutional rights of the accused. On the other hand, the *due-process model* stresses quality control. The emphasis here is on the rights of the defendant and the protection of the innocent. It is felt that the criminal process should respect the dignity of the accused—whether guilty or not—and that all constitutional rights of an accused should be fully protected at all times.

When the FBI's *Uniform Crime Report* indicates each year that crime in the United States is increasing dramatically, it is understandable why a large segment of the population might react in favor of the crime-control mode. Yet the overall price that we as a society might have to pay to implement such a value system would be very high in terms of the loss of our fundamental freedoms and rights.

1.02 NORMS AND BEHAVIOR

The concept of deviance can only be understood in relation to another sociological concept: that of norms. *Norms* determine which human acts are defined as acceptable, proper, tasteful, and—more important—legal. Ways of acting and reacting which are considered "normal" in the ordinary sense of that term—i.e., expected or approved—are said to fit the norm.

One way of determining the social values attached to certain forms of social behavior is to study the sanctions or penalties that attach to normative deviation. If an individual in a society fails to follow a norm, what should be the result? In American society, failure to shake hands when one is introduced may result in social disapproval and being labeled rude. Taking property by breaking into the dwelling of another, however, can bring the offender many years in the penitentiary. Ours is a society which greatly values private property, and there are stringent penalties for theft.

By contrast, a communist society might have lighter penalties for the theft of private property (theft of government property is often a capital offense) but much more rigid sanctions against "thought crime"—criticisms of the state by writers, intellectuals, playwrights, and professors.[5] Although all norms serve the purpose of regulating and directing human behavior, they are not all enforced *equally.* Using possible penalties for their violation as a criterion, norms may be classified as folkways, mores, and laws.

1.03 FOLKWAYS, MORES, AND LAWS

Folkways are those preferred and expected norms which are enforced through informal sanctions like ridicule, gossip, and possible ostracism by one's peers. Any twelve-year-old Brooklyn boy who aspired to the ballet and let himself be seen in leotards by the neighborhood gang would find his resolve tested by taunts, jeers, insults, and laughter because he would be flaunting the norms of the streetcorner society.

Mores are demanded standards of behavior which are enforced by threat of expulsion from the group. Mores are considered essential for the survival of the group or for the continued maintenance of its most central values. If, for example, a colony of nudists permitted the wearing of clothes on their premises, their reason for organizing would soon be gone.

When the mores of a group are backed by the police powers of the state, they have been crystallized into laws. Laws are legislatively enacted rules of behavior, the violation of which can result in a fine, imprisonment, execution by the state, or other formalized sanctions. Law evolves as an expression of the moral sentiments of a society, which in turn reinforces the same mores. Laws are most effective when supported by the mores. For example, the legal requirement that citizens of the United States wear appropriate clothing in public and not be indecently exposed needs relatively little enforcement. The population has so internalized this norm that its breach is a rarity.

However, the United States is not a monolithic culture. It is a federation of diverse subcultures, with varying religious and social attitudes, held together by a common belief in the democratic processes for decision making and conflict resolution. The values which unite the United States are stronger than the forces which divide it. In a pluralistic society, one would seldom expect any national legislation to be in complete harmony with the folkways and mores of all the groups in that society. The noble experiment with the prohibition of alcohol in the 1920s failed because it was an attempt to enforce laws that were too much at variance with societal norms. (Westbrook Pegler once observed that the nation, having given prohibition a halfhearted try, was now trying saturation.)

Before discussing the sources of the criminal law, we will briefly address ourselves to some legal definitions of what constitutes a crime in the United States.

1.04 DEFINITIONS OF CRIME

In our American system of jurisprudence, it is axiomatic that there can be no punishment for a harmful act unless it was clearly prohibited by some law in existence at the time it was committed. Although the doctrine *nulla poena sine lege* ("no punishment without a law for it") has not been universally recognized, it is an integral part of our criminal philosophy. Accordingly, the definition of what constitutes a crime is important to an understanding of the criminal law.

When a criminal statute or ordinance is so vague that "men of common intelligence must necessarily guess at its meaning and differ as to its application," a conviction based on that law is an unconstitutional denial of due process.[6] This is known as the "void for vagueness" doctrine.[7] Accordingly, various statutes or ordinances have been held by courts to be unconstitutionally vague; for example, those which purport to criminalize "vagrancy,"[8] "opprobrious words or abusive language, tending to cause a breach of the peace,"[9] or an act which "publicly . . . treats contemptuously the flag of the U.S.,"[10] to forbid "three or more persons to assemble on any sidewalks . . . and there conduct themselves in a manner annoying to persons passing by . . .,"[11] or "to curse or revile . . . a police officer. . . . "[12]

While most criminal statutes and ordinance probably do not run afoul of the due process requirements, the definitions of "crime" vary from jurisdiction to jurisdiction and among legal writers. For example, the well-known English legal historian William Blackstone defined "crime" as "an act committed or omitted, in violation of a public law either forbidding or commanding it."[13] Bishop offered this suggestion: "A crime is any wrong which the government deems injurious to the public at large, and punishes through a judicial proceeding in its own name."[14] The above definitions caused Clark and Marshall to combine the two: "A crime is any act or omission prohibited by public law for the protection of the public, and made punishable by the state in a judicial proceeding in its own name."[15] More recently, Perkins offered the following definition: "Crime is any social harm defined and made punishable by law."[16] An example of a legislative definition is found in a Louisiana statute which states that "A crime is that conduct which is defined as criminal in this Code (La. Rev. Statutes), or in other acts of the legislature, or in the Constitution of this state."[17]

Regardless of the definition suggested, it can readily be ascertained that no conduct may be deemed criminal if there is no express provision against it in the law at the time of the alleged offense. In order to further develop our discussion of deviance and crime, we will address ourselves to the sources of the criminal law.

1.05 SOURCES OF THE CRIMINAL LAW

The modern trend is for jurisdictions (local, state, and federal) to have comprehensive criminal codes in the form of statutes or ordinances. That is, no act (or omission) is a crime unless it is specifically so defined in an applicable constitution, statute, or ordinance. To date, about twenty states have comprehensive criminal codes. However, such codes are by no means the only source of our criminal law. Administrative regulations often prohibit certain conduct. For example, the Food and Drug Act prescribes certain criminal penalties for the violation of its provisions (e.g., those against adulterated foods or misbranded drugs).

Another source of the criminal law is our constitutions (state and federal). Article II of the United States Constitution defines the crime of treason (the only crime specifically noted in that document). Constitutions, however, represent the least usual source of our criminal law.

An additional major source of our criminal law is the *common law,* which is presently applicable in about thirty states. Here, conduct that is not prohibited by a statute, ordinance, or constitution may nevertheless be criminal if it was a crime under the common law. In order to appreciate how this can happen and what the implications are a brief discussion of the history and development of the common law is necessary.

1.06 THE COMMON LAW

The original colonists in America brought with them the English common law (criminal and civil). The term "common law" is used to distinguish the science of jurisprudence prevailing in England and America from other legal systems, such as the law of Continental Europe (civil law) or the Roman law.[18] As noted by a California appellate court, the common law represents "all the statutory and case law background of England and the American colonies before the American Revolution."[19]

From the centuries following the Norman Conquest (1066) to the middle of the nineteenth century, the English Parliament rarely met on a regular basis. Consequently, the English judges played a major role in the creation and development of crimes. If they considered certain conduct to be antisocial and harmful, they made it a crime (even though no statute existed).

By the seventeenth century, the English judges had created and defined the nine original felonies.[20] This judicial legislation continued to create additional crimes until the 1850s, when Parliament began to sit on a regular basis. Since that time the English judges have rarely added new crimes—the criminalization of conduct has been left to Parliament.[21] In short, the common law represents habits and customs derived from England which have become so integrated into our society that they are acceptable norms of behavior.[22] Thus, these norms became the source of our common law and have had a great impact on American jurisprudence.

Apart from its historical interest, why is the common law important today to the American system of criminal justice? As noted above, thirty states have retained common-law crimes (all federal crimes are statutory). This allows those jurisdictions to declare certain conduct criminal—if it was a common-law crime—even though it is not prohibited by a specific statute, or constitution.

For example, in a well-known state case,[23] the defendant, for more than a month, telephoned a married woman (a stranger to him) approximately three times a week at all hours of the night and day. The defendant asked her repeatedly to have sexual intercourse with him as well as to commit certain acts of sodomy. At that time, no Pennsylvania statute forbade this conduct.

However, the Pennsylvania Supreme Court affirmed the defendant's conviction of a common-law misdemeanor which prohibited any act which "directly injures or tends to injure the public." The court noted that the defendant's language was "obscene, lewd, and filthy" and suggested that such persons should not escape punishment simply due to the absence of a state statute. The court further noted that other persons were in a position to overhear the defendant's language (e.g., the telephone operator, persons using his four-party telephone line, and other persons in the victim's household). Thus, it is not entirely accurate to say "There's no harm in asking."

Admittedly, the case cited above is unusual. The modern trend is away from creating new crimes by way of the common law. Even in those states (twenty) that have abolished common-law crimes and have comprehensive codes, the local courts interpret common-law terms (often found in the statutes) in light of the common law. In the majority of states, it is not enough simply to read the criminal statutes in order to ascertain what conduct is criminal.

In those states, researchers or curious persons must investigate the local jurisprudence (case law), the criminal statutes (and ordinances where applicable), the common law, the local constitution, and the administrative regulations before venturing forth and comitting acts which might be held to be criminal. Yet it is a common-law principle that "Every man is presumed to know the law"; the maxim *ignorantia legis neminem excusat* ("ignorance of the law excuses no man"), although somewhat overstated, has led many states to adopt comprehensive criminal codes so that their citizens may know in advance, with reasonable certainty, what conduct is criminal. It has been suggested that the law plays an unfair game when citizens are forced to read common-law cases in advance of their conduct or act at their own peril.

In summary, the common law is an important source of the criminal law, and it continues to influence our American system of criminal justice. In order to further develop our discussion of deviance, crime, and the attendant legal sanctions, we will next address ourselves to purposes and basic premises underlying our criminal law.

1.07 BASIC PREMISES OF THE CRIMINAL LAW

The purpose of the criminal law is to prevent harm to society and to control behavior within legally acceptable boundaries. In order to accomplish this purpose, lawmaking bodies must (1) decide what conduct is to be made criminal and (2) prescribe a punishment appropriate for such offenses. In the drafting of such statutues, Anglo-American legislators rely on the following basic premises for guidelines.[24]

First, before behavior can be called a crime, there must be some *act*—often referred to as the *actus reus* (criminal act)—which results in external or threatened harm. A mental or emotional state is not sufficient to be called a crime.[25] Suppose, for example, an irate premed student, furious and frustrated that his chemistry professor has "given him" a C (professors "give" C's, students "earn" A's) decides to kill the professor for eliminating his chances to enter medical school. Aware that Professor Know-It-All always drinks a cup of coffee before each class, the outraged student purchases some deadly poison from a local drugstore, intending to eliminate his former mentor. If the police intercept the student while he is making his purchase, he has committed no crime. The law of attempted crimes requires a "dangerous proximity to success"[26]; mere preparation will not suffice. The threatened harm has not come close enough for the criminal law to intervene. You cannot be put in jail for what you are thinking or for merely preparing to commit a crime.

The crime of conspiracy would appear to be an exception to this general rule, but the *agreement* itself is the act which forms the essence of the crime. As noted in a famous early English case, "The gist of conspiracy is the agreement, and thus the agreement is punishable even if its purpose was not achieved."[27] Conspiracy statutues are sanctions against group activity because persons acting in concert are thought to represent a greater threat to the public than does an offender acting alone. Criminal conspiracies are, by their very nature, clandestine and often difficult to prove. How, then, do we know when two or more minds have met in agreement to commit a criminal act? In about half the states, the crime of conspiracy is complete at the time of the agreement; in the other states and in the federal courts, some *overt act* in furtherance of the agreement is required before a criminal conspiracy has been completed. The overt act, however, may be lawful and need only be performed by one of the parties to the conspiracy.

Suppose, for example, two men meet in a bar and decide that the best way to make this country "safe for democracy" would be to kill one of the candidates for President. They pound each other on the back, make rude noises, fill the air with oral slaughter, and end the conversation only when the bartender pours them out on the street at closing time. Have they committed the crime of conspiracy to kill the presidential candidate, or is it just "beer talk"? In those states which require only a verbal agreement, the defendants' criminal liability would be a question of fact for the jury. In those states requiring a substantial step toward the fulfillment of their plot (overt act), the men would have to take an additional step, such as buying a scope rifle and/or renting a room over a parade route. Although this is largely a question of fact for the jury, the jury in those jurisdictions would have to find *both* an unlawful agreement *and* an overt act in furtherance of the conspiracy in order to convict the would-be patriots.

A second basic premise underlying the criminal law is that the harm sought to be prevented must be legally forbidden. That is, a person cannot be convicted of a criminal charge for an act which was no offense at the time it was performed. This rule finds support in the United States Constitution, which prohibits criminal laws which contain ex post facto provisions.[28]

For example, if someone were known to have experimented with LSD prior to its being outlawed, that person could not be convicted for those acts, since they were committed prior to the criminalization of the conduct. However, if you were arrested for selling "bathtub gin" during prohibition and sent to jail, you would not be released simply because the act for which you were jailed had been "decriminalized."

No legislative body or court can enact a law or change the procedural guidelines which ex post facto increase the punishment or increase the burden of proof required for a criminal conviction. American society greatly values fair play, and one cannot change the rules of the game in the middle of the contest in either the criminal law or in football. Under our Constitution, due process forbids this.[29] The above principle does not, however, prohibit a legislature from *lessening* a punishment retroactively or from changing the mode of execution from hanging to lethal gas (the result is the same for the offender).

Third, the criminal act must be *voluntary.* Acts that are held to be involuntary (e.g., sleepwalking, involuntary intoxication) are affirmative defense to almost all crimes. A cabdriver forced at gunpoint to drive a would-be robber to a bank for the purpose of committing a bank robbery is not guilty of any crime, since he acted under duress. Duress is generally held to be a defense in lesser crimes (e.g., burglary and malicious mischief); but most states do not allow the defense of duress for capital offenses. Thus, it would not be a defense that A killed B because a third party threatened him with death if he did not do so.

A fourth basic premise underlying the criminal law, and applicable to most crimes, is the concept known as *mens rea* ("guilty mind"). This concept refers to the mental element in the commission of a crime. As neither judges, lawyers, nor juries have invented scientific instruments which accurately measure what is in the mind of a criminal actor, we must often depend on a logical inference from overt acts. We reach conclusions about motive and intent by moving from the seen (acts) to the unseen (thoughts).

In a criminal investigation, the toxicologist can measure for us, in most cases, the poison in the bloodstream of a deceased husband who has just enjoyed his last birthday cake (which, unfortunately for the husband, was laced with poison). How can we determine whether his wife, who baked this devil's food surprise, intended his death with malice aforethought?

Contrast what inference we might draw from the following hypothetical set of facts. First, suppose that the husband had recently taken out a $1 million life insurance policy with his wife as the beneficiary, and that the wife's torrid love affair with the butler was common knowledge. Or suppose that the couple enjoyed a good relationship and that the widow's ophthalmologist certified that her rare eye disease made the skull-and-crossbones warning on a poison label look like the sign for cake coloring. In the absence of an admission or confession, the state of mind of any defendant must be inferred from the facts that surround the case. For most crimes, the general formula for determining whether a person is guilty of a criminal offense is guilty intent (*mens rea*) and voluntary act or omission of an act (*actus reus*).

There are, however, criminal offenses which involve no mental element but consist only of forbidden acts (or omissions of acts). These are classified as *strict liability* or *public welfare* offenses. As a general rule, there can be no crime without some criminal intent, but this is by no means a universal rule. A killing which occurs during the commission of a dangerous felony may, in some jurisdictions, be murder regardless of whether such death was intended or not.

For example, should a bank robber become engaged in a gunfight with a nearsighted bank guard during the course of the robbery and the guard accidentally shoots an innocent customer, the robber might be guilty of felony murder (California and several other jurisdictions hold that a robber is not liable on a felony murder charge for death which results from a bullet from the gun of anyone other than the robber or his co-felon). In most jurisdictions, it is no defense that the defendant did not intend, with malice aforethought, to kill the victim. In one state case,[30] the defendants, driving a stolen car, attempted to outrun a police car. They drove through an intersection and caused an accident resulting in the death of an innocent third party. The defendants were convicted on second-degree murder. The appellate court reasoned that the death here was not a freak coincidence; a foreseeable result followed from the original crime.

Essential to the application of the doctrine of *mens rea* is that the actor be capable of forming a criminal intent. By law, certain classes of persons are not capable of committing a crime. Thus, children under the age of seven (at common law), mental defectives, persons acting under coercion or intimidation, or those—in some cases—whose actions were accidental are not held criminally liable since the element of criminal intent is missing. (In Chapter 11 we will discuss the troublesome problem of insanity as a defense to a criminal charge.) Whether persons legally incapable of committing a crime (as described above) are nevertheless criminally liable for "strict liability" offenses (where no criminal intent is required) is presently unclear in the criminal law.

But suppose the offender was so drunk that he "didn't know what he was doing" and therefore could not form a criminal intent? Does the law hold an offender whose mind was affected by alcohol accountable for acts committed while drunk? Offenders often attempt to avoid personal responsibility by blaming the whiskey and offering the excuse: "I was drunk out of my mind." For most crimes, voluntary intoxication is no defense for a crime, though "settled alcoholism" (delirium tremens) has been held to be a defense.[31] If you are insane, you are not criminally liable, and the law does not care if you got that way through a social disease, social stress, or twenty years of dedicated drinking (although the cause may be important in convincing the jury of your insanity).

A fifth premise underlying the criminal law is that the *mens rea* (intent) and the criminal conduct (act) must concur at the same time. In the parlance of lawyers, there must be a concurrence between the *actus reus* (act) and the *mens rea.* We do not punish people for having evil thoughts after they have committed an otherwise innocent act. For example, if one accidentally picks up the wrong umbrella at a restaurant and later realizes the mistake but nevertheless decides to keep it, one is not at that moment guilty of larceny. That crime requires an intent to steal (*mens rea*) at the *time* of the taking and carrying away (*actus reus*) of the property. Likewise, breaking and entering into the dwelling of another with the intent to escape a storm will not support a burglary conviction at common law. The alleged burglar must have an intent to commit a felony at the *time* of the breaking and entering. This is true even though, after entering, the accused decides to steal the owner's household goods (although he would be guilty of larceny). However, the intent of the person entering the dwelling is a question of fact for the jury; therefore the defense of lack of intent may not be believed.

Sixth, there must be a *legally causal relationship* (proximate cause) between the voluntary misconduct and the legally forbidden harm. The harmful consequences must be related to the intentional felonious action. Suppose, for example, a burglar who is surprised by a policeman shoots the policeman and leaves him lying in a blizzard. If it can be shown that the forces set in motion by the shooting (weakening of the policeman, his exposure to the cold) were causally related to the final harmful consequences (death by pneumonia), then the offender may be guilty of felony-murder in some jurisdictions. The policeman's demise under these conditions could be held to be a foreseeable and proximate consequence of the harm.

However, should the policeman, well on the road to recovery, contract syphilis from a friendly nurse and die from the disease, the burglar is not criminally liable for the death. The policeman's code of ethics and poor judgment would have led to his demise and the elements of foreseeability and proximate cause would be absent.

Finally, citizens must be given *advance notice* as to the punishment for a given criminal act. Citizens must be able to contemplate the consequences of their actions. In determining the actions to be criminalized and the severity of the punishment for such actions, legislators tend to reflect the moral sentiments of their constituents. Generally, the prescribed punishment for a given offense is found in the appropriate criminal statutes.

Should "victimless crimes," such as prostitution, be decriminalized?

1.08 LAW AND MORALITY

A leading Catholic bishop once told a Boston Protestant minister, "Gambling in moderation is not a sin." "Perhaps," replied the Protestant minister, "but in this state, it is a crime."

Not all crimes are sins and not all sins are crimes. Often the areas of criminal and sinful conduct overlap, but they are not the same.

When we apply the principles and premises of the substantive criminal law to human behavior, we encounter much lively debate over those acts which come under the heading of "victimless crimes": prostitution, gambling, marijuana usage, vagrancy, and the like. (These crimes will be discussed in detail in Chapter 4.)

Some argue that private morality should be the concern of the individual and his or her spiritual advisers and is not an appropriate subject of the criminal law. From this point of view, every individual is entitled to make personal moral choices freely and alone as long as these decisions bring no harm to others.

Advocates of this view argue that victimless crimes should be decriminalized. The result would be that, legally, the prostitute would become a businesswoman practicing the world's second-oldest profession (the priesthood being the oldest); a gambler would simply be a speculator in the grand old American tradition of the Wall Street broker who "bets" that a share of common stock will rise; a marijuana user would be regarded as one who uses drugs for recreation and is hurting no one's chromosomes but his or her own; and the vagrant would be seen not as a criminal but as a hapless chap who is too lazy to work and too nervous to steal.

Opposing this position are those who argue that the criminal law should lead public opinion in some areas and fortify our beliefs about morality in others. The law is seen as protecting the moral life of a society, just as it protects physical life and property. That is the official position of the legislature in the many states that make adultery a crime; yet if the *Kinsey Report* is accurate, it would be difficult to throw a handful of rocks into a group of these lawmakers without hitting an adulterer. If we decriminalize offenses such as adultery and other victimless crimes, it is argued, we give tacit approval to their "normalcy" and open the door to, for example, the spread of venereal disease; the seduction of the young by aggressive homosexuals; the impoverishment of the family through gambling losses; and an increase in the number of useless drones who refuse to work.[32]

A slightly different point of view sees these laws as repressive and unenforceable, claiming that their flagrant violation only breeds a cynical attitude toward the law. Prostitution has proved to be among the hardiest of institutions, gamblers are always with us, sex remains a favorite indoor sport, and marijuana has become part of the collegiate way of life. By attempting to control the uncontrollable, we actually weaken respect for the law and thereby diminish its ability to serve as an effective means of social control in other areas.[33]

Victimless crimes remain a controversial area in the United States. As noted above, one method of determining whether a defendant has committed a criminal act and is therefore liable is to infer her mental processes (*mens rea*) from her acts (*actus reus*) in the absence of an admission or confession. Another method of determining the criminal liability of an accused, utilized by the courts, is the concept known as the "reasonable man" test.

1.09 THE LAW AND THE "REASONABLE MAN"

In order to measure whether a specific act or a general area of conduct is to be viewed as malicious or negligent, lawful or prudent, courts sometimes use the "reasonable man" test. In general, this approach asks the question: Would a person of ordinary prudence and experience have behaved in such a manner? If so, should the defendant nevertheless be held criminally liable?

The "reasonable man" is a person of workaday affairs; the one who carries a lunch bucket and rides the transit to work. This is the person who must deal with this troublesome world in such a reasonable way as to avoid the turnkey on the one hand and the psychiatrist on the other while somehow earning a living in the process. It is a definition that excludes the extremes of our society: geniuses and lunatics, heroes and cowards. By imagining how the woman in the beauty parlor or the man on the tractor would behave, the law, in seemingly endless debate, tries to hone out a standard as to what conduct will be punished and what conduct will be excused.

In the criminal law, the "reasonable man" test is most often utilized to determine whether the charge for an intentional killing (which would ordinarily be murder) may be reduced to manslaughter. The criminal law permits a "heat of the blood" killing, although intentional, to be reduced to manslaughter under certain circumstances. In most jurisdictions, a defendant must overcome four hurdles in order to have a charge reduced from murder to manslaughter: (1) There must have been a *reasonable provocation* for the defendant to have acted; (2) the defendant must *in fact* have been provoked (actual provocation); (3) a reasonable person would, under the circumstances, not have "cooled off" between the provocation and the fatal blow; and (4) the defendant must not *in fact* have cooled off during the interval.[34]

The "reasonable man" test is utilized in items 1 and 3 above. That is, we ask the question: Would a reasonable person, under the circumstances, have lost normal self-control? If so, would such a person have regained self-control between the provocative act and the fatal blow? The criteria in items 1 and 3 are mixed questions of law and fact, while items 2 and 4 are questions of fact for the jury.

Because the "reasonable man" test is an objective standard, a defendant's own particular traits are not considered (e.g., bad temper, easy to provoke). The only issue is whether a reasonable person would have been provoked under the circumstances. However, notions of what is reasonable change with the times, and juries sometimes disregard the instructions of law and find defendants not guilty even with the criteria for the "reasonable man" test have not been met.

The "reasonable man" test is also utilized in other areas of the criminal law, especially when certain defenses are offered by defendant's (e.g., mistake of fact, self-defense). Further, the test is no stranger to tort (civil) law, where a defendant's civil liability might depend on a "reasonable man" standard. While the "reasonable man" test has often been criticized (reasonable people don't lose their tempers or kill), it has played a major role in the development of American jurisprudence. This classification of conduct has led the courts to decide that some actions harm society, and are therefore matters for public concern, while others are private disputes between individuals.

1.10 CRIMES AND CIVIL WRONG

In the days before the development of a formalized judiciary, every individual was his or her own sheriff and meted out justice insofar as this was possible. But, in the settling of disputes, people tended to overreact and to kill or maim each other for trivial reasons. Indeed, the *lex talionis* (law of equivalent retaliation) was applied in an attempt to mitigate such reactions and replace retaliatory murder with "an eye for an eye."

A major step toward civilized jurisprudence was taken when citizens were persuaded to accept the payment of fines for damages. This substitution of gold for "a pound of flesh" as compensation harbingered the development of tort or civil law. As the legal system evolved and became more complex, it eventually divided along two lines: (1) those forms of conduct to be treated as criminal offenses by the state and (2) those acts which are regarded as private disputes between individuals. In short, a crime is a wrong against society, whereas a tort is a civil wrong against an individual.

While tort law and the criminal law overlap, there are some important distinctions in purpose, allowable defenses, and requirements of proof for successful litigation.[35]

The purpose of tort law is to compensate a citizen, in order to resolve conflicts between individuals, for damages suffered. A tortfeasor (person who commits a tort) does not incur the same moral condemnation as one convicted of violating a criminal statute. Under tort law, unlike criminal law, both infants and the insane are liable for the damages they incur. So if your impish six-year-old son intentionally or negligently pulls the chair out from under Aunt Maybelle, she may sue you for resulting damage to her spine (and obtain a judgment against you). Likewise, if your half-wit brother-in-law (for whom you are responsible) amuses himself by burning his doctor's expensive medical bag, you may be liable to compensate the doctor for his loss (conversion of chattel). Such liability is based on the premise that persons in charge of children and the insane will be more watchful. Neither your young son nor half-wit brother-in-law would be open to criminal charges, for it is presumed that they would be incapable of *mens rea* (criminal intent); therefore their acts could not be deemed crimes. However, insanity is a defense for a certain class of torts, such as defamation of character.

Criteria for level of proof required in tort and other civil cases are not as stringent as those that apply in criminal cases. In most civil cases, the plaintiff need only convince the judge or jury that there is a *preponderance of evidence* in his or her favor, rather than the heavier quantum *beyond a reasonable doubt* required in all criminal cases.[36] In a few civil cases, the quantum of proof required is *clear and convincing evidence* (e.g., civil fraud, impeachment of public officials).

The burdens of proof outlined above have never been defined in a manner that pleases all minds, but it is helpful to think of "preponderance of evidence" as requiring 51 percent of the evidence; "clear and convincing evidence" as requiring about 75 percent; and "beyond a reasonable doubt" as requiring better than 90 percent certainty. The last of these burdens of proof is discussed in detail in Chapter 13.

Some acts are both crimes and torts. That is, a person may be a tortfeasor and criminal at the same time. For example, a mugger is both civilly and criminally liable. The principal reason that victims do not sue their assailants more often is that most street criminals are indigents; they are, in effect, "judgment-proof." Not only have the courts separated civil and criminal conduct, but criminal conduct is classified according to different criteria.

1.11 CLASSIFICATION OF CRIMES

Crimes are classified into various groupings for certain purposes. These classifications include (1) felonies, (2) misdemeanors, (3) *mala in se* crimes, (4) *mala prohibita* crimes, (5) crimes involving moral turpitude, (6) "infamous" crimes, (7) petty offenses, (8) major crimes, and (9) crimes based on the type of social harm caused.[37]

The classification of a crime may be important for several reasons: (1) a trial court may have jurisdiction only for felonies; (2) in the federal system, grand jury indictments are only required for "infamous" crimes; (3) in the majority of states, the impeachment of a witness (on cross-examination) is restricted to prior felony convictions; (4) habitual criminal statutes (which authorize a greater sentence) are usually restricted to felonies: (5) in the federal system, there is no right to a jury trial for petty offenses; and (6) the loss of certain civil rights (e.g., holding public office or the right to vote) is generally applicable only to felony convictions.[38]

At common law, crimes were classified into treason (which was further divided into high and petty treason), felonies, and misdemeanors. The English Statute of Treasons (1350) defined high treason as (1) an intent to kill the king, queen, or prince; (2) levying war against the throne; or (3) giving aid and comfort to the enemies of the king.[39] Petty treason (abolished by statute in 1825) consisted of the killing of a husband by his wife, of a master or mistress by a servant, or of a high-ranking member of the clergy. Petty treason has never been recognized as a separate classification in the United States—such killings have always been dealt with under our homicide statutes.

In the United States, the principal distinction between crimes is based on a felony-misdemeanor dichotomy. Under this classification, felonies include treason. The usual definition of a felony (in statutes or constitutions) is "any crime punishable by death or imprisonment in a prison."[40] Misdemeanors are defined as all other crimes punishable by fine or jail. Thus, felonies and misdemeanors are generally distinguishable by the *place* and *length* of imprisonment.

Felonies	*Misdemeanors*
Prison (state or federal) more than 1 year	Jail 1 year or less

How does one know whether a conviction is for a felony or a misdemeanor? Suppose, for example, a defendant, convicted of an offense which carries a maximum prison sentence of 5 years, is given only 6 months in the county jail. Is this a conviction for a felony or a misdemeanor?

In the overwhelming majority of states, it is the *possible* sentence, not the actual sentence imposed, which governs whether the conviction is for a felony or a misdemeanor.[41] In our example, the defendant would be a convicted felon in most states.

In some jurisdictions, however, it is the *actual* sentence imposed that marks the distinction. California and the federal courts utilize this classification. It is not a distinction without a difference, for there are important implications for the life of the offender if he or she is a convicted felon.

Conviction of a felony may carry with it certain civil disabilities, e.g., loss of the right to vote, to marry, to enter into contracts, or to enter certain professions and trades (e.g., a felon cannot be licensed to practice law or medicine or to operate a beauty parlor). Indeed, in some jurisdictions, a sentence to life in prison is considered to be a sentence to "civil death." The civil disabilities that are incurred vary from state to state and will be discussed in detail in Chapter 20.

Sometimes courts classify crimes according to a *mala in se-mala prohibita* dichotomy. *Mala in se* crimes are those which are inherently wrong; i.e., they are wrong in themselves and include dangerous crimes such as murder, robbery, burglary, and the like. On the other hand, *mala prohibita* crimes are wrong only because they are prohibited by law. They are not inherently dangerous or wrong and include gambling, public intoxication, violation of income tax laws, and the like. As a general rule, common-law crimes and dangerous crimes are classified as *mala in se.* All other crimes are *mala prohibita.*

Sometimes a violation of a criminal law can be either *mala in se* or *mala prohibita,* depending on the degree of the violation. For example, speeding slightly over the speed limit would be *mala prohibita.*

In most cases, the *mala in se–mala prohibita* dichotomy is important to the crimes of manslaughter and battery. Thus, if one engages in *mala in se* behavior and causes a foreseeable death or injury, one may be guilty of manslaughter (for the death) or battery (for the injury). However, if death or injury results from *mala prohibita* conduct (so that the death or injury is less foreseeable), the actor may only be civilly—not criminally—liable.

Another classification separates crimes into those that involve moral turpitude (vileness, inherent baseness, depravity) and those that do not. It is not unusual for a jurisdiction to provide for certain additional legal consequences if one is convicted of a crime involving moral turpitude. For example, such conviction may provide for (1) deportation of aliens, (2) disbarment of attorneys, (3) revocation of certain other occupational licenses, and (4) impeachment (discrediting) of witnesses at trial. As a general rule, crimes involving moral turpitude are *mala in se* crimes.

Another classification frequently found in state constitutions as well as the Constitution of the United States is "infamous" versus "noninfamous" crimes. The Fifth Amendment (United States Constitution) requires grand jury indictments for "infamous" crimes. As a general rule, if imprisonment or punishment at hard labor is authorized, it is an "infamous" crime. "Infamous" crimes are usually felonies.

Another classification separates petty offenses from major offenses. In the federal system, if an offense may be tried by a United States magistrate (as opposed to a United States district court judge) or the possible sentence is less than 6 months in jail, it is deemed a petty offense.[42] As a general rule, petty offenses are misdemeanors and major offenses are felonies.

A final classification divides crimes according to the type of social harm caused. Such a classification may be as follows: (1) offenses against the person (e.g., robbery, murder); (2) offenses against habitation (e.g., burglary); (3) offenses against property (e.g., larceny); (4) offenses against morality and decency (e.g., open profanity, prostitution); (5) offenses against the public peace (e.g., disorderly conduct); and (6) offenses affecting the administration of criminal justice (e.g., several of the Watergate crimes, perjury, obstruction of justice).[43]

Once a body of lawmakers have decided to criminalize certain actions, their next task is to ascertain an appropriate punishment. Our whole approach to the use of the criminal law as a means of social control is predicated on certain assumptions or theories about the deterrent effects of punishment.

1.12 THEORIES OF PUNISHMENT

In order to gain conformity to the criminal law, specific penalties are used to enforce these laws. An underlying premise is that if we take the joy out of crime, we will deter people from committing it. There are a number of theories which justify this approach.[44]

The first theory of punishment assumes that it will serve as a *general deterrence* to crime in society. The fundamental premise here is that the example of the punishment of criminals will deter others, for they will not wish to imitate the proscribed behavior. At early common law, executions were public, so that the "advertisement" would get wider audience. Offenders guilty of noncapital offenses were placed in stocks in the town square, where children amused themselves by throwing rocks at them. Does it work? It is impossible to measure with scientific precision how much crime is deterred by persons considering, in moments of calm reflection, the consequences—of being punished by the state—and then deciding against a criminal act.

The classic example quoted by those arguing against the effectiveness of capital punishment is the story of its use against pickpockets in England at early common law. Hangings were public affairs, and the excitement would draw crowds of onlookers. As the crowd pressed together for a good view of the thief about to drop to his death, other pickpockets would mill through the crowd, plying their trade.

A central question becomes: Who are the deterrables? For there are certain classes of persons to whom punishment is a meaningless event. We cannot deter the insane by placing rigid penalties on the statute books. A psychotic, homicidal maniac, or otherwise irrational person cannot make his or her behavior conform to the requirements of the criminal law. Also, there are sane people who nevertheless are so reckless and impetuous by nature as to seldom, if ever, contemplate the consequences of their behavior. Although they behave like young children, they are legally sane and therefore responsible for their actions; they are almost impossible to deter. Finally, it is impossible to deter a person who operates on the assumption that the penalty will not be inflicted. A professional "hit man" does not reason: "Now, I'm going to kill my mark, then the police are going to catch me, and the consequences of this action will be that I increase the misery in my life." Rather, he concludes: "Because I am so clever and my bail bondsman and mouthpiece so shrewd, I will collect my payoff after I murder this person, buy a fine car, and date beautiful women." In short, he reasons: "What will be the consequences of my committing a murder? Nice things will happen to me."

Who, then, do we deter with criminal penalties? The answer; sane, cautious, and forward-looking people who assume that they will be caught.

A second theory of punishment refers to the *specific deterrence* of an individual offender. By imposing an unpleasant experience (fine, prison), we deter the lawbreaker from further criminal acts. Reflecting this philosophy, an associate warden (and fundamentalist minister) with whom one of the authors once worked enjoyed telling incoming prisoners: "Prisons were not meant to be nice places; if they were, you might want to come back."

Are offenders deterred by fines and imprisonment? Those reformers who argue that prisons have no effect or only negative effects often tend to exaggerate the recidivism (return) rate. One of the most systematic reviews of the recidivism rate of convicted felons placed the figure at between 35 to 45 percent.[45] Whether a fine or prison experience effectively deters an offender from continuing in crime varies with the age of the offender, the offense for which the offender was arrested, and his or her prior criminal record. Recidivism is positively correlated with youth (ages fifteen to twenty-five), certain property offenses (such as car theft), and the length of time the offender has been involved in a criminal career.[46]

From the point of view of society and the individual offender, however, there are some negative aspects to the punishment approach. Simply punishing and warehousing offenders does not teach them new behaviors; it merely suppresses old behaviors for the time during which absolute control of the person is maintained. Punishment as an end in itself has the additional side effect of creating resentment and bitterness in those who are subjected to it. This leads to the possibility that the offender will return to society (98 percent of inmates eventually get out of prison) transformed into a much more dangerous person than before.

A third theory of why we punish offenders is that it serves to *protect* society. In this view, some persons are so dangerous to the life and property of others that they must be quarantined for the protection of society. The federal penitentiary on Alcatraz Island was a classic example of this approach.

A fourth theory of punishment, and the one which currently has the most support among those involved in the correctional process, is that we separate an offender from society in order to effect his or her *rehabilitation.*

The basic premise underlying this theory is that offenders are capable of change (for the better). From changes in the architecture of prisons to the introduction of treatment programs, the thrust is away from the old Georgia "chain gang" approach to one in which the offender is counseled and educated. The goal is to provide inmates with the social and work skills they need to get along in a modern industrial society.

The punitive reaction looks backward and reacts to the criminal in terms of the crimes that have been committed; the rehabilitation model looks forward, to the future, and focuses on the individual's capacity for improvement.

The fifth theory of punishment is that the arrest, trial, and imprisonment of offenders serves as a tool to educate the general population, especially about lesser (*mala prohibita*) offenses. The general population probably does not need to be told that murder and robbery are criminal acts, but widely publicized trials such as those accompanying the Watergate offenses did much to educate the ordinary citizen about the nature of conspiracy and the obstruction of justice.

The last, oldest, and perhaps most popular theory of punishment is that "evil deserves evil"—the *retribution* reaction. This approach makes no effort to rehabilitate the offender; it simply exacts revenge.

A secondary argument for the retributive response is that if the state failed to punish offenders, citizens would take the law into their own hands and we would be faced with lynch-mob justice.

There is an inherent conflict between these competing theories. Theories based primarily on retribution, deterrence, and prevention clash with those that place the greatest value upon rehabilitation of the offender. What has emerged is an attempt at rehabilitation within a context of punishment. In trying to implement these theories, legislators, judges, wardens, and parole boards must rank their priorities before making their decisions. A sentencing judge may be reluctant to send a youth to a tough prison, but if the protection of society is placed above what may be in the best interests of rehabilitation, the youth will go "inside." Likewise, parole boards must balance the protection of society against the value of early release in making their decisions.

SUMMARY

In this chapter we have discussed the nature of crime. We noted that wherever people live in groups, there are deviants—persons who either cannot or will not conform to the rules. Society attempts to control behavior through folkways, mores, and laws. Those who violate laws are labeled criminals and harsh sanctions are applied to gain conformity.

Our laws are greatly influenced by our British heritage and the English common law. We base our laws on certain premises such as (1) that there must be external harm (act) and (2) that the offender must have possessed a guilty intent (motive). The debate as to what acts should be criminalized centers around those offenses known as victimless crimes, where the offender may be a satisfied customer (gambling, sexual deviance).

In order to judge whether a specific act is malicious or negligent, courts sometimes use the "reasonable man" test, which simply asks: Would an ordinary person have acted in this manner under these circumstances? Crimes are separated from civil wrongs, which are called torts, though at times the two overlap. There are a number of other classifications of crimes, the most important being the separation of offenses into *felonies* (serious crimes) and *misdemeanors* (less serious offenses).

Underlying our system of criminal justice are several theories of punishment. These range from the belief that fines and imprisonment serve as a general deterrent to crime to the hope that offenders will, in some way, be rehabilitated by these measures. Judging from the rising crime rate, which will be discussed in Chapter 2, we have not yet hit upon the correct formula.

Chapter 2

The Extent of Street Crime

It should be acknowledged at the outset that attempts to arrive at an accurate appraisal of the extent of crime and the characteristics of criminals in the United States have proved to be frustrating. Crime is not easily measured, for secrecy is its essential characteristic. Offenders are hardly likely to identify themselves occupationally to a census taker as a "mugger" or "rapist." The accuracy of crime statistics varies from near perfection for bank robbery to anybody's guess in those "victimless crimes" where the "victim" is a satisfied customer (gambling and sexual deviance).

Concerning the latter offenses, Geis[1] estimates there are probably only about 20 convictions for every 60 million homosexual acts performed. Similarly, of crimes where the victim gets the criminal he deserves—e.g., confidence games where the victim willingly participates in hopes of easy money—less than 10 percent are reported to the police.

We shall begin our discussion of the extent of crime in the United States with a review of "crimes known to the police" and the official incidence rates published by the FBI in its annual publication the *Uniform Crime Reports (UCR)*. The Crime Index will be reviewed in some detail and the characteristics of known offenders will be examined by age, sex, race, and residence. An attempt to achieve some independent assessment of the validity of these official statistics will be made by reviewing prevalence studies, the social behavior of citizens as it relates to crime, and risk-insurance rates as an index of property crime. Finally, the limitations of official statistics will be discussed and some areas in need of improvement will be suggested.

2.01 THE UNIFORM CRIME REPORTS (UCR)

Many crimes go undetected, others are detected but the victims choose not to report them, and still others are reported but never recorded by the police. Thus, any attempt to measure the absolute number of crimes committed in a particular locale by such yardsticks as "crimes known to the police," "arrests," "convictions," or "prison commitments," can only be viewed as rough approximations.

Although the statistics presented in the *UCR* represent only a portion, and probably a small portion in some categories, of the total crimes committed, police records are closer to the actual crime and are a superior measure of the actual number of crimes committed than are court records or prison statistics.

Since 1930, the FBI has published "crimes known to the police" and arrest statistics in the *UCR.* These data are voluntarily submitted by law enforcement agencies from all parts of the United States. Despite its limitations, which will be discussed in detail later, this information is considered the most authoritative summary indicating the extent of criminality in American society. From the Wickersham Commission report on criminal statistics (1931) to recent textbooks on criminology, all regard police statistics as the best source for the measurement of street crime.

The *UCR* utilizes seven crimes as an index to measure the trend and distribution of crime in the United States. These seven crimes—murder, forcible rape, robbery, aggravated assault, burglary, larceny, and auto theft—are selected because, as a group, they are serious offenses and therefore are among the crimes most consistently reported to the police. The reasoning is similar to that of the economist who uses Standard & Poor's 500 Index as a device to measure the fluctuations of the stock market.[2] Obviously other crimes—kidnapping, arson, and perjury—are serious crimes, but they are omitted from the Index either because of the difficulty in measuring their occurrence or because they occur less frequently.

During 1975, the *UCR* received data from 13,000 contributing agencies; there were 400 when it began in 1930. The offenses reported are violations of the criminal law of the separate states; no violations of federal law are included in the *UCR.*

2.02 THE EXTENT OF KNOWN CRIME

As noted earlier, the FBI Crime Index is constructed from the voluntary reporting by the police of the seven index offenses. From these statistics a crime rate is derived.

It is important in dealing with *UCR* statistics to distinguish between the "volume" of crime and a crime "rate." "Volume" simply refers to the absolute number of crimes committed in a particular locale during a specified time interval. A crime rate, however, relates the number of crimes to the number of inhabitants. As in baseball statistics, it is not as important to know that a player got ten hits (volume) as it is to relate the number of hits to the number of times the player came to bat (rate). By relating a player's hits to times at bat, we can make predictive statements about the probability of his getting a safe hit (e.g., if he comes to bat thirty times and gets ten hits, his batting average is .300 and the probability is that he will get a hit three out of ten times).

Similarly, if a community has 100 crimes committed in one year and 200 the following year, the volume of crime has doubled; but unless you relate this volume to population growth or decline, these figures can be misleading. It is not unusual for newspaper headlines to read: "Crime increases 50 percent in the last 5 years." Before we become too alarmed, it is important to know whether this percentage refers to the volume of crime or to a crime rate.

A crime rate tells you the probability, within limitations, that a person in a particular community will be a victim of a crime. According

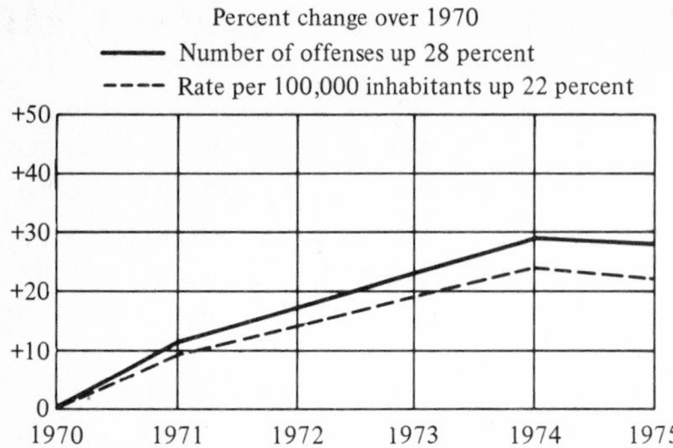

Figure 2-1 Murder, 1970–1975. *UCR, 1975.*

to the 1975 *UCR,* the national crime rate, or risk of being the victim of one of these crimes, has increased 179 percent since 1960. Next, we will discuss in some detail the seven offenses which constitute the *UCR* Crime Index.

Murder

"Murder" is defined by the *UCR* as the willful killing of another human being. In 1975, there were an estimated 20,510 murders committed in the United States. This crime represents approximately 2 percent of all violent crimes and less than one-half of 1 percent of the total crime index offenses.

The Southern states lead the nation in both volume and rate of murders. Georgia possessed the highest murder and nonnegligent manslaughter rate in the nation, a rate five times higher than that of Vermont. Montgomery, Alabama, and the surrounding counties was the "murder capital of the United States" in 1975. Most of the homicides in 1975 occurred during the month of December.

Until recently, criminologists discussing the homicide rate were quick to point out that, although this rate was increasing, we still had not reached the high rates achieved during the frustrating Depression years. With the rates achieved in the mid-seventies, we have slightly surpassed the violent days of the Depression thirties.

The homicide rates of 1975 would have been much greater except for the advances in medicine. Politicians may not have learned much from the four major wars fought by the United States in this century, but physicians have learned a great deal about how to treat gunshot wounds. The following is a reply to our query for information in this area from Dr. Francis C. Nance, professor of surgery and physiology at Louisiana State University Medical Center:

> With respect to mortality from gunshot wounds of the abdomen, I can provide accurate data. There has been a marked decrease in mortality since 1930. In 1930, mortality rate for penetrating wounds of the abdomen was approximately 50%. This has dropped to 12% for the period 1967–1974. The factors contributing to this improvement in mortality are primarily the availability of blood and plasma, of the introduction of antibiotics, improved postoperative care, and better-trained surgeons.[3]

Nationally, homicide is the thirteenth most common cause of death. Males outnumber females as victims of murder by more than three to one, with approximately 51 out of 100 murder victims being white, 47 black, and 2 percent "other races." Firearms continue to be the predominant weapon used in murder (66 percent). As in the past, the handgun was the principal instrument used, accounting for 51 percent of all murders. Japan, by contrast, prohibits the private ownership of handguns, with the result

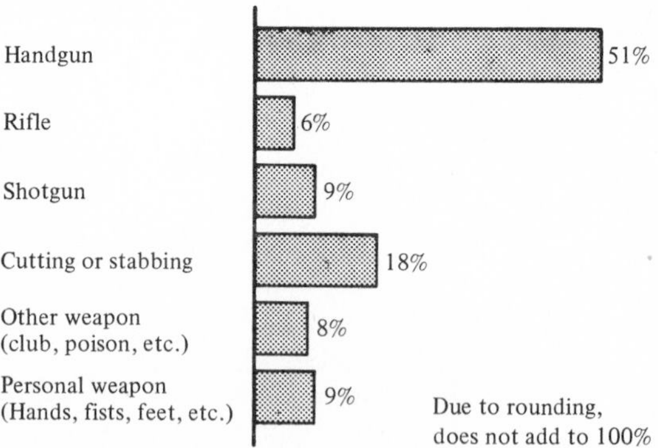

Figure 2-2 Murder by type of weapon used, 1975. *UCR, 1975.*

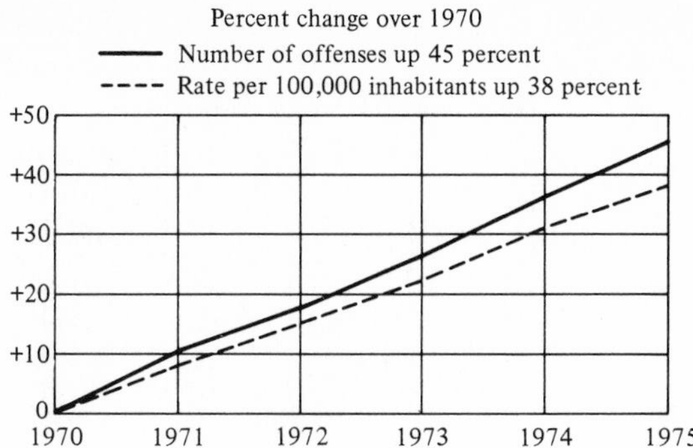

Figure 2-3 Aggravated assault, 1970–1975. *UCR, 1975.*

that the gun homicide rate in the United States in 1968 was 221 times that of Japan in the same year.[4]

Murders tend to be committed by relatives or close associates of the victim. In 1975, killings within the family made up approximately one-fourth of all murders. Over half these family killings involved spouse killing spouse. These facts have caused some to see criminal homicide as a social problem which is beyond the control of the police.

Nationally, police continue to be successful in clearing by arrest a greater percentage of homicides than any other Crime Index offense. In 1975, 78 percent of homicides were cleared by arrest. Of the adults prosecuted in 1975, 44 percent were found guilty as charged and 14 percent were convicted on some lesser charge.

Aggravated Assault

"Aggravated assault" is defined by the *UCR* as an unlawful attack by one person upon another for the purpose of inflicting severe bodily injury, usually by the use of a weapon. In 1975, there were an estimated 484,710 aggravated assaults in the United States. Regionally, Southern states led the nation, reporting 36 percent of the total. Tyler, Texas, was the SMSA (standard metropolitan statistical area) with the nation's highest aggravated assault rate. Most offenses occurred during the summer months. The rate of aggravated assaults per 100,000 inhabitants rose 38 percent from 1970 to 1975. Most aggravated assaults occur within the family unit or among neighbors and acquaintances.

Law enforcement agencies were able to "clear by arrest" 64 out of each 100 cases of aggravated assault in 1975. Because of the close family, or other relationship between the victim and offender, convictions are often difficult to obtain. The victim simply refuses to cooperate with the police.

Of persons arrested for this offense tried in 1975, 41 percent were either acquitted or let go because the charge was dismissed. Persons involved in these altercations tend to view their fights as family affairs and do not choose to resolve their conflicts through the courts. Settling these feuds is hazardous to the responding officer as well, 157 law enforcement officers having lost their lives between 1966 and 1975 in the course of trying to restore neighborhood peace.

Forcible Rape

Forcible rape, as defined in the *UCR,* is the carnal knowledge of a female through the use of force or intimidation. During 1975, there were an estimated 56,040 reported rapes. Again, the Southern states led the nation with 31 percent of the volume. Lawton, Oklahoma, was the SMSA reporting the highest rape rate. During the period 1970–1975, the rate of forcible rape increased 48 percent. Women living in

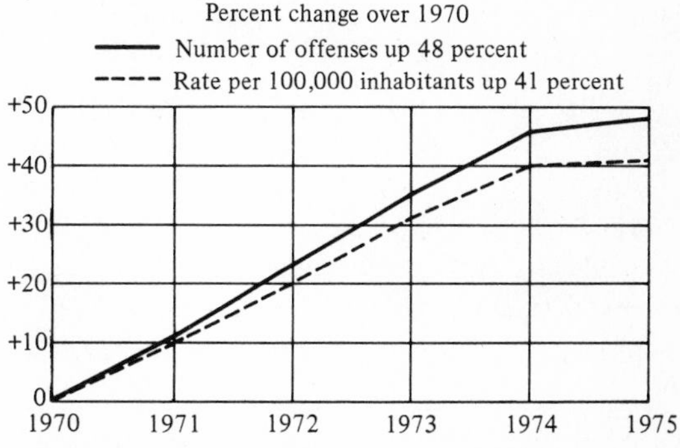

Figure 2-4 Forcible rape, 1970–1975. *UCR, 1975.*

large cities (with populations over 250,000) run a risk of being raped that is three times greater than that faced by women residing in rural areas.

Statistics on rape remain among the most unreliable of all crime statistics. Rape is one of the most underreported crimes partly because of the potential public embarrassment and partly because of the fear of reprisal from the offender. Nationally, 15 percent of all claims of forcible rape were discovered to be unfounded. A report of rape may, for instance, be turned in by a prostitute who is angry over a customer's failure to pay and is seeking revenge. As one vice-squad officer observed: "Hell hath no fury like an unpaid prostitute."[5]

Of rapes reported to the police in 1975, 51 percent were cleared by arrest. Of this number, about 58 percent were brought to trial. Of the adults prosecuted, 42 percent were found guilty of the substantive offense and 12 percent of a lesser charge.

Robbery

Robbery is defined by the *UCR* as the taking of money or other items of value by the use of force or intimidation. Unlike burglary or larceny-theft, robbery takes place in the presence of the victim. In 1975, there were an estimated total of 464,970 robberies committed in the United States. This represents an increase in the robbery rate of 27 percent since 1970. Robbery rates tend to increase in proportion to the density of the population. The Northeastern states in general and New York City (SMSA) in particular led the nation in 1975 in the rate of robberies per 100,000 population.

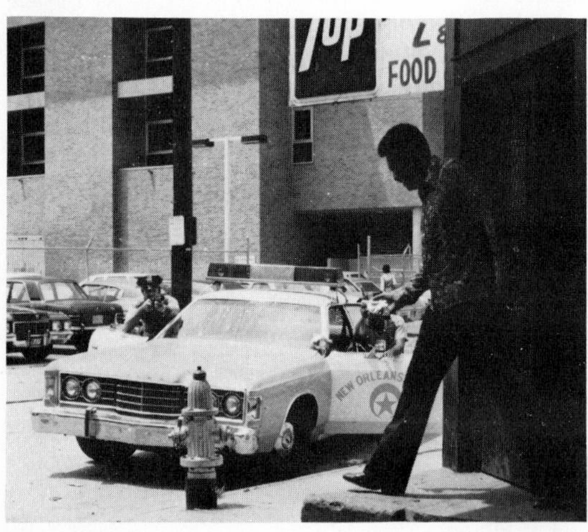

Law enforcement agencies are successful in making an arrest in about one out of four robbery offences which are reported.

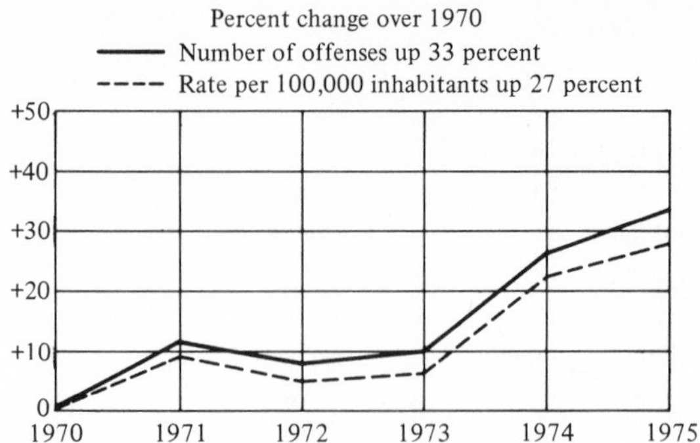

Figure 2-5 Robbery, 1970–1975. *UCR, 1975.*

The volume of bank robbery has increased dramatically since the days when Bonnie and Clyde were redistributing the wealth. However, when the factors of inflation, population increase, and the increased number of banks available to be robbed are considered, the difference is not so vast.

Armed robbers are referred to in prison argot as "heist men" and considered stupid. The FBI reports that the typical bank robber is "young and dumb." Some write holdup notes on the back of their own utility bills or run out of a bank so excited that they cannot find their get-

Table 2-1 Bank Robberies—1932 vs. 1975

Year	Banks held up	Dollar losses
1975	4,180	$18,179,140
1932	609	$ 3,400,000

Source: 1975 *UCR* and J. Bennett, "A Cool Look at 'The Crime Crisis,'" *Harper's Magazine*, April 1964.

away car. Based on the amount of prison time served, the average bank robber makes about 40 cents an hour.[6]

The most famous bank robber of modern times is "Willie the Actor" Sutton, so named because of the theatrical disguises he used in holdups and jailbreaks. When asked why he robbed banks, Willie is reported to have said, "Because that's where the money is." Ironically, after spending the larger part of his adult life either in banks or in jail, Willie now has a job as a consultant to a bank. His role: He advises them on how to stop holdups, which is rehabilitation of a sort.

In 1975, law enforcement agencies were successful in making arrests in 27 percent of the robbery offenses reported, with 58 percent of the adults arrested being prosecuted. Slightly over half those prosecuted were found guilty of the substantive offense.

Burglary

Burglary is defined by the *UCR* as the unlawful entry of a structure to commit a felony or theft. Forcible entry is not required to make the crime a burglary; an unauthorized entry is sufficient.

In 1975, the burglaries in the United States totaled an estimated 3,252,100. The most popular month for burglaries during 1975 was January. In 1970–1975, the burglary rate increased

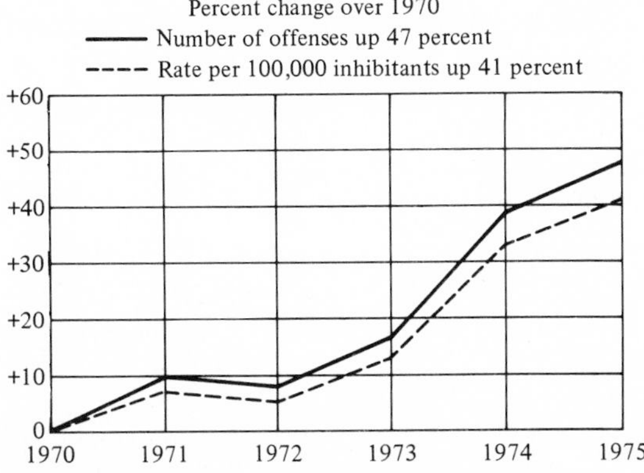

Figure 2-6 Burglary, 1970–1975. *UCR, 1975.*

41 percent, with the Western states experiencing the highest rates. Las Vegas, Nevada (SMSA), once again led all American cities in the burglary rate.

Daytime burglaries of residences accounted for over half of the residential burglaries, since more homes and apartments were left unguarded with the increased number of working wives. Police were successful in making an arrest in 18 percent of total burglary offenses reported. Of the adults prosecuted for burglary in 1975, 60 percent were found guilty of the substantive charge.

Larceny-Theft

Larceny-theft is defined by the *UCR* as the unlawful taking or stealing of property without the use of force, violence, or fraud. It includes such offenses as shoplifting, pickpocketing, purse-snatching, thefts from autos, and bicycle thefts.

In 1975 there were 5,977,700 larceny-thefts reported, an increase of 35 percent since 1970. The average value of goods stolen in 1975 was placed at $166, with the combined total loss to victims estimated at $992 million. Fort Lauderdale–Hollywood, Florida (SMSA), was the number-one city in the nation in 1975 in the rate of larceny-thefts per 100,000 population.

The tremendous volume of these crimes and a lack of witnesses make larceny-theft a difficult offense for police officers to solve. Only about one out of every five larceny-thefts reported was cleared by arrest in 1973, and 31

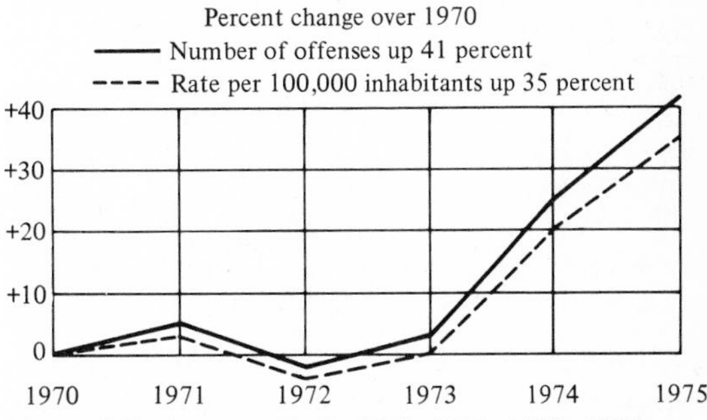

Figure 2-7 Larceny-theft, 1970–1975. *UCR, 1975.*

percent of those taken in were females. Women were arrested more often for larceny-theft than for any other offense in 1975. Of adults prosecuted for this offense in 1975, 73 percent were found guilty.

Motor Vehicle Theft

The *UCR* defines "auto theft" as the unlawful taking or stealing of a motor vehicle, including attempted theft. Temporary use by persons having lawful access to the vehicle is excluded from this definition.

In 1975, 1,000,500 motor vehicles were reported stolen, an increase of 3 percent in the auto theft rate since 1970. Nationwide, 1 out of every 130 registered automobiles was stolen. The heavily populated Northeastern states experienced the highest auto-theft rates, with Boston again the nation's leading city for auto theft.

Law enforcement agencies were able to solve 14 percent of the motor vehicle thefts by arresting the offender. Of all persons formally processed, 63 percent were referred to juvenile court jurisdiction. This was the highest percentage of juvenile referrals for a Crime Index offense.

The discussion of auto theft completes the review of the seven *UCR* index crimes. Crime continues to rise. Some observers have argued that the rise only reflects better reporting techniques. While that is an interesting hypothesis, one cannot prove a negative. Later in this chapter we will look at changed social behavior as an index of crime—a change which tends to support the conclusion that the rise in crime is genuine and not just a by-product of the computer age. Having gained some idea of the nature and extent of the major street crimes in the United States, we will now examine how these crimes are related to age, sex, race, and residence.

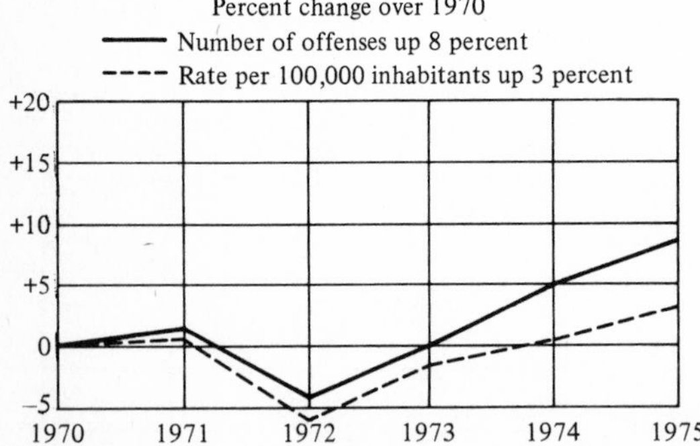

Figure 2-8 Motor vehicle theft, 1970–1975. *UCR, 1975.*

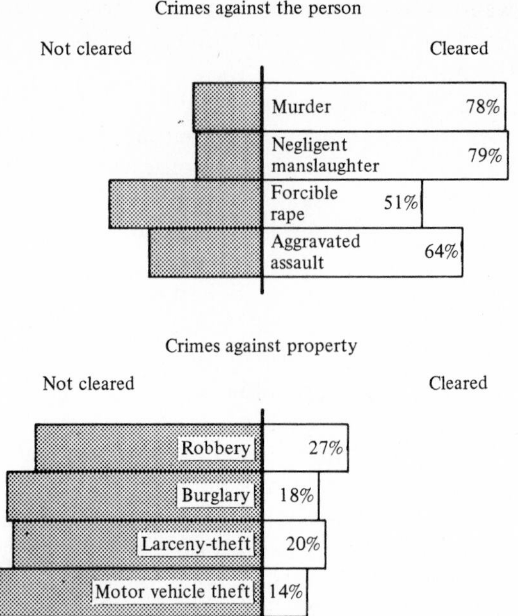

Figure 2-9 Crimes cleared by arrest, 1975. *UCR, 1975.*

2.03 CHARACTERISTICS OF KNOWN OFFENDERS

Age

Crime is a young man's game. Over half the total number of people arrested by the police in 1975 were under the age of twenty-five, Table 2-2 shows the relationship between the crime index offenses and the age of the arrested offender.

Table 2-2 Arrests in Relation to Age

Offense charged	Percentage of arrests by age	
	Under 18	Under 25
Murder and nonnegligent manslaughter	9.5	44.9
Forcible rape	17.6	58.0
Robbery	34.3	77.0
Aggravated assault	17.6	49.6
Burglary	52.6	85.2
Larceny-theft	45.1	75.4
Motor vehicle theft	54.5	84.6

Source: Adapted from *UCR, Uniform Crime Report*, 1975, p. 190.

The relationship of youth to crime is a reflection of the special problems of youth in adapting to American society as well as the unique personality traits of young people. Criminal acts require a certain amount of daring, vigor, and rebellion—qualities which the young possess in abundance. Society is not often plagued by daring, vigorous, rebellious old people.

Why some youths express these traits through criminal acts and others through social-approved channels is a problem for criminological theory. The role of theory is to make sense of facts, and the fact which criminological theorists must explain is why from half to three-fourths of all serious street crime in America is committed by persons under the age of twenty-five.

Sex

Male arrests outnumbered female arrests by five to one in 1975. Crime continues to be overwhelmingly a male phenomenon, though crime rates among women are rising. Table 2-3 shows the relationship between arrests for the seven index offenses and the sex of the offender.

Women are comitting more and more serious crimes than ever before. According to the *UCR*, arrests of females for violent crimes during the years 1960–1974 rose 160 percent, and arrests for property crimes rose 375 percent. There was a greater proportion of women involved in crime in 1975 than at any time since World War II. The modern female criminal is less likely to be a gun-wielding Bonnie Parker than a shrewd white-collar offender adept at double-entry bookkeeping.

The increase in crimes by women is most dramatic in the areas of forgery, fraud, and embezzlement—not in the traditional female crimes of prostitution or child abuse. Criminologists are predicting that, if present trends continue, in 20 years women will account for over 50 percent of these crimes.[7]

It is one thing to arrest a woman; it is quite another to put her in the slammer. While 1 in every 6.5 arrests is a woman, women represent only 1 in 9 convictions and only 1 in 30 of those are sent to prison. Women stand a better chance than men of being acquitted when charged with murder, robbery, theft, or forgery. When the charge is a drug violation, the conviction rates are about equal for both men and women.

On a typical day, the woman facing a judge will be poor, black, and a school dropout; she will be supporting several children. These women are picked up on charges of shoplifting, drug abuse, or "blowing away" a cheating husband, lover, or "other woman." When a woman is involved in a crime that requires several persons, she tends to be the accomplice of a burglar boyfriend or "hustler" husband.

Historically, the law has tended to view women as subordinate creatures. The common

Table 2-3 Arrests and Sex of Offender

Offense charged	Percentage of arrests by sex	
	Male	Female
Murder and nonnegligent manslaughter	84.4	15.6
Forcible rape	99.0	1.0
Robbery	93.0	7.0
Aggravated assault	86.9	13.1
Burglary	94.6	5.4
Larceny-theft	68.8	31.2
Motor vehicle theft	93.0	7.0

Source: Adapted from *UCR, Uniform Crime Report*, 1975, p. 191.

law of England, except in cases of murder or treason, would not hold a married woman accountable for a crime if she acted under the coercion of her husband. One early English case held that the husband's mere command was sufficient to prove coercion. Times, as they say, have jolly well changed.

This patronizing view of women carried over into theories of criminality. Women were pictured as pathetic creatures. The female criminal was perceived as a psychological child caught in a web of unfortunate circumstances. Police officers and judges were admonished to respond to women caught in the net of the law with leniency and chivalry. Women were assumed to be naturally purer than men; if they were in trouble, it was felt, there was a good chance they had been led astray by some wicked man.

Today, criminologists argue that women are no more naturally endowed with morality and decency than are men. The traditional roles assigned to women are those which assume a certain goodness and charity—nurse, teacher, and mother. Even in these roles—as in the case of the kindly nurse who poisoned the elderly widow for her fortune—female criminals were common enough to cast doubt on the purity thesis. As contemporary women begin to play roles formerly reserved for men, their crimes become more like those of men. In the past, women have preferred to use deceit in their crimes, choosing poison and blackmail over guns and fists.

The chivalrous treatment of women by police and judges in the past probably existed more in criminology textbooks than in reality, but in any event the women's liberation movement opposes any such special treatment for women by judges and juries. It is argued that women should stand up and take their punishment like a man. The movement's motto is "A woman's place is everywhere," and that apparently includes prison.

Race

When crime rates are analyzed by race, it becomes readily apparent that certain violent crimes in America are overwhelmingly committed by blacks. While blacks are overrepresented in all seven index offenses, it is in the area of violent crime that the rates for blacks reach epidemic proportions. One exception to this trend is kidnapping, a violent crime committed primarily by whites.

It would be a gross error to infer from high black crime rates that black people have some genetic predisposition toward crime. We must emphasize that black crime rates vary by sex, socioeconomic status, and geographic region. Criminologists generally consider race to be a significant factor in the explanation of crime rates insofar as it affects the nature of social experiences and social interaction.

Residence

Thus far we have seen that crime is associated with youth, maleness, and the experiences associated with being black in American society. Now we turn to the relationship of crime and residence. Persons living in large core cities (with populations over 250,000) run a risk being the victims of serious crimes that is three to ten times the risk experienced by persons who reside in rural areas.

Table 2-4 Arrests in Relation to Race

Offense charged	Percentage of arrests by race: White	Black
Murder and nonnegligent manslaughter	42.9	55.5
Forcible rape	46.6	50.8
Robbery	35.1	63.0
Aggravated assault	57.9	40.2
Burglary	72.0	26.1
Larceny-theft	70.5	27.5
Motor vehicle theft	74.8	22.2

Source: Adapted from *UCR* 1975, p. 193. Percentages do not equal 100 percent due to omission of other races. White and black are, of course, colors; the anthropological classification of these races is Caucasian and Negroid.

What is it about life in large cities that creates pressures toward deviance and crime? Certainly the speed, anonymity, crowded living conditions, and general spirit of alienation which characterize life in a metropolitan area must play a part.

Nor is the future bright for American cities. The middle class has voted with its feet and solved the crime problem in the cities by moving to the suburbs. But with the moving van goes the tax base, and with the tax base goes the support for police and public services. As Newman observes:

> Our central city areas are lived in now primarily by low income populations, minority groups—black, Puerto Rican—and suburbs have become white, middle-class havens.
>
> The word "haven" is an accurate one. One of the simplest, most obvious forms of crime prevention is to move your family out of a high crime area and into the suburbs.[8]

The actress Lee Remick describes the tension of life with crime in New York City:

> In London, she told newsmen, I can put my 11-year-old daughter into a taxi and send her off to a party and be reasonably sure that nobody is going to chop her up into little pieces before she gets there.
>
> In New York it's nerve-wracking to give children any degree of freedom at all. Until we moved here [London], I'd lived in New York City all my life, and towards the end it wasn't very pleasant. It's such a violent city, so tense and angry. You can feel anger everywhere.[9]

Table 2-5 Relationship of Crime to Resistance

Offense	Crime rate (per 100,000), 1975 SMSA	Rural
Murder and nonnegligent homicide	10.6	8.1
Aggravated assault	254.9	123.7
Forcible rape	31.3	12.0
Robbery	284.0	23.5
Burglary	1747.9	785.9
Larceny-theft	3195.6	941.6
Motor vehicle theft	586.2	102.4

Source: Adapted from *UCR*, 1975. SMSA refers to a standard metropolitan statistical area generally made up of a core city with a population of over 50,000 inhabitants and the surrounding counties which share certain metropolitan characteristics.

Table 2-6 Social Variables Associated with High Crime Rates

Status	Relatively high rates of crime	Low rates
Sex	Male	Female
Age	Young (15 to 25)	Older (over 50) and very young (below 12)
Race	Bl ck	White
Marital status	Single	Married
Residence	City (over 250,000 pop.)	Rural
Religion	Protestant	Jewish
Income	Low	Middle and high

Source: Adapted from discussion and sources cited in text.

Summary and Discussion

Social categories tend to be additive in predicting the probability that one will be involved in a crime. The street-crime problem in the United States is located among young black males from low-income big-city backgrounds.

2.04 PREVALENCE STUDIES

In an attempt to achieve some independent assessment of the validity of the data presented by the *UCR* the National Opinion Research Center (NORC) took a random sample of 10,000 households: asking people what crimes had been committed against them during 1965, the preceding year.

In an attempt to overcome the difficulties posed by police statistics, the NORC decided to survey the individual victims of crime. The central focus of the study was on crimes against the person and against property.

Half the people interviewed were victims of crimes they did not report to the police. The NORC sample revealed an estimated rate of crime twice that of the *UCR* index; nevertheless, in the case of homicide and car theft, there was close agreement between the two sources of crime data. Murder is second only to bank robbery as the crime most likely to be discovered and reported, and people apparently believe the police can do something about recovering a stolen car. Approximately 85 percent of stolen cars are recovered, though many of them have been stripped. Other factors affecting the accuracy of car-theft statistics include the high value of autos and the fact that cars must be registered and insured. From 7 to 10 percent of stolen cars recovered are owned by fleet or rental agencies.[10]

Since the advent of the Law Enforcement Assistance Administration (LEAA), there have been a number of prevalence studies. In 1973, the Census Bureau's National Crime Panel, in cooperation with LEAA, interviewed a random sampling of 60,000 households (125,000 persons age twelve or above) and 15,000 businesses.[11] The major findings:

1 The number of rapes, robberies, aggravated assaults, and burglaries is triple the number reported to the police.

2 Men are more likely than women to be the victims of personal crimes, blacks more than whites, and the young more than old.

3 The most prevalent type of crime is personal larceny, which accounts for about 40 percent of all victimizations.

4 The victimization rate for personal larceny is 47 per 1,000 persons; for a crime of violence (rape, robbery, or assault), 17 per 1,000.

5 New Yorkers are victims of violent crime less frequently than residents of Chicago, Detroit, Los Angeles, Philadelphia, and several other large cities.

2.05 SOCIAL BEHAVIOR AS AN INDEX OF CRIME

If, as the *UCR* and independent surveys indicate, crime is increasing (in some areas in epidemic proportions), the behavior of citizens should indicate that they are being affected by the increased likelihood of becoming victims of crimes. By doing some people watching, we can play the role of sidewalk sociologists and get some clue as to whether crime exists in the streets or only in the scare headlines of yellow journalism.

One sign of the increase in crime and criminals, especially in our large cities, has been the proliferation of the number of private security and guard agencies. The Detroit *Yellow Pages* list 108 private security agencies advertising that they will guard hospitals, plants, stores, offices, and your daughter's birthday party, or that they will meet you at your door when you return home.

Apartment-house ads reassure potential tenants that security guards are always on duty and that closed-circuit television systems monitor the exits. Burglar-alarm firms are on the increase. These firms utilize everything from police dogs to automatic telephone dials so that citizens may achieve a degree of safety in their homes. Stores have installed elaborate multilens television systems designed to deter shoplifting, holdups, and warehouse pilferage.

That crime has created an economic impact on the business world is shown by the increased demand for dead-bolt locks, Mace, and doors with peepholes. One New York commuter told this writer that the way he measures the spread of crime from the inner city to the suburbs is to notice how far out from the center city merchants must put up chain fences to protect their stores.

Various community groups have been formed as a direct result of citizen concern over crime. Merchants in the French Quarter of New Orleans have requested that a state police troops be placed in the middle of the tourist area to protect them. Organizations such as Women Against Crime have sought ways to make the streets safer.

In Washington, D.C., secretaries who must

work late park on guarded lots and are escorted to their cars by armed guards. Drivers of city buses carry no change in order to avoid attracting thugs. Taxidrivers normally cannot change large bills, for as soon as their cash builds up, they stop off and deposit it with a central office. In 1975, for the first time, the *UCR* listed crimes on campus. The dean of a Southern university, noting the ubiquity of campus security officers, sighed: "I can remember when all we needed was an old man to go around and make sure all the doors were locked."

2.06 RISK INSURANCE AS AN INDEX OF CRIME

For crimes against property, there is another independent measure: the premium rates on the various sublines of burglary insurance. Price[12] tested the accuracy of the statistics for crimes against property as reported in the *UCR* by cross-sectional comparisons with the premium rates for insurance against robbery, burglary, larceny, and auto theft. He observes: "Crime rates for crimes against property are highly correlated with premium rates on the most appropriate insurance coverages."

There is growing evidence that the urban businessperson cannot get adequate coverage without paying extremely high insurance rates. Even with increased premiums, one insurance man conceded that the only insurance risk he would be willing to take in certain inner-city areas would be "pig iron under water."

2.07 LIMITATIONS OF OFFICIAL STATISTICS

The method of reporting utilized by the *UCR* has been the subject of analysis by a number of sociologists and criminologists since its inception in 1930. Some of these criticisms used to anger the late J. Edgar Hoover. To the claim that FBI summaries "weren't worth the paper they were written on." Hoover responded by calling these critics "illogical and inane."[13] The criticisms have proved beneficial however, for over the years, the *UCR* has improved the quality of its reporting.

The student will recall some of the limitations of the *UCR* which were noted at the beginning of this chapter; for example, that not all crimes are reported and that some which are reported never get recorded. Also, it should be remembered that the FBI only *gathers* the statistics. The actual figures are volunteered by local and state law enforcement agencies. Just as a computer cannot purify bad data but is only as accurate as the information it processes, so the FBI summaries are no better than the accuracy of its reporting units.

In interpreting these statistics, the student should keep in mind that each index offense is assigned the same weight in police department reporting. Thus, the report of a larceny is counted as equal to a murder in determining the overall crime rate. Also, it is not possible to analyze the relationship of offense to offenders. The arrest of one person may clear several crimes, or the arrest of a gang may solve one crime. Thus, if 100 crimes are committed in a community, there may be 100 individual criminals or only a single very energetic one. Whatever the answer, it cannot be determined from the figures in the *UCR*.

The wide discretionary powers granted to district attorneys also affect the reliability of crime statistics. Prosecutors may decline to prosecute a case or may bargain with the accused to plead guilty to a lesser charge. Thus, an offender actually guilty of the sale of narcotics may plea-bargain to a charge of simple possession. Reasons for these practices may range from the strength of the district attorney's case to the prosecutor's appreciation of the accused's political connections.

Finally, crime rates are a function of police activity. When the police are efficient, energetic, and motivated, they make more arrests; this activity, in turn, creates a rise in the crime statistics.

SUMMARY

In this chapter we have attempted to locate the frequency and distribution of street crime in the social structure of American society. Using the incidence rates furnished by the FBI's *Uniform Crime Reports,* we learned that the crime rate in the United States increased 179 percent from 1960–1975. Street crime is associated with youth, maleness, the social experience of being black in American society, and urban living.

Some observers have denied that there is any real increase in crime in American society, arguing that the increased crime rates can be explained by better reporting techniques; they discount the fear expressed by citizens, claiming that crime exists more in scare headlines than in reality. These are interesting hypothesis, but when *UCR* statistics, independent surveys, risk-insurance rates, and social behavior are analyzed, the evidence seems to support the contention that we have a real street crime problem in this country which is changing the daily lives of American citizens.

Chapter 3

Victimless Crimes

"Crimes without victims" is as beguiling a misnomer as "sins without sinners," but it has become to be the rubric under which such offenses as drug addiction, alcoholism, prostitution, sex offenses, homosexuality, and gambling are discussed. As noted in Chapter 1, there is a fierce debate as to whether many of these offenses should be considered crimes at all. Some authorities argue that these behaviors are private consensual acts and therefore none of the law's business. Their contention is that the police should stop meddling in matters of morals and medicine, and that such acts should be decriminalized. But as we shall see, the issue is not all one-sided, for behavior does not occur in a social vacuum, and the law usually holds citizens responsible for the consequence of their acts.[1]

In this chapter we will discuss (1) drug addiction, (2) alcoholism, (3) prostitution, and (4) homosexuality.

3.01 ADDICTION AND DRUG ABUSE

From a medical point of view, a drug may be defined as "any substance other than food which by its chemical nature affects the structure or function of the living organism."[2] The discussion of drugs and drug abuse is fraught with value judgments which blur a scientific perspective. Certainly both alcohol and tobacco are psychoactive substances, yet in the public mind they are not "drugs."

If we concentrate on the medical benefits of a drug, we are interested in the therapeutic effects of the substance: i.e., did the drug improve the patient's general health? From a sociolegal point of view, we are interested in the

Table 3-1 Victimless Crimes–Total Estimated Arrests, United States, 1975*

Offense	Total estimated arrests
Drunkenness	1,217,000
Driving under the influence	947,100
Violation of liquor laws	601,400
Prostitution and commercialized vice	68,200
Sex offenses (except forcible rape and prostitution)	64,400
Gambling	62,600
Total	3,300,800

Source: Asterisk from *UCR*, 1975.
*In 1975, there were an estimated 9,273,600 arrests; thus one of every three arrests in the United States in 1975 was in the area of victimless crimes. There has been a slight but definite decline in victimless crime arrests: from 48.8 percent of all arrests in 1970 to 40.4 percent in 1974.[3]

risks that might be incurred by taking the drug. How toxic (poisonous) is it? We might logically assume that drugs which are legal—and can be bought without prescription—are safe, and that the reason for outlawing certain "street drugs" is their toxicity. But this assumes that we live in a totally rational society.

"Drug addiction" is defined by the World Health Organization as:

> . . . a state of periodic or chronic intoxication detrimental to the individual and to society, produced by the repeated consumption of a drug (natural or synthetic). Its characteristics include: 1) an overpowering desire or need (compulsion) to continue taking the drug and to obtain it by any means, 2) a tendency to increase the dosage, and 3) a psychic (psychological) and sometimes physical dependence on the effects of the drug.[4]

Although the term "addiction" is commonly understood to refer to the excessive use of narcotic drugs, the term properly encompasses any substance upon which the individual has become dependent.

The four most commonly used terms which refer to the use and abuse of drugs are "habituation," "dependence," "tolerance," and "addiction." Becoming *habituated* to a drug simply refers to developing the "habit" of using a drug, just as one might get into the habit of putting on the left shoe first. We talk about developing good and bad habits. The human being is a creature of habit, and William James referred to habit as the mechanism by which one achieves a stable phase in the development of personality.[5] One can be habituated to a drug to the point of not wishing to give up the habit; yet if it is merely a feeling of deprivation and not physiological or psychological dependence, a person cannot at this stage be called addicted.

Dependence is distinguished from habit by the degree of support the drug furnishes to the functioning of the individual. If I sprain my ankle and depend upon a crutch to walk, I can truly be described as being in a state of dependence upon the crutch for support. Similarly, a person may come to be dependent upon a drug for sleep, to reduce anxiety, or to restore some chemical imbalance in the body, as insulin does for a diabetic.

A distinction is often drawn between physical and psychological dependence, but this is somewhat arbitrary, since both elements are present to some extent in a person's dependence. Certainly a person who must take Seconal (a trade name for a barbiturate) to sleep would be classified—in the absence of any physical infirmities—as primarily psychologically dependent. A diabetic would ordinarily be physically dependent on insulin in the absence of any neurotic symptoms.

The term "tolerance" has a more precise meaning than "habituation" or "dependence." It refers to the ability of the body to build up an immunity to a drug, so that increasing amounts must be taken to achieve the same effects. Student nurses are instructed to watch closely a patient's reaction to the prescribed dosage to see if a condition of tolerance is developing.

Some drugs, because of their pharmacological properties, cause profound changes in the working of the body chemistry.

> It is as if the natural chemicals of the body move over to accommodate the interloper, the addictive drug, so that near normal bodily functions can go on only when a continual supply of the drug is pumped into the system.[6]

After the body has accommodated to the use of a narcotic, the drug's absence creates an abstinence syndrome commonly known as *withdrawal symptoms.* Narcotics are those drugs which produce tolerance and both psychological and physical dependence. A narcotics addict is "one who cannot be normal without a drug."

Arrests for narcotics offenses declined slightly from 642,100 in 1974 to 601,400 in 1975. Despite a more tolerant public attitude toward the use of marijuana, the arrests for possession or use of this drug represented more than two-thirds (416,000) of all arrests for narcotics offenses in 1975.[8] Given this vigorous legal reaction to marijuana, what is its nature?

Marijuana

The term "marijuana" is probably a corruption of the Portuguese term *maran guango,* meaning "intoxication." It was first applied to *Cannabis sativa* in Brazil.[9] The flowering tops, stems, and leaves of the female Indian hemp plant are dried, shredded, and ingested for the hallucinogenic effects. Marijuana is usually smoked in a pipe or cigarette (called a reefer or joint). It may also be baked into brownies. The Western variety of marijuana is relatively mild when compared with varieties from other countries. Western marijuana is considered to be about one-tenth as potent as *hashish.* This latter substance is the pure resin of the plant. The principal psychoactive substance in cannabis is thought to be delta-9-tetra-hydrocannabinol (THC), but some researchers question this.[10]

The psychoactive effect of cannabis is a subtle mood change not easily perceived by the uninitiated. Depending on the circumstances and mental set of the user, the typical reaction is a general sense of euphoria, giggling and hilarious laughter, distorted perception, a heightened sensitivity to sensual stimuli (e.g., colors and music), and increased hunger (called "the munchies"). In rare cases users have reported adverse reactions of paranoia and depression.

A professor of social work described his initiation into marijuana use as follows:

> We were at a party celebrating one of my students' successful defense of his doctoral dissertation. Most of the members of the group were sitting in a dimly lit room smoking marijuana. I tried it and could perceive no immediate effect. Then other members of the group began to laugh and point out my eyes were red. Somehow the music seemed clearer and I felt almost Guru-like and began to ruminate about the meaning of life. I felt a warm sense of oneness with others in the room. On the way home, my wife, who also was "stoned," asked me how fast I thought I was going. "About 35 m.p.h.," I replied. She doubled over in laughter. I was going 8 m.p.h. As cars passed us, it seemed the silliest thing in the world that people would care to pass us. We laughed until tears came in our eyes. Once home, I asked her if we had anything to eat. She had a German chocolate cake. We ate the entire cake. Each mouthful was the *pièce de résistance.*[11]

Users of marijuana do not acquire a physical dependence upon the drug and there are no withdrawal symptoms. Unlike drinkers, marijuana users do not suffer from hangovers. In some cases. extended marijuana use may induce psychological dependence. This, however, need not be seen as pathological except in rare cases. In every life-style we become "psychologically dependent"; that is, we desire certain things in order to achieve joie de vivre—a positive joy in living.

One unusual characteristic of marijuana is the property of "reverse tolerance." Researchers have discovered what had been conventional wisdom for some time—that regular users of marijuana acquire a greater sensitivity to it and need less of the substance to attain a "high."[12]

A chief criticism of marijuana use is the

"stepping-stone theory," i.e., that it leads to heroin use. The LeDain Commission report found that rather than marijuana users going on to heroin, it is persons who have a history of heavy alcohol or barbiturate consumption who are more likely to go on to opiates. Alcohol, barbiturates, and heroin are all central nervous system depressants, and that sequence is a more logical progression than a switch from marijuana, which is a hallucinogen.[13]

Among mind-altering drugs, marijuana seems to rank fourth in worldwide popularity, preceded by caffeine, nicotine, and alcohol.[14] In the early 1950s, a United Nations report estimated the number of marijuana users worldwide at approximately 200,000,000.[15] Marijuana was practically unknown in the United States before the 1920s. It was probably introduced by Mexican laborers in the Southwest and by merchant seamen from Latin America on liberty in the port of New Orleans.[16] The practice of smoking marijuana spread to the slums of big cities and found acceptance among jazz musicians, artists, and the general bohemian elite. Marijuana use was given a literary boost by the writings of the beat generation in the fifties. In his book *On the Road,* Jack Kerouac, the "hip Homer of the beat generation," provided a literary boost and guidelines for those who wished to "drop out."[17]

During the early sixties, marijuana use began to gain currency on college campuses. According to a 1972 Gallup poll, the proportion of college students who have tried marijuana at least once has grown from 5 percent in 1967 to 51 percent in 1972. Students whose fathers have had college training are more likely to be users than students whose fathers have not gone beyond high school. Students majoring in social science are more likely to use marijuana than are those specializing in other areas. Nationally, it is estimated that 24 million persons have experimented with marijuana.[18] Smoking pot is now a part of the collegiate way of life; judging from surveys and general references on television and in national magazines, it is as much a part of the American culture as alcohol was during prohibition.

The drive to outlaw marijuana was spearheaded by a federal bureaucrat named Harry J. Anslinger. A commissioner of the newly formed Federal Bureau of Narcotics (1932), a unit of the Treasury Department, Anslinger lobbied for the criminalization of this "lethal weed."[19] Atrocity stories attributing ax murders to marijuana usage began to appear in national magazines. Some of these preposterous stories and posters are now a source of amusement to college students. The immediate result, however, was that, by 1937, forty-six states had passed laws against marijuana, often the same Draconian penalties applied to heroin. Marijuana, in the public mind, was a narcotic in the same class as heroin. Thus, as heroin penalties escalated through the years, marijuana penalties rose with them.

The Marijuana Tax Act of 1937, modeled after the Harrison Narcotic Act of 1914, did not on its face ban marijuana. It recognized the medicinal usefulness of the substance and allowed physicians and others to continue prescribing cannabis if they paid a license fee of $1 per year. Only the nonmedical, untaxed possession or sale of marijuana was outlawed. One of the results of the criminalization of marijuana was to create new criminals and thus increase the demand for the law-enforcement services of a minor tax collection agency. By his "moral entrepreneurship" (to use Becker's phrase), Anslinger had used misinformation and propaganda to transform his department from a third-rate tax-collection agency into a viable crime-fighting force.[20]

Having achieved both state and federal antimarijuana legislation, the indefatigable Anslinger's next goal was to eliminate marijuana from legitimate medical practice, despite the clear stand of the American Medical Association approving its use. He was successful. By 1964 only seven persons remained registered under the Marijuana Tax Act for permission to use the drug in research or analysis.[21] Various forms of harassment had made researchers and doctors avoid the suspicious eye of the authorities.

Unlike some controversial drugs, marijuana has been thoroughly studied. Writers who report that "little is known about the psychological and physiological effects of marijuana" are simply revealing their ignorance of the contents of libraries. In addition to hundreds of papers on the subject, five major investigations have been made regarding the nature of marijuana. They are represented by

The Indian Hemp Drugs Commission Report (1894)
The Panama Canal Zone Military Investigations (1916–1929)
The LaGuardia Committee Report (1933–1944)
The Baroness Wootton Report (1968)
The Canadian government's *LeDain Commission Report* (1970)

All five investigating bodies are in substantial agreement on all major points of substance. Among the more important facts to be found in these exhaustive investigations are these:

> Marijuana is not a narcotic.
> Marijuana has no lasting physiological effect on the body or mind, and no deaths have been reported due to its use.
> Marijuana use is not a stepping-stone to heroin addiction.
> For adolescents, especially those of passive-dependent personality type, there is the danger of psychic dependence.
> Marijuana use gives rise to "reverse-tolerance," that is, habitual users report a lesser quantity is needed to achieve a "high."
> In essence, marijuana is a mildly intoxicating drug, best taken in confortable surroundings when one is in a recreational mood.

In summary, we have conflicting attitudes in American society concerning marijuana use. There can be no doubt that the use of marijuana has increased and that it is here to stay as part of the American scene. Yet despite a growing tolerance on the part of the general public, marijuana arrests rose from 18,185 in 1965 to 416,100 in 1975.[22] As to what the future holds, the college students of today will be the state legislators of tomorrow, and it may well be that they will concur with the reasoning of the Alaska Supreme Court when it ruled that smoking marijuana in the privacy of one's home should not be a crime:

> The right of privacy, the court said, is more precious than the marijuana prohibition, and what the marijuana smoker does in the privacy of his home is none of the state's business as long as no other person is harmed.[23]

Amphetamines

The long-distance "over the road" truck driver who wants to drive through the night, the weary overweight housewife who wants to drop a few pounds, the college student who is trying to cram an entire semester's learning into one night, the athlete who wants to bring an extra burst of energy to his body, and the immature teen-ager who "will try anything once"—are all susceptible to the lure of amphetamines or "uppers."

Amphetamine, first synthesized in 1887, was first used medically around 1930 to treat narcolepsy, a rare disorder characterized by an uncontrollable desire for sleep. The drug was marketed in 1932 under the trade name Benzedrine. Taken orally, it produces wakefulness and alertness; depresses appetite by lessening the sense of taste and smell; creates a sense of euphoria; and increases powers of concentration, motor activity, and speech activity.[24] Commercially, amphetamines are sold under the trade names of Benzedrine, Dexedrine, Methedrine, Desbutal, Desoxyn, and Dexamyl.

The body can acquire astonishing tolerance for amphetamine, so that users can take it at astronomical levels. A prescribed dose of amphetamine might be between 2.5 and 15 milligrams per day. "Speed freaks" have reported injecting as much as 1,000 milligrams every two or three hours.[25]

During World War II, the American, British, German, and Japanese armies used amphetamines to counteract fatigue. Today, medical uses of amphetamine have been limited to psychotherapy, where they are used to make a patient more talkative, for appetite control, in the treatment of obesity, in the treatment of narcolepsy, and to control hyperactivity in children.

Prolonged use of the drug is followed by depression. As one coed told this writer, "The higher up you go, and the longer you stay, the harder you fall." Despite the popular antidrug slogan that "Speed kills," death from amphetamine overdose is a rarity. Based on experiments with monkeys, a lethal dose would be somewhere above 800 milligrams in a 150-pound man. Amphetamines are dangerous for persons with a history of heart trouble.[26]

Simply because the lethal dosage is high, one should not underestimate the grave implications of using these drugs. As Brecher writes: "The intravenous injection of large doses of amphetamines . . . is among the most disastrous forms of drug use yet devised."[27] Misinformation about the nature and effects of marijuana use led to a skepticism on the part of many youths that the "establishment" could not be trusted to tell the truth about any drug. Warnings about the possible toxic effects of amphetamines—if not dismissed as propaganda—merely served to advertise them and whet the appetities of the curious.

Not all users of amphetamines escalate their dosage, but many do and eventually learn to gulp whole handfuls of tablets. Why one person will stay within tolerable limits and another react to amphetamine as "the pearl of great price" is a problem of personality theory. One explanation is that for the person with a poor-self image, the instant relief from these negative feelings provides the incentive to continue using the drug. For this individual, a sense of confidence is only a few pills away.

A particularly dangerous form of amphetamine abuse is the practice of injecting Methedrine (methamphetamine) intravenously. As it flows immediately into the bloodstream, the drug produces its unique euphoria (called a rush or flash) almost instantaneously. Methedrine users compare this reaction to a sexual orgasm. The drug also acts to delay sexual orgasm itself.[28]

Long-term amphetamine and/or Methedrine abuse results in a paranoid psychosis. Users report feeling that "people are out to get them," delusions of omnipotence, and hallucinations. "Speed freaks" often have open, running sores as a result of scratching imaginary "crank bugs." Under the influence of these drugs (when they are "wired"), speed freaks do bizarre things which alienate them even from the other types of drug users. Often the speed freak becomes an "outcast in a society of outcasts."[29]

Amphetamine addiction is difficult—in fact, nearly impossible—to break. Forced abstinence either through a prison sentence, civil commitment, or admission to a mental hospital can interrupt drug use, but the relapse rate is very high.

In order to control the sale and possible abuse of amphetamines, quotas were established in 1972. At that time there were approximately 100 manufacturers marketing the product; by 1975 this number had dwindled to fewer than 40, the other companies having found that the quantity allocated to them made it unprofitable to remain in this line of business. To counteract this decline in legitimate production, illicit "speed laboratories" or "bathtub labs" have sprung up, some capable of producing as much as 1,125,000 ten-milligram doses each week.

The drug scene seems to have something for everyone, and for those whose tastes do not incline them to "uppers," their very opposite—"downers," or barbiturates—are available.

Barbiturates

Julian is middle aged, college educated, and unemployed. He staggers and falls off the bar stool he has occupied for the past hour. He climbs up again, tries to speak to the bartender, and goes to sleep in midsentence. The bartender shakes him awake and tries to get him to eat. The food misses his mouth. He turns to a sailor sitting next to him and says something insulting and stupid. The sailor "decks" him.[30]

This story portrays a man who is a barbiturate addict, though he is capable of poly-drug abuse. Barbiturates are hypnotic and sedative derivaties of barbituric acid (malonylurea). These derivates act to depress the central nervous system, Taken in small doses, they effectively relieve tension and anxiety. In larger doses, they cause drowsiness and sleep.

The first hypnotic barbiturate was issued in 1903 (Veronal). It was followed in 1912 by Luminal, and since then over 2,500 derivatives of barbituric acid have been synthesized.[31] Barbiturates are classified as ultrashort acting and short-, intermediate-, and long-acting. Three of the most widely used (and abused) drugs are of the short-acting and intermediate category. They are sold under the trade names Nembutal, Seconal, and Amytal. At the normal therapeutic dose (100 to 200 milligrams a day), physical dependence does not develop. A lethal (deadly) dose is considered to be between 1,000 and 2,000 milligrams.

Barbiturates are a favorite means of committing suicide. An estimated 3,000 persons, mostly females, choose this method each year. Insomnia may be a symptom of an underlying depression, and doctors may unwittingly prescribe barbiturates for a suicide-prone individual. Persons who escalate to taking barbiturates in large amounts to fall asleep may also require amphetamines in the morning to wake up. Their lives become a drug-induced teeter-totter.

Some barbiturate users mix "barbs" with alcohol for a sedative and relaxing effect. The internally famous author and playwright Tennessee Williams tells in his memoirs of a time in his career when he seemed unable to write and utilized this practice:

> Strong coffee no longer sufficed to get the creative juices to flow. For several weeks I endured this creative sterility, then I started to wash down a Seconal with a martini. And I was "hooked" on that practice. That summer of 1955 in Rome this creative state of abandoment resulted in the film *Baby Doll,* the script of which has a wanton hilarity to it.[32]

Having discussed marijuana, amphetamines, and barbiturates, we now turn to perhaps the greatest challenge in the area of drug abuse: heroin.

Heroin

Heroin is an opium-derivative narcotic. The term "heroin" comes from the German *heroisch,* meaning "powerful." It is a semisynthetic derivative of morphine and was developed in 1898 by the Bayer Company in Germany. When it was discovered that heroin relieved morphine withdrawal symptoms, observers erroneously concluded that they had found a cure for morphine addiction.[33]

Like morphine, heroin can either be sniffed or injected under the skin or into a muscle. For maximum effect, the drug may be injected directly into a vein; often the large vein in the arm is used. This practice is known as "mainlining." Heroin acts on the central nervous system. It relieves pain and produces sedation, sleep, and a tranquilizing effect. It is ironic and especially tragic that heroin and other drugs which were designed to relieve pain and suffering have been the cause of such widespread human misery.

The drug scene upon which heroin appeared could well be called a dope fiend's paradise. Physicians regularly prescribed opiates to patients, drugstores sold opiates over the counter without prescriptions, mail-order houses did a brisk business dispensing drugs, and there were countless patent medicines available which contained liberal doses of opium or morphine.[34]

The social characteristics of the users who sought out this "paradise" were almost the exact opposite of those identifying the typical user of the 1960s and 1970s. The number of women taking various drugs for menstrual and menopausal discomforts were so large that they outnumbered males in the use of narcotics. Users also tended to be older (over forty), in the higher income brackets, and white.

Drug users around the turn of the century lived in a different legal world than do their present-day counterparts. While opiate use was seen as immoral and frowned upon as a vice, the nineteenth-century addict was not forced to hide from the authorities, driven into a deviant addict subculture, arrested, fined, imprisoned, and generally cut off from the world of respectability. Whatever unfortunate consequences resulted from opiate abuse were solely the result of the pharmacological properties of the drug and rather than the outcome of being hounded as a common criminal and suffering the fate of a social outcast.

The popular image of the drug addict in a state of degeneration as a result of drug abuse is misleading. The ravages of a life dedicated to drug taking are principally the result of "ripping and running" to steal the money needed to support an ever-increasing habit. If an addict has to choose between spending money on a nutritious meal or on a "fix," he or she simply goes without proper food. For the addict who is a member of the hard-core drug subculture, life is a desperate attempt to obtain money to feed his or her habit. Addicts are constantly fearful that the effects of the latest "fix" may wear off or that they may be "busted."

If such an addict were hospitalized in hygienic surroundings, given measured doses of the same drug, and put on a proper diet, he or she would be very different from the miserable street addict we so often see.

Thus, in analyzing the effects of heroin drug abuse, we must measure the effects of the drug itself and also take into consideration the lifestyle of the person who is addicted to an illegal substance.

If the drug user's legal milieu could be described as paradise (around the turn of the century), this state of bliss quickly ended with the passage of the Harrison Act (1914), when the user was suddenly consigned to a legal purgatory; today, with the impact of fifty-five additional federal laws affecting the use of drugs, the addict's legal position is like that of one exiled to the inner circles of a Dantean inferno.

The passage of the Harrison Act spelled the end of the moral and medical control of addiction and marked the beginning of the police control of opiates. On its face, the Harrison Act looked like a simple tax act providing for the orderly marketing of opium. It was

> An Act to provide for the registration of, with collectors of internal revenue, and to impose a special tax upon all persons who produce, import, manufacture, compound, deal in, dispense, sell, distribute, or give away opium or coca leaves.[35]

The "catch-22"[36] was the restriction that physicians registered under this act could prescribe opiates in the course of their professional practice only. This provision was interpreted by law enforcement officers to mean that opiates must be a part of a treatment plan which eventuated in making the patient drug free. Any treatment plan which simply sought to ease the addict's "disease" by providing maintenance doses would subject the physician to criminal penalties. The result has been to put a wide gulf between physicians and drug addicts. As one physician confided to this author: "When I took the oath of Hippocrates, I took another: never treat an addict." Thus an ethical and medical problem was transformed into a problem for the police.

Heroin is the principal drug of addiction in the United States. Estimates as to the number of active heroin addicts range from a low of 150,000 nationally to 300,000 in New York City alone. Presently, heroin is utilized mainly by the lower classes; it is generally accepted that over half the heroin addicts in the United States reside in the poverty areas of New York City.[37]

Approaches to the control and treatment of heroin addiction have included (1) jail sentences, (2) hospitalization, (3) therapeutic communities, and (4) methadone maintenance.

The criminal penalties for the trafficking in and use of controlled substances can only be termed Draconian.[38] Indeed, some future historian may well note that the drafters of these laws should be remembered more for the harshness of their punishments than for the wisdom of their laws.

3.02 LEGAL RESPONSE TO DRUG ABUSE

The two principal agencies responsible for enforcing the Controlled Substances Act (CSA) are the Food and Drug Administration (FDA) in the Department of Health, Education, and Welfare and the Drug Enforcement Administration (DEA) in the Department of Justice. The purpose of the CSA is to reduce the quantity of drugs that might become available to persons prone to abuse them.[39]

The CSA provides for nine control mechanisms. These are (1) registration of handlers, (2) record-keeping requirements, (3) quotas on manufacturing, (4) restrictions on distribution, (5) restrictions on dispensing, (6) limitations on imports and exports, (7) conditions for storage of drugs, (8) reports of transactions to the government, and (9) criminal penalties for illicit trafficking. We will now briefly discuss the requirements of each of these control mechanisms.

Each legitimate handler of controlled drugs—importer, manufacturer, wholesaler, hospital, pharmacy, physician, and researcher—must register with the DEA and be assigned a number. Companies that fail to take adequate steps to prevent diversion are handled by administrative hearing and risk being put out of business.

Full records must be kept by each handler of all manufacturing, purchases, sales, and inventories of the controlled substance. There are some exemptions available for researchers and physicians. With these records, it is possible to trace the flow of any drug from its origin to the patient.

The DEA, along with the FDA, sets limits upon the quantity of controlled substances, listed in schedules I and II, which can be produced during any calendar year. The purpose is to reduce gross overproduction of drugs by eliminating marginal manufacturers. This practice, of course, made the government an ally of established pharmaceutical firms in eliminating competition. There is further danger that government estimates may be overly conservative and that there will be an insufficient supply available for medical use,

The distribution of a controlled substance is carefully restricted. From one manufacturer to another, from manufacturer to wholesaler, from importer to wholesaler, and from wholesaler to dispenser, orders of schedule I and II drugs are recorded on special order forms in triplicate. The supplier is held accountable for any drugs which are shipped to a customer who does not have a valid registration.

Restrictions on the dispensing of a controlled substance vary with its place (between I and V) in the schedule classification. Schedule I drugs have no current accepted medical use in treatment in the United States and are used only in research situations. Drugs falling into schedules II, III, and IV require a prescription. Schedule II prescriptions must be written and signed by the physician; they may not be telephoned to the pharmacy. Further, the prescription may not be refilled. Schedule III and IV drugs may be prescribed either in writing or orally, and the patient can have the prescription refilled upon request up to five times within 6 months from the date of the initial prescription. Schedule V drugs are over-the-counter narcotic preparations, such as antitussives and antidiarrheals. The purchaser must be at least eighteen years of age and have his or her name entered into a special log by the pharmacist.

In an effort to control the import and export of narcotics, any international transaction involving a schedule I or II controlled drug must have the permission of the DEA. The exportation of schedule I and II drugs is severely limited and care is taken to ensure that the drugs are going to a country where they will not be reexported.

There are strict requirements for the storage of schedule I and II drugs. Among the security measures required are a specially constructed vault with reinforced concrete walls and steel gate, a 24-hour alarm system, and immediate availability of security guards. These expensive special storage requirements apply only to manufacturers, importers, exporters, and wholesalers who handle controlled substances in large amounts. Neighborhood pharmacies, hospitals, and physicians are not held to these rigid requirements. It should be noted, however, that the epidemic of drugstore holdups by addicts seeking drugs has caused many pharmacies to resemble banks with bulletproof windows, guard dogs, and security guards.

In order to monitor all drugs listed in schedules I and II and all narcotic drugs in schedule III, each manufacturer and wholesaler of any of these drugs must report all manufacturing activities, all importation and exportation, and all distributions to the DEA.

Finally, we come to the criminal penalties for trafficking in and using controlled substances. "Trafficking" is defined as:

> . . . the unauthorized manufacture, the unauthorized distribution (i.e., delivery whether by sale, gift, or otherwise), or the possession for unauthorized manufacture or distribution of any controlled substance.[40]

Federal penalties for violating the restrictions on narcotics in schedules I and II are punishment by up to 15 years in prison and a fine of up to $25,000 for the first offense. Trafficking in or illicit use of a schedule V substance is classified as a misdemeanor punishable by up to a year in prison and a fine of up to $5,000. Laws of the states vary, but generally they carry some of the stiffest penalties imposed by our system of justice.[41]

3.03 THERAPEUTIC COMMUNITIES

Despite enormous amounts of money and effort expended on such medical centers as the National Institute of Mental Health at Lexington, Kentucky, attempts to keep the street addict totally abstinent have failed. Addicted physicians and nurses or patients who have become addicted through careless medication respond well to conventional treatment, but the street addict poses a special problem. One would expect good results from the removal of the physical dependence by gradual withdrawal of drugs, followed by psychiatric treatment; but this approach has not worked. Relapse rates from these centers run as high as 90 percent, and "many of the addicts treated at these excellent medical facilities do not even show the simple respect for their . . . treatment by waiting forty-eight hours after release before taking a shot of heroin."[42]

Therapeutic communities such as Synanon, Phoenix House, Odyssey House, and Daytop Village were conceived as an alternative to conventional medical treatment.

The approach of these various therapeutic communities combines toughness with consideration. The motivation of any new arrival is thoroughly tested in order to screen out all but the highly motivated. The essence of the concept is a community of adults who come together in "tender loving care" to offer each other emotional support as they try to achieve a responsible way of life. Individuals are held responsible for their actions and addiction is seen not so much as a medical problem but as "self-chosen stupidity."

The founders and supporters of these therapeutic communities were highly evangelistic in their enthusiasm for the potential of their creations. Yablonsky said of Synanon: "The first real breakthrough in the history of prisons, from the viewpoint of the prisoner, has come from Synanon." He referred to the concept as a "vital new social movement." Supporters dreamed of the concept being applied to all the various mental health problems, with therapeutic communities being strung across the United States like Holiday Inns. *Time* magazine prematurely reported that the concept was so successful that only 10 percent of the addicts treated at Synanon relapsed.[43] Throughout the 1960s, Synanon was heralded as evidence that heroin addiction is curable. The supposed secret was that "only an ex-addict can cure an addict."

But under the piercing eye of scientific evaluation, the bubble burst. It was extremely difficult to find any abstinent alumni of these programs. One such center, Liberty Park Village in New Jersey, was designed to serve an area containing 4,000 addicts. Despite liberal funding (a budget of over $1½ million per year) and strict adherence to the principles of a therapeutic community, at the end of one year only twenty-two addicts had "graduated" from the program. Only four of these alumni could be located, and they were either on heroin or in jail. The rest had "split."[44]

The most incredible part of the story is the manner in which these communities present an image of success when in fact they are a dismal failure. At any given moment a cadre of twenty or so bright, articulate "ex-addicts" who are doing well at the moment are trotted out to talk eloquently about the benefits of the program.

State officials, Rotarians, sociology classes, and the like would go away with the warm feeling that the answer to one of America's most pressing social problems had been found. But the "success" statistics issued by these therapeutic communities refer almost entirely to the continuing community members—those who have become professional ex-addicts and remain in some administrative capacity with the centers. Therapeutic communities achieve a temporary success with addicts in residence, but their record when addicts return to the community is no better than that of public hospitals.

3.04 METHADONE MAINTENANCE

An alternative to programs which define "rehabilitation" as leading a drug-free life are those which treat heroin addiction as a metabolic disease and seek to stabilize the addict with a drug which acts as an antagonist to heroin.

Research using methadone—a dependency-inducing morphinelike analgesic—was begun in 1964 by Dr. Vincent Dole and Dr. Marie Nyswander at Rockefeller University in New York. Methadone works on the same brain centers as heroin and involves a cross-tolerance. Drs. Dole and Nyswander have utilized the drug to stabilize the life of the addict.

Heroin addicts are functionally disabled. They live on a seesaw or elavator. At one end, they are "high" or euphoric—sedated, tranquilized, absorbed in themselves, and completely irresponsible. At the other extreme, when they are "strung out" (sick), they become desperate in their need for drugs. Their symptoms are nausea, perspiration, tremors, and cramps. Their lives oscillate between "high" and "strung out," with little time to lead a normal existence.

During the first 6 weeks of a methadone maintenance program, the patients get a medical work-up, are withdrawn from heroin, and receive methadone in increasing doses until they are stabilized. After tolerance to the medication has been established, the dose (from 80 to 120 milligrams per day) can be held constant, without escalation or euphoria, for years.

When methadone is administered in this fashion, the patient does not experience euphoria and, because of the cross-blockage effect, cannot get high if he or she shoots heroin.

The second phase of the program lasts about a year, patients come to the clinic to drink their methadone (given in a glass of Tang to preclude injection) and leave urine specimens, which are checked to determine whether other drugs are being injected. In the final phase, patients become functioning, self-supporting members of the community and may pick up their supply of methadone for a week at a time. If abuses occur, they are most likely to do so at this stage of treatment.

Methadone is not a cure for addiction but a stabilizing agent. It is seen as a normalizer rather than a narcotic; its use is comparable to that of insulin for the diabetic, digitalis for the patient with heart disease, or cortisone for the arthritic. Critics of the methadone program compare the switch from heroin to methadone to an alcoholic's switch from scotch to bourbon. This is a false analogy, for an alcoholic who is given a shot of whiskey of any sort will be disabled.

From the point of view of criminology, the success or failure of drug treatment programs must be gauged in terms of their impact on the criminal involvement of the participants. By 1971, some 37,500 patients were receiving care in methadone maintenance programs. A follow-up study of 17,500 patients (1964 to 1971) revealed that

> . . . patients who volunteer for methadone maintenance and remain under treatment show a marked decrease in antisocial behavior as measured by arrests.[45]

Relaxation of admission criteria has led to an increase in the proportion of patients with problems of multiple-drug abuse and a corresponding increase in abuses and attempted abuses within the programs.

Methadone is not a panacea for the ills of the drug problem. No drug can give a person values or instill habits of industry and honesty where none existed before. What methadone does accomplish is to take the addict off a not-so-merry-go-round of being sick, high, or in jail, so that genuine rehabilitation can take place.

The criminal justice system spends more time arresting, jailing, and sobering up drunks than it does on any other non-traffic law enforcement activity.

What becomes apparent in all treatment for addicts is that whatever the approach—be it hospitalization, therapeutic community, or methadone maintenance—those addicts with the most stable social histories respond best, while the hard-core members of the addict-criminal subculture remain obstinately resistant to change.

3.05 ALCOHOLISM

Over 9 million Americans are alcoholics. As a sociomedical problem, alcoholism ranks third, surpassed only by heart disease and cancer in the number of lives disabled.[46] This figure of 9 million alcoholics is a conservative estimate, for many persons are not aware they are alcoholics, would vehemently deny it, and would be insulted if a physician were to diagnose them as such.

Some idea of the extent of the problem may be gained by noting that America has over ten times as many alcoholics as there are persons confined in all our jails, penitentiaries, and mental hospitals combined. The absolute number of alcoholics in America has more than doubled since 1960, when Keller, using the Jellinek estimation formula, estimated the number of alcoholics to be 4,470,000.[47]

There are more arrests for drunkenness than for any other nontraffic offense—1,217,000 in 1975.[48] When we add the total for alcohol-related offenses—driving under the influence, liquor law violations, and disorderly conduct—the figure reaches an astronomical 3,252,600 arrests in 1975. This does not include the number of family disturbance calls, homicides, rapes, and assaults that are alcohol-related. Considering its profound effect on human behavior, what is the nature of this substance?

Pharmacology of Alcohol

Alcohol is a drug. To a chemist, the label "alcohol" is a generic term referring to a whole family of related chemical substances; but to the drinker it implies one particular alcohol: ethyl alcohol. The World Health Organization has held that ethyl alcohol is a compound whose pharmacologic action is somewhere between that of addictive drugs (heroin) and habit-forming ones (nicotine). As a drug, ethyl alcohol may be bought without prescription and used to alter behavior without medical supervision. The amount users can buy is limited only by their pocketbooks.

The chief effects of alcohol are on the central nervous system and the brain. They are impairment of vision (seeing double), muscular incoordination, lengthened reaction time, euphoria, and removal of inhibitions. If a research scientist were determined to discover a substance that would undermine every skill necessary for safe driving, it would be difficult to find a better one than ethyl alcohol.

The Alcoholic Syndrome

An alcoholic may be defined as one whose drinking interferes with any compartment of his or her life. Thus, if a person looks around and discovers, as a result of his or her drinking, reduced work efficiency, marital dysharmony, impaired health, or disturbed social relations, he or she may be classified as an alcoholic.

Two key words in the understanding of alcoholism are "progression" and "insidious." The nature of alcoholism is such that it proceeds inconspicuously but with grave effect; as the ancients noted, "at last it biteth like an adder."[49]

It is difficult to draw a line and say at what point one ceases to be a controlled social drinker and moves to that obsessive compulsion we call alcoholism. Navigators charting the flight of planes from Hawaii to the mainland notify the captain when they have reached the "point of no return," which means that the plane is closer to the mainland than to the point of origin. Similarly, somewhere along the line, those who are alcoholics of the "gamma" type, the most common pattern in the United States, reach a point of no return. Once they begin drinking, they experience the phenomenon of craving and loss of control.

If we could take a full-blown alcoholic and run his or her life backwards, as a movie reel can be rerun, we could see the developmental stages clearly. In the prealcoholic phase, some of the danger signals are blackouts, or alcohol-induced amnesia, and excessive rationalizations about drinking. In the early stages of alcoholism, there is a loss of control, and the alcoholic begins to sneak drinks. The "morning drink" is considered one sure sign that trouble lies ahead. It should be emphasized, however, that alcoholics do not pass through a predetermined course, and these progressions apply only generally. We have no hard data on the number of persons who experience these symptoms and then gain control of their drinking versus those who continue headlong to full-blown alcoholism.[50]

Late-stage alcoholism is marked by drinking bouts, social collapse, and finally tremors, hallucinations, and—barring some interdiction—death.

Social Correlates of Drinking

Men are more likely to be heavy drinkers than women, and the ratio of male alcoholics to their female counterparts is estimated to be about 5 to 1. Bailey and coworkers, however, put the ratio of men to women in urban areas at 3.6 to 1.[51] Alcoholism has traditionally been a disorder of middle to later life, with male admissions to psychiatric facilities for alcoholism having the heaviest incidence between ages thirty-five and sixty-four.[52] However, school authorities report a trend away from the phenomena of the 1960s—i.e., experimentation with exotic drugs—to the use of a more familiar drug, alcohol, by young persons. This trend toward increased teen-age drinking may lower the age of the model alcoholic.[53]

Blacks and whites have proportionately about the same percentage of drinkers, but blacks experience more difficulties as a result of drinking. The alcoholism rate for blacks is from two to four times that of whites.[54]

Rates of alcoholism and problem drinking show up dramatically in the differences in group rates when charted by ethnicity. As one Irishman put it, "You don't have to be an Irishman to be an alcoholic, but it helps." The incidence of alcoholic problems among Irish-Americans runs two to three times higher than it does in any other ethnic group in America.[55] By contrast, approximately 90 percent of Jews "take a drink," yet they consistently have the lowest alcoholism rate of any major American ethnic group. One explanation for these differences in rates of alcoholism among various ethnic groups lies in the different cultural meaning drinking has for these groups. The Irish are motivated to drink for the sake of conviviality, and—under certain circumstances—drunkenness is highly valued among them. By contrast, Jews learn to drink in a controlled manner and to associate wine with religious observances.[56]

The percentage of drinkers increases as socioeconomic status increases. However, rates of heavy drinking, escape drinking, and problem drinking are highest among the lower socioeconomic groupings. The lower classes are more likely to drink to escape, while the upper classes tend to drink for recreational and social reasons. Alcoholism, however, is no respecter of persons, and alcoholics are found in all social classes.

As density of population increases, so does the percentages of drinkers in the area. The heavy drinking patterns associated with urban living have been attributed to the stresses of city life. Of more importance however, are the demographic profiles of urban areas. Cities contain a larger proportion of those social groups—lower-status men, Irish Catholics, Latin Americans, and blacks—who tend to drink heavily.[57]

Sociocultural factors tend to be additive. In the United States, the person most likely to be a drinker would be Catholic, college-educated male, thirty-one to thirty-five years of age, who is living in an urban area. The person most likely to be an abstainer would be a female with a grade school education, over age sixty-one, who lives on a farm and regularly attends the Methodist church.

Theories of Alcoholism

Research into the causes of alcoholism has proceeded along three lines: biological, psychological, and sociological. Biologists have hypothesized that alcoholics have a unique metabolic makeup and suffer from certain nutritional deficiencies. To date, no data have been presented which show conclusively whether these deficiencies in confirmed alcoholics preceded and caused their disorder or resulted from their long-term habit of drinking their lunch. Psychologists have searched for a "prealcoholic personality," but it appears that persons of varying personality types go on to lose control of their drinking. Sociologically, alcoholism rates are higher in those groups which do not provide strong sanctions against heavy drinking.

Treatment for alcoholism has been attempted by traditional psychiatric "talk therapy," aversive drug therapies, and Alcoholics Anonymous. Psychiatrists have reported little success in treating alcoholics; the use of drug therapies has met with some success; AA appears to have done the best job with those whose lives have become unmanageable because of alcohol.

Legal Response to Alcoholism

The principal approach to the problem of drinking and drunkenness in the United States has been a punitive legal response. The criminal justice system of the United States spends more time arresting, jailing, and sobering up drunks than it does on any other nontraffic law enforcement activity. Public drunkenness, vagrancy, and related criminal arrests account for almost 40 percent of the total nontraffic arrests in this country. This has been a consistent pattern for many years.

Ross located ten men who served more than 90 years behind bars and had been arrested a total of 1,023 times, at a total cost to the taxpayers of $300,000. These men were not hardened criminals but skid-row drunks to whom life was a revolving door between the jail and the closest barroom. The futility of this approach is personified by the thoughtful wino who, upon release from jail, would leave his false teeth with the jailer, knowing he would be back. In big-city "drunk courts," it is not unusual to watch a judge mete out "justice" to sixty drunks in 45 minutes.[58] The legal problems associated with alcoholism are covered in Chapter 11.

3.06 PROSTITUTION

The greatest task for morality and law is the control of sex and aggression. The French dramatist Pierre Beaumarchais (1732–1799) observed that the human being differs from the animal in eating without being hungry, drinking without being thirsty, and making love at all seasons.

The "oldest profession" is comparatively young according to Durant. It appears with the concept of property and the disappearance of premarital freedom. In its earliest form, we see it practiced as a method for helping a frugal girl to raise a dowry or for providing monies for the maintenance of temples.[59]

Herodotus (484–425 B.C.) noted that the Babylonians obliged every native woman, once in her life, to sit in the temple of Venus and have intercourse with a stranger. Those whom nature had endowed with beauty found their religious obligations swiftly and enthusiastically fulfilled, but the deformed and homely were known to have extended vigils.[60]

The idea that prostitution is inevitable and should be regulated by the state is at least 2,700 years old. The Assyrians utilized this method, and in India, around 300 B.C., there was appointed a superintendent of prostitution who looked after public women, controlled their fees and expenses, and appropriated their earning for 2 days each month. The concept of rules importing prostitutes for entertainment and intelligence service dates back to this time.[61]

During the time of Marco Polo (1254–1324), the Chinese made no effort to maintain chastity in single men. Rather, it was considered normal that a healthy youth should visit brothels. Sex was viewed as an appetite, like hunger, that should be regulated only by one's sense of moderation. Virginity and chastity have for centuries been virtues which men prized in women without making strenuous efforts to impose it on themselves.[62]

The Japanese of this period agreed with the Chinese that the desires of the flesh were best looked upon as natural, and thousands of men—including many respectable married men—crowded the Flower District of Tokyo.

> There in the most orderly disorderly houses in the world, fifteen thousand trained and licensed courtesans sat of an evening behind their lattices, gorgeously attired and powder-white, ready to provide song, dance and venery for unmated or ill-mated men.[63]

The Greek lawgiver Solon (ca. 638–558 B.C.), whose name is synonomous with legal wisdom, legalized and taxed prostitution, established public brothels, and even erected a temple to Aphrodite Pandemos (the Goddess of Love) from the revenues. Prostitutes, like priests and professors, have always been ranked. The highest class of Greek courtesans was composed of the *hetaerae,* which literally means "companions." Like the Japanese *geishas,* they mixed promiscuity with poetry and literature with love; but being businesswomen, they regulated their lovers by an hourglass.[64]

The Roman Emperor Caligula (A.D. 12–41) levied a tax on the earning of prostitutes equal to the amount each received for one "embrace." But with characteristic intemperance, Caligula had the law provide that those who left the profession to enter marriage would nevertheless remain subject to this tax forever after.[65]

The Romans, condoning the resort of men to prostitutes, legalized and restricted the profession. Brothels were kept closed during the day and were maintained outside the city walls. Prostitutes were registered and required to wear the toga instead of the stola. (The toga signified professional status rather than life as a married woman.)

With the rise in power of the Christian Church, a single standard of morality was demanded. The result was the beginning of the war between law and morality on the one hand and a recalcitrant human nature on the other.

> Paganism had tolerated the prostitute as a necessary mitigation of an arduous monogamy; the Church denounced prostitution without compromise, and demanded a single standard of fidelity for both sexes in marriage. She did not quite succeed; she raised the morals of the home, but prostitution remained, driven into stealth and degradation.[66]

Kingsley Davis argues that prostitution is condemned in contemporary industrial societies because it fulfills no recognized goal. He sees the moral condemnation rising, not so much from the selling of sexual favors in an attitude of emotional indifference, but from the prostitutes' promiscuity in unstable relationships.[67]

There is evidence that a change is taking place in the attitude of Americans toward prostitution. This attitudinal change is the result of efforts on the part of the women's rights movement, the contemporary legal emphasis on the right to personal privacy, and the tendency among many prosecutors to restrict the prosecution of victimless crimes.[68]

Presently, thirty-eight states outlaw prostitution by forbidding the performance of sexual acts for pay. Forty-four states and the District of Columbia have laws that make solicitation illegal. In six states—Iowa, Michigan, Missouri, Montana, parts of Nevada, and Rhode Island—solicitation is illegal but prostitution itself is not. The mere status of being a prostitute is a crime under vagrancy laws in Washington, Montana, New Hampshire, Nebraska, Oklahoma, and Texas.[69]

Prostitutes change with the times, and sex for pay can be found in most large cities from bar girls, call girls, the "hostesses" of massage parlors, "encounter group" members, and occasionally housewives supplementing budgets strained by inflation. Estimates of the number of full-time prostitutes in the United States range from 250,000 to 500,000.[70]

Prostitution and the Law

Why should society punish a transaction between a willing buyer and a willing seller? In the case of prostitution, it is not so much a sale as it is renting. As the sailor exclaimed when a hooker announced her price: "Honey, I don't want to buy it, just rent it for awhile." If a woman wishes to rent out her body, and since it is obviously *her* body, what interest does the state have in it—and what right to deny her this fee-for-service entrepreneurship?

At least four major objections are advanced to the decriminalization of prostitution: (1) it is offensive to all womankind; (2) it is a health hazard, spreading venereal disease; (3) the state should not allow a degrading vice to become appealing; and (4) the state has an obligation to protect its citizens even from self-chosen harm.[71]

One of the principles guiding the criminalization of acts is that there must be measurable external harm. There can be no doubt that the sight or thought of women renting themselves sexually is offensive to some other women. This psychic pain is a secondary one, however; for they are not directly affected, as in a robbery. If we admit the principle that there is a legitimate basis for criminal penalties when one segment of society is offended by the consenual acts of another segment, we open the door to the criminalization of almost anything. Everyone is offended by something. The present writer has never been thrilled to hear girls popping gum, but banishment to a penitentiary does not seem the appropriate response.

Although one may be reluctant to admit the principle that "secondary psychic pain" is a sound basis for criminalization, this does not mean that citizens should go unfettered with regard to what they may do with their bodies. Taken to a logical extreme, such a position might allow us to sell ourselves into slavery. Private acts often have public consequences.

It is somewhat ironic that the women who are most vocal about a woman's right to do as she pleases with an unborn fetus are outraged by the suggestion that women also have the right to do as they please with their sexual lives. Discussions of prostitution and abortion make strange bedpersons.

A good Marxist would be quick to point out that it is usually poor women who are forced to gain employment by becoming prostitutes. To a Marxist, prostitution is a clear example of the exploitation of the working classes by an unfeeling ruling class. The law punishes the poor vendor and excuses the rich purchaser. Their solution, of course, is to eliminate private property and usher in the workers' paradise.[72] Yet, prostitutes are easily spotted around the Astoria Hotel in Leningrad, for they affect the most stylish clothes, impressive coiffures, and best dentures.

Not all prostitutes seem so "exploited." At least one, calling herself the "happy hooker," received $100,000 advance for her sexual autobiography. (Considerably more than professors of criminal justice get for their insights.) No one seems to have topped the popular courtesan in Ptolematic days (the third century B.C.) who was reputed to have built a pyramid with her savings.[73]

In our own country, John Humphrey Noyes would have a different solution: eliminate private sexual property so that no one could "own" the sexual rights of another; in such a sexually liberated community, prostitution could not exist. Noyes's experiment, the Oneida Community, disappeared with his death, but the silverware which bears its name remains as a reminder of the colony.

While women may be offended by the fact that their sisters rent their bodies, it is not unknown for an attractive woman to agree to marry an older man who can provide security and prestige if not romantic attraction. This exchange, sanctioned by the state (though not by romantic poets), involves a long-term exchange between a woman marketing her beauty and sexual favors and an enthusiastic buyer.

It may not be a perfect analogy, but it brings to mind the story of the man who offered a "respectable" woman $100,000 to go to bed with him. She mused a moment and accepted. He then tendered a counteroffer of $1. Indignant, she protested: "What kind of a girl do you think I am?" "Madam," he replied, "We have established what you are; we are now merely haggling over the price."

It is impossible to know exactly how much venereal disease is spread by prostitutes, but if the Nevada experience is typical, it does not appear to be a great deal. In some areas, venereal disease actually declined with the legalization of prostitution. The earliest known regulation of venereal disease was an act of Parliament in 1161 which forbade the brothel keepers to keep women suffering from the "perilous infirmity of burning."[74]

Legalized prostitution—with the threat of criminal penalties removed—would perhaps make the occupation more attractive. It is difficult to say whether this would lead to the recruitment of girls into a profession which they would ordinarily find repugnant. There remain strong informal sanctions against promiscuity among women, let alone prostitution. Indeed, at least one observer feels it is this very loss of status that fixes the price of prostitution. The woman is paid for her loss of social standing more than for the "work" she performs.[75]

Under the doctrine of *parens patriae,* the state is the ultimate parent of all. Just as parents do not allow their children to play in the traffic, eat dirt, or quit school in the first grade, so the state has an obligation to protect its citizens from self-chosen harm. Thus, even if a woman is willing to sacrifice her social standing, the state "resists for her."

The central issue, however, is this: Can we reasonably expect to eradicate consensual sexual crimes through criminal penalties? Louis IX, in 1254, decreed the banishment of all prostitutes from France, and all he appeared to accomplish was to drive the practice underground.[76] Four hundred years later, Louis XIV decreed that all prostitutes found with soldiers within 5 miles of Versailles should have their noses and ears cut off.[77] Despite these Draconian measures, prostitution, like Christianity, survived persecution, and recently a group of unhappy hookers organized and actually staged a strike outside French churches.

The British, always sticklers for decorum, have taken a slightly different approach. The English make *solicitation* a crime. The idea is that if prostitution cannot be eliminated, it can at least be made less visible. The British, perhaps more careful students of history than we, seem more interested in discretion than prohibition. Thus, British prostitutes carry unobtrusive business cards.

In the United States we have various tactics for suppressing prostitution: policewomen pose as prostitutes and vice-squad members engage in various undercover operations, The strategies employed seem, at times, more shabby and repugnant than the practices they seek to control. Madam Nhu, the famed Dragon Lady of Vietnam and a devout Catholic, conceived of a most severe response to prostitution. Any man caught with a prostitute would be held in jail until his wife bailed him out. Surely, our Eighth Amendment provision against cruel and unusual punishment would preclude this measure.

Finally, the life of a prostitute is not always happy. Xaviera Hollander's autobiography notwithstanding, prostitutes make up less than three-tenths of 1 percent of the national population, yet they account for 15 percent of all suicides brought to public hospitals.[78] Most of their earnings are ripped off by parasitic pimps. A girl making $800 in a 5-day work week may get to keep only $100. Prostitutes risk being arrested and being beaten either by their pimps or by sadistic customers. The famed "Minnesota Strip" in New York (so called because women from Minnesota migrated here to avoid stringent antiprostitution laws) has been the scene of brutal murders of young (fifteen-year old) girls. Where there is prostitution, hotel burglaries increase, and prostitution also seems to be related to drug abuse.[79]

3.07 HOMOSEXUALITY

Probably no form of sexual deviance (with the possible exception of child molesting) arouses such strongly negative responses as does homosexuality. While prostitution breaks the rules, it is considered natural since it involves a man and a woman. But sexual activity between members of the same sex is seen as being "against nature." Western civilization, probably due to its Judeo-Christian heritage, has viewed homosexuality as especially degenerate, repulsive, and depraved. During the medieval period, the homosexual was believed to be possessed by devils. Today, in the minds of many, homosexuality is a sickness in which the choice of sex object affects every other aspect of life negatively. The homosexual is suspect at best and a repulsive degenerate at worst; in the legal codes of every state except two, he or she is also a criminal.

Many ancient societies, including Greece, accepted and promoted homosexuality. It was felt that men, as moral and intellectual equals, could more readily understand and admire each other than partners of opposite sexes would be able to do so. Women, who were held to be inferior to men, had no place in this elite company. The good life for the fortunate male involved both a wife, who would tend to practical matters while producing his children, and a young man whom he could love.

The Puritan attitude toward homosexuality was translated into moralistic English common law and became the basis of laws regarding homosexuality in the United States. Conviction for homosexual behavior carries the threat of life imprisonment in five states, 20 years in thirteen states, and between 10 and 15 years in another twenty states. A 1969 Harris poll revealed that 63 percent of the American people considered homosexuals harmful to American life. In the Netherlands, by contrast, homosexuality between consenting adults has not been a crime for 160 years.[80]

SUMMARY

In this chapter we have reviewed some of the activities that are called victimless crimes. Drug addicts in America have had their milieu changed from a legal paradise to one in which they are hounded and hunted. Marijuana has become increasingly popular, and concomitantly, there has been a steady rise in the number of marijuana arrests. Some states have begun to decriminalize the substance that Anslinger had called the "lethal weed"; and when the college students of today become the legislators of tomorrow, marijuana will undoubtedly become legal. Heroin remains the principal drug of addiction in the United States.

There are an estimated 9 million alcoholics in the United States and as much as 40 percent of police time is spent arresting, booking, and processing them. Prostitution remains a hardy institution, surviving centuries of attempts to eradicate it. Homosexuality remains relatively constant, and gambling is ever with us. Overall, the number of arrests for victimless crimes is falling slowly, but they still take up an inordinate amount of police energy as law enforcement tries valiantly to come between willing buyers and willing sellers. As one mayor of New Orleans is reputed to have said: "You can make prostitution illegal, but you can't make it unpopular." Durant reminds us that human vices are as old as man:

> History offers some consolation by reminding us that sin has flourished in every age. Even our generation has not yet rivaled the popularity of homosexualism in ancient Greece or Rome or Renaissance Italy. "The humanists wrote about it

with a kind of scholarly affection, and Ariosto judged that they were all addicted to it." Aretino asked the Duke of Mantua to send him an attractive boy. Prostitution has been perennial and universal, from the state-regulated brothels of Assyria to the "night clubs" of West-European and American cities of today. In the University of Wittenberg in 1544, according to Luther, "the race of girls is getting bold, and run after the fellows into their rooms and chambers and wherever they can, and offer them their free love." Montaigne tells us that in his time (1533–92) obscene literature found a ready market; the immorality of our stage differs in kind rather than degree from that of Restoration England; and John Cleland's *Memoirs of a Woman of Pleasure*—a veritable catena of coitus—was as popular in 1749 as in 1965. We have noted the discovery of dice in the excavations near the site of Nineveh; men and women have gambled in every age. In every age men have been dishonest and governments have been corrupt; probably less now than generally before. The pamphlet literature of sixteenth-century Europe "groaned with denunciations of wholesale adulteration of food and other products." Man has never reconciled himself to the Ten Commandments.[82]

Chapter 4*

Organized Crime: Business as Usual

If you have a lot of what people want and can't get, then you can supply the demand and shovel in the dough. In other words, that's what we ought to do with whiskey—get plenty of it, good uncut stuff right off the boat and then sell it at a high price to a bunch of people who don't have brains enough not to drink it.[1]
—"Lansky's Law:" advice from Meyer Lansky to Lucky Luciano on the eve of Prohibition.

Deal with the government and the rest of the squawkers the way you deal with a buyer in a seller's market. If the buyer wants to buy, he has to meet your prices. Nineteen hundred and twenty-nine to nineteen hundred and forty-two was the buyer's market—we had to sell on their terms. When the war [World War II] is over, it will be a buyer's market again. But this is a seller's market. They want what we've got. Good! Make them pay the right price for it.[2]
—Statement made at a meeting of the National Association of Manufacturers during World War II.

On March 4, 1974, Clarence M. Kelley, Director of the FBI, made an address before the Inland Daily Press Association in which he recited a litany of evils ascribed to "silent societies [which] have built and operated their illicit enterprises—gambling, loan-sharking, concocting stock swindles, peddling stolen goods, pandering women."[3] The remarks by Director Kelley do not seem to represent mind-blowing revela-

* *Henry W. Mannle, Criminal Justice Program, Tennessee Technological University.*

tions concerning heretofore unimagined phenomena. What may be significant about this address is that the "cry of wolf" was soothingly balanced with an admonition that "the war against organized crime not only can be won, but *is* being won."[4] Such optimism has come less than a decade following the work of the President's Commission on Law Enforcement and the Administration of Justice, published in *Task Force Report: Organized Crime.* This document, notwithstanding some hope on the part of the commission, generally reflected an attitude of pessimism.[5] However, to argue the merits of the stated accomplishments in the fight against "silent societies" may be about as enlightening as reevaluating the efficacy of strategies employed by civil authorities during the fictitious invasion of the New York metropolitan area by "Martians" in 1938.[6] Specifically, the student of crime may find it more intellectually productive to ignore, for the moment, those exciting episodes of Elliot Ness, the "conclusions" of the Kefauver hearings, the widely touted testimony of Joe Valachi, and —instead—reflexively consider some very basic, unresolved questions concerning "organized crime."

While alternative ideas have surfaced, the prevailing notions about the nature of organized crime (found in academic sources, law enforcement circles, and journalistic accounts) are highlighted by the *Task Force Report: Organized Crime* of 1967.

> Organized crime is a society that seeks to operate outside the control of the American people and their governments. It involves thousands of criminals, working within structures as complex as those of any large corporation, subject to laws more rigidly enforced than those of legitimate governments. Its actions are not impulsive but rather the result of intricate conspiracies, carried on over many years and aimed at gaining control over whole fields of activity in order to amass huge profits.[7]

Solutions to this problem, as identified above, range from the creation of new laws and centralized data banks (for gathering information on this "sinister force") to the recommendation that newspapers appoint qualified journalists to continually expose the "intricate conspiracies" of mobsters or, more in line with current concepts, the "Mafia."[8]

Such conventional wisdom forms the basis of much of our thought and action toward organized crime in that it is frequently and uncritically employed as a documented reality upon which to build an analysis of the problem.[9] Perhaps it is not a mere coincidence that a rather high level of consensus is accorded a paradigm that is propagated by official government sources. One of the few and more recent attempts to take the Task Force definition to task is found in the work of Frederick Homer.[10] Accordingly, a paramount concern of Homer's is that the task force approach represents a conclusive statement having the tendency to advance hypotheses and research restricted to post hoc speculation.[11]

The current conceptualizations about organized crime further limit our scholarly horizons by promoting ethical biases that inhibit objective research. More specifically, the thread that seems to bind together most of the literature on organized crime is one which holds that the phenomenon is inherently and independently (from other social forces) pathological, i.e., evil events arising from the behavior of evil people who have no redeeming qualities. A more objective inquiry aimed toward a balanced appraisal of the matter would be one that begins by assuming that organized crime, although deplorable at times, is a normal product of certain socioeconomic environments. By proceeding in this manner, one may be favorably disposed to seek explanations which are more substantive than the notion that "Organized crime is the product of a self-perpetuating criminal conspiracy."[12]

Rather than accept, in a carte blanche fash-

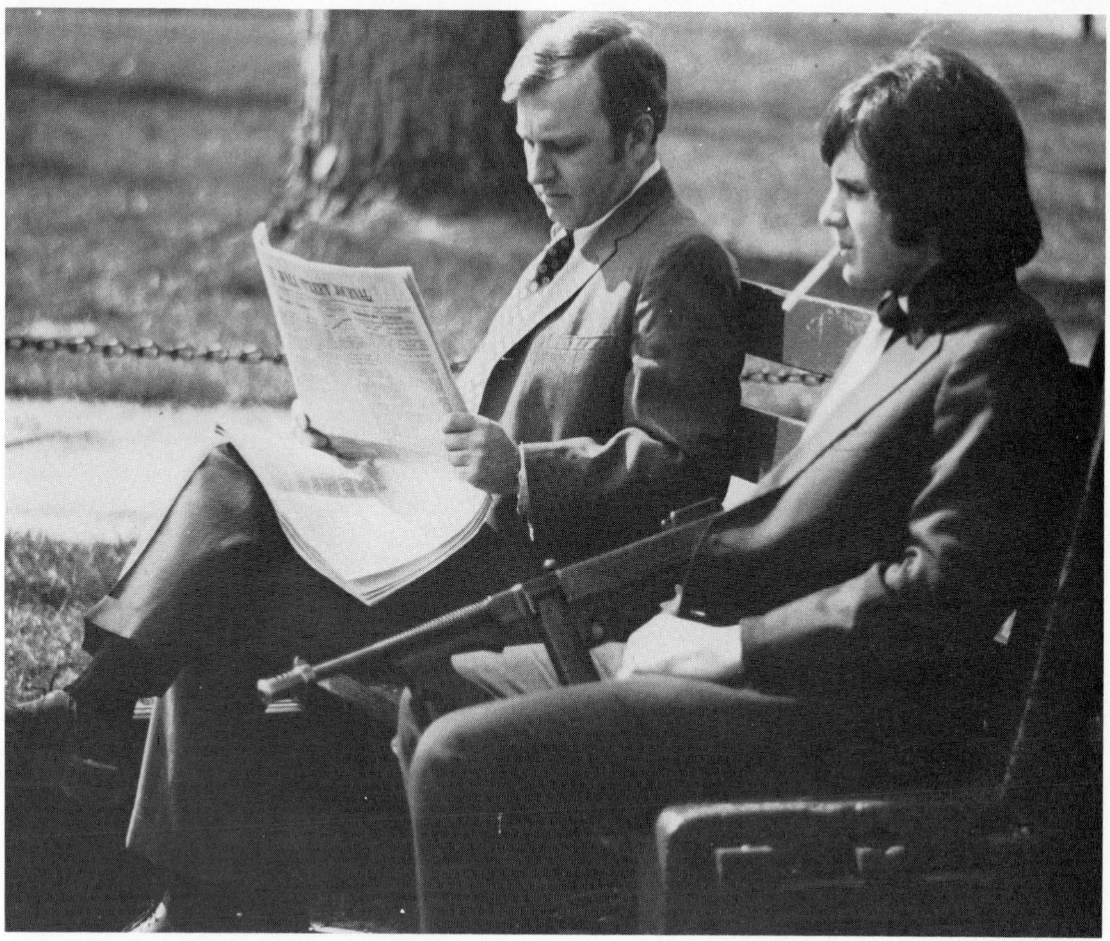

Organized crime: in the executive suite and on the street.

ion, the conventional notions about organized crime, let us open up the inquiry by considering issues that are pivotal to the subject.

4.01 DEFINITION OF ORGANIZED CRIME

While there may be disagreement as to the existence of the "Mafia"[13] or motivations behind the recent killing of Sam "Momo" Giancana (a former chieftain of organized crime in Chicago with reputed CIA connections),[14] few have lingering doubts about the existence of organized crime in American society. Nevertheless, a comprehensive and completely accurate definition of organized crime is lacking.

The often cited Task Force definition (noted previously in this chapter) contains statements that explicitly or implicitly give rise to serious questions. For example, the commission concludes that "Organized crime is a society that seeks to operate outside the control of the American people and their governments,"[15] an observation which implies, as noted by Homer,[16] that participants in organized crime are hard-core antagonists who relentlessly do battle against the "American way of life." Past and present events suggest that this is not the case. The "noble experiment" known as Prohibition may serve as a glaring example of the mutually supportive activities pursued by the public and organized crime as consumers and producers. While it is doubtful that Prohibition created organized crime, there is good reason to argue that the public's demand for booze combined with other prevailing social forces to refine the structural efficiency of organized criminal activity. One such social force which influenced the development of organized crime on a larger scale in the area of bootlegging and, somewhat later, racketeering was the urban political machine.[17]

A more fundamental question, originating from the same Task Force statement, raises the issue of whether organized crime represents values and activities which are in opposition to those of the American people themselves. While the dominant view seems to be that organized crime is a crippler of our domestic economy,[18] others (as does the writer) conceive of it as being pretty much in harmony with the practices of a free enterprise ideology. As Quinney notes:

> The economy of American society not only creates and perpetuates criminal activity in business and corporate enterprise, but fosters a kind of crime organized for the explicit purpose of making economic gain by criminal activities.[19]

Further, one widely accepted reason why organized crime appears to defy attempts to suppress it is that its services are desired by a substantial portion of the public. Could organized crime continue in some of its present spheres of activity if people suddenly quit gambling or purchasing "pornographic" materials? In addition, common values such as seeking preferential treatment through financial influence (for example, giving a corrupt traffic cop "the fine" in advance so as to avoid the hassles of a speeding ticket or DWI charge) seem to be shared by both the public and organized criminals.

In defining the problem, the Task Force also specified that "It [a society] involves thousands of criminals, working within structures as complex as those of any large corporation, subject to laws more rigidly enforced than those of legitimate government."[20] From this statement, three more "facts" are presented that should concern the unbiased student of organized crime. The first, and most crucial (because the other two are dependent upon its acceptance), is the Task Force's persistent claim that organized crime *is* "a society." When speaking in terms of a society, it then follows that one can logically assume the elements of a tight, clandestine structure with ritualized methods of internal control. But, is it correct to view organized crime as a society? May it not be more appropriate to think of organized crime as *including,* but not limited to, groups that have qualities of a "silent society"? Perhaps such thinking would be disappointing to the media and much of the public, since it would prompt us to reconsider the wars against Frank Nitti (Eliot Ness's archrival) and Francesco Castiglia (Frank Costello, Kefauver's prime target) as minor skirmishes with a much larger foe. Nevertheless, this chapter will attempt to provide a more inclusive definition of the problem.

A second fact that the Task Force implies in the above statement is that the similarities between the behavior of corporations and the criminal society end with their structural makeup. The Task Force bolsters this corporate analogy with an organizational chart[21] of crime groups that has been reproduced in almost every textbook dealing with organized crime. The question remains, why did this analogy between organized crime and the corporation end here? Could it be that to do otherwise would be unacceptable to many members of the President's Crime Commission (63 percent of the commission members had alliances with corporations, primarily as legal advisers)?[22]

Finally, the observation that "the society" imposes a more rigid code upon its members than that of bona fide governments creates the impression that there is some sort of a formalized legal structure within organized crime societies. Typically, the cornerstone of the code has been identified as *omerta* (a Sicilian word meaning "manliness" and interpreted as emphasizing silence). However, as we shall see, silence is golden regardless of whether we are considering executives conspiring to fix prices, presidential aides attempting to "bug" the offices of political rivals, or criminal societies scheming for other reasons. Quite possibly, under a new definition of organized crime, the so-called code may be relevant to diverse forms of organized activity—just as it may have been for the Three Musketeers.

If the Task Force definition of organized crime is so fraught with sources of criticism, what factors may have contributed to the provision of such a perspective for the President's Commission and, ostensibly, the public? One explanation suggests that the Task Force was hastily convened and given a limited budget.[23] Such limitations could conceivably hinder a serious creative effort. It is noteworthy that several of the Task Force members had attended a previous series of meetings on organized crime—the Oyster Bay Conference[24]—which appears to have influenced their new mission.[25] On the other hand, Smith[26] and Messick[27] point out that, in their eagerness to generate public understanding and anxiety, both the Oyster Bay conferees and the Task Force members were prompted to oversimplify the problem at the expense of objectivity.

It was the Task Force, as no other governmental commission before it had done, that gave an official stamp of approval to the "fact" that the " 'Mafia' (or 'Cosa Nostra') and 'organized crime' were one and the same."[28]

Because our knowledge about organized crime is limited, a definition necessarily flows from sketchy sources. It is much easier (and probably more accurate) to first see a live elephant and then define it than it is to have people who have perceived bits and pieces collectively go about the job of defining the entire creature. It follows then, that objectivity urges that one avoid, in defining organized crime—an area lacking a great deal of irrefutable documentation—the use of pejorative conclusions and, simultaneously, encourage comprehensive coverage. In hopes of doing this, the following definition will be utilized as a basis for our discussion of organized crime.

> Organized crime consists of illegal acts, executed by five or more "producers" with varying degrees of participation, to directly or indirectly secure a system of recurring financial rewards through the provision of goods and services for consumer groups differing in size and knowledge of involvement.[29]

To specify the exact number of participants necessary to constitute organized crime, in this case five, is a bit capricious. However, one should set some bondaries for the sake of discussion if nothing else. Five was chosen as a common denominator more for its legal precedence in the Crime Control Act of 1970 than its proved validity.[30] Significant, perhaps, is that the above definition says nothing of a society. This is intended, for to get at the nature of organized crime two essential concepts need to be explored: criminal societies *and* criminal alliances that are involved in the business of organized crime.[31]

4.02 THE NATURE OF ORGANIZED CRIME

Within the context of organized crime, *criminal societies* are groups of individuals united by bonds of ethnic origin, personal allegiance, or other common identities in addition to economic concerns. The financial ventures of criminal societies are varied and may entail both legal and illegal enterprises. *Criminal alliances* include persons for whom the attachment to others is based mainly upon specific and primarily illegal economic pursuit(s) that may be occupationally related, Both forms are organized, both are economically motivated, both are much more costly than conventional street crime (burglary, robbery, etc.), and both have an abundance of customers (willing or unwilling) to pay for their goods and services. However, the consumers of some criminal alliances may be less willing to pay than are the bulk of a criminal society's clientele.

Our definition thus prompts us to examine the activities of groups which have been labeled historically as Mafia, Black Hand, Unione Siciliana, and La Cosa Nostra (criminal societies). Further, we are beckoned to consider corporate crimes, political corruption, and other crime compacts having an economic base (criminal alliances). It also becomes relevant for us to examine how these two categories overlap when criminal societies or their members work in cooperation with a criminal alliance. Finally, we are encouraged to deal with related phenomena such as gambling and the stock market, narcotics and the legitimate drug industry, loansharking and usurious banking practices, and agents of crime versus crime-fighting agents.

4.03 CRIMINAL SOCIETIES AND ORGANIZED CRIME

In 1881, New Orleans policeman David Hennessey arrested Giuseppe Esposito, a reputed mafioso, who was being pursued by Italian authorities. Nine years later, during the evening of October 15, 1890, Hennessey, then police chief, was mortally wounded. On the way out, the dying chief reportedly uttered the word "Dagos" in an effort to indicate who was responsible for the attack. Unfortunately, the man who supposedly heard Hennessey's indictment failed to testify at subsequent proceedings against the accused killers.[32] Many citizens felt that there was a direct link between Esposito's previous arrest and Hennessey's murder and that the crime was a Mafia-ordered retaliation.

In the aftermath of the chief's murder, the police set up a dragnet which focused upon "Dagos." In spite of the Italian consul's protests, principles of due process were ignored. The local press made no secret of the Mafia issue. Eventually nine men were brought to trial as codefendants on a charge of murdering Hennessey. The final outcome was a mistrial for three of the defendants, while the remaining six were found not guilty of the murder charge. The "New Orleans Nine" were then remanded to the local jail pending a trial on other charges.

All hell broke loose. Angry citizen groups demanded that this travesty of justice be somehow rectified. Rumors of jury tampering by the Mafia spread rapidly. A large meeting of concerned citizens was held on the day after the trial ended. Unfortunately the gathering coincided with the birthdate (March 14) of Italy's King Umberto I. As was the tradition, residents of the Italian section of the city displayed the Italian flag in recognition. Much as a red flag has certain meanings for a bull that has been deprived of light, hostile citizens mistook this gesture of ethnic pride as a symbol of the Italian community's celebration of the previous day's verdict.[33] With little restraint from local authorities, an enraged mob charged the parish prison and executed the defendants, plus two more "Dago" prisoners for good measure. Where justice in the courtroom had failed, the "good" citizens of New Orleans had succeeded. The label "Mafia" was now a part of the vernacular. Quite possibly certain social and economic undercurrents in New Orleans predisposed much of the populace to favor the notion of a Mafia conspiracy.

Around the turn of the century there was growing concern over the mounting number of immigrants, particularly from southern and southeastern Europe, who were coming to settle in America's urban areas. The nativistic Know Nothing party had been popular in New Orleans in spite of that city's substantial Catholic population.[34] Beyond ethnic prejudice, there may have been considerable resentment based upon the increasing economic success of some men whose names ended in a vowel. Given these conditions, the Mafia could have served as a convenient scapegoat for venting deep-seated hatreds.

The seed had been planted. Through media coverage of the events in New Orleans, Americans were now informed of a sinister alien force in their midst. Since few Americans had even heard of the Mafia prior to 1890, citizens having a lingering interest in the subject were dependent upon European writings as their primary source of information. Now that we have located the Mafia's nominal introduction to the American public, let us turn to its cultural origins.

The birth of the word "Mafia" is subject to many interpretations, some of which are rather humorous. One account locates the origin of the word in 1282, when a Sicilian girl was raped on her wedding day. The girl's mother is supposed to have cried out "ma fia, ma fia" ("my daugher, my daughter").[35] Another story has it that the word "Mafia" is an acronym for the phrase: "Morte Alla Francia Italia Anela" ("Italy desires death to France"), used in 1282 by a band of Sicilian insurrectionists protesting the French occupation of the island.[36] Ianni notes a more credible explanation of the word's origin by pointing to the Sicilian adjective *mafiusu,* meaning "beautiful."[37] Beauty is said to be in the eye of the beholder, and it may have appeared to many village peasants that the activities of early Mafie were, indeed, beautiful—given the island's sociopolitical history.

Sicily is part of an area that includes the mainland south of Rome known as the Mezzogiorno. While the island is somewhat distinct from other provinces in the south, the differences are more a matter of degree than of kind. The Mezzogiorno is a very poor area, where it is not uncommon for over 50 percent of the labor force to be unemployed.[38] Upon returning to his home village of Lercara Friddi, the recently exiled Lucky Luciano was struck by the abject poverty of this typical Sicilian village.

> So he took me inside, and they had fixed up half of the second floor [the town's only hotel] as an apartment for me. It would've fit into a corner of my place at the Waldorf Towers. But I tried not to show how I felt, and I smiled and thanked him.
>
> They finally left me alone to take a little rest. I unpacked my suitcases and put some things away. Then I noticed somethin' really cute: the bathroom had an old fashioned iron tub, and there was a note on the wall in Italian which said "American shower"—there was a rubber tube with a flower sprinkler as a head, and it was hangin' on the wall above the faucets. Well, how can you feel blue when you see a thing like that? You realize how hard these people are tryin' to make you feel like an American who didn't come to a country of barbarians.[39]

The southern Italian is bound by the traditions of family loyalty, honor, and a deep respect for power. Personal identity begins, first and foremost, with the family (especially blood relatives), then it extends to the local village and seems to terminate at the boundaries of one's province. Somewhere within this hierarchy stands the Church—a strong institution but, nonetheless, one that is never placed before the family, The Mezzogiorno is, strictly speaking, a man's world. However, males occupy a bittersweet status, since power and privilege are intertwined with duty and harsh social commitments. For the southerner, behavioral infractions can spell a decades-long blood-letting vendetta, while for his urbane countryman to the north under similar circumstances, little more than a night's lost sleep might be involved, The family and its honor is above all else.[40] What we have said about the Mezzogiorno as a region is highly accentuated in Sicily,

A sustained nationalistic spirit of loyalty to the central government has hardly ever captured the heart of the southerner. Much of Sicily's inwardness is due to the fact that the armies of many nations have marched across its soil. In the face of these invasions, the acting "occupational" governments have been replete with corruption and repressive measures of control. Thus, the Sicilian tradition of provincialism is, at least in part, of external derivation. Such sentiments also found expression among immigrants to the New World. Trust only those that share (or have shared) your local values and customs—outsiders, even those from an adjoining province, may be the enemy.

As most Sicilians would agree, the charge that the Mafia exists in their province is correct. However, it is a society that is woven into the social fabric of the island (only in the western region, particularly around Palermo) as more than an organization. The modern adjective "mafia" imparts a sense of pride that embodies the virtues of honor and family loyalty—it *is* the cultural ideal of Sicily. In Sicily the proper noun "Mafia" (plural, "Mafie") is understood to mean a secret society (locally called the Onorata Societa[41]) or organization possessing much power and the ability to influence daily life. "To a Sicilian, the (lower-case) state of mafia and the (upper-case) powerful organization, Mafia, are two sides of the same coin."[42]

When the drive for Italian unification crystallized in 1860, groups of Mafie provided armed support for the forces of General Guiseppe Garibaldi against the repressive Bourbon establishment. As a political power in Sicily, the Mafie were able to satisfy the interests of the central government in Rome (House of Savoy) by providing a surplus of votes when popular elections were held. Thus, a symbiotic relationship was created that strengthened the hands of Mafia bands. At the turn of the century, many of the local Mafia families began to join together in a loose alliance to pursue mutual illegal interests (mostly extortion), forming what Ianni cites as a *cosca.* It is the grouping of *cosche* (plural for *cosca*) into various *consorterie*—not a rigidly centralized organization[43]—that make up the Mafia, or Onorata Societa, in Sicily today. The present structural pattern of the Mafia is pretty much the same as in the past, but the illegal activities and social functions of the society are changing. Trafficking in narcotics competes with extortion, and the people of Sicily now seem to be aware of alternatives to Mafia-enforced behavior codes. Before returning to the United States, another society that was spawned in the Mezzogiorno merits our attention at this point.

In Naples (which is now part of the province of Compania), an organization known as the Camorra was widely known during most of the nineteenth century.[44] While some Neapolitans still identify themselves as Camorristi, the society seems to have disappeared long ago. Unlike the Mafia, the Camorra existed as an association with some trappings of a highly structured, centrally organized grouping. Unlike the Mafia in Sicily, the Camorra did not begin as an organization that had the initial support of the people by performing certain social functions (providing order, symbolic idealism, etc.). Rather, it originated as a corrupt prisoners' union in the dungeons of Naples. Where the early Mafiosi tended to branch off into more pronounced illegal activities with increased political success, the Camorristi began as ex-convicts and like-minded recruits carrying out strong-arm crimes. By the mid-1800s, due to political conditions similar to those in Sicily, the Camorra gained power and influence as a "second government." As we have noted, the Mafia was able to survive several changing governments (including Mussolini's) because of its ability to change with a shifting environment. The Camorra, on the other hand, did not have the "staying-power" or the flexibility needed to perpetuate itself.

The label "Camorra" has never dominated the American consciousness of organized crime conspiracies as has "Mafia." There were periods in the early 1900s when American newspapers ran stories of the Camorra's exploits in Italy. However, attempts to establish the reality of the Camorra's existence in America never took hold. Perhaps the "Mafia" label won out because much more of the immigrant-Italian population came from Sicily than from Naples. A more subtle explanation, advanced by Smith,[45] is that the Camorra came to be identified in the American mind with open political corruption while the Mafia conjured up images of secrecy and violence. With that in mind, the Mafia became a far better candidate for the conspiracy-bound "fans" of the Hennessey incident. Linked with more general fears of immigration policy—over 1.6 million southern Italians immigrated to this country between 1900 and 1910[46]—was the concern that Italian ships were steaming to American ports loaded with *agents provocateurs* from Palermo. Shortly after the murder of Hennessey, the newspapers of New Orleans played upon these fears of the public by announcing the arrival of the ship *Elysia,* thought to be transporting a cargo of Mafia infiltraters.[47]

How strong is the case that the Mafia, as an organization, arrived in the little Italies of American cities as transplants from the soil of Sicily? No doubt some of the new arrivals did include (or perhaps could have included) those with a Mafia connection. However, it is doubtful that the ships docking included large numbers of Mafiosi or, more significantly, those possessing crucial leadership experience. There are at least two reasons why the transplant theory does not hold water. First, after a considerable period of struggle, the Mafia was successful in Sicily at the time we are speaking of and so, one might ask, why should there be an urge to migrate to the uncertainties of America? After all, Prohibition was at least 20 years away! Second, Italians who did come to the United States were embarking upon a venture to improve their lot largely as individual, and previously unassociated, families. In fact, many men came alone in hopes of making enough to enable a quick return to their families at home (*paesi*) with dreams of a better life. How could the Mafia, a rural phenomenon, take hold in the teeming cities of America with this lack of an established social network?[48] Evidence does indicate that years later some Mafiosi did come to this country to escape Mussolini's campaign—a program which included tactics that would hardly be endorsed by the U.S. Supreme Court—against the Onorata Societa.

> Although the Italian gangs had been noticeable for many years, their numbers increased during the 1920's when Mussolini's orders to exterminate the Sicilian Mafia spurred a mass migration of Mafiosi and other Sicilian leaders to the United States.[49]

While most Americans forgot the "Mafia" label after the New Orleans affair lost its sensational appeal, they did not forget the concept of a "Dago" crime problem. Another sinister force was gnawing at the American dream, or, more appropriately speaking, contributing to a nightmare for the estranged Italian immigrant. This problem was real and its victims were confined to places with names like Mulberry Street and Dago Hill. The new label was the "Black Hand" and it was identified by its Italo-American victims.

As we have noted, the Mafia and the Camorra had roots at one time or another in the Mezzogiorno region of Italy. The Black Hand was, however, as American as chop suey.[50] There is no evidence that any organization by that name had a Sicilian precedent. The closest tie between the Black Hand and native Italian groups may rest with the practices of some extortionists operating in the Mezzogiorno (perhaps they were Mafiosi or Camorristi, perhaps not) who would sign a threatening note with a black hand to intimidate the victim. The so-called Black Hand was never an organized society in any sense of the word. It appeared as a device used by loosely bound and usually small independent gangs of southern Italians preying upon the fears and traditions of their immigrant countrymen. Black Hand operations (mostly extortion) were able to succeed because they were perpetrated against people who brought to America a "primeval 'sense' of mafia."[51] The activities of the Black Hand almost never went beyond the Italian ghettoes.

> Can you imagine my father going uptown to commit a robbery or a mugging? He would have had to take an interpreter with him to read the street signs and say 'stick 'em up' for him. The only time he ever committed a crime outside Mulberry Street was when he went over to the Irish section to steal some milk so that my mother could heat it up and put it in my kid brother's ear to stop an earache.[52]

Thus, in the words of a second-generation Italian-American whose father was involved in Black Hand schemes, Ianni captures the parameters of early—and unorganized—Italian-American crime in this country.

The term "Black Hand" seems to have jelled in Italian-language newspapers, rather reluctantly, as a spin-off from the previous events in New Orleans. Italian-Americans "tended to view the New Orleans affair as part of a general pattern of anti-Italian attitudes on the part of Irish policemen and English-language newspapers in New Orleans, Chicago, and other American cities.[53] Ethnic pride combined with a mounting recognition that crime was becoming a large-scale problem in Italian communities to produce the "Black Hand" label in Italian papers. By 1904, the term "Mafia" had been replaced with "Black Hand" in the popular press as well.[54]

Leading speakers for Italian-Americans soon realized the potential dangers of admitting to an Italian crime problem—a problem which was already a firmly established reality in the public mind. To counter strongly fueled prejudices, the White Hand Society was formed in 1907 to improve the public's image of Italians (particularly southern Italians). A major goal of the society was to curb Black Hand crime by educating the less assimilated immigrants (*cafoni*) in ways to fight community crime.[55] Within a short period of time, it became obvious that the White Hand Society was not receiving the necessary grass-roots support from the Italian community. Black Hand activities were to survive another decade because of "benign" neglect and corruption on the part of the police and city hall.

> "Southerners" knew that crime pervaded their communities; they knew also that authorities could or would do little to terminate it. They believed the White Hand to be powerless in the face of official corruption or tolerance of corruption, and they had no desire to involve themselves with it.[56]

Black Hand crimes seemed to dissipate between the years 1915–1920. As the number of unassimilated immigrants began to dry up, so did the pool of potential victims. More significantly, the politics of moral entrepreneurship led to the official "drying up" of America's legitimate sources of booze with the passage of the Volstead Act (i.e., Prohibition). The immigrant Italian was not averse to having a "cooker" at home to be used in the production of illegal booze. Some Italian families were able to catapult (with the help of city hall connections) their Black Hand operations into bootlegging by organizing "mom and pop" distilleries. This was the case with the Genna brothers, who paid their tenement-dwelling producers as much as $15 per day—a considerable amount of money for an immigrant family on the South Side of Chicago during 1920.[57] By and large, due to their cultural handicaps (language, customs, lack of connections), it was next to impossible for the immigrants to really capitalize through big-time distribution.

Eventually, though, the Italians *began* to organize. Some writers have suggested that the Sicilians were predisposed to succeed during Prohibition because of their "ethnic cohesion and group loyalty."[58] These qualities—conducive to organized crime—no doubt helped the Italians to become involved in the large-scale production and distribution of illegal booze. However, other dimensions need to be examined before one passes lightly over this observation. For the sons of immigrants, family loyalty and Sicilian identity came after their commitment to the social environment of the tenement areas. Youth gangs of Sicilian (and other Italian) boys were more concerned about the raids on their turf by "outside" kids than with the ideal of Sicilian ethnic consciousness. As one of Ianni's subjects said, "the Irish and Jewish kids used to beat the living shit out of us until we got smart enough to fight together in gangs like they did."[59] It was the second-generation offspring that gave Italians the impetus to move into the more powerful roles of organized crime, especially after 1930. As Ianni further notes:

> The role-model ideal for these newly mobile and aspiring underlings was the Jewish gang-leader, and not the old-country-oriented mafiosi they comtemptuously called "greenhorns," "greasers," "handlebars," or "Moustache Petes."[60]

Prohibition was definitely a seller's market. As with any other commodity that is so much in demand and in such short supply, competition was very keen (to say the least). Those who had been shrewd enough to take notice of the fact that over half the states had gone dry prior to the Volstead Act were ready for business. Still, "everyone" wanted to get in on the act, and violence in the street became a common occurrence. Before Joe Saltis introduced the "Chicago piano" (machine gun) to gang warfare—which was later to be combined with Hymie Weiss's "one-way ride" tactic—some rather interesting approaches were used to reduce competition. For example, two of the Gennas's "hit men" (Albert Anselmi and John Scalise) would dip their bullets in garlic in the belief that, if they did not get a clean shot at the victim, the garlic would cause him to die later from gangrene poisoning.[61] In Chicago, organized crime also had assistance from the corrupt administration of Mayor Bill Thompson.

New York City was similar to Chicago in that it had its share of corrupt politicians, police officers on the take, and "the best judges that money could buy." In 1921, Al Capone had predicted that Lucky Luciano would become "the King of Booze in New York."[62] Before a coronation could be held, Luciano would have to reckon with some old-country "greasers" who didn't quite understand the ways of this second-generation upstart. Men like Salvatore Maranzano and Giuseppe ("Joe the Boss") Masseria had carved empires out of the little Italys by cornering the market on ice and Italian staples such as artichokes and olive oil. With encouragement from the Volstead Act, they—as the Gennas had done in Chicago—collected and distributed the products of the mom and pop stills. To up-and-coming second-generation men like Luciano and Costello, the old-country "greasers" were an anachronism with their demands for tribute and filial loyalty. This intraethnic conflict came to a head in the Castellamarese war, which lasted from 1930 to 1931.

Accounts of this period in the history of criminal societies invariably mention an event known as the "Night of the Sicilian Vespers." Accordingly, it has been reported that Luciano ensured the success of the new order by engineering the deaths of several old-country "Mafiosi types" on the same evening that Maranzano was killed.[63] While Luciano and company's original plan had included the simultaneous murder of other old-country types across the nation, this second phase of the plan was *not,* according to its architect, carried out.

> Plenty of people got eliminated *before* the day Maranzano got his, and it was all done as part of the plan. But all that stuff them writers always printed about what they called the "Night of the Sicilian Vespers" was mostly pure imagination. Every time somebody else writes about that day,

> the list of guys who was supposed to have got bumped off gets bigger and bigger. The last count I read was somewhere around fifty. But the funny thing is, nobody could ever tell the names of the guys who got knocked off the night Maranzano got his.[64]

It is important to note that during the twenties and early thirties the "Mafia" label was absent and, instead, men like Capone and Luciano were called gangsters. The ganster image was a favorable and more appropriate one in the eyes of the public. The style of the second-generation Italian gangster, along with his Jewish and Irish associates, was more that of a business entrepreneur than that of an old-country Mafioso. The contradiction, as suggested by Smith,[65] is that this shifting public image (Mafiosi to business people) was accompanied by apparently more violent behavior. In terms of the economic and social conditions of the time, this seemingly paradoxical condition may not be a true enigma. *The gangster produced and distributed goods and services for knowing and involved consumers in an essentially "criminogenic market structure."*[66]

During the 1930s, the gangster suddenly became a racketeer in the eyes as well as on the lips of the public. Racketeering itself was not new; neither was the name of the often-cited "silent" society that was a part of it. The Unione Siciliana had roots in Chicago at the turn of the century, where it began as a fraternal organization that also sold conventional insurance policies. In the early 1900s the Unione also helped to sponsor—along with notables such as Guido Sabetta, the Italian consul—the formation of The White Hand, previously discussed.[67] The Unione soon included members who were involved in bootlegging and other Black Hand-type ventures, in addition to many law-abiding old-timers who were simply looking for a place to play cards or boccie, drink a little wine, and discuss "the good old days" in their native villages. In time, the Unione Siciliana grew in size and was perhaps controlled by Black Handers for purposes of extorting the insurance funds or using its increasing political clout.[68] Following the Castellamarese war, it appears that the *name* "Unione Siciliana" was chosen (not necessarily the organization) at the suggestion of a Jew [Lansky] for purposes of expediency in dealing with residual sentiments from the Masseria-Maranzano days. At a meeting in Chicago, held for purposes of establishing some order following Maranzano's death, Luciano was cautioned by Lansky about an oversight:

> During a break late in the afternoon, Lansky took Luciano aside. He [Lansky] was worried. "We missed something, Charlie. Unless you straighten it out before tonight, you could blow the whole thing. There are lots of these guys who ain't able to give up all the old ways so fast. You gotta feed 'em some sugar that they'll understand. You've got to give the new setup a name; after all, what the fuck is any business or company without a name?"
>
> The more Luciano thought about Lansky's statement the more he agreed. "But the name has to be simple, somethin' that'll have a real meaning for these particular guys." he said.
>
> "That's right," Lansky said. "And I'd like to suggest you call it the Unione Siciliano."[69]

Such a happenstance, if it did actually occur as Luciano's biographers claim, could, first, explain how non-Italian organized criminals (Lansky, Siegel, etc.) came to be closely associated with the Unione Siciliano and, second, avoid the conspiracy theorists' premise that the old Unione Siciliana had been hijacked as a front for a forthcoming criminal cartel dominated by swarthy Sicilian immigrants. Nevertheless, the name "Unione Siciliano" stuck in the public mind and served as an ethnic link between the gangsters of the Prohibition era and the Mafiosi at home on the New Frontier of the 1960s.[70]

In 1951, the term "Mafia" was resurrected and received top billing over the more casual and vaguely used label of the "Unione Siciliano." The Special Senate Committee headed by Senator Estes Kefauver was charged with a mandate to investigate interstate gambling and political corruption. The stars of the popularly televised hearings were Frank Costello and New York City Mayor William O'Dwyer, along with a supporting cast that included Lansky, Willi Moretti, and Virginia Hill.[71] The committee stated that the country was the victim of "a crime syndicate known as the Mafia operating nation-wide under centralized direction and control,"[72] yet admittedly failed to offer proof of its existence. The lack of proof was less noticed than the reliance of some of the participating witnesses on the Fifth Amendment privilege against self-incrimination. Costello was a bit more candid with the committee than others, but when questioned about his financial affairs, he refused to answer for fear of incriminating himself. He was later to be cited for, and convicted of, contempt charges arising out of the Senate hearings.[73] Could it be that men who failed to answer pointed questions (by exercising their Constitutional rights) were hiding a crime-conspiracy network generically identified as the Mafia? In the meantime, the Federal Bureau of Narcotics was waging a campaign to alert the public to the growing menace of drugs.

Beginning in the 1950s, the media started to devote a considerable amount of attention to an "alarming" drug problem. Parents were warned through the popular press that dope pushers were lurking in the shadows of the neighborhood malt shop waiting to hook their kids on a wide variety of narcotics. Under the leadership of Harry Anslinger, pressure was eventually brought to bear on the McClellan committee (which would investigate a flushed meeting of criminal entrepreneurs at Apalachin, N.Y., in 1957) to tie narcotics into a Mafia conspiracy.

Congress responded to the mounting public concern by passing the Boggs Amendment (1951) and, five years later, the Narcotics Control Act. Both measures were designed to crack down on drug trafficking by providing stiff penalties for violators.[74] Thus, the narcotics trade was visualized as a violent, dirty business. More importantly, illicit drugs were thought to be (by Anslinger and others) distributed by a sinister *organized* force striking at the roots of America's strength: her youth. As Smith points out, it was the narçotics issue that helped the "Mafia" label resurface under the alias of "La Cosa Nostra."[75] In 1963, Joe Valachi testified before Senator McClellan's committee and reaffirmed existing beliefs that there was, indeed, a Mafia. Even though Valachi used the term "La Cosa Nostra," the committee and the press frequently substituted the word "Mafia." After all, the Mafia by any other name is still the Mafia—or is it? The committee (and public) felt that it was and became even more assured when Valachi (a convicted narcotics trafficker) provided elaborate organizational charts, descriptions of past events, and confirmation that a major source of income was gambling and narcotics. It was this background that prompted the President's Task Force Commission on Organized Crime to convincingly state:

> Today the core of organized crime in the United States consists of 24 groups operating as criminal cartels in large cities across the Nation. Their membership is exclusively men of Italian descent, they are in frequent communication with each other, and their smooth functioning is insured by a national body of overseers. To date, only the Federal Bureau of Investigation has been able to document fully the national scope of these groups, and FBI intelligence indicates that the organization as a whole has changed its name from the Mafia to La Cosa Nostra.[76]

Criminal societies do form a part of the organized crime phenomenon. But, is there a Mafia? In tracing the development of the "Mafia" label, an attempt has been made to point out that it is highly unlikely that the Sicilian version of the Mafia was transplanted in this country by a cadre of "shock troops" or dons receiving directives from Palermo. More likely is the notion that some Italian-Americans utilized criminal opportunities created by social forces in this country (as had other ethnic groups before them) to achieve mobility or success.[77] On a more subtle level, an effort was made to illuminate the theme that the "Mafia" label has been used at various times to support certain sociopolitical concerns, e.g., ethnic prejudice and the immigration issue, bureaucratic growth premised upon the trumpeting of a narcotics problem, or simply the temptation to attribute many of our social ills to an organized conspiracy predicated upon violence and a foreign, criminal value system. It is reasonable to assume that a condition of *mafia* (state of mind, not organization) existed among some Italian-American immigrants during the early 1900s. This cultural residue from the old country gave rise to both victims and predators through unorganized (in a structural sense) Black Hand exploits. As future generations came into contact with American values and social conditions, old-world values were displaced. The organization of Italian-American criminal societies for purposes of profiting from Prohibition was dependent upon the American social conditions of corrupt political machines and a criminogenic market structure. Further, the Italian-American crime "family" soon encompassed "stepchildren" (non-Sicilians, non-Italians) whose economic worth has increased interactions with the societies. Men like Lansky, Siegel, and Jake Guzik established such positions of trust, influence, and friendship that, for all practical purposes, they became members of criminal societies having an Italian flavor. To conclude that they were never "members" because, for example, they could never vote or sit on "the commission" (a subject that we will consider shortly) is to soft-pedal certain facts because they do not fit a reified concept of the Mafia folklore ("only Sicilians need apply") relevant to nineteenth-century Sicily but not twentieth-century urban America.

The Valachi testimony did much to sharpen existing perceptions of organized crime, but its authenticity has been challenged on several grounds.[78] Valachi's story "confirmed" not only organized crime's Italian background but also the organizational complexity that would befit a criminal master plan. Accordingly, "La Cosa Nostra" (a term one criminal society informant, Vincent Teresa,[79] found amusing) was structured along corporate lines with a board of directors (the commission). There were family units—a reputed carryover from Maranzano's reign—each of which had a boss (*capo*), advisers (*consigliere*), underboss (*sottocapo*), middle managers (*caporegima*), and salesmen (*soldati*).[80] The key to the validity of the conspiracy theory may lie in the disputed existence of the commission. Using that premise as a springboard, Ianni questions such an existence, at least as portrayed by the Task Force Report.

> For a national commission to operate as a legislature, judiciary, and executive in the way Cosa Nostra's rulers are said to do would require an elaborate corporate structure, but there is no indication that any such unit exists. Thus, if there is a commission, its real function seems to fall outside the sphere of the consciously constructed and rationally operated organization.[81]

Ianni's contention parallels those of Bell[82] and Hawkins.[83] However, there is evidence that following the Castellmarese war a commission was established by Luciano primarily as a mediation board for the Unione Siciliana.[84] Accounts of Italian-American criminal societies of later periods reinforce the proposition that a commission exists.[85] If a commission does in fact exist, it does not follow, necessarily, that it functions as a "national body of overseers" guiding and directing a criminal society in this country. As criminal societies have diversified in terms of membership (ethnically and numerically), locale, and activities (legitimate and illegitimate), the case for a powerful commission becomes weaker. Such recent episodes as the

Gallo-Profaci feud indicate the commission's lack of ability to keep the peace (or perhaps its lack of interest in doing so). In addition, it is difficult to imagine a commission, centered around New York City families, being able to control activities in places like Chicago, Miami, or New Orleans when it apparently cannot or will not do so on the home front. The idea of a powerful, authoritarian commission, with a flexible composition as implied by the Task Force, simply does not make sense if one is willing to accept evidence that successful criminal societies of the 1920s and beyond have been based upon a Yankee ideology of individualism buttressed by the southern Italian's propensity to reject centralized governments. It may be, as Luciano intended, that the commission stands for mediation rather than supreme authority—and it may be that its limited role as an arbitrator is weakening.

In conclusion, criminal societies having a significant but not exclusively Italian-American composition do exist. Further, they appear to be relatively autonomous and, at best, are joined in a loose confederation. In the course of their legitimate and illegitimate pursuits, these societies may interact with others operating as free agents or criminal alliances (individuals joined together primarily for specific, illegal economic activities rather than on the basis of common societal identities that coexist with economic bonds). Thus, there is little support for the notion that a tightly structured, ethnically homogeneous entity called the Mafia controls twentieth-century organized crime in America. Some societies are identified as families, but—as the fourth- and fifth-generation descendants of the original Black Handers take their place in suburbia—the family may be breaking up, being reduced to no more than a nominal vestige of the past. Finally, as the outgroup becomes more a part of the in-group, i.e., as these people become more involved in legitimate concerns and a middle-class life-style—the term "criminal society" may be losing its descriptive value.

4.04 ACTIVITIES OF CRIMINAL SOCIETIES AND ALLIANCES

When laws are passed that either prohibit access to desired commodities and services or limit their distribution to the public, a market structure is created that encourages organized crime. Primary illegal activities such as gambling, narcotics, loan-sharking, and sporadic violence have resulted from such criminogenic (crime-producing) market structures.

Gambling has been documented as having existed since antiquity. One could philosophize and conclude that life itself is a gamble. The colonists appeared to be more concerned with witchcraft than with moderate drinking and outlawing public lotteries. However, as morality came to be identified with austerity, colonial ruling bodies took steps to prohibit lotteries. While a majority of states presently allow for some form of legal gambling, for many the issue of legality is a moot point. Today gambling provides the single greatest source of *illegal* revenue for criminal societies and alliances. Legal and illegal wagering (cards, dice, slot machines, numbers, and racing), unlike hard narcotics, cuts across a broad spectrum of the population. The matter of legitimacy, however, is often a function of social class. That is, the higher one's social class, the more easily one can find legitimate gaming opportunities. How often does one read or hear about the police arresting executives for shooting craps on a streetcorner during their lunch period? Individuals who can afford to gamble legally either do so at appropriate locations (Reno, for example) or in private clubs and residences where the police do not venture. Lower-class people obviously do not have these opportunities. Poor police-community relations with minority groups are frequently a consequence of the differential enforcement of gambling laws. Minority groups know that "everybody" gambles and resent the presence of police patrols that scoop up corner crap games and numbers runners on the pretext of offering protective services in a high-crime area (robbery, murder, etc.).

For gambling to offer recurring rewards to criminal groups as well as legal operators, customers must be satisfied. If the games are on the up and up (not rigged), people will play no matter who is behind them. Criminal societies and alliances are rationally oriented in a business context. Thus, their gambling concerns are typically operated on the premise that—given the odds in most games of chance—the house is always a favored winner, so why bother to jeopardize business with extensive rigging? This is not to suggest that "the fix" has never been in; we have evidence of rigged sporting events that have involved organized crime. Rather, the point is that gambling with organized crime societies or alliances is generally as straight a proposition as one would find at state-sponsored off-track betting offices. Further, the contention that a winner is likely to be paid off with a pistol whipping from "the mob" is a bit far fetched. One does not keep customers when word gets out that bets are not being paid off. After all, no one can force another to gamble. It is a matter of choice, and dissatisfied or maimed customers will very likely choose to take their business elsewhere. In fact, a common strategy among bookies is the parlaying of resources among themselves in order to cover heavy winners ("numbers") that may hit simultaneously.

While narcotics and occasional violence are not likely to be condoned by many people in law enforcement, gambling is. If illegal gambling is to operate successfully, some palms in city hall and law enforcement agencies must be greased. Corruption and illegal gambling form a compatible, reciprocal relationship because of the nature of law enforcement, public sentiments, and the legal structure. Laws are sometimes made which prohibit very profitable services such as gambling. Those who enforce the law are comparatively low-paid functionaries who also have a great deal of enforcement discretion. Given this admixture—low pay, much discretion, a lot of money to be made from bribes, and public sentiments that favor gambling—a cop can easily justify turning the other way. When several officers and politicians organize to receive regular, sustained payoffs for not enforcing gambling laws, the situation constitutes (according to our definition) a *criminal* alliance. *Corrupt officials are, most definitely, a part of organized crime,* whether their names are Giuseppe or Mike! The Knapp Commission uncovered just such a criminal alliance only recently in the New York City area.[86] We can extend this example and surmise that if gambling became legal in some places, there would be a lot of unhappy officials having to look elsewhere for their pocket money.

In conclusion, gambling is a common experience. It may be permitted legally through licensing, of it may be outlawed entirely. Paradoxically, if society were to prohibit *all* forms of gambling, the place that would be first to feel the shock waves is Wall Street. Given the present state of the economy one would be just as wise to place bets with a bookie as with a stockbroker.

The selling of drugs, like gambling, has not always been considered illegal. Whether a drug is given an illegal status may be determined more by politics than by the nature of the substance. It is fairly well known that alcoholic beverages can be as biologically harmful and criminogenic as are many of the substances classified by officials as dangerous drugs. Yet alcohol is consumed by a rather large portion of the population and (as demonstrated clearly during Prohibition) cannot be effectively outlawed. Qualities ascribed to drugs may shift with time and social cirumstance. For example, LSD, peyote, and other currently used psychedelics would, had they been widely employed earlier, have been classified with alcohol, ether, chloroform, and nitrous oxide (laughing gas) in the nineteenth century. Oliver Wendell Holmes advocated the use of ether as a method of developing altered states of consciousness. To demonstrate the mystical powers of ether,

Holmes kept a scratch pad with him while under the influence of the vapors. Upon awakening from one experiment, he read his ether-induced insights to anxious colleagues. Holmes's message of revelation: "A strong smell of turpentine prevails throughout."[87]

Numerous studies have provided analyses of the sociopolitical background of the criminalization of drugs.[88] The legal prohibition of drugs has created a market structure that is supportive of organized crime (not exclusively of a societal type) and a subculture of pushers and users. The process of manufacturing, selling, and distributing controlled substances is complex and requires cooperation on the part of many factions. American criminal societies play a relatively small role in this trade when the total operation is considered. Books like *The Heroin Trail*[89] give testimony to the intricate arrangements among growers (Turks or Mexicans), refiners (Corsicans), transporters (Cubans, Corsicans, French, Americans), distributors (American crime societies and criminal alliances of blacks, Puerto Ricans, and Cuban exiles), and peddlers (free agents and lower-level members of criminal alliances). Because of market conditions, the illegitimate narcotics business is clearly a criminal matrix of international proportions.

Today's illegitimate drug market shares the competitive spirit that surrounded bootlegging during Prohibition; i.e., it is violent and contains many "comers" trying to hit it big. Unlike booze during Prohibition, hard drugs do not possess a broad base of public appeal. Second, drug dealers are not likely to be viewed as benign "gangsters–business people" as were some of the more flamboyant bootleggers of the 1920s. We might note, however, that some of today's dealers (and users) are able to avoid the image of the dope fiend or pusher by virtue of their professional mystique. Collusion between physicians and pharmacists to sell narcotics, barbiturates, and amphetamines illegally is not unknown.[90] When such collusion arises in these professions as part of an established moneymaking pattern, it constitutes organized crime, i.e., a criminal alliance whose members wear white smocks instead of pinstripe suits. Given the competition, violence, pressure from law enforcement, and the abundance of "rookies" in the trade, it would appear that criminal societies are backing off from drug distribution in favor of other legitimate and illegitimate interests.[91] Much of the business is being handled (at both managerial and worker levels) by urban minority groups that make up criminal alliances.[92]

Loan-sharking (the "juice racket") derives in practice and in name from the past business of shylocking: the lending of money outside of state-restricted interest rates. It has been estimated that crime societies obtain large amounts of illegitimate revenue, second in value only to that gained from gambling, through loan-sharking.[93] The lending of money at usurious rates (vigorish)—estimates run from 5 percent to 20 percent on a weekly/monthly basis—is typically combined with a threat of violence for nonpayment of the principal and interest. More important than actual violence is the strong implication that force will be used if necessary.

A profitable moneylending business depends on a steady and increasing cash flow at work on the streets. Therefore, customers who cannot pay the combined principal and accrued interest are rarely killed or even injured in ways that would permanently impede their earning capacity (dead or crippled borrowers may mean a loss of the original investment). Typically, a bargain is arranged whereby the customer pays an agreed-upon amount (less than the actual combined value of the principal and interest) and is told, with more or less sincerity, to "never come back." The working capital for loan-sharking may come from gambling, narcotics, legitimate businesses, or even from banks (borrowed) and put on the streets for those willing to pay usurious rates.

People from a variety of social circumstances

may avail themselves of the services of a loan shark. The need for quick money can arise from gambling debts (incurred in a straight or rigged game that is calculated to produce indebtedness for a specific victim) or business ventures (legitimate or illegitimate) requiring seed money to get started. When a proposed business venture is unable to qualify for a standard bank loan, the alternative can be a loan shark. It is in regard to legitimate needs that Schelling has suggested the creation of new avenues of legal lending that will compete with loan-sharking.[94] Participants in the juice racket are frequently independents with only nominal ties to crime families. However, independents will indicate mob connections in order to intimidate the customer and encourage payment.

Legitimate banking practices sometimes include procedures (legally derived) that closely parallel the commonly cited features of loan-sharking. When borrowers cannot pay their debts, the bank is legally empowered to foreclose, thus depriving the customer of home or livelihood if certain tangibles have been used as collateral. Lending institutions were known to be less than sympathetic during the Depression, when many people were displaced through foreclosures on farms and homes that later became prime investments (when oil was discovered in places like Oklahoma and Texas). Stories abound concerning the banker who foreclosed once too often on homesteads, causing angry citizens to finally lynch the "bloodsucker" who had left families with nothing but the clothes on their backs. In addition, the principle of maintaining a steady cash flow (juice) is articulated in bankruptcy laws that permit borrowers to erase their debts, keep some of their vital property, and immediately begin borrowing again with the stroke of a pen and the clap of a judge's gavel. Finally, there is the matter of what constitutes a usurious loan and, by definition, loan-sharking. One state legislature has recently introduced a bill that will eliminate a set legal interest rate on loans over $15,000 (most home loans). This proposal, if approved, will allow banks to charge any interest rate that the borrower is willing (through ignorance or lack of an alternative) to pay. The rationalized check on potential abuses is that "it will be controlled by the free enterprise system,"[95] in that banks will not be "too usurious" because they will be competing for customers. While this rationale sounds plausible, it does not seem to be logically related to the legislation's original purpose. Namely, the prohibition of restricted interest rates (so it is reasoned) will draw money from other states (with lower set rates) into the state where investors can receive a larger return from banks where no state restrictions exist. The end result is that the borrower is no longer protected (because of legal default) from usurious interest rates. This, by definition, constitutes loan-sharking. Put another way, such practices amount to state-sanctioned shylocking. They also may mark the development of a criminogenic market structure. This practice, if approved, will escape the tag "criminal alliance" only because the law is used to legitimate it! One wonders who is behind such legislation. Could it be the Mafia?

Criminal societies and alliances are involved in other illicit businesses (black marketing, extortion, criminal monopolies, and "scam" operations, i.e., the gaining of control over an established business, using its presumably good credit to overpurchase, volume selling of merchandise at low prices, then declaring bankruptcy). If we were to examine these activities closely—a task that is beyond the scope of this chapter—we would likely find relationships between criminal societies or alliances and legitimate business procedures, since both are products of very similar market conditions.

A further look at criminal societies would, as the *Task Force Report* notes, prompt us to observe that many of the crime families are involved in legitimate concerns. According to one recent article, legitimate ventures are becoming a dominant activity of groups that were identified by Valachi as being part of La Cosa Nostra.[96] If the families are concentrating on legitimate businesses, then (it would appear) our chief efforts against organized crime should be governed by a generalized notion of the phenomenon, one that includes illegal corporate behavior.

4.05 CORPORATE CRIMINAL ALLIANCES

In this chapter, a great deal of attention has been devoted to only a part of organized crime; criminal societies and criminal alliances involved in illegal activities. This partial emphasis has a purpose, namely, to (1) explore the mythology of the "crime conspiracy" and (2) encourage the reader to observe that the behavior and activities of criminal societies and alliances are outgrowths of socioeconomic forces that stimulate another major part of organized crime—corporate criminal alliances.

Our economic system stresses competition in the marketplace. Extreme competitiveness, in turn, produces pressures to succeed that often encourage the rationalization of illegal shortcuts. The corporate world represents a criminogenic market structure in that laws designed to curb such crimes as monopolistic enterprise, illicit advertising, and product adulteration are rarely enforced effectively enough to counter the pursuit of illegal profits, both individual and collective. Concern about corporate crime is not new. Attempts to formulate a conceptualization of the problem have met with difficulty from both the perspectives of advancing the issue and enunciating an operational definition of corporate crime.

In the late 1800s, both rural and urban America were becoming uncomfortable with the growing power of the corporation. Farmers and city dwellers alike were anxiously concerned over the feeling that the financial "strings" in this country had moved from the local bank to Wall Street. An early target of the muckrakers was the railroad empire. Citizens, aroused over the rebate policies of railroads that favored meat packers and the oil companies,[97] demanded action, and this culminated in the passage of the Interstate Commerce Act of 1887. Sociologist E. A. Ross maintained an uncompromising position in his criticisms of the railroads' exploitation of Chinese workers on the West Coast. Unfortunately, he made his remarks as a faculty member of a university that was founded by a leading railroad entrepreneur of the day, Leland Stanford. Within a short time, after refusing to back off of his stance, Ross was dismissed from Stanford University.[98]

One of the more widely cited academic works on corporate crime is a contribution by Edwin Sutherland. His book *White Collar Crime* was instrumental in attacking the notions that crime belongs exclusively to the victims of poverty and that the law is administered apolitically without regard for the offender's power or social status. Sutherland defined "white-collar crime" as "a crime committed by a person of respectability and high social status in the course of his occupation."[99] Some have taken issue with the definition by noting that it is too restrictive in the sense that it (1) is more concerned with the status (corporate level) of violators than the nature of violations, (2) ignores business-related crime that is not integral to one's occupation, and (3) does not concentrate adequately on various confidence games.[100] A definitive study of white-collar crime should, perhaps, go beyond the corporation and its executives into the shady side of the aluminum siding business, correspondence school rip-offs, and coupon swindles. Collectively, this is costly crime and often involves several participants. However, in terms of annual cost, the ability to evade criminal prosecution, the total effect on daily life, and the lack of attention from authorities, corporate criminal alliances should have a higher priority within the parameters of organized crime. Many police departments have "bunko" squads assigned to investigate con games and local consumer fraud, but to whom do citizens turn (assuming, of course, that they are aware of illegal activity) in response to executives who have "ring around the collar"? The Better Business Bureau?

Although Sutherland identified white-collar crime (corporate crime) as organized crime almost three decades ago,[101] today a distinction is frequently made between corporate criminals and organized criminals. What appears to be a distinction is in actuality a distortion that further helps to reduce the crime stigma for errant executives. Reputed criminal-society figures have sought the commonly afforded leniency that courts extend to corporate criminals through appeals made by their defense counsels.[102]

The Sherman Act (1890) was passed to inhibit, among other monopolistic practices, price fixing among corporations. Violators may be dealt with in a civil or criminal manner, the former approach being the predominant one. Criminal violations are classified as misdemeanors, with the punishment ranging from fines to jail sentences or a combination fine/jail term. Like the Interstate Commerce Act discussed previously, the Sherman Act arose in response to public fears that collusive behavior on the part of the big corporations was getting out of control. Accordingly, it is illegal to restrain trade by conspiring to fix prices.

In 1961, forty-five executives became defendants to the criminal charge of price-fixing in the electrical industry. These men had carried out their illegal business over an 8-year period by rigging prices of commodities valued at $1.75 billion annually.[103] Defense attorneys pleaded before the judge that their clients (who included vice-presidents from General Electric, Westinghouse, and the Carrier Corporation) were pillars of the community, were not as cutthroat in their competitiveness as the Gulf Coast shrimpers.[104] Ironically, the attorneys used a rather poor choice of analogy for a trial that was based upon the crime of inhibiting competition through price fixing. Given the purposes of the Sherman Act, it would seem that ideally—if not in practice—it is desirable for corporations to relate to one another as cutthroat competitors. One can hardly imagine the defendants preferring to see *their* suppliers in competition, price wise, for their business!

Judge Ganey apparently perceived the contradiction and sentenced seven executives to prison terms (less than a year), with twenty-three others receiving suspended sentences and/or fines. General Electric, the pivotal corporation in the conspiracy, received the largest fine of the firms involved in the crime ($437,500). GE was able to avoid the possibility of further litigation in the form of civil suits by being allowed to plead nolo contendere on thirteen of the original indictments. Thus, the episode had symbolic value (striking back at the big guys), but as a practical matter it clearly demonstrated that crime *does* pay (recall the estimated value of illicit business over an 8-year period) if one goes about it properly. Following the verdict, several of the defendants returned to their old jobs convinced that they had been scapegoats for doing what "everyone" knew was necessary to succeed in the corporate world. When asked by an interviewer whether the electrical industry had benefited from this experience, an executive replied rather smugly: "One thing I've learned out of all this, is to talk to only one other person, not to go to meetings where there are lots of other people."[105] By definition, those who were in on the "incredible electrical conspiracy" formed a criminal alliance involving secret deals between/among several parties that produced recurring illegal profits. It was organized crime with a "take" that would have caused Legs Diamond to sit up, take notice, and feel rained upon.

When the drug problem is discussed, visions of Mafia distributors, black pushers, and doped-up youth usually come to mind. The drug problem also has another dimension that is frequently overlooked—corporate crime in the otherwise legitimate drug industry. Because of their close relationship to a comfortable existence and, life itself, pharmaceuticals have a rather inflexible source of demand. People do not just quit buying prescription drugs in order to cut down on expenses; they sometimes do without other essentials in order to buy necessary pharmaceuticals. In addition, the highly technical nature of the product precludes any reasonable amount of control over the industry through the consumer's informed choice of purchase. It is unreasonable to expect pharmacists to advise less expensive drugs when their profits are related to higher-priced items. Assuming that the public *could* exercise intelligent discretion through the advice of concerned pharmacists, prescription regulations and state substitution laws *prohibit* the dispensing of cheaper alternative drugs (drugs having the same therapeutic qualities) if a brand name is used in the prescription.[106] The key intermediary in the drug industry racket is the physician. Drug companies spend enormous amounts of money bombarding the physician's office with promotional materials that proclaim the superiority (rarely the economy) of their latest discovery. Weary physicians are likely to prescribe a drug by its brand (trade) name rather than its more complicated generic handle. For example, Shaw points out that physicians are more likely to recall Warner-Chilcott's "Peritrate" (brand name) than the the generic designation "pentaerythritoltetranitrate."[107] Thus, the consumers are bound to pay the going rate (for mundane reasons and because of legal reinforcement) when, as is typically the case, their prescriptions are by brand name.

The marketplace for legitimate drugs has monopolistic features that reduce competition within the industry. The case of the electrical conspiracy was chosen to illustrate the weak enforcement of laws enacted to reduce restraint of trade in a pressurized, competitive market. There is evidence that provisions in the law effectively promote monopolistic behavior in the drug industry, wherein 7 percent of the companies capture 80 percent of the sales annually.[108]

> . . . large corporations, in spite of their protestations regarding the value of free enterprise and the competitive system, dislike free enterprise and competition. They have used the patent system, which grants to the inventor a monopoly for a period of years, as a device for destroying the system of free enterprise and competition.[109]

Patent laws were originally intended to promote the advancement of science and technology by guaranteeing the inventor rewards, through protection against infringements, on a particular discovery for a specified time.

In many instances very minor modifications on an original invention are all that is needed for a patent. It is possible, then, for one to exploit patent laws by introducing insignificant changes to a basic, patented product. It is difficult to believe, for example, that over a thousand patents on the toothbrush have been approved.[110] The issues of patent abuse and monopolistic practices are joined when one corporation obtains exclusive rights on almost every conceivable modification of a product—thus avoiding price competition and promoting restraint of trade. The large drug companies reduce competition by juggling the chemical structure of a pharmaceutical just enough to obtain a patent for one or more "new" derivatives having the same healing properties. This procedure, referred to as "molecular manipulation,"[111] allows the parent company to get a large share of the market on a related drug grouping. For example, several cephalosporin compounds have been marketed under differing brand names: Kafosin, Keflin, Kefzol (Eli Lilly Company, Velosef (Squibb), and Ancef (Smith, Kline and French). All these drugs are therapeutically *equivalent* but have had their original compound structure (cephalosporin) altered enough to qualify for patenting and to be sold under a brand name. In addition to varying in their molecular structure, they also vary in price!

Attempts have been made to curb monopolistic practices in the "legitimate" drug industry. Efforts to control the drug corporations have met with heavy resistance, largely at the hands of a collusion between the Pharmaceutical Manufacturers Association (PMA) and the American Medical Association (AMA). Physician-entrepreneurs invest heavily in certain drug company stocks and, quite naturally, have a vested interest in prescribing the brand names that are manufactured by companies in which they have holdings. In return for this convenient arrangement, drug companies have been known to provide physicians with all sorts of "gifts." Reforms that would attest to public welfare interests—e.g., legislation that would affect patent registration, the exploitive use of brand names, and quality control over production and advertising—have been rewritten in an acceptable form by the combined workings of the PMA and the AMA. Under the mystique of the "healing art," drug companies and physicians have hoodwinked the public into believing that, as Eli Lilly would have you believe, "For years, we've been making drugs as if someone's life [not necessarily ours or the pocketbooks of the stockholders] depended upon them."[112] The above activities smack of corporate criminal alliances (monopolies) and criminal alliances between physicians and drug companies. No one really knows how much these actions cost the public—they escape criminal sanctions because the law provides for their existence.

Giant corporations such as General Motors occasionally come under the scrutiny of the Justice Department for practices in restraint of trade. Unlike street criminals in danger of apprehension, corporations are usually well prepared in advance to defend their interests against those "who would destroy the free enterprise system." The auto industry, for example, has its own paid political analysts in the capital who keep them well informed as to pending legislation and the currents of public policymaking. But when caught by surprise, the industry is capable of committing acts that appear to have been copied from a grade B movie. Ralph Nader was the victim of some rather pedestrian harrassment by GM, the company that helped to "put America on wheels," when he was appearing before a Senate subcommittee on auto safety. Nader had written a well-received book, *Unsafe at Any Speed,*[113] that was highly critical of GM's now defunct (as a result of Nader's efforts) Corvair automobile. The head of GM's legal department hired a private detective to trail Nader on the pretext that he (Nader) was using his book and public appearances to prime potential jurors for pending negligence suits in which Nader would assist the plaintiffs. Detectives were instructed to probe for flaws in Nader's private life that could be used to discredit him. Nader further charged that he was plagued by constant phone calls while preparing testimony before the subcommittee and also annoyed by girls hired to catch him in a compromising situation. The affair ended after Nader sued GM for invasion of privacy and received a public apology from GM's president.[114]

As one of four major auto manufacturers, GM makes over 50 percent of the cars sold annually in this country. It is a corporation that has absorbed more than a hundred companies and has its own financing (GMAC) and insurance (Motors Insurance Corporation) subsidiaries.[115] Corporations possessing similar characteristics have been successfully prosecuted under the Sherman Act, most notably DuPont and Standard Oil. Lawyers from the Antitrust Division of the Justice Department began to look into GM's holdings during the latter part of the Eisenhower administration, but they have so far failed to exert any significant influence on the corporation's activities.

Corporate monopolies are more than a response to criminogenic market conditions—i.e., weakly interpreted antitrust laws as well as the absence of legally established restraints—in a competitive economic environment. Diffuse illegal behavior may also be an *effect* of markets dominated by oligopolist enterprises. Studies of the automobile industry (an oligopoly) reveal that lawful policy directives from the corporation place undue financial pressures upon dealers, promoting illegal behavior. Farberman found that auto manufacturers pressure dealers to sell a high volume of cars at a small margin of profit. This directive, in turn, places a burden on the dealers to amass enough working capital to avoid borrowing high-interest funds with which to purchase automobiles from the manufacturer. Refusal to buy a quota can result in one's franchise being revoked by the company. Faced with small profit margins from new-car sales, the dealer rationalizes various illegal activities that supply the needed cash flow. Crimes directly related to the corporate directives include the submission of phony warranty receipts by the dealer to the manufacturer and repair swindles plied against buyers.[116]

The used-car market is also affected by Detroit's directives in that a shortage of used cars (a trend that has grown in response to new-car prices) prompts new-car dealers to accept kickbacks from independent lots in return for a supply of marketable "preowned" automobiles.[117] Finally, the independent used-car dealer rationalizes the practice of "short sales"[118] as a necessary source of cash to meet the expense of kickbacks to the franchised dealer. Given the above complicated matrix (originating in Detroit rather than Marseilles), one may muse at the shortsightedness of attacking white-collar crime at the corner auto repair shop without looking beyond, to where the cars are distributed under conditions that influence crime on main street.

Examples of corporate-level criminal alliances are revealed frequently. We have heard of the ITT scandal and "the milk fund" (reminiscent of Watergate), collusion within the "military-industrial complex," the marketing of unsafe drugs, the tainted processed-food industry, and so on. We are told that citizens are cynical about high-level corporate crime and that judicial policies of lenience may be in harmony with public indifference. To the contrary, it may be that as our economic and political institutions have come increasingly under fire,[119] the public has become more sensitive to the issue of corporate crime. Almost twenty years ago, Newman investigated the attitudes of Americans toward violators of pure food and drug laws. The study revealed that respondents chose substantially harsher sentences for violators than were actually given in selected cases.[120] If the matter could be explored, one would likely find that "the Godfather" has more voluntary customers than do corporate criminal alliances.

SUMMARY

Organized crime is a complex problem encompassing behavior that is more generalized than the images protrayed in, for example, a James Cagney movie. Whether it be the workings of a criminal society, a criminal alliance, or more specifically, a corporate criminal alliance, the content and objectives of the activities are the same, namely:

> illegal acts designed to directly or indirectly secure a system of financial rewards through the provision of goods and services for consumer groups differing in size and knowledge of involvement.[121]

Central to our concept of organized crime is the existence of a criminogenic market structure wherein competition for excessive profits acts as a catalyst for crime. The competition itself, and resulting illegal acts, may spring from laws that prohibit certain goods and services (e.g., Prohibition). The profit motive may also generate organized crime when laws, through absent or weak legislation, fail to curb the drive for inordinate profits by allowing illegal business practices to continue and proliferate (e.g., restraint of trade). A distinction that is frequently drawn between corporate crime and other forms of organized crime concerns violence. The implication is that corporate criminals may get a little shady at times but are too refined to stoop to the violence associated with criminal societies or noncorporate criminal alliances. It is the element of violence that often serves to justify the belief that criminal societies are held together in a structured, totalitarian fashion.[122]

While citing distinctions between corporate crime and the so-called Cosa Nostra, Tyler observes the similarities between early capitalism and the developing criminal societies of the 1920s.[123] One need only reflect on the company "goon squads" used to break up union organizational meetings just a few decades ago. State police units, now commonly called the highway patrol or state troopers, were used extensively to suppress rioting miners and factory workers. The original submachine gun (before it filtered down for use in gang warfare) was promoted for use by police departments on the basis of its being able to 'humanely' disperse labor rioters with special bird-shot cartridges."[124] Today, there are whole industries that depend upon the tools of violence (weapons, war chemicals, electrical gadgetry for combat) for their profits.

Violence among criminal societies is still present (over a dozen deaths followed the attempted assassination of Joe Colombo in 1971), but it is relatively less frequent. It may be decreasing, or at least becoming more sporadic, as criminal societies move from the streets into suites. Criminal societies can assume, as do corporate criminal alliances, that pressures from law enforcement are minimal, prosecution is rare, and penalties are slight. There is no longer the need to silence threats on a wholesale basis. As Gordon observes:

> . . . corporate crime does not require violence because it is ignored by the police; corporate criminals can safely assume they do not face the threat of jail and do not therefore have to cover their tracks with the threat of harming those who betray them.[125]

Current strategies to combat organized crime are tied to conventional wisdom as espoused by the *Task Force Report*; that is, organized crime represents a conspiracy (Italian-dominated silent societies) that seeks to wrench enormous profits through illegal acts which have violence as a hallmark. With this as the perceived essence of the problem, public law enforcement policy has responded with control measures that are congruent with the conspiracy approach. The use of conspiracies to explain diffuse social problems may reify threats that are nonexistent. Additionally, when the enemy is cast up as a sinister, secretive force, the door is opened for abusive law enforcement practices that may endanger such civil liberties as the right to privacy, freedom from unreasonable searches, and so on. The danger lies in the public's belief that they are immune from such practices and that only the "bad guys" need be concerned.

Title III of the Omnibus Crime Control and Safe Streets Act (1968) provided for wiretapping to be used in gathering evidence on suspected organized criminals involved in specified crimes such as gambling, illicit narcotics trade, and so on. In its original form, the Act placed restraints on bugging (limits on duration and frequency) in order to prevent abuses.[126] The final form of Title III, however, increased the initially recommended limits and also stipulated that only crimes (in general) that threatened the commonweal, and for which a penalty of *more* than a year imprisonment was provided, could qualify for wiretapping permits. Interestingly, criminal prosecution of Sherman Act violations are treated as misdemeanors. Misdemeanors provide for possible imprisonment for *less* than a year. Some corporate executives may have breathed a sigh of relief over this amended provision of the act!

The Task Force strongly urged that tactical approaches (short-term suppression) to organized crime be replaced by more sophisticated strategic information gathering that would facilitate long-term control over crime cartels. A model intelligence-gathering program had been established previously by the state of New York. The NYSIIS (New York State Identification and Intelligence System) is a good illustration of a noble concern for civil liberties deteriorating under pressure for access to information of questionable value. Sensitive to some growing public concern over unbridled information systems and data banks, the head of NYSIIS cautioned that "the public is concerned, and rightfully so, about such things as 1984. It is getting awfully close—1984 is obviously only six years away, and some of the predictions of George Orwell are holding up pretty well. We had better be concerned about this because people are beginning to get mighty nervous."[127] Heeding the director's advice, NYSIIS has built in controls—aimed at protecting privacy and civil liberties—which restrict users, restrict the type of information to be entered and released, and provide that data will be gathered and stored only on actual or "probable" recidivists.[128] It would seem the NYSIIS has not held fast on its first provision (restriction of users) in that Gerth charges that information has been bought by, among others, American Airlines and Retail Credit Company. Further, state law provides that the New York Stock Exchange shall have access to NYSIIS data relative to its employees.[129] In an article on criminal justice information systems, Niederhoffer cites further differentials between NYSIIS principles and practices.[130]

Prior to 1961, the FBI was relatively uninvolved in the campaign against organized crime. The usual explanation for the lack of activity during this period was that the bureau did not have jurisdictional prerequisites. In addition, Hoover had his forces tied up with suppressing the Communist party, and toward the mid-1960s, the Ku Klux Klan. Some have humorously observed that the Communist party and the Klan were able to remain financially solvent because of the dues paid by FBI undercover agents. Whether the absence of jurisdictional power and the existence of other commitments were the only reasons why the FBI was reluctant to join in the fight against organized crime is another matter. At any rate, beginning in 1961, Attorney General Robert Kennedy pushed for legislation that would expand the bureau's role in the investigation and prosecution of organized crime. Table 4-1 lists the various bills enacted to facilitate the FBI's pursuit against the underworld activities of gambling and loan-sharking.[131]

Year of Enactment	Convictions to Date	
1961 Bills banning; Interstate Transportation of Wagering Paraphernalia (ITWP); Interstate Transmission of Wagering Information (ITWI); Interstate Transportation in Aid of Racketeering (ITAR)	ITWP ITWI ITAR	101 308 1,612
1964 Sports Bribery Statute		12
1968 Extortionate Credit Transactions (ECT)	ECT	215
1970 Provisions of the Organized Crime Control Act: Illegal Gambling Business Statute (IGB); Racketeer Influenced and Corrupt Organizations Statute (RICO)	IGB RICO	2,419 1

The concern of the FBI and, more generally, various strike forces with the revenue sources (gambling, loan-sharking, etc.) of criminal societies and alliances symbolizes the overshadowing apprehension that the crime conspiracy is eroding our basic political and economic values. Therefore, it is reasoned, these income sources must be crippled in order to save our democracy. The assumption is that the underworld wants to destroy government and the so-called free-enterprise system. One should really pause and wonder whether organized crime, at all levels, wants to destroy a system that has proved so profitable. Would it not be more practical to support a system of laws and government that creates or perpetuates profitable market structures—a system in which corruption and collusion are more than occasional signs of petty venality? Would it not be more efficient to exploit the weaknesses of an existing system rather than destroy it and risk the alternative of a reformist government?

In terms of the "legitimate" economy, criminal societies and alliances (rarely thought of as including corporate criminal alliances) are viewed as a threat when they use their illegally acquired funds (gambling, etc.) to promote legitimate businesses. If these businesses are run on a legitimate basis, provide reputable goods and services at competitive prices (probably some do), and happen to be in the hands of those identified as La Cosa Nostra, so what? If, to the contrary, these legitimate businesses (laundries, car-rental agencies, vending-machine operations, etc.) are conducted by illegal means, then the law should step in to prosecute them vigorously, as it should any other illegally operated legitimate business regardless of who owns the controlling interest. However, the emphasis is commonly placed on stopping the illegal business practices of criminal societies/alliances rather than those of more established, "respectable" entrepreneurs.

If organized crime is to be controlled (since it is not likely to be eliminated), solutions will have to originate from fundamental reconsiderations as to human nature and our social, political, and economic arrangements. The control of organized crime will not come from wiretapping provisions, data banks, and one-sided law enforcement alone. We must first come to grips with the idea that some activities (most notably gambling) are widely desired, regardless of whether we consider them to be patently immoral or simply forms of recreation. To criminalize gambling is to invite the development of organized groups ready to meet the demands of a profitable business as well as to provide tainted revenue for corrupt governments. Prostitution has a seamier side in that it stems from basic sexual inequality and exploitation. To criminalize the prostitute is to multipy social injustice and exacerbate allied problems (venereal disease, muggings, and extortion). The issue of drugs is complicated indeed. Encouraging people to use substances that can only reduce still further their ability to break from an already narrow opportunity structure is criminal behavior. A solution of the drug problem, however, rests with a consideration of the social forces behind drug use and the issue of public welfare versus profiteering in the legitimate drug industry. Gambling and prostitution more likely represent public consensus, either overt or covert. They should be legalized. If groups identified as having connections with organized crime become involved in these businesses and conduct them lawfully, so be it. If not, equitable prosecution should be applied for predatory and monopolistic violations.

The control of organized crime also depends on acceptance of the notion that this is a broad problem which encompasses images not usually associated with the Mafia stereotype. Dealing with organized crime also involves criminalizing those corporate criminals that make a mockery of the free enterprise ideology. Tough, enforceable antitrust legislation should be combined with strike forces on corporate criminal alliances. One might reflect on the token attempts to get at white-collar crime by noting that LEAA's 1973 budget was set a $1.75 billion;[132] of that, a mere *$532,000* was earmarked for the fight against white-collar crime.[133] If the crime-busting resources of wiretapping, surveillance, infiltration, and data banks were applied to suspected illegal corporate activities, the war against organized crime would at least have integrity. Monopolistic behavior—whether it represents corporate greed or the interests of organized criminal societies—is socially destructive. Smith hits the nail on the head when he observes that:

> As long as we countenance violence, consider personal gain to be more important than equity, are more interested in holding out the goal of success than in providing sufficient opportunities to achieve it, and are willing to bend the law for ourselves in the pursuit of wealth, power, and personal gratification and to persuade government officials, through corrupt dealings, to cooperate in that process—to that extent we will have a society receptive to illicit enterprise generally.[134]

As it began, this chapter has ended with a quotation that is intended to highlight the deeper meanings of the problem that we call "organized crime." Through viewpoints expressed by the author and a number of other students of the subject, we have attempted to assimilate interpretations about organized crime that approach the reality of the situation. Thus, the paradigm has been presented. Acceptance of this broadened concept of organized crime is, of course, the reader's choice. However, choosing not to accept the above analysis could be altered should someone in a pinstripe suit "make you an offer you can't refuse."

Chapter 5

Law Enforcement in America

Louis is a thirty-year-old police officer in a large metropolitan area. He has been on the force for 5 years now and plans to make law enforcement his career. He has gripes though. This week has been especially tough. He unbuckles his Smith and Wesson .38 service revolver, slumps his large frame in an overstuffed chair, pops the top of a beer, and recalls the week.

> Monday, we are serving a summons on a heroin pusher. When the son of a bitch sees us on the porch, he starts shooting. My partner drops him. I was too busy to be scared then, but two hours later I was shaking like a leaf. And Tuesday. Jesus, some nut shoots out the dome light on the blue-and-white. We finally locate the rooftop where this dude is taking target practice. It turns out he's an ex-mental patient who hates the police because he thinks the FBI is tapping his phone. Last night a drunk vomited all over my uniform, and to top off the evening we get a family disturbance call. The husband is beating the hell out of his wife over an argument about who gets the rest of a hamburger. We pull him off her. She gets mad because she thinks we are too rough with "her man" and bites me. Just as we were going off watch I spot this young guy working over an old lady for her purse. I chase him three blocks and when I catch him he tries to knee me in the groin. I broke his nose. Turns out he's big for his age. He's only fifteen. The Captain ain't gonna like that. Tonight I gotta go listen to my sociology professor explain to me how the police are just the tools of the ruling class to keep poor people oppressed and that most of what we do is reassure nervous old ladies about prowlers and coax cats out of trees. I'd like to coax him out of his ivory tower.[1]

The same or similar opinions could have

been repeated in interviews with police officers throughout the country. It reveals at least three things about police work in America. First, the nature of law enforcement ranges from controlling the use of drugs to keeping the peace within families. Second, as a highly visible symbol of the authority of society, the police attract the hostility and resentment of various segments of society from Marxist intellectuals to frustrated misfits. Finally, the police themselves often feel misunderstood and unappreciated.

The police, whose task is the preservation of public order and the prevention and detection of crime, are a relatively recent development in cultural history. Before analyzing law enforcement in this modern era, we will take a look at law and order in primitive societies.

5.01 LAW AND ORDER IN EGALITARIAN SOCIETIES

"Law comes with property, marriage and government," writes Will Durant. "The lowest societies manage to get along without it."[2] But the absence of law does not mean a permissive society free of control, since primitive socieites are ruled by a custom as uncompromising as any law. The glue which holds any society together is custom; it guarantees order and stability. Our elaborate bureaucracy of law enforcement is conspicuous by its absence in the lives of primitive people. The Eskimo, the Bushmen of the Kalahari, and the Australian aborigines, among others, managed to live for hundreds of thousands of years with only the most elementary forms of law and virtually no provisions for law enforcement.[3] Why are contemporary societies so dependent on their law-and-order specialists?

The maintenance of order finds it roots in the common interests of the populace. The greater the amount of common interest, the less need there is for law-and-order specialists. When people are wedded together by their common interests, they do not need an external force to compel them to cooperate. In primitive societies—where rivers, oceans, soil, pasture, are all open to members of the band or tribe—there is no need to protect these natural resources, since they belong to all. However, when one segment of a society has greater control over access to natural resources, when there are marked distinctions between the rich and the poor, when the ruler and the ruled arise, then some means of law enforcement is required to compel conformity.

With the rise of modern societies, there evolved stratification by social classes; along with this separation came the concept of private property. No longer are rivers, streams, and pasturelands open to all. Indeed, the wealthy mark off large sections of land and flaunt their nonuse of it in such a way that the economist-sociologist Thorstein Veblen (1857–1929) would refer to these spacious, manicured lawns as "unused pasture" and "conspicuous consumption." With the arrival of the concept of private property came the need for a paramilitary organization to protect the interests of landlords and the propertied classes.

Think for a moment of the sprawling megalopolis that comprises the New York–New Jersey area. On any humid summer evening there is on the average 5,000 people crowding every acre of land. Now picture the swimming pools of the country club set, encircled by gracious ladies in their bikinis, and this scene surrounded by vast unused pasture where middle-aged men amuse themselves by trying to hit tiny white balls into small holes in the ground. Why do you think the crowded poor allow the wealthy their Byzantine delights? Because in New York there are over 30,000 armed bluecoats who enforce the laws governing private property.

It is not within the scope of this brief introduction to cover all the facets of law enforcement. We shall, however, attempt to introduce the student to some of the current issues. We begin by examining the origins of modern law enforcement with the development of the London police and the influence of the English system on the structure of American law enforcement. Next we discuss police discretionary powers, police-community relations, the "police personality," and the use of women on patrol. Finally, we will examine some of the equipment utilized by the police: K-9 dogs, dumdum bullets, the polygraph, and forensic odontology.

5.02 THE DEVELOPMENT OF THE LONDON POLICE

The hostility that equated American police with "pigs" during the 1960s looks like mild antipathy compared with nineteenth-century attitudes toward the early Metropolitan Police—or "Scotland Yard"—of England. Today Scotland Yard is justifiably proud of its reputation as the most efficient and incorruptible police force in the world. During its early days, however, its members were attacked on all sides. They occasionally wore collars with iron spikes so that they could not easily be strangled or garroted. There was even a case in which the death of a policeman during a riot was adjudged justifiable homicide on the ground that the victim was, after all, a police officer, for whom such a fate was to be expected.[4]

This widespread hatred of the police is even more surprising when one considers that crime was then far more prevalent than it is today, with whole districts of London being prey to daily daylight robberies. To understand this animosity, we must retrace the development of the British police system. The creation of the Metropolitan Police in 1829 came about after more than two hundred years of resistance to the idea of an organized police force. The British believed that all the countries which then had police forces were despotisms, as indeed they were. At that time, every European police system, including the French, was a government instrument for espionage and tyranny, and nobody in England, from members of Parliament to illiterates, could see how any English police force might be any different. There was also simply a deep-seated resistance to change. Britons had gotten along without police during the period following feudalism, when the other European countries had developed such forces, and they saw no reason why they should develop a force.

The French police *(gendarmerie)* had been established by the rulers of the small postfeudal nation-states, each of whom needed a force to protect his state's boundaries. When these men at arms *(genŝ d'armes)* were not needed at the borders, it was obviously good business to use them to keep the peace at home. Britain, however, had no land frontiers needing guards and so did not develop such a force. The system using the amateur parish constable—in which the parish, county, or village would appoint one person to act as volunteer peacekeeper—had been sufficient since the late Middle Ages. Each village or county was thereby autonomous, and none wanted to lose that independence to any "central police." The only attempt at change had come in 1655, when Oliver Cromwell had divided England and Wales into police districts guarded by mounted soldiers. But this brought such hatred and resistance from the citizens that, after 18 months, even Cromwell gave up.

Clearly, then, as British scholar Patrick Pringle observes: "The main reason for opposition to the police idea in Britain was not love of freedom but hatred of change. France had a police force in the eighteenth century because France had always had a police force. England had no police force because England never had a police force. . . . The police was as difficult to introduce in England as it would have been to abolish in France."[5]

The earliest crime fighters arose in the late 1600s: self-styled detectives called "thief takers" and "common informers." Simply as a citizen, one could appoint oneself thief taker and hand highway robbers, burglars, and murderers over to the law. Rewards were outlandishly unfair by today's standards: a typical reward to the thief taker for conviction of a highway robber was £40 plus the robber's horse, weapons, and property. Obviously, such a profession drew many practitioners and quickly became boundlessly corrupt.

This free-for-all "system" was made possible by the official assumption that government responsibility ended with setting harsh punishments and carrying out sentences, leaving it to "the public" to bring in evildoers. This philosophy of strong punishment as a deterrent to crime led to the quadrupling of the number of crimes punishable by death, which went from about fifty to over two hundred by 1820.[6] But despite strong penalties, the situation was becoming intolerable by the middle of the eighteenth century, leading Justice of the Peace Henry Fielding (better known today as the author of *Tom Jones*) to decide that something had to be done about it. He convinced the government that London, by then the only major city on earth without a police force, could no longer get by without one, and was given enough money to hire a dozen assistants. Because Fielding's court was in Bow Street, his helpers were immediately dubbed the Bow Street Runners. At pay of 1 shilling a week, they were supposed to observe, to disguise themselves and visit the dens of criminals, to recruit informers, and to remember faces—in short, to give a more realistic picture than the corrupt and self-serving thief takers were doing of just who the criminals were. Of course, since Fielding kept the numbers small—never more than fifteen men—they were at a considerable disadvantage against the countless London criminals. And though there was still frequent misuse of authority and rampant dishonesty, the Bow Street Runners were fairly successful, in part due to Fielding's compilation of a register of known criminals complete with "word descriptions" of each one.[7]

When Fielding died in 1754, his half-brother John took over and headed the Runners until his death in 1780. In 1785, William Pitt tried to organize a central London police, but the mayor and aldermen of the City begged him to "relieve them from the dread of being reduced under the scourge of such a system."[8] And this was in a city' in which it was reckoned that there was a criminal for every 822 citizens, and that some 30,000 people made their living exclusively by robbery and theft![9]

Crime continued to increase through the early years of the nineteenth century. While the wealthier London citizenry hired private guards, a Select Committee of the House of Commons explained in 1818 why London should never have a police force: "In a free country, such a system would of necessity be odious and repulsive, and one which no government could be able to carry into execution. . . . It would be a plan which would make every servant of every house a spy on the actions of his master, and all classes of society spies on each other."[10]

In the 1820s, Home Secretary Robert Peel began a massive reform and consolidation of the existing common-law code, finally convincing Parliament that despite better laws, crime would never be brought under control without an organized police force. So in 1829, in defiance of popular opinion, the Metropolitan Police Act gave London a detective force of 1,000 men.

From the first, these Metropolitan Police, taking as their motto "Softly, softly," were intent on convincing the public that they were not going to be a repressive force like the French Sûreté. Since the French police ultimately drew their strength from their power to coerce, they could always rely on fear to get results. But the British police had to be fair and straightforward to continue in existence at all.[11]

Because of the strengh of public hatred, the early "bobbies" avoided the stigma of an obvious uniform by wearing ordinary tailcoats, trousers, and top hats. They carried truncheons instead of guns and kept them hidden, in order not to inflame public enmity even more. But the first "coppers" had a terrible time of it—they were thrown into the river, tossed onto spiked railings, assaulted, and kicked to death. It is not surprising that during the first 10 years of the Metropolitan Police, over six thousand recruits quit.[12]

What *is* surprising is that over five thousand recruits were fired. Peel and the first commissioners of the new police (nicknamed Scotland Yard for its headquarters building, which had formerly housed Scottish kings on state visits) were determined to win public trust on the basis not only of amicable behavior but also of demonstrated honesty. Recruits were given stringent rules of conduct, their powers were severely limited, and they were liable to fines and imprisonment for the slightest abuse of their powers.

Official dislike of the police continued for awhile: the central City of London occasionally gave asylum to wanted criminals and the courts often opposed the police. Rural constables often refused to give the Metropolitan Police necessary information in the investigation of cases. But officialdom gradually began to cooperate, and the public gradually began to trust the police. By the 1850s and 1860s when Charles Dickens began writing short pieces about the detective force for the popular *Household Words* magazine, the public followed the police adventures with pleasure. In 1869, a new police commissioner would still complain of the "suspicion . . . of the majority of Englishmen [of the police],"[13] but the public had begun to see itself as more on the side of the police than the "underdog" criminal.

Within a few more decades, the British police had become a cornerstone of the free government its opponents had feared it would undermine. By the twentieth century, Scotland Yard had become a synonym for incorruptibility and great detective work, and "bobby" had become a term more of fondness than denigration.[14]

5.03 LAW ENFORCEMENT IN AMERICA

The colonists who came to the American continent in the seventeenth and eighteenth centuries naturally brought, as part of their culture, the law enforcement structure with which they were familiar in England. The offices of constable and sheriff are direct cultural transplants from our English heritage. In America as in England, when towns grew in size and population, they began to develop organized metropolitan police forces of their own.

The earliest police forces were divided into two-shift systems; one for day and one for night. Since these shifts were separately administered, rivalries quickly arose and there was little cooperation between the two. Responding to this situation, the New York Legislature passed a law in 1844 creating the first unified day-and-night police.

These early police forces faced many of the

The police are responsible for everything from conducting the annual dog census to controlling crowds during a Mardi Gras parade.

problems that plague modern departments: poor public relations, low salaries, and political control.[15] From these early beginnings, we have seen the rise of various agencies of law enforcement that reflect the complex nature of our urban, industrial society. It is more precise to speak of "law enforcement" than "police," since the job of seeking conformity to the complex legal system of the United States has now been spread over a number of departments and organizations. More than ½ million people are employed by approximately forty thousand agencies in the service of law enforcement. About fifty of these agencies are at the federal level; the states account for about two hundred more; and the remainder are scattered throughout the counties, cities, and townships at the local level of government. Law enforcement in the United States tends to be fragmented and decentralized. As a nation, we have distrusted and resisted the establishment of a "national police force."

This fragmentation leads to questions of jurisdiction. At the time President John F. Kennedy was assassinated, it was not a federal crime to kill a President unless it happened on federally owned property. Thus Lee Harvey Oswald, had he lived, would have been tried by the state of Texas for homicide. The closest thing to a national police force that we have is the FBI, which has the authority to deal with about 180 federal crimes. Some idea of the specialization in law enforcement may be gained by looking at the numerous agencies on the federal level.[16]

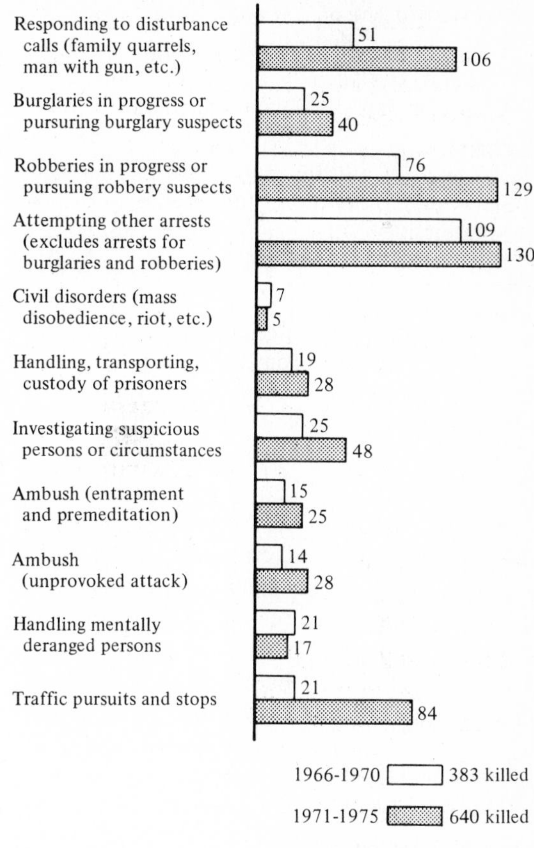

Figure 5-1 Situations in which law enforcement officers were killed, 1966–1975. *UCR, 1975.*

Federal Law Enforcement Agencies

The Department of Justice
Immigration and Naturalization Service: Border Patrol
    United States Marshal: Civil Rights
    Federal Drug Enforcement Administration
    Federal Bureau of Investigation

The Department of the Treasury
Bureau of Customs
Internal Revenue Service
Secret Service
Treasury Guard Force
White House Police Force
Bureau of Alcohol, Firearms, and Tobacco Tax

The Department of Defense
Office of Special Intelligence (OSI), United States Air Force
    Office of Naval Intelligence (ONI), United States Navy
    Criminal Investigation Division (CID), United States Army

The Post Office Department
Bureau of Postal Inspection

The Department of Transportation
United States Coast Guard

Units of law enforcement are also maintained within the following Departments: State; Interior, Labor; Agriculture; Commerce; and Health, Education, and Welfare. The following independent agencies of the federal government also maintain law enforcement units:

Atomic Energy Commission (AEC)
Civil Aeronautics Board (CAB)
Federal Communication Commission (FCC)
Interstate Commerce Commission
United States Civil Service Commission

State and Local Law Enforcement

The whole system of criminal justice begins with the police, and the array of things for which the police are responsible is mind-boggling. In addition to patrol and detective functions, the police may be called upon to license taxi drivers, regulate dance halls, conduct the annual dog census, control alcoholic beverages, run crime labs, and sponsor Police Athletic League contests. While television glamorizes the police's detective function, most police officers are in the patrol divisions. It is their duty to "keep the peace."

Keeping the peace does not, as is suggested by the movies, mean that the police race around having gunfights on a daily basis. Indeed, many police officers go from rookie to retirement without firing their weapons anywhere but on the range. As an agent of conflict resolution, the police officer is invested by society with the right to use "nonnegotiable force." Social workers, ministers, and psychologists may counsel, persuade, advise, suggest, or otherwise make recommendations to persons involved in various conflict situations, but the police officer *demands* conformity. A concerned social worker may plead with a drunken husband not to beat his wife and may be ignored. The police, however, "lay down the law" and can say to the husband, "One more word outta you, and we go downtown." Because we invest such power in the police, it is important that they use discretion in applying it.

5.04 POLICE DISCRETION

Discretion is the power or right to decide or act according to one's own judgment. It is the quality of being discreet and prudent. When we advise someone: "Use your own discretion," we imply "Use your own best judgment." The implication is that we expect cautious, judicious actions.

The discretionary power of the police resembles an inverted pyramid. Police officers on the beat have such "low visibility" that they are, by virtue of this position, enabled to exercise greater discretion than their supervisors. The police commission, who is constantly covered by the searchlight of the press, is in the position of having the most power and the least discretion. The rule is "the higher the visibility of the decision, the less discretion allowed to the decider."

Suppose a police officer stops a young law student for a traffic violation and discovers that the student has a marijuana cigarette. The officer may choose to arrest the student or, reasoning that society would not profit from ruining a budding career, just suggest that the student "eat the cigarette."

On the other hand, suppose the officer makes the arrest and the district attorney, discovering that the arrested student is the mayor's nephew, refuses to file charges. The press might then charge the D.A. with favoritism and build the incident into a public issue. Streetcorner justice is accomplished without this fanfare and at the discretion of the officer on the beat.

Discretion in Three Styles of Policing

Wilson describes three styles of policing which he calls the watchman style, the legalistic style, and the service style.[17] The watchman style is characteristic of those police departments with little professionalization and of politicians who appeal primarily to blue-collar workers. This approach leads to underenforcement of the law, corruption, and decisions based primarily on each patrol force member's private sense of justice.

In the legalistic style, there is greater professionalization and specialization as well as stricter adherence to the letter of the law. Traffic tickets are issued at a high rate, and the entire thrust of the department is an attempt to apply a single standard of law enforcement to all members of the community. Because of the emphasis on professionalism, this approach appeals to the middle class. Lower class citizens tend to resent its inflexibility and to see the police as "uptight."

The third style of enforcement, the service style, requires the police to intervene frequently but not always formally. The service style seeks a middle ground between the legalistic and watchman styles of policing. In applying informal sanctions, it is less sloppy than the watchman style and less uptight than the strictly legal approach to law enforcement. In order to observe at first hand how the police exercise their discretion, this writer rode along a patrol car in one of the New Orleans districts which has a high crime rate.[18]

One Saturday Night in a Patrol Car

11:02 P.M. We notice three men in the doorway of a drugstore. We make the block, park the blue-and-white out of sight, and the officers confront the men. One of the men is on the methadone program; he has a weekend "take-out" and is probably trying to sell it to the other two men. All are addicts. The officers confiscate the methadone and tell the addict he can get it back at the clinic. One of the other men is so "stoned" he has to be told three times he can leave.

11:35 P.M. Spot a teen-age (15-year-old) girl walking past a bar. The officers pick her up and take her home. "Her mother gives us tips on what's going down," they explain. "She has four kids and we try to help her keep track of them."

Midnight Answer a burglar alarm at a nurses' dormitory. Turns out it went off by itself.

1:00 A.M. Pass a lower-class bar. About a dozen black men are standing outside; most are drinking wine out of bottles wrapped in paper sacks. We stop. The officers line everyone up, take their IDs, tell them to go inside to drink, and we leave. "If we don't do this, pretty soon they'll decide to get into some mischief or they'll hassle people coming down the sidewalk. This way, they know we have an eye on them. Prevention."

2:13 A.M. A youth is running down the sidewalk being chased by two others. We stop them. Seems they were all sniffing glue and drinking wine and got into an argument. Officers confiscate the glue, break the wine bottles, take IDs, and send the youths off, all in separate directions.

3:30 A.M. Family disturbance call. Husband and wife are in a beef over who is going to eat the last piece of birthday cake. Actually, they are not married, but are living together "common law." Since the woman owns the house, officers advise her that she could throw him out and eat all the cake she wants.

4:02 A.M. Stop a car with a broken tail light. "Some guys love to give tickets," explains one officer. "I just stop these nit-picking things when I'm bored." Driver is warned to get it fixed.

4:45 A.M. Woman comes running down the street wearing only a cheap housecoat, screaming she has been raped. She leads the officers to her apartment, where she says the rapist has passed out drunk. Officers wake a sleeping man by placing a revolver in his ear. The stunned man explains she is a prostitute and, since he didn't feel he got his money's worth, he refused to pay her price. Officers send him on his way, look at the irate prostitute, and just shake their heads.

Rest of Evening Uneventful. Spend an hour "cooping" (dozing in the car).

5.05 Police-Community Relations

When former President Nixon was campaigning for office in 1972, he stopped at the shoeshine stand of a little black boy, leaned over, and asked in his most unctuous voice: "And what would you like to be when you grow up?" "Well," replied the youngster, "I know one thing. I don't want to be no police."[19]

The police have problems maintaining good public relations with the community at large and with minority groups in particular. A graphic illustration of mutual mistrust and misinformation followed the police raid on a Black Panther headquarters in Chicago. Two Black Panthers were killed in the raid, and an erroneous charge was widely disseminated that twenty-eight Panthers had been systematically murdered by the police. The unjustified rumor spread what has come to be known as "the black genocide myth." The Reverend Ralph Abernathy stated: "There is a calculated design of genocide in this country. . . . For too long black people have been in the hands of white America, and America is doing everything within her power to destroy us and to kill us."[20] The theme of these statements was that "the Panthers are the bullseye, but all blacks are the target."[21]

Good police-community relations is a vital ingredient in effective law enforcement. Recognizing this, two policemen, who are taking courses in criminal justice, attempt to establish rapport with a fellow student.

Violent street crime in this country is centered among, young, poor, black urban males (see Chapter 2), and it is with this group that the police must deal most forcefully. No areas have greater need of police protection than the poverty zones of the inner city, and good police relations in these communities are essential. Yet the police consistently get a bad black press. Take, for example, the issue whether a policeman should be required to live in the city he protects.

Proponents of this policy argue that officers will take better care of a city in which their own families walk down the streets they protect. For example, 55 percent of Atlanta's 1,835 police officers live outside the city. This not only reduces the number of 24-hour-a-day protectors but also decreases a tax base which is already shrinking rapidly because of the white flight to suburbia.[22]

Police in Cleveland and Chicago are required to live within the city limits. Police in Miami, Washington, D.C., and Gary, Indiana, may live no farther way than the surrounding county. Said one disgruntled taxpayer: "Do you think Dodge City would let Marshall Dillon live out of town?"

Police officers who oppose residency requirements argue that after 10- to 12-hour shifts, they deserve a rest, and that the cost of living in the city is prohibitive. As in the black genocide myth, blacks are skeptical and mistrustful of the motives of white police officers, as can be seen in this editorial from *Ebony* magazine:

> These arguments sound respectable enough, but in too many cases they mask the real reasons many white policemen, in particular, have moved outside of their cities. Like other fleeing whites, they seek escape from the apparently menacing fact that cities are becoming blacker and blacker. They seek the psychological security that they believe life in a suburban cocoon will give them while they maintain the financial security of a job on a big-city police force.[23]

The International Association of Police Chiefs has recommended, as a minimum, that police do not live at such distances from their duty posts that it would take more than an hour to mobilize them during emergencies.[24]

No major American city has a black police representation proportionate to the black population. Many blacks consider the police as essentially occupation forces rather than officers who serve and protect. Young blacks who aspire to careers in law enforcement may be viewed as turncoats by some segments of the black community. The result is that when they seek positions in law enforcement, young blacks may choose to migrate away from their home town.

Minority groups view the official representatives of government in a different light because their experiences with government has often caused them a personal "hassle." When Margaret Clark began her research among Spanish-speaking people in Sal si Puedes (San Jose, California), she found much resistance. The people were afraid she was a government worker in disguise. When Dr. Clark made a list of strangers who were most likely to appear at the door, she included the following: truant officer with the news that a child has been playing hookey from school, a depty sheriff or other representative of the juvenile court notifying a mother that her teen-age child is in trouble with the law, an immigration authority checking on documents, a representative of the health department checking substandard sanitary facilities, a building inspector making sure no code was being violated, tax assessors, FBI agents, and so on. Virtually every contact these *barrio* people have with government is some kind of hassle. The police mission to "serve and protect" is viewed as some sott of Kafka fantasy.[25]

The police find themselves in the role of "repressor-helper." Historically, they have been required to perform such varied tasks as regulating the employment of foster mothers and reading ponderous theological works for signs of heresy.[26] Police are called upon either to accomplish tasks that ordinary citizens find repugnant or to do jobs that other public services are not equipped to handle.

Take, for example, the unpleasant task of getting a reluctant paranoid schizophrenic to the state mental hospital. A study in Baltimore revealed that almost 50 percent of mentally ill patients and their families utilize the police as a community resource. Other, more appropriate community services simply were not willing to deal with recalcitrant patients. The hospital and the family may perceive the police as helpers in these sticky situations. But when an armed police officer forces a paranoid schizophrenic to go to a mental hospital, it does little to relieve the patients' persecution complex. What more evidence does the patient need that malevolent forces are out to get him than the experience of being dragged off kicking and screaming to the funny farm by some ham-fisted police officer?[27]

In addition to the unwelcome task of taking unwilling patients to mental hospitals, another especially thankless task facing the police is the "family disturbance call." Police feel that answering a call to a liquor-store holdup is more predictable than trying to restore peace in a family. In a family dispute, the officers may be greeted at the door with a brandished frying pan or have lye thrown on them. More police officers are assaulted in answering family disturbance calls than in any other area of law enforcement.

According to the FBI's *Uniform Crime Reports,* of 44,867 assaults on police officers in 1975, 12,563, or 28 percent, occurred in the course of answering disturbance calls. Even the handling, transporting, and custody of prisoners is not as dangerous as a husband-wife donnybrook.[28] Boston police answer forty-five such calls every day, and in Atlanta 60 percent of all calls during the morning watch are of this nature. The typical pattern is hard drinking followed by a husband beating his wife, and this seems to occur more frequently during the summer months when tempers are frayed by hot weather.[29] Several large-city police departments have developed specially trained "crisis-intervention teams" who deal exclusively with family disturbance calls.

Attempts to improve police-community relations have included such training as "operation empathy." In order to give the police a better understanding of what it means to be arrested, the officers themselves are "arrested," handcuffed, and jailed overnight. Police in-service training has utilized psychologists in sensitivity training and encounter groups in order to increase the officers' awareness of the meaning of their activities. One especially dramatic police–community-relations move occurred in Detroit when a newly appointed chief of police issued a St. Valentine's Day appeal for a 100-day love-in for the police.[30]

Since the police normally operate by negative reinforcement—that is, the application of fines and various punishments to increase law-abiding behavior—one psychologist decided it would help police-community relations if they offered a little positive reinforcement (rewards). In Atlanta, Georgia police started giving "positive tickets." When police spotted courteous drivers, the drivers were ticketed. But this time the ticket was a pass to an Atlanta Braves baseball game. The assumption was that rewards would increase law-abiding behavior without arousing the resentment that is elicited by punishment.[31]

Another attempt to improve police-community relations is the "neighborhood police team" concept. Police meet with the citizens they protect and advise them on various methods of coping with crime. This advice ranges from what type of lock is the most secure to how to react when confronted with a robber (stay calm) or how to repel a rapist (vomit on him).

Police Brutality

Any discussion of police-community relations must deal with police brutality—the most controversial issue in this area. Thirty-six people working for the Center of Research on Social Organization observed police-citizen encounters in the cities of Boston, Chicago, and Washington, D.C., for 7 weeks[32] to find some answers to these questions: How widespread is police brutality? Do the police mistreat blacks more than whites? In 37 of 3,826 police-citizens encounters, the police used undue force. Other findings were:

1 The rate of excessive force for white-citizen encounters with the police is twice that for black citizens.
2 There is little difference between the rate of force used by white and black policemen.
3 About one in every ten policemen in high-crime-rate areas of cities sometimes uses force unnecessarily.
4 The most likely victim of excessive force is a lower-class man of either race.
5 Police are likely to use force in settings they control (they select their own turf).
6 Police officers do not restrict their fellow officers.

One continuing debate over who should "police the police" turns on whether civilian review boards should handle citizen complaints or whether the police themselves are best qualified to keep their house in order. Police officers argue that only they can understand the nature and subtleties of police work. The Internal Affairs Division (IAD), which handles complaints about the work of 13,000 police officers in Chicago, received 5,251 complains from citizens who alleged police abuse in the years 1967–1972. The IAD sustained only 144 (2.7 percent) of these.[33]

The Chicago experience is not unusual. As Reiss writes:

> National and state civil-rights commissions receive hundreds of complaints charging mistreatment—but proving these allegations is difficult. The few local civilian-review boards, such as the one in Philadelphia, have not produced any significant volume of complaints leading to the dismissal or disciplining of policemen for alleged brutality.[34]

Police brutality is a topic on which commissioners of police typically issue routine statements to the effect that wrongdoing will be punished and the rank and file often view the charges as part of mentality that opposes law and order.

Perhaps the most extreme example of the police becoming a law unto themselves occurred in Brazil. Frustrated by their inability to contain or diminish crime, the police formed the *Esquadrao da Morte* ("Death Squad"). During is 14 years of existence, the Death Squad, composed of self-appointed teams of off-duty police officers, killed about a thousand "undesirable" citizens. Example: a veteran thief would—with the informal blessings of higher officials—be caught, driven down a lonely road at night, tortured with cigarette burns, slowly strangled, shot, and dumped into the river.[35]

One protection available to United States citizens against police brutality is to be found under section 1983 of Title 42, U.S. Code:

Is there a typical police personality?

> Every person who, under color of any statute, ordinance, regulation, custom or usage, or any State or Territory, subjects or causes to be subjected, any citizen of the United States or other person within the jurisdiction thereof to the deprivation of any rights, privileges or immunities secured by the Constitution and laws, shall be liable to the party injured in an action at law, suit in equity or other proper proceeding for redress.

Records of the Administrative Office of the United States Courts show that 8,267 cases involving section 1983 were filed in 1971—an increase of 700 percent since 1967. This increase has caused such persons as Congressman Ichord (D-Mo.) to become concerned that this law would be used to initiate frivolous or malicious suits against law enforcement officers.[36]

Given that the police exercise such enormous control over the lives of ordinary citizens, what is the typical police personality?

5.06 THE POLICE PERSONALITY

Is there a typical police personality? Critics of the police accuse them of being paranoid, having no faith in their fellow human beings, and being attracted to the police role because they want an opportunity to express their essential brutality under cover of the law. Police are often described as possessing an authoritarian personality. Between 60 and 70 percent of the recruits in the New York Police Department come from working-class homes.[37] Police cadets have not normally forsaken careers in medicine or the law to ride in a black-and-white. There is, in fact, a relationship between being socialized in the working class and an authoritarian attitude. It may be that police departments do not attract particular personalities but tend to recruit members from a relatively authoritarian class of people.

From a sociological perspective, it is more important to measure the expectations of a role within a social system than the dimensions of a unique personality. And it is entirely possible that a unique police personality may develop *after* recruits have spent some time playing the police role.

Police training increases one's readiness to perceive violence. It must have some effect on the police to see Black Panther Christmas cards featuring uniformed pigs with knives in their bellies. Balch found that although police officers verbalize discriminatory and prejudiced statements against minorities, aggressive discriminatory behavior is more typically a response to citizens' demeanor than to their race. Humility is a great virtue when one is facing possible arrest.

Police are no more or less prejudiced than the community as a whole. A police cadet recruited from south Boston is more likely to be prejudiced against blacks than a person socialized in a more tolerant milieu. Police tend to get the label "bigot" more than other segments or occupations in our society because their behavior is so *public.* Each cadet brings a unique personality constellation to the social role of police officer. The actual social behavior will be the result of that unique personality constellation as it combines with the demands of the social role.

In discussing the police, the student should keep in mind that we are attempting to make generalizations about 40,000 police departments in a nation of 220 million persons covering a land area of 3,615,241 miles stretching from the sunny sands of Miami Beach, Florida, to the icy wastes of Anchorage, Alaska.

Different kinds of work situations demand different behavioral styles from the workers. We do not, for example, counsel extraverted loudmouths to become reference librarians. Nor would we encourage timid souls who faint at the sight of blood to seek out the paramilitary role of the police. Asking a police officer to be nonauthoritarian is like asking a Green Beret to be a conscientious objector.

Trojanowicz describes the police personality profile more or less as follows: Police officers have a preference for working in structured settings, like orderliness, believe in moral absolutes, and believe that moral principles come from a power above humanity. They tend to prefer direct leadership and control in guiding the behavior of people rather than relying on the intrinsic motivation of the individual. They tend to be social conformists and political conservatives, are cautious about accepting abrupt changes, and prefer conventional avenues for social change. They tend to be systematic, methodical, competitive, self-assertive, mechanically adept, and like outdoor sports. They tend to prefer to preserve the status quo, since that is what they are sworn to protect.[38]

The law is conservative. It reinforces the status quo. Therefore it should not be surprising that those who enforce these laws are conventional persons, political and social conservatives. The police officer's role appears unattractive to political radicals.

What Policing Does to the Police

Skolnick has addressed himself to the analysis of how the features in the police officer's environment interact with the paramilitary police organization to generate what he calls a "working personality."

The danger present in their environment makes the police suspicious people. Because of their preoccupation with potential violence, they develop a stereotyping perceptual shorthand to identify possible assailants; e.g., "black equals danger."[39] The individual police officer's "suspiciousness" does not necessarily derive from personal experience but may stem from an identification with fellow officers who have been the victims of violence in the line of duty.

The police—socially isolated from the community and, in ghetto sections, actually viewed as a hostile army of occupation—band together with a solidarity and protective "blue-curtain clannishness" that surpasses the closeness existing in most other lines of work. Police are a closed fraternity, for they share unique risks.

The authority invested in police officers' roles isolates them from the public, who resent the regulation of their activities and morality. The police may be charged with hypocrisy, for they have probably engaged in some of the activities they forbid (smoking marijuana).

By way of contrast, the British police are more impersonal in their approach to offenders than their American counterparts because the role of the police officer in British society is more clearly defined and confers authority in a wider range of situations. American police officers cannot rely solely upon the authority of their badges and must develop effective public relations skills for handling such sticky situations as domestic disputes.

The typical Britisher is less likely than the American to challenge the authority of the police. Secure in their roles, the bobbies on the beat are much more likely to behave in a deferential manner to a wider range of persons. (No one likes to be given a ticket, however; and even in the rigid Soviet Union, citizens grumble over traffic tickets.) American police officers who behaved in an overly respectful manner would almost certainly be misunderstood by their colleagues and skeptical public.

After comparing the relative respect ascribed to the role of the police in Britain and America, Banton concluded that the police were a "sacred" (less open to satire and ridicule) sort of institution in Britain. He explains that this is a reflection, in part, of the values of the British social system, which is more integrated, less pluralistic, and more traditionally oriented than the American social system. British police symbolize the social order of their country to a greater extent than do American counterparts.[40]

Sociologists have argued that it is the requirements and expectations of a role within the social system that allow us to predict behavior, and that the impact of a personality in a given role is secondary.[41] Various studies and commissions have recommended higher educational requirements for the police officer. Suppose a police officer had a Ph.D., the highest academic degree awarded in the American educational system? How would such an educational background affect behavior on the beat? One professor turned cop describes his experience:

> As a college professor, I had grown accustomed to being treated with respect and deference, and I somehow assumed that this would carry over into my new role. Now I had learned that my badge and uniform, far from shielding me from disrespect, often acted as a magnet which drew toward me many individuals who hated what I represented.[42]
>
> I found that there was a world of difference between sitting in my air-conditioned office calmly discussing with a rapist or armed robber his past problems and encountering such individuals as the patrolman must: when they are violent, hysterical, desperate.[43]

Professor Kirkham also reported that he became so aggravated at times that he "lost his temper" and behaved in the very manner he had criticized from the "Ivory Tower" of the college campus. The *mea culpa* of Professor Kirkham is remarkable, not only because of the extreme naïvete he confesses but also for the overwhelming applause he received from the law enforcement community upon admitting that there are lessons that can only be learned in the streets. Kirkham's experience is valuable not only because it illustrates the primacy of role over personality but also because it revealed the strong feeling of anti-intellectualism that pervades American society in general and the working classes in particular.

The police role is a frustrating one, as demonstrated by the high suicide rate among police officers. Even in relatively rural and placid Wyoming, the suicide rate (1960 to 1968) for police was twice that for physicians, the next highest occupational group. In the asphalt jungle of New York City, the police suicide rate is twice that for the white male urban population in general. New York from 1960 to 1972 experienced seventy-four recorded police suicides. The London police, by way of contrast, had only sixteen police suicides in the same period.[44]

Among the reasons advanced for this high suicide rate are these:

1 Police work is a male-dominated profession, and males have higher suicide rates than females.
2 Firearms are easily available to the police.
3 The psychological repercussions of being constantly exposed to death are considerable.
4 Irregular working hours strain family relations.
5 The police are often exposed to criticism.
6 Judicial decisions negating police work create a sense of alienation and frustration.

Given that the police role is one which requires stability, maturity, and the capacity to use force judiciously, how can we weed out immature or potentially brutal police candidates? Dr. Robert B. Mills, a psychologist and police personnel expert, has made the following observations about police recruits:

1 Candidates who want to "enlist in the crusade against crime," often imposing their authoritarian views upon citizens or bolstering their masculinity with a police uniform, are questionable prospects.
2 Self-assertiveness in recruits proved a positive quality despite the images it conjures up of police brutality and using excessive force.
3 During role-playing exercises, some candidates collapsed into complete immobility under stress while others simulated gunfire on an unarmed crowd.
4 Black recruits had especially difficult problems as they were often the objects of hostility from other members of the black community and in some cases even received hostility from their own families.[45]

The discussion thus far has centered on the personality of the police officer. We turn from this to a discussion of a new variable injected into the role of those legally empowered to serve and protect: the policewoman.

5.07 WOMEN IN BLUE

The first policewoman in the United States was Lola Baldwin, who in 1905 was hired to protect young women at the Lewis and Clark Exposi-

Despite early favorable reports, the police world is still ambivalent about women patrol officers.

tion in Portland, Oregon. Los Angeles appointed women to its police force in 1911, but their duties were limited to protecting women, finding runaway girls, or preventing the sale of liquor to juveniles. Traditionally, policewomen have been assigned duties consistent with the male stereotype of a woman's role: they have been matrons for female prisoners, juvenile officers, or file clerks. Women have traditionally not only been restricted to specialized duty but also denied the opportunity to take promotional qualifying exams and barred from training courses which would have qualified them for advancement.[46]

This picture is changing slowly. Women are no longer mere meter maids. Females are being used as "patrol persons," complete with guns, nightsticks, and supplies of tear gas. Of the 166, 000 police officers in this country, 2,859 (2 percent) are women.[47] New York City, which has the world's largest police force (30,000), employs 733 women. Twenty-five of these women are investigators in the nation's first sex-crimes analysis unit. Sergeant Margaret Powers became the first woman desk sergeant. She had made over 300 arrests during her 9 years as a plainsclotheswoman and once dressed in a nun's habit to catch an extortionist. Captain Vittoria Renzullo was named to head a New York City police precinct in 1976—a city first. The role of policewomen has been expanded to include homicide investigations, narcotics, and civil disobedience.

By 1973 the FBI had fifteen female "untouchables" who operated without restrictions. The United States Secret Service waited 106 years to hire its first woman; now, of its 1,220 special agents, 7 are women. The famous Pinkerton private detective agency includes 4,000 women among its 36,000 employees.[48]

How well are these women performing in a rugged role formerly designated "for men only"? In Washington, D.C., a major evaluation study was conducted comparing the performance of eighty-six male and eighty-six female patrol officers. These men and women were evaluated by ride-along observations, citizen-satisfaction interviews, academy and department performance ratings, and interviews with command personnel. Policewomen handled generally similar calls and were equally effective in managing angry and distraught citizens. Although they made fewer arrests, there were no critical incidents where women were reported unable to perform the patrol function satisfactorily.[49]

Other general findings of this study were that women's policing style seems to differ significantly from that of men and that women tend to be less aggressive. It remains to be seen whether this approach will result in greater public satisfaction and citizen cooperation.

Citizens feel that policewomen can handle their service calls and domestic quarrels better than men due to their greater sensitivity. As Sherman observes:

> Aggressive policing may not be the sole criterion of good policing; perhaps sympathetic listening, compassionate understanding and human responsiveness are the policing characteristics that the public really desires and, indeed, deserves.[50]

One of the most common objections to policewomen made by policemen was that "the public would refuse to accept them." Citizen attitudes refuted this assertion, which may have been simply a rationalization of the male officers' own negative feelings. Citizens also reported that they felt no less safe when their calls for assistance were answered by women.

Most police work is essentially nonviolent and service-oriented. A woman may be more effective in defusing a potentially explosive situation than a more aggressive male would be. An ancient proverb advises that "A soft answer turneth away wrath," and it is a law of physics that for every action there is an equivalent reaction. It would be consistent, then, with both philosophy and science, to predict that diplomatic police behavior can encourage diplomatic reactions in citizens. There are examples of policewomen "charming" a 250-pound drunk into going to the drunk tank without the public brawl that sometimes occurs in such a situation.[51]

There are some differences between the performances and attitudes of policewomen and policemen. Policewomen had a significantly higher automobile accident rate than did men. (Male chauvinists loved this.) It also took women longer to quality on the weapons range. Women seem less dedicated and less committed to policing as a long-term career than do men. This is consistent with the attitudes of all married working women, for women tend to have "jobs," not careers.[52] The married women in this sample said they would leave policing any time it conflicted with home and family life.

Critique

The bottom line of the evaluation of the performance of women as police officers is this: "Sex is not a bona fide occupational qualification for doing police patrol work."[53] Women can do the job. With an increase in the number of female law enforcement officers, one hopes that we will also experience greater compassion, empathy, and sensitivity. It will be interesting to track the impact of policewomen to see if they are able to influence "the system" or if the system will change and "defeminize" the women.

The finding that women do as well as men in the role of police should come as no surprise. For, other than bearing children and feeding them at the breast, there is no task that everywhere in the world is considered to be exclusively "women's work."[54]

Despite these early favorable reports, the police world is still ambivalent about women patrol officers. Chief Robert Hanson of Seattle was quoted by *The Washington Post* as saying that the presence of women officers has endangered marriages in his department. Chief Dan Byrd of Dallas, Texas, was quoted in the same *Post* article as remarking, "If you put two women together [in a squad car], they fight. If you put male and female together, they fornicate."[55] Other concerns expressed are the much higher cost of injuries sustained by women ($890) than by men ($54) during training and the sharply higher attrition rate among female field officers (18.5 percent) than among males (6.67 percent). Concern is continually expressed about a woman's relative lack of physical strength, but it should be kept in mind that less than 0.1 percent of all police-citizen contacts involve violence.[56]

Thus far we have concentrated on the social characteristics of the persons who occupy the role of law enforcement officer. Now we turn to an examination of certain aspects of police technology.

5.08 CRIMINALISTICS AND POLICE EQUIPMENT

Criminalistics, an applied science, is principally concerned with the identification and individualization of persons and objects. Because physical evidence of an infinite variety may require examination in the course of a criminal investigation, criminalistics is necessarily eclectic and borrows from all relevant sciences. Criminalistics may be defined as the evaluation of physical evidence by the application of the natural sciences for the purposes of law enforcement. It involves physical evidence—some of it from the crime scene—which may include blood, hair, ammunition and firearms, soil, the human voice, and latent fingerprints. In this section we take a brief look at police records, K-9 dogs, police ammunition, the polygraph, and forensic odontology.

Police Records

Technology has created a new police weapon: computers against crime. The FBI's National Crime Information Center (NCIC) is a high-speed information-retrieval data bank. The NCIC possesses, among other data, computerized criminal histories of more than 400,000 persons. By 1984, according to projections, it will contain 8 million histories. This information is available to police via 187 control terminals throughout the country. Armed with this system, police are able to make an estimated 900 "hits" a day—positive identifications of either stolen property or wanted persons. The FBI also has the fingerprints and arrest records (or "rap sheets") of 20 million individuals in its criminal files.[57]

These records cause concern among civil libertarians, for the records sometimes do not indicate whether the arrestees were found innocent or guilty or whether they were released without being charged with a crime. These 20 million fingerprints are available on request to 3,750 local police departments, 1,420 sheriff's officers, and 390 federally insured banks. Once the FBI furnishes these data to local agencies, it "disavows responsibility." Thus information can end up in the hands of private businesses, insurance companies, and sources totally unrelated to law enforcement.[58]

Having identified a suspect with the help of the space-age computer, the police may have to track down the suspect with everything from a "bear in the air" (helicopter) to dogs.

Police Dogs

The training of dogs for police work originated in Ghent, Belgium, about 1900.[59] Today, over 350 city police departments in the United States and numerous state police units have K-9 squads and another 3,000 dogs serve with the Armed Forces. The principal breed of dog used is the German shepherd because of its keen sense of smell and its eagerness to cooperate with humans. These dogs can detect concentrations of scent as small as one-millionth of that which would be discernible by the human nose. In 1973 the U.S. Customs Service "pot hounds" sniffed out contraband narcotics worth an estimated $192.5 million.

These dogs are also used to locate explosives. They are more accurate than bomb-detecting machines (which cost around $20,000 each) and do not complain about the hazardous work. These German shepherds are a good investment from the taxpayer's point of view. The average cost of training a dog is $3,800, and the animal can be maintained for only $3 per day. These four-legged cops never go out on strike, take kickbacks, drink on the job, or exhibit racial or ethnic prejudices. Their handlers feel that the sight of the dogs in a squad car is a deterrent to criminals.[60]

The Dumdum Debate

"We don't shoot to wound," says Connecticut State Police Commissioner Cleveland B. Fussenich.[61] "We shoot to kill."[62] The surest way to stop fleeing suspects is to equip the police with hollow-point dumdum bullets and high-velocity .357 magnum pistols. These bullets were developed in the late nineteenth century by a British officer attached to the munitions works at Dum Dum, near Calcutta, India.

The soft-nosed bullet expands on impact, flattens out as it enters the body, cuts a 3-inch-wide path, and lodges in the body. Its use in warfare was prohibited by the Hague Conference in 1899.

Because of the bullet's expansion on impact, it is far less likely than the standard, round-nosed bullet to pass through a victim's body and hit an innocent bystander. Dumdums do not ricochet off buildings or automobile windshields as readily as do standard, jacketed bullets. A hollow-point fired from a .357 magnum has nearly twice the velocity of a bullet from a regular .38 service revolver. Those who are opposed to dumdums call their use inhumane and inconsistent with rehabilitation.

There has been a long-standing interest in the development of nonlethal weapons which will incapacitate suspected lawbreakers but will not kill or injure them permanently. Some of the devices so far contrived include weapons that deliver an electric shock, nonlethal "beanbag" projectiles, and various chemical agents that incapacitate the victim.[63]

The Taser shoots a tiny barb containing a hair-thin wire that links weapon and suspect. From a battery in the handgrip, a 50,000-volt shock is delivered. If sustained for 10 seconds, this charge will render a man unconscious.

The Stun-Gun fires a shot-filled beanbag that weights ⅓ pound and has a range of 250 feet. The impact is said to be twice that of a fast-pitched baseball. Syringe darts, long used by dogcatchers and game wardens, are being developed for use with nausea-inducing drugs. To deter skyjackers, stewardesses may be equipped with a repellent device which causes blinding pain for 30 minutes if it hits near the eyes. For riot control, police are considering using a hollow plastic "water ball" to knock people down and a high-bounce "superball" to ricochet stingingly through a crowd. All these James Bond contraptions are considered supplemental to firearms.

Having discussed some types of police equipment which aid the police in the apprehension of suspects, we now turn to two technological methods which aid in the interrogation and identification of suspects: the polygraph and forensic odontology.

The Polygraph (Lie Detector)

An Asian precursor of the modern lie detector involved scientific principles based on the fact that salivation is lessened when a person is subjected to nervous tension. The mouths of several suspects were filled with dry rice; the suspect having the greatest difficulty in spitting out the rice was judged guilty. Another forerunner of the modern lie detector was employed in India. Suspects were ordered into a dark room where a sacred ass was stabled and were directed to pull the animal's tail. They were warned that if the ass brayed, it was a signal of guilt. The ass's tail had been dusted with black powder; those with a clear conscience pulled the tail, whereas the guilty one did not. An inspection of suspect's hand quickly revealed the person with the guilty conscience.[64]

The modern polygraph, popularly known as the lie detector, evokes a range of reactions. Some view the device as an infalliable measure of truthfulness. Others arch an agnostic eyebrow and feel that such a mechanism is more appropriate for those whose minds are inclined to tinker with science-fiction than for a court of law. The truth, as is so often the case, lies somewhere between these extremes.

As an instrument, the polygraph measures changes in (1) respiration; (2) blood pressure and pulse; and (3) galvanic skin reflex, which is related to the activity of sweat pores in a person's hands. The polygraph technique requires a diagnostic procedure, and its effectiveness depends on the competence of the examiner.

The present judicial status of polygraphic evidence is generally one of inadmissibility. The technique has not gained sufficient scientific recognition to warrant the acceptance of the results as competent legal evidence. Judicial recognition is dependent on general acceptance by specialists within a profession or field of science. One of the questions left to be resolved is which field of science is best qualified to pass judgment upon the polygraph. Physiology? Psychology? Or should polygraph examiners themselves be the final judges of their own creation? Is the polygraph more art than science? The courts have avoided too hasty an acceptance of the device for fear that abuses might outweight its usefulness.[65]

Forensic Odontology

When bodies have been so badly burned or mutilated as to render identification by fingerprints or physical characteristics impossible, they can often be identified by the teeth. Dentists estimate that there are over 2½ billion possibilities in measuring the human mouth; given this variance, they have assumed that no two mouths have identical characteristics.

The concept of identifying bodies by teeth, tooth fillings, bridgework, or dentures is not a

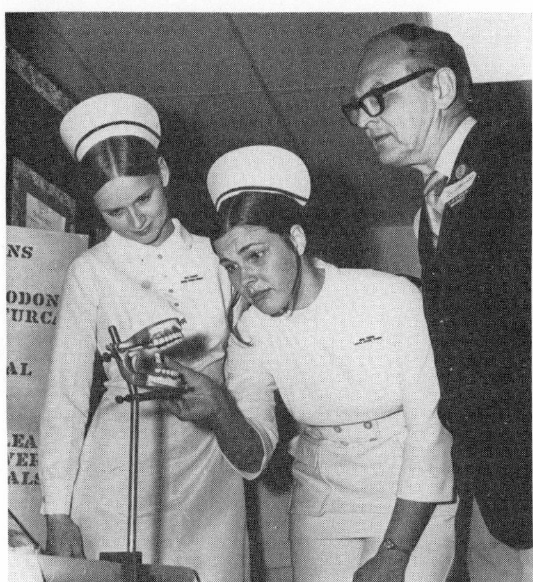

Your teeth can tell a forensic ondontologist a lot about you.

new one. A young dentist named Paul Revere identified a former patient killed in the battle of Bunker Hill through the bridgework he had constructed for the deceased. Adolph Hitler and Eva Braun, whose bodies were burned after they committed suicide in the last days of World War II, were identified in part through dental characteristics. Offenders have also been identified by teeth marks or bite marks left in victims.

Dental identification has been accepted by the courts as evidence and as a valid means, when there is a dental record of that person available for comparison by an expert, of identifying a deceased person who is otherwise unrecognizable *(People v. Mattox 1968 Ill. App. 2d).* Any licensed dentist is competent to give evidence as an expert on dental identification, though there exists a subclass of forensic odontologists. A dental technician who has sufficient practical experience would probably also qualify as an expert witness.[66]

SUMMARY

The police, who are charged with the task of preserving public order, are a relatively recent development in cultural history. Law-and-order specialists appear with the rise of class distinctions and the concept of private property. The police are placed in the role of repressor-helper and generally have a difficult time maintaining good public relations, especially with minority groups. The police are assigned the thankless tasks in society, e.g., taking reluctant mental patients to the hospital and settling family feuds. When police brutality occurs, it is most likely to occur against a lower-class male. Internal-affairs divisions which handle complaints against the police have a very low percentage of sustained complaints.

The typical police officer tends to be conventional and conservative. The role of the police is unattractive to political radicals; it is also a frustrating one, as demonstrated by the high suicide rate among police officers. Females are being used as patrol persons, and their performance compares favorably with that of their male counterparts.

Police technology now includes computers for quick suspect identification, K-9 dogs to sniff out narcotics, nonlethal and superlethal weapons, and lie detectors to aid in interrogation. The police need all the help they can get, since, as shown in Chapter 2, the United States is losing the war on crime. As one police academy commencement speaker put it: "the Barbarians are upon us, and you are the only guardians at the gate."[67]

Chapter 6

The Institution of Bail

Joe Lucas, a family man, distraught, and black, has been sitting in a small, filthy jail cell for 5 months awaiting his trial for possession of stolen property. During this period his former employer notified him that his services as a clerk in a small grocery store would no longer be required. Joe's wife, unable to continue paying the rent and utilities, has moved to a cheaper apartment in a large project complex. The family car has been repossessed, and Joe's wife has not visited him at the jail in over 4 weeks. Joe has heard that his wife has taken up residence with one of his best friends. He has also heard that one of his children has been arrested by juvenile authorities. Despite these depressing events, Joe has never been convicted of any criminal offense and is legally presumed to be innocent of the immediate charge. What has happened?

Joe's status is that of *pretrial detainee*—and the plight of Joe and his family is not atypical for many accused defendants unable to afford bail in America. In Joe's case the magistrate set his bail at $10,000 because of two prior arrests involving unrelated charges (which were ultimately dismissed). In simple terms, Joe could not afford to buy his way out of jail. The ransom could not be paid.

In more jurisdictions and for most offenses, if an accused can come up with the cash for 10 percent of the bail, a professional bondsman will provide a surety bond (guarantee) for the remaining 90 percent—and the accused can be released until trial.[1] The maximum fee that is chargeable by a professional bondsman is governed by state law and may be as high as 20 percent.[2] However, bondsmen often require that an accused put up additional *collateral* (property, subject to a security interest, which is placed within the legal control of the lender; it may be sold in the event of a default and applied to the amount owing). This collateral serves the bondsman as insurance against the possibility that the accused should fail to appear at the next stage of the criminal process.[3] Often an accused's friends or relatives will put up the required collateral (e.g., personal property such as a car or real property such as land).[4]

In Joe's case, he did not have the initial $1,000 (10 percent) or sufficient collateral to obtain the services of a bondsman—and he has been sitting in jail ever since his arrest 5 months earlier. If conditions were not bad enough for Joe, his attorney (a public defender who has just graduated from law school) has just obtained a second continuance so that Joe's new trial date is another 6 weeks away. In addition, the newly elected prosecutor has recently announced that he is discontinuing plea bargaining (see Chapter 13). And the U.S. Supreme Court had recently announced that credit for "good time" (time spent in jail awaiting trial) is not constitutionally required.[5] That is, a sentencing judge need not credit a convicted defendant with the time already served in jail (i.e., subtract it from the ultimate sentence). Joe has been informed by his attorney that the judge before whom he is to be tried does not believe in giving good-time credit.

Yet the Supreme Court has consistently stated that the Equal Protection Clause protects the rich and poor alike.[6] And the Eighth Amendment prohibits "excessive bail."

The institution of bail in America illustrates most dramatically that the rich receive preferential treatment over the poor under our system of criminal justice.[7] Bail practices are the clearest examples of *economic discrimination* in our system of justice. The poor languish in jail and its often cruel environment for weeks, months, or even years, awaiting trial and unable to purchase their freedom. But the more affluent defendants, after buying their freedom, remain free from the constraints of jail and are permitted to carry on most of the activities of other citizens. Yet an affluent defendant is not presumed to be more innocent of the immediate offense than a poor defendant.

"Selling freedom, we never close."

Bail, as presently practiced in America, is in essence a type of *legal ransom.*[8] The familiar adage "the rich get richer, and the poor get poorer" seems to be solidly based with regard to our unjust bail practices. In short, those who can afford a bondsman go free; those who cannot, remain in jail.

The courts have consistently held that the only legitimate purpose of bail is to *ensure the presence of the accused* at the next stage of the criminal process.[9] Based on this rationale, most jurisdictions (about forty states and the federal system) provide by statute that bail may be denied an accused altogether in capital cases.[10]

The risk of flight by a defendant charged with a capital offense is considered to be too great; no amount of money can guarantee a defendant's presence at trial under such circumstances.

Rule 46(c) of the Federal Rules of Criminal Procedure governs the standards for admission to bail as follows:

> If the defendant is admitted to bail, the amount thereof shall be such as in the judgment of the commissioner or court or judge or justice will insure the presence of the defendant, having regard to the nature and circumstances of the offense charged, the weight of the evidence against him, the financial ability of the defendant to give bail, and the character of the defendant.

Thus, under the federal rules, four factors determine the amount of bail to be set in individual cases: (1) the seriousness of the offense charged, (2) the amount of evidence in the prosecutor's favor, (3) the economic resources of the defendant, and (4) the defendant's character. But in most cases, the magistrate who sets bail knows the charge against the defendant and sometimes also the defendant's police record. The recommendations of the prosecutor are accorded great weight, and little information or inquiry is made for individual differences between defendants.[11]

The problems and injustices which beset the American bail system have been identified by many critics.[12] One New York study found that persons unable to post bond were: (1) convicted more often, (2) more often given prison sentences (as opposed to probation), and (3) given longer prison sentences than persons released prior to trial.[13] In addition, the study revealed that first offenders who were unable to make bail were three times as likely to be convicted and twice as likely to receive a prison sentences as a recidivist with more than ten prior arrests who is released on bail.[14] Other difficulties may be faced by those who cannot make bail. As noted by Mr. Justice Douglas:

> An accused who is imprisoned prior to trial cannot aid or effectively investigate his own case, cooperate to the fullest with his counsel, and earn enough money to perfect other legal services.[15]

The vast majority of defendants freed on bail appear at trial.[16] Three principal reasons have been given: (1) the defendants know they will probably be caught if they flee; (2) evidence of a defendant's flight is admissible by the prosecution at trial; and (3) the defendants know that their chances of being acquitted are substantially diminished if they flee.[17]

Several important studies on bail practices in America have been conducted. Although these projects are not of recent date, their principal findings, as outlined below, are noteworthy. Two well-known researches on bail practices have remarked that "neither time nor location has altered the face of the system [of bail]."[18]

6.01 BAIL STUDIES IN CHICAGO, PHILADELPHIA, AND NEW YORK

In 1927, Arthur Lawton Beeley, in his classic study *The Bail System in Chicago,* examined bail practices in the Municipal Court and Criminal Court of Cook County.[19] Beeley found that the setting of the amount of bail in Chicago was based on arbitrary standards and that individual factors were rarely considered in assessing bail.[20] He also found that 50 percent of the pretrial detainees were too poor to pay the required bail.[21] Beeley discovered that pretrial detainees who were unable to post bail had the following characteristics:[22] (1) 90 percent were residents of Chicago at the time of arrest, and 33 percent had lived in Chicago all their lives; (2) 60 percent were living with their immediate familes or close relatives at the time of arrest; (3) 50 percent were first offenders; and (4) 50 percent were regularly employed.

Beeley concluded that 28 percent of these pretrial detainees should have been released prior to trial because of their close ties to the community[23] and that they were "good release risks."

In 1954, a study of bail practices in Philadelphia was conducted by Caleb Foote.[24] Among Professor Foote's findings were that (1) three-fourths[25] of all defendants charged with serious offenses were unable to pay bail;[26] (3) the majority of defendants unable to obtain pretrial release did not spend any time in jail after their trial (53 percent);[27] and (4) 20 percent of those unable to pay bail were found not guilty.[28] Foote concluded that an inability to obtain pretrial release was highly correlated with a finding of guilty at trial.[29]

In 1957, Professor Foote conducted another bail study, this time in New York City.[30] The results were similar to those of the Philadelphia study. For example, 58 percent of the pretrial detainees could not afford to pay the requisite bail;[31] 54 percent of the defendants who were released prior to trial on bail received suspended stentences; and only 13 percent of the pretrial detainees received suspended sentences.[32]

Perhaps the best known study of bail practices is the Manhattan Bail Project undertaken by staff members of the Vera Foundation and law students from New York University.[33] The study sought to explore the feasibility of *release on one's own recognizance* (ROR) in New York City (called *pretrial parole* in that city). The researchers hypothesized that more defendants could be released on this basis if verified information on their backgrounds were available to the courts at the time of bail determination. Offenders whose bail had not yet been set were interviewed to determine if they might be good risks for pretrial release. Five factors were utilized to make an initial determination: (1) present or recent residence at the same address for 6 months or more; (2) current employment or recent employment for 6 months or more; (3) relatives in New York City with whom the defendant is in contact; (4) no previous criminal conviction; (5) residence in New York City for 10 years or more.

If the defendant met one of the five criteria (or partially met two of the five), the information was verified. A final determination and recommendation for release on parole (ROR) was based on such factors as the defendant's past and present employment, family relationships, residence patterns, character references, present criminal charges, previous criminal record, and other ties to the community.[34]

Between October 16, 1961 and September 20, 1962, the researchers offered 363 recommendations for pretrial release (ROR) to the court. Of these, 215 (60 percent) were released. Only 14 percent of the offenders in the control group (no information or recommendations made to the court but qualifiable for ROR under the criteria for the study). Thus four times as many defendants were released because of the project than would have been possible without the verified information. Of the 215 defendants released on the basis of the project's recommendations, only 3 failed to appear (less than 1 percent). In contrast, of 1,395 bailed defendants randomly selected in 1960 (prior to this project), 101, or 7 percent, failed to show up at trial.[35]

Other findings by the Manhattan Bail Project were similar to those found in earlier studies. For example, 64 percent of the detainees were convicted and imprisoned, whereas only 53 percent of the defendants released prior to trial were convicted. Only 17 percent of those convicted were ultimately imprisoned.[36] The project concluded that (1) bail is used to punish defendants; (2) the principal criteria used by the courts in setting bail is the present crime charged—factors relating to the defendant's ties to the community are largely ignored; (3) bail is used to ensure detention in order to satisfy public and journalistic demands; and (4) a defendant's financial ability to afford bail is one of the factors least often taken into account by the courts.

In another New York study,[37] Anne Rankin found that only 17 percent of bailed defendants were ultimately imprisoned, while 64 percent of the defendants unable to make bail were imprisoned attendant to sentencing. In addition, 36 percent of bailed defendants received suspended sentences, while only 9 percent of the detained defendants received such sentences.[38]

The above studies clearly demonstrate that many defendants are unnecessarily detained in jail prior to trial because they are unable to afford bail. Most defendants released prior to trial, whether bailed or by ROR, show up at trial. And the studies demonstrate that when certain background information on detainees is verified and they are recommended as good risks for the court, these ROR defendants have a substantially lower rate of default than do cash-bailed defendants. Yet as noted in the Manhattan Bail Project, most judges, when setting bail, take into account factors other than the likelihood of flight. Several proposals for bail reform have been implemented in various jurisdictions. These alternative bail practices will be taken up later in this chapter.

Bail procedures, although not uniform in America, are sufficiently similar from place to place to permit certain generalizations.

6.02 BAIL PRACTICES

Under most circumstances, defendants accused of committing misdemeanors can be released on bail as soon as the booking process has been completed. Usually, the amount of bail is set via a *bail schedule*—also known as station house bail.[39] Here the amount of bail has been predetermined, with the cooperation of the prosecutor and magistrate, and is mechanically fixed on the basis of the offense charged. No allowance is made for individual differences between defendants, their ability to pay, or their likelihood to appear at trial. Thus, the more affluent defendants are immediately released and poor defendants usually remain in jail—although ROR is available to misdemeant defendants in most jurisdictions. In many jurisdictions, *master bond schedules* are utilized; in this case the booking officer sets bail according to a fixed schedule.[40]

If an accused is charged with a noncapital felony, only a magistrate may set bail in most jurisdictions; this is usually done at the initial appearance (see Chapter 9). As we have noted, this bail figure is usually based on little knowledge of a defendant's background. Fixed schedules are often used even in felony cases.

In many states, if a defendant is arrested for a noncapital felony via an arrest warrant, the warrant will specify the amount of bail. Thus those defendants who can afford it can be released prior to their first appearance before a magistrate. Finally, the amount of bail can be increased or reduced "for good cause" by the magistrate or any judge of the court where the charge is pending; and an appeal based on "excessive bail," where it is alleged that the court abused its discretion in setting bail, is permissible in most jurisdictions.

Bail is permissible pending an appeal after conviction in most jurisdictions. However, appeal bail is usually discretionary with the sentencing court and is often denied. In the federal system, a convicted defendant who is pursuing an appeal is entitled to bail

> unless the court or judge has reason to believe that no one or more conditions of release will reasonably assure that the person will not flee or pose a danger to any other person or to the community. If such a risk of flight or danger is believed to exist, or if it appears that an appeal is frivolous or taken for delay, the person may be ordered detained.[41]

Enter the professional bondsman. He is a business person whose financial success depends on the ability to predict which defendants will appear at trial. In the event of a default by the bailed defendant, the 90 percent or so loss falls upon the bondsman. As a practical matter, the bondsman cannot afford to make too many errors in judgment. Accordingly, bondsmen may refuse to post bond in doubtful cases, they may insist that defendants or their relatives provide some form of collateral to secure the risk. In the event of a default by the defendant (i.e., failure to appear at trial), the bondsmen may resort to methods not available to law enforcement officers in order to apprehend and return the fugitive.[42] In many jurisdictions, failure of the defendant to appear at trial is an additional criminal charge,[43] and most defendants who "skip" trial or default on bail are eventually caught.[44]

In recent years several alternatives to the present bail system have been proposed, including bail reform measures, the use of citations or summonses, and a court-administered bail system.

6.03 ALTERNATIVES TO THE PRESENT BAIL SYSTEM

Bail Reform

Under the present bail system, many defendants are detained in jail prior to trial without an adequate knowledge or consideration of the defendant's background, likelihood of flight, or potential dangerousness.[45] One study reported that only 17 percent of all defendants released prior to trial were rearrested on other charges (counting both felony and misdemeanor bail recidivism charges);[46] and most rearrests occurred more than 2 months after pretrial release.[47]

A number of states and the federal government have undertaken steps to reform bail practices in America. The Federal Bail Reform Act of 1966 is often cited as an excellent example of model legislation in this area.[48] The Act provides as follows:

THE FEDERAL BAIL REFORM ACT OF 1966, 18 USCA 3146–3152:

3146. Release in noncapital cases prior to trial

(a) Any person charged with an offense, other than an offense punishable by death, shall, at his appearance before a judicial officer, be ordered released pending trial on his personal recognizance or upon the execution of an unsecured appearance bond in an amount specified by the judicial officer, unless the officer determines, in the exercise of his discretion—that such a release will not reasonably assure the appearance of the person as required. When such a determination is made, the judicial officer shall, either in lieu of or in addition to the above methods of release, impose the first of the following conditions of release which will reasonably assure the appearance of the person for trial or, if no single condition gives that assurance, any combination of the following conditions:

(1) place the person in the custody of a designated person or organization agreeing to supervise him;

(2) place restrictions on the travel, association, or place of abode of the person during the period of release;

(3) require the execution of an appearance bond in a specified amount and the deposit in the registry of the court, in cash or other security as directed, of a sum not to exceed 10 per centum of the amount of the bond, such deposit to be returned upon the performance of the conditions of release;

(4) require the execution of a bail bond with sufficient solvent sureties, or the deposit of cash in lieu thereof; or

(5) impose any other condition deemed reasonably necessary to assure appearance as required, including a condition requiring that the person return to custody after specified hours.

(b) In determining which conditions of release will reasonably assure appearance, the judicial officer shall, on the basis of available information, take into account the nature and circumstances of the offense charges, the weight of the evidence against the accused, the accused's family ties, employment, financial resources, character and mental condition, the length of his residence in the community, his record of convictions, and his record of appearance at court proceedings or of flight to avoid prosecution or failure to appear at court proceedings.

(c) A judicial officer authorizing the release of a person under this section shall issue an appropriate order containing a statement of the conditions imposed, if any, shall inform such person of the penalties applicable to violations of the conditions of his release and shall advise him that a warrant for his arrest will be issued immediately upon any such violation.

(d) A person for whom conditions of release are imposed and who after twenty-four hours from the time of the release hearing continues to be detained as a result of his inability to meet the conditions of release, shall, upon application, be entitled to have the conditions reviewed by the judicial officer who imposed them. Unless the conditions of release are amended and the person is thereupon released, the judicial officer shall set forth in writing the reasons for requiring the conditions imposed. A person who is ordered released on a condition which requires that he return to custody after specified hours shall, upon application, be entitled to a review by the judicial officer who imposed the condition. Unless the requirement is removed and the person is thereupon released on another condition, the judicial officer shall set forth in writing the reasons for continuing the requirement. In the event that the judicial officer who imposed conditions of release is not available, any other judicial officer in the district may review such conditions.

(e) A judicial officer ordering the release of a person on any condition specified in this section may at any time amend his order to impose additional or different conditions of release: *Provided,* that, if the imposition of such additional or different conditions results in the detention of the person as a result of his inability to meet such conditions or in the release of the person on a condition requiring him to return to custody after specified hours, the provisions of subsection (d) shall apply.

(f) Information stated in, or offered in connection with, any order entered pursuant to this section need not conform to the rules pertaining to the admissibility of evidence in a court of law.

(g) Nothing contained in this section shall be construed to prevent the disposition of any case or class of cases by forfeiture of collateral security where such disposition is authorized by the court.

3147. Appeal from conditions of release

(a) A person who is detained, or whose release on a condition requiring him to return to custody after specified hours is continued, after review of his application pursuant to section 3146 (d) or section 3146 (e) by a judicial officer, other than a judge of the court having original jurisdiction over the offense with which he is charged or a judge of a United States court of appeals or a Justice of the Supreme Court, may move the court having original jurisdiction over the offense with which he is charged to amend the order. Said motion shall be determined promptly.

(b) In any case in which a person is detained after (1) a court denies a motion under subsection (a) to amend an order imposing conditions of release have been imposed or amended by a judge of the court having original jurisdiction over the offense charged, an appeal may be taken to the court having appellate jurisdiction over such court. Any order so appealed shall be affirmed if it is supported by the proceedings below. If the order is not so supported, the court may remand the case for a further hearing, or may, with or without additional evidence, order the person released pursuant to section 3146 (a). The appeal shall be determined promptly.

3148. Release in capital cases or after conviction

A person (1) who is charged with an offense punishable by death, or (2) who has been convicted of an offense and is either awaiting sentence or has filed an appeal or a petition for a writ of certiorari, shall be treated in accordance with the provisions of section 3146 unless the court or judge has reason to believe that no one or more conditions of release will reasonably assure that the person will not flee or pose a danger to any other person or to the community. If such a risk of flight or danger is believed to exist, or if it appears that an appeal is frivolous or taken for delay, the person may be ordered detained. The provisions of section 3147 shall not apply to persons described in this section: *Provided,* that other rights to judicial review of conditions of release or orders of detention shall not be affected.

3149. Release of material witnesses

If it appears by affidavit that the testimony of a person is material in any criminal proceeding, and if it is shown that it may become impracticable to secure his presence by subpoena, a judicial officer shall impose conditions of release pursuant to section 3146. No material witness shall be detained because of inability to comply with any condition of release if the testimony of such witness can adequately be secured by deposition, and further detention is not necessary to prevent a failure of justice. Release may be delayed for a reasonable period of time until the deposition of the witness can be taken pursuant to the Federal Rules of Criminal Procedure.

3150. Penalties for failure to appear

Whoever, having been released pursuant to this chapter, willfully fails to appear before any court or judicial officer as required, shall, subject to the provisions of the Federal Rules of Criminal Procedure, incur a forfeiture of any security which was given or pledged for his release, and, in addition, shall, (1) if he was released in connection with a charge of felony, or while awaiting sentence or pending appeal or certiorari after conviction of any offense, be fined not more than $5,000 or imprisoned not more than five years, or both, or (2) if he was released in connection with a charge of misdemeanor, be fined not more than the maximum provided for such misdemeanor or imprisoned for not more than one year or both or (3) if he was released for appearance as a material witness, shall be fined not more than $1,000 or imprisoned for not more than one year, or both.

Citations and Summonses as Alternatives to Bail

In many cases, the formal arrest of a defendant may not be necessary—especially if the charge involves property, traffic, or local code violations; if the alleged crime is not serious; or if there is little danger of flight by the accused.[49] One such form of pretrial release is the so-called *citation* or summons procedure. Here the arresting officer has the discretion of either giving an offender a citation or summons at the scene of the crime or making a formal arrest. This procedure has been developed and incorporated in several cities including Oakland,[50] New Haven,[51] and Evanston, Illinois.[52] Usually, the use of citations is restricted to nonviolent misdemeanors,[53] and evidence of the defendant's ties to the community are the most important factors in deciding whether or not to give a citation in place of making a formal arrest.[54] A defendant with close community ties is considered less likely to flee prior to trial.[55]

The advantages of a citation or summons procedure over formal arrest and its attendant consequences are as follows: (1) it eliminates the economic discrimination found in the bail system; (2) it assures the presence of the defendant at trial; (3) it allows defendants to be released shortly after their apprehension without judicial intervention; (4) it saves much police time, which is required for arrests; and (5) the no-cash-deposit system saves the offender money which could be used for other purposes.[56]

An empirical study was conducted to evaluate the citation system in Evanston, Illinois, between September 1971 and September 1972.[57] Although the police in that city had an essentially negative view of the citation system,[58] it was found that there was no significant difference between the "ship rate" for citation defendants and arrested-bailed defendants (15 percent of defendants failed to show up at trial).[59] Furthermore, the conviction rates for citation and arrested defendants were about the same (44 and 45 percent respectively).[60]

The citation-and-summons system appears to be a successful alternative to the present money bail system; many jurisdictions in the future are likely to consider its adoption.[61] The American Bar Association Project on Standards for Criminal Justice, *Standards Relating to Pretrial Release* (1968), is reproduced in the appendix at the end of this chapter.

Court-Administered Bail

Defendants charged with bailable offenses in most jurisdictions will be released on their own recognizance (ROR) or will have to pay professional bondsmen a percentage of the premium (usually 10 percent) in order to obtain their pretrial freedom. The state of Illinois employs a system in which the defendant puts up 10 percent of the bail with the clerk of the court; if the defendant shows up to trial, the defendant receives a refund of 90 percent of the deposit.[62] Thus, the cash-deposit system only requires that a defendant post 1 percent of the total bail (as opposed to 10 percent under the preexisting system involving professional bail bondsmen). Because of court-administered bail, professional bondsmen have practically disappeared in Illinois.[63] Thus bondsmen no longer control the workings of the bail system in Illinois. The major disadvantage under this system is that many defendants do not have the 10 percent of the bail to deposit with the clerk, even though 90 percent of that amount will be refunded if they appear at trial. However, under Illinois law, defendants can be released on their own recognizance if the court is of the opinion that they will appear.[64]

Preventive Detention

In 1971, Congress passed a new law in Washington, D.C., which allowed judges to deny bail to certain offenders charged with noncapital felonies—the so-called preventive detention laws.[65] Accordingly, preventive detention laws were given much attention in the literature and were both applauded[66] and criticized as being unconstitution.[67] However, since they were rarely utilized,[68] the preventive detention laws were repealed in 1974.[69] Because of the paucity of such laws in America, preventive detention and its pros and cons is, in legal terms, a most important issue.

In the next section we will examine Supreme Court pronouncements on bail.

6.04 THE SUPREME COURT AND BAIL

The Supreme Court has not interested itself extensively in the issue of bail. Only three pronouncements to date are noteworthy, and the Eighth Amendment provision prohibiting "excessive bail" is still not applicable to the states, although virtually all jurisdictions have similar provisions.

In *Stack v. Boyle* (1951),[70] the Supreme Court discussed the purpose of bail. Each defendant's bail was set at $50,000. Chief Justice Vinson, writing for a majority of the Court, stated that "the fixing of bail for any individual defendant must be based upon standards relevant to the purpose of assuring the presence of that defendant [in court]."[71] The Court went on to hold that $50,000 for each defendant was excessive in this particular situation, since the government was unable to demonstrate the unreliability of these particular defendants.

Mr. Justice Jackson wrote a concurring opinion and stated that bail is an absolute right in noncapital cases and that it serves the following functions: (1) it allows a defendant an opportunity to prepare an adequate defense; (2) it preserves the presumption of innocence; and (3) it prevents the infliction of punishment prior to trial.[72]

In 1960, Mr. Justice Douglas, sitting as an individual circuit justice, considered an application for a reduction in bail.[73] In criticizing the bail system, Justice Douglas observed:

> . . . this theory (of bail) is based on the assumption that a defendant has property. To continue to demand a substantial bond which the defendant is unable to secure raises considerable problems for the equal administration of the law. . . . It would be unconstitutional to fix excessive bail to assure that a defendant will not gain his freedom. . . . Yet in the case of an indigent defendant, the fixing of bail even in a modest amount may have the practical effect of denying him release. . . . Imprisoned, a man may have no opportunity to investigate his case, to cooperate with his counsel, to earn the money that is still necessary for the fullest use of his right to appeal.[74]

A recent pronouncement by the Supreme Court is *Schilb v. Kuebel* (1972).[75] There the Court upheld the constitutionality of the Illinois cash-deposit system (referred to earlier in this chapter). A divided Court held that such a system, whereby 1 percent of the bail is retained for administrative costs regardless of a judgment of guilty or innocent, did not violate either the Due Process or Equal Protection Clause. The Court, however, did not take an opportunity in *Schilb* to discuss bail practices and the needed reform in America—although it did approve of the Illinois legislation which was directed against professional bondsmen.[76]

Although the Supreme Court has been markedly slow in providing guidelines to the lower courts on the constitutionality of bail practices, cases involving the issue of bail are not frequently before the Court. Many of these bail cases become lost by the time they find their way through the lower courts and reach the Supreme Court. Reform should be implemented by the Congress and state legislatures and should not await court decisions that may be unpopular.

SUMMARY

In this chapter we have discussed bail practices in America and noted that the only legitimate purpose of bail is to ensure the presence of the defendant at trial. We indicated that many studies show that most poor defendants cannot afford the fixed bail. Consequently they are forced to sit in jail, sometimes for long periods of time prior to trial, even though they are presumed innocent. Collateral consequences often attend this state of affairs. For example, pretrial detainees often lose their jobs and families, are handicapped in aiding in their defense, and tend to be more readily convicted and to receive longer sentences than bailed defendants.

Several alternatives to the present system of money bail were proposed including (1) release on own recognizance, (2) the use of citations or summonses, and (3) court-administered bail. Bail studies have consistently shown that far more defendants than necessary are unable to post bail and that defendants released without the payment of cash bail are just as likely (or perhaps more so) to appear at trial.

Although "excessive bail" is prohibited by the Eighth Amendment, that provision of the United States Constitution is not presently applicable to the states, and Supreme Court pronouncements on bail practices are wanting. Finally, we concluded that bail, as presently administered in America, discriminates economically in favor of the rich and against the poor.

In the next chapter we will examine the grand jury and its status in the administration of justice.

APPENDIX

A.B.A. Standards—Pretrial Release (Approved Draft, 1968)

2.1 *Policy favoring issuance of citations.*
It should be the policy of every law enforcement agency to issue citations in lieu of arrest or continued custody to the maximum extent consistent with the effective enforcement of the law. A law enforcement officer having grounds for making an arrest should take the accused into custody or, already having done so, detain him further only when such action is required by the need to carry out legitimate legislative functions to protect the accused or others where his continued liberation would constitute a risk of immediate harm or when there are reasonable grounds to believe that the accused will refuse to respond to a citation.

2.2 *Mandatory issuance of citation.*
(a) Legislative or court rules should be adopted which enumerate the minor offenses for which citations must be issued. A police officer who has grounds to charge a person with such a listed offense should be required to issue a citation in lieu of arrest or, if an arrest has been made, to issue a citation in lieu of taking the accused to the police station or to court.
(b) When an arrested person has been taken to a police station and a decision has been made to charge him with an offense for which the total imprisonment may not exceed 6 months, the responsible officer should be required to issue a citation in lieu of continued custody.
(c) The requirement to issue a citation set forth in (a) and (b) of this section need not apply and a warrant may be issued:
(i) where an accused subject to lawful arrest fails to identify himself satisfactorily;
(ii) where an accused refuses to sign the citation;
(iii) where arrest or detention is necessary to prevent imminent bodily harm to the accused or to another;
(iv) where the accused has no ties to the jurisdiction reasonably sufficient to assure his appear-

ance and there is a substantial likelihood that he will refuse to respond to a citation;

(v) where the accused previously has failed to appear in response to a citation concerning which he has given his written promise to appear.

(d) When an officer makes an arrest pursuant to subsection (c) above, he should be required to indicate his reasons in writing.

2.3 *Permissive authority to issue citations in all cases.*

(a) Authority. A law enforcement officer acting without a warrant who has reasonable cause to believe that a person has committed any offense should be authorized by law to issue a citation in lieu of arrest or continued custody. The authority to issue citations in serious crimes should not extend to the patrolman in the field but should be limited to the appropriate supervising officer in the police station. The statute authorizing such action should require that the appropriate judicial or administrative agency promulgate detailed rules of procedure governing the exercise of authority to issue citations.

(b) Implementation. Each law enforcement agency should promulgate regulations designed to increase the use of citations to the greatest degree consistent with public safety. Except where arrest or continued custody is patently necessary, the regulations should require such inquiry as is practicable into the accused's place and length of residence, his family relationships, references, present and past employment, his criminal record, and any other facts relevant to appearance in response to a citation.

2.4 *Lawful searches.*

Nothing in these standards should be construed to affect a law enforcement officer's authority to conduct an otherwise lawful search even though a citation is issued.

2.5 *Persons in need of care.*

Notwithstanding that a citation is issued, a law enforcement officer should be authorized to take a cited person to an appropriate medical facility if he appears mentally or physically unable to care for himself.

3.1 *Authority to issue summons.*

All judicial officers should be given statutory authority to issue a summons rather than an arrest warrant in all cases in which a complaint, information, or indictment is filed or returned against a person not already in custody.

3.2 *Mandatory issuance of summons.*

The issuance of a summons rather than an arrest warrant should be mandatory in all cases in which the maximum sentence for the offense charged does not exceed six months imprisonment, unless the judicial officer finds that:

(a) the defendant previously has failed to respond to a citation or summons for an offense other than a minor one such as a parking violation; or

(b) he has no ties to the community and there is a substantial likelihood that he will refuse to respond to a summons or

(c) the whereabouts of the defendant are unknown and the issuance of an arrest warrant is necessary in order to subject him to the jurisdiction of the court; or

(d) where arrest is necessary to prevent imminent bodily harm to the accused or to another.

3.3 *Application for an arrest warrant or summons.*

(a) It should be the policy to issue a summons in any case except one in which there is reasonable cause to believe that unless taken into custody, the defendant will flee to avoid prosecution or will fail to respond to a summons.

(b) At the time of the presentation of an application for an arrest warrant or summons, the judicial officer should require the applicant to produce such information as reasonable investigation would reveal concerning the defendant's:

(i) residence,

(ii) employment,

(iii) family relationships,

(iv) past history of response to legal process, and

(v) past criminal record.

(c) The judicial officer should be required to issue a summons in lieu of an arrest warrant when the prosecutor's attorney so requests.

(d) In any case in which the judicial officer issues a warrant he shall state his reasons for failing to issue a summons.

Chapter 7

The Grand Jury

The president of a local teamsters' union is subpoenaed to appear as a witness before a federal grand jury which is investigating alleged corruption in the labor unions. The union official requests that his retained counsel be allowed to appear with him during the grand jury proceedings. The request is denied. At the hearing, the official is told to produce an exemplar of his handwriting and to speak certain words to be compared with a recording (obtained pursuant to electronic surveillance authorized by a valid search warrant). He is told that his refusal to do so on the grounds that it violates the Fourth Amendment (unlawful search and seizure) and Fifth Amendment (privilege against self-incrimination) is not legally cognizable—and can result in an adjudication of civil contempt if he refuses to comply. In addition, the union official refuses to answer questions from the grand jury on the grounds that such answers "might tend to incriminate him" under the Fifth Amendment. Accordingly, the official is given *use immunity* (limited immunity) so that his compelled testimony cannot be used against him in a subsequent criminal proceeding. Failure to answer questions can now result in a finding of contempt. The union official/witness reluctantly complies with the requests of the grand jury. Two weeks later he is arrested and informed that he has been indicted by the grand jury for illegal labor union practices. What has happened?

The indictment and arrest of the union official was brought about by our grand jury system, which is deeply rooted in the American system of law. Yet few persons understand the functions and significance of the grand jury.[1] And, as will become clear, few constitutional protections safeguard witnesses at this stage of the criminal process.

7.01 ORIGIN AND HISTORICAL DEVELOPMENT OF THE GRAND JURY

Although the origins of the grand jury are obscure,[2] most historians trace the English grand jury back to the Assize of Clarendon in 1166 A.D., during the reign of King Henry II.[3] There, bodies of the "most lawful" lay persons—called *assizes*—in each county were directed to report to the King's sheriffs anyone who was believed to be guilty of certain serious crimes.[4] Originally, these proceedings before the Grand Assize (grand jury) were held in public, and charges were often based on community hearsay rather than upon the personal knowledge of the assizes.[5] An indictment by the Grand Assize created a presumption of guilt (the burden was on the defendants, not the prosecutor, to prove their innocence) and a *trial by battle* (whereupon the defendant had to fight the accuser) or *ordeal* (e.g., placing the defendant's hands in boiling water) followed.[6]

In the thirteenth century, trial by ordeal or battle was abolished,[7] and the grand jurors functioned in a capacity similar to that of petit (trial) jurors.[8] That is, the grand jury indicted and also became the trier of guilt or innocence.[9] However, by 1352 an English statute was passed which prohibited persons from serving in the dual capacity of grand and petit jurors.[10]

Thus, the original function of the grand jury was to increase the power of the Crown—not to serve as a protector of individual rights designed to guard against unwarranted prosecutions.

Not until 1681 did the English grand jury become an independent body free from the influence of the Crown.[11] After that, the grand jury was allowed to conduct secret hearings and could refuse to indict despite extreme pressure from royal influence. Thus the grand jury developed into a protector of individual rights standing between the prosecutor and the accused,[12] and all felony prosecutions were initiated by indictment.

The grand jury was brought to America by the early English colonists, and the first formal grand jury was established in Massachusetts in 1635. By 1683, the grand jury was found in all the colonies.[14]

The United States Supreme Court has described the functions of the grand jury as follows:

> . . . this body (the grand jury) has been regarded as a primary security to the innocent against hasty, malicious and oppressive persecution; it serves the invaluable function in our society of standing between the accuser and the accused, whether the latter be an individual, minority group, or other, to determine whether a charge is founded upon reason or was dictated by an intimidating power or by malice and personal ill will.[15]

The responsibilities of the grand jury are fourfold: (1) to investigate crimes within its jurisdiction; (2) to identify persons suspected of committing offenses; (3) to determine if probably cause exists to charge a person with an offense; and (4) to publish its findings to the court, usually in the form of an indictment or report.[16]

Despite its historical underpinnings, the use of the grand jury in America has been attacked, especially within the last decade, by legal scholars, judges, and prosecutors. Before we consider those criticisms, it is necessary to examine several other aspects of the grand jury.

7.02 POWERS OF THE GRAND JURY

In America, the grand jury is a political subsystem which bridges the gap between law enforcement agencies and the judicial system.[17] Three principal actors make up the grand jury system: the grand jury itself, the prosecutor, and the court.

The grand jury has the power to accuse and

formally charge those persons thought to be guilty of crimes, and it normally hears evidence presented by the prosecutor. In addition to its accusatory power, the grand jury has the authority to initiate and conduct independent investigations (presentments). However, the investigatory power of the grand jury is, today, rarely exercised.[18] Rather, the grand jury plays, for the most part, a supervisory role as a part of the prosecutor's investigation.[19] Thus the grand jury, for all practical purposes, serves as an evaluator of the prosecutor's evidence and as an accuser.[20] Inherent in its dual accusatory-supervisory role, the grand jury also serves, at least in theory, as a buffer to protect citizens from unfounded charges by the prosecutor.[21]

The authority of the grand jury to investigate all criminal offenses committed within its jurisdiction is extremely broad.[22] Thus, a "fishing expedition" to some extent is tolerated,[23] although the scope of the investigation may infringe upon certain First Amendment rights[24] as well as other constitutional rights (to be discussed).

In its investigation, the grand jury is not required to hear any evidence for the accused,[25] nor is the prosecutor required to present evidence to the grand jury which tends to favor the accused.[26]

Witnesses subpoenaed to appear before the grand jury have a "duty to testify,"[27] but the grand jury cannot *compel* witnesses to answer questions as to matters which might incriminate them in subsequent criminal prosecutions.[28] However, a witness who is granted immunity must answer *all* questions.[29]In addition, nontestimonial identification procedures such as handwriting and voice exemplars are not within the Fifth Amendment Privilege.[30]

In general, grand jury witnesses may not object to the admissibility of evidence before the grand jury,[31] and a defendant can be indicted solely on the basis of hearsay testimony.[32] Finally, a grand jury witness does not have a right to be represented by counsel at the proceeding regardless of whether he or she is an ordinary witness or a potential defendant.[33] American jurisdictions apply two different standards for indictment to the grand jury in its accusatory role: the *probable cause* standard (the prevailing standard) and the *prima facie* standard.[34] Under the latter, more strict standard, the prosecutor must prove each element of the crime in order to make a prima facie case at trial.[35] The former standard requires only that the government establish a probability (more probable than not) that the accused committed a criminal offense.

In addition to being empowered to issue subpoenas for testimonial purposes (subpoena *ad testificandum*), grand juries may issue subpoenas for papers, records, and documents (*duces tecum*).[36] Although a grand jury witness is not required to respond to a subpoena *duces tecum* which is too broad and unreasonable,[37] in only a few cases has judicial relief been granted. In one case, the Borden Company was required to search its files for records dating back 20 years. The subpoena, which was held valid, produced *ten truckloads*—weighing over *50 tons*—of materials, which required the full time of twenty-eight of the company's employees over several months.[38] That case may have set an all-time record for volume of material subpoened by a grand jury.[39] Other burdensome subpoenas have also been held valid.[40]

Because grand juries now rely almost exclusively on the prosecutor to set the general direction of their investigations,[41] it is necessary to examine the role of the prosecutor.

7.03 THE PROSECUTOR AND THE GRAND JURY

The prosecutor has become the dominant figure in our grand jury system.[42] This is because, in most cases, the prosecutor alone determines what matters the grand jury will consider and what evidence they will hear. The prosecutor conducts the interrogation of subpoenaed witnesses and may request an indictment. In short, the prosecutor has a great deal of influence on the grand jury; statistical evidence suggests that a prosecutor can obtain an indictment at will.[43] In only a few cases does the grand jury refuse to indict.[44]

There are, however, some limitations on prosecutorial domination. For example, the prosecutor may not comment on the sufficiency of the evidence. The grand jury has the absolute authority to refuse to indict, and the prosecutor may not be present while the grand jury deliberates on the bill of indictment. In addition, the prosecutor must function as a legal adviser to the grand jury to ensure that the proceedings are conducted in an orderly and lawful manner.[45]

The prosecutor, who must attempt to prosecute all persons guilty of criminal offenses while at the same time acting as the grand jury's legal adviser, plays somewhat inconsistent roles. Many scholars argue that the power of the grand jury to counterbalance prosecutorial domination (e.g., refuse to indict) is rarely utilized. There is strong evidence that the grand jury spends only a minimum of time in its deliberations on the question of whether to adopt the prosecutor's bill of indictment.

A study of one state grand jury was conducted in Houston, Texas, between November 1971 and February 1972. During this period, the grand jury under study considered 918 felony cases.[46] Figure 7-1 reveals that the grand jury spent an average of only 7.4 minutes per case during its first six working sessions and only 5.9 minutes per case during the final six sessions. It spent a mean time of 7 minutes per case, and 80 percent of the cases were voted on with no discussion whatsoever.[47]

Although nearly two-thirds of the grand jurors felt that they were adequately informed to decide the fate of the accused after 5 minutes,[48] the study concluded that the inadequate training and preparation of the jurors for grand jury service, combined with the reluctance of the prosecutor to supply additional information, were primary factors in these quick verdicts.

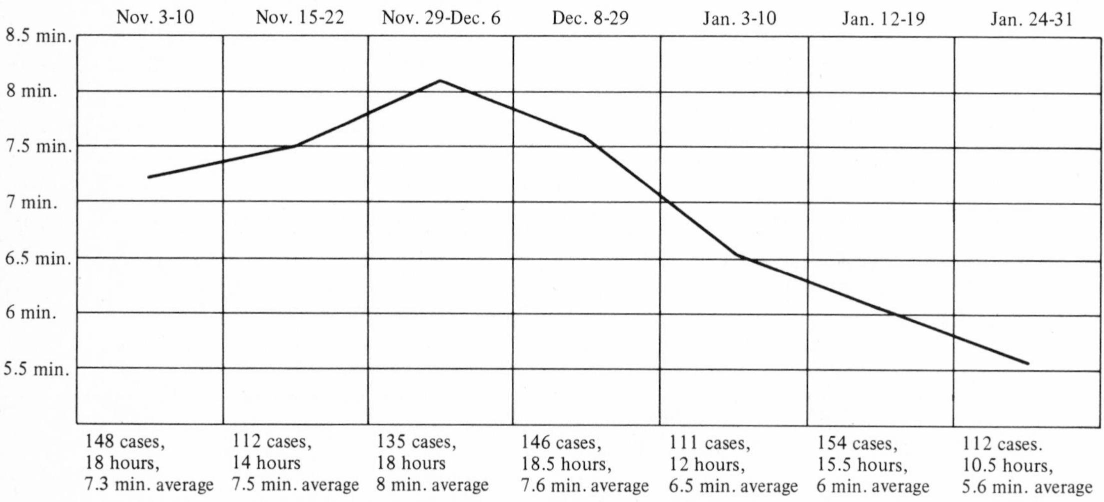

Figure 7-1 Number of minutes spent deliberating on cases by the 117th grand jury. Each of these time periods includes three working sessions except the period from December 8 through December 29, which includes five working sessions. In this figure as well as FIGURE 7-2, the 3-month session is divided into seven time periods, each of which includes an average of 131 cases. *Robert A. Carp,* The Harris County Grand Jury—A Case Study, *12 Houston L. Rev. 90, 102 (1974).*

Figure 7-2 reveals that the percentage of cases in which the grand jury did not follow the prosecutor's recommendations ranged from 11 percent during its first six sessions to only 2 percent during its last six working days. It would appear that, over time, the prosecutor became more influential with the grand jury—although this study concluded otherwise.

Because of the potential for prosecutorial abuse in grand jury proceedings, some courts have developed a prophylactic rule known as the *undue influence doctrine.*[49] It states that if the prosecutor has engaged in misconduct which usurps the independent decision-making process of the grand jury, any indictment returned must be quashed or expunged. However, a defendant may have substantial difficulty in proving an allegation of prosecutorial misconduct, since there is a strong presumption of the regularity of grand jury proceedings.

Some abuses of the grand jury by the prosecutor have been documented:

> Examples of prosecutorial behavior that have been the basis for a finding of undue influence include: making pleas, threats, or other coercive statements that may tend to induce the grand jury to indict a particular individual; expressing any opinion concerning the sufficiency and weight of the evidence, even if requested to do so by the grand jury; summarizing the evidence; making inflammatory speeches against individual indictees; using examination techniques that impugn the character of a prospective defendant; and in many jurisdictions, merely being present when the grand jury deliberates and votes.[50]

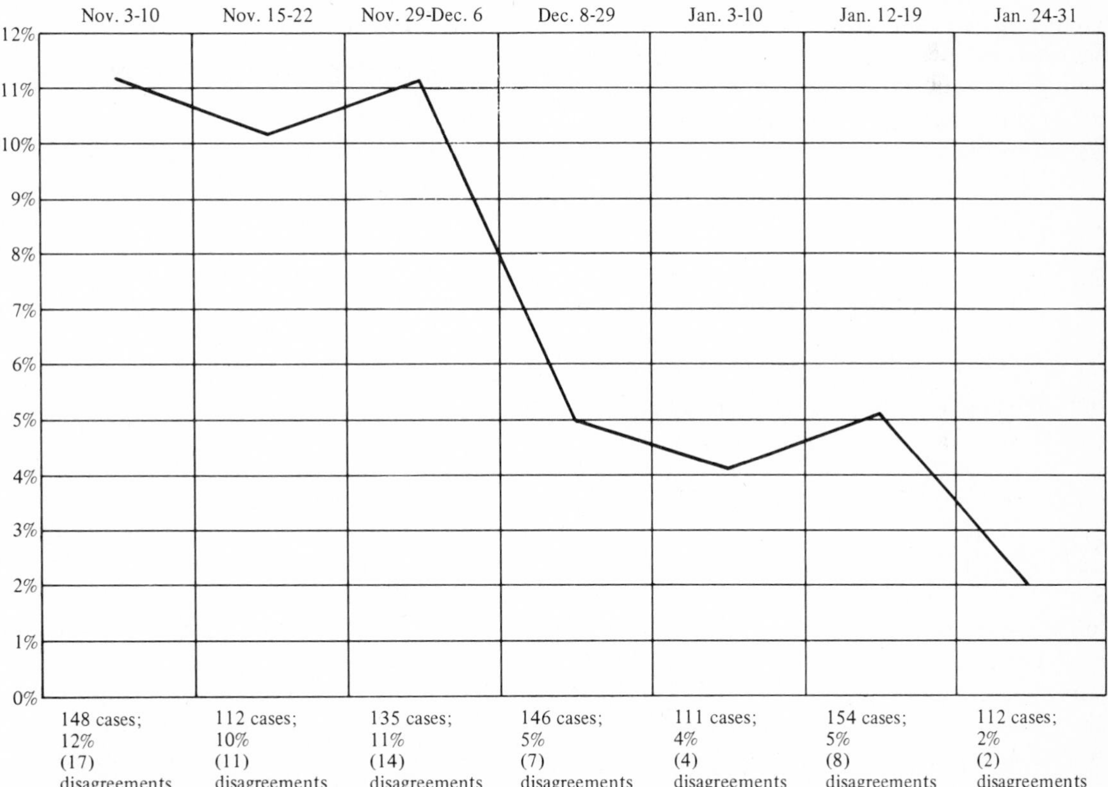

Figure 7-2 Percentage of cases on which the 117th grand jury did not follow the district attorney's recommendations. Robert A. Carp, The Harris County Grand Jury—A Case Study, *12 Houston L. Rev. 90, 117 (1974).*

Although conceptually the grand jury is premised upon the belief that a person suspected of committing a crime should not be subjected to the ignominy and expense of a trial unless members of the community find probable cause that the person has, in fact, committed the crime, prosecutorial discretion is susceptible to arbitrary and malicious use if the grand jury does not use its system of checks and balances on the prosecutorial process. Prosecutorial domination strikes at the heart of the theoretical base of the grand jury system; if the grand jury abdicates its role as a protector against unfounded charges and the jurors allow their powers to be usurped by prosecutorial process, the courts will have to take a more active role in the grand jury process.[51] The touchstone of the grand jury concept is to maintain a balance between the rights of the accused and the interests of the state to ensure that the element of fairness is omnipresent.

The court also plays a supervisory role in the grand jury system.

7.04 THE COURT AND THE GRAND JURY

The grand jury is an "arm of the court."[52] The court functions to enforce the powers of the grand jury and to make sure that its procedures are orderly and fair. The powers of the court and the grand jury process are summarized as follows: (1) the power to call the grand jury into existence;[53] (2) the power to dismiss the grand jury;[54] (3) the power to charge the grand jury as to its duties, and upon request of the grand jury, to furnish legal advice;[55] (4) the power to refuse to issue subpoenas (*duces tecum* and *ad testificandum*);[56] (5) the power to quash an indictment;[57] (6) the power to divulge the records of the grand jury only upon a showing of a "particularized need;"[58] and (7) the power to hold a witness in contempt upon refusal to testify.[59]

However, the court may have some difficulty in ensuring fairness during the grand jury process because the judge is barred from the grand jury room throughout the sessions and deliberations.[60] Moreover, it has been noted that most courts have been extremely reluctant to interfere with the grand jury's accusatory procedures,[61] and courts generally refuse to review the sufficiency of the evidence presented to the grand jury when an indictment is returned.[62] It is generally argued that such review would invade the secret province of the grand jury and cause intolerable delays in the criminal process.[63]

In summary, the checks and balances by the court on the possible misuse of the grand jury's power and the prosecutor's domination are often not exercised.

Next we will discuss the composition and selection of the grand jury.

7.05 COMPOSITION AND SELECTION OF THE GRAND JURY

The size of the grand jury as well as the minimum vote required to indict varies from jurisdiction to jurisdiction.[64] Federal grand juries are composed of from sixteen to twenty-three members.[65] Sixteen members are required for a quorum, and the votes of twelve members are necessary for an indictment.[66] ("The Federal Rules of Criminal Procedure" relating to the grand jury are presented in this chapter's appendix.)

Grand jury proceedings are conducted in secret, and the matters occurring before the grand jury may not be reported[67] (although a federal statute allows defendants certain grand jury testimony when necessary at trial[68]).

Grand juries in America are selected by three basic methods[69]: (1) the key-man system, (2) the single-list system, and (3) a combination of the two. The *key-man system* is triggered by jury commissioners sending letters to "key men" who supply the names of persons they think are qualified for grand jury service. After the names are gathered, the jury commissioners select the grand jury lists for the term. It has been noted that under the key-man system, most grand jurors have been selected on the basis of personal friendship with the jury commissioners or because they are associates with the commissioners' friends.[70] The statements of two former grand jury members have been recounted:

> One of Judge (X)'s jury commissioners goes to church, and I am good friends with his wife. I mentioned one or two times that I'd like to serve on the grand jury, and I guess she mentioned this fact to her husband because one day he called me and asked if I would like to serve. I talked it over with my husband and then called him right back and said that I'd be happy to be on the jury.[71]

Another former grand juror stated:

> I teach in the School of Social Work at the University. One day our department chairman came into my office and said that he had had a call from Dean (X) of the Law School who is one of Judge (Y)'s jury commissioners. The Dean had asked our department chairman if there was anyone in the department who would like to serve on the grand jury, and for some reason or other the chairman approached me about this. I told the chairman that if he didn't mind my missing a few of my classes now and then, I would be happy to serve. The chairman said he thought it would be good experience for me, and he then called back the Dean and had me put on the list.[72]

In Harris County (Houston, Texas), it was found that the average grand juror is Anglo-Saxon, male, and a college graduate of about fifty-one years of age who earns about $25,000 per year.[73]

Table 7-1 reveals that women, young people, Blacks, Mexican-Americans, and the poor are grossly underrepresented on grand juries. Yet most courts have held that grand juries must represent a fair cross-section of the members of the community,[74] and a grand jury may not be selected in a manner that deliberately and systematically excludes persons of a particular race.[75]

The second method of grand jury selection, the *single-list system,* involves the use of preexisting lists from which jury rolls, venires, and panels are drawn. In most jurisdictions the grand jury is selected by a random drawing from a list of all registered voters—the same method as is used in selection of petit (trial) jurors. Some jurisdictions utilize tax assessment rolls or the telephone directory as a source for the drawing of grand jury panels.[76]

The *combination system* utilizes aspects of the key-man and single-list system and includes the use of key men, telephone directories, tax rolls, and voter registration lists as well as other sources.[77]

In each of these three systems, a potential for an improper composition of the grand jury exists. Inherent in these systems is the possibility that all the significant groups in the community will not be represented on grand juries.

Alternatives to the present selection methods include (1) the use of canvassers who would call on individuals door-to-door to solicit potential voters; (2) the use of supplemental lists (e.g., membership rolls of Indian tribes); and (3) the use of a yearly mail census.[78]

The Congress has provided for supplemental lists in the Federal Jury Selection Act.[79]

7.06 GRAND JURY INDICTMENT VERSUS PROSECUTION BY INFORMATION

The grand jury is given recognition in the United States Constitution via the Fifth Amendment, which provides in part that:

> No person shall be held to answer for a capital, or otherwise infamous crime, unless a presentment or indictment of a Grand Jury, except in cases arising in the land of naval forces, or in the Militia, when in actual service in time of War or public danger. . . .

Thus, since 1791, the Fifth Amendment of the Constitution has required that federal prosecutions of "infamous" crimes be by *indictment* or *presentment* of the grand jury. Today,

Table 7-1 Socioeconomic Characteristics of Harris County Grand Jurors Compared with 1970 Census Figures (N = 156 for the Questionnaire Sample)

	Percentage of grand juries	Percentage of county
Sex		
Male	78	49
Female	22	51
Age		
21-35	10	23
36-50	43	18
51-65	37	8
Over 65	10	5
Median juror age, 51		Median adult age, 39
Income		
Under $5,000	1	16
$5,000-$10,000	3	31
$10,000-$15,000	25	29
$15,000-$20,000	16	9
Over $20,000	55	15
Median juror income, $25,000		Median family income in county, $10,348
Race		
Anglo	82	69
Negro	15	20
Mexican-American	3	11
Education		
Less than high school	0	24
Some high school	3	23
High school degree	8	25
Some college	34	13
College degree	32	Comparable data not available
Graduate degree	23	Comparable data not available
Median juror education, 16 years		Median county resident education, 12 years
Employment		
Business executive	35	
Proprietor	7	
Professional	20	
Employed worker	13	Comparable data not available
Retired	13	
Housewife	11	
Other	1	

Source: Robert A. Carp, "*The Harris County Grand Jury–A Case Study*," 12 HOUSTON L. REV. 90, 95 (1974).

an infamous crime is essentially the equivalent of a felony (involving possible imprisonment for more than a year in a prison or penitentiary—as opposed to a possible sentence of jail or fine).[80] Conversely, misdemeanors and petty offenses do not normally require the initiation of grand jury action.

An early pronouncement by the United States Supreme Court held that the Due Process Clause of the Fourteenth Amendment does not require the states to employ the grand jury process to initiate criminal prosecutions.[81] As a result, only about half the states and the federal courts today require that felony prosecutions be initiated through the grand jury process.[82] The remaining states permit most felonies to be prosecuted *either* by grand jury indictment or by a prosecutor's bill of information.[83] However, most "indictment jurisdictions" permit the use of informations where the requirement of an indictment is waived by the defendant.[84]

The history of the prosecutor's bill of information—a method by which the prosecutor assumes the role of the accuser[85]—dates back to the time of Edward I (1272–1307).[85] Although the information was originally used only infrequently and restricted to lesser offenses,[87] even in this role it was subject to much private and official abuse.[88] Finally, in 1692, the English Parliament passed tight legislative restrictions making civil accusers criminally liable for malicious accusations.[89]

As noted by one commentator:

> The king's council came to initiate prosecutions based on informations not only of the king, but also of private persons, and as a result, there were many false and malicious prosecutions started and then dropped. The procedure . . . came to be abused in that it was used for political prosecutions. . . . To check private persons from using information to initiate false and malicious prosecutions, a statute was passed in 1692 (4 W. & M., c. 18) which required that the informations of private citizens should be approved of by the court. . . . [90]

Today, the information is a charge filed by the prosecutor, usually after the defendant has been bound over for trial, without the use of the grand jury process.[91] Two important differences between these two procedures are noteworthy: (1) the use of the information is much faster and less expensive than the convening of a grand jury[92] and (2) a defective indictment must be dismissed and resubmitted to the grand jury, while a defective information may be amended by the prosecutor at or before trial.[93] The reason for the latter rule is that the jurisdiction of a criminal court where an indictment is required rests on the charge of the grand jury. If the indictment is amended—a so-called impermissible variance—it is no longer the charge of the grand jury, and the jurisdiction of the court ceases.[94] Like the indictment, the information must allege jurisdiction and charge an offense.[95]

Most surveys reveal that, in those jurisdictions which permit either indictments or informations, the latter procedure is overwhelmingly preferred by prosecutors. For example, an Iowa survey found that fewer than 10 percent of all felonies were initiated by indictment.[96] Similarly, a 1968 California survey revealed that only 4.3 percent of the 58,514 felony prosecutions were initiated via the grand jury process; only 1.0 percent of the prosecutions in Los Angeles were initiated by indictments.[97] Between 1965 and 1970, about 25 percent of federal defendants waived the grand jury process.[98]

The *presentment,* authorized by the Fifth Amendment, is an indictment initiated by the grand jury itself, whereas an indictment is initiated by the prosecutor.[99] As noted by the great legal historian Blackstone:

> A presentment . . . is the notice taken by a grand jury of an offense from their own knowledge or observation without any bill of indictment laid before them. . . . [T]he officer of the court must afterwards frame an indictment, before the party presented can be put to answer it.[100]

Today, in the federal courts, only prosecutions by indictment are permitted (unless waived by the defendant, whereas an information may be filed[101] in all but capital cases, which require grand jury indictments[102]). And earlier we indicated that presentments by state grand juries have fallen into disuse.[103]

Although many critics of the grand jury have

called for its abolition, the grand jury procedure offers certain advantages to prosecutors:

> . . . indictments are often sought: (1) when the accused has evaded apprehension and the statute of limitations would bar an information requiring the presence of the accused; (2) when the district attorney desires to avoid premature cross examination of emotional or reluctant witnesses; (3) when there is great public interest in the case and the district attorney, for political reasons, desires to share responsibility for prosecution with the grand jury; (4) when the investigative powers of the grand jury are useful, as in complex fraud cases or those involving corruption in public office; and (5) when the district attorney believes that employing the grand jury would be speedier than using preliminary examination procedures, as in cases involving multiple defendants or offenses.[104]

Professor Amsterdam has noted several situations in which a defendant might find it desirable to *waive* the grand jury process: (1) where the delay that might be involved in presenting the case to the next available grand jury would cause hardship or inconvenience (e.g., defendant is in jail); (2) where the defendant has decided to plead guilty and a waiver of the indictment will be helpful in plea negotiations with the prosecutors; (3) where a grand jury indictment would cause substantial adverse publicity; (4) where testimony before the grand jury is likely to alert the prosecutor to possible defects in the case that have gone unnoticed; (5) where testimony before the grand jury may alert the prosecutor to additional charges previously unknown; and (6) where it is likely that the prosecutor will call prospective defense witnesses before the grand jury in order to "freeze" their testimony (that is, any variance of their testimony at trial from their grand jury testimony can be used for impeachment purposes).[105]

The Preliminary Hearing

Most jurisdictions recognize the defendant's right to a preliminary hearing following the filing of a prosecutor's bill of information.[106] The purposes of the preliminary hearing are to (1) prevent unfounded charges by an overzealous or malicious prosecutor; (2) protect persons from unfounded open and public accusations of crime; (3) avoid the unnecessary expense of a trial; (4) save the defendant from the humiliation and anxiety inherent in public prosecutions; and (5) determine if there is probable cause to bind the defendant over to trial.[107]

Thus the preliminary hearing, like the grand jury process, is a screening process to determine whether there is probable cause to bring a defendant to trial. Although a preliminary hearing is not constitutionally required,[108] the Supreme Court has held that the Fourth Amendment requires a preliminary hearing as a prerequisite to an "extended restraint of liberty" prior to trial.[109] The Court did not indicate how extended the restraint prior to trial must be.

The preliminary hearing also serves to provide the defense with some degree of *discovery* of the prosecutor's case, since the latter must establish probable cause of the defendant's guilt before the defendant may be bound over for trial.[110]

In federal practice, defendants are allowed a preliminary hearing to determine whether there is a basis for holding them in jail or on bail until the grand jury can dispose of the matter.[111] If the grand jury has indicted the defendant, no preliminary hearing is permitted.[112] But if a preliminary hearing is permitted, it may nevertheless be waived by the defendant in most jurisdictions;[113] in fact, the waiver of the preliminary hearing may be as high as 80 percent in some jurisdictions.[114]

Most jurisdictions permit the defendant the right to confront and cross-examine prosecution witnesses at the preliminary hearing. There is constitutional right to counsel at the preliminary hearing where the prosecution is required to produce witnesses for cross-examination.[115] However, the Supreme Court recently implied (but did not hold) that the right to confrontation, cross-examination to produce witnesses, and counsel may not be constitutionally required at the preliminary hearing in all instances.[116]

F. Lee Bailey and Henry R. Rothblatt—two well-known criminal defense attorneys—suggest that a defendant should waive the preliminary hearing (when permitted) under the following circumstances: (1) when there is sufficient proof to warrant the magistrate's holding of the defendant, (2) when there is little likelihood that the magistrate will reduce or dismiss the charge, and (3) when nothing will be gained by perpetuating the unfavorable testimony of the prosecution's witnesses (especially if the latter might become unavailable at trial). Other reasons to waive the preliminary hearing include the wish (4) to avoid the unfavorable publicity which might result, (5) to avoid alerting the prosecutor to possible defects in his case prior to trial, and (6) to prevent alerting the prosecutor to more damaging evidence against the defendant which could strengthen the prosecutor's case or result in additional charges against the defendant.[117]

While some commentators advocate the abolition of the grand jury process in favor of prosecutor's informations,[118] others argue conversely.[119] Each procedure has its strengths and weaknesses, but it is altogether clear that there are fewer constitutional safeguards for a potential defendant in the grand jury procedure than there are in the prosecutor's information and preliminary hearings.

The value of the grand jury system has aroused considerable debate for more than a century.[120]

7.07 CRITICISMS OF THE GRAND JURY SYSTEM

Champions of the grand jury system have referred to it as a "shield" against malicious prosecutions,[121] a "sword" against criminals,[122] an "instrument of justice,"[123] and "a means of exposing criminal activity."[124] Conversely, critics of the grand jury system have attacked it as a "rubber stamp" for the prosecutor,[125] as "archaic, inordinately cumbersome and expensive,"[126] subject to "political abuse,"[127] and as a "tool of the executive"[128] which should be "abolished."[129] Regardless of its merits or negative features, the grand jury has become a household word because of its prominence in the public eye during the Watergate scandals.[130]

In this section we will briefly discuss some of the commonly asserted criticisms of the grand jury system (some criticisms were noted earlier in the chapter).

The "Rubber Stamp" Charge

Numerous studies have suggested that the grand jury is so ineffective in protecting citizens against unfounded prosecutions that the grand jury process has become a mere "rubber stamp" for the whims of the prosecutor. The study most often cited was conducted by Dean Wayne Morse of the University of Oregon School of Law (Morse, later to become a United States Senator, was then an associate professor).[131] In this study, Morse traced over 7,400 cases that had been decided by grand juries in twenty-one states.[132] Questionnaires were circulated to the prosecutors and judges involved in these cases.

Morse found that the grand juries indicted in 83 percent of the cases initiated by the prosecutor.[133] In addition, he found that in only 5 percent of the cases did the prosecutor disgree with the grand jury's disposition of the case,[134] and only slightly over 4 percent of the cases were initiated by the grand jury itself.[135]

Morse concluded that:

> Grand juries are likely to be a fifth wheel in the administration of criminal justice in that they tend to stamp with approval, and often uncritically, the wishes of the prosecuting attorney. At best the grand jury tends to duplicate the work of the committing magistrate and prosecutor.[136]

Table 7-2 Percentage of No Bills Returned in New York State from July 1, 1963 to June 30, 1964

County	Total defendants considered	No bills returned	Percentage of no bills returned
Bronx	2,116	176	8.32
New York	6,200	767	12.37
Kings	5,198	627	12.06
Queens	2,030	400	19.70
Richmond	427	76	17.80
New York State	27,436	3,476	12.67

Source: 10 N.Y. ADMIN. BD. OF THE JUDICIAL CONFERENCE ANN. REP., LEG. DOC. NO. 90, Table 31, 417 (1965).

Although Morse's study was conducted in 1931 and the information can be criticized as being dated, more recent studies suggest that a high incidence of indictments initiated by the prosecutor has continued to the present.

The data in Table 7-2 reveal that for the calendar year July 1, 1963, to June 30, 1964, "no true bill" (refusal to indict) was returned in only 12.67 percent of the cases presented to grand juries from five counties in New York State.

Table 7-3 contains similar information. The data in Table 7-3 reveal that for the calendar years 1970 and 1971, only 12.67 percent "no true bills" were returned in Cleveland, Ohio.

A former prosecuting attorney stated that:

> Almost without exception grand jurors know only the facts of the case that the state's attorney chooses to present, and almost invariably grand jurors follow the wishes of the prosecutor as to who shall be indicted and who shall not be indicted. In fact, it is now quite safe to say that the reliability of the grand jury runs just about parallel with the reliability of the state's attorney. This is not a criticism of either jurors or prosecutors and is not an attempt to indicate anything but a sincere effort on the part of either, but if the state's attorney is to so much govern the grand jury, why not let him exercise his discretion quickly by means of an information.[137]

Commentators who challenge the assertion that the grand jury is merely a rubber stamp of the prosecutor do so on two major grounds. They claim that (1) the high incidence of agreement between the grand jury and the prosecutor indicates that the latter is careful in the selection of cases—i.e., that there are few unfounded charges—[138]and (2) that a refusal of the grand jurors to indict despite the advice of the prosecutor alone justifies the existence of the grand jury.[139]

As long as the percentage of "no true bills" returned by grand juries is small, the rubber stamp charge is likely to remain at the forefront of the attack on the grand jury system.

Another criticism of the grand jury is the traditional secrecy of the grand jury minutes which may handicap the defense at trial.

The Charge of the "Unreasonable Rule of Secrecy"

Most jurisdictions have rules which specify that certain persons appearing before the grand jury must take an oath of secrecy. In general, the stenographer, prosecuting attorney, and jurors are prohibited from disclosing matters occurring before the grand jury except upon court order.[140] However, most jurisdictions do not impose an obligation of secrecy on grand jury witnesses;[141] the witnesses may disclose, privately or publicly, their testimony or whatever information they obtained during the proceeding.

The justifications for the traditional secrecy of the grand jury have been stated by Mr. Jus-

Table 7-3 Percentage of No Bills Returned in Cuyahoga County (Cleveland), Ohio, during 1970 and 1971

Year	Total cases filed with grand jury	No bills returned	Percentage of no bills returned
1970	4,151	305	7.35
1971	4,380	238	5.39

Source: Office of the Clerk of the Court of Common Pleas, Cuyahoga County, Ohio, 1970 and 1971 yearly reports.

tice Brennan of the United States Supreme Court:

> (1) To prevent the accused from escaping before he is indicted and arrested or from tampering with the witnesses against him. (2) To prevent disclosure of derogatory information presented to the grand jury against an accused who has not been indicted. (3) To encourage complainants and witnesses to come before the grand jury and speak freely without fear that their testimony will be made public, thereby subjecting them to possible discomfort or retaliation. (4) To encourage the grand jurors to engage in uninhibited investigation and deliberation by barring disclosure of their vitas and comments during the proceedings.[142]

The tradition of grand jury secrecy has been attacked as preventing defense counsel from presenting an adequate defense or an effective challenge to an improper indictment.[143] Without the grand jury testimony of the defendant and other witnesses, mounting an effective defense may present serious problems.

In 1958 and 1959, the Supreme Court seemed to relax the prohibition against the disclosure of grand jury testimony. In two cases decided during those years, the rule developed that disclosure would be permitted if the defendant was able to show a "particularized need" for discovery.[144] However, the "particularized need" rule still rendered difficult the discovery of grand jury testimony, since a defendant and counsel know little of what transpired at the grand jury proceeding.

In 1970, the Congress passed the so-called Jencks Act,[145] which generally provides that no statement or report made by a government witness and in possession of the United States shall be subject to discovery until after the government witness has first testified at trial. Under the Jencks Act, a defendant has an absolute right to discovery of a government witness's grand jury testimony without a showing of a "particular need." A major problem is that the grand jury testimony cannot be discovered by the defendant until *after* the government witness has first testified on direct examination. The defendant is left with little time to review the grand jury testimony for impeachment or other purposes.

A few jurisdictions require an *automatic disclosure* to the defendant, in advance of trial, of the grand jury testimony.[146]

The arguments in opposition to the traditional secrecy of grand jury proceedings have been summarized as follows:

> (1) Escape of accused—the escape of an alleged criminal who may be indicted will not necessarily be prevented by the secrecy of grand jury proceedings since, in most cases, he has already been arrested and has appeared at a preliminary hearing. He has either been released on bond or imprisoned before the grand jury's deliberations commence. (2) Harrassment of grand jurors—strict laws have been enacted to prevent the harrassment of grand jurors. (3) Voluntary disclosure of evidence—any reluctance that a prospective witness might have in testifying of his own volition before a grand jury should really not be dispelled by secret proceedings. The witness must realize that any testimony or evidence which he contributes to the case will eventually be made public at trial. (4) Defamation of accused—the good name of the accused will not, in the majority of cases, be protected by secret proceedings since, as was seen previously, most cases presented to the grand jury generally result in true bills. Thus, while the accused may have an excellent defense at trial and be subsequently acquitted, he must, nevertheless, bear the social stigma of having been indicted. (5) Tampering with witnesses—once a witness for the prosecution testifies at a preliminary hearing, the accused will know the substance of the prima facie case against him. Furthermore, since the defendant can obtain a pre-trial list of all the witnesses to be presented against him, it is, therefore, a simple matter to approach these witnesses. Secret grand jury proceedings will not prohibit tampering with the witnesses, if the defendant is adamant about doing so.[147]

The liberalization of discovery rules governing grand jury proceedings by the courts and legislatures has been markedly slow, and the traditional secrecy of the grand jury is likely to remain a subject of controversy.

Another source of considerable controversy is that present grand jury proceedings serve to undermine or "chill" certain constitutional rights of defendants.

The Charge of Undermining Constitutional Rights of Defendants

The constitutional protections which safeguard grand jury witnesses and potential defendants are few. The problems facing today's grand jury witness have been summarized as follows:

> The witness at today's grand jury faces a host of legal problems, many of which stem from rules established when the grand jury was truly a screening device and which now conflict with the more modern view of individual rights. Witnesses in early grand jury proceedings were denied the right to challenge the jurisdiction of the court or grand jury over the subject matter under inquiry, were required to answer questions even in the absence of a specific charge against a particular person, and were not permitted to contest the relevancy and materiality of the grand jury's questions. In general, witnesses were required to cooperate completely with the grand jury, unless the most fundamental constitutional rights were threatened.
>
> Today's grand jury witness is accorded very few of the basic rights which the greatly revamped, modern rules of waiver, privilege, and immunity so firmly safeguard. Most significantly, the witness must submit to virtually unlimited grand jury questioning with respect to criminal matters, his constitutional rights endangered, without the benefit of counsel. Our society has no comparable institution which sanctions such interrogations of a person "legally" denied counsel.
>
> Summoned before the grand jury, the witness is faced with "a barrage of questions, often improper in the normal judicial setting, thrown at him by a group of reasonably intelligent citizens excited at the prospect of playing both lawyer and detective." This questioning is conducted by a prosecuting attorney and thus embodies all of the characteristics of a judicial, criminal proceeding. Faced with such questioning, the witness, standing alone, is likely to become confused. Nevertheless, he is required either to invoke his fifth amendment right to remain silent, which may create suspicion and subject him to a contempt charge, or to make a statement which might be used against him in a subsequent trial. . . . [148]

First Amendment Rights

During the last decade, the expansive use of the grand jury process and investigations into allegedly dissident political groups has become a focus of concern to commentators and legal scholars.[149] Specifically, it is said that the subpoena power of the grand jury is being used to subvert the First Amendment rights of citizens.[150]

The First Amendment to the United States Constitution provides that:

> Congress shall make no law respecting an establishment of religion, or prohibiting the free exercise thereof; or abridging the freedom of speech, or of the press; or the right of the people peaceably to assemble and to petition the Government for a redress of grievances.

The Supreme Court has held on many occasions that First Amendment rights are preferred and fundamental[151] and that any "chilling effect" on these guarantees is subject to judicial intervention.[152] Yet is is said that "Federal grand juries have less than a clean slate with respect to the First Amendment."[153]

The grand jury investigations of Black Panthers, Weathermen, and other dissident groups have posed First Amendment problems because of the breadth and scope of their inquiries.[154] And it is said that the Nixon administration abused the power of the grand jury process to further the political status of the executive branch of government.[155] Perhaps most Americans do not feel concerned about these constitutional challenges and the grand jury process. After all, federal grand juries indicted all the

Watergate defendants and played an active role in the eventual demise of the Nixon administration,[156] and most citizens are not the subject of grand jury investigations. Yet First Amendment encroachments on the rights of citizens pose serious constitutional challenges.

The most celebrated case involved a clash between the First Amendment, the right of a newspaper reporter to protect his news sources, and the necessity for grand jury investigation.[157] Earl Caldwell, a black reporter for *The New York Times,* had obtained confidential information about the Black Panther party. He was subpoenaed by a federal jury and ordered to testify before it; he was also asked to bring with him notes and tape recordings given him for publication by officers and spokesmen of the Black Panther party. Caldwell and the *Times* moved to quash the subpoena on the grounds that it had a "chilling effect" on First Amendment freedoms. The government responded, in opposition, that the grand jury was investigating possible violations of federal statutes including threats against the President, interstate travel to incite a riot, mail frauds, and swindles.

The district court denied the motion to quash on the grounds that *every person* is required to testify upon being properly summoned. Nevertheless, the court ordered Caldwell to appear before the grand jury under a protective order which forbade the grand jury from requiring him to reveal his confidential sources of information without "a showing by the Government of a compelling and overriding national interest. . . ."[158]

Caldwell refused to appear before the grand jury and subsequently was held in contempt of court and jailed until such time as he complied with the court's order or until the expiration of the term of the grand jury.

Caldwell appealed the contempt order and the United States Court of Appeals for the Ninth Circuit reversed.[159] That court held that the First Amendment provided a qualified testimonial privilege to journalists and, absent a showing of a compelling necessity by the government, Caldwell was not required to appear before the grand jury because of the potential impact of such an appearance on the flow of news to the public.

The Supreme Court decided *Caldwell* and two similar cases[160] on the issue of whether the compulsory attendance of journalists before state or federal grand juries violates the freedom of speech and press guarantees of the First Amendment.

Mr. Justice White, writing for a five-to-four Court, rejected the arguments supporting a journalist's privilege. The Court held that (1) citizens generally owe their testimony before grand juries,[161] (2) journalists are not exempt from appearing before grand juries,[162] and (3) there is no reason why "the public interest in law enforcement and in insuring effective grand jury proceedings is insufficient to override the consequential, but uncertain, burden on news gathering. . . ."[163] As noted by the Supreme Court:

> . . . we cannot seriously entertain the notion that the First Amendment protects a newsman's agreement to conceal the criminal conduct of his source, or evidence thereof, on the theory that it is better to write about crime than to do anything about it. Insofar as any reporter in these cases undertook not to reveal or testify about the crime he witnessed, his claim of privilege under First Amendment presents no substantial question. The crimes of news sources are no less reprehensible and threatening to the public interest when witnessed by a reporter than when they are not.[164]

Justice Powell, concurring, suggested that journalists may not be required to supply information to the grand jury if (1) the information sought only has a "remote and tenuous relationship to the subject of the investigation" or (2) if the journalist believes that the revelation of confidential sources will not further a legitimate need of law enforcement.[165] Justice Douglas dissented and held that journalists have absolute immunity from the grand jury process.

Justice Stewart, dissenting (and joined by Justices Brennan and Marshall), stated that the Court's "crabbed view of the First Amendment reflects a disturbing insensitivity to the critical role of an independent press in our society."[166]

The *Caldwell* case and its progeny may well set judicial precedent that will remain undisturbed for many years. As noted by one commentator, the "courts should be especially careful of sanctioning the wholesale application of immunity by the government as a vehicle for unlimited and unchecked exploration into protected first amendment freedoms."[167]

Fourth Amendment Rights

For a long time, the Supreme Court asserted that one's Fourth Amendment rights need not be sacrificed in a grand jury investigation.[168] However, recent cases have underscored the conflict between the grand jury's investigative powers and a citizen's right to be free from unreasonable searches and seizures.[169]

Many of these cases have involved the illegal use of wiretapping and electronic surveillance. In 1970, Congress passed the Omnibus Crime Control and Safe Streets Act.[170] Title III of that act provided for judicial authorization of wiretapping but made unauthorized illegal search and its fruits (products) inadmissible in any proceeding, including grand jury hearings.[171]

In 1972, the Supreme Court held that if a witness is held in contempt of court for refusing to answer questions at a grand jury proceeding, it is a defense that the questions were based upon information illegally seized in violation Title III of the Omnibus Crime Control and Safe Streets Act.[172] Thus, a grand jury witness may refuse to answer questions which are the fruits (products) of illegal electronic surveillance.

In other Fourth Amendment cases, the Supreme Court has been less generous to grand jury witnesses. In one case, the Supreme Court held that compelling a grand jury witness to furnish a sample of his handwriting was not a "seizure" within the meaning of the Fourth Amendment[173] and that the government was not required to make a preliminary showing of "reasonableness" since one's handwriting is a physical characteristic constantly exposed to the public.[174]

Similarly, the Supreme Court has held that a witness cannot refuse, on Fourth Amendment grounds, to furnish an exemplar of his or her voice to a grand jury.[175]

Perhaps the most controversial case in recent times involving the Fourth Amendment and the grand jury process occurred in *United States v. Calandra* (1974).[176] There, a grand jury witness (petitioner) refused to answer questions on the ground that the questions were based on evidence obtained from an unlawful search and seizure at the witness's place of business.

The district court agreed with the witness, and the United States Court of Appeals for the Sixth Circuit affirmed, holding that the Fourth Amendment *exclusionary rule* (under which illegally obtained evidence and its fruits cannot be used in a criminal proceeding against the victim of an illegal search and seizure) was properly invoked by the grand jury witness to bar questions based on the evidence obtained in the search and seizure.

The United States Supreme Court disagreed. In an opinion by Justice Powell expressing the view of six members of the Court, it was held that the Fourth Amendment exclusionary role is not applicable to grand jury proceedings and that a grand jury witness may not refuse to answer questions on the ground that the information sought was the product of an unlawful search and seizure. As noted by the Court:

> [G]rand jury questions based on evidence obtained thereby involve no independent invasion of one's person, house, papers or effects, but rather the usual abridgment of personal privacy common to all grand jury questioning. Questions based on illegally obtained evidence are only a derivative

use of the product of a past unlawful search and seizure. They work no new Fourth Amendment wrong.[177]

The majority concluded that to allow a grand jury witness to invoke the exclusionary rule would "unduly interfere with the effective and expeditious discharge of the grand jury's duties."[178]

The three dissenting justices characterized the majority's holding as a "downgrading" of the exclusionary rule which threatens to make the Fourth Amendment a "dead letter."[179] (For a discussion of the exclusionary rule, see Chapter 9.)

Fifth Amendment Rights

The Fifth Amendment to the United States Constitution guarantees witnesses the privilege against self-incrimination. This protection applies whenever a witness's compelled answers might result in criminal proceedings, and it is applicable to grand jury proceedings.[180]

The enactment of immunity laws has been a source of considerable controvery in recent years. It is axiomatic that witnesses may refuse to answer questions that might incriminate them in a criminal proceeding. It is no less the rule that witnesses who are properly given immunity may not refuse to answer questions on self-incrimination grounds. The constitutional test for an immunity statute is this: Does the statute afford the witness immunity from criminal prosecution which is coextensive with the privilege against self-incrimination? In general, there are two types of immunity: *transactional* and *use.*

Use immunity (limited) only prohibits the government from *using* a witness's compelled testimony in a subsequent criminal proceeding. It does not prohibit the trial of a witness on the *transaction* to which the witness has testified if the later evidence is obtained from a *legitimate independent* source. The present federal *use immunity statute* provides that:

no testimony or other information compelled under the order (or any information directly or indirectly derived from such testimony or other information) may be used against the witness in any criminal case. . . .[181]

Thus, if defendants are granted *use immunity* at a grand jury or other proceeding, their compelled testimony may not be used against them directly or as an "investigatory lead" in a subsequent criminal proceeding; indeed, the prosecutor has an affirmative duty to prove that the evidence intended for use against the immunity-granted witness was derived from a legitimate source wholly independent of the compelled testimony.[182] For example, if a grand jury witness is given *use immunity* and his compelled testimony reveals that he was a participant in a bank robbery, he may nevertheless later be prosecuted for that crime if the prosecution is able to produce at trial evidence wholly independent of the witness's grand jury testimony. Thus, use immunity is not total and complete in that a witness could be prosecuted for any *transaction* (crime) to which he or she was compelled to testify.

Transactional immunity (completely prohibits the government from *prosecuting* any witness "on account of *any transaction* matter or thing" concerning that which he was compelled to testify after claiming his fifth amendment privilege."[183] Thus, if a grand jury witness is given *transactional immunity* and his compelled testimony reveals, for example, that he participated in several brutal homicides and a half-dozen bank robberies, he may not later be prosecuted for those crimes regardless of any independent evidence the prosecutor is able to procure.

Thus, the type of immunity that a witness receives can be important both to the witness and the prosecutor.

Although *transactional* immunity was formerly available to federal defendants in certain cases, the power of the federal government to authorize this type of immunity was lost under the Organized Crime Control and Safe Streets Act of 1970. Today, only use immunity is authorized in federal cases.

In two controversial cases decided by the United States Supreme Court in 1972, the Court held that only *use immunity* is constitutionally required, *not* transactional immunity.[184] Although a state or the federal government may constitutionally authorize either type of immunity, the prosecutorial limitations attending a grant of transactional immunity are obvious. And in view of those decisions by the Court, many states are likely to follow the more limited federal use immunity statute.[185]

The Supreme Court has yet to explore the applicability of the *Miranda* decision and the grand jury process. Specifically, the issue of whether a grand jury witness is entitled to full *Miranda* warnings is presently before the Supreme Court.[186] In view of the Court's most recent pronouncements regarding the Miranda decision, it seems unlikely that the scope of *Miranda* will be extended to the grand jury process (see Chapter 9). Most federal courts that have been faced with this issue have rejected the applicability of *Miranda* to the grand jury process.[187]

The Right to Counsel

In the federal courts, a witness's counsel is prohibited from being present in the grand jury room;[188] a similar rule exists in most jurisdictions. However, in most jurisdictions the grand jury witness is allowed to consult with an attorney outside of the grand jury room concerning his or her rights.[189] This rule is designed to prevent a disruption of the grand jury process by the witness's lawyer.[190] Federal Judge Wilkey has noted what a mockery the coming and going of a witness makes of the grand jury proceeding.[191] "At one point the witness left the grand jury room at 1:59 P.M., returned at 3:48 P.M., was asked the same question, again left the room, and finally, on her return, read a prepared statement raising every conceivable objection."[192]

The absence of counsel at the grand jury proceeding may lead witnesses, because of their lack of familiarity with the law, to inadvertently waive their constitutional rights.[193]

> When answering a question at a grand jury proceeding, the average witness may not be aware of his waiver of the privilege against self-incrimination. Once waiver occurs, however, even if it is inadvertent, the witness can be cited for contempt if he then claims privilege for an area that he has opened up in his testimony. The only exception is where an answer would increase the degree of incrimination.[194]

Although the right to counsel is constitutionally required at most stages of the criminal process (see Chapter 9), the Supreme Court has never held that this Sixth Amendment right is applicable to grand jury proceedings. A 1957 decision by the Supreme Court held that counsel is not constitutionally required when a witness is compelled to testify at a proceeding conducted by a state fire marshall.[195] Most courts have interpreted that decision as not requiring counsel at grand jury proceedings, largely as a result of the dictum (side remark by a court which is unnecessary to decide the case) of Mr. Justice Reed in which he stated that "[A] witness before a grand jury cannot insist, as a matter of constitutional right, on being represented by his counsel."[196]

As noted by one commentator, the grand jury witness without counsel is subjected to a "cruel trilemma" in which she can (1) incriminate herself, (2) risk a perjury prosecution, or (3) subject herself to a finding of contempt;[197] such a situation "patently unfair to the witness."[198]

Although other constitutional challenges to the grand jury system have been asserted,[199] it is clear that the present grand jury process is subject to much abuse of power. And a grand jury witness receives less procedural and constitutional safeguards at this stage of the criminal process than at any other stage. It is noteworthy that in 1933, England, the mother country of the grand jury, abolished that institution.[200]

SUMMARY

In this chapter we discussed the historical development of the grand jury, which originated in England during the twelfth century. The original function of the grand jury was to increase the power of the Crown—not to protect citizens from unfounded charges. Toward the end of the fifteenth century, the grand jury became an independent body as a protector of individual rights standing between the prosecutor and the accused. The grand jury was brought to America by the early colonists and, by 1683, was found in all the colonies.

Today's grand jury performs four major duties: (1) to investigate crimes in its jurisdiction; (2) to identify suspected criminals; (3) to determine if there is probable cause to charge a person with an offense; and (4) to publish its findings to the court, usually in the form of an indictment.

The *powers* of the grand jury are threefold: (1) accusatory, (2) investigatory, and (3) supervisory.

Witnesses before the grand jury do not receive many of the procedural safeguards that protect witnesses at other stages of the criminal process. Grand jury witnesses have a "duty to testify" unless they claim the Fifth Amendment privilege against self-incrimination. If immunity is granted, they must testify or face a finding of contempt. Nontestimonial identification procedures (e.g., handwriting and voice exemplars) are not subject to Fifth Amendment protections. The exclusionary rule is not applicable to grand jury proceedings; a defendant can be indicted solely on the basis of hearsay testimony. In general, the right to counsel is not applicable to grand jury proceedings.

Two standards govern indictments. Most jurisdictions apply the *probable cause* standard. A few utilize the *prima facie* standard.

The grand jury has the power to issue subpoenas (1) for testimonial purposes (subpoena *ad testificandum*) and (2) for records and documents (subpoena *duces tecum*).

The prosecutor is the dominant figure in the grand jury system because, in most cases, the prosecutor alone determines what matters and evidence the grand jury will hear. As the person in charge of the proceedings, the prosecutor has a great deal of influence on the grand jury, although there are also certain limitations, which were noted.

The grand jury is an "arm of the court" and, in this regard, the court plays a supervisory role to enforce the powers to the grand jury. The powers of the court were noted.

Although the size of grand juries varies from jurisdiction to jurisdiction, federal grand juries have from sixteen to twenty-three members. The votes of twelve members are required for an indictment.

Grand jurors are selected by three basic methods: (1) the key-man system, (2) the single-list system (the most common), or (3) a combination of the two.

Although the grand jury is recognized in the Constitution, indictments are only required in the federal system. About half of the states utilize the prosecutor's bill of information. The differences between the indictment and information procedures were discussed.

The grand jury has been the subject of much criticism in recent years. These criticisms were discussed.

The charge that the grand jury has become a rubber stamp for the prosecutor rather than a shield to protect citizens from unfounded charges is not without merit. As a result, many commentators advocate the abolition of the grand jury. However, that would require an amendment to the Constitution. Perhaps the criticisms of the grand jury could be abated by having the courts play a more active supervisory role in the grand jury system.

APPENDIX:
THE GRAND JURY
THE FEDERAL RULES OF CRIMINAL PROCEDURE

Rule 6. The Grand Jury

(a) *Summoning Grand Juries.* The court shall order one or more grand juries to be summoned at such times as the public interest requires. The grand jury shall consist of not less than 16 nor more than 23 members. The court shall direct that a sufficient number of legally qualified persons be summoned to meet this requirement.

(b) *Objections to Grand Jury and to Grand Jurors.*

(1) Challenges. The attorney for the government or a defendant who has been held to answer in the district court may challenge the array of jurors on the ground that the grand jury was not selected, drawn or summoned in accordance with law, and may challenge an individual juror on the ground that the juror is not legally qualified. Challenges shall be made before the administration of the oath to the jurors and shall be tried by the court.

(2) Motion to Dismiss. A motion to dismiss the indictment may be based on objections to the array or on the lack of legal qualification of an individual juror if not previously determined upon challenge. . . . An indictment shall not be dismissed on the ground that one or more members of the grand jury were not legally qualified if it appears from the record kept pursuant to subdivision (c) of this rule that 12 or more jurors, after deducting the number not legally qualified, concurred in finding the indictment.

(c) *Foreman and Deputy Foreman.* The court shall appoint one of the jurors to be foreman and another to be deputy foreman. The foreman shall have power to administer oaths and affirmations and shall sign all indictments. He or another juror designated by him shall keep a record of the number of jurors concurring in the finding of every indictment and shall file the record with the clerk of the court, but the record shall not be made public except on order of the court. During the absence of the foreman, the deputy foreman shall act as foreman.

(d) *Who May Be Present.* Attorneys for the government, the witness under examination, interpreters when needed and, for the purpose of taking the evidence, a stenographer or operator of a recording device may be present while the grand jury is in session, but no person other than the jurors may be present while the grand jury is deliberating or voting.

(e) *Secrecy of Proceedings and Disclosure.* Disclosure of matters occurring before the grand jury other than its deliberations and the vote of any juror may be made to the attorneys for the government for use in the performance of their duties. Otherwise a juror, attorney, interpreter, stenographer, operator of a recording device, or any typist who transcribes recorded testimony may disclose matters occurring before the grand jury only when so directed by the court preliminary to or in connection with a judicial proceeding or when permitted by the court at the request of the defendant upon a showing that grounds may exist for a motion to dismiss the indictment because of matters occurring before the grand jury. No obligation of secrecy may be imposed upon any person except in accordance with this rule. The court may direct that an indictment shall be kept secret until the defendant is in custody or has given bail, and in that event the clerk shall seal the indictment and no person shall disclose the finding of the indictment except when necessary for the issuance and execution of a warrant or summons.

(f) *Finding and Return of Indictment.* An indictment may be found only upon the concurrence of 12 or more jurors. The indictment shall be returned by the grand jury to a judge in open court. If the defendant is in custody or has given bail and 12 jurors do not concur in finding an indictment, the foreman shall so report to the court in writing forthwith.

(g) *Discharge and Excuse.* A grand jury shall serve until discharged by the court but no grand jury may serve more than 18 months. The tenure and powers of a grand jury are not affected by the beginning or expiration of a term of court. At any time for cause shown the court may excuse a juror either temporarily or permanently, and in the latter event the court may impanel another person in place of the juror excused.

Rule 7. The Indictment and the Information

(a) *Use of Indictment or Information.* An offense which may be punished by death shall be prosecuted by indictment. An offense which may be punished by imprisonment for a term exceeding one year or at hard labor shall be prosecuted by indictment or, if indictment is waived, it may be prosecuted by information. Any other offense may be prosecuted by indictment or by information. An information may be filed without leave of court.

(b) *Waiver of Indictment.* An offense which may be punished by imprisonment for a term exceeding one year or at hard labor may be prosecuted by information if the defendant, after he has been advised of the nature of the charge and of his rights, waives in open court prosecution by indictment.

(c) *Nature and Contents.*

(1) In General. The indictment or the information shall be a plain, concise and definite written statement of the essential facts constituting the offense charged. It shall be signed by the attorney for the government. It need not contain a formal commencement, a formal conclusion or any other matter not necessary to such statement. Allegations made in one count may be incorporated by reference in another count. It may be alleged in a single count that the means by which the defendant committed the offense are unknown or that he committed it by one or more specified means. The indictment or information shall state for each count the official or customary citation of the statute, rule, regulation or other provision of law which the defendant is alleged therein to have violated.

(2) Criminal Forfeiture. When an offense charged may result in a criminal forfeiture, the indictment or the information shall allege the extent of the interest of property subject to forfeiture.

(3) Harmless Error. Error in the citation or its omission shall not be ground for dismissal of the indictment or information or for reversal of a conviction if the error or omission did not mislead the defendant to his prejudice. . . .

Chapter 8

The Administration of Justice

8.01 AN OVERVIEW OF THE CRIMINAL JUSTICE SYSTEM

An eighteen-year-old boy sits outside his caseworker's office at a federal correctional institution in Tallahassee while serving a 5-year sentence for driving a stolen automobile from Jacksonville to Atlanta. A twenty-three-year-old first offender works 40 hours a week pressing license plates in a state prison while serving a 20-year sentence for armed robbery. A former college student separates linen in a Texas prison laundry while serving a sentence of 1,500 years for posession of marijuana. A mother and housewife sits in a jail cell reading the local newspaper, the headlines of which read: "Mother of four slays husband during family argument." A thirty-year-old black inmate and product of the ghetto gets up at 4:30 A.M. to begin a day's work in the prison kitchen while serving a life sentence as a multiple offender. A fifty-year-old man and former Cabinet member of the President heads for the dining hall in a minimum-security federal institution while serving a 30-month sentence for obstruction of justice. An inmate on death row reads that Claudine Longet has been sentenced to 30 days in jail for killing her lover.

What do all these persons have in common? They are bitter and disillusioned with the American system of criminal justice. The previous day, the President of the United States had announced that a recently resigned President was to receive a full pardon for all his unlawful activities during his 5-year tenure in office. The pardon of former President Nixon by President Ford did little to persuade the above subjects that our system of justice operates de facto under the lofty constitutional ideals of due process and equal protection of the law. In this chapter we will briefly describe the various agencies that make up our criminal justice system. Then we will trace the steps in the processing of a defendant charged with a felony in a typical large metropolitan area.

"The administration of criminal justice" refers to the processing of persons accused of committing crimes through the agencies which make up our system of criminal justice. In all modern nations, as the technological needs of societies have increased, governments have attempted to meet this challenge by changing their role and structure. The results have not always been good. In the United States, "criminal justice" is administered through massive bureaucratic components which literally grind out millions of cases a year. The very size of this system limits its effectiveness.

The word "processing" suggests that our system of criminal justice is largely bureaucratic. Indeed, millions of persons are involved in the system on a daily basis either as employees or products. Often the defendant is "forgotten" as the system grinds on, and this can present problems in terms of future rehabilitation. Many persons convicted of crimes leave jail or prison feeling angry and disenchanted, convinced that, in our system, criminal justice is more of an ideal than a reality. To some offenders, "justice" can only mean a finding of not guilty. Nevertheless, some of the complaints have merit and deserve systematic evaluation. The word "system" further suggests that there are strong bureaucratic overtones in our administration of criminal justice. It indicates that we attempt to mete out justice by asembly-line methods, just as we manufacture automobiles. The employees of our criminal justice system are the workers, and the defendants are the products.[1]

The adage that "a chain is no stronger than its weakest link" aptly applies to our system of criminal justice. That is, the agencies and personnel which make up the system determine the degree of "justice" that we, as a society, confer on persons accused of criminal offenses. It is little comfort to a defendant to know that, although he is entitled to a fair trial, the arresting officer modified the police report and his testimony to enhance the admissibility of evidence incident to a search and seizure. Another defendant, falsely accused by a correctional officer of committing an infraction of prison rules, may then be given a disciplinary hearing before an adjustment committee at a prison for a violation of prison regulations and find herself placed in solitary confinement for an indeterminate period.

First, we plan to describe briefly the various agencies of our system of criminal justice.

8.02 AGENCIES OF THE CRIMINAL JUSTICE SYSTEM

Law Enforcement Agencies

The primary function of our law enforcement agencies is to enforce the criminal laws through investigation, arrest, and aid in the prosecution of defendants. Discretion is the touchstone of these agencies. The police may or may not arrest a particular subject and the investigation of possible criminal offenses may range from a brief encounter with subjects incident to a family dispute to a lengthy, full-scale, intensive investigation of a multiple-victim homicide.

In the United States there are approximately forty thousand separate federal, state, and local law enforcement agencies. These agencies account for almost one-half million felony prosecutions a year.[2] In addition, more than 9 million persons arrested for crimes (felonies and misdemeanors) were processed by these agencies in 1976.[3]

Of these agencies, 200 are state agencies (e.g., state police) and 39,750 are local agencies (e.g., city police). Although there are over 2,800 separate federal offenses, these agencies deal with less than 10 percent of all felony prosecutions per year.[4] The overwhelming majority of criminal statutes are local ordinances against offenses ranging from public drunkeness to criminal homicides.

The size of our law enforcement agencies varies greatly from jurisdiction to jurisdiction. In some larger metropolitan areas—for example, Detroit—there may be three or four separate sheriff's departments in addition to over one hundred local police departments. For example, New York City alone has over 32,000 police officers (the largest police force in the world). In contrast, the rural town of Pervis, Mississippi, has a three-man police operation. All these agencies have the single common goal of enforcing the criminal law to keep peace in the community. However, the background, training, and policies of the various agencies are as diverse as their sizes. A few law enforcement agencies require prospective peace officers to have college degrees. Some require 2 years of college. Most agencies, at least in large metropolitan areas, require that their officers have high school diplomas. In a few areas, especially rural ones, the educational background of peace officers is not regarded as particularly important.

The training of law enforcement personnel in the United States varies from extensive schooling (up to 16 weeks) at a police or federal academy to virtually no formal training. In some places the rookie police officer may strap on a uniform complete with a gun, nightstick, and badge and be trained "on the street." A recent trend in many states is to require all peace officers to receive several hundred clock hours of formal law enforcement training before they are given the authority to enforce the law.

In summary, the size of the agencies and the background and training of the personnel involved in the enforcement of our laws are as diverse as the criminal laws which seek to implement conformity to our social values.

Prosecutors

The prosecutor, as the chief law enforcement officer in any jurisdiction, is the most important person in our system of criminal justice. Because the daily problems confronting prosecutors are manifestly different from those faced by other law enforcement personnel, the prosecutor is placed in a separate category among our agencies of criminal justice.

The prosecutor possesses a vast amount of discretion in the daily operations of law enforcement—even more than the peace officer. As noted by Robert Jackson, a former prosecutor and later an associate justice of the U.S. Supreme Court, "The prosecution has more control over life, liberty, and reputation than any other person in America. . . ."[5] By and large, it is the prosecutor who decides who will be formally tried, for what offenses, and whether to dismiss charges or offer a defendant an opportunity to plea bargain for a reduced charge or recommended lighter sentence. This discretion is subject to few constraints. The major limitation often depends on the amount of legally admissible evidence available for a prosecution. Some limitations on prosecutorial discretion are self-imposed as a matter of policy, not law. Many prosecutors will not prosecute a first offender charged with possession of a small amount of marijuana, nor will they prosecute an assault or battery charge resulting from a family dispute. These self-imposed policy restrictions are generally not made known to the public in most jurisdictions. Most prosecutors believe that public knowledge of their nonprosecutorial policies in the decision-making process would seriously undermine general deterrence of those crimes.

In the United States there are approximately 2,700 prosecutors (state and federal) with large staffs, especially in the larger metropolitan areas.[6] The official titles of these prosecuting officials vary from jurisdiction to jurisdiction; the prosecutor's office may be known as that of the county prosecutor, district attorney, state attorney, or some other title may be used.

In urban areas, misdemeanors and violations of city ordinances are usually prosecuted by an elected or appointed official often known as the city attorney. In many areas, especially rural ones, a committing magistrate (often called a justice of the peace) tries misdemeanor cases. It is not unusual for a magistrate in a rural area also to be the town mayor, whose responsibilities often include the maintenance of the town finances. Often the mayor's court forfeitures, costs, and fees provide a substantial portion of the town funds. In addition, it is not uncommon for the mayor-judge to receive, in addition to a regular salary, a percentage of the fines and costs levied against violators. These practices continue today in many rural areas of America, although the U.S. Supreme Court has, on at least two occasions, condemned these practices as violative of a defendant's right to a fair trial before an impartial judge.[7] As one magistrate in rural Mississippi recently noted, "We don't much care about putting these defendants in jail. We would rather fine them. Keeping them in jail costs the town money." In addition, most jurisdictions do not require that committing magistrates be members of the bar. Many magistrates have not completed high school or ever entered the halls of a law school. In contrast, almost all jurisdictions require that felony prosecutions be conducted by an official (e.g., a district attorney) who is a member of the local bar.

In the federal system, prosecutors (known as United States attorneys) are headed by the United States Attorney General under the Department of Justice. Presently, there are ninety-three United States Attorneys, one for each U.S. district court.[8] The attorneys are appointed by the President, usually at the recommendation of a local United States senator (if he or she is a member of the same political party) for a 4-year term; however, in theory and often in practice, such an appointment can result in a lifetime position.

Although prosecuting attorneys are the chief law enforcement officers in their communities, they have no formalized ties with the police or other law enforcement agencies. Sometimes the police actually resent the local prosecutor, as they feel that plea bargaining is a form of leniency or that the prosecutor is dismissing too many good cases for political or other reasons. Many police officers might say, "I had a good bust, and the D.A. dropped the charges." Often the functions of prosecutors go beyond merely prosecuting cases, since they may give legal advice to public officials, appear before legislative committees to recommend passage or abolition of a particular law, and, in many rural areas, defend against civil suits brought against the county or state. In large metropolitan areas, there are usually two legal departments concerned with governmental litigation: the prosecutor handles criminal cases and a city attorney handles civil matters.

Prosecutors' officers vary by size and by the method whereby the prosecutor obtains office (election or appointment). The majority of prosecutors' offices in the United States are typically small (as are most counties in America) and only have two or three attorneys. In addition, many prosecutors work only on a part-time basis, especially in the rural areas where the crime rate seems to be much lower than it is in our larger urban areas. At the other end of the scale is the Los Angeles District Attorney's Office (the largest in the country), which has over three hundred deputy district attorneys.

The majority of state (as opposed to federal) prosecutors are elected officials. Therefore, they must please their constituents in order to remain in office. Failure to convict a substantial number of persons brought to trial or the dismissal of too many cases can be politically disastrous. Most incumbent prosecutors are reelected. However, on occasion prosecutors will lose their bids for reelection because the public has decided, erroneously or not, that too many "dangerous criminals" have been allowed back on the street. Perhaps, this explains in part why the internal policies of a prosecutor's office are a well-guarded secret.

It is not unusual for the prosecutor's office to serve as a step up in politics. Thomas E. Dewey, for example, who convicted Lucky Luciano on ninety-seven counts comprising various criminal offenses, was eventually elected Governor of New York. Earl Warren, later the Chief Justice of the U.S. Supreme Court, was the attorney general of California before being elected governor of that state. The present Chief Justice of the Supreme Court, Warren Burger, was at one time an assistant United States attorney for the Department of Justice.

Both state and federal prosecutors have limited jurisdiction. The jurisdiction (the power of the prosecutor to bring a defendant to trial) is usually confined to one country or city, and the attorney general of the state has little control over the prosecutor's actions. On occasion the attorney general or governor will send in a "special prosecutor" to try or investigate a particular case. Otherwise, a prosecutor's discretion is largely unfettered. On the other hand, United States attorneys have, in principle, jurisdiction to try cases in any part of the country; in fact, however, their activities are usually confined to a particular area of a state (known as a district). Such jurisdictions may encompass several counties and cities (e.g., the Northern District of California, or an entire state such as Massachusetts).[9]

In summary, prosecutors in the United States enjoy maximum discretion in their roles as the chief law enforcement officers in their jurisdictions. Their major prosecutorial limitations are dependent upon the amount of legally admissible evidence secured by other law enforcement personnel, their self-imposed policy decisions, and their jurisdiction to try a case set by law. In most large metropolitan areas, plea bargaining constitutes most of the daily activity in a prosecutor's office. In Chapter 12, we will discuss plea bargaining more fully.

Opposing the prosecutor in our adversary system of criminal justice is the defense attorney. We will next turn to a discussion of the defense attorney's role in our overall system of justice.

Defense Attorneys

Criminal defense attorneys occupy a unique position in our American system of criminal justice because they often represent unpopular clients. In reality, probably only 2 percent of all attorneys practice criminal law on a regular basis. The major reason is one of economics. The typical criminal defendant is indigent and cannot afford to be represented by a private attorney. Few persons charged with a crime can afford to hire F. Lee Bailey, Melvin Belli, Percy Forman, Edward Bennett Williams, or others of similar stature to represent them, although almost all criminal defense attorneys occasionally represent poorer clients for minimal fees. More than 60 percent of all persons charged with state criminal offenses are too poor to hire their own attorneys. In contrast, in the federal system, only 40 percent of all persons charged with federal offenses are indigent. The difference in indigent rates between state and federal charges is generally attributed to the nature of the offense charged. In order to commit certain federal crimes with any hope of success, the offenders must possess certain skills and occupy positions of responsibility and trust. For example, violation of the Securities and Exchange Act, Anti-Trust Act, and Federal Bankruptcy Act (through fraud) all require that the offender have a certain level of education and occupy a fairly high position in an employment hierarchy. There are, however, some federal crimes which are committed largely by offenders who are indigent. For example, 76 percent of all persons charged with violating the Dyer Act (knowingly transporting a stolen automobile across states lines) are indigent, whereas only 7 percent of persons accused of federal income tax violations are indigent.[10] On the other hand, one does not have to be a college graduate or even employed to rob a local grocery store—armed robbers are usually neither. Like most persons engaged in a profession, defense attorneys expect reasonable compensation for their services; they cannot afford and do not desire to confine their business to indigents.

Representing an unpopular client can have serious effects on the future business of the defense attorney. How anyone could represent a Charles Manson, Richard Speck, or Sirhan Sirhan is incomprehensible to many people. These individuals, who are clearly unfamiliar with the Canons of Ethics of the American Bar Association, may be unwilling to employ such an attorney for their own, often more lucrative civil cases. Defense attorneys do not always receive their full fees even from nonindigent clients. As noted by the well-known criminal defense attorney F. Lee Bailey, about 30 percent of his cases wind up "in the red" either because the expenses outweigh the fees or because the client cannot afford to pay the bill.[11] Finally, representing defendants in criminal cases can be politically disastrous. As noted by F. Lee Bailey:

> Unlike the state prosecutor, the defender has always been at a marked disadvantage when it comes to protecting his professional status. Except in very unusual circumstances, almost no machinery exists for controlling a prosecutor who transgresses ethical, moral, or legal bounds in the exercise of his office. People are indicted for predominately political reasons most weeks of the year, but the prosecutors who contribute to this sort of miscarriage of justice are seldom brought to task. The defense lawyer who takes honest shots at official diddling doesn't have a grand jury to shield him, and he has no authority to take action against an individual. He is only sanctioned to defend those persons against whom action is taken. Consequently, he often winds up as the dart board.[12]

Bailey continues,

> Most advocates who have made news as criminal lawyers have either been prosecuted or scrutinized and threatened by bar associations.[13]

Two years after making these remarks, Bailey was criminally indicted for conspiracy to defraud by using the United States mails in connection with his role as counsel for well-known Florida business people. Finally, criminal defense attorneys who aspire to high political office may lose votes as a result of having represented unpopular clients. However, most defense attorneys do not become nationally known figures; they engage in the daily business of defending an accused and receive little notoriety.[14]

There are some advantages to being a criminal defense attorney. For example, many attorneys enjoy the widespread publicity surrounding a serious crime. Like prosecutors, defense attorneys sometimes give press conferences, appear on radio and television talk shows, and may appear as featured speakers at local community functions. Sometimes the defense attorney who becomes, in effect, a "hero" to the group he or she is defending may make new contacts and friends who admire the attorney's courage in defending freedom under our system of democracy.[15]

Persons charged with murder, rape, or other serious crimes are often difficult to defend because they are usually poor and uneducated. Furthermore, the heinousness of their alleged crimes creates a widespread public outcry for revenge. In these cases, even the selection of a fair and impartial jury can be a long and arduous task.

Unless they are appointed by the court, many attorneys are understandably reluctant to defend such unpopular clients, fearing the public backlash and potential loss of future clients. In addition, many attorneys hesitate to represent a criminal defendant on the ground that it is not their legal speciality—although any member of the bar can, regardless of legal expertise, legally defend an accused. Probably most attorneys who do not practice criminal law on a regular basis are unfamiliar with the sometimes complicated procedures which attend criminal trials; nor do they keep abreast of most appellate decisions (state and federal) in this area on a regular basis. We—or at least the defendant—would not want a tax attorney handling a defense for murder.

Chief Justice Burger has estimated that from one-third to one-half of lawyers who try serious cases are not really qualified to provide fully adequate representation.[16] Other problems confront the defense attorney. Suppose a defendant confides in the attorney that he is guilty of the crime charged. Why does the American Bar Association require an attorney to represent a defendant he knows or believes to be guilty? There are at least five basic reasons for this requirement: (1) As a basic principle of our system of criminal justice, everyone is presumed innocent and is entitled to an adequate defense. (There is some disagreement of the courts as to what adequate representation consists of). And the defendant's guilt or innocence should be decided by a judge or jury—not by attorneys or the police. (2) A defendant needs an attorney to protect his or her constitutional rights. (3) Even the factually guilty might be legally innocent, as in the defense of insanity. (4) The U.S. Supreme Court has held, in a long line of cases, that a defendant (rich or poor) has a constitutional right to be represented by counsel at the various stages of a criminal proceeding.[17] Finally, our system of criminal justice is premised upon a theory that it is better for ten guilty men to go free than for one innocent man to be convicted.

In summary, criminal defense attorneys do not always enjoy the prestige one commonly associates with being a member of the bar. Certainly they do not enjoy the public esteem accorded our judges. Often the defense attorney is seen as impeding justice and thwarting society's goal of punishing the guilty. Yet defense attorneys perform a necessary role in our adversary system of criminal justice. Regardless of some of the shortcomings of our system, we would not want to adopt another.

Next we turn to a discussion the places where judicial controversies are fought to a conclusion: the courts.

Courts

Our courts (state and federal) are diverse in nature and complex in structure. Those courts having proper jurisdiction are the beginning and the end of the formal legal process for most persons who are charged with crimes in which a decision to prosecute has been made.[18] We operate under a dual federal-state court system, with each type of court operating, to some extent, independently of the other. Further, federal and state courts are sovereign in that the former are established via the United States Constitution and by Congress and the latter are established by state constitutions via their respective state legislatures. The structure of our federal court system is uniform and precise. On the other hand, our state court systems vary considerably, especially in terms of basic jurisdiction, not only among the states but intrastate from county to county and district to district. In order to understand more fully how our dual system of courts operates, we shall first discuss the structure and jurisdiction of our federal courts.

8.03 THE FEDERAL COURTS

Article III of the United States Constitution

Section 1. The judicial power of the United States, shall be invested in one Supreme Court, and in such inferior Courts as the Congress may from time to time ordain and establish. . . .

Section 2. (2) The Judicial Power shall extend to all Cases in Law and Equity, arising under this Constitution, the Laws of the United States, and Treaties made, or which shall be made, under their authority; to all Cases affecting Ambassadors, other public Ministers and Consuls; to all

Cases of admiralty and maritime Jurisdiction; to Controversies to which the United States shall be a Party; to Controversies between two or more states; between a State and a Citizen of the same State claiming lands under the Grants of different States, and between a state, or the Citizens thereof, and foreign States, Citizens or Subjects.

(2) In all Cases affecting Ambassadors, other public Ministers and Counsuls, and those in which a State shall be a Party, the Supreme Court shall have original Jurisdiction. In all other Cases before mentioned, the Supreme Court shall have appelate Jurisdiction, both as to Law and Fact, with such Exceptions, and under such Regulations as the Congress shall make.

Judicial Review and the Supreme Court

It is well settled that federal courts do not have jurisdiction beyond that authorized by the United States Constitution. That is, federal courts have limited jurisdiction as opposed to state courts, which usually or often have general jurisdiction. Further, state courts also have concurrent jurisdiction. That is, they, as well as federal courts, can decide constitutional issues. For example, in a state criminal trial it is quite common for a criminal court to decide whether a search was unreasonable in light of the Fourth Amendment. Many other issues involving the United States Constitution are often decided by state courts. However, it is not unusual for these constitutional issues decided by state courts to be reviewed later by the federal judiciary. One might ask how it can happen that the lowest federal court (U.S. district court) can review and perhaps overturn a decision already decided by a state's highest court.

Article 6, section 2 of the United States Constitution provides, *inter alia,* that "This Constitution and the Laws of the United States which shall be made in Pursuance thereof . . . shall be the supreme Law of the Land. . . . (This statement is also known as the Supremacy Clause.) While the Constitution does not expressly provide which branch or agency of the government shall have the authority to interpret its provisions and enforce the Supremacy Clause, this issue was resolved early in our judicial history in the landmark decision of *Marbury v. Madison* (1803).[19] There, Chief Justice John Marshall, writing for the Court, held that the federal judiciary has the authority to hold acts of Congress unconstitutional and that it is the "duty of the judiciary department, to say what the law is." Thus the doctrine of judicial review was formally established and crystallized the role of the U.S. Supreme Court as the final interpreter of the Constitution with respect to all important federal issues. Indeed, *Marbury* has never been overruled; the principles announced in that case were reiterated as recently in *U.S. v. Nixon* (1974),[20] where a unanimous court[21] rejected a Presidential claim of an absolute, unqualified executive privilege of immunity from the judicial process. Although some legal historians have suggested that, shortly after the *Marbury* decision was announced, Marshall might have been willing to abandon judicial supremacy in the interpretation of the Constitution in return for security against impeachment, the doctrine of judicial review has survived the legal debates it was bound to generate and its demise is not likely to occur in the foreseeable future.

In the 50 years following the *Marbury* decision, not a single act of Congress was declared unconstitutional until the famous *Dred Scott* decision in 1857.[22] Shortly after the *Marbury* decisions was announced, in order to implement the supremacy of the United States Constitution, the Court held that the doctrine of judicial review was also applicable to the acts of state legislatures[23] and decisions of state courts.[24] From 1803 to 1857, only 36 state statutes were declared unconstitutional by the Supreme Court. However, these cases involved only a small number of contested statutes because acts of state legislatures and Congress are presumed to be constitutional and the burden of proving a constitutional defect lies with the part contesting a legislative flaw. The burden on a party seeking to persuade the Supreme Court to invalidate specific legislation (state, federal, or local) is heavy. Nevertheless, 177 cases were argued before the Court during the 1972–1973 term. Of these, 57 involved claims that a state or federal statute or city ordinance violated the United States Constitution, and many such claims were sustained by the Court. Today, the increasing number of unconstitutional claims before the Supreme Court has become a matter of concern to some noted legal authorities and particularly to Chief Justice Burger.[25] Although he obviously does not favor abandoning the doctrine of judicial review, since he wrote the opinion for a unanimous court in *U.S. v. Nixon,*[26] Mr. Burger's chief concern seems to be an overloaded docket. Mr. Justice Douglas, on the other hand, felt that the Court should review more cases.

It is clear from Article 3 that the Supreme Court is the only judicial tribunal specifically mentioned in the Constitution; its jurisdiction is established and defined in that article. Further, it is clear that the Congress can (and has) established inferior federal courts applicable to criminal justice, to wit: courts of appeals and U.S. district courts.[27] Article 3 also provides that the Congress can restrict the appellate jurisdiction of the Supreme Court. Since 1789, Congress has made a variety of "exceptions" and "regulations" governing the Courts' appellate jurisdiction, the Court designed to override some of its "unpopular" decisions through contrary federal statutes.[28]

Today, the basic jurisdiction of the Supreme Court is provided by federal statutes which give the Court jurisdiction to review all cases in lower federal and state courts involving the effect or meaning of a federal statute, constitutional right, immunity, or treaty where such an issue is properly raised.[29] Finally, it is clear that the Congress cannot confer jurisdiction on the Court greater than that authorized by Article 3.

Original Jurisdiction Article 3 makes it clear that the Supreme Court possesses two types of jurisdiction: *original* and *appellate.*

The *original jurisdiction* of the Supreme Court grants it the power to be the trier of fact and law in certain cases of controversies. This power is rarely exercised and almost never involves an issue relevant to criminal justice. The most numerous class of suits decided by the Supreme Court under its power of original jurisdiction involves suits by one state against another.[30] Most often the Court is asked to resolve disputes as to boundaries or water rights.[31] During the 1973–1974 term, the court decided only two cases involving its original jurisdiction on their merits.[32]

Under its *appellate jurisdiction,* a case may reach the Supreme Court in one of three principal ways: on certificate, on appeal, or by a writ of certiorari.

Certification On occasion, the U.S. Court of Appeals (intermediate federal appellate court) will make a request that the Supreme Court review a case where a point of law is unclear in the lower federal courts. *Certification* may involve instructions on any question of law in either a civil or criminal case and is governed by federal statutes.[33] It is generally accepted that only the Court of Appeals may request certification, not the parties to the lawsuit. Although the federal statutes governing certification purport to make it obligatory for the Supreme Court to decide cases sent up in this manner, there are many exceptions where the Supreme Court might find jurisdiction on certificate to be improper. Thus, the granting of review by the Court on certificate is in fact discretionary. Finally, certification is generally unimportant in the area of criminal justice. Few important criminal cases are reviewed by the Court on certificate.

Appeal (Direct Appeal) In some instances appellate review (as a matter of right) is made obligatory by the Supreme Court via federal statutes. This type of review is known as an *appeal* or *direct appeal* and may involve decisions from lower federal courts as well as others from final state courts. Some examples where the Supreme Court will review, on appeal, final judgments of a state's highest court (in which a decision could be rendered) include those:

1 Where state court has held a treaty or federal statute to be invalid
2 Where a state court has upheld a state law or provision in a state constitution against a challenge that it conflicts with a federal statute or the United States Constitution

In the federal system, the Supreme Court will review cases *on direct appeal* when:

1 A U.S. district court has held that a federal statute is invalid and accordingly dismissed an indictment or arrested a judgment upon which the indictment was founded
2 A court of appeals has held that a state law is repugnant to a federal statute or the United States Constitution
3 A Three-judge U.S. district court has granted or denied an interlocutory or permanent injunction in any civil action, suit, or proceeding
4 A federal court has held any act of Congress to be unconstitutional in any civil action, suit or proceeding in which the United States is a party

In each instance, review by the Supreme Court on direct appeal is available only when a substantial federal question is presented and at least four (out of nine) of the Justices agree. Otherwise, the appeal will be dismissed for a variety of reasons. Two commonly given explanations for the Court's refusal to consider a case on direct appeal are (1) for want or substantial federal question and (2) for want of jurisdiction. However, when a case presented for review is *on direct appeal,* a dismissal is a decision *on its merits.* That is, the judgment of the last court is a disposition on the case's merits. Thus, mandatory review by the Supreme Court on direct appeal is, to a large extent, discretionary, as is the final method of appellate jurisdiction by the Supreme Court, on writ of certiorari.

Writ of Certiorari Under its appellate jurisdiction, most cases decided by the Supreme Court occur by *writ of certiorari.* This is a discretionary writ authorized by the Congress in 1925. The major purpose of this method of appellate review is to allow the Supreme Court authority to control, to some extent, its own docket and to review only those cases presenting substantial constitutional or federal questions. In all but a few cases, the Court declines to accept for review those lower-court decisions (federal and state) brought up on certiorari. For example in 1973–1974, only 205 cases out of a total 3,876 filed with the Supreme Court were granted certiorari (5 percent). The reason is one of judicial economy (the large number of cases filed) or the absence of issues significant enough to deserve the court's attention.

As with cases filed on direct appeal, the "rule of four" prevails. That is, before certiorari can be granted, four Justices must agree that the case filed for appellate review by the Court presents a substantial federal or constitutional question. Unlike a dismissal on direct appeal, a dismissal from a writ of certiorari is *not* a decision on the merits of the case. The dismissal only has the legal effect of affirming the last lower-court decision on that case and is not a disposal on its merits. It does not mean that the Supreme Court is agreeing with the legal conclusions of the lower courts. Such a dismissal simply means that four Justices, for various reasons, were not willing to review *that* case.

Rule 19 of the Supreme Court Rules governs, in part, the purposes for which certiorari will be granted. However, there are instances where the Court does not adhere strictly to the rules, and it has decided cases of great social importance (e.g., state criminal abortion statutes).

> Rule 19:
> CONSIDERATIONS GOVERNING REVIEW OF CERTIORARI
>
> 1. A review on writ of certiorari is not a matter of right, but of sound judicial discretion, and will be granted only where there are special and important reasons therefore. The following, while neither controlling nor fully measuring the court's discretion, indicate the character of reasons which will be considered.
>
> (a) Where a state court has decided a federal question of substance not theretofore determined by this court, or has decided it in a way probably not in accord with applicable decisions of this court.
>
> (b) Where a court of appeals has rendered a decision in conflict with the decision of another court of appeals on the same matter; or has decided an important state or territorial question in a way in conflict with applicable state or territorial law; or has decided an important question of federal law which has not been, but should be, settled by this court; or has decided a federal question in a way in conflict with applicable decisions of this court; or has so far departed from the accepted and usual course of judicial proceedings, or so far sanctioned such a departure by a lower court, as to call for an exercise of this court's power of supervision.
>
> 2. The same general considerations outlined above will control in respect of petitions for writs of certiorari to review judgments of the Court of Claims, of the Court of Customs and Patent Appeals, or of any other court whose determinations are by law reviewable on writ of certiorari.

Lower Federal Courts

Article 3, section 2 of the United States Constitution provides for one Supreme Court and indicates that Congress may from time to time ordain and establish inferior federal courts. This was done under the Judiciary Act of 1789, so that today our federal court system is a three-level system. The eleven U.S. courts of appeals are intermediate appellate courts, and the U.S. district courts sit as trial courts. In addition, the Congress has provided for other specialized federal courts such as the U.S. Court of Claims, U.S. Tax Court, U.S. Court of Military Appeals, U.S. Court of Customs and Patent Appeals, and the U.S. Custom Court. These specialized federal courts are not important to the study of criminal justice. Most federal criminal cases begin at the district court level, and appeals from an adverse decision may be taken to the courts of appeals and/or the Supreme Court.

U.S. Courts of Appeals In 1891, the Congress created an intermediate federal appellate court known as the U.S. court of appeals. There are eleven courts of appeals, one each for the District of Columbia (known as the D.C. Circuit), and ten other circuits. These latter circuits include anywhere from three to ten states and territories. The work of the courts of appeals is largely appellate. Most often, in criminal cases, these courts review decisions of the U.S. district courts (trial courts). Further, the number of judges appointed to each circuit ranges from three to fifteen. The fifth and ninth circuits are the largest. Because of the heavy case loads in these latter circuits, there is a movement for the Congress to split these circuits and create two additional ones.

Normally, only three judges hear a case on appeal. However, in important cases, a majority of the judges of a circuit may order a hearing before the court *en banc* (full court). Usually the decisions of the courts of appeals are final. That is, the Supreme Court does not review most courts of appeals decisions—although review is always a possibility. Under some circumstances, a decision of a district court may be appealed directly to the Supreme Court by passing the court of appeals. Most often this occurs when a three-judge district court has been empaneled to hear an important issue. Finally, most final decisions of a district court are appealable (as a matter of right) to the appropriate court of appeals (civil and criminal).

U.S. District Courts The trial courts in the federal system are known as U.S. district courts. These are courts of general jurisdiction and are located in every state as well as the District of Columbia and in certain American territories such as Guam, the Canal zone, the Virgin Islands, and Puerto Rico. Presently, there are ninety-three district courts, with each state having at least one judicial district. Some larger states may have as many as four district courts (e.g., California, New York, and Texas). Normally a district will not extend across state lines.

Most districts have two or more judges, although a single judge sits in a few districts. The Southern District of New York (the largest district) has twenty-seven authorized judgeships. Normally a single judge will try a case, although in exceptional cases a three-judge court will empanel to hear a case. Finally, the district courts have original jurisdiction in most civil actions as well as jurisdiction to try persons accused of federal crimes. In most instances, an appeal from an adverse decision by a district court is taken to the court of appeals—although a direct appeal to the Supreme Court can occur in certain instances.

United States Magistrates In 1968, by passing the Federal Magistrates Act,[34] Congress created new positions for officials known as federal magistrates. These magistrates (formally called United States commissioners) are appointed by the federal district judges and may serve either full time or part time. Their functions are similar to those of committing magistrates (on the state level) and include (1) issuing warrants, (2) holding preliminary hearings, (3) fixing bail, (4) trying "minor" federal offenses—usually equivalent to misdemeanors on the state level, and (5) doing "such additional duties as are not inconsistent with the Constitution and laws of the United States." These additional duties include serving as special masters in civil actions and assisting district judges during pretrial or discovery proceedings. Recently the Supreme Court held in *Wingo v. Wedding* (1974)[35] that the Federal Magistrates Act does not grant a full-time magistrate authority to hold habeas corpus evidentiary hearings. Only a district judge may conduct such a hearing.

8.04 STATE AND LOCAL COURTS

Because of the diversity of state and local courts in the United States, any catagorization and generalization of these court systems is likely to be unsatisfactory. Most state court systems operate on three levels made up of appellate courts, courts of general jurisdiction, and courts of inferior jurisdiction.

State Supreme Courts

Each state has a highest appellate court—most often called the state supreme court. However, several states use a different generic description for their highest courts. For example, in New York, Maryland, and Kentucky, the highest appellate court is called the Court of Appeals. Elsewhere other titles are used, such as the Supreme Court of Errors or the Supreme Judicial Court. Whatever title is used, these highest state courts perform similar functions: they, as the final tribunal courts, rule on issues of law within their states. Most decisions do not proceed into the federal courts because these courts have limited jurisdiction. Only when a case presents an issue of federal or constitutional law will there be any review beyond the state courts.

In those states *without* an intermediate appellate court, the state supreme court (or its equivalent) will usually review criminal cases presented on appeal. Otherwise, these final courts have discretionary power to choose, usually by a writ of certiorari, the cases they will hear. In some classes of cases (e.g., capital cases), the state supreme court *must* review the conviction before the judgment is final.

Courts of Appeals

Many states have intermediate appellate courts called district courts of appeals. Most criminal cases in states that utilize this system end at this stage. Under this system, the state supreme court will usually deny certiorari in most cases. Again, some states use different generic descriptions (e.g., superior court) for intermediate appellate courts. The major purpose of intermediate appellate courts is to allow the state supreme court judicial economy to select those cases for review that present the most important questions of law. In certain types of cases (e.g., capital cases), review by the highest appellate state court is mandatory.

Trial Courts

In the United States, trial courts are either courts of general jurisdiction or courts of limited jurisdiction, often called inferior courts.

Courts of general jurisdiction usually try the more serious criminal cases (e.g., felonies) and, like appellate courts, have different generic titles throughout the United States. For example, in California felonies are tried in the Superior Court; in Detroit, felonies are tried in the Recorder's Court; in New Orleans, felonies are tried in criminal district courts; and interestingly, in New York, the felony trial court is called the New York Supreme Court. Whatever their title, these courts which try felonies are usually the lowest-level courts of record. (That is, there are the lowest-level courts in which a transcript of the proceedings is made by a court reporter.) There are more than 3,500 courts of record in the United States. On occasion, a court of record having general jurisdiction may function as an appellate court for lower inferior courts (not courts of record).

In the United States there are more than 12, 500 lower trial courts having limited jurisdiction (e.g., misdemeanors, traffic offenses). They are usually not courts of record. That is, the proceedings are not transcribed by a court reporter as with appellate courts and courts of general jurisdiction. Inferior courts go by a variety of names (e.g., Magistrate Court, Municipal Court, Police Court, etc.). A defendant can appeal a misdemeanor conviction from an inferior court to a court of general jurisdiction and obtain a new trial *de novo.* That is, a new trial is conducted (same witnesses, same evidence) before a different judge in a court of general jurisdiction instead of the usual presentation of briefs and oral arguments by attorneys before an appellate court. This is rarely done because of the time and expense involved.

Juveniles charged with offenses are usually tried in a court of limited jurisdiction called a juvenile court. Juveniles, like misdemeants, may usually appeal an adjudication of delinquency to a court of general jurisdiction and obtain a trial *de novo.*

In summary, the court structure in the United States is complex and jurisdiction is diversified under a variety of generic titles depending upon the locality involved. The criminal courts are the institutions in our system of criminal justice that implement the intent of the criminal process under governance of the law.

The work load of our correctional agencies is determined by the judgments and sentences given to defendants by our trial courts.

8.05 CORRECTIONS

The trilogy of our correctional institutions jails and prisons, probation, and parole is that aspect of our system of criminal justice which is the least known or understood by most people. Most people have never been in or visited a jail or prison; neither, most probably, have they associated with a person who is on probation or parole. Yet on any given day, two-thirds of all persons convicted of crimes are in the community, not in correctional institutions.[36] The major task confronting our correctional agencies is to effectively handle and rehabilitate those who are known to be our worst citizens. Because of the apparently soaring crime rate and the already overcrowded conditions in correctional institutions, sentencing judges often have little choice but to place nonviolent first offenders on probation; often, second offenders are also given probation.

Correctional institutions attempt to respond to overcrowded conditions by placing many offenders on parole (early release), in the hope that they will not return to the institution. Although the true rate of recidivism (repetitious of offences) is unknown, the President's Task Force on Law Enforcement and the Administration of Justice states that those who repeat their offenses represent one-third to one-half of all offenders.[37] For that group of recidivists, neither specific deterrence nor rehabilitation has been fruitful.

Deplorable conditions in the institutions contribute to the rate of recidivism. As noted by the President's Task Force:

> Life in many institutions is at best barren and futile, at worst unspeakably brutal and degrading. To be sure, the offenders in such institutions are incapacitated from committing further crimes while serving their sentences, but the conditions in which they live are the poorest possible preparation for their successful reentry into society, and often merely reinforce in them a pattern of manipulation or destructiveness.[38]

Although the major purpose of our correctional agencies is presumably rehabilitation, their actual task has been one of custody. At the present time, there are 400 prisons and over 5,000 city and county jails in the United States. The joint Commission on Correctional Manpower and Training states that more than 214, 000 adult offenders are confined daily in state and federal prisons.[39] These offenders are guarded and fed by more than 71,000 personnel in the correctional system. Eighty-seven percent of our correctional personnel perform essential custodial or administrative functions. The remaining 13 percent are vocational or academic teachers and persons involved in health services, social work, or counseling. The President's Task Force estimated that on any given day in 1965, our correctional system was responsible for 1.3 million offenders. It handles nearly 2.5 million admissions per year, yet only 1 percent of the total correctional budget is spent on research. Nearly 50 percent of the budget is spent on adult institutions, primarily for custodial and administrative tasks.[40]

Such an emphasis on custody results in a denial of differential treatment to convicted offenders and encourages a high rate of recidivism.

The correctional process will be examined in greater detail in Part Four. Now, however, we will examine the steps in the processing of a person accused of a felony in a large urban area.

8.06 STEPS IN THE PROCESSING OF A FELONY

The legal steps involved in the processing of a person accused of a crime vary according to the nature of the charge (i.e., felon or misdemeanor) and the jurisdictional requirements of the place of the offense (e.g., information state or grand jury state).

The processing of a person arrested for a misdemeanor is relatively simple in most jurisdictions. Upon being arrested, the accused is taken to a local lockup, booked, and given an opportunity to post bond; then a trial date is set. The trial itself is usually held in a court of inferior jurisdiction, often called the magistrate's court, city court, or police court. The presiding judge (magistrate) is called a justice of the peace, United States magistrate (federal system), or city judge. Usually the trial is *de novo* (no transcript of the proceedings transcribed). The defendant may be found not guilty at the completion of the trial or, if convicted, sentenced to a jail term not to exceed a year.

The defendant may also be fined or receive a suspended sentence. In most jurisdictions, the *possible* sentence for an offense usually distinguishes felonies from misdemeanors. That is, felonies are usually punishable by more than a year in prison and misdemeanors carry a possible jail sentence of up to 1 year. In a minority of jurisdictions (e.g., California), the *actual* sentence imposed determines whether the conviction is for a felony or misdemeanor. Persons convicted of misdemeanors have a right to an appeal in most jurisdictions. Usually this involves a new trial (*de novo*) in a court of general jurisdiction.

The processing of a person accused of a felony is quite different and varies from jurisdiction to jurisdiction. Basically, there are two types of felony procedures in the United States. One type—found in about half the states, especially in California and most Western states—involves the filing of a *bill of information* by the prosecutor; these states are sometimes collectively known as *information states.* Here, in all but rare instances, the decision to prosecute is left entirely to the prosecutor; the defendant does not benefit from the shield of a grand jury. In many states, a grand jury indictment is required before a defendant may be tried for a capital offense. This is because the crime charged and the possible sentence are matters too serious to be left entirely to the discretion of the prosecutor. It is considered more desirable to spread the responsibility to a group of sixteen to twenty-three citizens, called the grand jury, because these citizens bring to the decision a cross-section of experiences and viewpoints.

The other type of felony procedure found in the United States requires a *grand jury indictment* before a person may be brought to trial. The Fifth Amendment of the United States Constitution requires cases brought in the federal system to utilize a grand jury; but the states have an option, with about half using grand juries exclusively for felony prosecution. Most Eastern states are so-called *indictment states.* The functions of the grand jury were discussed earlier in the text.

Before discussing the thirteen or so possible legal steps involved in the processing of a felony, it should be noted that most defendants do not complete the full gamut of legal procedures permitted. Recall that 80 to 90 percent of all persons accused of a crime plead guilty, usually to a lesser offense or in return for a recommended lighter sentence. Such a guilty plea takes the defendant out of the criminal process at a much earlier stage. However, some defendants exhaust their legal remedies, and for them the entire process may take many years. We shall now discuss the various steps in a felony prosecution in a typical large city for a defendant charged with a serious crime.

Prearrest Investigation[41]

The investigation of a specific crime by the police may be initiated in a variety of ways. The police may become alerted that a crime has taken place by the complaint of a victim or a witness; the police may observe the commission of a crime during the course of patrol duty; the police may obtain information from an informer; or information may be obtained through the use of undercover agents or continued surveillance. Most violent and property crimes come to the attention of the police through a complaint by a victim or witness, whereas most "victimless crimes"—such as drug abuse, prostitution, gambling, and consensual deviant sexual behavior—require the use of informers and undercover agents. These latter crimes involve a transaction between a willing seller and buyer and are not normally brought to the attention of the police by one of the participants. The "victims" of these crimes are often satisfied customers, or they may be unwilling to report such transactions for fear of revealing their own deviant behavior. The married man who is the victim of larceny or robbery committed by a prostitute will carefully contemplate the consequences of reporting such crimes.

The majority of police-suspect encounters (1) relate to a possible misdemeanor (85 percent), (2) occur on the street, (3) do not involve an arrest, and (4) often detain the suspect for less than 5 minutes. In some large cities, the annual number of police-suspect encounters may exceed several hundred thousand (not including traffic offenses).

In one-third of all police-suspect encounters, the questioning goes beyond mere identification of the person. That is, the person detained becomes a bona fide suspect.

In certain high-crime areas, 20 percent of all encounters lead to some form of search. Of these, 85 percent involve a search of the suspect, which is usually justified by the police as a valid "stop and frisk." Only 15 percent of all searches involve a home or vehicle.

The majority of searches do not involve a search warrant. Usually the police seek to justify a warrantless search on the basis of the suspect's consent or as being incidental to a lawful arrest. Certain Fourth Amendment problems relating to these searches will be discussed in Chapter 9.

Arrest

The legal definition of "arrest" varies from state to state. The most common definition is the "taking in custody of a person for purposes of charging with a crime." As noted by Perkins,[42] no actual touching of the person is required. Only an assertion of authority and the subject's submission are necessary for an arrest.

Upon being arrested, a person is usually taken to a local police station to be booked.

Booking

"Booking" is essentially a clerical process conducted at the police station. Here the police record the charges against the person, who is fingerprinted, photographed, and subjected to an inventory search. Often charges are dropped at this point because of a procedural error by the police, such as an illegal search and seizure, or because probable cause for the arrest is wanting. Usually the decision to dismiss charges is made by an assistant prosecutor, although someone higher in the police hierarchy than the arresting officer may make this decision (e.g., the desk sergeant, especially if the suspect has been arrested for a misdemeanor).

If a person has been arrested for a felony without an arrest warrant (majority of cases), no bail is usually set until the "initial appearance" or the arraignment (a later stage); in any case, bail must be set by a magistrate. If a person has been arrested pursuant to an arrest warrant, the warrant should specify the amount of bail required, and the person can then be released upon paying the specified fee. If a person has been arrested for a misdemeanor, bail schedules are used and the person can usually be released immediately after the booking process.

Decision to Prosecute

At some point after the booking process, a decision must be made whether to prosecute the arrested person. This decision is entirely at the discretion of the prosecutor, who is almost never required by law to prosecute a given case. On rare occasions, however, a court may enjoin the prosecutor from pursuing a case in which the prosecutorial discretion has now been abused. It is not unusual in larger cities for 30 to 50 percent of all persons arrested for a crime not to be prosecuted, either because of a lack of evidence or for other reasons cited above.

In some cities, it is left to the police to decide whether to prosecute a minor misdemeanor. The cases that are pursued are prosecuted by a police officer before a magistrate. There, at the "initial appearance," a plea is made; if the defendant pleads not guilty, a trial is immediately held. In this sort of trial, the rules of evidence are frequently relaxed.

Initial Appearance (Presentment)

If a decision has been made to prosecute a person charged with a felony, the defendant is taken before a magistrate at a stage called the *initial appearance.* This is the defendant's first appearance before a magistrate. Often this stage is called the *arraignment* (federal system), but such a label may be technically wrong if no plea has been taken at this stage of the criminal process.

Statutes in many states require that an arrested person be taken before a local magistrate "without unnecessary delay," often within 10 days. Although the "unnecessary delay" rule is not constitutionally required, it is ridgidly followed in the federal system because of two U.S. Supreme Court decisions sometimes called the *McNabb-Mallory rule.*[43]

In these two cases, the Supreme Court invoked its supervisory power over the lower federal courts. Therefore the "unnecssary delay" rule is without a constitutional basis and Congress could ostensibly invalidate it. In June 1968, Congress abolished the McNabb-Mallory rule in the Omnibus Crime Control and Safe Streets Act, which provides that delay alone is not a controlling factor regarding the admissibility of a confession.[44] The constitutionality of that provision of the act has not yet been decided by the Supreme Court.

At the initial appearance, defendants are informed of the nature of the charges against them, their constitutional rights are given (e.g., *Miranda* warnings), they are informed of their right to counsel, and their right to a preliminary hearing is explained. At this time also, bail is sometimes set, often by a schedule, although bail may be delayed until the arraignment.

Preliminary Hearing

A defendant has a statutory right to a preliminary hearing following the initial appearance in most jurisdictions. Here the state must introduce evidence of "probable cause" that the defendant committed the crime for which he or she is charged.

The major purpose of the preliminary hearing is to protect defendants against unwarranted prosecutions. In a sense, a preliminary hearing performs a function similar to that of a grand jury (i.e., both stages require a finding of probable cause). However, a defendant at the preliminary hearing is given more legal rights than are granted to a potential defendant during a grand jury investigation. For example, the preliminary hearing is considered a "critical stage," during which the defendant has a constitutional right to be represented by counsel (*Coleman v. Alabama,* 1970).[45] Further, defendants may, at the preliminary hearing, cross-examine prosecution witnesses and introduce evidence on their own behalf (*Pointer v. Texas,* 1965)[46] pursuant to the Confrontation Clause of the Sixth Amendment. During this stage, the rules of evidence are more formally adhered to, as in a trial. Also, a transcript of the proceedings is often recorded for possible use at the trial.

In the majority of cases, the magistrate finds "probable cause" and binds the defendant over for a trial. It should be noted that the preliminary hearing is usually conducted by a magistrate of a court of inferior jurisdiction (e.g., a justice of the peace in municipal court). The defendant is actually tried in a court of general jurisdiction (e.g., criminal court).

Although a preliminary hearing is not constitutionally required,[47] most states provide for such a hearing pursuant to a statute or state constitution. A defendant can waive such a hearing; in large cities, it is not unusual for over 70 percent to do so. Where an indictment is brought by a grand jury, it is generally assumed that the defendant has no right to a preliminary hearing since both it and the grand jury perform the function of establishing probable cause.

There are several good reasons why a defendant may wish to have a preliminary hearing. First, there is always the possibility that the state lacks sufficient evidence to determine probable cause. Second, the defendant may use such a hearing as a discovery device. That is, the state will be required to produce some of its evidence in advance of trial. This discovery can be useful in preparing a later defense. Third, the defendant may wish to "freeze" the testimony of the prosecutions witnesses. That is, a prosecution witness who changes his or her testimony at trial (from testimony at the preliminary hearing) can be impeached; in other words, the witness's credibility is attacked.

Sometimes a defense attorney does not want a preliminary hearing. For example, if it appears that the prosecution witnesses are aged, ill, or likely to leave the jurisdiction, it may be desirable to waive the hearing. The reason is that testimony at the preliminary hearing may be admissible at trial if a witness is bona fide absent at the trial (*Mancusi v. Stubbs,* 1972).[48] A defendant has a right to face his or her accusers at trial with few exceptions. Another reason for waiving a preliminary hearing arises when a defendant has committed several criminal acts sufficient for a multiple court information but has been charged with only one count. By waiving the hearing, the defendant might persuade the prosecutor not to file the additional counts.

In the majority of states, the prosecution may demand a preliminary hearing even though the defendant wishes to waive it, such a prosecutorial request, however, is unusual.

If a magistrate dismisses charges at the preliminary hearing, a grand jury can still indict the defendant for the same crime without violating the defendant's Fifth Amendment protection against double jeopardy. Further, in the majority of states, hearsay evidence that would not be admissible at trial is admissible to establish probable cause at the preliminary hearing. Although the Supreme Court has not decided whether probable cause can be established entirely through hearsay evidence at a preliminary hearing, the Court has approved the use of hearsay at a federal administrative agency hearing (*Richardson v. Persles,* 1971).[49]

If a magistrate has found probable cause at the preliminary hearing, the defendant is "bound over" for trial and the prosecutor will file a bill of information.

Grand Jury Indictment

Recall that in about half the states as well as in the federal system, a bill of information is not allowed in the processing of a felony case. That is, every felony charge requires a grand jury indictment before the defendant can be tried. However, even in information states, the prosecutor can elect to take the case before the grand jury.

The grand jury is composed of citizens (sixteen to twenty-three in number) who meet behind closed doors in secret to consider evidence introduced by the prosecutor. As in the case of the preliminary hearing, the grand jury must find probable cause in order to formally charge a defendant. Usually a majority vote is sufficient.

During a grand jury hearing, the potential defendant has perhaps fewer legal rights than at any other stage of the criminal process. For example, people who are the subjects of grand jury investigation have no constitutional right to be represented by counsel, to present evidence in their own behalf, or to cross-examine the witnesses of the prosecution. Often persons being investigated are not notified that they are the subjects of a grand jury inquiry. While those subpoenaed to appear before a grand jury may bring their retained counsel, the counsel does not have a right to represent a client in the hearing room and must usually wait outside the closed doors. It should be noted that persons subpoenaed to appear before a grand jury do not lose their constitutional privilege against self-incrimination unless they waive it. They *can* refuse to testify. However, if witnesses are given immunity so that their testimony cannot be later used against them, they may be required to testify subject to contempt of court if they refuse.

The Supreme Court has held that a grand jury indictment can be based entirely on hearsay evidence that would not be admissible at trial (*Costello v. U.S.,* 1956).[50]

The functions of the grand jury have been attacked by legal commentators for many years. The grand jury has often been accused of being a "rubber stamp" or "sword" of the prosecutor, although historically its primary purpose was to act as a shield against unwarranted prosecutions.[51] In spite of this criticism, the Fifth Amendment of the United States Constitution expressly provides for grand juries; however, this provision of the Constitution is not presently applicable to the states (*Hurtado v. California,* 1884).[52] The grand jury is likely to be with us for many years.

Arraignment

After probable cause has been established at the preliminary hearing or by the grand jury, a defendant is brought before a trial judge for an arraignment. Here the defendant is informed of the charges and—if this has not been previously done— counsel is court-appointed and bail is set. Perhaps the most important function of the arraignment is the taking of the plea. The plea itself can take one of three general forms: (1) guilty, (2) not guilty, or (3) nolo contendere (no contest).

At the arraignment, 75 to 85 percent of defendants plead guilty—usually because of plea bargaining. About 15 to 30 percent of defendants plead not guilty, and often the prosecutor drops charges here (5 to 10 percent). A relatively uncommon plea is *nolo contendere,* which is a discretionary plea with the judge. Here the defendant is neither admitting guilt nor denying it. If this plea is accepted, the legal effect is one of guilt and the defendant can be convicted on that basis. The major purpose of the plea of nolo contendere is to prevent evidence of a criminal conviction from being admitted at any subsequent civil trial arising out of the crime committed. Because the majority of defendants convicted of a felony are poor, they need not worry about any subsequent civil litigation. They are in effect "judgment proof." Probably the best-known person who plead nolo contendere to a felon charge in recent times was former Vice-President Agnew; his plea resulted in his conviction for violating federal income tax laws.

Assuming a defendant has plead not guilty to the felony charge, the next step in the criminal process is the pretrial motions.

Pretrial Motions

Various pretrial motions are available to a defendant who has plead not guilty, although they are only filed in 12 to 20 percent of all cases. Of the four most common types of pretrial motions are (1) motion to quash indictment or information, (2) motion of a change of venue, (3) motion of a bill of particulars, and (4) motion to suppress evidence.

The motion to quash an indictment or information alleges that the indictment or information is insufficient for a variety of reasons. For example, the motion may claim that the indictment or information does not state a crime, that jeopardy has attached (in violation of the prohibition against double jeopardy), that the statute of limitations has run, or that the composition of the grand jury is improper (e.g., no racial balance).

The least commonly filed pretrial motion is for a *change of venue.* Here the defendant alleges that a fair trial is not possible in a particular district because of massive pretrial publicity, usually via the press, radio, and television. The defendant asks that the trial be moved to another area of the state where little or no publicity has tainted the case. The motion of a change of venue is rarely granted. Several of the Watergate defendants in Washington, D.C., requested a change of venue, which was denied by Judge Sirica; his decision was subsequently affirmed by the District of Columbia Court of Appeals.

Another pretrial motion is the *bill of particulars.* Here the defendant wishes to obtain information about the details of the charge in order to prepare a defense and avoid prejudicial surprise at trial. Often this motion is granted, although the decision lies in the sound discretion of the trial judge.

The most commonly filed pretrial motion is a *motion to suppress* evidence. Most often defendants will allege that the evidence to be used against them was illegally obtained, usually where some search has been made. In some large cities, up to 75 percent of these motions are successful and the case, after such a ruling, is often dismissed by the prosecutor for lack of evidence. For example, if a defendant is charged with the illegal possession of contraband and a judge has held, on a motion to suppress, that the contraband will not be admissible at trial, the prosecutor may have little choice but to *nolle prosequi* (dismiss) the case.

In many states, the prosecutor may taken an appeal to an appellate court, challenging a pretrial decision by a judge. This is called an *interlocutory appeal* and is rarely done.

Assuming that the pretrial motions of a defendant have either been denied or granted in part, the next step in the criminal process is the trial itself.

Trial

The trial of a person charged with a felony will be discussed in greater detail in Chapter 10.

Only a small percentage of persons charged with a felon actually go to trial in the United States. Because 80 to 90 percent of all defendants plead guilty prior to trial, the trial itself only affects 10 to 20 percent of all defendants. Of those defendants who plead not guilty and go to trial, about 60 percent request a trial by jury and 40 percent request a bench (judge only) trial.

Overall, the acquittal rate for felonies is less than 33 percent, but this varies by the offense. For example, over 90 percent of persons charged with forgery who go to trial are convicted, whereas less than 50 percent of persons charged with forcible rape are convicted. The overall acquittal rate of all crimes in the United States (felonies and misdemeanors) is less than 20 percent.

Finally, less than 20 percent of all trials last more than a few days. Often a criminal trial will last less than a day.

Assuming that a defendant has gone to trial and been convicted, the next step in the criminal process is that of sentencing.

Sentencing

The sentence imposed by the trial judge is the most crucial part of the judicial procedure to the convicted defendant. Relatively little hard research has been conducted in this vital area by comparison to other areas of the judicial process. The judge has much discretion throughout the criminal process with regard, for example, to the amount of bail, the power to admit or exclude evidence, and the speediness of the trial. However, the judge has the greatest discretion in the area of sentencing. As a general rule, a judge is restricted only to imposing a sentence within the limits of the applicable statute to which a defendant has been convicted, which can include jail, prison, probation, suspended stentence, or fine. In the majority of states, an appellate court will not overturn a sentence imposed by a trial judge unless the judge's statutory discretion has been abused.

The major discretionary issue before a judge is: What sentence should a particular defendant receive?

The imposed sentence will reflect the judge's own commitment to a particular sentencing philosophy: retribution or rehabilitation, isolation or deterrence. Some judges are especially tough on drunk drivers, others on "hot check" artists. Defense attorneys try to plea their clients before sympathetic judges.

A more detailed examination of sentencing will be presented in Chapter 12.

After sentencing, some defendants appeal their convictions to a higher court.

Appeals

Of the 80 to 90 percent of defendants who plead guilty, few appeal their convictions. As noted earlier, a guilty plea substantially reduces the legal grounds for a reversal of the conviction. Of the 10 to 20 percent who plead not guilty to a felony charge, two-thirds are convicted. Of these, 20 to 40 percent appeal their convictions to an appellate court. The rate of reversal varies by jurisdiction but may be 10 to 20 percent the inescapable conclusion is that the majority of defendants do not appeal their convictions and only a small percentage of persons convicted of a felony have their convictions reversed by an appellate court. In those instances where an appelate court has overturned a conviction, the case is usually reversed and remanded back to the trial court for a new trial.

The U.S. Supreme Court has held that if a state provides for an appeal by an indigent defendant in a criminal case, the defendant has a right to court-appointed counsel, at state expense, on the first appeal (*Douglas v. California,* 1963).[53] However, the Court rejected the argument that an indigent defendant has a constitutional right to counsel *beyond* the first appeal, even though subsequent appeals to a higher court may be allowed by a state (*Ross v. Moffit,* 1974).[54]

After exhausting their appeals, defendants may seek postconviction remedies.

In summary, the legal steps involved in the processing of a person accused of committing a misdemeanor are relatively simple in most jurisdictions. The suspect is arrested, usually booked, and given an opportunity to post bond. A trial is then held within a reasonably short time. On the other hand, the processing of a person accused of committing a felony can be quite complicated and lengthy. The procedures utilized depend in part on whether the accused is charged in an information or grand jury jurisdiction. The legal steps involved vary by jurisdiction and can range from a prearrest investigation through complicated postconviction remedies.

SUMMARY

In this chapter an overview of the American criminal justice system was presented. In particular, we described how the system, with many component agencies, a hugh bureaucracy processes millions of persons charged with various offenses each year. Often the process undermines effective law enforcement and rehabilitation efforts. Further, we described the five major agencies of the criminal justice system: law enforcement, prosecutors, defense attorneys, courts, and corrections. In particular we noted some of the major problems confronting these agencies and indicated the diversity and complexity of their structures in terms of both size and jurisdiction. Further, we traced the legal steps involved in the processing of a person charged with a crime; we indicated that the procedures utilized depended upon the nature of the offense charged and the jurisdictional requirements (i.e., information or grand jury) of the jurisdiction (federal or state) involved. Finally, we indicated that the ultimate decision to prosecute a person accused of a crime rests with the prosecutor. This power is called *prosecutorial discretion.*

Chapter 9

The Right to Counsel and Other Assistance Available to an Accused

The constitutional right of an indigent defendant to court-appointed counsel (at state expense) is of recent vintage. This is due, in large part, to the historical development of the United States Constitution and, for many years, the lack of U.S. Supreme Court decisions defining the scope of the right to counsel. Before specifically addressing the issue of the right to counsel in criminal cases, it is desirable to examine the historical development of and the relationship between the Fourteenth Amendment and the first ten amendments to the Constitution—known as the Bill of Rights.

9.01 APPLICATION OF THE BILL OF RIGHTS TO THE STATES (NATIONALIZATION)

When the present United States Constitution was written in 1787, few constitutional protections were afforded persons charged with criminal offenses. Recognizing this oversight and based on some abuses suffered by the colonists at the hands of the British, the framers of the Constitution later (in 1791) added ten amendments—as known as the Bill of Rights. Within the Bill of Rights are twelve specific provisions which relate to the criminal process, namely:

1 A prohibition against unreasonable searches and seizures (Fourth Amendment)

2 A requirement of grand jury indictments (Fifth Amendment)

3 A prohibition against double jeopardy (Fifth Amendment)

4 A prohibition against compulsory self-incrimination (Fifth Amendment)

5 A right to a speedy trial (Sixth Amendment)

6 A right to a public trial (Sixth Amendment)

7 A right to a trial by jury (Sixth Amendment)
8 A right to confront adverse witnesses (Sixth Amendment)
9 A right to defense witnesses (Sixth Amendment)
10 A right to counsel (Sixth Amendment)
11 A prohibition against cruel and unusual punishment (Eighth Amendment)
12 A prohibition against excessive bail and fines (Eighth Amendment)

The application of the Bill of Rights to the states has been substantially completed. Prior to the 1960s, comparatively few state criminal cases were reviewed by the U.S. Supreme Court. Those cases that did manage to draw the Court's attention were decided primarily on Fourteenth Amendment due process grounds. The Court, for many years, specifically declined to apply to the states those guarantees found in the Bill of Rights which relate directly to the criminal process. This was due, in large part, to the historical development of the United States Constitution and the various judicial philosophies of the justices on the application of the Bill of Rights to the states prior to the 1960s.

More than forty years after the Bill of Rights was ratified, the U.S. Supreme Court held (in a decision that did not at that time receive much attention) that the Bill of Rights was not applicable to state criminal proceedings.[1] Chief Justice Marshall, writing for the Court, stated that the provisions found in the Bill of Rights were applicable only to federal, not state trials. Marshall's views on the nationalization of the Bill of Rights remained a dominant force on the Court for over a century. Thus, a state could apparently deny to an accused any one of the aforementioned guarantees in the Bill of Rights without violating a federal constitutional protection.

During the next 35 years, few attempts were made by state criminal defendants to have the various guarantees in the Bill of Rights made applicable to the states.

In 1868 the Fourteenth Amendment was adopted. It provides, in part, that no *state* shall "deprive any person of life, liberty, or property, without *due process* of law, nor deny to any person . . . the *Equal protection* of the laws." The issue that slowly crystallized was whether a state could provide to an accused due process and the equal protection of the laws (as required by the Fourteenth Amendment) and still deny an accused those guarantees found in the Bill of Rights.

The first state criminal case in which this issue was decided by the Supreme Court occurred in 1884.[2] There the Supreme Court rejected the defendant's argument that a Fifth Amendment provision (which requires grand jury indictments for "infamous crimes") was applicable to the states. The defendant had been brought to trial on a charge of murder on a "bill of information" (filed by the prosecutor) as opposed to a grand jury indictment. The Supreme Court held that the due process requirement (Fourteenth Amendment) did not incorporate the Fifth Amendment and that a state could initiate a criminal charge by a prosecutor's bill of information without the prior screening of a grand jury required in the federal courts. That case has never been overruled, and today about half the states require grand jury indictments in all felony charges unless waived by the defendant.

Since 1884, the Court has had much difficulty interpreting the relationship between the Fourteenth Amendment limitation on the states and the Bill of Rights. During the next seventy-five years or so, four views on the nationalization of the Bill of Rights to the states were espoused by various justices of the Supreme Court. These views were (1) fundamental fairness, (2) total incorporation, (3) total incorporation plus, and (4) selective incorporation. These views will be discussed briefly, without an extensive examination of their merits or objections.[3]

Fundamental Fairness

The first view that developed on the nationalization of the Bill of Rights is known as the *fundamental fairness doctrine.* According to the adherents of this view, there is no necessary relationship between the Fourteenth Amendment and the Bill of Rights. The Amendment's Due Process Clause was viewed as incorporating "traditional notions of due process . . . as those principles implicit in the concept of ordered liberty."[4] Accordingly, it was not deemed fundamentally unfair for a state to try a defendant two times for the same murder (over the defendant's objections), with the second trial resulting in a death sentence. The Fifth Amendment prohibition against double jeopardy was held not to be applicable to the states.[5] Nor was it deemed fundamentally unfair for a state prosecutor to comment adversely (to the jury) on a defendant's failure to testify at trial. The Fifth Amendment privilege against self-incrimination was held not to be applicable to the states.[6] Under this view, a state is required to afford a defendant only "that fundamental fairness essential to the very concept of justice." Here the Court looks to basic fairness as viewed by the "totality of circumstances" of the case. A violation of a Bill of Rights guarantee may or may not indicate that fundamental fairness has been violated. This interpretation was the prevailing view of the Court for many years, but it is no longer accepted by a majority of the court.

Total Incorporation

A second view—the *total incorporation doctrine*[7]—held that the Fourteenth Amendment made all the Bill of Rights guarantees applicable to the state. This doctrine's proponents argued that support for its position is found in the legislative history of the Fourteenth Amendment and that such a view avoids the subjective approach of fundamental fairness by confining the issues to the specific language of the Bill of Rights. The total incorporation view has never commanded support from a majority of the Court.

Total Incorporation Plus

The *total incorporation plus* view holds that due process includes all the guarantees of the Bill of Rights *plus* any additional rights viewed as basic to society under a fundamental fairness test.[8] This view has always received the weakest support from the Court.

Selective Incorporation

The *selective incorporation* view combines aspects of both fundamental fairness and total incorporation. This view accepts the premise that the Fourteenth Amendment encompasses all rights "essential to the scheme of ordered liberty"[9] but holds that other rights, although not found in the Bill of Rights, may be fundamental. Once a guarantee within the Bill of Rights is found to be fundamental, that guarantee is incorporated "whole and intact," made applicable to the states, and enforced according to federal standards.[10] Under this view, the Court does not look to "the totality of circumstances" but examines the total right of the amendment.[11] Selective incorporation is the approach currently utilized by the Court in implimenting the Bill of Rights to the states.

Through a long line of decisions by the Supreme Court, ten of the twelve provisions in the Bill of Rights relevant to the criminal process are today applicable to the states. Only the Fifth Amendment provision requiring grand jury indictments and the Eighth Amendment prohibition against "excessive bail and fines" are not presently applicable to the states. The total incorporation view has almost been fulfilled. Nine of the ten provisions applicable to

Table 9-1 Application of the Bill of Rights to the States

Guarantee	Applicable to the states?	Case
Unreasonable searches and seizures	Yes	Wolf v. Colorado, 338 U.S. 25 (1949)
Grand jury indictment	No	Hurtado v. California, 110 U.S. 516 (1884)
Double jeopardy	Yes	Benton v. Maryland, 395 U.S. 784 (1969)
Compulsory self-incrimination	Yes	Malloy v. Hogan, 378 U.S. 1 (1964)
Speedy trial	Yes	Klopfer v. North Carolina, 386 U.S. 213 (1967)
Public trial	Yes	In re Oliver, 333 U.S. 257 (1948)
Trial by jury	Yes	Duncan v. Louisiana, 391 U.S. 145 (1968)
Confrontation clause	Yes	Pointer v. Texas, 380 U.S. 400 (1965)
Defense witnesses	Yes	Washington v. Texas, 388 U.S. 14 (1967)
Right to counsel	Yes	Powell v. Alabama, 287 U.S. 45 (1932); (capital cases) Gideon v. Wainwright, 372 U.S. 335 (1963); (noncapital felonies) Argersinger v. Hamlin, 407 U.S. 25 (1972); (misdemeanors)
Cruel and unusual punishment	Yes	Robinson v. California, 370 U.S. 660 (1962)
Excessive bail and fines	No	None

the states were decided by the Supreme Court in the 10-year period of 1962 to 1972. (See Table 9-1.)

9.02 STAGES WHERE THE RIGHT TO COUNSEL IS MANDATED

An indigent charged with a criminal offense does not have a constitutional right to court-appointed counsel at all stages of the criminal process. This is because of the general language of part of the Sixth Amendment, which says that "In all criminal prosecutions, the accused shall . . . have the Assistance of Counsel for his defense."

It is well-settled that although the constitutional right of an indigent defendant to appointed counsel is not restricted to the trial itself, it does not include all stages of the criminal process. Through a long line of decisions, the United States Supreme Court has held that the right to counsel is applicable at "critical stages" of the criminal process. A critical stage occurs where "substantial rights of a defendant are affected."[12] A poorly educated defendant is no match for a highly skilled prosecutor at the trial or other critical stages of the criminal process.

At what points in the criminal process does (or should) the right to court-appointed counsel be constitutionally required: pretrial? trial? posttrial?

Most of the cases involving the right to court-appointed counsel decided by the Supreme Court have involved the failure of a state to provide, at state expense, counsel for an indigent defendant. The Court has accepted the premise that more affluent defendants could have retained counsel (at their own expense) and that it is unconstitutional to deny defendants the assistance of their *retained counsel* at trial.

In at least two cases, the Court has suggested that the right to court-appointed counsel may be required independent of the Sixth Amendment.[13] In a leading case, Mr. Justice Black, writing for the Supreme Court, noted that "there can be no equal justice where the kind of justice a man gets depends on the amount of money he has."[14] Although the above case involved the right to a transcript (stenographic recording of the trial proceedings) by an indigent defendant on appeal from a felony conviction, the equal-protection argument advanced there was later applied in a right-to-counsel case.[15] The Court held that a state is required to appoint counsel to indigent defendants *on the first appeal* after conviction of a felony. The defendants, after being convicted of thirteen felonies (in a single trial) in a California state court, were denied court-appointed counsel on their first appeal, although wealthier defendants were permitted to receive the benefits of retained counsel. The Supreme Court noted that, although state appellate review is not constitutionally required in criminal cases, an indigent defendant is entitled to equal treatment, at least on the first appeal, as of right. The Supreme Court has not, to date, specifically ruled whether the same right to court-appointed counsel on a first appeal is applicable to indigent misdemeants. Presumably it is.

Most of the earlier right-to-counsel cases decided by the Supreme Court involved the issue of whether a denial of counsel violated due process under the Fourteenth Amendment. This was because the Court did not begin to significantly expand the scope of the right to counsel (in state cases) until the 1960s. A general right of court-appointed counsel to indigents accused of noncapital felonies, as described above, was not applicable to the states until 1963.[16]

In the celebrated Scottsboro (Alabama) case decided in 1932, a group of young, illiterate black youths were accused of raping two white women who were riding a freight car. Their request for court-appointed counsel at trial on the grounds that they were too poor to hire their own counsel was denied by the Alabama courts. They were convicted and sentenced to death. In that case, the Supreme Court first recognized the right to court-appointed counsel in a state criminal case. The Court held that an indigent has a constitutional right (as a matter of Fourteenth Amendment due process) to counsel in *state capital* cases.[17] The Court hinted that there might be a general right to counsel in all criminal cases but did not then decide the issue.

Six years later (1938), the Court held that indigent defendants charged with *federal felonies* have a Sixth Amendment right to court-appointed counsel.[18] Subsequently, in 1942, the Court first considered the issue of the right to appointed counsel in *all state felony* cases. In this instance the defendant, a farmhand charged with robbery, requested that a lawyer be appointed to represent him as he was too poor to retain his own counsel. His request was denied and he was convicted. On appeal, the U.S. Supreme Court held that there is no constitutional right to court-appointed counsel in state noncapital felony cases absent "special circumstances."[19]

During the next 20 years, the Court, on the case-by-case basis, found a number of instances in which "special circumstances" required the presence of counsel in state felony cases. For example, in a later case the Supreme Court held that a charge under a Virginia habitual criminal statute, which carried a long sentence, was serious enough to warrant the assistance of court-appointed counsel.[20] Other instances where the Court found a need for counsel include the sentencing of a defendant,[21] the entering of guilty plea court at any time,[22] the arraignment of a defendant charged with a capital offense,[23] and arraignments in general.[24] By 1963, the Court had found so many instances of "special circumstances" requiring the presence of appointed counsel that the earlier rule generally denying appointed counsel in noncapital felonies was no longer viable.

In *Gideon v. Wainwright* (1963)[25] the Court reexamined the issue of the general right to court-appointed counsel in state felony cases. Gideon, an indigent drifter, was charged with breaking into a poolroom, and he asked the trial court for counsel. His request was denied at that time since Florida law permitted court-appointed counsel only the capital cases. Gideon "conducted his defense about as well as could be expected from a layman,"[26] but he was nevertheless convicted. His petition for review to the Florida Supreme Court was denied and he appealed to the U.S. Supreme Court. The Supreme Court agreed to hear his appeal and appointed Mr. Abe Fortas (a well-known Washington D.C. attorney and later an associate justice of the Supreme Court) to represent him. Gideon's conviction was reversed and a unanimous Court held that indigents charged with a *felony* in a state case have a Sixth Amendment right (through the Due Process Clause of the Fourteenth Amendment) to court-appointed counsel. Mr. Justice Black, writing for the Court, stated that "in our adversary system of criminal justice, any person hauled into court, who is too poor to hire a lawyer, cannot be assured a fair trial unless counsel is provided for him."[27]

During the next 10 years the Court found other stages in the criminal process where indigent defendants were entitled to appointed counsel at state expense. In *Miranda v. Arizona* 1966),[28] the Court held that the prohibition against compulsory self-incrimination (Fifth Amendment) requires that a suspect is entitled (as a constitutional right) to the *presence* of counsel during custodial interrogation. Although *Miranda* involved the issue of involuntary confessions and was not decided on Sixth Amendment grounds, the right to counsel was deemed necessary in order to protect a defendants' Fifth Amendment rights.

In the following year (1967), the Court held that a *postindictment lineup* is a "critical stage" for an accused at which the presence of counsel is constitutionally required.[29] The Court was concerned with the inherent dangers of misidentification of lineups and felt that the guiding hand of counsel would reduce such risks. The Court at that time left open the question whether a *preindictment lineup* requires the presence of counsel. This issue was resolved in 1972, when a majority Court held that counsel was not constitutionally required at this stage of the criminal process.[30]

In 1967, the Court held that an indigent defendant has a right to court-appointed counsel at a *probation revocation hearing* where *no sentence* was pronounced at the time of conviction.[31] Subsequently, the Court held in another decision that there is no general right to court-appointed counsel at a *probation revocation hearing* where a sentence *had been* imposed at the time of conviction.[32] However, the Court did hold that court-appointed counsel may be required at such hearings where defendants cannot adequately defend their cases. The Court noted that the right to counsel at such hearings would be determined on a case-by-case basis similar to the approach taken prior to the *Gideon* decision.[33]

Whether an indigent defendant is entitled to court-appointed counsel at a *parole revocation hearing* was recently left open by the Supreme Court. There the Court held that a defendant must, in accord with due process, be afforded certain procedural rights at such a hearing, to wit: a determination of probable cause for the revocation of parole in a *preliminary hearing* at the place where revocation is sought and, if probable cause is determined, a revocation hearing on the *merits* of the claim seeking to revoke parole at the correctional institution to which the parolee has been returned.[34] (The constitutional rights of convicted offenders are presented in Chapter 15.)

In another case, the Supreme Court has held that the "guiding hand of counsel" at a *preliminary hearing* (not the same type of hearing as noted above in parole-revocation proceedings) is essential to protect an accused against an erroneous or improper accusation.[35] Although the Court acknowledged that a preliminary (pretrial) hearing is a "critical stage," it also held that a denial of counsel at such a stage could be a "harmless error."[36] In an earlier case, the Court had held that "before a federal constitutional error can be held harmless, the court must be able to declare a belief that it was harmless beyond a reasonable doubt."[37] Where a defendant alleges a constitutional error, the burden of proof is on the state "to prove the error did not contribute to the verdict obtained."[38]

Although the Court has found "harmless constitutional errors" at other stages of the criminal process, it has never held that a denial of counsel at the *trial* itself is subject to the "harmless error" rule.[39]

In *Argersinger v. Hamlin* (1972)[40] the Court extended the rationale of *Gideon* to include the right to court-appointed counsel to indigent defendants in cases where the imposition of a jail sentence is a possibility.

Another stage at which the right to court-appointed counsel is constitutionally required involves the juvenile justice process. *In re Gault* (1967)[41] held that "Due process . . . requires that in respect to proceedings (juvenile delinquency) which may result in commitment to an institution in which the juvenile's freedom may be curtailed, the child and his parent must be notified of the child's right to be represented by counsel retained by them, or if they are unable to afford counsel, the counsel will be appointed to represent the child."[42]

More recently the Court refused to extend the right to court-appointed counsel beyond the first appeal after conviction of a *felony.* The Court held that a constitutional right to court-appointed counsel does not extend to *discretionary state appeals* and for application for review in a state supreme court beyond the first appeal as of right.[43] Further, the Court has recently held that inmates subjected to prison disciplinary hearings do not have a constitutional-right to counsel at such administrative proceedings.[44]

Those stages deemed critical—where "sub-

Table 9-2 Stages Where Court-Appointed Counsel May Be Required

Stage	Right to court-appointed counsel?	Case
1. Pretrial custodial interrogation	Yes	Miranda v. Arizona, 384 U.S. 436 (1966)
2. Preliminary hearing	Yes	Coleman v. Alabama, 339 U.S. 90 (1970)
3. Arraignment	Yes	Hamilton v. Alabama, 368 U.S. 52 (1961); (capital cases)
		White v. Maryland, 373 U.S. 59 (1963); (felonies)
4. Preindictment lineup	No	Kirby v. Illinois, 406 U.S. 682 (1972)
5. Postindictment lineup	Yes	U.S. v. Wade, 388 U.S. 218 (1967)
		Gilbert v. California, 388 U.S. 263 (1967)
6. Guilty plea in court	Yes	Moore v. Michigan, 355 U.S. 155 (1957)
7. Sentencing	Yes	Townsend v. Burke, 334 U.S. 736 (1948)
8. First appeal after conviction	Yes	Douglas v. California, 372 U.S. 353 (1963)
9. Beyond first appeal	No	Ross v. Moffitt, 94 S. Ct. 2437 (1974)
10. Probation revocation hearing—no sentence at conviction	Yes	Mempa v. Rhay, 389 U.S. 128 (1967)
11. Probation revocation hearing—sentence given at conviction	No, only in "special circumstances"	Gagon v. Scarpelli 411 U.S. 778 (1973)
12. Parole revocation hearing	No (not fully decided)	Morrissey v. Brewer, 408 U.S. 471 (1972)
13. Juvenile delinquency proceeding	Yes	In re Gault, 387 U.S. 1 (1967)

Table 9-2 Stages Where Court-Appointed Counsel May Be Required (continued)

14. Trial (state felony)	Yes	Gideon v. Wainwright, 372 U.S. 335 (1963)
15. Trial (state capital case)	Yes	Powell v. Alabama, 287 U.S. 45 (1932)
16. Trial (federal felony)	Yes	Johnson v. Zerbst, 304 U.S. 458 (1938)
17. Trial (misdemeanors) and petty offenses	Yes	Argersinger v. Hamlin, 407 U.S. 25 (1972)
18. Grand jury hearing	No	In re Groban, 352 U.S. 330 (1957)
19. Taking of a blood sample from a suspect	No	Schmerber v. California, 384 U.S. 757 (1966)
20. Taking of handwriting exemplars	No	Gilbert v. California, 388 U.S. 218 (1967)
21. Taking of voice exemplars	No	U.S. v. Dionisio, 410 U.S. 1 (1973)
22. Showing of photographic displays	No	U.S. v. Ash, 413 U.S. 300 (1973)
23. Taking of fingerprints	No	None
24. Prison disciplinary hearings	No	Wolff v. McDonnell, 418 U.S. 539 (1974)
25. High school disciplinary hearings	No	Goss v. Lopez, 419 U.S. 565 (1975)
26. Summary counts martial	No	Middendorf v. Henry, 425 U.S. 25 (1976)

stantial rights of a defendant may be affected"—require a constitutional right to counsel. "Special circumstances" found in the pre-*Gideon* progeny and future cases involving parole revocation hearings and other issues may involve a right to court-appointed counsel. These latter determinations are likely to be made on a case-by-case basis. The stages at which the constitutional right to court-appointed counsel applies (unless waived) are outlined in Table 9-2.

Recently, a majority of the Supreme Court held that a defendant in a state criminal trial has an independent constitutional right to self-representation and that defendants who voluntarily and intelligently waive counsel may proceed to defend themselves at trial without the assistance of counsel.[45] As noted by the Court:

> To force a lawyer on a defendant can only lead him to believe that the law contrives against him. Moreover, it is not inconceivable that in some rare instances, the defendant might in fact present his case more effectively by conducting his own defense. Personal liberties are not rooted in the law of averages. The defendant, and not his lawyer or the State, will bear the personal consequences of a conviction. It is the defendant, therefore, who must be free personally to decide whether in his particular case counsel is to his advantage."[46]

The Court noted that the defendants who elect to represent themselves are expected to comply with the rules of procedural and substantive law. And such defendants who assume the risk cannot thereafter complain that the quality of their defense amounted to a denial of "effective assistance of counsel."[47]

The constitutional right of an indigent to court-appointed counsel is not included at certain other stages of the criminal process, including investigative proceedings such as grand jury and legislative hearings.[48] Other stages where appointed counsel is not constitutionally required include the taking of a defendant's fingerprints,[49] handwriting exemplars,[50] blood samples,[51] voice exemplars,[52] and during photograph sessions[53] where there is only a minimal risk of violating a defendant's rights.

In addition to the right of counsel at various stages of the criminal process, a defendant enjoys certain other constitutional protections such as the right to be free from unreasonable searches and seizures and the privilege against self-incrimination. These constitutional rights, as well as others, also have the effect of placing legal constraints on police practices.

9.03 LEGAL RESTRAINTS ON POLICE PRACTICES

Searches and Seizures

The Fourth Amendment to the United States Constitution provides that:

> The right of the people to be secure in their persons, houses, papers, and effects, against unreasonable searches and seizures, shall not be violated, and no Warrants shall issue, but upon probable cause, supported by Oath or affirmation, and particularly describing the place to be searched, and the persons or things to be seized.

Fourth Amendment problems have always been troublesome to the courts and law enforcement officials. This is perhaps due, in large part, to the general language of the amendment itself. The Fourth Amendment refers to three separate concepts without fully connecting them. First, the Fourth Amendment prohibits unreasonable searches and seizures. Second, the amendment suggests that on certain occasions a search warrant may first be required prior to conducting a search. Third, the amendment suggests that probable cause must precede the issuance of a search warrant or search.

The standards of "unreasonable searches and seizures" and "probable cause" are not self-defining, and the judiciary must ultimately decide the meaning of the Fourth Amendment. A literal reading of the Fourth Amendment might suggest that all warrantless searches are unreasonable, even with probable cause. However, this is not the case, as law enforcement would be impossible if search warrants were required in all situations. One need only imagine the risk to a police officer who was not permitted to search, without a search warrant, the person of a dangerous felon upon arrest.

Before we discuss the legal effects of an unreasonable search or seizure, a brief overview of the Fourth Amendment is in order.

Overview of the Fourth Amendment

The Fourth Amendment requirements of reasonable searches and seizures based on probable cause are "terms of limitation"[54] which place a restraint on governmental law enforcement activities. In the words of Professor Amsterdam, "The Bill of Rights in general and the Fourth Amendment in particular are profoundly anti-government documents."[55] The framers of the Constitution, mindful of the use of general warrants and writs of assistance in England and the American colonies prior to the American Revolution, "fashioned [it] against the background . . . that an unrestricted power of search and seizure could be an instrument for stifling liberty of expression."[56] Accordingly, the Fourth Amendment severely restricts the laudable goals of effective law enforcement, even in a democratic society. Against this background, the Court has had to judicially create "exigent circumstances" which relax the stringent standards of the Fourth Amendment and, at the same time, put some teeth into its provisions when the rules have been broken.[57] Further, the Fourth Amendment is applicable only to "*persons, houses, papers,* and *effects*"; and, in the case of search warrants, the *place, person,* or *things* to be searched or seized must be described with *particularity.*[58] Against these standards, it is no small wonder that the elusive terms of the Fourth Amendment have presented the Justices of the Court with some of their more pronounced vexations. In some of its earlier decisions, the Court formulated a standard that "the test . . . is not whether it was reasonable to procure a search warrant, but whether the search was reasonable."[59] More recently, the Court seems to have modified this flexible standard which eluded black letter law[60] and to be reaching those decisions in terms of a calculus model suggested in *Katz v. United States*[61] (although it would be sheer folly to suggest that the Court has abandoned these issues on a case-by-case analysis).[62] As noted by the *Katz* Court, "searches conducted outside the judicial process, without prior approval by judge or magistrate, are *per se* unreasonable—subject only to a few specifically established and well-delineated exceptions."[63] Thus, in order to justify a warrantless intrusion, "the burden is on those seeking the exception to show the need for it."[64] Because most searches and seizures conducted by law enforcement authorities occur outside the parameters of the judicial process,[65] the Supreme Court, through a long line of decisions, has upheld warrantless searches when any of the following are involved: a lawful arrest,[66] consent,[67] hot pursuit,[68] an emergency,[69] a border search,[70] a "stop and frisk,"[71] misplaced trust,[72] abandoned property,[73] the actions of a private citizen when not acting in concert with the law enforcement agents,[74] certain administrative searches,[75] and evidence found in plain view.[76]

In at least three of the above exceptions, the Supreme Court has judicially waived the constitutional requirement of probable cause prior to a search and seizure, even though the Fourth Amendment does not, on its face, make those distinctions. Most border searches or their "functional equivalents"[77] do not require a finding of probable cause prior to the governmental intrusion.[78] Except in the limited area of body intrusions,[79] no suspicion is required prior to a search of persons, their vehicles, or their property during border searches. Apparently the only limitation here is that the search must be *reasonable.*[80] In the area of stop-and-frisk law,[81] the Court has held that a stop and frisk of a suspect is a search and seizure;[82] only a reasonable suspicion—less than probable cause—that the person may be armed and dangerous is required prior to the intrusion.[83] However, the search is limited to a patting of the exterior of the suspect's clothing in looking for a dangerous weapon.[84] Finally, in certain administrative searches,[85] probable cause is not required prior to a warrantless search as long as it is not accompanied by any unauthorized force,[86] the lawfulness of the intrusion is not dependent upon the subjects' consent,[87] and the search is authorized by statute.[88]

Thus, the intent of the framers of the Constitution was to require law enforcement officials to have some objective, good reason before they conducted a search. Accordingly, the Fourth Amendment is generally thought to mean that (1) before the police can search and seize evidence, they must have *probable cause* that the person they are searching is guilty of some crime or, in the case of property, that the items seized are stolen, contraband, or otherwise qualify as criminal evidence. That is, all searches and seizures must be *reasonable;* and, in some instances, (2) a *search warrant* issued by "a neutral and detached magistrate" may first be required, even though the search was otherwise reasonable.[89]

The whole history of the law of search and seizure revolves around the tension between the two standards: Was the search reasonable? Was there a search warrant or some acceptable justification for a warrantless search?

The illusive standard of "probable cause" has been defined by the Supreme Court:

> Probable cause exists where the facts and circumstances within (the arresting officers') knowledge and of which they had reasonable trustworthy information (are) sufficient in themselves to warrant a man of reasonable caution in the belief that an offense has been or is being committed.[90]

The issues involving searches and seizures are often complex, and the attendant rules flowing from judicial decisions are so complicated that it is virtually impossible for any law enforcement official to be correct all the time. As noted by Chief Justice Burger in a recent case:[91]

> Policemen do not have the time, inclination, or training to read and grasp the nuances of the appellate opinions that ultimately define the standards of conduct they are to follow. The issues that these decisions resolve often admit of neither easy nor obvious answers, as sharply divided courts on what or what is not reasonable amply demonstrate. Nor can judges, in all candor, forget that opinions sometimes lack helpful clarity.[92]

Accordingly, our remaining discussion will not focus on the rules governing the laws of search and seizure. That subject is usually treated as a separate course and this work is not appropriate for such a task. Rather, we shall examine the methods of protecting and enforcing our Fourth Amendment rights when the police violate the rules.

The Exclusionary Rule

At common law and until recently in our judicial history, evidence that was illegally seized by state or federal law enforcement officials was nevertheless admissible at a subsequent criminal trial. Although persons against whom an illegal search and seizure had taken place were, in effect, the victims of trespass, their only legal recourse was to resist the officer and/or sue in a civil action for damages or prosecute for oppression (permitted in some states). Also, the violating officer was subject to disciplinary action or removal by superiors.

In *Weeks v. United States* (1914), the Supreme Court held that evidence illegally seized by *federal officers* is not admissible in a subsequent federal criminal trial.[93] That is, evidence illegally seized will be *judicially excluded* at the trial stage. This is known as the *exclusionary rule,* and *Weeks* has never been overruled. Mr. Justice Day, writing for the Court in *Weeks,* stated:

> If letters and private documents can thus be seized and held and used in evidence against a citizen accused of an offense, the protection of the 4th Amendment, declaring his right to secure against searches and seizures, is of no value, and, so far as those thus placed are concerned, might as well be stricken from the Constitution.[94]

Between 1914 and 1926, of 45 states that considered adopting the exclusionary rule announced in *Weeks,* 14 states adopted the rule and 31 rejected it. In 1926, the N.Y. Court of Appeals (the highest New York State court) for the first time considered that issue,[95] and the court unanimously rejected the newly formulated rule announced in *Weeks.* Judge Cardozo (later an associate justice of the U.S. Supreme Court), writing for the New York court, criticized the exclusionary rule announced in *Weeks* because "the criminal is to go free because the constable has blundered."[96]

During the next quarter of a century or so, the exclusionary rule announced in *Weeks* was fully applicable in federal cases. By 1949, thirty states had rejected the *Weeks* doctrine and sixteen had accepted it.

In *Wolf v. Colorado* (1949),[97] the police had illegally seized the appointment books of a physician (Wolf); he was subsequently convicted, on that evidence, of conspiracy to commit abortion. On review of his conviction, the U.S. Supreme Court held that while the Fourth Amendment is applicable to the states through the Fourteenth Amendment's Due Process Clause, the Fourth Amendment does not forbid the admission of evidence obtained by an illegal search and seizure at a state criminal trial. Mr. Justice Frankfurter, writing for a majority Court, stated:

> . . . we have no hesitation in saying that were a state affirmatively to sanction such police incursion into privacy it would run counter to the guaranty of the Fourteenth Amendment. But the ways of enforcing such a basic right raise questions of a different order. How such arbitrary conduct should be afforded, the means by which the right should be made effective, are all questions that are not be so dogmatically answered as to preclude the varying solutions which spring issues not susceptible to quantitative solution.[98]

In *Wolf,* the Court went on to suggest that remedies other than the imposition of the exclusionary rule were available. For example, the Court suggested that (1) an aggrieved person could sue the police for an action in trespass, (2) the internal discipline of the police would curb illegal searches and seizures, and (3) local community opinion would deter oppressive conduct by the police.[99] But the remedies suggested by the *Wolf* Court seemed ineffective, as noted by the California Supreme Court in a later case (1955), where that court judicially imposed the exclusionary rule on all California courts "because other remedies have completely failed to secure compliance with Constitutional provisions. . . ."[100]

The following year (1956), the U.S. Supreme Court held that evidence illegally obtained by federal agents would not be admissible in a state criminal proceeding;[101] and in 1960, the so-called silver platter doctrine was abolished, which had allowed evidence illegally seized by state law enforcement agents to be admissible in a federal criminal trial.[102]

By 1961, six new justices, including a new Chief Justice (Warren), had been appointed to the Court since the *Wolf* decision. In *Mapp v. Ohio,* (1961),[103] the Court reviewed the applicability of the exclusionary rule to the states. In a 5-to-3 decision (Mr. Justice Stewart wrote a memorandum opinion in which he declined to state his view on the merits of the Fourth Amendment issue), the Court overruled *Wolf* and held that evidence illegally seized in violation of the Fourth Amendment is inadmissible in a state criminal trial. The Court noted that at the time of *Mapp,* over half of the states that had passed on the issue of the exclusionary rule had accepted it (in whole or in part). Writing for a majority Court in *Mapp,* Mr. Justice Clark stated:

> . . . our holding that the exclusionary rule is an essential part of both the Fourth and Fourteenth Amendments is not only the logical dictate of prior cases, but it also makes very good sense. There is no war between the Constitution and common sense. Presently, a federal prosecutor may make no use of evidence illegally seized, but, a State's attorney across the street may, although he supposedly is operating under the enforceable prohibitions of the same Amendment. Thus, the State, by admitting evidence unlawfully seized, serves to encourage disobedience to the Federal Constitution it is bound to uphold. . . .
>
> The criminal goes free, if he must, but it is the law that sets him free. Nothing can destroy a government more quickly than its failure to observe its own laws, or worse, its disregard of the character of its own existence.[104]

Between the *Mapp* decision in 1961 and 1976, seven new justices were appointed to the Court, including a new Chief Justice (Burger). The present Court is sometimes referred to as the "Nixon Court,"[105] because the former President appointed four new justices during his first term in office. Only Justices Stewart and Brennan, on the Court at the time of *Mapp*, remained on the Court in 1977.

Today, the future of *Mapp* is somewhat in doubt. For example, Chief Justice Burger and Mr. Justice Blackmun have expressed doubts as to the effectiveness of the exclusionary rule as a deterrent to illegal police action.[106] More recently, the Court held that the exclusionary rule is not applicable to evidence presented to a federal grand jury.[107]

Although the exclusionary rules does not deter all illegal searches and seizures, its demise could cause a marked increase in illegal police conduct. Perhaps the rule should be restricted to only the most serious crimes or to intentional police misconduct. However, the Fourth Amendment does not make those distinctions, and anything other than "good faith" on the part of the police might be difficult to prove. The pros and cons of the judicially created exclusionary rule are likely to remain a source of controversy among law enforcement personnel, judges, and legal writers, regardless of the future interpretation given it by the Supreme Court.

In addition to the prohibition against unreasonable searches and seizures, there are other legal restrictions on police practices.

The Privilege against Self-Incrimination

One of the most controversial but important constitutional rights is the privilege against self-incrimination. The Fifth Amendment to the United States Constitution provides, in part, that "no person . . . shall be compelled in any criminal case to be a witness against himself."

The Fifth Amendment privilege guarantees that defendants need not testify at their trials or subject themselves to cross-examination. The prosecutor must prove the charges against a defendant absent the voluntary testimony of the defendant. Nor may a prosecutor comment (to the jury) on a defendant's failure to take the stand and testify.[108] Further, the privilege guarantees that no person may be compelled to answer any questions if the answers could be used to convict or implicate that person in a crime.

Historical Development of the Privilege against Self-Incrimination

The Fifth Amendment is a product of seventeenth-century England, where political and religious prosecutions were common. The questioning of suspects, even upon mere suspicion and without evidence, was a regularly accepted practice. Suspects could be tortured or otherwise punished for refusing to answer questions. After a long and bitter struggle, the principle developed in England that no person could be brought in and questioned about any alleged wrongdoing without that person's voluntary consent or be given immunity from prosecution arising from his or her answers.[109]

This privilege against self-incrimination was brought to the United States by the colonists and has become a basic part of our American criminal law. Today, the Fifth Amendment privilege is applicable to both federal[110] and state proceedings.[111]

In the first case of importance involving the issue of searches and seizures (1886), the Supreme Court noted that *both* the Fourth and Fifth Amendments guarantee a constitutional right of privacy, and that those amendments run into each other.[112] The Court held that the doctrines of those amendments:

> apply to all invasions on the part of the government and its employees of the sanctity of a man's home and the privacies of life. It is not the breaking of his doors, and the rummaging of the offense; but it is the invasion of his indefeasible right of personal security, personal liberty and private property. . . . Breaking into a house and opening boxes and drawers are circumstances of aggravation; but any forcible and compulsory extortion of a man's own testimony or of his private papers to be used as evidence to convict him of crime or to forfeit his goods is within the condemnation . . . (of those Amendments).[113]

Scope of the Privilege against Self-Incrimination

The scope of the Fifth Amendment privilege applies in most situations where the government demands information from citizens through calling them to answer questions if their testimony could lead to a criminal prosecution. The privilege is not restricted to defendants in a criminal trial. It is also applicable to witnesses before a grand jury or legislative committee or witnesses in civil and criminal trials. However, the burden of establishing the applicability of the privilege rests upon its beneficiary. As a general rule of evidence, a privilege may only be asserted by a party whom the privilege is designed to protect. That is, the privilege cannot be asserted on behalf of a friend, relative, or acquaintance.[114] However, the privilege is not applicable in many other situations (which will be discussed later in this chapter).

Many of the legal issues raised in criminal cases concerning the privilege against self-incrimination involve involuntary confessions. Prior to 1936, the Supreme Court had never reversed a state court where it was alleged that a conviction was the product of an involuntary confession. Because the Fifth Amendment was not then applicable to the states,[115] the Supreme Court allowed the state courts to determine the voluntariness of confessions in its criminal cases. In *Brown v. Mississippi* (1936), the U.S. Supreme Court reversed the murder convictions of several blacks on due process grounds.[116] As an investigative technique, several deputy sheriffs hung Brown from a tree and whipped him with steel-studded leather belts until he confessed to murder. The deputy sheriffs admitted torturing the defendant, and his extrajudicial confessions was the only evidence admitted at his trial. The defendants were convicted and sentenced to death, and the Mississippi Supreme Court affirmed the convictions. The U.S. Supreme Court had little difficulty finding reasons to reverse these convictions on due process grounds.

Subsequently, after *Brown,* the Supreme Court decided many cases involving alleged involuntary confessions in state criminal cases. The test for the admissibility of confessions became the *voluntariness of the confession* measured by the "totality of circumstances."[117] In determining the voluntariness of a confession, the Court examined several factors including the defendant's age, educational background, prior experience with the criminal justice system, and mental and physical condition as well as the length of the interrogation by law enforcement officers.[118]

By 1957, in the federal courts, a rule had developed that any "unnecessary delay" between an arrest and an initial appearance before a magistrate by the defendant (called an "arraignment" in the federal system) would render a confession involuntary and therefore inadmissible at trial (a decision known as the *McNabb-Mallory rule*).[119] The McNabb-Mallory rule has never been made constitutionally binding on the states, and no rigid doctrinal measures were developed by the Supreme Court on the voluntariness of a confession beyond the "totality of circumstances" test for many years. Exactly 30 years after the *Brown* decision, the Supreme Court, in *Miranda v. Arizona* (1966),[120] formulated a set of procedural guidelines which attempted to control police conduct. By 1966, the privilege against self-incrimination was applicable to the states[121] and the Court for the first time held (in *Miranda*) that the privilege applies to police interrogations. The Court, in a 5-to-4 decision, laid down a set of procedural safeguards which required the police to give a suspect four warnings prior to any "custodial interrogation." The four warnings include informing suspects or defendants that (1) they have a right to remain silent; (2) anything they say can be used against them; (3) they have a right to the presence of an attorney during questioning; and (4) if they are too poor to retain counsel, the Court will appoint a lawyer for them (at state expense).[122]

"Custodial interrogation" was defined by the Court as being interrogation "in custody or [when the defendant is] deprived of his freedom of action in any significant way."[123] Evidence obtained without the *Miranda* safeguards is subject to exclusion at trial.[124]

Even the exclusionary rule makes illegally

seized evidence inadmissible as an affirmative part of the prosecutor's case-in-chief (on the issue of guilt or innocence). However, illegally obtained evidence (in violation of *Miranda*) can, under some circumstances, be introduced on cross-examination to impeach (discredit the credibility of) a witness-defendant.[125] Subsequently, the Supreme Court held that statements obtained in violation of *Miranda* may be admissible to impeach a defendant who takes the stand and gives testimony inconsistent with his or her prior statements (obtained in violation of *Miranda*).[126] The Court was concerned that *Miranda* could be used as a vehicle for perjury by defendants. Whether a violation of *Miranda* can be a "harmless error" has not yet been decided by the Supreme Court. Based on the present composition of the Court, it would seem that such an error could be held harmless or that *Miranda* may someday be overruled.

The *Miranda* decision caused some police to become alienated from the courts. The decision was made when there was a marked increase in violent crimes (see *UCR,* 1966). Some politicians and law enforcement officials attributed the increase in the crime rate to the fact that the Supreme Court was "handcuffing the police"[127] by making decisions like *Miranda.*

Several empirical studies have indicated that *Miranda* warnings have not significantly reduced the number of confessions by suspects.[128] One study reported that the clearance and conviction rates remained about the same before and after *Miranda.*[129]

Several reasons have been advanced why *Miranda* has not made a great deal of difference in the obtaining of confessions. First, *Miranda* warnings are usually read from a card in bureaucratic tones. Second, often even highly intelligent, well-educated suspects fail to appreciate the nature of the constitutional rights at stake. Third, many suspects are asked incriminating questions before being warned. Finally, in some instances the police simply lie about the giving of the warnings.

Whether the *Miranda* decision should be viewed as providing judicial control over the police or as a guarantee of a person's constitutional rights, it has caused considerable controversy among the public, the lower courts, and law enforcement agencies. Because *Miranda* was a 5-to-4 decision and six new justices have been appointed to the Court post-*Miranda* (including, recently, Justice John Paul Stevens), the judicial future of this landmark decision is uncertain. For example, in a recent decision (1974), the Court held that evidence obtained as a result of a pre-*Miranda* interrogation conducted with the Miranda safeguards could be used by the prosecution in a post-*Miranda* trial.[130]

The privilege against self-incrimination is not applicable in all instances where a person might be subjected to a criminal prosecution. For example, where the police have probable cause that a suspect is intoxicated and has committed an offense, a sample of blood may be taken from the suspect at the direction of the police by a physician, even over the suspect's protest, without violating his or her Fifth Amendment privilege.[131] The Supreme Court held that the privilege:

> . . . protects an accused only from being compelled to testify against himself, or otherwise provide the State with evidence of a testimonial or communicative nature and that the withdrawal of blood and use of the analysis in question did not involve compulsion to these ends.[132]

Further, the Court has held that compelling a suspect to stand in a lineup and utter specified words or to put on some item of clothing does not violate the privilege against self-incrimination.[133] Such acts are not deemed "testimonial or communicative in nature."[134] Also the Fifth Amendment does not protect one from being compelled to give voice[135] or handwriting exemplars[136] before a grand jury. Voice and handwriting exemplars are physical characteristics which are constantly exposed to the public. Fingerprints are also generally considered physical characteristics exposed to the public, and a suspects in lawful custody may be compelled to provide exemplars of their prints for identification purposes. However, if fingerprints are obtained during the *illegal detention* of a suspect, the prints are not admissible for evidentiary purposes.[137]

The taking of photographs for identification purposes is not impermissibly suggestive and does not violate any constitutional rights of a suspect. The Supreme Court has held that the right to counsel does not apply at this stage (photograph sessions) of the criminal process.[138] Further, the Fifth Amendment privilege is not applicable to drivers involved in traffic offenses who refuse to stop and show their identification.[139] The Supreme Court rejected a driver-defendant's claim that, if he was required to stop and report his name and address, there would be a real danger the he would be prosecuted for a traffic offense and that therefore his Fifth Amendment privilege would be violated.

More recently, the Court held that where an accountant was subpoenaed to produce his client's records, the client's Fifth Amendment privilege was not violated.[140] A majority of the Court reasoned that the client had no possessory interest in the property and the subpoena did not involve compulsion against *him* (the accountant).

In most situations, a person who has been granted immunity may not refuse to testify. Transactional and use immunity were discussed in Chapter 7 ("The Grand Jury").

While the Fifth Amendment privilege often protects the guilty as well as the innocent, it is an important constitutional right that is jealously protected by the courts.

Another aspect of the criminal process where a defendant's constitutional rights are protected involves certain pretrial and in-court identification procedures.

Pretrial and In-Court Identification Procedures

The police use a variety of procedures to verify that a suspect may or may not be guilty of a particular crime. These include lineups, showups, on-the-scene identifications, in-court identifications, and the examination of photographs for identification purposes. Previously we discussed the right to counsel, the prohibition against unreasonable searches and seizures, and the Fifth Amendment privilege against self-incrimination at various stages of the criminal process. Quite apart from these specific constitutional rights, a defendant may allege and prove that a pretrial or in-court identification procedure was so inherently unfair that due process of law was denied.

In 1967, the Supreme Court (for the first time) held that evidence obtained from a pretrial identification procedure "was so unnecessarily suggestive and conducive to irreparable misidentification that (the defendant) was denied due process of law."[141] That case involved a *showup* where, for the purposes of identification, only one suspect was brought before a witness to a crime. Although showups have been generally condemned by the courts, nevertheless the Supreme Court approved of the limited use of this procedure in a hospital room where the death of the victim-witness occurred after the defendant had allegedly stabbed her eleven times. The Court stated that the test for an alleged violation of due process at pretrial identification procedures "depends on the totality of circumstances surrounding it."[142] These guidelines were used by the Court in the following year (1968), when the showing of photographs ("mug shots") of suspects to witnesses was in issue.[143] In this case the Court held that such photographs might be used as long as the pictures are not "impermissibly suggestive." Mr. Justice Harlan, writing for the Court, stated that the practice of showing photographs of suspects not yet in custody

> has been used widely and effectively in criminal law enforcement, from the standpoint both of apprehending offenders and of sparing innocent suspects the ignominy of arrest by allowing eyewitnesses to exonerate them through scrutiny of photographs.[144]

The only case to date in which the Court has found identification procedures to be violative of due process occurred in 1967. There a defendant was subjected to two suggestive lineups and a showup before he was finally identified by a witness. The Court held that the identifications were "impermissibly suggestive" and therefore inadmissible at trial.[145]

The above cases did not resolve the issue of whether unnecessary suggestiveness *alone* requires the exclusion of the tainted evidence. In 1972, the Court held that while suggestive confrontations and unnecessarily suggestive ones are to be condemned, these violations *alone* do not require the exclusion of the evidence, at least to confrontations which occurred prior to 1967.[146] The Court reiterated that the "totality of circumstances" (of the procedure) must be considered. However, the Court left open the question of whether a strict exclusionary rule would be applicable to later confrontations (post-1967). When examining the "totality of circumstances," the Court held that there must be a "very substantial likelihood of irreparable misidentification" before a conviction based on eyewitness identification will be overturned.[147] The Court noted that the factors to be considered in evaluating the likelihood of misidentification include (1) "the opportunity of the witness to view the criminal at the crime, (2) the witness's degree of attention at the time of the crime, (3) the accuracy of the witness's prior description of the criminal, (4) the level of certainty demonstrated by the witness at the confrontation, and (5) the length of time between the crime and the confrontation."[148]

An in-court identification may be admissible, though a pretrial identification procedure is shown to be tainted by a denial of counsel or a violation of due process if the in-court identification is shown to be derived from a source *independent* from the illegal pretrial identification.[149] Thus an in-court identification will not be permitted unless it is shown that a pretrial identification was illegal *and* there is no independent source for the in-court identification.

In general, the legal issues arising from pretrial and in-court identifications require an examination by a reviewing court of the overall fairness of the procedures. The determination of such fairness is based on the "totality of circumstances" surrounding the identification. Probably, in a majority of cases, a defendant raising these issues will not be successful because of the heavy burden of establishing a "very substantial likelihood of irreparable misdentification.

SUMMARY

In this chapter we discussed some constitutional rights available to persons with or suspected of committing a criminal offense. In particular, we focused on certain Fourth, Fifth, and Sixth Amendment protections. We noted that the right to appointed counsel evolved rather late in the constitutional development of our criminal process. We indicated that this was because of the different views held by the justices of the Supreme Court on the nationalization of the Bill of Rights. These views were discussed at the beginning of the chapter.

Next we traced the development of the right to counsel and indicated that various stages where it is constitutionally required. In general, the right to court-appointed counsel is applicable to "critical stages" where "substantial rights of a defendant may be affected."

Next we discussed the Fourth Amendment prohibition against unreasonable searches and seizures and the requirement of probable cause. We indicated that illegally seized evidence is inadmissible at a criminal trial (exclusionary rule) at both state and federal proceedings.

Next, we examined the Fifth Amendment privilege against self-incrimination, traced its historical development, and indicated the scope of the privilege. Further, we discussed the types of immunity available to witnesses in order to protect their constitutional rights.

Finally, we discussed certain pretrial and in-court identification procedures and indicated that inherently unfair lineups, showups, photograph sessions, and on-the-scene identifications constitute a denial of due process. We further discussed in-court identifications and indicated that such testimony would be admissible if based on a source independent of the tainted evidence, even if the original identification procedure had been unfair or otherwise denied due process.

Most of the rights discussed in this chapter involve constitutional protections available to a defendant prior to trial. A defendant perhaps enjoys more constitutional rights at trial than at any other stage of the criminal process.

Chapter 10

The Criminal Trial

Suppose an accused is on trial for selling marijuana and and he curses and throws an object at the judge in full view of the jury. Further, suppose repeated admonishments by the judge are ignored by the accused and he is found in contempt of court and ordered bound, shackled, and gagged for the remainder of the trial. If the defendant is convicted, can he successfully argue on appeal that he was denied a fair trial? Or must a trial be discontinued until a defendant promises to behave himself? In this chapter we will discuss these and other issues relating to American criminal trials.

10.01 FUNCTIONS AND PURPOSES

The trial of a defendant charged with a criminal offense is that aspect of our criminal justice system which draws the closest public scrutiny. There have been many eventful criminal trials, such as those of Socrates and Christ in ancient times and the trials of the Watergate defendants, Patricia Hearst, and Claudine Longet in recent years.

Even though only 10 to 20 percent of all criminal cases actually go to trial (probably closer to 10 percent),[1] the criminal trial is an integral part of our criminal justice system. The major functions of a criminal trial are (1) to produce reliable facts and (2) to separate the guilty from the innocent under strict rules of evidence in an atmosphere of fairness to the defendant and the government. Unlike certain other stages of the criminal process which occur behind closed doors (e.g., grand jury hearings), in a criminal trial the government is required to *openly* produce evidence before *impartial* fact finders (judge or jury). Secret

Only 10 to 20 percent of all criminal cases actually go to trial.

trials not open to the public are a violation of due process.[2]

Yet a public criminal trial serves to do more than ascertain the guilt or innocence of an accused. The trial allows a defendant's constitutional rights (e.g., to confront witnesses, to avoid self-incrimination, to be protected by the exclusionary rule) to be exercised and safeguarded. In other words, the trial has the symbolic effect of preserving the defendant's constitutional rights. Further, the criminal trial serves to educate the public about the level of conduct that is socially forbidden and criminal. The trial, perhaps, has less of an educational effect with regard to *mala in se* (inherently wrong or dangerous) crimes than those offenses classified as *mala prohibita* (not inherently wrong but nevertheless criminal). Most adults probably do not have to be taught that murder, robbery, rape, and the like are socially unacceptable and are criminal offenses. But trials for certain *mala prohibita* crimes—for example, possession of stolen property—may serve to educate many of our less informed citizens.[3]

Criminal trials also perform, to varying degrees, the function of general deterrence of crime in our society. Because criminal trials are often reported by the mass media, the general public is made aware of the possible criminal liabilities for engaging in certain prohibited conduct. For example, the Justice Department often arranges to try its income tax evasion cases in the spring of each year. A musician tempted to overestimate the value of a gift of musical papers might well place a lower value on them after having witnessed the example of bandleader Skitch Henderson and his jail sentence.

The U.S. Supreme Court has, in recent years, addressed itself to some crucial constitutional issues which affect the rights of defendants in a criminal trial. These issues include the following: (1) Does the constitutional guarantee to a trial by jury apply to any offense, however minor? (2) Does a jury verdict have to be unanimous to convict, or is a simple majority sufficient? (3) Is the common-law twelve-person jury constitutionally required in criminal cases or will a six-person jury suffice? (4) Does the constitutional admonition that an American citizen has a right to a trial by a "jury of his peers" mean that blacks must be judged by blacks, women by women, and striptease artists by other striptease artists? In the next section we will focus on some constitutional protections available to an accused at the trial stage of the criminal process.

10.02 SOME CONSTITUTIONAL PROTECTIONS AT TRIAL

The Sixth Amendment to the United States Constitution provides in part that:

> In all criminal prosecution, the accused shall enjoy the right to a speedy and public trial, by an impartial jury of the State and district wherein the crime shall have been committed . . . and to be informed of the nature and cause of the accusation; to be confronted with the witnesses against him; to have compulsory process for obtaining witnesses in his favor. . . .

Article 3, section 2, clause 3 of the United States Constitution provides in part that "The trial of all Crimes, except in cases of impeachment, *shall be by jury*. . . ."

Accordingly, an accused charged with a serious federal offense is entitled to a trial by jury.[4] In *Duncan v. Louisiana* (1968), the Supreme Court held that the Sixth Amendment provision guaranteeing a trial by jury is incorporated by the Fourteenth Amendment Due Process Clause and is applicable to state criminal trials for "serious offenses."[5] Although the *Duncan* Court did not define a serious offense (as opposed to a petty offense), it noted that the *nature of the offense* and the *maximum potential sentence* are of major importance in determining whether a crime is serious or not. Duncan was convicted of simple battery in Louisiana, a misdemeanor punishable by 2 years' imprisonment and a fine. His request for a trial by jury was denied because the Louisiana Constitution, at that time, granted jury trials only in cases in which capital punishment or imprisonment at hard labor could be imposed. In reversing the conviction, Mr. Justice White, writing for the Court in *Duncan,* held:

> . . . in the American States, as in the federal judicial system, a general grant of jury trial for serious offenses is a fundamental right, essential for preventing miscarriages of justice and for assuring that fair trials are provided for all defendants. . . .[6]
>
> It is sufficient for our purposes to hold that a crime punishable by two years in prison is, based on past and contemporary standards in this country, a serious crime and not a petty offense.[7]

Two years later, in another decision, the Supreme Court defined a serious offense.[8] Writing for the Court, Mr. Justice White held that "no offense can be deemed 'petty' for purposes of the right to trial by jury *where imprisonment for more than six months is authorized.*"[9]

Contempt of Court and the Disruptive Defendant

Most of the cases involving the right to trial by jury decided by the Supreme Court in recent years have been those of defendants charged with contempt of court. There are two types of contempt: civil and criminal. The differences depend upon whether the purpose is to punish or to coerce the defendant into performing some act ordered by the court. Where defendants can *purge* themselves of contempt by performing the act ordered by the court, the contempt charge is *civil* in nature. For example, a divorced husband-father who refuses to pay child support or alimony (and has the ability to pay) can be sentenced to jail for contempt. Usually, he can purge himself and be released by complying with the order of the court.

Criminal contempt of court is designed to "preserve the power and vindicate the dignity of the courts, and to punish for disobedience of their orders."[10] Thus, for one to throw an object (such as a brick) at the judge or at someone in the courtroom or to behave in a disrespectful manner in court (such as cursing the judge) is punishable as criminal contempt. On the other hand, to refuse to perform some act after being enjoined (forbidden) by the court not to do so is usually civil contempt. Imprisonment is authorized by either type of contempt but, to reiterate, defendants can purge themselves of civil contempt (and thereby be released from jail or be relieved from paying a fine) by complying with the order of the court. However, there is no constitutional right to a trial by jury for civil contempt.[11]

The right to a jury trial in criminal contempt cases depends upon the *authorized punishment* or the punishment *actually imposed.* In a series of decisions, the Supreme Court has held that where the *maximum punishment* authorized for criminal contempt is less than 6 months' imprisonment, no right to a jury trial is required.[12] Where the punishment *imposed* is 6 months or less[13] or when probation is granted up to 5 years and the defendant could receive no more than 6 months imprisonment,[14] no Sixth Amendment right to a trial by jury is required.

More recently, the Supreme Court has had to decide cases in which the defendant has repeatedly engaged in disruptive conduct and made insulting and slanderous remarks to the judge. In a leading Illinois case,[15] the defendant was allowed to conduct his own defense against a charge of armed robbery without court-appointed counsel. During the course of the trial, the defendant argued with the trial judge "in a most abusive and disrespectful manner."[16] After repeated admonishments from the judge, the defendant continued, saying, "There's not going to be no trial, either. I'm going to sit here and you're going to talk and you can bring your shackles out and straightjacket and put them on me and tape my mouth, but it will do no good because there's not going to be no trial."[17] At another point during the trial, the defendant told the judge, "when I go out for lunchtime, you're [the judge] going to be a corpse here."[18] Finally, the trial judge ordered the defendant removed from the courtroom and the trial continued in his absence. He was convicted of armed robbery and received a sentence of 10 to 30 years in prison. Thirteen years later, after appellate remedies had been exhauseted and a writ of habeas corpus had been filed in the federal courts, the case reached the U.S. Supreme Court. The Supreme Court held that defendants can lose their constitutional right to be present at their own criminal trials if, after being admonished by a trial judge to discontinue their disruptive behavior, they nevertheless continue to be disruptive, so that the trial cannot be carried on with the defendant in the courtroom. The Court further held that there are at least three constitutionally permissible ways in which trial judges may deal with obstreperous defendants during criminal trials: (1) bind and gag them, thereby keeping them present; (2) cite them for contempt; or (3) take them out of the courtroom until they promise to conduct themselves properly.

In a later case,[19] a defendant, charged with prison breach and holding hostages in a penal instutition, called the trial judge during the course of the proceedings a "dirty sonofabitch," "dirty tyrannical old dog," "stumbling dog," and "fool," charging him with running a "Spanish Inquisition" and telling him to "go to hell" and "keep your mouth shut."[20] The defendant was convicted by a jury of the substantive (original) charges and, at sentencing, the trial judge cited him guilty of eleven counts of criminal contempt during the course of the trial. The accused was sentenced to 11 to 22 years in prison for contempt. On review of his conviction, the U.S. Supreme Court reversed and remanded the criminal contempt conviction, holding that the trial judge could have acted instantly as the defendant's outbursts occurred and immediately sentenced him for his criminal contempt. But because the insults involved were such as to "strike at the most vulnerable and human qualities of the trial judge's temperament,"[21] the defendant was entitled to a public trial before *another judge* on the criminal contempt charges. In other words, a trial judge faced with an obstreperous defendant must "strike while the iron is hot" lest the contempt case be lost to another judge.

In a related case,[22] two accused persons were codefendants with the defendant in the case noted above. Consistent with that decision (above), they were also tried for criminal contempt arising from their criminal trial before another judge. Both requested jury trials at the contempt proceeding. Their requests were denied; the judge found them both guilty of criminal contempt and imposed consecutive sentences aggregating close to 3 years' imprisonment. In reviewing their convictions, the U.S. Supreme Court held that in postverdict adjudications for acts of criminal contempt committed during a trial, a defendant has a Sixth Amendment right to a trial by jury if the sentences imposed aggregate more than 6 months imprisonment, even though no sentence for more than 6 months was imposed for any single act of contempt. That is, *absent an express waiver of a jury trial* by the defendant, a judge trying a criminal contempt case postverdict (from the substantive charges) may not sentence a defendant to more than 6 months total imprisonment. In a companion case decided the same day, the Supreme Court reaffirmed the rule that a crime carrying more than a six-month sentence is a "serious crime" triable by a jury; it, however, held that an alleged contemnor (person who commits contempt) is not entitled to a jury trial even where there exists a strong possibility that upon conviction the defendant will face a substantial term of imprisonment regardless of the punishment actually imposed.[23] That is, the trial judge at sentencing for criminal contempt is restricted to a maximum sentence of 6 months imprisonment absent an express waiver of a jury trial by the defendant.

More recently, the Supreme Court has held that an attorney is not subject to the penalty of contempt of court for advising a client to refuse to produce materials demanded by a subpoena when the attorney believes "in good faith" that the material (obscene magazines) may tend to incriminate the client.[24] The Court noted that such an order violated the Fifth Amendment priviledge against self-incrimination, especially since no state law (Texas) guaranteed that the magazines under subpoena would not be inadmissible against the client at a later criminal proceeding.

An accused has a constitutional right to a trial by jury for serious offenses.

Unanimous Verdicts, Twelve-Person Juries, and Reasonable Doubt

Other Sixth Amendment issues regarding the right to a jury trial have recently been decided by the Supreme Court. In a leading case, the Court held that it is not unconsitutional for a state to allow less than twelve jurors to sit on a noncapital felony case.[25] In that case, a divided Court specifically approved Florida's use of six-person juries in noncapital trials. Writing for a majority Court, Mr. Justice White stated:

> . . . the number (of jurors) should probably be large enough to promote group deliberation, free from outside attempts at intimidation, and to provide a fair possibility for obtaining a representative cross section of the community. But we find little reason to think that these goals are in any meaningful sense less likely to be achieved when the jury numbers six, than when it numbers 12—particularly if the requirement of unanimity is retained. And, certainly the reliability of the jury as a fact-finder hardly seems likely to be a function of its size.[26]

Whether a criminal conviction can be based on less than a unanimous verdict of the jury was resolved by the Supreme Court 2 years later. In a Louisiana case, the Court affirmed a noncapital felony conviction (robbery) based on a 9-to-3 jury verdict.[27] Mr. Justice White, writing for a majority Court, stated that:

> Disagreement of three jurors does not alone establish reasonable doubt, particularly when such a heavy majority of the jury, after having considered the dissenters' views, remains convinced of guilt. . . . But the fact remains that nine jurors—a substantial majority of the jury—were convinced by the evidence.[28]

In a companion case, the Court affirmed felony convictions based on 11-to-1 and 10-to-2 verdicts of the jury allowed in Oregon for noncapital cases.[29] The Court stated that:

> . . . the purpose of trial by jury is to prevent oppression by the Government by providing a "safeguard against the corrupt or overzealous prosecu-

> tor and against the complaint, biased or eccentric judge." Given this purpose, the essential feature of a jury obviously lies in the interposition between the accused and his accuser of the commonsense judgment of a group of laymen. . . . A requirement of unanimity, however, does not materially contribute to the exercise of this commonsense judgment.[30]

The dissenting Justices in the above cases (Marshall, Douglas, Brennan, and Stewart) argued, in part, that less than unanimous verdicts in criminal cases violate the rule of evidence requiring conviction *only* by proof beyond a reasonable doubt, as constitutionally required by *In re Winship* (1970).[31] *Winship* held that "the Due Process Clause protects the accused against conviction except upon *proof beyond a reasonable doubt of every fact necessary to constitute the crime with which he is charged.*"[32] Although *Winship* involved the adjudicatory stage of a state juvenile delinquency proceeding, the Court made it clear that proof beyond a reasonable doubt is constitutionally required for a conviction in all criminal cases. The next year (1971), the Supreme Court held that there is no constitutional right to a trial by jury in juvenile proceedings. The Court reasoned that the adjudication of juvenile offenses is "quasicriminal" in nature, so that the full panoply of rights given to adult offenders is not applicable.[33]

The above cases and discussion make it clear that an accused has a constitutional right to a trial by jury for "serious offenses"; that juries made up of fewer than twelve persons are not unconstitutional in noncapital state cases; that less than unanimous verdicts in noncapital state cases are permissible; and that proof beyond a reasonable doubt is the constitutional standard for conviction in all criminal cases.

On a number of occasions the issue has arisen whether a defendant can waive his or her Sixth Amendment right to a jury trial over the prosecutor's objections or without the court's permission. There is some evidence that defendants tried and convicted by a jury receive heavier sentences than those tried by a judge alone.[34] Sometimes the prosecutor may desire a jury trial to avoid the trying of a case (over the defendant's objections) before a judge with a reputation for being "defense oriented"; or a trial judge may wish a jury trial in a highly publicized case to preserve the role of the fact-finding process by the jury; or the judge may want to avoid criticism for an unpopular result.[35]

In the federal system, all cases are to be tried by a jury unless the defendant waives such a trial in *writing* and obtains the *consent* of *both* the prosecutor and the court.[36]

The Supreme Court has held that in federal trials there is no federally recognized right to a criminal trial before a judge sitting alone.[37] However, in some instances, the Court has noted that a defendant can waive his right to a trial by jury.[38] The Court went on to hold that the prosecutor, under the Federal Rules of Criminal Procedure, does not have to articulate reasons for demanding a jury trial absent some compelling reasons stated by the defendant. Although a waiver of a jury trial by a defendant is permissible even absent advice by counsel,[39] a few states prohibit jury waivers altogether in felony cases. In the majority of states, the withdrawal of a voluntary and intelligent waiver by a defendant of a jury trial is discretionary with the trial court.[40]

Assuming that defendant has elected to be tried by a jury, the next stage in the criminal process is the trial itself.

10.03 STAGES OF THE TRIAL

> We have a criminal jury system which is superior to any in the world, and its efficiency is marred only by the difficulty of finding twelve men every day who don't know anything and can't read.
>
> Mark Twain
> *Roughing It*

Voir Dire

The selection of the jurors to actually hear the

evidence and attempt to reach a verdict is known as the *voir dire* ("to tell the truth"). During this process, each attorney attempts to prepare potential jurors to support the case and to prepare them for certain evidentiary events that will occur during the course of the trial. For example, during the voir dire a defense attorney may inquire of a prospective juror whether she will hold it against the defendant if he (the defendant) invokes his Fifth Amendment right not to testify. This defense tactic is designed to prepare the jury for the fact that the defendant will not be testifying (to minimize the potential harm). Jurors could reasonably infer that defendants do not testify because they have something to hide, and defense attorneys wish to neutralize this inference as much as possible. At the end of this trial, the defense attorney may again remind the jury of their promise not to condition their verdict on the basis of the defendant's absent testimony.[41]

The potential jurors are called the *veniremen* and are usually selected by elected or appointed jury commissioners who draw their names from the voter registration lists or lists of actual voters from the political subdivision within the district of the court. It has been suggested that voter registration lists do not provide a representative cross-section of the community and that census data should be utilized.[42]

All states have certain minimal qualifications for eligibility to serve on a jury. These include United States citizenship, residency in the locality, a stated minimum age, a reasonable fluency in English, good character, and ordinary intelligence.[43] Most states disqualify convicted felons and insane persons. Further, all states provide statutory exemptions from jury service for certain occupational groups such as attorneys, physicians, law enforcement personnel, housewives with very young children, certain governmental officials (e.g., the Secretary of State), and the like. Such exclusions have generally been upheld by the Supreme Court.[44] On the other hand, the Sixth Amendment requirement of an "impartial jury" is not violated by a jury made up entirely of federal employees.[45]

It is often said that a defendant in a criminal case has a right to be tried by "a jury of his peers." Today, a jury of one's peers means a *random cross-section of the community*.[46] However, the Supreme Court has held that "neither the jury roll nor the venire (the jury actually selected) need be a perfect mirror of the community or accurately reflect the proportionate strength of every identifiable group."[47] Thus, an accused police officer is not entitled to a jury of police officers and a black defendant is not entitled to be tried by a black jury nor to representation of the black race on any particular jury panel.[48] However, it is a denial of equal protection (Fourteenth Amendment) to arbitrarily and intentionally discriminate and eliminate members of a defendant's race from a jury panel.[49]

Many of the cases decided by the Supreme Court on the issue of discriminatory jury selection have dealt with blacks alleging that they were systematically excluded from grand and petit juries on the basis of race. Recently, the Supreme Court held that a white defendant is entitled to federal relief upon proof that blacks had been systematically excluded from state grand and petit juries that indicted and convicted him.[50]

In a series of decision dealing with discriminatory jury selection, the Supreme Court has held that (1) minority groups excluded from juries may file a class action suit charging discriminatory exclusion from grand and petit juries;[51] (2) where a defendant shows a prima facie case of systematic discrimination of grand and petit juries, the burden is on the state to disprove the alleged discimination;[52] (3) the use of questionnaires by jury commissioners in selecting a venire list which includes a space for racial designation may present a prima facie case of discrimination;[53] and (4) a state statute requiring grand jury members to be "upright" and "intelligent" may be so subjective a criterion as to present a prima facie case of discrimination.[54]

The usual practice of selecting the jury during the voir dire is to summon the veniremen in groups of twelve to ascertain their competency to sit on the final jury selected. The purpose of the examination is to ascertain whether each member is free of all interest, bias, or prejudice and can render a true and just verdict.[55] The usual order is for the trial judge to present questions to the group or in some cases to question individuals to determine whether they are qualified to sit on the case. Next, the prosecutor conducts the voir dire, followed by the defense attorney. The practice and order of the voir dire examination varies from jurisdiction to jurisdiction. In the federal system and in about ten states, trial judges have discretion to either conduct the voir dire themselves or permit counsel to do so.[56] In the Patricia Hearst trial in San Francisco for federal bank robbery, the federal judge took the unusual step of questioning the prospective jurors in secret (in chambers) to avoid any possible influence by the press on the prospective jurors. In about half of the states, both the judge and counsel have a right to examine prospective jurors.

Veniremen (prospective jurors) can be disqualified from sitting on a jury in two ways: (1) peremptory challenges and (2) challenges for cause.[57]

The *peremptory challenge* allows an attorney (prosecutor or defense attorney) to have a prospective juror excused from sitting on the instant case where *no reason is required.* A juror may be excused because of the color of her blouse, because he has a beard, or for any reason, rational or not, that the attorney may choose. Each side has a *limited* number of peremptory challenges depending on the seriousness of the offense charged. Cases where the imposition of the death penalty or life imprisonment is a possibility usually provide for a greater number of peremptory challenges for each side.

The second method of disqualifying veniremen is known as the *challenge for cause.* After the peremptory challenges have been exhausted, a potential juror may be excused by one of the attorneys only for cause. That is, a legally sufficient reason must be articulated by the attorney seeking to excuse the prospective juror. In most cases, few challenges for cause are invoked. Under this type of challenge, a prospective juror would virtually have to admit prejudice against one side or admit to having information about the case which would preclude that juror from reaching a fair verdict based solely on the evidence presented in court. Other grounds for legally sufficient challenges for cause include (1) a history of mental and/or physical infirmities, (2) prior service on a jury with respect to the same charge, (3) relationship to one of the parties or witnesses to the case, and (4) conscientious convictions which may preclude impartiality.

The personality, occupation, and general temperament of a prospective juror influences (perhaps subconsciously) that person's attitude of sympathy or antagonism toward an accused. In defending a person charged with a crime of passion, it is advisable for defense counsel to get jurors who understand emotion—jazz musicians, artists, and actors. Such persons, when hearing that the defendant, at the time of the crime, was "out of it" with rage or frustration, can be emphathetic, for they have "been there." Bankers, accountants, and scientists—persons whose jobs require a computerlike approach to facts—are less likely to be understanding of the undisciplined and hotheaded.

A prosecutor who wishes to increase the likelihood of obtaining a conviction would be wise to line the jury box with persons who deeply believe in an absolute right and wrong, good and evil, heaven and hell, and in the efficacy of the swift and sure administration of punishment to wrongdoers. Persons who have strong fundamentalist Protestant backgrounds often adhere rigidly to such beliefs. In a rural Louisiana case, the district attorney had done so effective a job of picking the jurors that, when the trial was about to begin, one juror blurted out: "Bring the guilty sonofabitch in and we'll give him a trial!"

The situation is different when the case involves a civil action (e.g., tort) and requires the careful measurement of damages in terms of money. Here the plaintiff (person seeking damages) needs jurors who know "the worth of money." The no-nonsense banker and the hard-nosed accountant are more likely to give a client adequate compensation for losses than would a group of musicians who tend to think of life as a "loaf of bread, a jug of wine, and thou."[58]

In short, the purpose of the voir dire examination is to (1) ascertain whether a challenge for cause exists and (2) determine whether it would be prudent to exercise one of the limited peremptory challenges.[59] In selecting the jury, counsel want veniremen who will be sympathetic to their cause.

In certain types of cases, especially capital ones and those that are highly publicized, challenges for cause are frequently utilized. Sometimes a defendant or group of defendants is accused of committing a serious crime that has been the subject of much nationwide publicity by the mass media for weeks or months. How do we guarantee that such defendants will receive a fair trial by an impartial jury?

Although the problem of pretrial publicity is raised in only a small number of cases, this issue presents a conflict between two important constitutional rights: the right of the press to print the news (First Amendment) and the right of a defendant to receive a fair trial by an impartial jury (Sixth Amendment). The major problem in highly publicized cases is that the jurors are already familiar with the case. What percentage of the population had not heard of Charles Manson, Sirhan Sirhan, James Earl Ray, Richard Speck, Jack Ruby, Patricia Hearst, or Watergate at the time of their trials? What percentage of the population did not see television films of the killing of Lee Harvey Oswald or the shooting of Governor George Wallace? Such persons must have been few in number.

Because the freedom of the press guaranteed by the First Amendment is a *fundamental constitutional right,* it would be difficult, if not impossible, to stop the press from reporting the news even to ensure a defendant a "fair trial." As noted by the Supreme Court, "Any prior restraint of expression comes to this Court bearing a heavy presumption against its constitutional validity, and a party who seeks to have such a restraint upheld thus carries a heavy burden for showing justification for the imposition of such a restraint."[60] Suppose *The Washington Post* had been prevented from reporting Watergate?

Again, how do we guarantee a defendant a fair trial by an impartial jury in a highly publicized case? Perhaps we cannot. That is, under our system of criminal justice, we cannot *guarantee* a fair trial by an impartial jury. We can only *attempt* to do so. Otherwise defendants who have been the subjects of much publicity could never be tried and would have to be turned loose.

The Supreme Court has dealt with the issue of prejudicial publicity in several cases. In a leading case,[61] the defendant was charged with a brutal murder which was the subject of much pretrial publicity throughout the state of Indiana. On voir dire, almost all the jurors examined admitted that they were familiar with the case or had heard something about it. Of those jurors questioned on this point, 90 percent expressed some preconceived notion as to the defendant's guilt. Nevertheless, a jury was impaneled and the defendant was convicted of murder. The U.S. Supreme Court, in reviewing the case, struck down for the first time a state conviction solely on the basis of prejudicial pretrial publicity. The Court recognized that in highly publicized cases it may be impossible to find a jury without some knowledge of the case. The Court stated that:

> It is not required . . . that jurors be totally ignorant of the facts and issues involved. In these days of swift, wide-spread and diverse methods of communication, an important case can be expected to arouse the interest of the public in the vicinity, and scarcely any of those best qualified to serve as jurors will not have formed some impression or opinion as to the merits of the case. This is particularly true in criminal cases. To hold that the mere existence of any preconceived notion as to the guilt or innocence of an accused, without more, is sufficient to rebut the presumption of a prospective juror's impartiality would be to establish an impossible standard. *It is sufficient if the juror can lay aside his impression or opinion and render a verdict based on the evidence presented in court.* [Author's emphasis].[62]

Thus, it is not required that all veniremen be totally ignorant of the facts surrounding a highly publicized case. If potential jurors on voir dire state that they are willing to set aside their preconceived notions of guilt or innocence and reach a verdict based solely upon the evidence presented, a challenge for cause based on the grounds of prejudicial publicity may properly be denied by the court, and those jurors may be allowed to sit on the case.

There are at least three other viable remedies for handling highly publicized cases: (1) a continuance, (2) a change of venue, and (3) "gag orders."

A decision by the Supreme Court on prejudicial publicity surrounding a criminal trial occurred in the well-known case of *Sheppard v. Maxwell* (1966).[63] There the defendant, Dr. Sam Sheppard, was convicted in Ohio of brutally murdering his pregnant wife.

In reviewing Sheppard's conviction (the well-known defense attorney F. Lee Bailey represented him on his appeal), the U.S. Supreme Court held that a trial judge has an affirmative duty to protect a defendant against the effects of highly publicized cases. The Court stated that trial judges should adopt stricter rules (called "gag orders") governing the use of the courtroom by the press, should insulate witnesses, and should control the release of information to the press by the various parties and witnesses for both sides. Mr. Justice Clark, writing for a majority Court in *Sheppard* (only Mr. Justice Black dissented), held that:

> Where there is a reasonable likelihood that prejudicial news prior to trial will prevent a fair trial, the judge should continue the case until the threat abates, or transfer to it another county not so permeated with publicity.[64]

One purpose of a *continuance* (delay) in a highly publicized case is to delay the trial so that prospective jurors will have an opportunity to forget the news accounts detailing the facts surrounding the crime charged. However, continuances are not always effective because, as soon as the case is reinstated on the trial calendar, the press will recapitulate its earlier stories. Also, too long a delay without the defendant's consent may arguably result in a denial of the speedy trial guaranteed by the Sixth Amendment.

Another remedy for massive pretrial publicity is a *change of venue.*[65] That is, the trial is moved to another area of the state or county. In state cases, the case can be transferred to another county but not to another state. The jurisdiction of the courts in state criminal cases is restricted to the state in which a defendant is lawfully charged. In federal cases, the case can be transferred to any part of the United States, although the accused is usually tried in the district where the crime was committed. In some highly publicized cases, a change of venue will not be helpful. If Lee Harvey Oswald had lived to be tried for the killing of President Kennedy, what venue would have guaranteed him an "impartial jury"? The Watergate defendants (John Mitchell and the rest) requested a change of venue outside the area of Washington, D.C., because of pretrial publicity. In what area of the United States could they have been tried by a jury unaffected by the new accounts surrounding the case? Perhaps only in some remote area of Alaska where television sets are scarce and interest in politics is secondary to fighting the elements.

Other Supreme Court cases involving prejudicial publicity are those where jurors were exposed to news accounts detailing a defendant's prior criminal record or giving other inadmissible, prejudicial, or immaterial evidence. Such exposure alone may be a basis for a reversal of a conviction.[66] In other decisions, the Supreme Court has reversed convictions where (1) a change of venue was denied after the people of a community (Baton Rouge, La.) were repeatedly exposed by television to a defendant's personal, detailed confession of the crimes with which he was later charged;[67] (2) a trial is dominated by a mob so that there is an actual interference with the course of justice[68] (e.g., a courtroom filled with hooded KKK members at a trial of a black defendant accused of killing one of their own); and (3) the trial judge has a direct pecuniary (out of pocket) interest in the outcome of the trial[69] (e.g., the judge's income is dependent upon the fines assessed). The Court has further held that the probability of prejudice is inherently suspect where (4) a jury deliberates in the custody of a deputy sheriff who had given key testimony against the defendant[70] or (5) a baliff, assigned to shepherd a sequestered jury during deliberations, suggests to the jury that the defendant is guilty. The latter instance is a violation of the Sixth Amendment right to confront witnesses.[71] The Supreme Court has also held that where (6) a state statute restricts a change of venue to felony cases (excluding misdemeanors) and prejudicial pretrial publicity has been alleged, there is a denial of a fair trial by an impartial jury.[72] Finally, the Court has ruled that (7) a criminal trial that is televised may alone be a denial of due process even though no actual prejudice is shown.[73]

The above discussion makes it clear that the major purposes of voir dire are to determine the competency of the veniremen and to allow the attorneys for both sides an opportunity to select jurors who they feel will be favorable to their side of the case. On the issue of prejudicial publicity, the selection of the jury and the events surrounding the trial itself may determine whether a defendant receives a fair trial by an impartial jury.

After the jury is impaneled and sworn, the indictment or prosecutor's bill of information is read by the clerk of the court to the jury; the stage is then set for the opening statements by the prosecutor and defense counsel.

Opening Statements by the Prosecutor

Before evidence is formally presented in court, the prosecutor is permitted to address the jury. Thse opening remarks are "limited to a statement of facts which the government intends (or in good faith intends) to prove. It should not be argumentative in character, nor should it be designed to destroy the character of the defendant before the introduction of any evidence on the crime charged. . . ."[74] The major purpose of the opening statement by the prosecutor is to explain to the jury the issues to be tried.

On occasion, the prosecutor will overstate the case. That is, the prosecutor will promise more to the jury in the way of evidence than can be delivered. The prevailing view is that if the prosecutor, during opening remarks, states more than can be proved, it is not a reversible error *if* such remarks are made *in good faith* (e.g., a claim to have eyewitnesses who change their testimony at trial). It is improper for the prosecutor during *opening* to state that certain evidence will be admitted during the course of the trial when the prosecutor already knows (or should know) that such evidence will be inadmissible. Whether a prosecutor acted "in good faith" is discretionary with the trial judge.[75]

Opening statements by the prosecutor also serve as a discovery device to the defendant.

That is, such statements may put the defendant on notice as to the scope of the issues that may have to be defended. It has been held that "improper suggestions, insinuations, and . . . assertions of personal knowledge" by a prosecutor on *opening* are improper.[76]

Reversals of convictions based on improper opening statements are uncommon. Such errors are generally cured by the trial judge's admonition and instructions to the jury to disregard the improper remarks. However, a defendant who fails to object to erroneous opening statements at trial may be deemed to have waived such errors unless they rise to a level of "plain error."[77]

The prosecutor who overstates a case during opening statements may be rebutted by the defense attorney during closing arguments that the prosecutor failed to keep "promises" made during the course of the trial. In that respect, the prosecutor may suffer a loss of credibility with the jury. In short, it may be a tactical advantage for the prosecutor on opening statements to make only succinct general statements as to what the prosecution intends to prove and to state the elements of the crime charged without going into much detail.

The amount of time allocated to opening statements is discretionary with the trial judge. Such remarks are not evidence to be considered on the issue of guilt or innocence, and the jury will be so instructed.[78] Finally, in most jurisdictions, opening statements by the prosecutor are not required in nonjury trials.[79] When the prosecutor's opening remarks are completed, defense counsel will make some opening statements.

Opening Statements by the Defense

Upon completion of opening statements by the prosecutor, the defendant (or defense counsel) is permitted in most jurisdictions to address the jury immediately and to state the defense's theory of the applicable legal issues.[80] The major purpose of such opening statements is to allow the defense to outline the facts by which an acquittal is sought. Here, as in the prosecutor's opening statement, the defense's opening may also serve as a discovery device for the prosecutor. That is, in those jurisdictions which deny full discovery of the prosecutor's case against a defendant (a majority), the defense attorney's opening remarks may give the government advance notice of the intended defense.

The rules governing the scope of opening statments by the defense are similar to those imposed on the prosecutor. Remarks must be made "in good faith" as to what the defense intends to offer as a matter of evidence. It is proper for defense counsel to assert ("in bad faith") that certain evidence will be introduced when the counsel knows, or should know, that it is inadmissible, and to complain to the jury that the trial judge's ruling prevented a fair defense.

Because the defense attorney might promise the jury a defense or evidence that cannot be delivered later, during the trial, opening remarks are frequently superficial or waived entirely.[81] However, it is best not to waive opening remarks, as the prosecutor's opening remarks will otherwise go unchallenged.[82] Sometimes, for tactical reasons, opening remarks will be delayed until the close of the prosecutor's case. However, such defense delays are discretionary with the trial court in most jurisdictions; it is within the judge's discretion to require the defense's opening statement immediately after that of the prosecutor or not making one at all.[83]

On occasion defense counsel will, during the defense's opening statement, make flagrant, erroneous, and misleading remarks designed to divert the jury's attention from the issues of the trial (e.g., opening defense statements making personal attacks on the judge or the prosecutor—statements that are irrelevant to the issues being tried), and the jury may subsequently acquit the defendant. It is important to recall that the state cannot normally appeal an acquital and, because of the Fifth Amendment prohibition against double jeopardy, the defendant cannot be retried for the same offense.[84] In view of these circumstances, what would prevent an unscrupulous defense attorney from employing such tactics? Probably the only sanctions available against such improper conduct are for the trial judge to find the attorney in contempt of court and impose proper punishment or for the state bar association to institute disciplinary action (e.g., official reprimand, suspension, or disbarment), although the latter sanction is an unlikely event.

In this connection, the *American Bar Association Standard* on the opening statement provides the following:

> In his opening statement the prosecutor (or defense attorney) should confine his remarks to evidence he intends to offer which he believes in good faith will be available and admissible and a brief statement of the issues in the case. It is unprofessional conduct to allude to any evidence unless there is a good faith and reasonable basis for believing that such evidence will be tendered and admitted in evidence.[85]

Upon completion of opening statements, the next stage of the trial is the presentation of the evidence by the prosecutor—known as the case in chief.

The Prosecutor's Case (Case in Chief)

It is well settled in our American system of criminal justice that a defendant charged with a criminal offense (state or federal) is *presumed innocent,*[86] and an accused is protected against a criminal conviction "except upon *proof beyond a reasonable doubt* of every fact necessary to constitute the crime with which he is charged."[87] Thus, a prosecutor seeking to convince a jury of a defendant's guilt bears a heavy burden of persuasion. Unlike civil proceedings where the burden of proof on the plaintiff is by a preponderance of evidence, the more rigid standard of proof beyond a reasonable doubt is designed to protect an accused from "unjust convictions, with resulting forfeiture of life, liberty and property."[88] As noted by the Supreme Court:

> The requirement of a proof beyond a reasonable doubt has (a) . . . vital role in our criminal procedure for cogent reasons. The accused during a criminal prosecution has at stake interests of immense importance, both because of the possibility that he may lose his liberty upon conviction and because of the certainty that he would be stigmatized by the conviction. Accordingly, a society that values the good name and freedom of every individual should not condemn a man for commission of a crime when there is reasonable doubt about his guilt. . . . Use of the reasonable doubt standard is indispensable to command the respect and confidence of the community in applications of the criminal law. . . . It is also important in our free society that every individual going about his ordinary affairs have confidence that his government cannot adjudge him guilty of a criminal offense without convincing a proper factfinder (judge or jury) of his guilt with utmost certainty.[89]

How then is "proof beyond a reasonable doubt" defined? A frequently cited definition of this burden of proof is found in an early case decided by the Massachusetts Supreme Court (1850):[90]

> . . . It is a term (reasonable doubt) often used, probably pretty well understood, but not easily defined. It is not mere possible doubt; because everything relating to human affairs, and depending on moral evidence, is open to some possible or imaginary doubt. It is that the state of the case, which, after the entire comparison and consideration of all the evidence, leaves the minds of the jurors in that condition and *they cannot say they feel an abiding conviction, to a moral certainty, of the truth of the charge.* [Author's emphasis.][91]

Thus, in the order of procedure at a criminal trial, the prosecutor must introduce evidence of a defendant's *guilt beyond a reasonable doubt* in order to obtain a conviction. Questions on the legality or admissibility of the prosecutor's evidence do not require proof beyond a reasonable doubt in most jurisdictions. For example, the Supreme Court has held that the burden of proof in establishing the voluntariness of an extrajudicial confession in a state criminal case by the preponderance-of-evidence standard.[92]

The forms and types of evidence that a prosecutor may produce in open court to obtain a conviction under our rigid standards of proof are best reserved for a course in the law of evidence.[93]

Motion for a Directed Verdict

At the conclusion of the prosecutor's case, the usual practice in most jurisdictions is for the defense attorney to request that the jury be removed from the courtroom. Once the jury has gone, the defense attorney will make a *motion for a directed verdict by the court.* That is, the judge is asked to find the defendant not guilty because the prosecutor has not produced sufficient evidence for the case to go to the jury. (The jury is removed from the courtroom in order to eliminate the possibility of prejudicing it against the defendant in the event the motion is denied.)

The directed verdict is almost always requested by defense counsel to preserve some rights in the event that there should be a subsequent conviction and an appeal by the defendant. Such an appeal may be made even if a confession by the defendant has been admitted in evidence, the defendant's fingerprints were discovered all over the scene of the crime, and fifty Catholic priests have testified that they saw the defendant commit the crime. The motion for a directed verdict is usually not granted even in close cases where reasonable people could disagree as to the sufficiency of the evidence produced by the prosecutor.

Occasionally, a motion for a directed verdict is granted when the prosecutor has not been able to prove one vital element of the crime charged. For example, at common law a burglary required *both* a breaking and entering in addition to a dwelling at night with intent to commit a felony. Failure of the prosecutor to introduce evidence of *all* these elements (e.g., if there is no evidence of entry) cannot result in a legally sufficient burglary conviction; a directed verdict would be proper under these circumstances.

Sometimes, in a multiple-count indictment, *certain counts* (charges) will result in an acquittal of those counts on a motion for a directed verdict. However, the trial will proceed on the remaining counts.

It is the duty of the trial court to direct an acquittal when there is insufficient evidence of the defendant's guilt. The standard on a motion for a directed verdict is whether a reasonable fact finder (judge or jury), interpreting the evidence most favorably to the prosecution, could not find that the defendant was guilty beyond a reasonable doubt. But the trial judge (even in a nonjury trial) does not have the authority to direct a verdict of guilty at the end of the prosecutor's case before the defense has had an opportunity to present its case.

Assuming that the motion for the directed verdict has been denied, the next stage of the trial is the case by the defense.

The Defendant's Case

The Fifth Amendment to the United States Constitution provides, in part, that: "No person . . . shall be compelled in any criminal case to be a witness against himself." As noted earlier in the text, the privilege against self-incrimination is applicable to the states[94] and is coextensive in both federal and state criminal proceedings.[95]

Because of the Fifth Amendment, defendants are not required to testify personally in their own behalf or to present any defense during the course of the trial.[96] Accordingly, the defense attorney may elect to "rest" a case and allow the prosecutor's evidence to go to the jury unrebutted because (1) it may be felt that the prosecutor's case is simply too weak to sustain a conviction (that is, the defense will rest on the unfulfilled proof of the prosecutor), (2) the defendant has a prior criminal record which will be brought out by the prosecutor on cross-examination if the defendant testifies, (3) there are no reliable witnesses available to testify on behalf of the defendant, or (4) the defendant simply does not have a good defense to the crime charged. It may be felt that offering a generalized, vague defense might be more damaging than helpful. Also, in some states, the defendant has a right to open and close final arguments, as outlined above, if no defense has been offered in evidence.

In most criminal cases that go to trial, the defendant will offer some evidentiary defense to the crime(s) charged. These defenses may take the form of an outright denial of guilt in the defendant's testimony (general denial) or the production of character witnesses who attempt to exculpate the defendant through testimony as to the defendant's good reputation in the community for truthfulness and veracity. Other defenses which may be asserted include: (1) alibi evidence, (2) self-defense, (3) insanity, (4) entrapment, and (5) lack of intent (mistake of fact or involuntary acts). When applicable, there are many other defenses available to defendants; these, however, will not be discussed in this work. For information on other defenses, the reader should refer to appropriate criminal law texts.[97]

After the defense has presented its case, the next stage of the trial is the prosecutor's rebuttal.

Prosecutor's Rebuttal

In all jurisdictions, the prosecutor is permitted to *rebut* any new evidence or new matters gone into during the defendant's case.[98] The purpose of rebuttal is to weaken the defendant's case. Why is the prosecutor allowed to rebut the defendant's case? The basic reason is one of fairness. That is, the prosecution has a heavy burden of proof—i.e., beyond a reasonable doubt—in order to obtain a conviction. If there were no opportunity for the prosecutor to rebut, the defendant might present new evidence which, if uncontested, might suffice to sustain a reasonable doubt and hence to acquit a defendant who would otherwise be found guilty. For example, in those states that do not provide for a notice-of-alibi rule, the unanticipated alibi witness might leave the prosecutor at a serious disadvantage were there no opportunity to offer rebuttal evidence. Cross-examination of the alibi witness might prove ineffective, so that the prosecutor could require additional state witnesses to weaken the credibility of the "surprise" defense witness. The testimony of most witnesses ends on cross- or redirect examination (without recross).

The next stage of the trial is the defendant's rejoinder.

Defendant's Rejoinder (Surrebuttal)

If the prosecutor has introduced new evidence or gone into new matters during the *rebuttal* stage of the trial, the defense, at the discretion of the court, may be allowed to rebut this new evidence, called the defendant's *rejoinder* or *surrebuttal.*[99] However, rejoinder evidence is limited to new evidence which is offered to counter the prosecutor's rebuttal. As a practical matter, rejoinder evidence is not usually introduced by defense counsel and is typically limited to cases involving complex issues where many witnesses have testified. The court's decision to preclude rejoinder evidence is not a basis for a reversal of a conviction in most cases.

When both sides have exhausted their case, the evidentiary part of the trial is over.

In summary, the evidentiary part of a criminal trial may pass through four stages: (1) the prosecutor's case (case in chief), (2) the case of the defendant, (3) the prosecutor's rebuttal, and (4) the defendant's rejoinder. Further, the examination of each witness may pass through four stages: (1) direct examination, (2) cross-examination, (3) redirect examination, and (4) recross-examination.

During the next stage of the trial, the attorneys for both sides work out the judge's instructions on the law to be given to the jury.

Working Out Instructions on the Law

Before the jury retires to deliberate, the trial judge must "charge the jury." That is, the judge will explain to the jury the applicable law, indicate the essential elements of the crime charged, and outline the applicable defenses in context with the evidentiary issues presented. Each attorney would like the judge to instruct the jury on the law most favorable to the side that attorney is representing. Accordingly, prior to closing arguments (the next stage of the trial), The attorneys may request that the judge include certain points in the charge to the jury. Sometimes each attorney will submit written instructions to the trial court at this point, and usually the judge will rule on each requested instruction prior to closing arguments. Such motions are designed to given counsel for both sides advance notice of the details of the charge in order to make a proper closing argument around the charge.

A modern trend in state courts is for jury instructions to be taken from a uniform work entitled *Standard Jury Instructions,* which has been approved by the State Supreme Court in the jurisdictions where it is utilized.[100] Standardized instructions are designed to implement the objectives of accuracy, to save time, and to avoid partiality in an intelligible and uniform manner.[101]

Rule 30 of the *Federal Rules of Criminal Procedure* governs jury instructions in the federal courts. This rule allows the parties to file suggested written instructions at the close of the evidence, although they are not required to do so. After the instructions on the law have been worked out between the judge and the attorneys, the next stage of the trial is the closing arguments.

Closing Arguments

Usually, the last opportunity for counsel to address the jury personally occurs at that stage of the trial known as *closing arguments.*[102] As with the opening arguments, such statements on closing are *not evidence* to be used by the jury in deciding the guilt or innocence of the defendant, and the jury will be so instructed by the court.

The time limit for closing arguments is discretionary with the courts and can vary from a few minutes to several hours or, in extreme cases, to days.

Usually the prosecutor begins the closing arguments, and the defense arguments follow. In most cases the prosecutor is allowed to rebut the closing arguments of the defense because of the heavy burden of proof placed on the prosecutor. However, the prosecutor's rebuttal is usually restricted to those areas argued on closing by the defense, so that no new lines of argument may be introduced by the prosecutor during the rebuttal. In a few states (e.g., Florida), the defense is entitled to first and last closing arguments if no defense witnesses have testified.

During closing arguments, each side attempts to convince the jury why that side's position should prevail. Sometimes great emotion and histrionics are displayed, and it is not unusual for counsel to engage in Bible readings, the recitation of poems, and the like. Although such presentations should be somehow relevant to the issues in question, most judges permit much latitude here. For example, in the famous Leopold-Loeb case, Clarence Darrow, in arguing for a prison sentence for the defendants (as opposed to capital punishment), was allowed to argue his position for 3 days, and he completed his argument by reading a verse from Omar Khayyam.[103]

As a rule of thumb for defense attorneys on *closing,* it has been said that "When the facts are against you, tell the jury about the law. If the law is against you, stress the facts to the jury. If both the law and the facts are against you, attack the prosecutor."[104] Attacking the prosecutor is specifically condemned by the *American Bar Association Standards* (7.8) unless justified by the record.

Some guidelines on closing arguments for defense attorneys have been suggested by F. Lee Bailey in his excellent work *Successful Techniques for Criminal Trials*:[105] (1) stress to the jury their responsibilities regarding the presumption of innocence and reasonable doubt; (2) present the facts in a manner most favorable to the defendant; (3) anticipate and counter the prosecutor's arguments; (4) pose questions for the prosecutor to answer so that the opposition will spend more time answering you than developing their own arguments; (5) encourage the jury to reject speculation and suspicion of the defendant; (6) lead the jury to conclusions most favorable to the defendant; (7) minimize the prosecutor's antics and histrionics; (8) highlight favorable evidence for the defense; (9) discredit unfavorable witnesses; (10) personalize and humanize the defendant; (11) be colorful, frank, and sincere; (12) emphasize the good characteristics of the defendant; (13) explain any weaknesses in the defense; (14) implore each juror to think individually; and (15) describe the prospective fate of the defendant if convicted.

Bailey suggests the following closing statement establishing self-defense where a defendant is accused of murder:

> Let me suggest to you that a person has a right to shoot and kill in the defense of his home and family—not when these vital things are in danger, but when he *thinks* they are in danger. The court will tell you that the accused has the right to decide upon appearances, and if he did, even though mistaken, he is not guilty. You are twelve persons sitting here months after the incident occurred, listening to the evidence, truthful and otherwise, to determine whether the defendant acted too hastily.
>
> No person need wait to see just how far an aggressor will go before he takes a life. The first instinct of a human being is to save his own life or the life of a loved one. He hasn't time to gamble. When he thinks it is time to save his life or the life of a loved one he has the right to act. Every man's home is a castle which even the government may not enter. Every man has the right to kill to defend himself, his family, his home or others.
>
> You must prove that the defendant premeditated, that he deliberated. You must prove the intent to kill; you've got to prove that this accused did not have the right to kill. You must prove it by the evidence, not mere guesswork, not by how he seemed to act afterwards, or any other unfavorable factors that have developed against the accused. You must prove the point that the shooting was wrongful—that's the law. Where has the prosecution proven that the defendant had no right to shoot?[106]

One of the major concerns of the prosecutor on *closing* is to avoid violating the so-called *Griffin rule.* Recall that a prosecutor may not comment to the jury on a defendant's failure to testify. However, the *Griffin* rule is not absolute. That is, the prosecutor may summarize the evidence presented by the government and note that it was unrebutted by the defense without specifically drawing attention to the fact that the defendant has not testified; and, of course, an adverse inference is there to be picked up by the jury.

If the defendant has testified but refused to answer certain questions where not privileged to do so, the prosecutor may properly comment on the defendant's failure to answer *those* questions. Further, if defense counsel argues on closing as to what the defendant *would have* testified to (when the defendant did not testify at all), the prosecutor may properly comment on the defendant's failure to testify. Other permissible comments by the prosecutor at closing include (1) an accurate summary of the evidence presented, (2) a noting of discrepancies and conflicts in the testimony of defense witnesses, (3) an argument that the evidence in the record supports and justifies a conviction, (4) statements as to the evil of crime in society, (5) arguments for a fearless administration of law and order, and (6) comments on the *conduct* of the defendant.[107]

It is improper for the prosecutor to make statements not based directly on the evidence or which cannot be reasonable inferred from the evidence. Statements that are irrelevant to the issues being tried or that misstate the evidence in the record are improper. For example, in a recent Illinois case,[108] the prosecutor's remark during closing argument that "I am just the thirteenth juror in the case, ladies and gentlemen, nothing more" was held to be prejudicial to the defendant since it tended to convey the impression that the prosecutor was impartial.

Although improper arguments alone can be a basis for a reversal of a conviction on appeal, only 10 percent of all cases appealed are reversed on this basis.[109] In most jurisdictions, few improper remarks on closing are per se reversible error. The prejudicial effect of improper statements on the defendant must be evaluated in light of its context within the facts of a particular case.

The U.S. Supreme Court has held that a violation of the Griffin rule can be "harmless error" if the improper comment by the prosecutor did not affect the verdict beyond a reasonable doubt.[110]

Sometimes counsel for one side will make an improper comment on closing. In order to cure this error, the other side must make a *timely and specific objection* to the improper comment. Failure to do so *waives* the objection unless the error is such that it could not be cured (i.e., "plain error"). Usually, an improper remark is cured if the objection is sustained and the trial judge properly instructs the jury to disregard it. However, if the improper remark is so prejudicial that the defendant cannot get a fair trial, a motion for a mistrial should be sustained.

Following the closing arguments, the next stage of the trial is the charge to the jury by the trial court.

Charge to the Jury

During this stage of the trial, the judge will read to the jury instructions on how to reach a verdict; this is the *charge to the jury*. The major purpose of the charge (instructions) is to inform the jury what rules of law apply to the case. That is, the jury is instructed to apply the law to the facts that were presented during the evidentiary stage of the trial. The instructions usually include such matters as the presumption of innocence, the burden of proof, the elements of the crime charged, how to evaluate the credibility of the witnesses, and the applicable defenses and procedures to be followed while deliberating.

The instructions should be given as clear and concise statements of law. Inaccurate instructions of law are a basis for reversible error;[111] it has been said that erroneous instructions to the jury are the most common *single* source of reversible error in criminal cases.[112] However, erroneous instructions must be *prejudicial* to the defendant in order to be reversible. In determining prejudicial error, appellate courts generally focus on the *charge as a whole* rather than upon an isolated instruction.

In about fifteen states and in the federal courts, the trial judge, in instructing the jury, may *summarize* or *comment on* the evidence.[113] However, the judge's comments must not reflect or impose the judge's personal opinions and conclusions on the jury. Such comments are designed only to aid the jury in seeking the truth, and the members of the jury must be informed unequivocally that they are the final decision matters on the facts. It is improper for a judge, while commenting on the evidence, to be an advocate or urge a personal view of the defendant's guilt or innocence.

At the conclusion of the charge, the jury is excused from the courtroom and taken to the jury room to begin deliberations.

The Jury Deliberates

Once the jury have entered the jury room and

begun their deliberations, nobody can "check on them." They can receive coffee, but the jury room cannot be "bugged." The secret nature of jury deliberations has made them difficult to research.[114]

It is well settled that a *juror* cannot *impeach* his or her own verdict and is *incompetent* (unqualified) to testify as to facts which inhere in the verdict.[115] After returning a verdict of guilty, members of a jury cannot later attempt to overturn that verdict because "they changed their minds" with regard to the evidence presented. Thus, a juror may not testify postverdict as to matters which necessarily inhere in his or her own consciousness. This is because jurors are *presumed* to have done their duty in accordance with their oaths. However, jurors are competent to testify as to improper acts or prejudicial external influences on the jury during their deliberations (e.g., prejudicial newspaper article in the jury room, threat by baliff urging them to reach a certain verdict, rolling of dice for a verdict, bribery of jury, etc.). In short, in the absence of jury misconduct, a jury cannot impeach its own verdict (change its mind after the verdict).

What happens when a jury is unable to reach a verdict after deliberating many hours or days? The trial judge has discretion to declare a mistrial (hung jury) and the defendant can be tried again by a new jury. Otherwise the jury may be ordered to continue its deliberations.

In many jurisdictions, before declaring a mistrial because of a "hung jury," the trial judge will stress to the jury the importance of reaching a verdict through a supplemental instruction known as the *Allen charge* ("dynamite charge"). The *Allen* charge, in effect, encourages deadlocked juries to reach an agreement. The jurors are informed that no juror is expected to yield a conscientiously held opinion, but if a majority of the jury is for either conviction or acquittal, the minority ought to consider whether the majority view be reasonable and correct.

The original *Allen* charge was approved by the U.S. Supreme Court in 1896,[116] but it has been criticized by legal writers and has recently come under attack by some federal courts as being coercive on the minority members of the jury.[117] Although no federal court has held the *Allen* charge to be unconstitutional, some state and federal courts have prohibited its future use. These courts recommend that trial judges conform to the *American Bar Association Standards, Trial by Jury,* which provides that:

> **a** Before the jury retires for deliberation, the court may give an instruction which informs the jury:
>
> **i** that in order to return a verdict, each juror must agree thereto;
>
> **ii** that jurors have a duty to consult with one another and to deliberate with a view to reaching an agreement, if it can be done without violence to individual judgement;
>
> **iii** that each juror must decide the case for himself, but only after an impartial consideration of the evidence with his fellow jurors;
>
> **iv** that in the course of deliberations, a juror should not hesitate to reexamine his own views and change his opinion if convinced it is erroneous; and
>
> **v** that no juror should surrender his honest conviction as to the weight or effect of the evidence soley because of the opinion of his fellow jurors, or for the mere purpose of returning a verdict.
>
> **b** If it appears to the court that the jury has been unable to agree, the court may require the jury to continue their deliberations and may give or repeat an instructions as provided in subsection (a). The court shall not require or threaten to require the jury to deliberate for an unreasonable length of time or for unreasonable intervals.[118]

Once the jury has reached a decision, the trial judge and counsel are notified that a verdict has been reached. The verdict is the next stage of the trial.

The Verdict

The types of verdicts that a jury may lawfully reach in a criminal trial depend upon several factors such as the plea given by the defendant (e.g., not guilty or not guilty by reason of insanity). Other factors include the number of offenses charged (counts), the number of defendants, whether a lesser included offense is a responsive verdict (e.g., a finding of guilty of second-degree murder when the accused has been charged with first-degree murder).

The foreman of the jury (selected by other jurors at the beginning of its deliberations) or the clerk of the court will read the verdict(s) in open court. Possible verdicts can range from a finding of not guilty to each charge to guilty to all charges or from not guilty on some counts or not guilty by reason of insanity (if plead) to responsive verdicts (lesser included charges). If the verdict of the jury is one of not guilty, that ends the case as far as the prosecutor is concerned. The acquitted defendant may not be tried a second time for the same offense because of the double jeopardy bar. However, a defendant may appeal a verdict of guilty in all jurisdictions.

Once the verdict(s) has been read in open court, either counsel or the court may request that the *jury be polled.*[119] Each juror is asked by the judge or clerk of the court if that verdict "was then and is now" that juror's verdict. Jurors, however, are not asked to state the basis for their verdict. In all jurisdictions, the defendant has a right to have the jury polled. Under *American Bar Association Standards Relating to Trial by Jury,* if the result of the poll is not a unanimous concurrence, the court may order a mistrial or require the jury to deliberate further.[120]

At this point, the trial ends. Subsequent proceedings may occur, such as a motion for a new trial, sentencing, appeals, and certain postconviction remedies.

SUMMARY

In this chapter we have discussed the various rules of evidence that attend each stage of the criminal trial. These rules are designed to ascertain reliable facts, separate the guilty from the innocent, and allow our constitutional values to be exercised in an atmosphere of fairness to all parties.

Although only 10 to 20 percent of all criminal cases actually go to trial, the criminal trial is an integral part of our system of criminal justice. During the trial stage of the criminal process, an accused perhaps enjoys more constitutional rights than at any other stage. An accused at trial is guaranteed the right to *due process,* which includes the right to a public trial, the right to a trial by jury, and the protection against a conviction except by proof beyond a reasonable doubt. In most jurisdictions and in the federal courts, unanimous jury verdicts are required. Further, an accused is entitled to a fair trial in a jurisdiction free from extensive publicity, to an impartial judge, and to a jury made up of a random cross-section of the community. In addition, an accused does not have to testify and has a right to counsel, to confront prosecution witnesses, to call defense witnesses, to fair and accurate instructions by the judge (charge to the jury), to opening and closing arguments, and to an appeal.

Because the prosecutor (state or federal) is also entitled to a fair trial, the government too enjoys certain rights. For example, in many jurisdictions and in the federal courts, the prosecutor can demand a jury trial over the objections of the defendant. Further, in highly publicized cases, jurors with preconceived notions as to the guilt or innocence of the defendant may be allowed to sit on the case under some circumstances. Because the burden of proof is very heavy on the government, the prosecutor is permitted to rebut the defendant's case as well as, in most jurisdictions, to have first and last closing arguments. Also, the government, in many jurisdictions, is entitled to advance notice of certain defenses (e.g., alibi, insanity).

In short, both the accused and the government are entitled to certain substantive and procedural rights which are designed to enhance the reliability of the fact-finding process.

Certain other constitutional rights inhere at the trial stage of the criminal process, including the right to a speedy trial, the right to confront witnesses, and the right to produce defense witnesses. These constitutional guarantees will be fully explored in the next chapter.

Chapter 11

Some Additional Constitutional Guarantees at Trial

A defendant is brought to trial for armed robbery in Florida more than seven years after the date of the crime.[1] A defendant on trial for murder in Texas is not allowed to introduce the favorable testimony of his accomplice.[2] An informer, testifying for the prosecution in the narcotics trial of a defendant in Illinois, refuses on cross-examination to reveal his true name and address.[3] In Missouri, a defendant is convicted along with others of raping his wife after the trial judge denied a continuance for a psychiatric examination, a denial made even though (1) the defendant attempted suicide the second day of the trial and was absent during the remaining proceedings and (2) additional evidence suggested that he was incompetent to stand trial.[4]

What do all these defendants have in common? They were all convicted of the substantive charges. But the U.S. Supreme Court reversed their convictions, since they were found to have been denied certain constitutional rights. In this chapter we will focus on some additional but important constitutional guarantees granted an accused under our adversary system of criminal justice.

In the two previous chapters we noted that an accused is entitled to certain constitutional protections prior to, during, and after the trial. Some of these guarantees include the right to counsel at most stages of the criminal process, the prohibition against unreasonable searches and seizures, the use of the exclusionary rule, the right of the defendant *not* to testify, the prohibition against being tried twice for the same offense, the requirement of fairness during pretrial identification procedures, the right to a fair trial, and the use of certain defenses available to an accused in most jurisdictions.

In this chapter we will discuss some additional constitutional safeguards which are designed to further protect an accused against an unjust prosecution and enhance due process during the fact-finding process at trial. One of these safeguards—the right to a speedy trial—prevents the accused from being tried at all if it is violated.

11.01 THE RIGHT TO A SPEEDY TRIAL

The Sixth Amendment to the United States Constitution provides, *inter alia,* that "In all criminal prosecutions, the accused shall enjoy the right to a speedy . . . trial."

Two important clauses in this guarantee are noteworthy. First, the right to a speedy trial is applicable only to criminal prosecutions, not civil proceedings. Second, the amendment plainly states that this guarantee is a matter of right, not the prosecutor's discretion. Yet not until 1967, in the landmark case of *Klopfer v. North Carolina,*[5] was this constitutional safeguard made applicable to the states. Recall that the provisions of the Bill of Rights have always been binding on the federal courts.

The defendant in *Klopfer,* a professor of zoology at a major university, had been tried in 1964 for criminal trespass because he had allegedly failed to leave a restaurant after being ordered to do so. His first trial resulted in a mistrial as the jury was unable to reach a verdict. Thereafter the prosecutor filed a motion to take a *nolle prosequi,* which was granted by the trial court. The effect of a *nolle prosequi* does not permanently discharge defendants, since they are subject to retrial, at a later date, at the discretion of the prosecutor. Eighteen months after Klopfer's indictment, the trial judge denied the defendant's motion for a speedy trial, and his case was twice continued. On appeal, the North Carolina Supreme Court affirmed on the ground that a defendant does not have a right to compel the state to prosecute, notwithstanding the right under North Carolina law to a speedy trial.

On certiorari, the U.S. Supreme Court reversed and held that the right to a speedy trial is one of the most basic rights under our Constitution and is therefore applicable to the states. Chief Justice Warren, writing for the Court in *Klopfer,* noted that an unjustifiable delay by prosecuting officials in bringing a defendant to trial may have dire consequences:

> The pendency of the indictment may subject him to public scorn and deprive him of employment, and almost certainly will force curtailment of his speech, association and participation in unpopular causes. By indefinitely prolonging this oppression, as well as the "anxiety and concern accompanying public accusation," the criminal procedure condoned in this case . . . clearly denies the petitioner the right to a speedy trial. . . .[6]

Most of the right-to-speedy-trial decisions by the Supreme Court have involved unconscionable delays by prosecuting officials. For example, in *Smith v. Hooey,*[7] the defendant, while a prisoner in a federal penitentiary in Kansas, was indicted in Texas for theft. For the next 6 years the state of Texas refused to bring Smith to trial, even though he made repeated requests that they do so. Finally, Smith filed a motion to dismiss in the Texas trial court for want of prosecution. No action was taken on the motion. Thereafter the defendant filed a writ of mandamus (a motion asking for an order to show cause why the pending charge should not be dismissed) in the Texas Supreme Court. The latter court refused to issue the writ.

On certiorari, the U.S. Supreme Court set aside the order of the Texas Supreme Court and held that a state has a constitutional duty to try defendants who have repeatedly demanded that they be brought to trial. In addition, the Supreme Court held that the Sixth Amendment right to a speedy trial cannot be dispensed with by a state court simply because the defendant is serving a sentence in another jurisdiction. That is, a state has a constitutional duty to make a diligent, good-faith effort to bring the defendant to trial.

In another decision involving an unusually long delay between the filing of formal charges and trial,[8] the defendant was convicted in Florida of federal bank robbery and eventually was imprisoned at Alcatraz. In the meantime, state officials in Florida secured an arrest warrant and detainer against the defendant for an unrelated state charge of armed robbery. During the next several years, the defendant requested that the Florida officials either dismiss the pending charges or return him to Florida for trial. Seven years later, a state prosecuting attorney secured the defendant's return to Florida; he was brought to trial over his objections and convicted of armed robbery. His claim that he was denied a speedy trial was denied by the Florida courts.

On certiorari, the U.S. Supreme Court reversed the conviction. It found that the defendant had been denied a speedy trial in that (1) there was no valid reason for the delay by the state; (2) such a delay resulted in *actual prejudice* to the defendant, since two of his potential defense witnesses had died and another potential witness was unavailable; and (3) the police records had been lost or destroyed. But as noted by the Supreme Court:

> The right to a speedy trial is not a theoretical or abstract right but one rooted in hard reality in the need to have charges promptly exposed. If the case for the prosecution calls on the accused to meet charges rather than rest on the infirmities of the prosecution's case, as is the defendant's right, the time to meet them is when the case is fresh. Stale claims have never been favored by the law, and far less so in criminal cases. Although a great many accused persons seek to put off the confrontation as long as possible, the right to a prompt inquiry into criminal charges is fundamental and the duty of the charging authority is to provide a prompt trial.[9]

What happens when the federal government learns of possible crimes committed by a suspect but a grand jury fails to indict until 3 years later? Has the suspect been denied a speedy trial? The Supreme Court has answered no.

In *United States v. Marion,*[10] federal investigators discovered that the defendants were engaged in a fraudulent home-improvement business in Washington, D.C., from 1965 to 1967. They were not indicted until 1970. A U.S. district court dismissed the indictment for "lack of speedy prosecution,"[11] and the United States appealed directly to the Supreme Court. In rejecting the defendants' claim, the Court held that the Sixth Amendment guarantee of a speedy trial is not applicable until the "putative [potential] defendant" has become an "accused"; thus this guarantee is *inapplicable* to preindictment delays. The Court noted that if a preindictment delay causes *substantial prejudice* to the defense—e.g., loss of alibi witnesses—then the indictment could be dismissed as a denial of due process (not because of a denial of a speedy trial). As noted by the Supreme Court:

> Invocation of the speedy trial provision thus need not await indictment, information, or other formal charge. But we decline to extend the reach of the amendment [Sixth] to the period prior to arrest. Until this even occurs, a citizen suffers no restraints on his liberty and is not the subject of public accusations: his situation does not compare with that of a defendant who has been arrested and held to answer. Passage of time, whether before or after arrest, may impair memories, cause evidence to be lost, deprive the defendant of witnesses, and otherwise interfere with his ability to defend himself. But this possibility of prejudice at trial is not itself sufficient reason to wrench the Sixth Amendment from its proper context. Possible prejudice is inherent in any delay, however short; it may also weaken the Government's case.[12]

In summary, the right to a speedy trial is not applicable to preindictment delays; a defendant must first become an accused before the

Sixth Amendment guarantee is applicable; however, a preindictment delay which causes *actual prejudice* to a defendant at trial *can* be a denial of due process resulting in a dismissal of the charges.

Rule 48(b) of the *Federal Rules of Criminal Procedure* governs the enforceability of the speedy trial provision of the Sixth Amendment in federal cases. The rule authorizes a dismissal of an indictment, information, or complaint "if there has been an unnecessary delay in presenting the charge to a grand jury or in filing any information against a defendant who has been held to answer to the district court, or if there is unnecessary delay in bringing a defendant to trial. . . ." But the rule has been held to be applicable only to *postarrest* situations.

Suppose a defendant has been arrested but is not brought to trial for several years. Must she affirmatively prove that the delay caused *actual prejudice* to her case in order to successfully argue that her Sixth Amendment right to a speedy trial has been violated? The Supreme Court has held that a showing of *actual prejudice* by a delay between arrest and trial is *not* required.[13] The Court noted that a showing of actual prejudice is only one factor to be considered in balancing the interests of the defendant against the conduct of the prosecution.[14] A showing of prejudice to the defendant caused by the delay is neither a necessary nor a sufficient condition for a finding of a deprivation of a defendant's right to a speedy trial.

What other factors are to be considered in balancing the interests of a defendant's constitutional right to a speedy trial against the conduct of the prosecutor? Recently, the Supreme Court answered this question.

In *Barker v. Wingo,*[15] the Court refused to assert an inflexible rule governing the criteria by which the speedy trial guarantee is to be judged. There the defendant, Barker, was not tried for 5 years following his arrest for murder. During this period, the prosecutor obtained numerous continuances in an attempt to convict the defendant's accomplice, so that if the latter were convicted, his testimony would be available at Barker's trial. Barker did not object to the continuances until 3½ years after his arrest. Subsequently, Barker was convicted of murder and eventually his appeal, on the ground of a denial of a speedy trial, reached the U.S. Supreme Court. The Supreme Court affirmed Barker's conviction and held that he had not been denied his right to a speedy trial, especially in light of the fact that he did not want a speedy trial. The Court found only a *minimal prejudice* to the defendant by the delay.

The Court noted that the right to a speedy trial is generically different from other constitutional rights protecting an accused and cannot be quantified into any precise number of days or months. Accordingly, a claim by a defendant of the denial of the right to a speedy trial is subject to a balancing test. The Supreme Court in *Barker* identified the following four factors to be controlling in assessing the right to a speedy trial: (1) the length of the delay, (2) the government's reasons for the delay, (3) the defendant's assertion of the right, and (4) the prejudice to the defendant caused by the delay.

The *Barker* Court noted that the length of the delay is dependent upon the particular circumstances of each case. For example, a complex conspiracy case might justify a considerably longer delay than an ordinary street crime. In addition, the Court noted that the reasons asserted by the prosecutor for the delay are to be assigned different weights. For example, a purposeful delay by the government in an attempt to handicap the defense would weigh heavily against the government, whereas a more neutral reason (e.g., overcrowded court docket or a missing witness) should be weighed less heavily. Although it is not absolutely necessary that a defendant assert the right to a speedy trial, the Court indicated that absent such an assertion, the defendant will have difficulty proving a denial of a speedy trial. Finally, the Court noted that the prejudice to the defendant caused by the delay should be assessed in light of the interests that the speedy trial right is designed to protect: (1) to prevent oppressive pretrial incarceration, (2) to minimize anxiety and concern of the defendant, and (3) to limit the possibility that the defense will be hampered.[16] The greatest weight is assigned to the latter category, since an unusual delay can result in a denial of a fair trial in violation of the Due Process Clause. The *Barker* Court further noted that:

> We regard none of the four factors identified (above) as either a necessary or sufficient condition to the finding of a deprivation of the right of speedy trial. Rather, they are related factors and must be considered together with such other circumstances as may be relevant. In sum, these factors have no talismanic qualities; courts must still engage in a difficult and sensitive balancing process. But because we are dealing with a fundamental right of the accused, this process must be carried out with full recognition that the accused's interest in a speedy trial is specifically affirmed in the Constitution.[17]

More recently the Supreme Court, in *Jackson v. Indiana,*[18] held that an indefinite commitment of a defendant solely on the ground that the latter lacked the capacity to stand trial violates due process. In this case the defendant—a mentally defective deaf mute who could not read, write, or otherwise communicate except through limited sign language—was charged with two separate robberies. This trial judge set in motion the Indiana procedures for determining the defendant's capacity to stand trial. Two examining psychiatrists were appointed by the court and reported that Jackson was unable to understand the nature of the charges against him or to aid in his own defense. His medical prognosis was regarded as "rather dim." The trial court found that Jackson was incompetent to stand trial, ordered the trial delayed, and committed him to a state psychiatric institution. Under the Indiana law, other citizens who were committed (e.g., the feeble-minded or the mentally ill) but not charged with criminal offenses could be released "at any time" at the discretion of the superintendent of the institution. But under Indiana procedures, Jackson could not be released until he "became sane."

Jackson's counsel filed a motion for a new trial, contending that (1) there was no evidence that Jackson was "insane," (2) that there was little reason to believe that Jackson would ever be competent to stand trial, and (3) that the Indiana commitment procedures as applied to Jackson amounted to a life sentence without any conviction of a crime.

The trial court denied the motion and the Indiana Supreme Court affirmed. On certiorari, the U.S. Supreme Court reversed and held that a criminal defendant cannot be held more than the reasonable period of time necessary to determine whether there is a *substantial probability* that the defendant will be competent to stand trial in the foreseeable future. If it is determined that the defendant is not likely to become competent, the state must either institute civil proceedings for indefinite commitment applicable to those not charged with a crime or release the defendant. Although the Court did not decide the case on Sixth Amendment grounds (Jackson's counsel did not raise that issue), it noted that such grounds might be available to an incompetent accused who will never have an opportunity to prove his or her innocence.

What are the legal consequences when it is determined that a defendant (after conviction) has been denied a speedy trial—may there be a retrial if the accused was otherwise granted a fair trial? The Supreme Court has answered no.

In *Strunk v. United States,*[19] the defendant, convicted in federal court of transporting a stolen automobile across state lines, was sentenced to a 5-year term in prison. Prior to his trial, the district court denied the defendant's motion to dismiss the charges, alleging a denial of a speedy trial (10-month delay). The court of appeals reversed the district court, finding that the defendant had been denied a speedy trial but that the "extreme remedy of dismissal of charges was not warranted."[20] The court of appeals remanded (returned) the case back to the trial court with instructions to reduce the defendant's sentence by 259 days in order to compensate for the unnecessary delay between indictment and arraignment.

On certiorari, the Supreme Court unanimously reversed the court of appeals and held that the conviction must be reversed, the sentence vacated, and the indictment dismissed. As noted by Chief Justice Burger writing for the Court in *Strunk*:

> . . . dismissal of an indictment for denial of a speedy trial (is) an "unsatisfactory severe remedy." Indeed, in practice, "it means that a defendant who may be guilty of a serious crime may go free, without having been tried." But such severe remedies are not unique in the application of constitutional standards. In light of the policies which underlie the right to a speedy trial, dismissal must remain . . ."the only possible remedy."[21]

More recently, the Congress has passed into law the Speedy Trial Act of 1974, which governs federal trials.[22] The provisions of this act, which take effect over a 5-year period, impose gradually declining time limits between arrest and indictment, indictment and arraignment, and arraignment and trial. At the end of the fifth year, a federal defendant who has not been brought to trial within 100 days after arrest may move for a dismissal of the charges. However, one section of the act provides the district court judge with discretion to determine whether or not the dismissal shall be with prejudice.[23] A dismissal of charges under the provisions of the act apparently does not preclude a reindictment on the same charges, since jeopardy does not normally attach prior to trial. Finally, the act provides that the federal judge shall consider the following factors in determining whether to dismiss the case with or without prejudice: (1) the seriousness of the offense, (2) the facts and circumstances of the case which led to the dismissal, and (3) the impact of a reprosecution on the administration of justice.

In summary, the Sixth Amendment right to a speedy trial is necessarily relative and is dependent on the particular circumstances of each case. While some delay is permissible in prosecuting a criminal case, inordinate, purposeful, or oppressive delays are unconstitutional. Although it is not absolutely essential that a defendant assert a denial of a speedy prosecution prior to trial, the absence of such an assertion weighs heavily against a defendant who later claims these Sixth Amendment grounds for relief. Other factors include the length of the delay, the reasons given, and the prejudice to the defendant. No single factor is controlling; a final determination is based on a balancing of the defendant's interests protected by the Sixth Amendment against the prosecutor's justification for the delay. Finally, once it has been determined that a defendant has been denied a speedy trial, the only available remedy is to dismiss the conviction and/or the charges.

The speedy trial provision of the Sixth Amendment is only applicable once a defendant has been arrested; preindictment or prearrest delays are not controlling. Finally, the Speedy Trial Act of 1974, which will be implemented over a 5-year period, provides that a federal defendant must be brought to trial within 100 days after arrest.

In addition to the right to a speedy trial, an accused has the constitutional right to call witnesses in his or her defense.

11.02 THE RIGHT TO DEFENSE WITNESSES (COMPULSORY PROCESS)

The Sixth Amendment to the United States Constitution provides, *inter alia,* that "In all criminal prosecutions, the accused shall enjoy the right . . . to have compulsory process for obtaining witnesses in his favor. . . ." That provision of the Sixth Amendment guarantees that criminal defendants be provided with an opportunity to present defense witnesses on their own behalf. In addition, it guarantees the right of a defendant to present a defense as well as to testify for the defense.

The leading case on the right to compulsory process is *Washington v. Texas,* decided by the U.S. Supreme Court in 1967.[24] There the defendant, Jackie Washington, had been tried and convicted of murder in Texas. At his trial, the prosecutor's evidence showed that Washington became jealous when his girlfriend began dating another young man, the victim. Washington and several other youths, including one Charles Fuller who owned a shotgun, drove to the girl's house where she, her family, and the victim were having supper. Some of the young men threw bricks at the house while Washington and Fuller were left in front of the house with the shotgun. When the victim rushed out of the house to investigate, the shotgun was fired by either Washington or Fuller. The victim was fatally wounded and Washington and Fuller were arrested. The latter was convicted of murder and sentenced to 50 years in prison.

At his trial for the same murder, Washington testified that he had tried unsuccessfully to persuade Fuller to leave before the shooting and that Fuller had shot the deceased. Washington's attempt to offer Fuller's testimony in support of this defense was rejected by the trial court in light of two Texas statutes which then provided that persons charged or convicted as coparticipants in the same crime could not testify for one another[25] (although coparticipants in a crime could testify for the prosecution). Washington's conviction followed, and he also was sentenced to 50 years in prison. The Texas Court of Criminal Appeals affirmed and the U.S. Supreme Court granted certiorari.

The Supreme Court unanimously reversed Washington's conviction and held that the right of an accused to have compulsory process for obtaining witnesses in favor of the defense is applicable to the states. As noted by the Court:

> The right to offer the testimony of witnesses, and to compel their attendance, if necessary, is in plain terms the right to present a defense, the right to present the defendant's version of the facts as well as the prosecution's to the jury so it may decide where the truth lies. Just as an accused has the right to confront the prosecution's witnesses for the purpose of challenging their testimony, he has the right to present his own witnesses to establish a defense. This right is a fundamental element of due process of law.[26]

Thus, the right to defense witnesses includes more than the power to subpoena them. The right to compulsory process includes the right of defendants (and their witnesses) to present their own versions of the facts.

What happens when a trial judge intimidates the only defense witness and thereby drives the witness off the stand? Is the accused denied a right to present his or her own defense? This happened in *Webb v. Texas.*[27]

There, during the defendant's trial for burglary and at the end of the prosecutor's case, the defendant called his only witness, one Leslie Mills, who had a prior criminal record and was then serving a prison sentence. The trial judge, on his own initiative and out of the presence of the jury, admonished the defense witness Mills that (1) if he lied under oath, he (the judge) would personally see that the witness was indicted for perjury, (2) he would probably be convicted, (3) he would serve additional years in prison, and (4) he did not have to testify at all.

Not surprisingly, the defense witness refused to testify. Webb's counsel objected that such an admonition deprived the defendant of his right to present his only defense witness and that none of the state's witnesses had been so admonished. The defendant's motion for a mistrial was denied and Webb was subsequently convicted of burglary. The Texas Criminal Court of Appeals affirmed his conviction and the U.S. Supreme Court granted certiorari.

In a per curiam decision, seven members of the Court held that the defendant's conviction must be reversed. The majority of the Court held that the trial judge's threatening remarks effectively drove the sole defense witness from the stand, thereby denying the defendant his due process right to present his own witnesses in order to establish a defense. Justices Blackmun and Rehnquist dissented and stated that the judge's admonition, although improper, was not sufficiently prejudicial to the defendant in light of the overwhelming evidence of his guilt, as he had been caught in the burglarized building by the owner.[28]

What happens when a defendant seeks to introduce evidence or an oral confession by a third-party witness (not a party to the lawsuit) and the trial judge excludes that testimony is inadmissible hearsay under the local rules of evidence? This happened in *Chambers v. Mississippi* (1973).[29]

Chambers, the defendant, was tried for the murder of a police officer, convicted, and sentenced to life imprisonment. On appeal, Chambers claimed that he was denied a fair trial because the trial judge prevented him from introducing evidence favorable to his defense. Shortly after the killing, one Gable McDonald, a lifelong resident of the local area, made a written confession to Chamber's attorneys and subsequently confessed the killing (orally) to three friends. Later, McDonald denied making these inculpatory statements; he was never brought to trial. Chambers called McDonald as his own witness (because the state refused to do so) and introduced McDonald's written confession. During cross-examination by the state, McDonald denied making the confession. Chambers moved to have McDonald declared an adverse witness so that he could impeach (discredit) McDonald's testimony by introducing evidence of McDonald's three oral confessions. Chambers's motion was denied because, under Mississippi law, a party may only impeach adverse witnesses (the "voucher rule" whereby parties calling witnesses as their own may not impeach such a witness unless he or she is declared by the trial court to be a "hostile witness"). That is, a party calling a witness vouches for his or her testimony and may not impeach the witness. The trial court held that the testimony of the three witnesses to whom McDonald had confessed was inadmissible hearsay. The Mississippi Supreme Court affirmed Chambers's conviction, and the U.S. Supreme Court granted certiorari to decide whether the defendant had received a fair trial.

In an opinion by Justice Powell, the Supreme Court reversed and remanded. The Court held that the application of the Mississippi rules of evidence which precluded Chambers from cross-examining the witness who had confessed and the exclusion, as hearsay evidence, of the latter's oral confessions violated Chambers's due process rights to a fair trial, including his right to present witnesses on his own behalf. As noted by the *Chambers* Court:

> The right of an accused in a criminal trial to due process is, in essence, the right to a fair opportunity to defend against the State's accusations. The rights to confront and cross-examine witnesses and to call witnesses in one's own behalf have long been recognized as essential to due process.[30]

Thus, a trial judge's exclusion of evidence which is vital to a defense impairs an accused's right to present a defense, even though the offered evidence is inadmissible under local rules of evidence.

More recently, in *Cool v. United States* (1972),[31] the defendant, Marilyn Cool, was convicted in a federal court of "possessing and concealing, with intent to defraud, counterfeit obligations [money] of the United States." The defendant introduced the exculpatory (self-serving) testimony of an admitted accomplice that "neither the petitioner [Marilyn Cool] nor her husband had anything to do with the crime." The trial court instructed the jury that if it was convinced that the accomplice's testimony was true "beyond a reasonable doubt," it should not "throw this testimony out," implying that such testimony should be disregarded unless the jury was convinced it was true beyond a reasonable doubt. The U.S. Court of Appeals affirmed. On certiorari, the U.S. Supreme Court reversed and remanded.

In a per curiam opinion expressing the views of six members of the Court, it was held that the instruction by the trial judge was erroneous. In the Court's view, the judge erred first in impermissibly restricting the defendant's Sixth Amendment right to present exculpatory evidence to the jury. Furthermore, he made the mistake of requiring, in effect, the defendant to establish his innocence beyond a reasonable doubt contrary to the rule formulated in *Winship*[32] (Chapter 10), constitutionally establishing a presumption of innocence. As noted by the *Cool* Court:

> Accomplice instructions have long been in use and have been repeatedly approved. . . . No constitutional problem is posed when the judge instructs the jury to receive the prosecution's accomplice testimony "with care and caution." But there is an essential difference between instructing a jury on the care with which it should scrutinize certain evidence in determining how much weight to accord it and instructing a jury . . . that as a predicate to the consideration of certain evidence, it must find it true beyond a reasonable doubt.[33]

In summary, the Sixth Amendment to the United States Constitution guarantees, in part, the right of accused parties to testify on their own behalf as well as to present their own defense witnesses; any undue interference with this constitutional right—whether by local rules of evidence, by procedure, or by the trial judge—is a violation of due process.

An addition to the right of a speedy trial and to call defense witnesses, an accused has the right to confront witnesses testifying for the prosecution.

11.03 CONFRONTATION CLAUSE

The Sixth Amendment to the United States Constitution provides, *inter alia,* that "In all criminal prosecutions, the accused shall enjoy the right . . . to be confronted with witnesses against him. . . ."This statement is also known as the *Confrontation Clause.* Essentially, it guarantees the right of an accused to cross-examine the witnesses brought in by the prosecution; it almost always involves the right to challenge witnesses who are appearing on behalf of the government (federal, state, or local). As noted by the U.S. Supreme Court, the purposes of the Confrontation Clause are threefold in that it:

> (1) insures that the witness will give his statement under oath—thus impressing him with the seriousness of the matter and guarding against the lie by the possibility of a penalty for perjury; (2) forces the witness to submit to cross-examination, the "greatest legal engine ever invented for the discovery of the truth"; (3) permits the jury that is to decide the defendant's fate to observe the demeanor of the witness in making his statement, thus aiding the jury in assessing his credibility.[34]

The leading case on the Confrontation Clause is *Pointer v. Texas* (1965).[35] There, the defendants were arrested for a robbery in which $375 was taken by force from the victim. At the preliminary hearing, the state introduced the testimony of certain witnesses who implicated the defendants. Neither defendant was represented by counsel, nor did either one have an opportunity to cross-examine the chief state witness. Subsequently, Pointer was indicted for robbery. At the trial, the state offered evidence that the prosecution witness had moved to California and did not intend to return to Texas. Furthermore, over the defendant's objections that he was denied the right to confront the witnesses against him, the prosecution introduced in evidence the transcript of the testimony of the chief prosecution witness at the preliminary hearing. Pointer was convicted and his convictions was affirmed by the Texas Court of Criminal Appeals.

On certiorari, the U.S. Supreme Court reversed and remanded. In an opinion by Justice Black, it was held that the Sixth Amendment right to confront witnesses was made applicable to state criminal trials by the Due Process Clause of the Fourteenth Amendment. As noted by the Court:

> It cannot seriously be doubted at this late date that the right of cross-examination is included in the right of an accused in a criminal case to confront the witnesses against. him. And probably no one . . . would deny the value of cross-examination in exposing falsehood and bringing out the truth in the trial of a criminal case. The fact that this right appears in the Sixth Amendment of our Bill of Rights reflects the belief of the Framers of those liberties and safeguards that confrontation was a fundamental right essential to a fair trial in a criminal prosecution. Moreover, the decisions of this Court and other Courts throughout the years have constantly emphasized the necessity for cross-examination as a protection for defendants in criminal cases.[36]

Since *Pointer,* the Supreme Court has decided more than twenty cases involving the Confrontation Clause. One of the more noteworthy decisions on this issue involves the so-called *Bruton rule* decided in *Bruton v. United States* (1969).[37]

In *Bruton,* the defendant and one Evans were jointly tried in a federal court for armed postal robbery. During the trial, a postal inspector testified that Evans (who did not testify) had orally confessed to having committed the robbery with Bruton. The trial judge instructed the jury that Evans's confession was admissible against Evans (as an exception to the hearsay rule) but that the confession was inadmissible hearsay evidence as to Bruton. The trial judge held, therefore, that the codefendant's references to the defendant must be disregarded as to the latter's guilt or innocence. Evans and Bruton were convicted. The U.S. Court of Appeals affirmed Bruton's conviction because of the trial judge's limiting instructions to the jury.

On certiorari, the U.S. Supreme Court reversed Bruton's conviction. In an opinion by Justice Brennan, the Court held that an accused's Sixth Amendment right to confront witnesses (right to cross-examine) is violated if a codefendant's confession implicates a second codefendant and the confessor (first codefendant) does not testify at the trial, even though the jury had been instructed that the confession was only admissible against the confessor.

The *Bruton* rule is clearly applicable to *joint trials* (more than one defendant) and does not bar joinder of accomplices even where the prosecution intends to use a confession. However, by joining accomplices in a single trial, the prosecution may pay a heavy price if the confessor does not intend to testify and be subjected to cross-examination. Apparently the *Bruton* rule would be applicable even though the codefendants were tried individually if the confessor (codefendant also implicating the accomplice) did not testify and therefore were not subjected to cross-examination at the accomplice's trial. Here the confession of a codefendant (not on trial) would be admissible under traditional rules of evidence (known as a declaration-against-interest exception to the hearsay rule). However, this admissible hearsay might become incompetent because of the Confrontation Clause. That issue remains to be decided by the Supreme Court.

In other important cases decided by the Supreme Court on the issue of the Confrontation Clause, the Court has held that:

1 Prior inconsistent statements made by a witness at a preliminary hearing are admissible at trial if that witness testified *at trial* and undergoes a full cross-examination, even though the accused did not have an opportunity to cross-examine the witness at the earlier hearing (and such prior inconsistent statements are admissible to prove the truth as the matter asserted).[38]

2 An accused's confrontation rights are not violated if the accused is voluntarily absent during the course of the trial and the trial continues during such absence.[39]

3 An unruly defendant may be removed from the courtroom until the trial judge is assured that the accused will observe the rules of proper conduct.[40]

4 A witness is not deemed "unavailable" so as to allow the prosecution to introduce former testimony absent a *good-faith effort* by the prosecutor to obtain the witness's presence at trial.[41]

5 A mere showing that a witness was incarcerated in a federal prison outside the state at the time of trial is not a good-faith effort to show "unavailability."[42]

6 A showing that a witness is bona fide absent (e.g., moved to another country) is sufficient to show "unavailability."[43]

7 The *Bruton* rule is not applicable where a codefendant testifies but denies making the confession (thereby testifying favorably for his or her accomplice) and the codefendant's confession is later admitted.[44]

8 A state rule permitting the use against the accused of out-of-court statements made by a coconspirator *after* the commission of the crime (and not in *furtherance* of the crime) where there is some *indication* of *reliability* is not a violation of the Confrontation Clause.[45]

9 Witnesses for the prosecution must reveal their *true identity* and *address* (in order to aid the defense in cross-examining for possible impeachment purposes.[46]

10 An accused must be allowed to cross-examine a witness as to any matters which may indicate possible bias by the witness testifying against the accused (e.g., showing that the witness was, at one time, on probation as a juvenile delinquent.[47]

11 A violation of the *Bruton* rule may be "harmless error" if there is other "overwhelming evidence" of the accused's guilt.[48]

12 The Confrontation Clause is applicable to juvenile proceedings.[49]

13 The Confrontation Clause is not applicable to investigative proceedings (e.g., grand jury hearings).[50]

14 An accused has a constitutional right to cross-examine all adverse witnesses (whether the adverse witness is called by the prosecution or the defense).[51]

15 An accused at a probation[52] or parole[53] revocation hearing has a Sixth Amendment right to confront and cross-examine all adverse witnesses.

16 An inmate at a prison disciplinary hearing does not have a constitutional right to confront and cross-examine any witnesses at the hearing.[54]

17 A convicted defendant at sentencing has no constitutional right to cross-examine persons who have supplied information to the court relative to sentencing.[55]

Although the above list of decisions by the Supreme Court on the Confrontation Clause is not exhaustive, it does suggest that the Court, at least since *Pointer,* views the Confrontation Clause of the Sixth Amendment as an integral part of an accused's constitutional rights and that local or state rules which unduly interfere with this constitutional safeguard must give way to this Sixth Amendment safeguard.

In the next section we will discuss the problem of mental illness and the criminal offender. As noted by Abraham Goldstein, "the insanity defense has attracted more attention than any other issue in criminal law."[56]

11.04 INSANITY AS A DEFENSE TO A CRIMINAL CHARGE

A long-term alcoholic is arrested for the seventieth time on a charge of public intoxication. A man with a shovel attacks a police officer screaming, "I love you." A heroin addict robs a liquor store to maintain his habit. A sex-crazed man rapes a woman because he "can't help himself." A distraught and unemployed husband butchers his wife and four children to save them from "evil forces." A man sets off a bomb aboard a commercial airplane and 150 passengers are killed.

What do all these acts have in common? They all involve criminal acts to be sure. But each of the offenders may or may not be criminally liable. In this section we will focus on an important but controversial defense to a criminal charge: insanity.

Insanity is an *affirmative defense* to all criminal charges; defendants invoking this defense have an affirmative duty to offer evidence creating some reasonable doubt as to their sanity. In addition, the burden of proof as to a defendant's alleged insanity varies from jurisdiction to jurisdiction, and that burden may ultimately fall on either the prosecutor or the defendant.

One of the most frustrating problems in criminal law is what to do with persons whose behavior becomes intolerable. Who is criminally responsible, what is the role of psychiatry in law, and what is the function of the jury? The treatment of the mentally ill, alcoholics, and drug users is one of the most troublesome problems in our legal order and invites controversy and frustration.[57]

But as noted by Kittrie, "some of history's most illustrious figures have been prey to what now may be called insane delusions, manic depressive states, or paranoia."[58] Mary Baker Eddy (the founder of the Christian Science Church) was at one time committed to a mental hospital.[59] Earl Long, the former and controversial Governor of Louisiana, was certified insane in 1959 and placed in a mental asylum.[60] Other notable historical figures who have fallen prey to what would today be diagnosed as a mental illness include Hegel, the German philosopher; King Saul; Martin Luther; Goethe, Dante, and Mozart.[61]

An overriding issue in today's legal order is to what extent an accused's criminal liability may be excused by virtue of a mental disease. The solutions have not invited a consensus of opinion and have presented our judicial system with some of its most vexing problems. As noted by Wales, cases using insanity as a defense have resulted in a "judicial tug-of-war" over which psychiatric maladies qualify.[62] The purpose of this section is not to engage in a detailed discussion of the philosophical-medical debates surrounding the imposition of criminal responsibility in relation to mental illness. Rather, our intent is to present a summary of the existing law and to outline the various procedures attending insanity as a defense to a criminal charge.

The word "insanity" has a variety of meanings that often apply outside the context of criminal responsibility.[63] For example, a civil commitment embodies the notion that a disturbed person may be subjected to institutionalization for reasons other than his or her alleged criminal acts. It is well settled that an insane person cannot make a valid will. The test is often stated whether the *testator* (person making the will) is able to understand the nature of the property involved and its disposition. Another commonly asserted test for a civil commitment for insanity is whether the person sought to be committed is capable of proper self-care and can look after his or her affairs. As will be seen, neither of the above tests can determine whether a person may be excused for alleged criminal acts. In general, a person found to be civilly insane in most jurisdictions (1) cannot incur contractual obligation, (2) is an incompetent witness in court, and (3) cannot serve on a jury. Interestingly, insane persons are liable for their torts (civil injuries independent of contract), but not for their crimes.

The various tests for insanity depend upon the circumstances for which the defense is employed. As noted by LaFave and Scott, the term "insanity" serves various functions in the criminal law. It is used (1) in defending a person accused of a crime and in determining whether an accused (2) is competent to stand trial, (3) is competent to be executed, (4) is to be committed to a mental institution following a successful insanity defense, and (5) is competent to be released following a commitment.[64]

In this section our discussion is limited to the first two functions (i.e., insanity as a defense to a crime and competency to stand trial). Following that, we will briefly discuss criminal responsibility, alcoholics and other drug users, and the doctrine of "diminished capacity."

Tests for Insanity as a Defense

In American jurisprudence there are four prevailing definitions of insanity for the purposes of the criminal law: (1) the M'Naghten rule, (2) the irrestible impulse test, (3) the Durham (product) test, and (4) the substantial capacity test.[65] Some jurisdictions utilize a combination of the above or have developed modifications of them.

The oldest and probably most controversial of these tests for criminal insanity is the so-called M'Naghten rule.

M'Naghten (Right-Wrong) Rule The right-wrong (M'Naghten) test can be traced to early Hebrew and Roman law, Greek moral philosophy, and the literature of the Church in the Middle Ages. But as it exists in contemporary American law, it originated in an 1843 English decision by the Queen's Bench known as *M'Naghten's case.*[66] This was the case of Daniel M'Naghten, who had shot and killed Edward Drummond, private secretary to Sir Robert Peel (the founder of Scotland Yard). M'Naghten erroneously believed that Peel was the principal organizer of a conspiracy to kill M'Naghten. He intended to shoot Peel, *not* Peel's secretary.

At his trial for murder, M'Naghten claimed that he was not responsible for his acts because he was insane and suffering from delusions. The jury acquitted him, finding that he was "not guilty by reason of insanity." The jury's decision was not a popular one in England because of the importance of the intended victim. Because English jurisprudence had never attempted to clearly delineate the standards for acquitting a defendant because of insanity, the English Parliament (House of Lords) posed five questions regarding such standards to the Justices of the Queen's Bench for their deliberation.

The answers to these questions were attached to an appendix of the original decision are today considered a part of that opinion. A majority of the judges formulated the following test, now known as the M'Naghten rule, for insanity against a criminal charge:

> [T]o establish a defense on the ground of insanity, it must be clearly proved that, at the time of committing the act, the party accused was laboring under such a defect of reason, from disease of the mind, as not to know the nature and quality of the act he was doing, or that he did not know what he was doing was wrong.[67]

Thus, the M'Naghten rule states that a successful insanity defense requires that the accused overcome two hurdles: (1) that he or she suffered a disease of the mind affecting the ability to reason and (2) that the accused understand the nature and quality of the act *or* understand that the act was wrong.

Today, the M'Naghten rule is the sole test for insanity in more than half of the American jurisdictions. Not surprisingly, the M'Naghten rule has been, and continues to be, a source of debate and criticism by legal commentators and psychiatrists alike. Its critics far outnumber its defenders. Yet the M'Naghten rule or a modification of it remains in full force in about thirty American jurisdictions. Perhaps this is partly because insanity as a defense is only raised in a small percentage of criminal cases,[68] most often homicide, and is rarely successful. This is not surprising, since few people suffer from a mental disorder which blocks their ability to distinguish right from wrong. In addition, even if juries do believe that an accused is "crazy," they are reluctant to find such persons not guilty by reason of insanity, seeing them as too dangerous to be set free. After all, "a crazy person may repeat that behavior." There is little evidence to support this popular notion, but it nevertheless persists. In addition, in most jurisdictions a finding by a jury of not guilty by reason of insanity results in an automatic civil commitment of the defendant to a mental institution. Often juries are not informed of this in the judge's instructions, thereby increasing the likelihood that the insanity defense will not be successful, especially if the defendant has been charged with a violent offense.

Without an extensive discussion of the merits, the following criticisms are often made of the M'Naghten rule:[69]

1 The test does not state what *type* of mental disease is required to satisfy the M'Naghten rule (e.g., psychosis, neurosis, organic disease, character disorder).

2 The element of "knowledge" implies intellectual awareness and ignores "free will."

3 The element of knowledge of the "nature and quality of the act" is unclear and repetitious.

4 The element to "know" does not clarify legal wrong from moral law and is usually given to the jury without explanation.

5 The M'Naghten rule does not differentiate between partial or complete insanity.

6 The M'Naghten rule is at variance with modern principles of psychiatry.

7 The right-wrong test is inconsistent with the purposes of the criminal law because it takes account only of the impairment of reason, not of the capacity to take voluntary action.

8 An accused's knowledge of right and wrong is a moral and ethical question which psychiatrists cannot answer.

9 The jury is largely left to decide the criteria for the elements of the defense without adequate instructions.

Other objections to the M'Naghten rule have been raised,[70] but this test continues to be the dominant one for insanity in most American jurisdictions.

Irresistible Impulse Test Of the thirty or so states that adhere to the M'Naghten rule, approximately fifteen have adopted, in addition, the *irresistible impulse* test, also known as the *lack-of-control test.* Although the notion of irresistible impulse was first suggested in an English case prior to *M'Naghten,*[71] it was expressly rejected by the English courts after *M'Naghten.*[72] The term "irresistible impulse" was first used in the United States in 1844 in a Massachusetts case,[73] and a few states adopted that test in the 1860s and 1870s. However, the leading case in the United States where "irresistible impulse" was first freely defined was tried in 1887 in Alabama.[74] The Alabama court held that the jury should receive the following instructions where insanity is imposed as a defense:

> **1** Was the defendant at the time of the commission of the alleged crime, as a matter of fact, afflicted with a *disease of the mind,* so as to be either idiotic, or otherwise insane?
>
> **2** If such be the case, did he know right from wrong as applied to the particular act in question? If he did not have such knowledge, he is not legally responsible.
>
> **3** If he did have such knowledge, he may nevertheless not be legally responsible if the two following conditions concur.
>
> > **a** If, by reason of the duress of such mental disease, he had so far lost the *power to choose* between the right and wrong, and to avoid doing the act in question, as that his free agency was at the time destroyed.
> >
> > **b** And if, at the same time, the alleged crime was so connected with such mental disease, in relation of cause and effect, as to have been the product of it *solely.*[75]

Broadly speaking, the irresistible impulse test permits a verdict of not guilty by reason of insanity if it is found that the defendant had a mental disease which caused a loss of self-control (even if the defendant knew what he or she was doing and knew that it was wrong). That is, the mental disease need not satisfy *both* the M'Naghten and irresistible impulse tests. Thus, it is not necessary that the defendant's impulse be *sudden* or that the acts involved be *totally* irresistible.

Despite the fact that the irresistible impulse test was a subjective improvement over the M'Naghten rule, it has not escaped criticisms. Some of these are briefly discussed below.

Some critics have suggested that the word "impulse" is too restrictive because it suggests that the defense covers only impulsive acts.[76] However, most instructions to the jury indicate that any evidence tending to show loss of control is admissible; thus a sudden, unplanned act is not required.[77] A second criticism of the irresistible impulse test is that the rule requires total impairment of voluntary control: that an absolute inability to resist is required.[78] This criticism is without merit since juries are not so instructed, and any defendant suffering from a complete loss of control would undoubtedly meet the stricter M'Naghten test. Finally, the irresistible impulse test is said to be too vague, uncertain, and difficult to prove or disprove. More likely, as noted by the 1844 Alabama court, the inherent difficulty lies in the definitions of insanity itself, not in the rule.[79]

Despite its shortcomings, the irresistible impulse test is the dominant test for insanity in many American jurisdictions.

Durham Product Test In 1869, the New Hampshire Supreme Court became the first state court to completely reject the M'Naghten rule. In *State v. Pike,*[80] the New Hampshire Court held that the jury should decide what constitutes mental disease. Two years later, in *State v. Jones,*[81] the New Hampshire Court held that a defendant was to be found not guilty by reason of insanity *if the crime involved was the product of a mental disease.* Although the *Pike-Jones* decisions were praised by many authorities, no other state or jurisdiction adopted the new product test during the next 83 years.

In 1954, the U.S. Court of Appeals for the District of Columbia decided the case of *Durham v. United States.*[82] In an opinion written by Chief Justice David L. Bazelon, the Court held that "an accused is not criminally responsible if his unlawful act was the product of mental disease or mental defect."[83] The Court noted that the broader *Durham* rule was preferable to the narrower M'Naghten or irrestible impulse tests in light of modern "psychic realities and scientific knowledge."[84] The Court suggested the following jury instruction under the new product test:

> If you the jury believe beyond a reasonable doubt that the accused was not suffering from a diseased or defective mental condition at the time he committed the criminal act charged, you may find him guilty. If you believe he was suffering from a disease or defective mental condition when he committed the act, but believe beyond a reasonable doubt that the act was not the product of such mental abnormality, you may find him guilty. Unless you believe beyond a reasonable doubt either that he was not suffering from a diseased or defective mental condition, or that the act was not the product of such abnormality, you must find the accused not guilty by reason of insanity. Thus your task would not be completed upon finding, if you did find, that the accused suffered from a mental disease or defect. He would still be responsible for his unlawful act if there was no causal connection between such mental abnormality and the act. These questions must be determined by you from the facts which you find to be fairly deducible from the testimony and the evidence in this case.[85]

The response to *Durham* was divided, with most psychiatrists generally approving the new test[86] but the legal profession generally viewing it with some skepticism.[87] For one thing, no effort was made in *Durham* to define or explain the meaning of "product"; nor were mental disease or mental defect explained. In addition, the jury was not provided with any standards by which to judge the evidence. But the jury had to find that the accused had a mental disease or defect and that his or her unlawful act was the product of such a malady *beyond a reasonable doubt.*

During the next 18 years, over a hundred appellate decisions involving the insanity issue were written by the U.S. Court of Appeals for the District of Columbia. The court attempted to overcome some of the more substantive criticisms of Durham by defining "product" and "mental disease or defect" and providing the jury with some guidelines to govern expert testimony on the issue of insanity. For example, shortly after the *Durham* decision, Chief Judge Bazelon (who has written more opinions on the insanity defense than any other federal judge, largely because the District of Columbia Court of Appeals has confronted this issue more often than all the other courts of appeals combined)[88] substituted the term "abnormal mental condition" for "mental disease or defect."[89]

In 1962 the Durham rule became known as the Durham-McDonald rule,[90] in which the court redefined "mental disease or defect" as "any abnormal condition of the mind which substantially impairs behavior controls."[91] Other attempts by the District of Columbia Court to define mental illness and criminal responsibility adequately were less than successful. Finally, in 1972, the court agreed to make a complete review of the insanity defense.[92]

In *United States v. Brawner,* the court rejected the older *Durham* rule and adopted the Model Penal Code's substantial capacity test, which had been accepted by all but two of the eleven U.S. Courts of Appeals.

Substantial Capacity Test In 1955, the American Law Institute's (ALI) Model Penal Code project proposed another test—known as the *substantial capacity test*—The ALI test is as follows:

> **1** A person is not responsible for criminal conduct if at the time of such a conduct as a result of mental disease or defect he lacks substantial capacity either to appreciate the criminal wrongfulness of his conduct or to conform his conduct to the requirements of law.
>
> **2** As used in this Article, the terms "mental disease or defect" do not include an abnormality manifested only by repeated criminal or otherwise anti-social conduct.[93]

Thus, under the substantial capacity test, there must be (1) proof of a mental disease and (2) proof that a defendant was substantially unable to appreciate the wrongfulness of the act. The more narrow *Durham* rule was rejected because of the term "product." Further, section 2 indicates that persons with personality or character disorders (e.g., psychopathic personality, sociopathic personality, antisocial personality) cannot successfully invoke an insanity defense under this test in more jurisdictions.[94]

The substantial capacity test has been criticized in that the words "substantial capacity" and "appreciate" do not have common, absolute meanings among expert witnesses and jurors. This lack of precise definition is likely to encourage the use of different standards by persons assessing a defendant's degree of impairment or awareness.[95] But by and large, the substantial capacity test has been praised by most commentators in view of the unhappy results of other tests.[96] As noted by LaFave and Scott, this test "will probably be adopted by many jurisdictions in the years ahead."[97]

The defense of insanity to a criminal charge is closely related to another legal issue: incompetency to stand trial.

11.05 INCOMPETENCY TO STAND TRIAL

It is axiomatic in American jurisprudence that a person who is incompetent at the time of trial may not be tried for a criminal offense. Here an accused's criminal responsibility is not an issue (on the insanity defense at trial). Rather, an initial determination must be made as to the accused's ability to meaningfully participate in the proceedings. As noted by the U.S. Supreme Court:

> . . . it is not enough . . . that the defendant [is] oriented to time and place and [has] some recollection of the events . . . the test must be whether he has sufficient present ability to consult with his lawyer with a reasonable understanding—and whether he has a rational as well as factual understanding of the proceedings against him.[98]

Thus, it must be determined whether the accused (1) is able to sufficiently aid counsel in preparing a defense and (2) understands the nature of the charges.[99] Conviction of an accused who is legally incompetent to stand trial is a violation of the Due Process Clause of the United States Constitution;[100] but the issue of incompetency to stand trial may be raised by the accused, the prosecutor, or the court.[101] In the federal system and in most states, defendants are usually given a mental examination to determine competency if there is a reasonable doubt of their capacity to stand trial.[102]

In the federal system, 18 U.S.C. §§ 42244–4248 governs the issues of incompetency and insanity. It provides that a defendant found incompetent to stand trial may be committed "until the accused shall be mentally competent to stand trial or until the pending charges against him are disposed of according to law." However, the federal courts have held that these statutes could not withstand constitutional scrutiny if interpreted to authorize indefinite commitments. Thus, without a finding of dangerousness, one committed as incompetent to stand trial can only be held for a *reasonable period of time* necessary to determine if the accused has a *substantial chance* of attaining the capacity to stand trial in the *foreseeable future.* Otherwise the accused must be released or given a new competency hearing.[103]

The above rule was intended by the U.S. Supreme Court to prevent any inherently unfair procedures from being used against an accused who may be incompetent to stand trial. Without some safeguards, an accused (1) could serve a longer period of confinement than would be authorized if he or she were found guilty of the substantive charge, (2) might be not guilty of the substantive charge, (3) could be committed to a mental institution for years without receiving adequate psychiatric treatment, or (4) might be held unnecessarily. (Not all defendants found incompetent to stand trial need to be held in custody, especially if not found to be dangerous to themselves or the community.) In addition, an indefinite commitment based on an incapacity to stand trial raises other constitutional issues in light of the right to a speedy trial, the presumption of innocence, and the Eighth Amendment prohibition against cruel and unusual punishment.[104]

A recent decision by the U.S. Supreme Court on the issue of incompetency to stand trial is found in *Drope v. Missouri* (1975).[105] In this case, James Drope, the defendant, was indicted with two others for the forcible rape of the defendant's wife. Prior to trial, Drope filed a motion for a continuance to provide time for a psychiatric examination and treatment, attaching a psychiatrist's report that indicated his need for psychiatric treatment. The trial court denied the motion on the ground that the form of the continuance was improper. The case proceeded to trial and the prosecution called the defendant's wife as the state's first witness. She testified that her husband (the defendant) had "participated with four of his acquaintances in forcibly raping her and subjecting her to other bizarre abuses and indignities, but that she had resumed living with him . . . so that her children would be taken care of."[106] Further, she testified that her husband often engaged in "strange behavior," but that she had changed her mind about not wanting to testify as the defendant had tried to kill her a few days prior to the trial and she no longer believed him to be sick.

On the second day of the trial, the defendant attempted to commit suicide by shooting himself in the abdomen. Despite his absence, the trial court denied a motion for a mistrial because, in its view, the defendant had voluntarily absented himself. The trial continued. Subsequently, the defendant was convicted of rape and sentenced to life imprisonment. The Missouri Court of Appeals and Missouri Supreme Court affirmed.

On certiorari, the U.S. Supreme Court unanimously reversed and remanded. In an opinion written by Chief Justice Burger, the Court stated that:

> It has long been accepted that a person whose mental condition is such that he lacks the capacity to understand the nature and object of the proceedings against him to consult with counsel, and to assist in preparing his defense may not be subjected to trial . . . the prohibition is fundamental to an adversary system of justice.[107]

The Court concluded that the trial judge's failure to suspend the trial pending a psychiatric examination to determine the defendant's competence to stand trial denied the defendant's due process rights to a fair trial in light of (1) the wife's testimony, (2) the psychiatric report, and (3) the defendant's attempted suicide. The above evidence was regarded as *sufficient indicia* of the defendant's incompetency to stand trial. As noted by the Supreme Court:

> Even when a defendant is competent at the commencement of his trial, a trial court must always be alert to circumstances suggesting a change that would render the accused unable to meet the standards of competence to stand trial. . . . that in light of the evidence of petitioner's behavior including his suicide attempt, and there being no opportunity without his presence to evaluate that hearing in fact, the correct course was to suspend the trial until such an evaluation could be made.[108]

The Supreme Court did not decide whether an accused can voluntarily waive the constitutional right to be present at trial because of a self-inflicted wound. Presumably an accused *can* do this under some circumstances.

Another troublesome area related to insanity and incompetence to stand trial involves the treatment of alcoholics and drug addicts. In Chapter 3 we discussed alcoholism and drug addiction as "victimless crimes." In this section we will discuss some of the constitutional questions associated with these maladies.

11.06 ALCOHOLISM, DRUG ADDICTION, AND CRIMINAL RESPONSIBILITY

The issue of alcohol, drugs, and criminal responsibility has received much attention in the literature within recent years[109] but has largely been ignored by the U.S. Supreme Court.

Alcoholism and the Criminal Law

The President's Commission on Law Enforcement and the Administration of Justice reported that up to half of all national nontraffic arrests are for alcohol-related offenses.[110] The sheer volume of these arrests places inexorable strains on the police and the courts while also overcrowding correctional institutions. Yet, as noted by the President's Commission on Crime in the District of Columbia, "resort to the criminal sanctions has completely failed."[111]

The federal courts have generally rejected the view that the imposition of punishment on chronic alcoholics is a violation of the Eighth Amendment prohibition against "cruel and unusual punishment" or of the Due Process Clause. But at least two circuits of the U.S. Court of Appeals have accepted this rationale.

In *Easter v. District of Columbia* (1966),[112] decided by the U.S. Court of Appeals (D.C.), it was held that a District of Columbia law forbade the imposition of criminal sanctions because of an alcoholic's public intoxication and that civil commitment was the appropriate treatment. Easter, who was a chronic skid-row alcoholic, had been arrested seventy times for public intoxication or alcohol-related offenses. His counsel, on the seventieth arrest, argued that because of Easter's chronic alcoholism, he could not resist drinking and was therefore not capable of the voluntary conduct or *mens rea* that is required for criminal responsibility. Although the majority of the judges of the District of Columbia Court of Appeals rejected this defense, four of the judges, including Chief Judge David Bazelon, concluded that "one who is a chronic alcoholic cannot have the *mens rea* necessary to be held responsible criminally for being drunk in public"[113] and that therefore punishment was forbidden by the Eighth Amendment. In *Driver v. Hinnant* (1966),[114] the U.S. Court of Appeals for the Fourth Circuit reached a similar conclusion.

In 1968 the U.S. Supreme Court decided *Powell v. Texas.*[115] This case concerned Leroy Powell, who had been tried and convicted of public intoxication in violation of a Texas statute. On appeal and at trial in the county court, the defendant argued unsuccessfully that chronic alcoholism is a defense to public intoxication because of the Eighth and Fourteenth Amendments to the United States Constitution.

When the U.S. Supreme Court considered Powell's case on appeal, five members of the Court agreed that his conviction should be affirmed, but they could not agree on an opinion.

Four members of the Court held that there is no consensus as to the definition, manifestation, or treatment of alcoholism as a disease and that Powell was being punished for his *act* of being drunk in public—not for his "status" or "condition" of being a chronic alcoholic. Mr. Justice White concurred in the affirmance of the conviction on the grounds that the defendant had failed to established that it was impossible for him to (1) resist drunkenness and (2) avoid public places when intoxicated. Four members of the Court dissented on the ground that criminal sanctions should not be imposed on persons who are in a condition that they are powerless to change.

The *Powell* decision represents the only attempt by the U.S. Supreme Court to date to grapple with the vexing problem of alcoholism and criminal responsibility. The *Easter* decision remains in full force in the District of Columbia because Congress passed a law in 1967 (D.C. Code) implementing that decision.[116] In view of the *Powell* decision, most federal and state courts disallow chronic alcoholism as a defense to an offense involving intoxication. Next, we will briefly discuss drug addiction and the criminal law.

Drug Addiction and Criminal Responsibility

Not since 1962 has the U.S. Supreme Court ruled on the issue of whether narcotic addiction precludes punishment under the Eighth Amendment. According to the leading pharmacological text in the field, addiction is as "a behavioral pattern of compulsive drug use characterized by overwhelming involvement with the use of a drug, the securing of its supply, and a high tendency to relapse after withdrawal."[117] In general, state and federal laws and the courts have treated drug addicts more harshly than alcoholics, especially since the addict who possesses, uses, or buys narcotics may be caught up in state or federal regulatory schemes along with the drug sellers.

In 1962 the U.S. Supreme Court decided *Robinson v. California,*[118] involving a California statute which made addiction to narcotics a misdemeanor punishable by 90 days to 1 year in jail. Under this statute, the Los Angeles Municipal Court convicted Lawrence Robinson, the defendant. His conviction was affirmed by the Appellate Department of the Los Angeles County Superior Court (the highest court in the State in which a decision could be had on Robinson's appeal).

On appeal, the U.S. Supreme Court reversed. In an opinion by Justice Stewart, the Court held that the California statute violated the Eighth Amendment prohibition against cruel and unusual punishment. As noted by the *Robinson* Court:

> This statute . . . is not one which punishes a person for the use of narcotics, for their purchase, sale or possession, or for antisocial or disorderly

> behavior resulting from their administration. . . . Rather we deal with a statute which makes the "status" of narcotic addiction a criminal offense. . . . It is unlikely that any State . . . would attempt to make it a criminal offense for a person to be mentally ill, or a leper, or to be afflicted with a venereal disease. . . . a law which made a criminal offense of such a disease would doubtlessly be universally thought to be an infliction of cruel and unusual punishment. . . .[119]

Thus, a statute making a misdemeanor of the *status* of drug addiction without any proof of an *act* is unconstitutional. After *Robinson,* it was inevitable that addicts would attempt to frame their defenses against prosecutions for possession and use by claiming that their acts were involuntary, caused by pharmacological stress. The federal courts have not been receptive to this defense. In general, the federal courts have found the *Robinson* rationale to be inapplicable to possession of drugs by an addict.[120]

Finally, in 1973, the U.S. Court of Appeals for the District of Columbia decided *United States v. Moore.*[121] There, the defendant, a forty-year-old addict who had been a user for 24 years, had been convicted for possession of heroin. On appeal, his counsel relied primarily on the defense of pharmacological duress, maintaining that the defendant's acts were involuntary (although it was conceded that he did not suffer a mental illness that would bring him within the parameters of the insanity defense).

In a per curiam decision, the court, sitting *en banc* (with all the judges of the circuit present), rejected the defense of pharmacological duress largely on the grounds that, if allowed, the defense would inevitably be extended to excuse other possession-related crimes (e.g., robbery to obtain money to buy drugs). The court also ruled that medical evidence was too imprecise to show that heroin addiction resulted in an "uncontrollable compulsion." Further, the court declined to apply the *Robinson* rationale to drug addiction.

Four of the judges dissented (including Chief Judge Bazelon), stating that the common-law defense of compulsion should be applicable to heroin addiction. The *Moore* dissenters argued:

> [T]he development of the common law of *mens rea* has reached the point where it should embrace a new principle: a drug addict who, by reason of his use of drugs, lacks substantial capacity to conform his conduct to the requirements of the law may not be held criminally responsible for mere possession for his own use.[122]

The dissenters argued that the criminal law has long recognized that accused persons are not criminally responsible unless their acts were voluntary or the product of a "free will"; that evidence of duress, insanity, somnambulism, unconsciousness due to a physical malady, or involuntary intoxication are commonly accepted defenses to criminal charges.

In 1973, the Supreme Court denied certiorari in *Moore,* thereby declining to settle the applicability of *Robinson* to prosecutions of addicts for possession of drugs.[123]

Only three of the justices who decided the *Robinson* case remain on the Burger Court,[124] and the present court has repeatedly denied invitations to decide the applicability of criminal responsibility, drug addiction, and the Eighth Amendment prohibition against cruel and unusual punishment.

Next we will discuss the doctrine of *diminshed capacity.*

11.07 PARTIAL INSANITY (DIMINISHED CAPACITY)

What is the criminal responsibility of an accused who is suffering from some abnormal mental condition which is *not* of a character to afford a successful insanity defense in that jurisdiction? Suppose the defendant is only "partially insane" and can distinguish right from wrong in a M'Naghten jurisdiction—should the jury be allowed to consider that evidence on the issue of guilt or innocence or whether the defendant had the requisite mental competence to be held responsible for other lesser offenses?

In some jurisdictions (a minority), evidence of a defendant's abnormal mental condition (not amounting to legal insanity) is admissible on the issue of guilt or innocence or to negate the requisite mental state of the crime which is charged.[125] Thus, a showing of partial insanity (or partial responsibility) can result in a verdict of not guilty of the crime charged or a finding of guilty on a lesser offense, often referred to as the doctrine of *diminished capacity*. However, it should be noted that a showing of diminished capacity is quite different from the defense of insanity. The latter defense, if successful, usually results in a commitment to a mental institution, whereas a showing of diminished capacity will result in a verdict of not guilty (and subsequent release of the defendant) or imprisonment following conviction of a lesser grade of an offense.

In most jurisdictions, the insanity defense is viewed as an all-or-nothing proposition, so that the defendant must establish complete insanity or be fully responsible for the offense charged.[126] The better view would seem to admit evidence of diminished capacity, since there are fundamental differences between insanity as a defense and diminished capacity. As noted by LaFave and Scott, "there is no inconsistency in the conclusion that a defendant undeserving of a finding of not guilty by reason of insanity might nonetheless have lacked that mental state."[127]

Most of the jurisdictions that have accepted the doctrine of diminished capacity have involved situations where the defendant was charged with first-degree murder. Because premeditation and deliberation are common forms of first-degree murder (all other murders being second degree), evidence of a defendant's diminished capacity is usually offered to negate the requisite *mens rea* (premeditation and deliberation) required for first-degree murder. In that sense, the doctrine serves as a defense to the higher offense, but the defendant nevertheless may be fully responsible for the lesser offense (second-degree murder).[128]

A few jurisdictions permit a showing of diminished capacity sufficient to reduce a charge of murder to a finding of guilty of manslaughter. In even fewer jurisdictions, the doctrine of diminished capacity has been applied so as to result in a complete acquittal, especially in the case of crimes requiring a specific intent (e.g., attempted crimes, conspiracy, robbery, larceny, burglary, etc.) where the evidence indicated that the defendant lacked the requisite mental state.

The doctrine of diminished capacity has not been without criticism. There is some concern that it will result in *compromise verdicts* by the jury.[129] That is, the jury may be divided on the issue of insanity and may reach a consensus upon the middle ground of the "diminished capacity" defense so that defendants will serve shorter prison sentences for lesser offenses or be fully acquitted.[130] In the case of homicide trials, this fear is probably exaggerated. As noted by Goldstein, the sentences for these lesser homicide offenses (e.g., second-degree murder, manslaughter) are "usually long enough to keep the offender in custody until he is "cured" or has reached an age when the criminal tendencies of even the most dangerous are likely to have disappeared."[131] However, the danger may be real where the offense charged is serious and the doctrine results in a complete acquittal or a short prison sentence.[132]

In summary, the doctrine of diminished capacity, although rejected in most jurisdictions, is generally applicable to homicide trials, especially those for first-degree murder; if successful, a defense based on this doctrine usually results in a conviction for second-degree murder. In a very few jurisdictions, successful use of the doctrine can result in a finding of guilty to a lesser offense (e.g., manslaughter) or a complete acquittal. Arrangements for a civil commitment should be made for the few "dangerous offenders" who have been acquitted under the doctrine.

The ALI Model Penal Code accepts the doctrine of diminished capacity in the following terms:

> Evidence that the defendant suffered from a mental disease or a defect is admissible whenever it is relevant to prove that the defendant did or did not have a state of mind which is an element of the offense.[133]

SUMMARY

In this chapter we have focused on some important constitutional rights granted to all persons accused of committing a criminal offense. In addition, we discussed some of the legal ramifications attending insanity as a defense, incompetency to stand trial, alcoholism, drug addiction, and criminal responsibility. Finally, we discussed the doctrine of diminished capacity.

Among the constitutional rights granted an accused under the Sixth Amendment is the right to a speedy trial. We indicated that this constitutional safeguard is today binding on state criminal trials; that, in general, an accused must first be formally accused before the speedy trial provision is applicable. However, on a preindictment delay which causes *actual prejudice* to an accused's defense, there may be a denial of due process. Further, we indicated that the Supreme Court has been unwilling to set definite criteria, in terms of months or days, on the speedy trial provision. Instead, the Court has identified four factors to be controlling in assessing a defendant's right to a speedy trial, to wit: (1) the length of the delay, (2) the government's reasons for the delay, (3) the defendant's assertion of that right, and (4) the prejudice to the defendant caused by the delay. We also indicated that a finding of a denial of a speedy trial constitutionally requires a dismissal of the charges. Finally, we indicated that the federal courts now operate under the Speedy Trial Act of 1974 (which is to be implemented over a 5-year period), so that a federal defendant who has not been brought to trial within 100 days postarrest may move for a dismisal of the charges.

The Sixth Amendment guarantees defendants the right to testify on their own behalf as well as to present defense witnesses; this is known as the provision for *compulsory process.* We indicated that this Sixth Amendment provision is today applicable to state criminal trials as well as federal trials. Finally, after examining several recent Supreme Court decisions involving compulsory process, we indicated that any *undue interference* in the defense of an accused is a violation of the Due Process Clause. Next, we examined the Sixth Amendment right known as the Confrontation Clause.

The Confrontation Clause guarantees the right of an accused to cross-examine adverse witnesses. We indicated that this Sixth Amendment right is today applicable to both state and federal criminal trials. Further, we noted that the Supreme Court, in recent years, has decided more than twenty cases on the issue of the Confrontation Clause, including the case giving rise to the well-known but often confusing *Bruton* rule. Finally, we summarized some of the recent holdings of the Supreme Court on this Sixth Amendment provision.

The problem of mental illness and criminal responsibility was next examined. We indicated that there are four major tests for criminal insanity in American jurisprudence, to wit: (1) the *M'Naghten* (right-wrong) *test,* (2) the *irresistible impulse* (lack of self-control) *test,* (3) the *Durham* (product) test, and (4) the test of *substantial capacity* (ALI Model Penal Code). We defined these tests and indicated some of the more common criticisms surrounding each.

In considering the rules surrounding *incompetency to stand trial,* we indicated that such a defense is quite different from that of insanity.

We noted that the test for incompetency is generally (1) whether the accused can aid counsel in the defense and (2) whether the accused appreciates the nature of the proceedings. Finally, we indicated that an incompetent accused cannot be tried or convicted as long as the condition of incompetence continues.

We then briefly discussed alcoholism, drug addiction, and criminal responsibility, noting that the Supreme Court has not played a major role in shaping legal ramifications in this often controversial area. We discussed the *Robinson* and *Powell* decisions and indicated that neither decision permits chronic alcoholism or drug addiction to be used as a defense to a criminal charge where the status of addiction is not being charged. However, it was noted that the U.S. Court of Appeals for the District of Columbia, in the *Easter* decision, permits chronic alcoholism as a defense to intoxication-related offenses, although the *Moore* decision rejected drug addiction as a permissible defense to drug-related offenses.

Finally, we briefly discussed the doctrine of diminished capacity. We indicated that although it is a minority view and is usually employed in first-degree murder trials, a small number of jurisdictions permit the doctrine to result in an acquittal or a finding of guilty to a less serious offense.

In the next chapter we will discuss some of the rules and legal ramifications involving plea bargaining, sentencing, appeals, and postconviction remedies.

Part Two

Plea Bargaining, Sentencing, Appeals, Postconviction Remedies, and the Correctional Process

Chapter 12

Plea Bargaining and Sentencing

In the previous three chapters we discussed, at some length, many of the constitutional rights which protect criminal defendants *before* and *during* their trials. Despite these procedural safeguards, it is well recognized that up to 90 percent of all defendants plead guilty,[1] almost always in exchange for some benefit or consideration promised by the prosecutor.[2] Further, upon judgment of conviction (whether by trial or guilty plea), the defendant is *sentenced* by a court of competent jurisdiction. After sentencing, the defendant may elect to *appeal* the judgment of conviction or the sentence itself to a higher tribunal(s), although appeals based on sentences within the legal limits are not subject to appellate review in most jurisdictions. Finally, the convicted defendant may, after exhausting the normal appellate route, attempt to have his conviction overturned by resorting to what are called *postconviction remedies.*

In this chapter, we will first discuss the plea-bargaining process and guilty pleas, and then deal with the sentencing process.

12.01 THE PLEA-BARGAINING PROCESS AND GUILTY PLEAS

Although plea bargaining originated in seventeenth-century England,[3] its widespread use in the United States was not officially recognized until quite recently in our history.[4] Few American courts discussed the practice, and most that did condemned it.[5] Today, the process of plea bargaining is our principal method of disposing of criminal cases, although a higher percentage of misdemeanants plead guilty than do accused felons.[6]

After a defendant has voluntarily plead guilty to a criminal charge and the plea has been accepted by a competent court, certain legal consequences follow.

Consequences of Pleading Guilty

First and foremost, a plea of guilty to a criminal charge results in a *conviction,* and a conviction of a felony in most jurisdictions results in the loss of certain civil rights (see Chapter 15). As noted by the U.S. Supreme Court, "A plea of guilty . . . is itself a conviction. More is not required; the court has nothing to do but give judgment and sentence."[7]

In addition, a guilty plea in most jurisdictions *waives all nonjurisdictional errors.* That is, a plea of guilty is a waiver of any defects in the prior proceedings, such as the legality of an arrest or search and seizure.[8] However, a minority of states allow collateral attacks on the methods by which evidence was obtained against the defendant notwithstanding a plea of guilty, and such claims are cognizable in a federal habeas corpus proceeding.[9] As noted by the U.S. Supreme Court:

> In most States a defendant must plead not guilty and go to trial to preserve the opportunity for state appellate review of his constitutional challenges to arrest, admissibility of various pieces of evidence, or the voluntariness of a confession. A defendant who chooses to plead guilty rather than go to trial in effect deliberately refuses to present his federal claims to the state court. . . . Once the defendant chooses to bypass the orderly procedure for litigating his constitutional claims . . . the State acquires a legitimate expectation of finality in the conviction thereby obtained. . . . Ordinarily a "guilty plea represents a break in the chain of events which has preceded it in the criminal process."[10]

Finally, a plea of guilty is a *waiver of certain constitutional rights:* (1) the right to a jury trial, (2) the right to confront adverse witnesses, and (3) the right to remain silent.[11]

Why, under these circumstances, do most criminal defendants plead guilty, especially when the possibility exists that they might be acquitted if they plead not guilty and go to trial?

The Plea-Bargaining Inducements

The successful implementation of the plea-bargaining process normally requires a *quid pro quo* arrangement between two parties (prosecutor and defendant) each in a position to exchange benefits. Most frequently, the prosecutor offers the defendant a *charge reduction* (e.g., burglary reduced to attempted burglary or first-degree murder reduced to second-degree murder or manslaughter) in exchange for a plea of guilty.[12] In most cases this automatically reduces the possible maximum sentence which may be imposed.

The second most common promise offered by a prosecutor is the *charge dismissal.*[13] Here the prosecutor, in exchange for a plea of guilty to one charge, may drop one or more related charges against the defendant. The inducement to the defendant is to avoid the possibility of multiple convictions and longer consecutive sentences. Sometimes the promise is not to press additional charges under a habitual-offender statute which might subject the defendant, if convicted, to severe punishment.

The third most common promise given by prosecutors in exchange for a plea of guilty is the *sentence recommendation.*[14] Here the prosecutor agrees to *recommend* to the sentencing judge a particular sentence such as probation, fine, or other disposition. However, in most instances the recommendation is not binding on the judge; an element of risk for the defendant is involved.[15]

Other inducements by the prosecutor may include a promise (1) not to prosecute other codefendants, (2) to allow the defendant to serve in the military in place of being prosecuted, (3) not to oppose probation, (4) to allow the defendant to serve in a particular prison, or (5) to have the defendant tried in the juvenile court.[16] The range of inducements available to prosecutors is broad. But as noted by Davis, most defendants are willing to forego their constitutional right to a trial and its attendant rights as a *mitigation of punishment.*[17] It is well known that the average defendant who pleads guilty usually receives a lighter sentence than he would have had there been a trial and subsequent conviction.[18]

Several rationales have been advanced for this disparity in sentencing:[19] (1) the belief of some courts that an acknowledgment of guilt by an accused is the first step in rehabilitation; (2) the belief of many judges that any defendant who has testified at trial and been convicted has probably committed perjury; and (3) the view that, in the face of overwhelming evidence of guilt, dilatory, frivolous defenses will be deterred if a heavier sentence is imposed. Consequently, most defendants who plea bargain successfully do so in the hope of minimizing the punishment, and most are successful.

Sometimes the mitigation of punishment through plea bargaining is of secondary interest to defendants. For example, they may wish to begin serving their sentences immediately, thus avoiding long pretrial dealys and hastening the date of their release; or they may wish to minimize the social stigma of a public trial (e.g., sex offenders).[20]

If the defendant is out on bail pending trial, the prosecutor usually must make a better deal, since these defendants are often not willing to give up their freedom in exchange for a guilty plea[21] and they may be reluctant to plea bargain at all.

Delaying the trial may have certain advantages: (1) a substantial delay between arrest and trial may weaken the state's case as memories fade, witnesses disappear, etc.; (2) while on bail the defendant may be able to build a good record of employment and behavior; and (3) many defendants who are able to make bail often have retained counsel who do not feel administrative pressures to plea bargain, as do public defenders.[22] The latter group must work with the prosecutors on a daily basis and are interested in maintaining good working relationships.

Whatever inducements are offered by the prosecutor, the bargain is usually attractive enough to prompt most defendants to accept the offer. However, in most jurisdictions, a prosecutor need not ever plea bargain in general or with reference to any particular defendant; the policies of the prosecutor usually dictate the degree of plea bargaining practiced in any particular jurisdiction.[23]

The U.S. Supreme Court has made several pronouncements on the issue of plea bargaining.

12.02 THE CONSTITUTIONALITY OF PLEA BARGAINING

Although the precise question of the constitutionality of plea bargaining has never been decided by the U.S. Supreme Court, its *dictum* (side remarks by a court which are unnecessary to decide the resolution of the case) has suggested that such practices will be upheld under appropriate safeguards.[24]

In the federal system, rule 11 of the *Federal Rules of Criminal Procedure* governs the plea bargaining process:

RULE 11. PLEAS (FEDERAL RULES OF CRIMINAL PROCEDURE)

a Alternatives—A defendant may plead not guilty, guilty, or nolo contendere. If a defendant refuses to plead or if a defendant corporation fails to appear, the court shall enter a plea of not guilty.

b Nolo Contendere—A defendant may plead nolo contendere only with the consent of the court. Such a plea shall be accepted by the court only after due consideration of the views of the parties and the interest of the public in the effective administration of justice.

c Advice to defendant—Before accepting a plea of guilty or nolo contendere, the court must address the defendant personally in open court and inform him of, and determine that he understands, the following:

1 the nature of the charge to which the plea is offered, the mandatory minimum penalty provided by law, if any, and the maximum possible penalty provided by law; and

2 if the defendant is not represented by an attorney, that he has the right to be represented by an attorney at every stage of the proceeding against him and, if necessary, one will be appointed to represent him; and

3 that the defendant has the right to plead not guilty, or to persist in that plea if it has already been made, and that he has the right to be tried by a jury and at that trial has the right to the assistance of counsel, the right to confront and cross-examine witnesses against him, and the right not to be compelled to incriminate himself; and

4 that if he pleads guilty or nolo contendere there will not be a further trial of any kind, so that by pleading guilty or nolo contendere he waives the right to a trial; and

5 that if he pleads guilty or nolo contendere, the court may ask him questions about the offense to which he has pleaded, and if he answers these questions under oath, on the record, and in the presence of counsel, his answers may later be used against him in a prosecution for perjury or false statement.

d Insuring That The Plea Is Voluntary—The court shall not accept a plea of guilty or nolo contendere without first, by addressing the defendant personally in open court, determining that the plea is voluntary and not the result of force or threats or of promises apart from a plea agreement. The court shall also inquire as to whether the defendant's willingness to plead guilty or nolo contendere results from prior discussions between the attorney for the government and the defendant or his attorney.

e Plea Agreement Procedure

1 In General—The attorney for the government and the attorney for the defendant or the defendant when acting pro se may engage in discussions with a view toward reaching an agreement that, upon the entering of a plea of guilty or nolo contendere to a charged offense or to a lesser or related offense, do any of the following:

a move for dismissal of other charges; or

b make a recommendation, or agree not to opposethe defendant's request, for a particular sentence, with the understanding that such recommendation or request shall not be binding upon the court; or

c agree that a specific sentence is the appropriate disposition of the case.

The court shall not participate in any such discussions.

2 Notice of Such Agreement—If a plea agreement has been reached by the parties, the court shall, on the record, require the disclosure of the agreement in open court or, on a showing of good cause, in camera, at the time the plea is offered. Thereupon the court may accept or reject the agreement, or may defer its decision as to acceptance or rejection until there has been an opportunity to consider the presentence report.

3 Acceptance of Plea Agreement—If the court accepts the plea agreement, the court shall inform the defendant that it will embody in the judgment and sentence the disposition provided for in the plea agreement.

4 Rejection of Plea Agreement—If the court rejects the plea agreement, the court shall, on the record, inform the parties of this fact, advise the defendant personally in open court, or on showing of good cause, in camera, that the court is not bound by the plea agreement, affort the defendant the opportunity to then withdraw his plea, and advise the defendant that if he persists in his guilty plea or plea of nolo contendere the disposition of the case may be less favorable to the defendant than that contemplated by the plea agreement.

5 Time of Plea Agreement Procedure—Except for good cause shown, notification to the court of the existence of a plea agreement shall be given at the arraignment or at such other time, prior to trial, as may be fixed by the court.

6 Inadmissibility of Pleas, Offers of Pleas, and Related Statements Except as otherwise provided in this paragraph, evidence of a plea of guilty, later withdrawn, or a plea of nolo contendere, or of an offer to plead guilty or nolo contendere to the crime charged or any other crime, or of statements made in connection with, and relevant to, any of the foregoing pleas or offers, is not admissible in any civil or criminal proceeding against the person who made the plea or offer. However, evidence of a statement made in connection with, and relevant to, a plea of guilty, later withdrawn, or a plea of nolo contendere, or an offer to plead guilty or nolo contendere to the crime charged or any other crime, is admissible in a criminal proceeding for perjury or false statement if the statement was made by the defendant under oath, on the record, and in the presence of counsel.

f **Determining Accuracy of Plea**—Notwithstanding the acceptance of a plea of guilty, the court should not enter a judgment upon such plea without making such inquiry as shall satisfy it that there is a factual basis for the plea.

g **Record of Proceedings**—A verbatim record of the proceedings at which the defendant enters a plea shall be made and, if there is a plea of guilty or nolo contendere, the record shall include, without limitation, the court's advice to the defendant, the inquiry into the voluntariness of the plea including any plea agreement, and the inquiry into the accuracy of a guilty plea.

The Supreme Court has indicated that the purposes of Rule 11 are twofold: (1) to assist the district judge in determining whether the defendant's guilty plea is truly *voluntary* and (2) to produce a *complete record* at the time the plea is entered on the factors relevant to voluntariness.[25] In addition, the Supreme Court has held that a failure to comply with the requisites of the Rule may constitute reversible error entitling the defendant to plead anew.[26] That is, the trial judge must *personally address* a defendant wishing to plead guilty, determining whether (1) the plea is made voluntarily, (2) the defendant understands the nature of the charge, and (3) the defendant is aware of the minimum and maximum penalties. Failure to do so is reversible error even though the defendant was represented by counsel.

Although Rule 11 is applicable only to federal trials, it is clear that a state conviction based on a guilty plea is invalid unless accompanied by appropriate safeguards. The leading case on the voluntariness of a state conviction based on a guilty plea is *Boykin v. Alabama* (1969).[27]

In *Boykin,* the defendant plead guilty in an Alabama court to five counts of armed robbery which carried a sentence of 10 years imprisonment to death in the electric chair. Under Alabama law, the jury determined the punishment even pursuant to a guilty plea. Boykin was sentenced to be executed for each of the robbery counts. His appeal to the Alabama Supreme Court that a sentence of death for robbery was cruel and unusual punishment was unanimously rejected. However, four of the seven justices of the Alabama court discussed, on their own motion, the constitutionality of plea bargaining, and three of the justices dissented from the affirmance of Boykin's conviction.

On certiorari, the U.S. Supreme Court reversed. In an opinion written by Justice Douglas, it was held that a conviction based on a guilty plea cannot stand unless the record of the proceedings affirmatively establishes that the defendant *voluntarily* and *intelligently* waived three constitutional rights: (1) right to a trial by jury, (2) the right to confront adverse witnesses, and (3) the privilege against self-incrimination.[28] As noted by the *Boykin* Court:

> It was error . . . for the trial judge to accept petitioner's guilty plea without an affirmative showing that it was intelligent and voluntary. . . . Ignorance, incomprehension, coercion, terror, inducements, subtle or blatant threats might be a perfect cover-up of unconstitutionality.[29]

However, the *Boykin* decision did not indicate whether the trial judge must *expressly* inform the defendant which constitutional rights are lost by pleading guilty. It is arguable that this is required, as the Supreme Court has often noted that there can be no presumption of a waiver or a constitutional right from a silent record.[30]

In 1970, the Supreme Court decided several cases dealing with the issue of the voluntariness of guilty pleas; these cases are known collectively as the *Bradey-McMann-Parker* trilogy.

In *Brady v. United States,*[31] the defendant was indicted in New Mexico in 1959 for kidnapping in violation of federal statutes which provided a maximum penalty of death only if the jury recommended so. In the event that the defendant was convicted without a jury trial or plead guilty, the federal kidnapping statute authorized a maximum sentence of life imprisonment. At first Brady, represented by competent counsel, plead not guilty. But the trial judge was unwilling to try the case without a jury. Upon learning that his codefendant had confessed to the crime and would be available to testify against him, Brady changed his plea to guilty. The trial judge thrice questioned Brady as to the voluntariness of his plea in compliance with Rule 11, and his plea of guilty was accepted. He was given a sentence of 50 years prisonment, which was later reduced to 30.

Eight years later, Brady sought postconviction relief on the ground that the federal kidnapping statute providing for the death penalty only at the recommendation of the jury operated to coerce his plea of guilty (so as to avoid a possible death sentence) and that his counsel exerted impermissible pressure on him by representations with respect to a reduced sentence or clemency.

The district court, after a hearing, denied relief and found that no impermissible pressures had been put on Brady by his counsel to plead guilty. It found further that he had not plead guilty because of the federal kidnapping statute but because his codefendant was available to testify against him if Brady plead not guilty and went to trial. The court of appeals affirmed and the U.S. Supreme Court granted certiorari.

In a unanimous opinion by Justice White, the Supreme Court affirmed and held that a plea of guilty is not invalid merely because a defendant seeks to avoid the possibility of a death penalty; that the voluntariness of a guilty plea is to be determined by "all of the relevant circumstances surrounding it;"[32] and that one of these circumstances is the possibility of a heavier sentence following a guilty verdict after trial. As noted by the Court:

> The State to some degree encourages pleas of guilty at every important step in the criminal process. For some people, their breach of a State's law is alone sufficient reason for surrendering themselves and accepting punishment. For others, apprehension and charge, both threatening acts by the Government, jar them into admitting their guilt. In other cases, the post-indictment accumulation of evidence may convince the defendant and his counsel that a trial is not worth the agony and expense to the defendant and his family. All of these pleas of guilty are valid in spite of the State's responsibility for some of the factors motivating the pleas; the pleas are no more improperly compelled than in the decision by a defendant at the close of the State's evidence at trial that he must take the stand or face certain conviction.[33]

The Court went on to find that Brady's plea of guilty was voluntarily, knowingly, and intelligently made notwithstanding that he might have been partially motivated by fear of the death penalty.

In 1968, in another case, the Supreme Court had struck down the death penalty provision of the federal kidnapping statute as unconstitutional because the death penalty could be imposed only at the recommendation of a jury.[34] Thus, although a plea of guilty precluded the imposition of the more severe sentence, the statute did operate to impose an impermissible burden upon the exercise of the constitutional right to a trial by jury. However, *Brady* was distinguished because there was no real evidence that the fear of the death penalty under the kidnapping statute induced his plea of guilty.

In *McMann v. Richardson* (1970),[35] decided the same day as *Brady,* the Court was faced with the issue of the extent to which an otherwise valid guilty plea may be attacked by assertions that the plea was motivated by a prior coerced confession.

In each of the three consolidated cases decided in *McMann,* the defendants plead guilty in New York State courts to various felonies including murder, rape, and robbery prior to the Supreme Court's decision in *Jackson-Denno* (1964).[36] There the Court held that the *trial judge* (not the jury) must make a preliminary determination of the voluntariness of an alleged coerced confession, that the judge must hold a hearing (so-called *Jackson-Denno* hearing) outside the presence of the jury on the voluntariness of the confession, and that only if the judge finds the confession to be voluntary may the jury consider that as part of the state's evidence against the defendant.

The defendants in *McMann* claimed that the guilty pleas were tainted by coerced confessions, but the state courts denied relief. The district courts, without granting hearings, denied federal habeas corpus relief, but the court of appeals reversed and remanded each case back to the district courts to hold evidentiary hearings on the connection between the confessions and the guilty please since, prior to *Jackson-Denno,* the procedures employed by New York to treat the voluntariness of a confession had been unconstitutional.

On certiorari, the U.S. Supreme Court vacated and remanded. In an opinion by Justice White, the Court held that defendants who allege that they plead guilty because of a prior coerced confession are not, without more, entitled to a hearing on a petition for federal habeas corpus and that such defendants are bound by their pleas of guilty unless it can be shown that "serious derelictions on the part of counsel"[37] resulted in a plea which was not a knowing and intelligent act.

As noted by the Court:

> For the defendant who considers his confession involuntary . . . tendering a plea of guilty would seem a most improbable alternative. The sensible course would be to contest his guilt . . . at trial . . . and win acquittal, however guilty he may be. . . . If he nevertheless pleads guilty the plea can hardly be blamed on the confession which in his view was inadmissible evidence and no proper part of the State's case. . . . a guilty plea in such circumstances is nothing less than a refusal to present his federal claims to the state court . . . surely later allegations that the confession rendered his plea involuntary would appear incredible. . . .[38]

The Court noted that a showing that a guilty plea that was induced by ineffective or incompetent counsel is subject to relief. However, the test is not whether counsel's advice was erroneous but "whether the advice was within the range of competence demanded of attorneys in criminal cases."[39] The Court indicated that the matter should be left, for the most part, to the sound discretion of the trial judge.

In *Parker v. North Carolina,*[40] decided the same day as *Brady* and *McMann,* the defendant was indicted for first-degree burglary, an offense then punishable by death under North Carolina law unless the jury recommended a penalty of life imprisonment. However, a competent plea of guilty to this offense would result in a mandatory sentence of life imprisonment.

Parker confessed shortly after being taken to the police station. He informed his counsel that the confession was not prompted by threats or promises and had been voluntary. Because his attorney believed that the defendant's confession would be admissible at trial, he recommended that Parker plead guilty. The defendant signed written statements authorizing his plea of guilty and the prosecutor and the trial judge accepted the plea.

On appeal, Parker asserted, *inter alia,* that his plea of guilty was invalid because it was induced by the North Carolina statute which authorized a lower penalty for burglary pursuant to a guilty plea than if he went to trial and was convicted. This claim was rejected by the Supreme Court on the basis of the *Brady* decision. In addition, Parker asserted that he had received "bad advice" from his attorney with regard to the admissibility of his confession. This claim was rejected by the Supreme Court.

As noted by Justice White writing for a majority Court in *Parker*:

> . . . even if Parker's counsel was wrong in his assessment of Parker's confession, it does not follow that his error was sufficient to render the plea unintelligent and entitle Parker to disavow his admission in open court. . . . We think the advice he received was well within the range of competence required of attorneys representing defendants in criminal cases. Parker's plea of guilty was not open to attack on the grounds that counsel misjudged the admissibility of Parker's confession.[41]

The *Brady-McMann-Parker* trilogy indicates that voluntary pleas of guilty are not subject to federal relief notwithstanding the possibility of a greater imposition of a sentence if the defendant is convicted at trial or alleges that a prior coerced confession induced a guilty plea. Further, guilty pleas are not subject to collateral attacks absent some showing that there was a dereliction of duty on the part of counsel. A simple showing of "bad legal advice," without more, is not sufficient to render an otherwise guilty plea invalid.

In 1970, the Supreme Court was faced with another issue of first impression on plea bargaining. What happens when a defendant voluntarily pleads guilty to an offense and the plea is accompanied by a protestation of innocence? Is the plea of guilty valid if accepted by the trial judge? This happened in *North Carolina v. Alford.*[42]

Alford was indicted in North Carolina for first-degree murder, which authorized the death penalty unless the jury recommended life imprisonment. Faced with substantial evidence of guilt, Alford's appointed attorney recommended that the defendant plead guilty, but the decision was left to Alford. The prosecutor and Alford agreed to a plea of guilty to second-degree murder punishable by a maximum of 30 years' imprisonment.

Before the trial judge accepted the guilty plea to the reduced charge, several state witnesses summarized the state's case, which strongly suggested Alford's guilt. Alford testified that, although he had not committed the murder, he was nevertheless pleading guilty to avoid the possibility of a death sentence if he went to trial and was convicted. The trial court determined that Alford was cognizant of the difference between first- and second-degree murder and that he knew the consequences of his plea and the rights waived thereby. The plea was accepted.

Based on Alford's prior criminal record—which included convictions for murder, armed robbery (nine times), transporting stolen property, forgery, and carrying a concealed weapon—the trial court sentenced him to 30 years' imprisonment, the maximum penalty for second-degree murder.

Alford's earlier attempts to obtain postconviction relief failed in the state in federal courts. In 1967, Alford filed a petition for federal habeas corpus in the district court which denied his claim that the plea was involuntary. On appeal, the court of appeals reversed and held that Alford's plea of guilty had been involuntary.

On appeal, the U.S. Supreme Court vacated and remanded. In an opinion written by Justice White, a majority Court, relying on *Brady,* held that the fact that a defendant pleads guilty to avoid a possible more severe sentence "does not necessarily demonstrate that the plea of guilty was not the product of a free and rational choice, especially where the defendant was represented by competent counsel. . . ."[43]

With regard to Alford's protestation of innocence at the time of the plea, the Court stated:

> . . . while most pleas of guilty consist of both a waiver of trial and an express admission of guilt, the latter element is not a constitutional requisite to the imposition of criminal penalty. An individual accused of crime may voluntarily, knowingly, and understandingly consent to the imposition of a prison sentence even if he is unwilling or unable to admit his participation in the acts constituting the crime.[44]

In addition, the *Alford* Court indicated that criminal defendants do not have a constitutional right to have their guilty pleas accepted by the court, and that the states could prohibit the acceptance of guilty pleas from defendants who also assert their innocence.[45] However, the Court did not delineate the constitutional scope of discretion permitted by trial courts in accepting guilty pleas.

In other cases relevant to plea bargaining decided by the U.S. Supreme Court, the Court has held that:

1 A plea of guilty is subject to attack if the defendant was unrepresented by counsel at the time of the plea.[46]

2 Unless the attorney's advice was clearly incompetent, a criminal defendant who pleads guilty on the advice of counsel is not automatically entitled to federal habeas corpus relief simply on proof that the indicting grand jury was unconstitutionally selected.[47]

3 If a defendant knowingly and voluntarily pleads guilty to a criminal charge, it is not an error for the trial court to deny a defendant's motion to withdraw the plea prior to sentencing simply because counsel was representing other codefendants and there was an alleged conflict of interest.[48]

4 The failure of a prosecutor to keep a promise inducing a guilty plea renders the plea involuntary.[49]

5 When a state law permits a defendant to plead guilty without forfeiting the right to judicial review of certain constitutional issues such as the voluntariness of a confession, these claims are cognizant in a federal habeas corpus proceeding.[50]

6 There is no constitutional right to have a guilty plea accepted; this is at the discretion of the trial judge.[51]

Although the above list is not exhaustive, it is clear that once the safeguards which accompany a plea of guilty are fulfilled (e.g., voluntary, knowing, intelligent waiver of certain constitutional rights), the Supreme Court, in an effort to preserve the finality of a judgment based on a guilty plea, has upheld federal judicial review only in limited circumstances. The results of the Supreme Court pronouncements on plea bargaining have been designed to curtail attacks following a valid judgment and sentence. Yet plea bargaining is necessary under our adversary system of justice, and its benefits are not limited to the defendant who pleads guilty. As noted by Chief Justice Burger:

> The disposition of criminal charges by agreement between the prosecutor and the accused, sometimes loosely called "plea bargaining," is an essential component of the administration of justice. Properly administered, it is to be encouraged. If every criminal charge were subjected to a full-scale trial, the States and the Federal Government would need to multiply by many times the number of judges and court facilities.[52]

The benefits of plea bargaining have been described by the Supreme Court as follows:

> . . . It leads to a prompt and largely final disposition of most criminal cases; it avoids much of the corrosive impact of enforced idleness during pretrial confinement for those who are denied release pending trial; it protects the public from those accused persons who are prone to continue criminal conduct even while on pretrial release; and, by shortening the time between charge and disposition, it enhances whatever may be the rehabilitative prospects of the guilty when they are ultimately imprisoned.[53]

Although "negotiated justice"[54] may be a cheap way to promote judicial efficiency, the increasingly heavy caseloads and backlogs in the courts leave little room for bureaucratic functioning and reform under our present system of adversary justice without the use of plea negotiations. Although the National Advisory Commission on Criminal Justice Standards and Goals called for totally abolishing plea negotiations by 1978,[55] it is likely, despite the inherent problems which attend this process, that the courts will continue to protect the plea-bargaining system. Perhaps if certain offenses were "decriminalized" and the allocation of judicial resources were markedly increased, the extent of plea bargaining could be substantially reduced or altogether abolished. But the proponents of abolition should not forget that, because of the numerous procedures and safeguards which attend the plea-bargaining system, the defendants have had their "day in court."

Following a judgment or conviction, whether by a finding of guilty at trial or via a guilty plea, the defendant is sentenced.

12.03 SENTENCING

In previous chapters we noted that intricate constitutional doctrines protect the rights of an accused at almost every stage of the criminal process. Although the sentencing process may be the most crucial part of the criminal justice system to the defendant,[56] few common-law and constitutional protections attend this stage and the convicted are left to the "mercy of the sentencing judge."[57] In most jurisdictions, no legal standards have been developed to ensure that decisions are rational or sentencing is fair. In most states, the judge may have little or no background information concerning the defendant being sentenced. A presentence report may be available, but the judge is not bound by the recommendations of the probation officer. And there is no constitutional right for a defendant or counsel to have access to the information in that report as a check on its validity.[58] In most jurisdictions, the sentence imposed is dependent upon (1) the limitations of punishment imposed by the applicable criminal statute and (2) the judge's personal morality and judgment.[59] And a particular sentence imposed, if it is within the legal boundaries, is not subject to appellate review in most states. Because of a lack of uniform standards and guidelines, gross disparities have resulted in the sentencing process; such disparities serve to undermine what little rehabilitation occurs in our correctional process.

Sentencing decisions—as well as the frequency, length, and types of sentences that are handed out to the convicted[60]—have been found to be based on such extralegal factors as the socioeconomic and racial characteristics of the defendant.[61] Table 12-1 indicates that nonwhites receive, on the average, longer sentences to federal prisons than whites; this disparity in sentencing has put a blemish on our system of criminal justice.

Table 12-1 Average Sentences of Court Commitments to Federal Prisons, by Race and Offense (Fiscal Year Ended June 30, 1972)

Offenses	Average sentences (in months)	
	Whites	Nonwhites
Offenses in which nonwhites have longer average sentences than whites:		
Assault	51.1	81.2
Burglary	41.8	43.1
Drug laws	51.9	73.5
Embezzlement	26.9	31.0
Escape	20.1	46.0
Forgery	34.1	40.1
Immigration	10.4	14.0
Income tax	14.2	30.7
Juvenile delinquency	35.0	36.1
Selective service acts	29.3	38.6
Offenses in which whites have longer average sentences than nonwhites:		
Counterfeiting	45.3	44.0
Extortion	56.0	51.4
Firearms	44.9	37.8
Fraud	34.5	33.0
Kidnapping	248.8	219.0
Larceny	39.5	33.3
Liquor laws	20.4	14.8
National security laws	66.9	24.0
Robbety	138.3	130.3
Securities	45.9	44.9
Average sentence for all offenses	43.3	58.7

Source: U.S. Department of Justice, Federal Bureau of Prisons, *Statistical Report*, Fiscal Years 1971 and 1972, Washington, D.C., pp. 60-61.

Quinney notes that other extralegal factors influence the sentencing process. These include (1) the personality of the sentencing judge, (2) the geographical distribution, (3) the local sentencing customs, (4) the recommendations of the probation officer, and (5) local bureaucratic considerations.[62] The dilemma is one of increasing concern to criminologists and the judiciary[63] and solutions do not come easily.

The National Advisory Commission on Criminal Justice Standards and Goals has recommended the use of *sentencing councils of judges.*[64] Here the sentencing judge consults with two or more colleagues over the appropriateness of a sentence in order to reduce sentence disparities. Alternatives include the convening of *sentencing institutes* to bring together judges, prosecutors, and other specialists such as criminologists, psychiatrists, and correctional experts to promote uniformity in sentencing objectives.[65] Another possibility is the use of *mixed sentencing tribunals*[66] composed of a panel of three: (1) the judge, (2) a psychiatrist or psychologist, and (3) a criminologist or educator who would assess individual sentences. Other suggestions include the use of *appellate review of sentences* and *legal reform measures* largely through the *Model Penal Code* of the ALI (American Law Institute), the *Model Sentencing Act* (proposed by the National Council on Crime and Delinquency), and the *American Bar Association Standards Relating to Sentencing Alternatives.* Without examining the merits and pitfalls of the above proposals, it is clear that sentencing practices in the United States today vary considerably and are often the capricious and arbitrary product of the judge's personal philosophy. As noted by federal Judge Marvin E. Frankel , the sentencing process in the United States is literally "lawless."[67]

In this country we have the distinction of handing out some of the most severe prison sentences in the world.[68] But as we have noted, "even-handed justice" is not one of the byproducts of our system. The defendant who is sentenced to 25 years for bank robbery must feel a sense of injustice when his codefendant, who testified against him, is put on probation or given a suspended sentence. And yet severe sentences, despite the favor they find among many, seem to have relatively little effect on the rate of recidivism. For example, a recent work suggests that the recidivism rate in the United States is between 50 and 80 percent and that the average inmate is returned to society within 3 years but repeats crimes within a year.[69]

Although we were the first country to substitute incarceration for capital punishment, the first to systematically employ parole, and the first to divert the young into the juvenile justice system,[70] it is surprising that innovations in our sentencing practices are wanting.

We shall next consider the *forms* of sentences and commitment in the United States, which are diverse and complicated.

Forms of Sentences

Three major *forms* of sentences are employed in our criminal justice system—the definite, the indeterminate, and the indefinite[71]—although some recent works dichotomize our sentencing structures into only the first two types.[72]

Definite Sentences Originally, and especially in the Eighteenth Century, the definite sentence meant a flat term of years which was fixed and invariable according to the established law. The definite sentence deprived the judge of any discretion in sentencing. Mitigating factors such as a defendant's age, mental condition, prior criminal record, or social history were deemed immaterial. Thus, in theory at least, the unfettered discretion of judges and the associated potential for abuse in sentencing was eliminated. This view of classical criminology soon gave way to a more enlightened view, espoused by the neo-classical school of criminology, that some variation in sentencing should remain within the discretion of the judge in light of the circumstances of the individual offender and the immediate offense. The definite sentence, without possibility of parole, is rarely used today.

Indefinite Sentence The indefinite sentence is one in which a minimum and maximum time is set by the legislature (e.g., 5 to 10 years); here the offender can be released early by an administrative agency, usually called the parole board. This theory of sentencing represents a compromise between the definite sentence which removes all discretion in sentencing from the judge and the indeterminate sentence which originally meant an open-ended commitment until the offender was "cured." The so-called indefinite sentence of today is a variation of the indeterminate sentence.

Indeterminate Sentences The theory of the indeterminate sentence is a product of the late-nineteenth-century positivistic criminology of Italy. Originally, an indeterminate sentence meant no minimum or maximum. The offender was sent to an institution to be "reformed," and release was predicated upon the therapeutic medical model. The date of release was left in the hands of physicians and correctional authorities. Today, the indeterminate sentence has come to mean, in most jurisdictions that employ it, a *partially indeterminate sentence* in which minimum and maximum penalties are fixed by the legislature.[73] But the offender can be released whenever it is decided that the rehabilitation process has been effective.

Other variations are employed under indeterminate sentencing structures.[74] Such sentences are sometimes used for "sexual psychopaths" in lieu of fixed sentences and, in theory, can result in a life sentence.

The most common variation of the indeterminate sentence is found in several Western states (e.g., California), where the trial judge sentences the offender to a maximum term provided by statute but the release date is determined by a parole board or Adult Authority (California).

Another variation of the indeterminate sentence occurs where the trial judge selects minimum and maximum terms but the correctional authorities are given discretion to release the offender within this range.

In some jurisdictions, a minimum sentence must be served for all offenses regardless of the maximum term imposed by the judge. Finally, it has been noted that the determinate sentence (described above) is really a variation of the indeterminate sentence. Although a fixed term is set by the judge, the offender can be released by the parole authorities prior to the expiration or the maximum term.[75] Today, thirty-six jurisdictions employ some form of indeterminate sentencing structure.[76] But as noted by Saul Rubin, the terms "definite," "indeterminate," and "indefinite" are "opaque and confusing."[77] And indeterminate sentences have been subjected to a great deal of criticism, since those states with the greatest indeterminacy in their sentences also have the longest sentences.[78]

Next we will consider the *types* of sentences available to judges in the United States.

Types of Sentencing Alternatives

Most jurisdictions, in the interest of fairness, require that a defendant be sentenced soon after his conviction. For example, in the federal system, sentence is to be imposed "without unreasonable delay,"[79] and many jurisdictions specify a time limit for imposition of sentence.

The types of sentencing alternatives available to the judge are diverse. It should be noted that at least twelve states permit jury sentencing in certain types of noncapital cases;[80] the constitutionality of such sentencing has been upheld by the Supreme Court.[81] Sentencing alternatives include (1) suspended sentences, (2) probation, (3) fines, (4) imprisonment and (5) capital punishment.

Suspended Sentences In most jurisdictions, a conviction for many nonserious offenses permits the judge to impose a suspended sentence, although such a sentence is not allowed following a conviction for some serious offenses (e.g., first-degree murder). Most often, when this sentencing alternative is utilized, the judge will impose a sentence—for example, imprisonment or fine—and suspend the imposition of the sentence provided that the offender complies with the conditions which often accompany this type of sentence. Sometimes the offender is placed under the supervision of a probation officer and told to "stay out of trouble" or to make restitution to the victim of the crime. If the offender fails to comply with the accompanying conditions, the judge may reinstate the original sentence. Sometimes the constitutionality of these conditions is questionable (e.g., "Stay out of this city" or "Leave this state and never return").

Perhaps the most common type of sentencing alternative utilized by judges is the imposition of probation.

Probation Probation, in which the offender is placed under the supervision of a probation officer for a term of years, is used in the United States in more than half the cases.[82] However, probation can be imposed without supervision. Former Vice-President Agnew was sentenced to 3 years' unsupervised probation following his conviction for violating federal income tax laws. Conditions usually accompany a probationary sentence, and offenders can avoid imprisonment altogether if they comply with these requisites.

Goldfarb and Singer have listed the following conditions accompanying probation as more or less typical in many jurisdictions:

1 Reporting to the probation officer on a regular basis
2 Maintaining lawful behavior
3 Making restitution to the victim
4 Paying fines
5 Serving a short jail term prior to probation
6 Making restricted use of automobiles
7 Not leaving the jurisdiction of the court without permission
8 Abstaining from the use of alcohol
9 Avoiding establishments where liquor is served
10 Avoiding the company of known criminals or ex-convicts
11 Attending church regularly
12 Marrying the mother of the offender's unborn child[83]

Usually only a few conditions are imposed on a single probationer. But some specified conditions of probation have been held to be unconstitutional and lawless; one study reported that probation revocation rates increase as more conditions are imposed.[84]

Failure of the probationer to comply with the conditions of probation can result in a revocation, and the offender may then be imprisoned (see Chapter 15).

Fines are frequently used as alternative sentences for nonserious offenses.

Fines The use of fines for punishment is common for nonserious offenses, although they are also authorized for many serious crimes in most jurisdictions (e.g., a manslaughter conviction in Missouri authorizes imprisonment or a fine of $500).[85] In considering the utility of fines as a type of punishment in light of the four major theories of punishment (deterrence, retribution, imprisonment, and rehabilitation), one commentator noted that "fines serve almost no function other than satisfying the community's desire for revenge against the criminal."[86] Yet in forty-seven states and the federal system, offenders who cannot pay the imposed fine may be imprisoned; thus failure to pay fines has become a major cause for imprisonment.[87] Many jurisdictions operate on a philosophy of "pay or go to jail." Although debtor's prison was long ago abolished in the United States, the inability of "men of straw" to pay fines results in something like a debtor's prison. Yet the U.S. Supreme Court stated, over 20 years ago, that "[t-]here can be no equal justice where the kind of trial a man gets depends on the amount of money he has."[88]

In recent years, the Supreme Court has on occasion reviewed the constitutionality of imposing fines on offenders. In *Williams v. Illinois* (1970),[89] the defendant was convicted of petty theft (a misdemeanor) and sentenced to a maximum term of a year's imprisonment and a $500 fine. Court costs of $5 were also imposed. Under the law then in effect in Illinois, any defendant who was in default in payment of the fine and court costs at the end of the year's sentence was required to remain imprisoned to work off the monetary obligation at a rate of $5 per day. Williams fell into this category, being unable to pay the $505 assessed. This brought him an additional 101 days' confinement beyond the maximum term authorized for the offense. The Illinois courts rejected the defendant's allegations that he was denied the equal protection of the law because of his inability to pay.

On appeal, the U.S. Supreme Court vacated and remanded. In an opinion by Chief Justice Burger, the Court held that the Equal Protection Clause of the Fourteenth Amendment precluded the imposition of an aggregate punishment on an indigent offender which exceeds the maximum sentence fixed by the statute governing the offense involved. As noted by the Court:

> The mere fact that an indigent in a particular case may be imprisoned for a longer time than a non-indigent convicted of the same offense does not, of course, give rise to a violation of the Equal Protection Clause. Sentencing judges are vested with wide discretion in the exceedingly difficult task of determining the appropriate punishment in the countless variety of situations that appear. The Constitution permits qualitative differences in meting out punishment and there is no requirement that two persons convicted of the same offense receive identical sentences.[90]

The Court went on to state that, under appropriate circumstances, a state may enforce judgments against indigents unable to pay fines. It declined, however, to discuss the constitutionality of the available alternatives.

The next term, in *Tate v. Short* (1971),[91] the Court was faced with a "pay the fine or go to jail" situation.

Tate was convicted in a Texas municipal court of nine traffic offenses punishable by fine only. His fines totaled $425, which he was unable to pay. He was sentenced to a municipal prison farm, where he was required to remain until he paid off the fine at a rate of $5 a day (or 85 days). The Texas courts rejected Tate's petition that the imposition of the sentence was unconstitutional because of his indigency.

The U.S. Supreme Court, on the basis of the *Williams* decision (above), reversed and remanded. In an opinion by Justice Brennam, the Supreme Court held that a defendant's imprisonment was based solely on his indigency, in contravention of the Equal Protection Clause (Fourteenth Amendment). As noted by the Court:

> Imprisonment in such a case is not imposed to further any penal objective of the State. It is imposed to augment the State's revenues but obviously does not serve that purpose; the defendant cannot pay because he is indigent and his imprisonment, rather than aiding collection of the revenue, saddles the State with the cost of feeding and housing him for the period of his imprisonment.[92]

The *Tate* Court did not decide the constitutionality of alternative sentencing provisions whereby defendants are imprisoned because they refuse or neglect to pay a fine although they have the means to do so.

A few jurisdictions permit the paying of fines in installments (e.g., California and New York).[93] Such procedures have been widely endorsed, as they avoid the expense of maintaining the offender in jail and the offender's family on state welfare.[94] The laws of some countries require that fines be imposed according to the ability of the defendant to pay (e.g., Cuba and Sweden).[95] Such an arrangement implies a simple, cheap, and effective method of punishment. But it could, arguably, result in a type of *inverse discrimination* where the rich might pay heavily and the poor little or nothing for the same offense. Ultimately, this could lead to an elimination of fines as a form of punishment, and all offenders who did not receive suspended or probationary sentences would go to jail. But, as we have noted, our jails are already overcrowded.

Except for probation, the most common type of sentencing alternative utilized in the United States is imprisonment.

Imprisonment The term "imprisonment" refers to incarceration in jail *or* prison. In the United States—unlike European countries—sentences for terms of more than 5 years are common and those of more than 10 years are not uncommon.[96]

The underlying premise upon which imprisonment is based is that some offenders are too dangerous to be free in society, that they will repeat further crimes if not incarcerated, and that such punishment is necessary to protect the public.[97] Accordingly, we sentence our offenders to some of the longest terms in the world.[98] Yet the validity of incarceration as a mode of punishment depends on the accuracy of our predictions.[99] As noted by Herbert Packer, "this proposition is highly dubious,"[100] and our judges tend to overpredict dangerousness.

The American Bar Associations's Advisory Committee on Sentencing and Review stated that long prison sentences are necessary in only a small minority of cases (10 to 15 percent). One well-known study concluded that the longer offenders remain incarcerated, the more likely they are to commit further crimes upon release.[101] Alternatives to institutional commitment (discussed in Chapter 14) are probably more effective for most offenders, at least in terms of recidivism. Probably a lot of long-term sentences result from nothing other than the desire for vengeance. But according to law in the United States—unlike many European countries—our judges do not have to give the defendant with reasons for the sentence imposed.[102] The judge at sentencing may refer, for the record, to the ideals of rehabilitation or the "dangerousness of the offender"; but in many instances a harsh sentence may reflect a judge's personal philosophy of punishment, predicated on revenge; and in most jurisdictions there are no or few remedies available to offenders.

Because most state judges are elected officials, they must "please the public" to some degree. The sentencing policies of a judge are one of the most visible measures of his work product on the bench. The general public is not trained to determine whether a judge's legal rulings on a day-by-day basis are correct. But the sentences imposed, especially those that are harsh, have *high visibility.* In a law-and-order society, the imposition of long prison sentences can and does influence votes. This is not to suggest that federal judges do not impose unusually harsh sentences. Some do, but not for the sake of reelection. And even unusually long sentences imposed in the federal system and in two-thirds of the states are, for the most part, not subject to appellate review. Yet in almost every jurisdiction in the United States, a $2,000 judgment in a civil case is subject to at least one review by an appellate court, and in many cases two appellate reviews. The sentencing power of our judges is the most unrestricted in the free world.[103]

Today, the sentence least often imposed in The United States is capital punishment.

Capital Punishment Between 1967 and 1977 there has only been one public execution in the United States. Gary Gilmore was executed in Utah in January, 1977. In view of the Supreme Court's most recent pronouncements on the constitutionality of capital punishment, it seems likely that this form of sentencing and punishment will become of greater significance in future years. In any case, the imposition of the death penalty, when compared with other sentencing alternatives, has always been, historically, of statistical insignificance.

Meltsner, in his book *Cruel and Unusual Punishment: The Supreme Court and Capital Punishment* (1973, p. 75) indicates that 3,859 persons were executed in the United States between 1930 and 1967, and that more than half these executions involved nonwhite persons. (See the lists below for exact figures.) To many scholars, these statistics present a prima facie case of discrimination based on race especially when capital punishment for the crime of rape is considered.[104] Nevertheless, a Gallup poll taken in 1972 indicated that 57 percent of Americans favor the imposition of the death penalty.[105]

One prisoner consoles another.

	Murder	*Rape*	*Other*	*Totals*
White	1,664(49.9%)	48(10.6%)	39(55.7%)	1,751(45.4%)
Black	1,630(48.9%)	405(89.0%)	31(44.3%)	2,066(53.5%)
Other	40(1.2%)	2(0.4%)	0(0.0%)	42(1.1%)
Totals	3,334(100%)	455(100%)	70(100%)	3,859(100%)

Several arguments have been advanced for and against the imposition of the death penalty.[106]

Arguments Favoring Capital Punishment Hugo Bedau notes that most support for capital punishment comes from law enforcement personnel, most notably the police and prosecutors.[107] The major arguments favoring the death penalty are that:

The realities of death row: Prison counselors advise inmates.

1 The Scriptures support this form of punishment; e.g., "He who kills a man shall be put to death" (Lev. 24:7).[108]

2 It has a deterrent effect on murder and other serious crimes.

3 Most states and the majority of the world's nations provide for the death penalty.

4 Certainty of punishment is essential to deterrence.

5 It costs more to keep people in prison for long terms than to execute them.

6 Rehabilitation is not an effective substitute.

7 Life sentences do not mean "natural life" but rather a varied term of years.

8 Society has a right to exact revenge from vicious criminals.

9 Intricate legal safeguards virtually preclude the innocent from being executed.

10 There are no effective alternative penalties.

11 Its imposition does not constitute "cruel and unusual punishment."

The electrocutioners' box.

Much of the support for capital punishment is based on emotionalism rather than empirical scientific evidence. Nevertheless, its proponents are zealous in their views—nothing short of some executions will dissuade them—and we concede that some of their arguments are somewhat academically attractive.

Those favoring the abolition of capital punishment are equally zealous in their views.

Arguments against Capital Punishment Bedau notes that a large majority of contemporary social scientists (e.g., criminologists, correctional authorities, social workers) are opposed to the death penalty.[109] A summary of the arguments against capital punishment would include the observations that:

1 It is not a measurable deterrent to murder or to other serious crimes.

2 Its application has favored the rich and white.

3 The per capita cost of execution is higher than imprisonment.

4 It is based on primitive notions of revenge.

5 Innocent people could be and have been executed.

6 A civilized society upholds the sanctity of human life.

7 Paroled and pardoned murderers are the least likely to repeat their crimes.

8 It undermines rehabilitation and sound penal reforms.

9 It is unthinkable that death, as a legal sentence, should be subject to human discretion.

10 It violates the Fifth Commandment "Thou shall not kill."

11 It constitutes cruel and unusual punishment.

And so the arguments go; some, both pro and con, are attractive. Although the U.S. Supreme Court, in 1976, upheld the constitutionality of the death penalty for first degree murder in some instances, capital punishment will probably remain highly controversial among both scholars and the public. And even a clear pronouncement by the Supreme Court is not likely to resolve the academic debates.

Because the "cruel and unusual punishment" argument currently looms at the forefront of

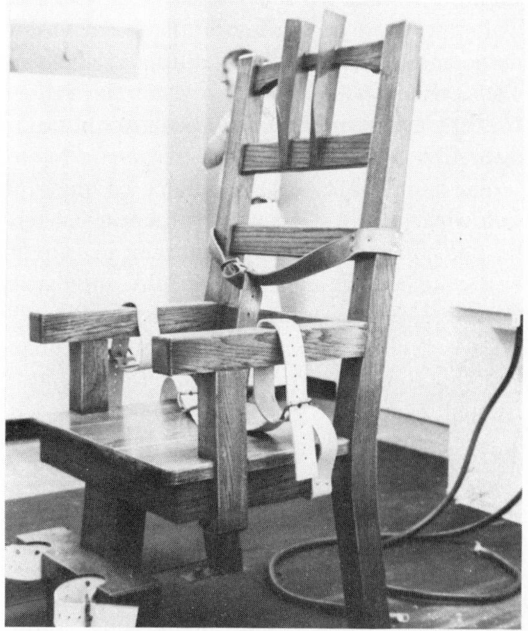

The electric chair.

the debate on capital punishment, we will discuss the historical interpretation of that provision of the Eighth Amendment by the Supreme Court.

"Cruel and Unusual Punishment" The constitutionality of capital punishment in America is inexorably intertwined with the Eighth Amendment prohibition against cruel and unusual punishment. In 1962, the Supreme Court held that this constitutional provision is applicable to the states,[110] but its scope has not, to date, been clearly delineated by the Court.

Historically, the Supreme Court has made several pronouncements on the issue of cruel and unusual punishment. It has held that the term "punishment" includes imprisonment,[111] the death penalty,[112] and a deprivation of citizenship.[113]

Almost from the beginning, the Supreme Court has stated that this provision of the Eighth Amendment does not lend itself to a precise definition. As noted by the Court, "The [Eighth] Amendment must draw its meaning from the evolving standards of decency that mark the progress of a maturing society."[114] Thus, this constitutional provision is a fluid concept apparently subject to reinterpretation over time.

The Supreme Court has indicated that the following factors determine whether a particular punishment is cruel and unusual: (1) whether the method of punishment is inherently cruel or severe,[115] (2) whether the punishment is excessive,[116] (3) whether the punishment is unacceptable to society,[117] and (4) whether the punishment is inflicted arbitrarily.[118]

Accordingly, the Supreme Court has said with regard to cruel and unusual punishments that:

1 It is unconstitutional to imprison a person merely on the ground of narcotics addiction.[119]

2 It is not cruel and unusual punishment to imprison people for being publicly drunk, even though they are alcoholics.[120]

3 The imposition of the death penalty by means of electrocution is not cruel and unusual.[121]

4 It is not cruel and unusual punishment to subject a defendant to electrocution a second time after the first attempt has failed.[122]

5 Public shooting as a means of execution is not cruel and unusual punishment.[123]

6 It is not unconstitutional, in some instances, for judges to hold people in contempt of court and order them to jail until they comply with an order of the court.[124]

7 A state statute which authorizes more severe sentences for habitual criminals is not unconstitutional.[125]

8 The loss of United States citizenship as punishment of one who had been convicted as a deserter and dishonorably discharged from the military service is cruel and unusual.[126]

9 A sentence of imprisonment *plus* a fine is not per se cruel and unusual punishment.[127]

10 Punishments of torture or unnecessary cruelty are unconstitutional.[128]

11 The imposition of a harsher sentence on one of several codefendants for the same offense is not cruel or unusual.[129]

The above list is not exhaustive, as the Supreme Court has touched on the issue of cruel and unusual punishment in at least twenty cases. However, it shows that the issue of such punishment is not limited to the death penalty. It is also clear that, at least until recently, the Supreme Court did not view the imposition of the death penalty as cruel and unusual. The pronouncement of the Supreme Court in *Furman v. Georgia* (1972)[130] did not, unfortunately, settle the issue of the constitutionality of the death penalty.

In *Furman,* each of the three defendants were black; they were convicted in a state court, after a trial by jury, and sentenced to death. Two of the defendants were convicted of rape and the other of murder. The Supreme Court reversed the state court judgments in each case and held, in a brief per curiam opinion expressing the view of five members of the Court, that "the imposition and carrying out of the death penalty *in these cases* constitutes cruel and unusual punishment in violation of the Eighth and Fourteenth Amendments."[131] Each of the nine justices wrote a separate opinion. A close reading of the nine opinions (covering 131 pages) indicates that the *Furman* decision did not resolve the issue of the constitutionality of capital punishment in the United States.

After *Furman,* thirty-five jurisdictions enacted revised capital punishment statutes providing for the imposition of the death penalty upon conviction in a limited number of offenses.[132] The legislative intent was obvious: to eliminate the apparent discrimination found by the majority of the Court in *Furman.* Only Justices Brennan and Marshall held that the imposition of the death penalty is per se unconstitutional; four of the justices were of the opinion that the death penalty *as presently applied* did not constitute cruel and unusual punishment. Therefore it seemed that any future decisions by the Court on the death penalty in the United States would rest with the votes of Justices White, Stewart, and Stevens (assuming that the opinions of the other justices remained constant).

During the 1975–1976 term, the Supreme Court granted certiorari in five cases in which the issue of capital punishment was again raised. The death penalty was upheld in three of the cases, in the states of Georgia, Texas, and Florida, where legislative guidelines were provided for either the jury or the judge during the sentencing process.[133] In a 7-to-2 decision, the Court held that the death penalty for murder is not per se cruel and unusual punishment provided that (1) there is controlled discretion on the part of the sentencing authority and (2) the rights of the defendant are protected against arbitrariness and caprice by appellate review. However, in 5-to-4 decisions, the Court struck down mandatory death statutes in Louisiana and North Carolina, holding that the history of mandatory capital punishment schemes in the United States reveals that the mandatory approach "has been rejected as unduly harsh and unworkably rigid" and that such schemes do not conform with the "evolving standards of decency" required under the Eighth Amendment.[134] Justices Brennan and Marshall adhered to the view that capital punishment is per se unconstitutional. The Court did not decide the issue of whether the death penalty is constitutional where (e.g., in cases of rape) the victim has not died.

There is one additional topic relevant to the sentencing process that deserves attention: allocution. We shall consider that next, before concluding this section.

Allocution At common law and in most jurisdictions today, a convicted defendant has a right to address the court personally prior to the imposition of sentence. This practice, known as *allocution,* is observed so that:

1 "[T]he defendant might be identified by the court as the real party adjudged guilty."
2 The defendant may have a chance to plead a pardon.
3 The defendant may move in arrest in judgment.
4 The defendant may have an opportunity to say why judgment should not be given against him or her.
5 The example of being brought up for the animadversion of the court and the open denunciation of punishment might tend to deter others from the commission of similar offenses."[135]

Rule 32(a) of the *Federal Rules of Criminal Procedure* governs the sentencing of federal defendants. That rule provides in part that "Before imposing sentence the court shall afford the defendant an opportunity to make a statement in his own behalf and to present any information in mitigation of punishment."

The U.S. Supreme Court has held that federal judges, before imposing sentence, should afford defendants an opportunity to make, in person and not merely through counsel, statements in their own behalf.[136] But the failure of a federal judge to address a defendant personally prior to sentencing is not an error of constitutional dimensions, and such errors are not cognizable in federal habeas corpus proceedings.[137] Presumably the procedural effect of a denial of allocution requires a remand of the case for resentencing.

After judgment and the imposition of a sentence, the defendant may appeal the decision of the court to a higher court, called an appellate court.

SUMMARY

In this chapter we discussed two major areas which have become integral albeit controversial parts of our system of criminal justice: plea bargaining and the sentencing process.

The plea-bargaining process accounts for 80 to 90 percent of convictions in the United States. A valid plea in open court has certain legal implications: (1) it is followed by a conviction, (2) it restricts the avenues of appeal in most jurisdictions, and (3) it constitutes a waiver of three important constitutional rights (the rights to trial, to confront witnesses, and to remain silent).

In order to encourage defendants to plead guilty, the prosecutor usually must offer the defendant a deal. Most often the prosecutor agrees to (1) a charge reduction, or (2) a charge dismissal, or (3) a sentence recommendation. However, other inducements are available to the prosecutor. Most defendants plead guilty to mitigate their punishment.

Although the plea-bargaining process has been both applauded and criticized, the U.S. Supreme Court has (in its dictum) approved of its constitutionality. However, the Court has insisted on certain safeguards to ensure that a guilty plea is a voluntary, intelligent, and knowing waiver of certain constitutional rights.

Following conviction, a defendant is sentenced. We indicated that few constitutional protections attend this stage of the criminal process. An appeal on the sentence itself is not permitted in most jurisdictions, and often the sentencing judge has little background information about the convicted defendant prior to sentencing. In addition, we noted that our present system of sentencing results in gross disparities that are often the product of the judge's personal moral philosophy. Several legal reforms in sentencing were noted.

We noted that there are three major *forms* of sentencing in the United States: (1) definite, (2) indefinite, and (3) indeterminate. Further, we indicated that the five major *types* of sentencing include (1) suspended sentences, (2) probation, (3) fines, (4) imprisonment, and (5) capital punishment.

The pros and cons of capital punishment were stated and the Supreme Court's recent pronouncements on the death penalty were discussed.

Following sentencing, a defendant has a right to appeal a conviction in every jurisdiction, although the dictum of the Supreme Court has suggested that the right to appeal is not of a constitutional dimension.

In the next chapter we will take up some important concepts that underlie the correctional process: probation, pardon, and parole.

Chapter 13

Probation, Parole, and Pardon

Since the days of ancient Rome—when the law provided that if a condemned man encountered a vestal virgin en route to the gallows, his life was to be spared—the law has contained a variety of provisions for the imposition and mitigation of sentences. Persons convicted of crimes in the United States may (1) be placed on *probation* instead of being incarcerated, (2) be *paroled* prior to the maximum expiration of their prison sentences and released from prison under supervision, (3) have their sentences and/or fines *suspended* or *commuted* to a lesser term of years, or (4) receive a full or conditional *pardon*, which usually carries with it the restoration of civil liberties. A fifth method of mitigating the full force of legal sanctions deals with groups rather than individuals and is called *amnesty* (group pardon).

13.01 HISTORICAL BACKGROUND OF PROBATION

To avoid a mechanical and mindless application of the punitive criminal law, there have evolved a number of legal practices which lend flexibility to its requirements. Here the common thread is the idea of a conditional suspension of punishment dependent upon "good behavior."

These legal devices assume that the individual offender is capable of *social rehabilitation;* they reflect the broader cultural trend, initiated during the Enlightenment, away from a purely punitive response and toward the *humanitarian treatment* of offenders.

One of the first methods used for this purpose arose in the thirteenth century.[1] Criminals could "secure sanctuary" by seeking refuge in a church for 40 days, after which they were forced to leave the area by a designated road or port. By the sixteenth century, the practice had been altered so that a criminal who secured sanctuary might be compelled to remain in an assigned region for life, having the name of the locality branded on a thumb. In the later part of the fifteenth century, certain offenses—such as murder, rape, burglary, and arson—no longer carried the right of sanctuary. The entire sanctuary concept disappeared with the break-up of the monasteries.

A second early system for the mitigation of penalties grew out of the ecclesiastical courts and reflected the influence of religion upon law in the Middle Ages. The Church demanded a "right of clergy," by which it sought to try its own officers. In practice, this was primarily a device to avoid capital punishment; church courts were not permitted to impose the death penalty and, except in heresy and witchcraft, generally imposed less severe penalties than did secular courts. The designation of those who qualified as clergy evolved from a strict definition of the term to include, eventually, all who could read, literacy being defined as the ability to comprehend the first verse of Psalm 51: "Have mercy upon me God, according to thy loving kidness: according unto the multitude of thy tender mercies blot out my transgressions."

Finally this right was extended to the peers of those who could read. Thus, those who shared cultural similarities to the lawmakers were exempt from the more stringent penalties. Although the absolute number of persons who could claim the right of clergy increased, the number of times one could claim this right and the number of offenses for which the right could be claimed were reduced. The application of the law gradually came to be little different for those under the protection of the right of clergy than for those in the general society. By the eighteenth century, with the religious sector's loss of dominance over the secular community, the right of clergy meant nothing.

An early English device which is a forerunner of today's probation was the English courts' practice of releasing minor offenders on their *own recognizance*. This procedure—with or without the addition of sureties (or bail)—is of major historical importance in the evolution of probation, for it adhered to the fundamental principles of probation: (1) suspension of penalty, (2) conditions, and (3) supervision.

13.02 ORIGIN OF PROBATION IN THE UNITED STATES

Probation as we know it in this modern era began in the state of Massachusetts.[2] When offenders received suspended sentences or were released on their own recognizance, volunteers began to assist them during the time of their suspended sentences. The most famous of these volunteers was John Augustus, a Boston cobbler, who began his career, while in attendance at the local police court, by offering to put up bail for a chronic drunkard. When the defendant reappeared after 3 weeks, the judge was so impressed with his sobriety and apparent rehabilitation that he imposed only a nominal fine of 1 cent and costs ($3.75). Thus the man avoided serving time in the House of Correction. For the next 17 years, Augustus acted as surety for over two thousand men and women and had a high proportion of successes. He is generally considered the first probation officer.

The first legal provision for probation officers to be employed by a state was the Massachusetts law of 1878. Under this act the mayor of Boston was authorized to hire a probation officer and the municipal court was allowed to place offenders on probation. In 1880, the legislature extended this authority to all mayors of the state; by 1891, it had become mandatory for lower-court judges to appoint probation officers.[3]

By 1925, all states had juvenile probation

laws; but it was not until 1956 that they all had similar laws for adult offenders as well (Mississippi was the last state to pass a law creating an adult probation department). Probation had existed in Mississippi prior to 1956, but then it was handled by the welfare department.[4]

The creation of a federal probation law did not come until almost fifty years after Massachusetts had pioneered this innovative concept. Thirty states and at least twelve countries already had probation laws before the federal probation laws for adults were passed in 1925. A sort of probation had existed in the forms of the sentence suspension practiced by U.S. district courts (federal trial courts), but this practice was frowned upon by the U.S. Department of Justice, which saw the suspension of sentence as an infringement on executive pardoning power and therefore as unconstitutional.[5] The position of the federal courts was that the power to suspend sentence had been exercised continuously by federal judges for many years and was the only ameliorative device available to them as long as there was no federal probation system.

The U.S. Supreme Court settled the constitutional aspects of the controversy in 1916, when it handed down its decision in *Ex parte United States* (242 U.S. 27). In a unanimous opinion delivered by Chief Justice Edward D. White, the Court held that Federal courts had no inherent power to suspend sentence indefinitely and that there was no reason nor right:

> To continue a practice which is inconsistent with the Constitution since its exercise in the very nature of things amounts to a refusal by the judicial power to perform a duty resting upon it and, as a consequence thereof, to an interference with both the legislative and executive authority as fixed by the Constitution.

As a remedy for this situation, probation legislation was suggested. But efforts to enact a probation law met with roadblocks never envisioned by its advocates. Finding a plan that would satisfy an entire nation proved far more difficult than finding a uniform plan for a single state. The concept was new and judges as well as members of Congress had only a fuzzy understanding of it; they would on occasion say "parole" when they meant "probation." Some judges saw no need for probation, arguing that the uniformity and severity of punishment would serve as a sufficient deterrent against crime.

The Volstead Act (prohibition amendment), passed by Congress in 1919, made it difficult to gain support for a probation law. Prohibitionists, then in control of Congress, were suspicious of any action which might enable judges to place violators of the prohibition law back on the streets rather than in jail. (Some idea of the zeal of prohibitionists can be gained by noting that the South Carolina legislature passed a law prohibiting the manufacture of men's trousers with pockets large enough to conceal a whiskey flask.) Prohibitionists in the Congress introduced a bill which provided for a prison sentence for everyone convicted of drinking.

Others opposed the passage of a probation law (the federal parole system had been established in 1919) on the grounds that it would fill the streets with lawbreakers and was just another soft-headed attempt to turn courts into reform associations. Nevertheless, proponents of a probation law were able to win support for their position by arguing the value of individualized treatment and—perhaps a more powerful argument—the economic advantages. Finally, 47 years after the enactment of the Massachusetts probation law, the federal courts were provided with similar legislation. Advocates of probation have argued that it is an enlightened form of individualized treatment; opponents of the concept describe probation as a form of unrealistic leniency; and the probationers themselves often complain that it is simply another form of punishment. What is the essential nature of probation?

13.03 PROBATION: TREATMENT OR PUNISHMENT?

Probation is a combination of both treatment and punishment. It is a legal disposition: An offender is sentenced to serve time on probation. At the same time, it is a process of treatment in the context of community-based corrections. Ideally, offenders receive guidance and counseling in an attempt to ensure their adjustment to free society. In reality, probation is punitive because restrictions are placed on the probationer. (Many authorities would deny the punitive aspects and would argue that all their policies are rehabilitative.)

Three methods of implementing probation are used: (1) the law may allow the trial judge to suspend the execution of sentence and place the offender on conditional probation; (2) a state statute may, on the other hand, require sentencing but permit the suspension of imposition; or (3) both alternatives may be left to the discretion of the trial judge.[7] When the judge has suspended the imposition of sentencing, violation of probation often results in a stiffer prison sentence than would originally have been imposed. By definition, probation implies that the offender has not served time in a penitentiary (at least on the offense at issue); the courts thus have little jurisdiction over parole except in matters of procedural due process. Courts normally cannot order a person to serve time in the state penitentiary and then set the date of release on parole.

Some states do allow judges to utilize "split sentencing" or "shock sentencing." Offenders are placed on probation with the stipulation that they be confined for a portion of their probationary period. The assumption is that a "taste of confinement" or the "shock" might lead to a modification of behavior.[8]

Unlike those subject to the federal "split sentence" provision, offenders in Ohio are sentenced to correctional institutions and must then file a petition to the court to suspend execution of sentence. The decision regarding early release is entirely up to the court, and early release may also be granted at the judge's initiative. In one study (575 cases) designed to determine who receives early release from incarceration, researchers found race to be the most important factor, followed by education and recommendations from the probation department. White felons who have been convicted of narcotics violations and who have some college education stand the best chance of early release on shock probation. It appears that, in the administration of justice, some offenders are more equal than others.[9] As to the effectiveness of this approach, of 1,674 inmates released on shock probation between 1966 and 1970, only about 10 percent have been reinstitutionalized.[10] Success rates on probation are due in part to the type of supervision offenders are given. We will now examine the complicated roles of probation officers.

The twin objectives of probation—protection of the community and rehabilitation of the offender—create a dilemma and role conflict for the probation officer.

Unlike the private counselor—e.g., privately retained psychiatrist—who operates as a fee-for-service entrepreneur and whose counseling is accomplished under the legally protective cloak of patient-client privilege, the probationer and probation officer are legally thrust into a potentially intimate relationship. The label of "client" for a probationer in this situation is a euphemism of the first order. Each participant—officer and probationer—defines the situation differently.

The probationer brings to the "counseling/supervision" situation a natural apprehension. Sitting on the other side of the desk is an official representative of the criminal justice system who has the power to further restrict the probationer's freedom and possibly initiate probation revocation preceedings which could result in a trip to the penitentiary. This is hardly a situation to inspire trust.[11] As one probationer put it, "A probation officer is just a wolf in sheep's clothing."

The probation officer is also apprehensive about the encounter. Will the probationer be cooperative or, by violating the conditions of probation, cause trouble? Past experience may put the officer on the defensive not to be conned and to watch for signs of rebelliousness on the part of the "client."

Given the ambiguity of their roles, there are two polar positions probation officers may take to reduce their anxiety. First, probation officers may see themselves as authority figures who can control probationers simply by showing them "who's boss." The structure of their interaction is defined by the legislatively enacted condition of probation. Given this role, the probation officer explains the rules firmly, issues a paternalistic admonition to "be good," and may end the interview with the old saw: "If you work with me, I'll work with you."

On the other hand, the probation officer may reject the role of authority figure and assume that of a helpful friend. From this stance, rules are seen as relatively unimportant and the probationer's approval as all-important. In effect, the probationer now controls the probation officer, for the latter can withdraw approval at any time. The "helpful friend" approach means that the probation officer will suppress any critical remarks or even overlook violations of probation rather than risk incurring the probationer's disfavor and perhaps damaging their "counseling relationship."

A middle position between these unsatisfactory extremes would be for the probation officer to try to show the client that power or dominance is not the issue but that, within the limitations of their legal relationship, the officer would like to find ways to help the probationer complete the terms of probation successfully. Reality is that the probation officer is a counselor-cop (or vice-versa), and it is always best to face reality.

Stratton points out that it is possible to turn a probationary interview into a session in which it is the officer who, perhaps unconsciously, cons the probationer.[12] When is a probation officer doing a con job? First, when the officer hides behind the bureaucratic wall and interprets rules and regulations in a manner that leaves no room for a meaningful relationship with those who are being supervised. Here, the probation officer assumes a role of detached noninvolvement, a "better than you" attitude. Then probationers find themselves interacting with rules rather than a fellow human being.

The probation officer may con clients with the "indirect no" by verbalizing interest at first and then finding some excuse not to become involved. A example would be, "I'd like to talk to your father" (interest) "but I only work until five" (the indirect no). Another self-deception is for the probation officer to become pseudo-hip by affecting street language, out-of-sight platform shoes, mod hairstyles, and elaborate handshake rituals that are not a true reflection of the officer's background and values. It is a dishonest image.

Then the probation officer may use the interview time to discuss social pleasantries, so as to get through the day without ever coming to grips with what is really happening to the probationer's life, feelings, and attitudes. It is "safer" to discuss the weather than to encourage an honest expression of thoughts and feelings. The probation officer is not responsible for the weather.

Finally, the probation officer may allow probationers to let appointments slip by, to miss restitution payments, and to delegate job-hunting tasks to others. Such attitudes reinforce dependency rather than initiative and responsibility.

Changes in the criminal justice system have brought changes in the various roles and expectations of the probation officer. Czajkoski has written about the various roles played by the probation officer. In addition to being a counselor, the probation officer also, according to

Czajkoski, functions as a judge, prosecutor, jailer-at-large, and criminal investigator.[13]

The probation officer has traditionally served a quasijudicial role in making sentencing recommendations to the judge. Various studies have shown a high correlation between the recommendations of the probation officer and the final disposition by the judge[14] (in some cases as high as 95 percent). One reason for this compatibility is the probation officers' practice of anticipating the judge's desires (or biases) and slanting their recommendations in that direction. A probation officer soon learns that it is pointless to recommend probation for a drunken driver if the judge is still angrily recalling the demolition of his own car by a drunken driver.

Czajkoski sees the emergence of a new role for probation officers with the more open practice of plea bargaining. Formerly plea bargaining was a kind of charade in which the defendant made a deal "offstage" to plead guilty to a lesser charge and then, for the benefit of the record, denied that any promises had been made.

Plea bargaining is now openly acknowledged by the Supreme Court, which had held that plea inducements are generally compatible with the goals of the criminal justice system. Czajkoski observes "it is evident that the judge's role in sentencing has shrunk almost to that of a mere announcer."[15] In reality, it is the prosecutor, the chief plea bargainer, who largely determines the sentence. Some prosecutors' offices have produced handbooks to help young assistant district attorneys fix sentences through bargaining. As these guidelines are based on the crime committed and not the individual characteristics of the offender, they represent a move away from the correctional philosophy of individualized justice.

Theoretically, the probation officer is supposed to make sentencing recommendations to the judge based on an estimate of offender's potential for rehabilitation. Now, according to Czajkoski, if probation is granted it is mainly a function of the offender's success in plea bargaining. With this change has come a change in the role of the probation officer.

The probation officer's job is to "cool out the mark"—to convince the offender that the decision to plea bargain was wise. In effect, the probation officer certifies the bargain.

In addition to being of help in sentencing and plea bargaining, the probation officer serves as something of a jailer-at-large by supervising probationers to protect the community. This role involves the talents of a criminal investigator, as the officer must discover if probation violations and/or crimes have been committed by those under supervision.

Despite changes in the administration of justice and the rising importance of the prosecutor's office, one of the probation officer's major social-work functions is the preparation of a presentence report.

13.04 THE PRESENTENCE REPORT

Information secured in a presentence investigation can be utilized at every stage in the administration of criminal justice: (1) by the courts in determining the appropriate sentence, (2) by the prison classification team in assigning custody and treatment, (3) by the parole board in deciding when the offender is ready to return to the community, (4) by the probation and parole officers as they help the parolee adjust to the community, and (5) by correctional researchers as they try to locate those variables which are associated with success on probation.[16]

The primary purpose of the presentence investigation is not to determine the guilt or innocence of the defendant, which has already been determined legally, but to give anyone who may be working with these people insights into their personalities and some understanding of the social milieu which produced them.

Some type of presentence investigation should be made in every case (at least in felony convictions), for to sentence offenders without regard to their unique personalities is like prescribing medicine without a preliminary diagnosis. Objectivity is a must in the preparation of the presentence report; the probation officer must see things as they are and not as one might wish them to be. Under our adversary system of justice, the district attorney and the defense counsel are committed to particular points of view, but the preparer of the presentence report is free to include all facts pertinent to the case.

Included in the report should be an official description of the offense and the defendant's own version of the events; statements of codefendants; the defendant's prior record; the defendant's family and marital history; a description of the neighborhood in which the defendant was reared; and facts regarding the defendant's education, religion, mental and physical health both past and present, employment history, and military service record. All these items are essential if the probation officer is to present a complete picture of the defendant. The officer may choose to include other optional data—such as "attitude of defendant toward arresting officers," and "amount of bond"—if this information seems to add substantially to the report.

The evaluative summary is the most difficult and significant aspect of the presentence report. It is here that professional probation officers are separated from mere fact-gathering clerks. It requires considerable analytical skill and understanding of human behavior to interpret the cold facts in a presentence report and on that basis make a meaningful recommendation to the court. A presentence report can be no better than the skills of the investigating probation officer. Many judges ask for recommendations for sentencing alternatives or—if the defendant is to be placed on probation—recommendations regarding the treatment plan that should be inaugurated. Offenders who are placed on probation do not just go "Scot free" but must abide by general and special conditions of probation.

13.05 PROBATION AND PAROLE CONDITIONS

Even though probation is managed by the courts and parole by an executive department of government, the general and special conditions are similar. The conditions of probation and parole are usually fixed jointly by the legislature, the court, and the probation and parole department. Some of these regulations are fixed by statute and affect all persons under supervision. These laws are usually general in nature and involve such reasonable conditions as admonishing the probationer to live a law-abiding life, not to leave the state without the court's consent, to report periodically to the probation or parole officer, and, perhaps, to pay the court costs.

Unique conditions may be applied according to the individual case. For example, an offender may be required to leave the county, to return home, to support minor offspring, to make restitution to the victim, or to attend meetings of Alcoholics Anonymous. Younger offenders may find themselves "encouraged" to join the Marines; this is a tactic for "giving the problem away."

Some conditions of probation and parole may be unfair and unrealistic. When this occurs, the probation officer may choose to enforce them selectively, thereby muting their effect in the interest of common sense justice. In the application of the required conditions, the concerned probation officer will ask: Are these rules reasonable? Are they effective? Do they serve the best interests of the individual and the community?

13.06 REVOCATION OF PROBATION

Similar to the disparities in sentencing are the disparities of the revocation of probation. Criteria for revoking probation are not uniform throughout the country and not even among judges in the same district court. The legal aspects of probation and parole revocation hearings will be taken up in Chapter 16.

Conditions of probation should be realistic and applied flexibly. Unrealistic conditions of probation only frustrate the offender further and may lead to additional violations. It is pointless to demand an excessive fine or restitution from an individual when financial problems were the genesis of the difficulty. To insist on compulsory church attendance or attempt to enforce total abstention from alcohol may only arouse the probationer's resentment. Conditions of probation should be guidelines that help the probationer lead a law-abiding life, not rigid vows of chastity and obedience which only the most disciplined cloistered monk could endure.

When a probationer violates the conditions of probation, care should be taken to determine whether the violation was the result of unrealistic probation rules or an arrogant and indifferent attitude on the part of the probationer. The probation officer should ask: To what extent is this violation reflective of deeper hostile attitudes? Or is it just symptomatic of the sort of floundering people do when they are trying to find themselves? Probation officers should be careful to remain objective and not revoke probationers because of a personal dislike for an argumentative "client." This writer has heard probation officers brag about being "out to get" a probationer they felt had not shown them proper "respect."

Revocation is justified only when probationers defy an order of the court or when they become threats to the community. In cases involving restitution, when probationers are sentenced to imprisonment, the victims of their crimes suffer the entire loss. Few violations should result in an automatic revocation of probation. One guideline question to ask is: How would we have responded to this act had the person not been on probation? For example, we do not sentence people to jail for losing or quitting their jobs. All violations should be judged in the light of the probationer's total adjustment to society.

13.07 SUCCESS RATES ON PROBATION

Advocates of probation justify its continued use on two central grounds: (1) that probation is an effective means of individual treatment and (2) that it is a tax bargain for the state. We will examine each of these assertions.

It is generally argued that it costs the state ten times as much to keep people in prison as it would to place them on probation. Nationally, the average cost of maintaining a prisoner is $10 a day (1975), the low being $1.90 (in Mississippi) and the high $23.69 (in Montana).[18] Nationally, the cost of placing 100 people in prison for a year would be $365,000; if these people were placed on probation, assuming a caseload of thirty-three per supervisor, the bill to the taxpayers could drop to approximately $35,000. The cost of imprisonment is so high in Montana there could be a different probation officer for each probationer. At the other extreme, Mississippi apparently has discovered how to keep people alive on a subsistence level, and the economic argument would have to be replaced with one based on humanitarian concerns.

Table 13-1 Cost per Day and by Year of Maintaining Prisoners (1975)

	Daily	Yearly
Nationally	$10.00	$3,650.00
Mississippi (lowest)	$ 1.90	$ 693.50
Montana (highest)	$23.69	$8,646.85

Source: Adapted from K. Lenihan, "The Financial Condition of Released Prisoners," *Crime and Delinquency*, July 1975, pp. 266-281.

Not only is probation less expensive from a supervision standpoint, but persons on probation and parole pay taxes, make restitution to victims, pay fines, and support dependents who might otherwise be on welfare. In Florida, for example, during 1968, persons under supervision paid over $6 million in taxes and made restitution to victims in the amount of $155,000.[19] There is considerable justification then, for the claim by probation and parole departments that their services represent one of the greatest bargains purchased by society's tax dollar. Granted that probation is less expensive than incarceration, is it effective?

Success on probation may be measured by a number of alternate measures ranging from percentage of probationers who have their probation revoked for technical violations to percentage of those who commit a subsequent misdemeanor or felony. The Florida Probation and Parole Commission's annual report (1968) boasted that from the beginning of its operation in 1941, 88 out every 100 persons placed on probation had successfully completed probation.[20] In Louisiana, of 9,092 offenders on probation and parole during 1973, only 83 had their parole or probation revoked by the commission of new felony. This figure must be placed in the context of each probation officer averaging a caseload of eighty-six, which means only minimal supervision.[21]

England analyzed the outcomes of eleven probation studies and found a success rate of from 60 to 90 percent.[22] In California, 11,683 adult probationers were followed up after 7 years, and 72 percent were found to be successful in terms of not having had their probation revoked.[23] While these figures are encouraging as to the successful adjustment of people placed on probation, there are some thorns in these official roses.

It would seem that any probationer committing a felony would automatically be subject to parole revocation. In a study of 814 federal offenders placed on probation between the years 1946 and 1960, however, Vasoli discovered that 155 of 622 probationers officially listed as successes had committed at least one felony during the probationary period. This failure to revoke was not the result of laxity on the part of the federal probation officers but occurred because these were federal probationers imprisoned for state offenses. Rather than filing detainers against them, the probation officers would terminate, surrendering jurisdiction to the state. District officers, in their monthly statistical reports, would fail to indicate why probation had been terminated; therefore the cases would be counted as successes. This errant system has been rectified somewhat by FBI "flash no-

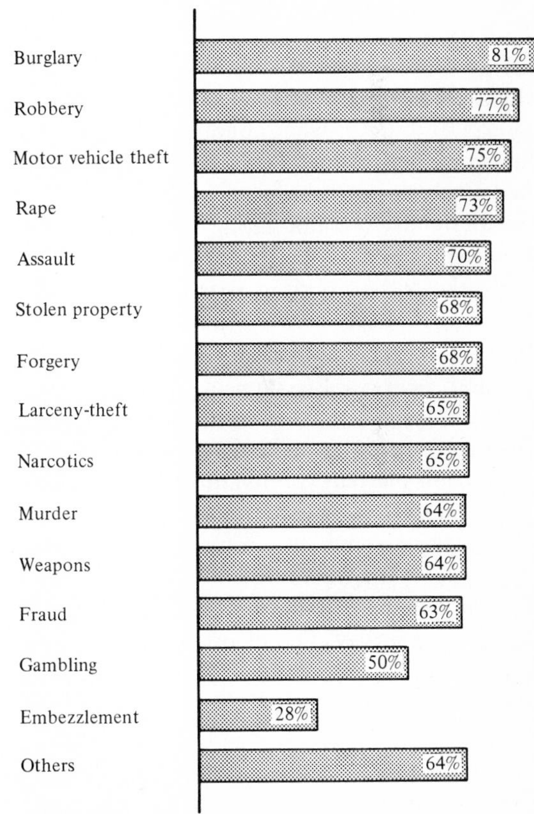

Figure 13-1 Percent of repeaters by type of crime in 1972. (Persons released in 1972 and rearrested within four years.)

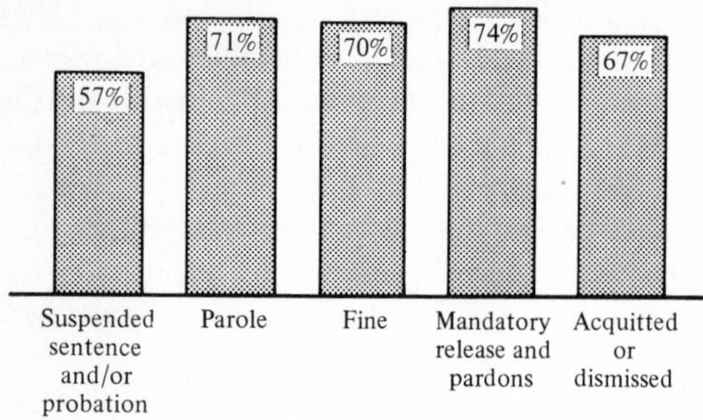

Figure 13-2 Percent of persons rearrested with four years by type of release in 1972.

tices." It is still possible, however, for offenses committed by probationers to go unrecorded in national statistics.[24]

The central issue of this discussion remains this: What types of offenders succeed on probation and under what conditions? In general, as people grow older they are correspondingly less likely to be rearrested. Aging is still the most effective "rehabilitating" factor in corrections, since crime takes energy. Maybe the formula should be "With increased physical debilitation, there is increased social rehabilitation." There is also a significant relationship between the type of offense and the probability of a rearrest: for example, embezzlers (older people) make good probation risks, while auto thieves (youths) do not. See Figures 13-1 and 13-2.

To determine whether probation, in practice, conforms to the high ideals it espouses in theory, the American Bar Association conducted a nationwide survey. The report listed the following criticisms:

1 Probation was granted without sufficient knowledge of the defendant and his background.

2 Presentation reports often may contain a bias either for or against the offender.

3 Sentencing sometimes becomes a public spectacle.

4 Probation is often used to clear the docket, to induce the defendant to plead guilty, and to alleviate crowded prison conditions.

5 Probation is often used as a collection agency to induce payment of fines, restitution, and alimony.

6 Cost of probation is sometimes borne by the probationer—in effect a "probation tax." The offender pays for the "privilege."

7 Probation officer's recommendations were ignored, neglected, or overruled in many jurisdictions.

8 There was inadequate supervision of probationers on the part of probation officers due to heavy caseloads or apathy.

9 There was an over-identification on the part of the probation officer with the social-work expectations of his role to the neglect of law-enforcement responsibilities.

10 There was inadequate and unreliable statistical research, making it nearly impossible to discover the success or failure of the system.[25]

Despite these shortcomings, probation remains a superior method of dealing with many offenders, especially as opposed to incarceration in a dehumanizing institution. Whenever practical, men and women should be treated in relative freedom. It is axiomatic that to function as a "normal" person, one must live in a relatively normal environment. Institutionalization should be utilized only when the offenders are dangerous to themselves and/or the community.

13.08 METHODS OF RELEASE FROM PRISON

Approximately 98 percent of all persons sent to prison will eventually be returned to free society. The question then, is not *whether* we will

Table 13-2 Savings of All Inmates Released in One Eastern State from March 1, 1972, to February 28, 1973

Savings	Number of releasees	Percentage of total released
$ 20 or less	479	17
$ 21-$50	1,115	39
$ 51-$100	523	18
$101-$150	212	8
$151-$200	97	3
$201-$300	126	4
$301-$400	77	3
Over $400	221	8
Total	2,850	100%

release offenders from prison but rather under what circumstances we will release them. Release may occur through expiration of sentence (serving "day for day"), commutation of sentence, reduction of time by earning "good time," parole, pardon, or successful appeal of conviction.

Sentences may be either determinate (fixed), indeterminate (1 day to life), or mixed (e.g., not less than 5 or more than 10 years). At one time criminologists who were attempting to individualize treatment felt that a strict indeterminate sentence was preferable for all offenders. The sentence, then, bore no relationship to the offense. Just as you do not "sentence" an individual to a hospital for a term of months per disease (a strict 2 years for cancer, regardless of progress toward health), so an offender was to be sentenced to prison until "rehabilitation" had been achieved. It was similar to medical reasoning—the so-called medical model. Although it was logical on its face, it has created a multitude of frustrations and inequities.

In practice, the indeterminate sentence can be oppressive. The inmate is punished for behavior in prison rather than for the crime. The sentence can be constantly reset if the inmate does not make what the board of corrections or parole board feels is appropriate progress. The system of indeterminate sentences is unpopular with inmates because of the uncertainty of their release date. Students may be able to gain some rapport with the situation of an inmate serving an indeterminate sentence if they imagine that, instead of completing a specifically outlined number of required courses, they had to take courses until a faculty board decided they "knew enough" for a college degree. The present writers feel a better approach (for most offenders) would be to diagnose what social skills were lacking in the repertoires of social responses available to the offender, to sentence the inmate to an institution until specific requirements had been completed (e.g., finish high school, serve at least 6 months with no disciplinary writeups, attend group counseling for a specified period), and then release the inmate under supervision. There is no guarantee that institutional adjustments will mean the released person will "go straight," but it is the principal criterion for release that is available to us.

Juvenile "commitments" are quasi-indeterminate; it is possible to keep delinquents in institutions until they reach their majority, normally at age twenty-one. Release of the criminally insane and of defective delinquents usually depends on the judgment of the medical profession; it is not strictly a matter regulated by the criminal law.

Prerelease Centers

If deep-sea or scuba divers surface immediately from a great depth, they experience severe cramps known as "the bends." Similarly, after being immersed in the confining atmosphere of a "total institution" (the Army, a religious order, or a prison), an individual suddenly released to the autonomy of the "free world" may experience what might be termed "psychological bends."

To ease the reentry of inmates into society, a number of modern prison systems have adopted the concept of the prerelease center. These centers are typically located within or near the institution. Here inmates spend their last month prior to release preparing for a society which may have changed dramatically during their time in prison. Some of the courses provided are as follows:

1 A driver-education course through which inmates obtain their licenses.

2 Discussions of dress styles led by a representative of the clothing industry so that inmates may have some idea of contemporary fashion.

3 Individual and group counseling sessions which address themselves to such potentially incendiary topics as: How will you react if you discover your wife/husband has been unfaithful?

4 Talks by representatives from groups like Alcoholics Anonymous, the department of welfare, insurance agents, banks, schools, and religious organizations.

If the center is funded federally through vocational rehabilitation, the inmate receives aid in obtaining a job, maintenance money, and transportation to his or her new home. "Maintenance money" is a broader concept than the traditional "gate money" ($10 and some new clothes); it represents a response to the total needs of the newly freed person. The benefits of a prerelease center are obvious. However, in many instances, only inmates granted parole (the "best risks") go through the prerelease center. "Flat timers" (those who have served their entire sentences) leave the institution with nominal gate money and a handshake. Thus, we have a situation in which those offenders considered most likely to be repeaters are given the least aid. Then, should the offender return (having committed a second crime), administrators can congratulate themselves with an "I told you he was a poor risk!" It is a self-fulfilling prophecy worthy of *Alice in Wonderland.*

Table 13-3 Summary of Gate Money Amounts, by Number of States–1971

Amount	Gate money regardless of savings	Gate money as a supplement to savings	Neither
Less than $20	9	1	
$20-$29	13	6	
$30-$39	2	–	
$40-$49	3	–	
$50-$59	6	2	
$60 or more	3	4	
Neither gate money nor a supplement			2
Total	36	13	2

Most of the offenders who enter prison are poor and lack any salable work skills. When they leave prison, they come out the same way. There is one difference, Now, in addition to being poor and without skills, they are ex-convicts. Every year over 80,000 men and women are released from state prisons in the United States. According to one estimate 40 to 60 percent of these persons will return for additional incarceration, the majority within 2 years of release.[26]

States use two methods to provide those who are released from prison with money. The first is an outright grant of a small amount—usually around $25—upon release. The other method is to supplement the prisoner's savings. Besides gate money, many states provide clothing and transportation. Releasees may be given bus tickets home or, if they are from out of state, bus tickets to the state line. In Connecticut, parolees are picked up by their parole officers and driven home. In Texas, only parolees (as opposed to flat timers) receive free transportation.

One of the "pains of imprisonment" is that there is little or no opportunity to acquire any substantial assets. The inmate's most common wage is between 50 cents and $1 per day. In many cases, the inmate must purchase toiletries

Table 13-4 States That Provide Transportation and Clothing—1971

	Number	States
Provide both transportation and clothing	36	Alabama, Arizona, Alaska, Colorado, Connecticut, District of Columbia, Florida, Georgia, Illinois, Indiana, Iowa, Kansas, Kentucky, Louisiana, Maine, Michigan, Mississippi, Missouri, Nebraska, New Hampshire, New Mexico, New York, North Carolina, North Dakota, Ohio, Oklahoma, Pennsylvania, South Carolina, South Dakota, Tennessee, Texas, Vermont, Virginia, Washington, Wisconsin, Wyoming
Provide clothing only	9	Hawaii, Idaho, Massachusetts, Minnesota, Montana, Nevada, New Jersey, Rhode Island, Utah
Provide transportation only	3	California, Delaware, West Virginia
Provide neither transportation nor clothing	3	Arkansas, Maryland, Oregon
Total	51	

Note: If the inmates pay for transportation or clothing out of their own money (gate money or other resources), the state is classified as "not providing such", even though the money is intended to cover the costs of transportation or clothing.

and cigarettes out of this money. There are some other sources of income for inmates, such as blood donations, medical experiments, and craft work. Then too, some inmates "strong-arm" their weaker companions into paying for the privilege of living there. They sell "insurance" to the weaker inmates to protect them from "slipping in the shower or falling down the stairs." Other deviant means of gaining money might include selling dope or gal-boys (passive homosexuals, also called "punks"). In Texas, inmates receive $5 a day for participating as subjects in medical research; in Illinois, inmates who volunteer to serve as research subjects in a malaria hospital are paid $50 a month. The use of inmates as medical guinea pigs is being phased out, however.

Most inmates who have savings have accumulated their money from jobs on work release, not from prison earnings. Work release began with the enactment of the Huber Law in Wisconsin in 1913. Other states did not follow suit until after World War II. Forty states now have work-release programs; however, less than 2 percent of inmates are ever on work release, and then usually for only 90 to 180 days before they leave prison. These programs represent a source of income for only a fraction of the inmate population; they constitute an almost negligible part of the institutional experience.[27]

When released prisoners are eligible for state welfare assistance, they usually receive emergency aid for only a day or two (half this time is spent waiting in lines and filling out forms). In eighteen states, loans are sometimes available from inmate welfare funds, but most institutions make loans to only three or four people per year. Michigan and Wisconsin are exceptions, furnishing loans to between 300 and 400 releasees.

Table 13-5 Inmate Wages From Institutional Earnings*—1971

	Number	States
No institutional earnings	6	Alabama, Florida, Georgia, Maine, Mississippi, Texas
Less than 50 cents a day	17	Colorado, District of Columbia (institutional work), Illinois, Indiana, Kansas, Louisiana, Massachusetts, Michigan, Montana, Nevada, New Jersey, North Carolina, North Dakota, Oklahoma, Virginia, West Virginia, Wyoming
50 cents to $1 a day	21	California, Connecticut, Delaware, Idaho, Iowa, Kentucky, Maryland, Minnesota, Missouri, Nebraska, New Hampshire, New York, North Dakota, Ohio, Pennsylvania, Rhode Island, South Carolina, South Dakota, Tennessee, Utah, Vermont
More than $1 a day	9	Alaska, Arizona, Arkansas, District of Columbia (prison industries), Hawaii, Illinois, New Mexico, Oregon, Washington
Total	53†	

*Institutional earnings are defined as jobs within or connected with prison maintenance or prison industries. Crafts and hobby items, sold at a piece rate, and blood donations are not included.

†Illinois and the District of Columbia are each included in two categories since they have two distinct wage ranges.

13.09 PAROLE

Parole is the conditional release, under supervision, of an offender from a correctional institute after a portion of the sentence has been served. The word is taken from the French and is used in the sense of *parole d' honneur,* or "word of honor." The concept has its roots in military history, referring to the practice of releasing a captured soldier on his *parole* (i.e., his word of honor that he would not again take up arms against his captors). Similarly, inmates are released to free society on their *parole,* or word of honor, that they will not again become enemies of society. Parole differs from probation because the former implies that the offender has "served time." Administratively, parole is a function of the executive branch of government, while probation is a judicial function of the court. Selection, supervision, regulations, revocation, and release procedures are similar, and the two kinds of conditional release are often confused by the public.

13.10 HISTORY OF PAROLE

Prisoners have always been released upon the arrival of their "mandatory release date." That is, sentences normally have a termination date. In inmate jargon, this is referred to as serving "flat time" or "day for day." Parole is a conditional release. Inmates who appear to be making genuine progress toward rehabilitation are selected to serve a final portion of their sentence, under some form of supervision, in the community.

Historical precedent for the modern practice of conditional release under supervision may be found in at least four areas: (1) the system of indenture and "transportation" in the eighteenth and nineteenth centuries, (2) Alexander Maconochie's "ticket of leave" system, (3) the Irish system which had incorporated the marks system, and (4) the prisoner aid societies which did philanthropic work with ex-convicts in the United States.

The practice of indenture, or binding children from institutions over to their employers, dates back to 1562 and originally had no relationship to the treatment of criminals. The terms of a contract of indenture are similar to the conditions of modern parole. For example, consider the conditions imposed upon Benjamin Franklin when he was indentured to his brother, as quoted by Newman from Van Doren's biography of Franklin:

> . . . During which term the said apprentice his master faithfully shall or will serve, his secrets keep, his lawful demands everywhere gladly do . . . At cards or dice tables or any other unlawful game he shall not play. Matrimony he shall not contract nor from the services of his master day or night absent himself but in all things as an honest faithful apprentice shall and will demean and behave himself toward said master all during said term.[28]

Through this method, children could earn their discharge from indenture. Failure to satisfy the demands of the employer could, however, result in return to an institution.

Dressler suggests that the British practice of deporting felons to the colonies was later translated into parole. The British government decided to grant stays of execution to convicted felons in response to the colonies' need for cheap labor. Deportation and placement of the offender in the free community under supervision then constituted a mitigation of prison sentence. By 1775, England was transplanting approximately two thousand felons annually to the colonies, but the practice ended abruptly with the advent of the American Revolution.

Alexander Maconochie, a captain in the Royal Navy and a prison reformer, is credited by Dressler with being, more than any other one man, the "father" of parole. Maconochie's contribution to parole was the mark (point) system. Prisoners in his Norfolk Island (Australia) prison earned their freedom by acquiring a required number of marks. In cases of a poor work record or insubordination, the convict was fined marks rather than lashed. As Dressler explains:

> Maconochie had struck on an idea that gave prisoners hope. They, and they alone, could reduce their sentences. They could hasten the day when they would be on ticket to leave. And when the time came, it was now understood, they might return to England. Declared Maconochie: "When a man keeps the key of his own prison, he is soon persuaded to fit it to the lock!" The prisoners responded.[29]

Under Maconochie's plan, offenders moved through degrees of freedom from strict custody to liberty. They were finally released on a ticket of leave. The program ended in 1867 when free settlers, competing with ticket-of-leave holders for the discovery of gold in Australia, demanded that they be deported.

Walter Crofton, head of the Irish prison system, added refinements to the ticket of leave Maconochie had devised. He agreed with Maconochie that the purpose of prison was to rehabilitate, and his prisoners moved through his system from solitary confinement to conditional release under supervision. However, Crofton devised a more careful program of supervision than had existed heretofore. He created the position of inspector of released prisoners, whose function it was to protect the community by checking on those who were released and further assisting them in their readjustment to society.

Ex-convicts have never had an easy time reentering the society which rejected them. The stigmatization of the prison experience makes them immediately suspect. In the nineteenth century, ticket-of-leave men were blamed for most of the crimes committed. The public complained (in England especially) that the ticket-of-leave system was simply a leniency which endangered the public safety.

Victor Hugo graphically describes the plight of Jean Val-Jean, the nineteenth-century French ex-convict with a "yellow passport," in this moving scene from *Les Miserables* (1862):

> "See here! My name is Jean Val-Jean. I am a convict; I have been nineteen years in the galleys. Four days ago I was set free, and started for Pontarlier, which is my destination; during those four days I have walked from Toulon. To-day I have walked twelve leagues. When I reached this place this evening I went to an inn, and they sent me away on account of my yellow passport, which I had shown at the mayor's office, as was necessary. I went to another inn; they said: 'Get out!' It was the same with one as with another; nobody would have me. I went to the prison, and the turnkey would not let me in. There in the square I lay down upon a stone; a good woman showed me your house, and said: 'Knock there!' I have knocked. What is this place? Are you an inn? I have money; my savings, one hundred and nine francs and fifteen sous which I have earned in the galleys by my work for nineteen years. I will pay. What do I care? I have money. I am very tired—twelve leagues on foot, and I am so hungry. Can I stay?"
>
> "Madame Magloire," said the bishop, "put on another plate."
>
> The man took three steps, and came near the lamp which stood on the table. "Stop," he exclaimed; as if he had not been understood, "not that, did you understand me? I am a galley-slave—a convict—I am just from the galleys." He drew from his pocket a large sheet of yellow paper, which he unfolded. "There is my passport, yellow as you see. That is enough to have me kicked out wherever I go. Will you read it? I know how to read, I do. I learned in the galleys. There is a school there for those who care for it. See, here is what they have put in the passport: 'Jean Val-Jean, a liberated convict, native of———,'you don't care for that, has been nineteen years in the galleys; five years for burglary; fourteen years for having attempted four times to escape. This man is very dangerous. There you have it! Everybody has thrust me out, Will you receive me? Is this an inn? Can you give me something to eat, and a place to sleep? Have you a stable?"
>
> "Madame Magloire," said the bishop, "put some sheets on the bed in the alcove."
>
> Madame Magloire went out to fulfill her orders.[30]

Prisoner aid societies arose with the idea of providing aftercare for discharged prisoners. The services they provided were similar to those furnished by contemporary parole departments: secure employment, housing, clothing, and other needs of the newly released. All prisoners given assistance by one of these societies were expected to report on their progress in readjusting to society.

Parole in its modern form was adopted first by New York State, when the 1869 law authorized the building of Elmira Reformatory. To be eligible for parole, prisoners at Elmira had to be able to show a good record of conduct for 12 months and to present a suitable plan for employment. Each parolee was given a new suit of clothes (symbolizing a new beginning) as well as transportation expenses and each was expected to report to an assigned "guardian" once a month. The parole period was limited to 6 months; a longer period was felt to be discouraging to the prisoner.

The first National Parole Conference was convened in Washington, D.C., in 1939 by President Roosevelt. At that time, parole was little more than an ideal. Over half the nation's parole officers were in five states, and the individual caseload in one state was 2,500! According to Wright, "aftercare" in those days was little more than "afterthought."[31] By 1941 parole as a concept had fallen into such public disfavor that, in a survey of 25,000 policyholders of the Northwestern National Life Insurance Company, 83 percent of the men and 88 percent of the women felt that pardon and parole should be abolished and that persons convicted of crimes should serve their full sentences.[32]

Despite its shaky beginnings, parole has demonstrated its usefulness as a correctional concept. Every state in the union has passed laws authorizing its use. Indeed, a few states are now extending the principle of parole to include all prisoners under mandatory conditional release programs, generally 3 months prior to the sentence expiration date. Presently mandatory condition release (MCR) is granted by "gain time" (reduction in sentence through good behavior) or expiration of sentence. Like parole, MCR is release under supervision. Those—generally considered the greatest threat to society—who serve to the expiration of their sentences are made to shift for themselves. According to the *UCR* (1970), 75 percent of those released without supervision will be rearrested within 4 years. In the interest of both individual rehabilitation and society protection, it is imperative that all prisoners released from our institutions be given some form of supervision.[33]

The Parole Board

American penal systems have devised a separation of powers over the destiny of the offenders under their jurisdiction. Our judicial system determines the guilt or innocence of the offender and may place limits on the time the convict must serve. Departments of correction are responsible for the custody and care of the inmate. Boards of parole determine if and when a prisoner should be released to the community prior to the expiration of sentence. Parole boards are organized according to three principal models: (1) a board composed of personnel from within a particular institution, (2) a state parole board housed within the division of correction with authority to release from all state institutions, and (3) a parole board administratively independent from the division of corrections with power to release from any state institutions.

Abuses and favoritism that existed in the early days of parole, under the Elmira system, have led increasingly to the establishment of parole boards independent of the department of corrections. This trend, however, has created a situation in which those who know the prisoners best, the custodial officers and correctional social workers, have little or no control over the release of the individuals with whom they work day after day. Boards must lean heavily on the sterile information contained in the convict's "record jacket" and perhaps a brief interview with the prospective parolee. Necessarily, their judgments are largely intuitive at best, and haphazard at worst.

Selection for parole and subsequent release from prison involves an interplay between a formal system of rules and the informal system of attitudes (predispositions to act) of parole board members. Thomas analyzed this process as exhibited by the Indiana parole board. (Thomas was himself a member of this board.[34])

During Thomas's period of service, parole hearings were held 2 months prior to the earliest release date. One month prior to the hearing, each board member received copies of the classification summaries for those who were to be considered. The monthly total of these summaries in Indiana averaged about five hundred. The Indiana parole board, during Thomas's tenure, consisted of three men. To be considered for parole, each applicant must have been on "good behavior" for a year. Two votes for or against an applicant determined the decision.

Other than the inmate and the board members, the only other person present at the form hearing was the institutional parole officer. The basic consideration in the parole process, from the point of view of the parole board members, was the protection of society. Factors considered by the board included (1) the nature of the inmate's offense, (2) the inmate's criminal record, (3) psychological reports, (4) reports on the inmate's institutional conduct, (5) a parole plan, (6) community sentiments, and perhaps (7) a prediction table.

Board members might disagree with the institutional recommendations and sometimes had firm opinions about releasing persons guilty of particular crimes (e.g., rape or homicide). Community pressures ("Does anyone on the outside want this man kept inside?") were also considered.

Thomas did not see the parole selection process as a scientific endeavor but rather a guessing game in which the members of the board tried to ascertain if the time were right to take a chance on the potential parolee "making it on the streets."

Gottfredson and Ballard,[35] in an attempt to discover whether differences in parole decisions were associated not only with the characteristics of the offenders themselves but also with the persons responsible for the decisions, analyzed, 2,053 cases in which parole was granted over a 2-year period. They concluded that the members of the paroling authority tended to make similar sentencing decisions when the different kinds of offenders considered were taken as a group. This result does not make the decision-making criteria scientific, but it does indicate consistency and uniformity.

Most parole boards in the United States find themselves in the position of the one in Connecticut which has recently been described by Jackson. The Connecticut board has nine members, each appointed by the governor; only three sit at a time. None are professional criminologists; they include people with such diverse occupations as retired minister, dentist, and dean of the University of Connecticut Law School. Decisions are made on what appear to the board to be appropriate responses to their questions. Any candidates for parole who are belligerent (humility is a great virtue in this situation) or who show resentment that society has locked them in a cage will jeopardize their chances. Smart inmates will attempt to convince the board that they are grateful for the opportunity to learn to be solid citizens. The situation is aptly summed up thus: "With little to guide them, three good men must say 'yes or no' as convicts plead for freedom."[36]

Four inmates of the Indiana State Penitentiary have described how parole candidates resent at least three aspects of the parole decision process (Griswold et al.).[37] First, the tendency of parole boards is to place great emphasis on the candidate's prior record:

> What is so frustrating to men who keep getting rejected for parole because of "past record" is that there is obviously nothing that the individual can do about it. It cannot be changed, it cannot be expunged. It, therefore, generates a feeling of helplessness and frustration, especially in men who take seriously what they are told about rehabilitation and perfect institutional records. These men cannot understand the rationale behind parole denials based on past records if the major goal of the correctional system is rehabilitation and if they have tried to take advantage of every rehabilitation program offered by the institution. The men know that merely serving another two or five years is not going to further the "rehabilitation process."

The second source of resentment for inmates is the attitude of parole boards that their principal responsibility is to protect society and that the rehabilitation of the offender is secondary. (For citizens, the resentment is reversed.) With this as their guide, parole boards are reluctant to release offenders who are considered risks, preferring to let them serve day for day and return to the community without supervision. This practice undoubtedly reduces the recidivism rate for those on parole and enhances the public image of parole boards. Its impact on the overall recidivism rate, however, should be the paramount consideration. "If the parole principle be sound for one prisoner," wrote James V. Bennett, "it is sound for all" (*Of Prisons and Justice*).[38] The issue is whether keeping poor parole risks in prison for a longer period of time makes them better parole risks. The answer for some is yes. The passage of time, more than anything else about the dehumanizing prison atmosphere, seems to mature a few people. But for most, the longer offenders are subjected to the crimogenic environment of a penitentiary, the more likely they are to absorb the values, techniques, and rationalizations of the criminal subculture.

Lastly, inmates are convinced that parole boards are more responsive to public opinion and political pressures than to the factual situation and record of the individual applicant. This feeling on the part of prisoners only adds to their cynicism toward the entire parole process.

At this point, it should be said that parole procedures are a constant source of grievance for both prisoners (too vague and strict) and the community (too lenient).

What are the most important factors to consider in selecting a candidate for parole? What if a candidate has a good institutional adjustment but a history of alcohol abuse? Which factor should outweigh the other? These parole decisions are quasijudicial, for they involve a form of deferred sentencing—a decision *when* to release.

Gottredson and others constructed guidelines of favorable factors that indicate a good risk on parole. They include the following: not guilty of auto theft, no prior incarcerations, high school graduate, at least eighteen years old at first conviction, employed or a full-time student for at least 6 months during the last 2 years in the community, and has plans to live with wife or family upon release.[39]

13.11 PAROLE SUPERVISION

As late as 1970, most state agencies did not allow officers to supervise "clients" of the opposite sex. By 1974, 46 of the 50 states allowed probation and parole officers to mix caseloads without regard to sex. In California and in the division of probation in New York, women officers supervise males, but male officers never supervise females. The reason given is that this rule protects male probation officers from false rape and paternity charges.

Caseload segregation by sex is inefficient because it creates an inbalance in caseload size. Male officers find themselves with an overload, and women officers with an "underload." This does not mean that some care should not be exercised in matching an offender and a supervisor; rapists, prostitutes, homosexuals, and lesbians should not be forced into a counseling relationship with an officer whose sex itself may present a problem. There is some preliminary evidence that aggressive male offenders tend to lose some of their aggressiveness when dealing with a female parole officer, as they do not feel the need to present a "macho" image with a woman.

For many years, large caseloads have been the probation and parole officers' most frequent excuse for failure. The logic was simple enough. Obviously, if you have a large caseload, it reduces the amount of supervision and counseling you can do, which in turn results in greater recidivism among your charges. The San Francisco Project (1969) shattered this hypothesis. In this study, four levels of work loads were established, ranging from "ideal" (50 cases) to maximal, or a caseload involving very little supervision (250 cases). The results revealed that the number of contacts between probationer and supervisor had little relationship to success of failure on probation. It is now felt that the concept of "caseload" is meaningless without some system of classification that matches type of offender with type of supervision.[40]

West Germany has developed a method reminiscent of Orwell's *1984* for monitoring parolees; it involves an electronic device which is buried under the parolee's skin. The device sends out a signal that can be picked up through walls of any kind. These "anthropotelemetric" units have batteries which last for 2 years (which is the longest period Germans are placed on parole). Each transmitter emits a signal, coded to the individual carrying it, which is transmitted at 30-second intervals to a central monitoring station that slots the parolees' whereabouts on a radarlike screen. The invention is unpopular with the ex-convicts. Said one: "At least when I was in my cell at night I could put my head under the blanket and feel that I had some privacy, but with this box actually inside of me, I'm never alone. Someone is always watching. It gives me the creeps. I feel like a robot." But the device fascinates West Germany's Director of Prisons Erik Horzberger, who predicted that eventually no one will get out on parole in Germany without first submitting to an operation in which a monitor is implanted under the skin.[41]

13.12 SUCCESS ON PAROLE

While parolees may be discharged from supervision prior to the date of their maximum prison sentences, they cannot be kept on parole beyond their mandatory release date. Violations of parole conditions tend to occur in the first months after release.[42] Those crucial days just after release are described as follows by one female parolee: "The one thing I hadn't counted on was being afraid! As I walked down the street amid crowds of people on their way to work, it seemed to me that every eye was upon me. Every face seemed ready to shout, 'get back in prison where you belong.' "[43] Civil rights are restored in some states upon release from prison on parole; in others, rights are restored after parole is satisfactorily completed. Certain other states restore one's civil rights only after a full pardon from the governor. This loss of certain civil rights is a source of great resentment on the part of parolees. As one college student (a criminology major) who has served time for marijuana possession put it: "I'll be a college graduate, and I can't even vote!" (The civil disabilities attending the conviction or a felony are discussed in Chapter 16.)

The success rate reported by parole commissions averages around 75 percent nationally. Local rates of success range from 60 to 90 percent. The *Florida Probation and Parole Commission Report* for 1968 stated: "The Commission proudly reports a current success ratio of 78.5 percent while under supervision, based on the release of 19,222 parolees since 1941, with revocation necessary in only 4,275 instances." The parole violation rate refers only to the period of parole and does not take into account those offenders who become recidivists after supervision is terminated. The *UCR* (1975) reports that 71 percent of inmates paroled will be rearrested within 4 years.

Glaser[44] analyzed six factors as being associated with the probability of an offender's return to prison: age, offense, criminal record, race, IQ, and physique.

1 *Age.* There is an inverse relationship between crime and recidivism. The older people are when released from prison, the less likely they are to return to crime. With the exception of alcoholics, inmates released after the age of fifty are more likely to commit misdemeanors than felonies should they return to crime. Further, the younger offenders are at first arrest or confinement, the more likely they are to persist in a criminal career.

2 *Offense.* Over 90 percent of the felony crimes reported to the police are economic offenses. Those convicted of larceny, forgery, and auto theft are high risks on parole.

3 *Prior Criminal Record.* All we know of the future is what we know from the past. When offenders have perpetrated a number of crimes, it is not unreasonable to assume that they are committed to a life of crime and will repeat their past behavior. The extent of an offender's criminal record will indicate the probability of more crimes being added to it. The exception to this is the four- or five-time loser who has reached the age of "criminal menopause." Such a person has either outgrown the desire to commit crimes or simply is too old and tired to stand the stress of that type of life.

4 *Race, IQ, and Physique.* Although significant differences exist between blacks and whites in overall crime rates, such differences are almost nonexistent among released prisoners. Race seems to be a greater factor in the commission of original crimes than in recidivist offenses.

IQ has not been found to be predictive of violation, and while a husky body build has been found to be related to delinquency, there is no research on the body builds of released prisoners.

Ultimately, the success or failure of a person on parole depends largely upon the type of people with whom he or she interacts. As one successful parolee put it: "If I hadn't a mother who could forgive and forget, or an employer who graciously told me we all make mistakes, what might have happened to me? Without encouragement from society and from those I love, no doubt I would have ended up a repeater."[45]

13.13 PARDON

Scott,[46] in his review of pardoning powers, points out that all Western nations make use of some form of pardon as a means of lending flexibility to the disposition of criminal cases. England has historically vested this power in the Crown. But in the United States, power is vested in the people, who can delegate it to whomever they please. On the federal level, the President holds this power, and the states normally vest it in the governor and a group of advisers. Pardon boards in the United States follow three models: (1) In about one-fourth of the states, the power of pardon is given to the governor alone, who may appoint a pardon attorney to assist in this function; (2) half the states have advisory boards that recommend pardons to the governor, who then has the final decision; and (3) another one-fourth of the states invest the pardon board with final authority, and the governor sits as an ex-officio member.

A pardon does not, as Cozard[47] points out, expunge the record of a conviction and establish the innocence of the person pardoned. A pardon granted specifically on the ground of innocence usually removes the guilty stigma in effect, but the record of the conviction remains.

A pardon really indicates guilt followed by forgiveness. The purpose of the pardoning power is to return convicted felons to the status they held prior to conviction. In some states, no rights are lost by conviction, so clemency is unnecessary.

There are three types of pardon in capital cases: (1) full pardon, (2) commutation to life or a term of years, and (3) reprieve or stay of execution. Full pardons are generally given only when the person was wrongfully convicted. Although there are many safeguards in our criminal justice system to ensure against wrongful conviction, judicial errors do sometimes arise from such factors as mistaken identity, perjured testimony of hostile witnesses, public pressures upon a district attorney, or the failure of an individual to testify on his or her own behalf for fear that the jury will learn of a previous criminal record.

After ex-President Nixon was granted his pardon, the number of federal prisoners' applications for commutation of sentence tripled by comparison to the average for the 5 years prior to September 8, 1974. Many of the applications informed President Ford that the applicants had "suffered enough." However, the number of pardons granted in the 2-month period following the Nixon pardon was below average.[48]

In most cases of innocence established some time after conviction, a pardon is the only effective way to rectify the wrong; courts generally have no power to grant new trials because of newly discovered evidence.

Commutation is the substitution of a lighter for a heavier punishment. Unlike pardon, it does not mean forgiveness and does not effect a restoration of civil rights. Generally, the authority to commute a sentence is assumed in the authorization of the pardoning power. The greater power (to pardon) by definition includes the lesser power (to commute). The power to commute is most often used to make a prisoner eligible for parole. Politically, it is a middle road and shifts the responsibility for release from the governor's office to the parole board.

Commutation is appropriate to lend spirit to the letter of the law when there are extenuating circumstances which do not affect the technical, legal question of guilt or innocence of a capital crime. The classical illustration in law (*Regina v. Dudley and Stephens,* 1884) concerned two men and a cabin boy cast adrift in a lifeboat, with almost no food, 1,600 miles from the Cape of Good Hope. After 20 days, having been without food and water for a week, the men killed and cannibalized the cabin boy. Four days later, they were rescued. All three would have perished had not the men resorted to "survival of the fittest." An English court convicted them of murder, and they were sentenced to death. However, their sentences were later commuted to 6 month's imprisonment because of the unusual circumstances.

Scott[50] estimated that of those who are sentenced to die, about one in four or five obtains a commutation to life imprisonment. Reprieves are used if new evidence is under consideration, if a woman prisoner is pregnant, if an inmate on death row becomes insane, or if a holiday season is approaching.

An amnesty is a general pardon. Literally translated, the word means "removal from memory." Historically, it has been used to restore citizenship to those who have taken part in a rebellion. Lincoln issued two such proclamations after the Civil War. It is generally held that the power to grant individual pardons includes the power to grant general pardons.

SUMMARY

A number of devices have been incorporated into the criminal justice system of the United States to lend flexibility to the rigid requirement of the criminal code. These measures typically reflect a desire to combine the twin goals of (1) protection of society and (2) the rehabilitation of the offender to a useful role in society. The older view was that justice meant extracting exactly the amount of pain from the offender as the offender had inflicted upon society, that is, "making the punishment fit the crime." This doctrine survives but is declining with the increasing impact of the behavioral sciences upon the law. Treatment of the offender takes place within the framework of criminal law, and conflicts inevitably arise between the goals of absolute protection of society and what is therapeutic for the individual.

Chapter 14

Institutionalization and Treatment of the Offender

The penitentiary is an American invention. The gentle Quakers played a role in this, since they exerted the greatest influence in the formation of the Philadelphia Society for Alleviating the Miseries of Public Prisons through which, in 1787, Philadelphia's Walnut Street Jail was transformed into the first American penitentiary. It is ironic that this institution—the penitentiary—which has become a symbol of oppression, brutality, and inhumanity, was conceived as a humanitarian enterprise.[1]

The Quakers hoped that the penitentiary would mark a movement away from the public flogging, executions, and degrading public labor which characterized the treatment of offenders in the eighteenth century. The Quakers themselves, when they sought self-improvement, simply reflected in solitude on whatever peccadilloes were nagging at their consciences. Then, having achieved an appropriate level of penitence, they went forth as "improved" people. Therefore they reasoned—by extension—that if reflection, self-examination, and Bible reading were of such great benefit to them, it should be useful to criminals as well. Thus the penitentiary would be a place where men and women would reflect on the error of their ways and become penitent. Unfortunately, benevolent motives do not always produce benevolent results, and today we have numerous scholars and humanitarians calling for either wholesale reforms or the abolition of the penitentiary as a correctional concept. From Jessica Mitford, in her *Kind and Usual Punishment*[2]—an analysis of the "prison business"—to our court judges, persons of varying academic backgrounds have come to see the penitentiary as a failure and an anachronism. Judge James E. Doyle, a federal district court judge, wrote in *Morales v. Schmidt* (1973):

> I am persuaded that the institution of prison probably must end. In many respects it is as intolerable within the United States as was the institution of slavery, equally toxic to the social system, equally subversive of the brotherhood of man, even more costly by some standard, and probably less rational.[3]

While one group of scholars are calling for an end to the penitentiary system, another equally distinguished group are arguing that a small proportion of offenders account for a large share of the crime statistics and that these persons should be incarcerated with long, disabling sentences. These scholars question the efficacy of "rehabilitation" and would seriously limit probation and parole while eliminating indeterminate sentences in favor of "flat sentencing."[4]

In order to better understand the modern debate over the future of corrections, it is necessary to take a brief and admittedly somewhat simplified view of the historical background of American corrections.

14.01 HISTORICAL BACKGROUND OF THE PENITENTIARY

Imprisonment, historically, has been used (1) to detain people awaiting trial, (2) as a means of forcing payment of fines, and (3) to hold, temporarily, those condemned to galley servitude.[5] Confinement was not the cornerstone of the system, as it presently is in America. It served merely as a way station to "transportation" (banishment) or to the gallows.

In the Middle Ages, petty offenders, vagabonds, the mentally ill, and various other public nuisances were either whipped or placed in public exhibition in the stocks. Those placed in stocks were made ready targets for the various missiles children and passers-by might choose to hurl at them. Often the punishment was intended to fit the crime. If a fish merchant was dishonest, he might be forced to wear a necklace of stinking smelt; and should a woman possess a sharp, scolding tongue, she risked being silenced with an iron bridle. More serious offenders faced a variety of fates including mutilation, branding, forfeiture of property, banishment, and death.[6] The role of the prison, however, was to serve merely as a holding house until the appropriate final punishment was selected.

In eighteenth-century England, convicts lived a grim life in "hulks" and "gaols." "Hulks" were abandoned or unusable transport ships which were used to confine offenders. The gaols, or early jails, gave us the word "gaolbird" (jailbird). The inmates were confined in large, cagelike cells and appeared to onlookers as birds in a cage.[7] Offenders were kept in congregate confinement, with men, women, and children brutally thrown together. These conditions shocked the conscience of John Howard (1726–1790), the sheriff of Bedforshire, who spearheaded a reform movement to end these abuses.

At about the same time in the United States, Dr. Benjamin Rush, Benjamin Franklin, and others interested in penal reform met to devise a humane program for the treatment of criminals. The history of state prisons in America since that time can be roughly divided into five historic periods. Each of these periods contributed something to the ideological history of American corrections, as penologists sought the proper formula for reformation of the offender.[8]

Historic Era	
1790–1830	The early American prison
1830–1870	The Pennsylvania and Auburn Systems
1870–1900	The reformatory system
1900–1935	The industrial prison
1935–1970	Corrections in transition

14.02 THE EARLY AMERICAN PRISON: 1790–1830

The early American prison system was established to punish offenders. The assumption was that reform would result from a combination of punishment and the repentance that would follow such chastisement. The formula was simple: penance through punishment.

Ideologically, this is an unlikely combination of the concepts of the French rationalists and American Revolutionary thinkers, influenced also by the theology of the Quakers and Puritans. It was a combination of the ideas of the English philosopher Jeremy Bentham (1748–1832) and his "hedonistic calculus" (calculating which behavior will result in the greatest pleasure) and the Puritan belief in the refining and reforming quality of punishment.

But these lofty philosophical concepts were soon lost in mundane politics, in the inept and ignorant policies of prison officers (which led to such abuses as overcrowding), and in the recalcitrance of criminals who persisted in their criminality despite the changed approach from corporal punishment to the more humane penitentiary system. Disappointed with these early results, penal reformers designed two competing penitentiary systems that were to dominate American penal philosophy for the next half century.

14.03 THE PENNSYLVANIA AND AUBURN SYSTEMS: 1830–1870

The basis of the Pennsylvania system was a "separate" and "silent" regime. The formula for rehabilitation was solitary confinement, silence, and labor in a little courtyard outside the cell. The emphasis was on keeping inmates from contaminating each other by spreading criminal ideas.

Its competing counterpart, the Auburn system, adopted a slightly different plan whereby all inmates were locked in separate cells at night but worked together silently in congregate workshops during the day.

With the element of noncommunication, something new had been added to prison discipline. Prisoners now walked to and from work or meals in lockstep and ate in silence "back-to-face." In time, the Auburn system prevailed over the Pennsylvania system because congregate work was better suited to industrial production. The legacy to corrections of these experiments was (1) a prison industries program and (2) the architectural concept of the interior cell block for isolating prisoners. The latter was deemed necessary for keeping a few dangerous prisoners, but it led, unfortunately, to the building of monstrous megaprisons that were both costly and debilitating to the personalities of the people caged in them.

By the 1860s the rule of absolute silence began to fall apart due to the need for communication to run the industries. Production and economics ruled over treatment ideology.

14.04 THE REFORMATORY ERA: 1870–1900

The American Prison Congress met in 1870 to try to devise a set of guiding principles for prison operations. Delegates at this congress were impressed with the ideas of Alexander Maconochie (1787–1860), a captain in the Royal Navy and prison reformer. Maconochie had installed the mark (point) system for his prisoners in his Norfolk Island, Australia, prison. By this system, inmates would earn their freedom by acquiring a required number of "marks." In cases of a poor work record or insubordination, the convict was fined marks rather than lashed. Thus, the amount of time prisoners had left to serve depended upon their ability to earn marks. Declared Maconochie, "When a man keeps the key of his own prison, he is soon persuaded to fit it to the lock."[9]

As an outgrowth of the principles agreed upon at this Congress, the first reformatory in America was built at Elmira, New York. It was designed as a first-offender institution for youths aged sixteen to thirty. Both academic and vocational education were provided. Discipline was built around a regimental military organization complete with swords for officers and dummy rifles for the rank-and-file prisoners. An institutional newspaper was established and entertainment provided, though "corrupting" vaudeville or minstrel shows were forbidden.

The Reformatory era gave corrections the concepts of the indeterminate sentence, parole, and positive reform through education. The idea of being released early on parole proved to be a powerful incentive to inmates to cooperate with institutional regulations, and it helped relax some of the old iron discipline which had held over from the "separate and silent era."

14.05 THE INDUSTRIAL PRISON: 1900–1935

Increasing prison populations led to increasing costs, which in turn created pressures for more emphasis on prison labor and industry. At the beginning of this period, there were approximately 50,000 convicts in state prisons. By the close of this era in American prison history, the convict population had grown to 126,258.[10]

During this period criminals were supposedly sent to prison at hard labor *as* punishment and not *for* punishment. In other words, the very pain of confinement was held to be sufficient punishment. Wardens were not supposed to view their charges as candidates for the lash simply because they were convicted felons. In time, the treatment-oriented reformatories of the preceding era became more like the industrial prisons, so that in practice there remained few differences except in the ages of the inmates. Reform gave way to economics as the United States prison system from 1900 to 1935 was guided by the watchwords "custody, punishment, and industry."

One outstanding feature of this fourth period of American penal history was the success of free industry in driving prison products from the open market. One industry after another sought protection from competition with "slave labor." Economics has been a ruling force throughout penal history. From the British experience, when capital punishment was opposed because business enterprises needed galley oarsmen, through the triumph of the Auburn over the Pennsylvania systems, to the rise and decline of prison industries, the guiding principle has been: What is the most economically profitable way we can deal with the criminal offender?

The story of prison industry's battle with organized labor is a history in itself and is too detailed to be covered here. The passage of two federal laws signaled the end of any realistic prison industry. The Hawes-Cooper Act (1929) defined prison products as subject to the laws of any state to which they were shipped, thus divesting them of their interstate status and cutting profits tremendously. The Ashrust-Sumners Act (1935) prohibited interstate shipment where state laws forbade it and required that all prison products shipped out of state be labeled with the prison name. The Depression years of 1929–1933 saw thirty-three states pass laws which prohibited the sale of prison products on the open market. By 1935, for the great majority of prisoners, the penitentiary industries were a memory, and the system had returned to those guiding principles with which it apparently feels most comfortable: punishment and custody.

14.06 CORRECTIONS IN TRANSITION: 1935–1970

The next 35 years might be labeled "Corrections in search of its soul." Correctional administrators were saddled with the architecture and principles of the past. Yet slowly, especially on the federal level, attempts were made to introduce effective treatment techniques.

Indeed, it was during this period that the term "corrections" came into usage to replace the older "penology." "Penology" derives from the Greek *poena,* meaning "punishment"; thus penology could be defined as the scientific study of the application of pain. The term is now generally reserved for references to studies of the institutional experience, with corrections being defined as that branch of criminology that studies any facet of the correctional process from probation to aftercare.

Changes in the philosophy and treatment of offenders in the United States—a society generally characterized by rapid advance in other areas—have been painfully slow. Correctional reform has moved with the speed of a "cautious glacier," to use Norval Morris's phrase. Clemmer collected the data for his study *The Prison Community* in the 1930s, yet in the reissue of that work in 1958, he would write in the preface: "Some 40 percent of American prisons appear little different today in basic organization, institutional program . . . than they were twenty years ago."[11] Of 187 fortress-type prisons in the United States, 61 were built before 1900.[12]

Clemmer estimates that 60 percent of the penal institutions in the United States have shown some progress—in such areas as providing inmates with recreation, group counseling, work release, etc.—since the Depression days. He attributes these improvements to increasing social concern in the general society, the influx of dedicated professionals choosing careers in corrections, and scientific advances.

But despite these hopeful signs, state prisons in the United States in the 1970s remain monotonous, stupefying warehouses of forgotten people. Homosexuality and virtually meaningless work assignments remain the hallmarks of prison life. As a symptom of the frustrations that are aroused by these conditions, Clemmer points to the 105 riots and serious disturbances which occurred in the American prison community during the relatively brief period 1950–1957.

The initial phase of this last era of corrections saw the erection of an experiment in the building of an "escape-proof" prison—the ultimate in maximum-security confinement: Alcatraz.

14.07 ALCATRAZ: CASE STUDY AND LANDMARK IN AMERICAN PENOLOGY

The French philosopher and mathematician Blaise Pascal (1623–1662) once observed that whenever civilized nations occupy an island, they turn it into either a fortress or a prison—in any event something that renders its occupants uncomfortable. When the Americans occupied Alcatraz, they did both: they converted it first into a fortress and then into a prison.[13]

"The Rock" was discovered in 1775, when its only inhabitants were flocks of pelicans, by a Lieutenant in the Spanish Navy. He christened it Isla de los Alcatraces, or Island of the Pelicans. When California became part of the United States, Alcatraz was first utilized as a military base. In 1907, it became the Pacific branch of the United States military prison system. During World War I, it was used to confine conscientious objectors.

By the 1930s, federal penitentiaries were jammed. The federal penitentiary at Atlanta had been built to hold 2,000 inmates, and its population had risen to 4,130. Federal prisons were not only overcrowded but wardens were plagued with riots and escapes. The Attorney General of the United States believed that most of the problem stemmed from a hard core of incorrigibles, professional gangsters of a type that ordinary prisons were not built to hold.

Thus he began to look around for a prison from which escape would be impossible. The army did not really need a prison and the federal government did. Alcatraz seemed a perfect solution. Its 12 acres did not contain a drop of fresh water or vegetation to offer shelter, and its rocks rose sharply 130 feet from the sea. The island was surrounded by cold water (average 51°F) and strong tides (6 to 9 knots), and the shoreline was regularly patrolled by an efficent

Coast Guard. Thus it was selected to be the site of the American Devil's Island (the "dry guillotine") for hardened criminals.

"The Rock" symbolized more than a safe lockup. It represented the ultimate punishment society could inflict upon federal offenders short of killing them. It was the point of no return for multiple offenders. Harassed federal prison wardens now had a new threat with which to intimidate unruly inmates. Troublemakers could be exiled to Alcatraz.

Alcatraz officially became a federal penitentiary on January 1, 1934. It was a place without privileges, trustees, commissary, sports, honor systems, or entertainments. Originally there was a rule of silence at meals. Newspapers and radios were also forbidden. To add to the discomfort of its inhabitants, yachts circled the island each day, carrying sightseers who were laughing and drinking. This made for a sharp and bitter contrast between freedom and prison. And at night, the glittering mosaic of San Francisco's lights would torment the caged prisoners.

There was no reward system for good behavior, simply quick and sure punishment for rule infractions. Guards were equipped with high-pressure water hoses, straight jackets, and special handcuffs that tightened with every jerk. This approach was called "death by regulation." The guard-inmate ratio was one to three, and each inmate was confined in a single cell. Like some Dantean inferno, Alcatraz might well have had a sign saying: "All hope abandon, ye who enter here."

Alcatraz housed some of America's most famous criminals, including Al Capone and Machine-Gun Kelly. Capone was not sent to Alcatraz because he was a troublemaker or an escape risk but because it was felt that he was running the penitentiary at Atlanta. Both Capone and Kelly were considered what Will Rogers called "rattlesnake normal"—they would not bite unless stepped upon. Capone was released from Alcatraz in 1939 under a federal prison regulation that covers inmates suffering from an incurable disease. He died in Florida 8 years later of syphilis.

There is no hard evidence that anyone ever escaped from America's escape-proof penitentiary. Eight men were shot or drowned while attempting to escape and thirteen others were recaptured, but another five are unaccounted for. The authorities officially listed them as dead from drowning, but no bodies were found.

During the 1960s, when Robert Kennedy was Attorney General, the decision was made to close Alcatraz as a penal institution. It was crumbling and renovation would have cost over $5 million (its original cost was $260,000). But apart from the expense that would have been involved, Alcatraz was not kept open because American penal philosophy was changing. During the 1960s, optimism ran high and maximum efforts at rehabilitation were being initiated. Alcatraz was seen as an anachronism, an ugly dinosaur of a punitive past, best left to decay and history.

Ironically, the pendulum in the 1970s has swung back toward skepticism about the possibility of rehabilitating offenders, and we may again hear the suggestion that we build an escape-proof prison.

14.08 PRISONERS IN STATE AND FEDERAL INSTITUTIONS (1973)

In terms of our total population (approximately 220 million), there are relatively few persons serving time in state and federal institutions. A 1976 poll by *Corrections Magazine* (see Table 14-1) placed the number at 249,538 inmates who had been sentenced as adults or youthful offenders and whose maximum sentence was a year and a day or longer. Of this number, 89 percent were confined in state institutions and the remainder were held in federal prisons.[14]

As in the past, prisons today are overwhelmingly populated by males. Male arrests outnumbered female arrests by 5 to 1 in 1975, but

Table 14-1 Survey of Inmates

	Number of inmates 1/1/75	Number of inmates 1/1/76	Percent change
Alabama	4,260	4,420	+ 4
Alaska	322	349	+ 9
Arizona	2,072	2,534	+ 22
Arkansas	2,007	2,338	+ 17
California	24,780	20,007	− 20
Colorado	1,968	2,104	+ 7
Connecticut	2,805	3,060	+ 9
Delaware	555	701	+ 27
District of Columbia	1,321	1,538	+ 16
Florida	11,420	15,709	+ 38
Georgia	9,772	11,067	+ 13
Hawaii	310	366	+ 18
Idaho	536	593	+ 11
Illinois	6,672	8,110	+ 22
Indiana	4,360	4,392	+ 1
Iowa	1,520	1,857	+ 22
Kansas	1,421	1,696	+ 19
Kentucky	2,958	3,257	+ 10
Louisiana	4,759	4,774	+ 0.3
Maine	527	643	+ 22
Maryland	6,128	6,606	+ 8
Massachusetts	2,047	2,278	+ 11
Michigan	8,702	10,882	+ 25
Minnesota	1,370	1,724	+ 26
Mississippi	2,117	2,429	+ 15
Missouri	3,754	4,150	+ 11
Montana	344	377	+ 10
Nebraska	1,254	1,259	+ 0.4
Nevada	854	893	+ 5
New Hampshire	285	302	+ 6
New Jersey	4,824	5,277	+ 9
New Mexico	979	1,118	+ 14
New York	14,387	16,056	+ 12
North Carolina	11,997	12,486	+ 4
North Dakota	173	205	+ 19
Ohio	9,326	11,451	+ 23
Oklahoma	2,867	3,435	+ 20
Oregon	2,001	2,442	+ 22
Pennsylvania	6,768	7,054	+ 4
Rhode Island	550	594	+ 8
South Carolina	4,422	6,100	+ 38
South Dakota	277	372	+ 34
Tennessee	3,779	4,569	+ 21
Texas	16,833	18,934	+ 12
Utah	575	696	+ 21
Vermont	387	393	+ 2
Virginia	5,635	6,092	+ 8
Washington	2,698	3,063	+ 14
West Virginia	940	1,213	+ 29
Wisconsin	2,591	3,055	+ 18
Wyoming	222	384	+ 73
Total States and District of Columbia	203,431	225,404	
U.S. Bureau of Prisons	22,361	24,134	+ 8
Total U.S	225,792	249,538	+ 11

Source: Information obtained by *Corrections Magazine* in a survey made January 1, 1976.

males in state and federal penitentiaries outnumbered females by 32 to 1. There has been a slight increase in the count of female prisoners, reflecting the gradually increasing female participation in crime punishable by prison sentences. Still, the total number of female prisoners in custody in all state and federal institutions was only 6,684 in 1973. California led the nation with 627 female inmates; North Dakota and New Hampshire did not have any females in custody in penitentiaries.

Regionally, the South's share of the total state prison population (1973) was 47 percent (its proportion of the national civilian population is only 32 percent). The five states listing the largest number of inmates in 1976 were California (20,007), Texas (18,934), New York (16,056), Florida (15,709), and North Carolina (12,486). North Dakota had the fewest prisoners—205.

14.09 THE CLASSIFICATION OF OFFENDERS

In the days when prisons served primarily as holding houses for persons awaiting trial, there was no segregation or classification of offenders. Men and women, murderers and petty thieves, first offenders and hardened criminals were all lumped together. With the rise of the treatment ideology and the belief that rehabilitation is enhanced by an individualized approach, attempts have been made to classify offenders into a typology, both for the good of the individual and to ensure efficient operation of the institution.

14.10 THE CLASSIFICATION PROCESS

Classification takes place within a bureaucracy, and as in all bureaucracies, there is a formal and an informal organization. Thus, decisions are made and justified according to "the book" (*Manual of Correctional Standards*). Yet on occasion, informal considerations may weigh heavier than formal ones in determining where an inmate is housed or works. The classification process, while it varies somewhat from state to state, generally has the following features: (1) the inmate is first assigned to a diagnostic and reception center where an elaborate case study and record jacket is constructed; (2) the inmate meets with a classification committee for a custody and work assignment; (3) at regular intervals during incarceration, the inmate may meet with a reclassification committee for a job or custody change; and finally (4) the inmate may be reviewed prior to meeting with the parole board for a preparole report.

14.11 THE CLASSIFICATION COMMITTEE

The initial classification committee and the "reclass" board is composed of officials representing major areas of the institution. (In some states, such as Florida, the inmate may first go to an independent diagnostic and evaluation center where type of institution—maximum-, medium-, or minimum-security—is decided. The inmate then meets an institutional classification committee for a second intrainstitutional classification.) A typical classification committee would consist of the associate warden for custody, the chief of security, the director of classification, the head of industries, and the classification officer presenting the diagnostic summary. In this way, the different interests of the institution are represented. As a practical matter, the overriding consideration is custody and the prevention of escapes; second is convenience with regard to institutional needs and the establishment of a work force for prison industries. The last consideration is treatment and assignment of the inmate to a position that will best serve rehabilitation.

14.12 THE DIAGNOSTIC SUMMARY

When an offender arrives at the reception center, a diagnostic summary is constructed which holds all the relevant information about the new prisoner. Among the items which may be included are medical records; school records; an FBI "rap sheet"; intelligence and school-placement tests; and letters from relatives, employers, and former teachers giving their opinion as to what motivated the offender to commit the crime. The record should give the inmate's version of the crime as well as the official report. After a personal interview, the classification officer constructs a summary profile of the inmate and concludes with a recommendation as to custody grade and job assignment based on a prediction regarding the inmate's probable institutional adjustment. The following is such a classification summary of a rather typical inmate incarcerated at the Louisiana State Penitentiary at Angola, Louisiana.

> Jerome R_____ is a 21 year old Negro male who was returned to this institution as a straight parole violator (simple robbery and probation violation), owing balance of term. He is officially classified as a second offender. He was previously received here on March 31, 1970, with a sentence of 6 years and was paroled on June 17, 1972. During his period of confinement, he was placed under medium and minimum custody. Job assignments included farm line and half-day butcher school. He had numerous disciplinary actions for fighting (over a pair of shoes), attempting to force another inmate to submit to sodomy, being in the wrong dormitory, breaking in the chow line, lying to a free man,

and disobeying a direct order. Subject presents himself as a pleasant individual, functioning in the fair range of intelligence with a tested IQ of 75. Minimum custody is recommended based on length of sentence. Employment is left to the discretion of the board.

One difficulty in the construction of diagnostic summaries occurs when understaffed penitentiaries utilize inmate-clerks in the administration of tests. "Con politicians" gravitate toward clerical roles where they are in a position to "deal." They may sell a high IQ score to an inmate who needs to qualify for vocational school so as to avoid the drudgery of farm work or the risk of losing a hand stamping out license plates. If inmate-clerks have access to inmate records, a second set of permanent records should be secured in files available only to staff members.

14.13 THE CLASSIFICATION INTERVIEW

After the construction of the diagnostic summary, the inmate meets with the classification committee. Each inmate is presented to the board by the classification officer. After reading the summary, each member of the board may question the inmate to get a first-hand evaluation as to attitudes and prognosis for institutional adjustment. At this interview, the director of classification will have a "want list" from industries indicating the skills needed in the labor force. From the background information and the interview, the committee attempts to answer two questions: "Where can this inmate work?" and "Where can he or she live?"

14.14 CLASSIFICATION BY CUSTODY

Inmates may be classified by the degree of control deemed necessary to prevent their escape and to maintain the peace and security of the institution. Offenders are sentenced by the courts to the division of corrections with the statutory mandate that corrections maintain custody of these prisoners. Custody is a necessary precondition to treatment, as obviously no rehabilitation can take place without inmates. Men and women who are sentenced to penitentiaries are assumed to be in need of external controls. Typically, the institution tries to provide stages of control, gradually reducing the number of external controls as the inmate demonstrates the capacity to handle greater amounts of freedom. As 98 percent of the men and women in prison will eventually return to society in complete autonomy, the institutional experience should provide a step-by-step experiment in self-control. As noted by Professor Fox:

> The long-range function of custody is to provide external controls for persons who have not internalized the social controls sufficiently well to get along without outside social forces. Enlightened custody attempts to provide only that amount of external control which is immediately necessary and to gradually reduce that external control as the individual is able to function in society on his own devices.[15]

Prisoners may be classified in terms of the following degrees of custody: (1) close or lockdown, (2) maximum, (3) medium, and (4) minimum. These classifications may seem somewhat confusing, since they are also used to describe different types of prisons in terms of their construction. It would be possible, for example, to be classified a minimum-security prisoner within a maximum-security penitentiary. While specific restrictions vary somewhat from institution to institution, it is possible to define the various prisoner classifications in board outline.

Close custody means that these inmates are segregated from the general inmate population and live in single cells. They are not allowed to go out on work details, are fed in their cells, and are under strict lockdown 24 hours a day. This custody classification is reserved for extreme escape risks, prisoners who may exhibit bizarre behavior patterns and are being held for psychiatric evaluation, prisoners who have turned "state's evidence" and must be held out of their population for their own protection, patients with tuberculosis who have violated the contagious disease act by refusing to go to a hospital, and younger prisoners who would be subject to homosexual attacks and must be protected. Other stages of custody range in degree of control from being "under the gun" to being a trusty who may travel statewide unescorted. After being classified, the inmates enter the prison community and learn the "pains of imprisonment."

14.15 GLOSSARY OF PRISON TERMS

These terms are frequently used at the Louisiana State Penitentiary at Angola, Louisiana, and at the Mississippi State Penitentiary at Parchman, Mississippi. Each prison develops its own terminology, but the roles these terms describe are more or less the same everywhere. Clemmer, in *The Prison Community,* identified 1,200 terms indigenous to prison life. The terms given here were selected because they identify key inmate roles.

Longlines: The labor gangs that work in the fields. They are guarded by inmate trustees (now being phased out with the help of LEAA grants) with .30-.30 rifles and directed by a prison employee who is referred to as "the driver."

Big-striper: Medium-security prisoner at Angola, who must be under a drawn gun at all times. Called a "gunman" at Parchman (always "under the gun").

Shooter: Inmate trustee, wears white pants, can carry a gun.

Free world: Anything or any person not of the prison.

Lay-in: An inmate given a lay-in (for example, because of illness) does not have to work.

Snitch: An informer; also called a snake or rat.

Catch: Any job on the prison other than the longline. There are "good catches" and "bad catches." Any job other than picking cotton or cutting cane in the longline is considered a good catch.

Cage Boss: Inmate who stays in the cage all day and serves as a sentry to keep people from stealing. A "cage" separates the guard from the men in the dorm.

Alcatraz: "The hole," maximum security unit (MSU), or punishment unit. There are two sections of Alcatraz at Parchman, the permanent side and the punishment side. Permanent-side inmates live in separate cells and are not allowed out. Punishment-side inmates remain in cells for up to 14 days (10 days at Angola).

Dark hole: Dark solitary-confinement cell.

Cooler: Punishment cell at the first-offenders' camp.

Buck: Refusal to work or follow orders.

Punk or gal-boy: Homosexual who plays feminine role. If promiscuous, may be called a whore.

Stud: Homosexual who plays male role.

Hogs: Tough prisoners who, on occasion, strong-arm other prisoners into paying them "insurance premiums" for their own protection against such "accidents" as falling downstairs or slipping in the shower.

14.16 THE PAINS OF IMPRISONMENT

Sykes has identified at least five aspects of punishment associated with losing one's status as a free citizen and taking on the status of a convicted felon.[16] These are the loss of (1) liberty, (2) goods and services, (3) heterosexual relationships, (4) autonomy, and (5) security.

The Loss of Liberty

This first and most obvious punishment means that the inmate's life is confined to one institution and, in all probability, to one section of that institution. His or her "life space" has shrunk to a narrow portion of the world. While letters from relatives and friends form one link with free society, these become less frequent with the passing months and years. Sykes found that 41 percent of the prisoners in the New Jersey State Prison had received no visitors in the previous year.

Letters do not always bring good news. They may tell of problems in the free world about which the inmate can do nothing: sick children, poverty, an unfaithful wife or husband. As Warden Hayden Dees, veteran of 25 years of prison work, told this author: "My experience has been that a woman will wait for a man about two or three years. Then one day he gets a letter informing him he is being divorced."[17]

Being separated from free society is painful, boring, and lonely. Added to these deprivations is the realization that the inmate has been ostracized from society and is considered a pariah. Military outposts are also lonely, but it is honorable and patriotic to serve one's country. Inmates must live with the knowledge that they have been found unfit for life in a free society. While some professional criminals may accept imprisonment as an occupational hazard, more typical inmates feel degraded by it. Therefore they find methods of "rejecting the rejectors," for example, by calling the correctional officers "screws" and telling tales of their stupidity.

The Loss of Goods and Services

It is true that most prisoners were poor "on the outside," but their material possessions within confinement reduce them to a Spartan existence. A cot, a set of uniforms, and perhaps some pictures are all that most inmates can call their own. When released, many inmates can take all their possessions with them in a shoe box.

Ours is a materialistic society; success and personal worth are measured in materialistic terms. The English once had a theory of "least eligibility," by which they meant that no convicted person should be any better off than a free citizen. The status of inmates generally conforms to this view. Since most state prisons pay inmates little or nothing, prisoners are at the bottom of the economic ladder. The effect of this economic failure is a sense of uselessness and humiliation.

The Loss of Heterosexual Relationships

Only the maximum-security institution located at Parchman Farm, Mississippi, permits sex through conjugal visits for *all* married men *throughout* their sentences. Most American penal institutions permit spouses and girl friends to visit within the prison, but these visits are restricted to about 2 hours twice a month. Sometimes the visitor is required to sit on one side of a plate-glass window and the prisoner on the other. They communicate by means of a phone, and their conversation is monitored by a guard.

Some writers have suggested that men under confinement experience a reduction of sexual drive, but the data on which such views are based often come from uniquely adverse, apathy-inducing situations like concentration camps, for example. In prison, sexual assaults occur daily, homosexuality is rife, and pornographic literature is widely circulated among inmates. These facts suggest that the prisoners retain a strong interest in sex.

An inmate who is a confirmed homosexual prior to entering prison does not usually miss members of the opposite sex. But, if the Kinsey report data are accurate, only 4 percent of males are exclusively homosexual. Thus, assuming randomness, the percentage of exclusive homosexuals in prison would be small.

Life in a single-sex society represents a severe and acute deprivation for most inmates. Someone once observed that "the last animal domesticated is man by woman." Women have a gentling effect on men, and their absence only creates a coarser, more brutal atmosphere.

Female inmates also feel the effects of living in a single-sex society. They tend to take less interest in their appearance than they did formerly, since they have fewer opportunities to validate their attractiveness as females.

The Loss of Autonomy

Inmates find their lives regulated down to the most minute details: the hours they sleep, the work they perform, the clothes they wear. In some state penitentiaries, if prisoners want more to drink at mealtime, they raise their cups like infants. All decisions are made for inmates. It may be that some welcome this external control, but others—who have been socialized in the relatively free atmosphere of a democratic society—typically feel only deep and abiding resentment. Petty regulations are often enforced, and inmates who object face the possibility of being "written up" as insubordinate. The psychological effect of this atmosphere is to undermine the inmates' self-image and make them grow to doubt their ability to run their own lives.

The Loss of Security

At first glance, it might seem that the inmate—although deprived of liberty, property, heterosexual relations, and autonomy—will at least benefit from the *security* of a total institution. Many people think of prison life as simply a matter of sitting in one's cell, reading quietly, and casually marking the passage of time by tearing off the pages on a calendar. This notion is nothing but a myth.

The *fact* is that, aside from the deprivations already mentioned, the inmate is sentenced to live in the company of frustrated misfits, sociopaths, and aggressive homosexuals. He will soon learn that the greatest physical danger in prison lies in potential violence from other inmates, not in the risk of being punished by some sadistic correctional officer. If a rumor circulates that an inmate is a "rat" (an informer), he may, when he goes to sleep, have lighter fluid thrown on his face and ignited. Or if an inmate is young, blond, and has no hair on his chest, he may find that he must either become a "gal-boy" or have his throat cut.

Faced with life in such a pathological environment, how do inmates adapt?

14.17 PRISON-ADAPTIVE MODES

How do convicts adapt to prison? How does one survive physically and psychologically intact in a society of captives? This writer once asked an old convict about the best way to adjust in prison. His answer: "Go into a cellblock, ask in a demanding voice: 'Who is the toughest guy here?' and when the guy steps forward, throw your arms around his neck and say: 'Daddy!' " In other words, become the gal-boy of the toughest "hog" in the joint.

Irwin has argued that early studies which identified two adaptive styles—withdrawal and/or isolation versus a collective style—overlooked important alternate styles.[18]

The question: "How shall I do my time?" assumes that one is *able* to cope with the situation. Some people crumble under the deprivations of the prison experience; they retreat into the private, unsharable world of schizophrenia. Those who can and do cope with prison life can be divided into two groups: (1) those who identify with a broader world than the prison and (2) those who orient themselves to the prison world.

Irwin identifies three patterns of adaption to the prison experience. Those convicts who tend to make the prison their whole world are "jailing"; they cut themselves off emotionally from the outside world. On the other hand, those who adapt by "doing time" try to maximize their comforts, minimize their conflicts, and get out of prison as soon as possible. A third adaptation, "gleaning," occurs when inmates attempt to improve themselves, taking advantage of prison facilities and rehabilitation programs to accomplish this.

Some inmates alternate among these adaptive modes during their time in the institution, while other inmates follow a single pattern consistently.

Doing Time

This approach, especially characteristic of professional criminals, is an attempt to take prison in stride. Serving time in prison is for them an occupational hazard of a life of crime, and the point of the prison experience is to get through a sentence as quickly and painlessly as possible.

Inmates doing time avoid trouble with correctional officers, find some activity to pass the time, try to secure a few luxuries, and generally do whatever they think will help them make parole or acquire "good time" (reduction in sentence based on good behavior).

"Getting along" means not violating the convict's normative system. If a stabbing occurs, the inmate doing time sees nothing, since each individual "does his own time." Conversely, the inmate tries to identify with those programs in the institution that increase the probability of making parole. From time to time, correctional administrators shift their allegiance from one particular treatment approach to another. The "smart" inmates become involved in the most fashionable program: group counseling, vocation training, Alcoholics Anonymous, reality therapy, or whatever is current. Inmates soon learn that counselors with backgrounds in social work respond to the phrase: "I have *insight* into my problem." So they learn to have "insight" which means agreeing with whatever the counselor's diagnosis may be.

While there is a sense in which it is appropriate to classify virtually all prisoners as people who are doing time, the ways in which they attempt to accomplish this vary. The professional thief—one who has learned the attitudes and techniques of the criminal subculture—has been subjected to "anticipatory socialization." In taking on the criminal life as a career, thieves assume that they will spend at least a portion of their lives in prison, and they are prepared for it. When such people "hit the gates," they already know enough to avoid troublemakers and stool pigeons, and they realize that it serves no purpose to buck the authorities. In short, their every move in prison is geared toward one goal: getting out.

Jailing

Just as doing time is characteristic of the professional thief, so "jailing" is the characteristic style of young people who have grown up in reformatories or other state institutions. Youthful socialization has prepared them well for institutional life. Raised in a world where "punks," "queens," "stud-broads," and "femmes" have replaced members of the opposite sex, where "bonaroos" are fashionable clothing and cigarettes have replaced money, state-raised youths are both street-wise and institution-wise; they know how to survive.

A youth so socialized knows everything from how to manipulate a social worker to the formula for potato vodka and the best way to steal drugs from the infirmary. The state-raised youth may have learned to use the typewriter so as to pass up the farm line for a job as an inmate-clerk. Such a job puts one in a better position to "deal" (for example, to help another inmate get a change of jobs in return for a carton of cigarettes).

Gleaning

Just as doing time is characteristic of the professional thief and jailing is the hallmark of the state-raised youth, "gleaning" is a style more characteristic of the hustler and the drug addict.

Correctional administrators have tried to introduce into prisons a variety of social programs designed to prepare the inmate for conventional life in free society. The manner in which inmates take advantage of these programs varies with their reference group.

Drug addicts tend to avoid practical programs like television repair workshops. Instead, they gravitate toward the creative arts—areas which seem to promise glamor and excitement. Their reference group is the drug subculture on the outside, and the way in which they "improve themselves" must be consistent with the values of the drug subculture. They may adopt an "intellectual," "bohemian," or "mystic" self-image and are likely to show a certain aimlessness in their pursuit of prison programs.

Since "hustlers" depend upon their skills in public relations, they would enroll in prison courses in public speaking, join the prison chapter of the Jaycees (Junior Chamber of Commerce), try to get selected for the team of prison speakers who go out to high schools to warn youngsters of the evils of a life of crime, and perhaps join the bridge club. At any rate, all this self-improvement is designed to sharpening the inmate's skills as a "con person." Sociologists call this an "unanticipated consequence of planned change." It has been suggested that prisons function as "colleges for crime," but today this function is broader than the simple transmission of overtly criminal attitudes and techniques.

The "square john" and the lower-class person do not glean in the true sense but often really seek to improve themselves. As the square john uses conventional society as a reference group, he enters those programs that will train him for acceptance in the free world. He may join Alcoholics Anonymous, seek out the counsel of the prison psychologists, attend group therapy, or turn to religion.

The lower-class person, typically older, may use the prison experience for self-improvement by finishing high school or enrolling in vocational training such as carpenter school. The state-raised youth, who by definition has had limited experience of the world outside of institutions, has the toughest job of all preparing for life in the free world. It is especially difficult for these young people to have any other reference group but "old buddies" from reform school, and their ideas of "making it" often comes from television and movies, which can create unrealistic expectations.

14.18 THE PRISON CODE

Prisoners enter a society with conflicting sets of expectations. On the formal level, they are expected to recognize their guilt and accept the justness of their punishment. The expectation of the correctional administrators is that the offender will obey prison regulations, treat correctional officers with respect, and utilize the time in prison to prepare for a law-abiding life.

The "inmate code" is the direct antithesis of these official expectations. The major rule of this code is to "do your own time." Essentially this means that you do not interfere in any other convict's affairs. If the convict in the next cell is making "home brew," to "rat" (inform) to a correctional officer would be a most severe infraction of the inmate code, and the offender would face swift and certain retribution. The only time an inmate is considered to have the right to react is when another prisoner's behavior infringes on the inmate's rights. The inmate is then expected to solve the problem personally—not by calling for help.

In addition to this general behavioral principle, the inmate code forbids admissions of guilt and assumes any sentence to be unjust. The prison is always to be referred to as harmful, and correctional officers are to be viewed as "screws" or "hacks"—stupid and untrustworthy. The time in prison should be devoted to exploiting every "free man" and prison program to one's own advantage.

14.19 PRISONIZATION

What should be readily apparent is that institutionalization means that the offender undergoes a resocialization or acculturation process.

The process by which an inmate takes on, in greater or lesser degree, the folkways and general culture of the penitentiary has been termed "prisonization." By participating in the subculture of the prison world, the inmate becomes acculturated and assimilates the prison mores, internalizing a set of norms based on the prison codes. It is no linguistic accident that new inmates are referred to by the host inmate population as "fresh fish."

There is no finer school for crime than a state or federal penitentiary. There, youthful offenders who have been sentenced for holding up a service station learn to rob banks—that is where the money is. Illiterate "B & E men" (those whose career was breaking and entering) who learn to read and write in prison are encouraged by fellow convicts to use their newfound skills to become "paper hangers" (hot-check artists).

Attitudes and ambitions are the result of associations. They are the products of group living. The recidivism rates of United States prisons are one test of Sutherland's theory of differential association. Sutherland contended that one becomes a criminal because of intimate contacts with criminal patterns and also because of isolation from anticriminal mores. From this perspective, our prison system could be called a "Sutherland box," similar to the famous "Skinner box" devised by psychologist B. F. Skinner for testing rats. Isolated geographically and socially from normal society, inmates spend most of their sentences in intimate association with burglars, robbers, drug addicts, and the like. Personality is, to a large extent, the subjective side of culture. As a result of this participation in a convict culture, the offender often emerges with a personality even more dedicated to a life of crime.

In order to combat the influences of the convict subculture, a number of treatment programs have been devised. Three will be discussed: (1) education, (2) religion, and (3) work release.

14.20 PRISON EDUCATION

Education for prisoners sprang from the efforts of religious workers to teach prisoners to read the Bible and other religious literature. From this beginning, the concept of providing secular education for offenders evolved, following the assumption: "If the good citizens are the educated citizens, then the education of bad citizens should make them good."[19] Opposing this concept were those who were skeptical of education for prisoners, arguing that it would simply transform burglars into check forgers.

The earliest attempts at prisoner rehabilitation were based on faith in stringent discipline, isolation, and regular labor. It was expected that a regimen including these would form habits of industry which would persist after release from the prison environment. These assumptions did not, however, bring the desired results. With the failure of the Pennsylvania and Auburn systems, American penologists began to look for more positive methods of changing inmate attitudes.

As a result of the principles agreed upon at the first American Correctional Association's Annual Congress at Cincinnati in 1870, the Elmira Reformatory, which opened in 1876, established a school of "letters" and a trade school. The reformatory era in general and the Elmira institution in particular saw the introduction of a number of innovations into American corrections: the mark system , the indeterminate sentence, parole, and a new type of prison employee: the full-time prison teacher.[20]

It would be difficult to imagine a milieu more antagonistic to the transmission of knowledge than that of the penitentiary. Prisoners are those who, chiefly because of the seriousness of their crimes, are filtered through the judicial process to incarceration. As pointed out in Chapter 2, in discussing the social characteristics of arrested persons, offenders tend to be young, male, poor, and from urban areas.

Education for these persons has been a painful, boring experience generally culminating either in dropping out or being expelled. The typical inmate tests at an average grade achievement of sixth or seventh grade, with an average tested IQ of about 95, or slightly below average.[21] To take these offenders—many of whom have their epitaph and self-image tattooed on their arms ("Born to Lose")—and transform them into eager students is a task that would call for powers approaching the miraculous.

Nor are all inmates enthusiastic about the prospects of returning to the schoolroom. An illiterate inmate of the Arkansas Department of Corrections was unsuccessful in attacking this form of rehabilitation. Claiming the right to remain ignorant, he protested compulsory school attendance. The court denied his claim, holding that a state may undertake to rehabilitate its inmates.[22]

Some insight into the educational background of inmates can be gained from this speech given by an inmate to a prison speech class:

> Good evening, class. The incident which happened to me in my childhood life was when I was at the age of five. In the first grade of school my teachers had a certain dislike for me. They never would assist me in any of my problems. They would always push me to the back of the class, but yet still I was promoted in grades for something that I did not deserve. It continued to the eighth grade where it became a task I could not cope with. It was so embarrassing until I dropped out of school and accepted life on my own as a man. I ended up in jailhouses and institutions.[23]

State prison systems in the United States have generally set aside one institution for youthful offenders which they designate as a reformatory or correctional institution. These institutions employ "free-world" teachers and make a good-faith effort to provide at least the opportunity for legitimate education. Penitentiaries, on the other hand, do not provide education of any sort to more than 10 percent of their inmates, and this instruction is of doubtful quality. As an inmate in the Indiana State Penitentiary wrote:

> In the area of vocational education and training we find, on paper, a number of prisons offering courses in printing, automotive body work, automotive mechanics, drafting, electricity, welding, sign painting, refrigeration, bricklaying, plastering, carpentry, radio, and television repair, typewriter repair, and machine shop.
>
> All well and good. But . . . in the three institutions I have been in, every course was being taught by an inmate, and most of them knew little about the trade they were assigned to teach. Carpentry was not taught by a carpenter but by a man who had "fooled around" with building construction as a day laborer. Brickmasonry was taught, not by a brick-mason, but by an inmate who had never had a brick in his hand until he came to prison.[24]

The use of inmate-teachers creates a number of problems. Inmate-students can challenge the authority of an inmate-teacher simply by observing: "You got a number on your shirttail too." Inmate-teachers are pressured to give good grades, overlook cheating, let the students "pool their ignorance" in the name of class discussion, or wander off into irrelevant topics. Inmate-teachers who resist these pressures face possible reprisals when they return to the dormitory or cellblock. Conversely, a con-politician can gravitate to the teacher role because it provides a strategic position from which to "deal."

In addition to taking formal classroom instruction, some inmates enroll in various correspondence courses. This system creates problems in the monitoring of the completed work. Inmates, like some college students, simply copy someone else's lessons, do the work in collaboration, or get an inmate-clerk to falsely note on their record jackets that they have successfully completed the assigned work. In one prison, one-third of 220 correspondence courses were completed in a week.[25]

Glaser found that when parolees were asked whether the schooling they had obtained in prison was of any use to them, slightly more than 25 percent said yes. Parole-violation studies comparing students with nonstudents indicate that—as measured by parole-revocation rates—students adjust slightly better after release. However, these former prison students tend to be younger first offenders, a group that consistently shows lower recidivism rates with or without educational experiences. Glaser's conclusion as to the overall inpact of prison education upon the failure rate was that "Academic education in prison becomes useful only with long confinement."[26]

Prison education in the federal system is vastly superior to that offered in most state systems. Persons convicted of federal crimes—for example, income tax evasion, or embezzlement—tend to be better educated than those who are incarcerated for state offenses. Still, from 15 to 20 percent of federal offenders are unable to read at the sixth-grade level.[27]

The Federal Bureau of Prisons has set three educational goals for its inmates:

> **1** Every inmate leaving the Federal Prison System will be able to read at the sixth grade level.
>
> **2** Every inmate capable of doing so will have earned a high school diploma or equivalency certificate by the time he is released.
>
> **3** Every inmate who does not have a work skill will have been given training that will qualify him for post-release employment in a relevant, career-oriented occupation.

To implement these objectives, the bureau operates twenty-nine schools located in the major institutions across the country. During 1974, the daily student load averaged 8,300 students, with 3,328 inmates completing high school equivalency programs. Almost four thousand federal inmates were enrolled in college-level courses in 1974, including 550 attending courses on campus in study-release programs in the community.

The federal system also offers a variety of vocational training programs, involving more than eight thousand inmates in such diverse fields as cabinetmaking, furniture reupholstering, diesel mechanics, pipefitting, plumbing, television repair, and cooking.

When Glaser inquired of 131 successful releasees as to the principal reasons for their shift away from crime, thirty-five (26 percent) mentioned their work supervisors. These men did not mention the technical skills transmitted as often as they did the *personal relationship* which evolved during their prison stay. Frequently, this was a paternalistic relationship between an older man and a younger inmate. In speaking of the chief engineer at Leavenworth's powerhouse, a releasee said:

> He was a nice old man and retired after I left. When I left he shook hands with me and said: "You big son-of-a-bitch, if you come back to this place I'll kill you, much as I like you. You don't belong in this place." Tears were in his eyes.[28]

This experience should underscore the principle that if rehabilitation is to take place, it is most apt to occur when inmates are brought into contact with law-abiding persons in a non-punitive situation where each may show concern for the other. In prison education, as in all education, it is the personal characteristics of the faculty, not the catalog description of the curriculum, that will determine the success or failure of the educational process.

14.21 RELIGION IN PRISON

It would be difficult to identify a more important influence on our modern concepts of crime and punishment than religion. Transgression and punishment, penitence and forgiveness, guilt and pardon, justice and mercy; the entire process of the administration of justice is heavily influenced by our Judeo-Christian heritage. As we have already noted, the concept of a "penitentiary"—a place where offenders might repent—was drawn from religious precepts.

The majority of inmates, however, choose not to attend chapel. Many, if not most, suspect that the chaplain is simply a tool of the establishment, endeavoring to convince them of the rightness of the punishments being inflicted upon them. As for those who do attend, Clemmer reported, "It is the opinion of numerous inmates that those who attend because of a religious drive are usually the intellectually dull, the emotional, the provincial, and the aged."[29] For some homosexuals, chapel provides a convenient rendezvous—especially in the winter, when it is too cold to go out into the recreation yard.[30] The percentage of sex offenders, murderers, and embezzlers in church seems to be larger than it is in the general prison population.[31]

Prisoners' attitudes toward religion range from belief to apathy—from "God never did anything for me" to outright hostility, as when Christ is sacrilegiously referred to as "Jerusalem Slim."[32] Some inmates attempt to use religion as a facade that helps them to feign rehabilitation and impress the parole board. This attempt at manipulation is referred to by prison staff and inmates as "jailhouse religion."

This is not to say that religion has no influence upon inmates. Certainly the psychological situation of inmates is such that they are in need of the consolation and forgiveness which religion offers. Glaser found that, of successful releases (N = 65) who credited a specific staff member with being a major influence in their reformation, one-sixth (N = 11) cited the prison chaplain and religious workers as being instrumental in their rehabilitation.[33] This is impressive in that religious workers make up less than 1 percent of the total prison staff. The Louisiana State Penitentiary is typical of many state institutions in employing two chaplains, one Catholic and one Protestant, to minister to the spiritual needs of over four thousand inmates.[34] Given this ratio, it is unlikely that the average inmate would have much contact with the chaplains.

The tradition of the prison chaplain is an old one. Chaplains were the first to play a role in helping and treating prisoners, and they have performed these functions consistently. They have, at various times, taught school, established prison libraries, and served a social-work function with the families of prisoners. But as the goal of penitentiaries changed from penance to rehabilitation,[35] the role of the prison chaplain was usurped by librarians, teachers, classification officers, and psychologists. Religion, one of the oldest traditions in American penal treatment (e.g., the efforts of the Salvation Army and the Society of St. Vincent de Paul), now finds itself playing only a minor role.[36]

With the prison system under attack as an evil, many chaplains are concerned about their proper role and how to validate their genuine concern for prisoners. Among the issues identified as of primary concern by the First National Conference of Jesuit Prison Chaplains were:[37]

1 Is the chaplain in intrinsic danger of being part of the "system," since he is being paid by the state?

2 Are prisons intrinsically evil? And therefore should the chaplain refuse to enter them as a form of protest?

3 Should the chaplain be a civil servant? Or should his denomination support him?

4 How may the chaplain remain free to criticize the establishment and defend the oppressed?

5 Are chaplains being used as the "opiate of the convicts," to sprinkle holy water on an evil system?

One of the freedoms which a citizen forfeits upon entering a penitentiary is the unfettered exercise of religious beliefs. The First Amendment reads: "Congress shall make no law respecting an establishment of religion or prohibiting the free exercise thereof . . ." In a prison environment, however, distinction is made between the freedom to believe, which is absolute, and freedom to exercise one's beliefs, which may be subject to certain restrictions. The courts have until recently taken a hands-off position on this issue, feeling that it was not for them to review the practical judgment of prison authorities in matters of prison discipline. Prisoner litigation in this area has ranged from frivolous suits asking for the right to worship the centerfold in *Playboy* magazine to the request of Black Muslims for the right to observe special dietary rules during the month of Ramadan. The courts have tried to achieve a balance of interests, allowing prisoners to practice their religion but limiting their freedom as required by the overriding interests of society.[38] (The constitutional rights of prisoners are discussed in Chapter 15.)

14.22 WORK RELEASE

The paradox of prison is that we are attempting to train men and women to function in a free society by socializing them in the normative structure of a society of captives. It is like attempting to prepare sailors for life at sea by sending them to boot camp in the Gobi desert.

Repeated studies have shown that the most important factors associated with postrelease success are the availability of a family for social support and a meaningful job.[39] One way of reintegrating offenders into the community is to place them on work release near the end of their sentences. These programs are also known as day parole, work furlough, day work, outmate programs, daylight parole, intermittent jailing, and private prerelease work.[40] The inmate is allowed to work in the community during the day and return to confinement at night. Some type of work release has been utilized by prison administrators since the colonial days, when women prisoners were placed with private families as indentured servants.

In 1913, the United States gained its first work-release program when the Wisconsin legislature passed the Huber Law, which allows selected misdemeanants to work in the community during the day and return to jail at night. Forty years passed before other states followed the example of Wisconsin. In 1957, North Carolina passed a similar law for felons.[41] By 1971, work-release programs in the United States had been adopted by 41 states, the District of Columbia, and the Federal Bureau of Prisons. In Europe, this system is utilized by Sweden, France, Scotland, Norway, West Germany, and Great Britain.[42]

Enabling legislation for work release normally contains restrictions on employment. Generally three conditions are necessary for acceptable employment. First, the work releasee must not compete in a skill area where there is already a surplus of free laborers. Second, prisoners' working conditions and pay must be equal to those of free workers. If the job involves a union, it must be consulted; and—finally—no work releasee can work during a labor dispute.[43]

Work release is not available to everyone. Inmates most often prohibited from participating in work-release programs—either by statute or administrative decision—are (1) violent offenders, (2) sexual offenders, (3) drug users, (4) individuals whose offenses have been accompanied by notoriety, (5) members of organized crime, and (6) those considered to be escape risks.[44]

Apart from being limited to certain types of offenders, selection is further restricted to those inmates with only a short time left to serve. The reasoning is that work release will serve the inmate best as a bridge to life in the free world. Time limits range from 3 months left to serve in Michigan to 24 months in Georgia, with the most common requirement being 6 months. Some state statutes require that a given proportion of the inmate's sentence be served before he or she is eligible for work release. North Carolina requires that all inmates who wish to become eligible for work release must first serve one-quarter of their sentences. When an offender is sentenced to less than a year, the sentencing judge may make the decision about assignment to a work-release program. In North Carolina, for example, if the offender is serving less than 5 years, the sentencing court may authorize work release; if the sentence exceeds 5 years, the responsibility falls to the board of parole.

Because inmates do not usually have salable

work skills, the types of jobs they can hold are on a rather low level. Institutional training seldom corrects this deficiency. Most federal work-releasees surveyed had jobs unrelated to their institutional training.[45] Root reports that his experience with a work-release program in the industrial area of New Jersey was that work-releasees usually were given the least desirable jobs and were paid the lowest wages.[46] Jessica Mitford, the muckraking critic of the United States prison system, has suggested that there is little reality in pictures on work-release brochures showing smartly dressed men and women striding purposefully to work with attaché cases in hand. She suggests that we would come closer to the truth by showing convicts engaged in "stoop labor" in the California farming industry.[47]

The majority of work-release prisoners appear to satisfy their employers' needs. A North Carolina survey reported that 76 percent of the 465 employers who responded found the performance of their work-release employees to be of the same quality as that of the average nonprison employee performing the same work at the same wage. Another 20 percent rated the work releasees' performance superior to that of others; only 4 percent said it was inferior.[48] If work release is considered "successful" when a prisoner remains in the program until the end of his or her prison term, success rates range from 66 to 90 percent. The principal reasons for failure and/or removal from the program are drinking, breaking regulations to be with women, and marital conflicts.[49]

There can be no question that work release is both a tax bargain and an economic asset to correctional administrators. In North Carolina, 6,080 inmates earned nearly $4½ million in the first 5 years of the program (1961–1965). From this amount, the prison department deducted $1,502,000 for their keep and another $370,000 for transportation. The 5,000 work-releasees in California during the fiscal year 1968 earned more than $2 million in after-tax income (an average of $400 per prisoner). It was disbursed in the following manner.

$650,000	Maintenance
$600,000	Support of dependents
$500,000	Paid to inmates at time of release ($100 per inmate)
$200,000	Inmates' personal expenses

A study of the District of Columbia's work-release programs found that it cost twice as much to keep an offender in an institution than to put him or her on work release.

Priorities for inmates' wages are as follows: (1) room-and-board payments, (2) travel and incidental expenses, (3) support of dependents, (4) payments of fines and debts, and (5) savings for release.[50]

In order to assess the general acceptance of work release, a questionnaire was sent to 492 sheriffs in forty-two states; 218 (37 percent) responded.

> The sheriffs cited the following advantages of the work program: It enables the prisoner to support his family; he is not a county burden; he is able to keep his job; he is able to support himself; the jail experience is not so demoralizing. The chief disadvantage, according to 68 percent of the sheriffs, was that work release defeats the punitive purposes of sentencing. Other disadvantages listed were the special handling required, loss of control over the prisoner, security problems, excessive administrative costs and resentment of work-release prisoners by prisoners not in the program.[51]

Jessica Mitford, the gadfly of American corrections, does not doubt that "rent-a-con" is a practical way of supplementing county jail and state prison budgets, providing "sinecures" (dead-head jobs) for guards, and supplying cheap labor to nonunion employers, but she doubts that it is beneficial to the inmate. To Miss Mitford, what is billed as "rehabilitation" and "inmate benefits" is, in actuality, designed to keep the prison business solvent.[52]

SUMMARY

Penitentiaries were conceived by religiously oriented reformers in an attempt to make the treatment of offenders more humane. The American prison system vacillated back and forth between various approaches, stressing treatment on the one hand and the simple warehousing of inmates on the other. Changes in penal philosophy tend to follow whatever is the most economical method of dealing with inmates. As an experiement in rehabilitation, the penitentiary has been a failure, and some scholars are calling for its total abolition. Ironically, other scholars have admitted that we do not know how to rehabilitate offenders; they see the necessity of maintaining prisons for those who are violent and dangerous to society. The penitentiary will, in all likelihood, be with us for some time to come.

Chapter 15

Constitutional Rights of Convicted Offenders

It is inaccurate to state that upon conviction a prisoner retains no constitutional rights or that the full panoply of constitutional rights safeguards prisoners notwithstanding a conviction. Both statements are erroneous. Prisoners *do* retain certain constitutional rights following conviction and imprisonment, and some rights *are* lost as a legal consequence of a valid criminal conviction. In this chapter we will discuss some of the legal disabilities which attend and are consequences of our criminal process. This will be followed by a discussion of recent litigation involving the rights of prisoners.

15.01 THE "HANDS-OFF" DOCTRINE AND ITS DEMISE

The law of corrections and especially that body of law dealing with the rights of prisoners is of recent vintage.[1] Only recently have our courts (especially the federal courts) been willing to turn their attention to the plight of prisoners with the recognition that not all one's constitutional rights are forever lost upon conviction. Traditionally, American courts adhered to a "hands-off" policy when inmates—especially those in state custody—complained of prison regulations or practices.[2] For many years the courts (federal and state) maintained that, since correctional authorities were experts in the processes of custody and institutionalization, the judiciary should refrain from undue interference in these matters except in the most unusual cases. This view came to be known as the "hands-off" doctrine.[3] As noted by the Supreme Court of Virginia in 1871, a prisoner is but a "slave of the state."[4] Several reasons were advanced in support of the "hands-off" doctrine: (1) the maintenance of the correctional system is an executive function and should not be subject to judicial review; (2) judicial review of the correctional system violates the doctrine of separation of powers; (3) the judicial branch lacks the expertise to review the decisions of correctional authorities; and (4) the judicial branch lacks jurisdiction to review such cases, since prisoners do not have any rights.[5]

Over time and especially since the adoption of the 1964 Civil Rights Act, the problem of prisoners' rights has received increased attention from the courts.[6] Sections of the Civil Rights Act give state prisoners direct access to the federal courts for the redress of their legitimate grievances on conditions and practices in prisons. Although there has been a steady decrease in the population of correctional institutions in recent years,[7] the number of lawsuits filed by inmates attacking the conditions of confinement and prison regulations (as opposed to attacks on the legality of conviction) has dramatically increased.[8] Although the U.S. Supreme Court did not respond as quickly as other federal courts to the demise of the "hands-off" doctrine, recent Supreme Court pronouncements give strong evidence that the earlier reasons given for judicial restraint are no longer viable.[9]

Before we discuss some of the legal problems associated with the rights of prisoners, a brief statement of some "facts" regarding our correctional institutions and its prisoners will be presented. Our discussion does not include alternatives to incarceration; these were presented earlier in the text.

15.02 SOME "FACTS" ABOUT CORRECTIONAL INSTITUTIONS AND PRISONERS[10]

There are approximately 400 institutions for offenders in the United States, ranging from maximum-security prisons to reception centers. Of these, 250 are prisons for adults, housing over two hundred thousand prisoners (federal and state). About 10 percent of all prisoners are confined in federal institutions, and about 3 percent of the adult prison population is made up of women.

Of the 77 maximum-security institutions in America, 45 were built before 1900 (12 were built before 1850); they employ over seventy thousand full-time employees. Of all correctional employees, 87 percent perform only custodial or administrative functions. Only the 31 prisons for women and 58 institutions for men are oriented primarily toward rehabilitation; the remainder are primarily custodial.

In the United States, there are over five thousand jails which house convicted misdemeanants, defendants awaiting trial, and a few people who are serving short felony sentences. More than half of all people in jail have not been convicted of any offense the majority being pretrial detainees who are unable to make bail. Our jails hold 3 to 4 million people, and in two-thirds of the jails there are no rehabilitation programs. Over a million people served jail sentences in 1965.

It has been estimated that between 20 and 50 million Americans have criminal records and that 50 to 90 percent of the males in high poverty areas have such records. However, only 28 percent of all convicted offenders are in institutions on any given day (72 percent are in community or juvenile programs such as probation, parole, or halfway houses).

The majority of convicted offenders are less than thirty years of age, poor, have less than a high school education, lack salable skills, and come from urban areas. But most of our major correctional institutions are located in rural areas, although there is a trend toward smaller institutions that are nearer urban areas.

A disproportionate number of institutionalized offenders are nonwhite. Blacks make up more than half the inmate population in many large prisons. All but 2 percent of institutionalized offenders are eventually released (either on parole or because they have served their full terms). Although we sentence our offenders to some of the longest prison terms in the world, several polls indicate that most Americans believe that our courts are too lenient with offenders. Yet our recidivism rate is estimated to run between 50 and 80 percent. In view of the above, it is not surprising that prisoners' litigation has continued to rise in recent years. In the words of Chief Justice Burger, our prisons are "a national disgrace."

Few Americans have any substantial knowledge of their prisons; an "out of sight, out of mind" philosophy is dominant in our society. But this attitude may change. One important development has been the suggestion that female criminality has dramatically increased in recent years.[11] Such a trend would make the proportion of incarcerated males to females more equal and would probably draw increased public attention to our correctional institutions.

In addition to giving one a criminal record—which is, at best, a socially undesirable acquisition—other legal consequences attend a criminal conviction, especially a felony.

15.03 CIVIL DISABILITIES FOLLOWING CONVICTION

A felony conviction can and often does result in long-term confinement, which restricts or eliminates many of the basic social amenities that go with personal freedom. Few jurisdictions permit conjugal visits (the state of Mississippi was the first to allow this); furthermore, money, alcohol, and drugs (not prescribed by a physician) are contraband in prison. There is even a rigidly enforced institutional dress code in most jurisdictions. Thus, many of the social freedoms taken for granted by free citizens are lost or restricted during confinement, up to and including mealtimes and the hours of sleep. But convicted offenders are subjected to other disabilities and disqualifications quite apart from the sentence imposed. These additional legal deprivations are known as the *collateral consequences*[12] or *civil disabilities*[13] following a criminal conviction. The additional rights which may be lost include the right (1) to vote; (2) to serve on a jury; (3) to hold public office; (4) to make or enforce a contract; (5) to sue; (6) to make a will or inherit property; (7) to collect insurance, pensions, or workmen's compensation benefits; and (8) to obtain a license for certain occupations.

The loss or retention of certain civil rights as a consequence of conviction is, for the most part, a question of individual state laws;[14] only the most generalized statements about civil disabilities can be made absent an intensive study of the law within a particular jurisdiction. Not all states provide for a loss of civil rights following a criminal conviction; in some only a few civil rights are lost, and in a few all civil rights are lost (permanently or temporarily).

The *Vanderbilt Law Review* has done an exhaustive study of the collateral consequences of a criminal conviction.[15] This study is often referred to as a primary source for such a topic;[16] and our discussion borrows, to some extent but not completely, from it.

The Right to Vote

The majority of states permanently deny convicted felons the right to vote.[17] The underlying rationale is that (1) such persons have no strong personal interest in the outcome of an election (especially those incarcerated,)[18] (2) it prevents electoral fraud,[19] and (3) it keeps former felons from the ballot box and thus prevents them from voting to repeal provisions of the criminal code.[20]

While denying the right to vote to *imprisoned* defendants might have some merit, legitimate grounds for permanent disenfranchisement are tenuous at best. As noted by the President's Task Force on Corrections, "there seems to be no justification for permanently depriving all convicted felons of the vote . . ."[21] and "Rehabilitation might be furthered by encouraging convicted persons to participate in society by exercising the vote."[22]

The constitutionality of state disenfranchisement of convicted felons was recently determined by the Supreme Court in *Richardson v. Ramirez* (1974).[23]

In *Richardson*, three ex-felons who had completed their sentences and paroles petitioned the California Supreme Court to compel California county officials to register them as voters. Under the California Constitution, persons convicted of "infamous crimes" were denied the right to vote. The California Supreme Court held that the provision of the California Constitution (denying the vote to all ex-felons whose prison terms and parole have expired) was in violation of the equal protection clause of the Fourteenth Amendment.

On certiorari, the U.S. Supreme Court reversed and remanded. In a majority opinion by Justice Rehnquist, the Court stated that the resolution of the case was, in part, dependent not only upon section 1 of the Fourteenth Amendment's Equal Protection Clause but also upon the less familiar section 2. Section 2 of the Fourteenth Amendment provides that:

> Representatives shall be apportioned among the several States according to their respective numbers, counting the whole number of persons in each State, excluding Indians not taxed. But when the right to vote at any election for the choice of electors for President and Vice President of the United States, Representatives in Congress, the Executive and Judicial officers of a State, or the members of the legislature thereof, is denied to any of the male inhabitants of such State, being twenty-one years of age, and citizens of the United States, or in any way abridged, *except for participation in rebellion, or other crime,* the basis of representation therein shall be reduced in the proportion which the number of such male citizens shall bear to the whole number of male citizens twenty-one years of age in such State. [Emphasis added.]

A majority Court in *Richardson* held that the express language of section 2 of the Fourteenth Amendment and the historical and judicial interpretation of the amendment do not preclude a state from disenfranchising convicted felons even though their sentences and paroles have been completed. As noted by the *Richardson* Court:

> The problem of interpreting the "intention" of a constitutional provision is . . . a difficult one. Not only are there deliberations of congressional committees and floor debates in the House and Senate, but an amendment must thereafter be ratified by the necessary number of States. The legislative history bearing on the meaning of the relevant language of § 2 is scant indeed; the framers of the Amendment were primarily concerned with the effect of reduced representation upon the States, rather than with the two forms of disenfranchisement which were exempted from that consequence by the language with which we are concerned here. Nonetheless, what legislative history there is indicates that *this language was intended by Congress to mean what it says.* [Emphasis added.][24]

Of course, a state may allow ex-felons the right to vote. The *Richardson* decision merely holds that such disenfranchisement does not violate the Equal Protection Clause of the Fourteenth Amendment.

The Right to Serve on a Jury

In at least a half-dozen states, jury service by a convicted defendant is prohibited by statute.[25] But in most states the right of an ex-felon to serve on a jury is denied in practice.[26] The President's Commission on Law Enforcement and the Administration of Justice[27] and the National Advisory Commission on Criminal Justice Standards and Goals[28] recommend the suspension of the privilege of serving on a jury only during *actual confinement.* Otherwise, according to these commissions, there is little justification for permanently disqualifying all convicted felons from serving as jurors. The criminal records of prospective jurors can be revealed during the voir dire and, if relevant, used as a challenge for cause (see Chapter 10).

The American Law Institute's *Model Penal Code* provides that a person convicted of "a crime be disqualified . . . from serving as a juror *until he has satisfied his sentence.*"[29]

The Right to Hold Public Office

In the majority of states and the federal government, a convicted felon may not hold public office.[30] In some states, this disqualification is permanent.[31] In others, the result is temporary.[32] The rationale for this disability is to protect the public against ex-felons running for or holding public office.[33] But as noted by the *Task Force Report: Corrections,* it is rarely necessary to provide automatic disqualification to hold public office.[34] Disqualification should be restricted to those crimes and offenders that would threaten the public if allowed to run for public office.[35] The National Advisory Commission on Criminal Justice Standards and Goals recommends that restrictions on the right to hold public office be applicable only during *actual confinement.*[36]

The Right to Make or Enforce a Contract

At common law, a convicted felon had a right to make a contract but could not sue to enforce it; although the other party to the contract *could* sue to secure performance.[37]

Today convicts may make and enforce contracts in thirty-seven states.[38] In the thirteen other states—the so-called *civil-death jurisdictions* (discussed below)—there is no uniformity regarding a convict's right to make or enforce contracts. In seven of these civil-death states, a convict has no right to enforce a contract; in Missouri, a convict has no right to contract at all.[39] In most of the civil-death states, convicts generally have a right to contract, but their power to enforce performance is limited.[40]

The National Adivsory Commission on Criminal Justice Standards and Goals recommends that all restrictions on the right of convicted offenders to contract or sue to enforce contracts be repealed.[41] As noted by the *Task Force Report: Corrections,* the blanket loss of contractual powers is inconsistent with the correctional goal of rehabilitation and reintegration of the offender into the community.[42]

The Right to Sue

Convicts may be sued in all states.[43] In a few, however, convicts either may not sue in their own names or are prohibited from bringing suit while imprisoned.[44] In some states, convicts must sue through personal representatives (retained or court appointed); in most states, prisoners may not personally appear in court to defend themselves against civil suits.[45]

Such rigidly enforced disabilities may serve to undermine rehabilitation, as they seriously impair the offender's right to execute and enforce valid legal instruments (e.g., wills, contracts). The National Advisory Commission on Criminal Justice Standards and Goals recommends the abolition of all restrictions on an offender's capacity to sue or be sued.[46]

The Right to Make a Will or Inherit Property

At early common law, the conviction of a felony meant death and forfeiture of one's property to the Crown.[47] Thus, there was no need for convicts to make wills or for anyone to make provisions for an offender to inherit property. Today, convicts may own property, and the capacity to make a valid will is determined by statute. In most states, a convict may make a valid will provided the testator (person writing the will) is of legal age and of sound mind.[48]

Today, in the majority of states, a convict may generally inherit property except under the "slaying statutes," which forbid an offender from inheriting from the person he or she is convicted of feloniously killing.[49] That is, killers may not inherit from their victims.

The Loss of Insurance, Pensions, Workmen's Compensation, and Other Benefits

Most insurance companies will not insure a convict.[50] The prospective insured is deemed a poor risk, as his or her future is too uncertain. The fact that most defendants are poor raises a substantial question, in the eyes of insurers, of their ability to continue making payments on premiums after release (when they will also be saddled with criminal records).

Most states and the federal government deny those convicted of certain offenses the right to participate in annuity, pension, or retirement programs even though other requirements such as age and length of service have been fulfilled.[51]

Most states forbid inmates from receiving workmen's compensation benefits as a result of injuries in prison.[52] The rationale is that inmates do not and cannot make contracts for hire for their services even though they may be paid for such services.[53] Although federal inmates are compensated for their in-prison injuries, the denial of benefits to convict-employees has been likened to a form of indentured servitude[54] and may be an unconstitutional denial of equal protection of the laws.[55]

The Right to Obtain a License for Certain Occupations

Perhaps the most deleterious civil disability accompanying a criminal conviction stems from those statutes and regulations which require governmental licensing for many occupations.[56] An ex-offender may be denied a license to practice as, for example, (1) a barber, (2) an architect, (3) an engineer, (4) a realtor, (5) a cosmetologist, (6) a physician, (7) an attorney, (8) a dentist, (9) a dry-cleaner, (10) a pharmacist, (11) a nurse, (12) an undertaker, (13) a notary public, (14) an insurance adjustor, (15) a liquor dealer, (16) a private detective, or (17) a law enforcement officer.[57] While the above list is not exhaustive and not all states prohibit the licensing of convicted offenders for certain occupations, almost all states prohibit the practice of *some* occupations by ex-offenders. Yet the unemployment rate for ex-offenders is three to four times higher than the national average.[58] Employers are reluctant to hire ex-offenders.[59] Even former Attorney General John Mitchell, now a convicted felon himself and no watery sentimentalist, has indicated a need for a public reevaluation of ex-offenders and employment opportunities.[60] Moreover, studies have shown not only that unemployment is a major factor in the increase in crime[61] but also that regular employment is directly related to a low recidivism rate.[62]

These additional barriers to employment are particularly significant, since most offenders have low employability (they are poor and uneducated, have few salable skills, etc.).[63] Employment problems also undermine the parole process, since in order to be paroled an inmate must, traditionally, secure a job before being released.[64] Otherwise the inmate must remain in prison waiting to obtain employment even after parole has been granted.

It is at best, a cruel hoax for a state to train an inmate in a certain occupation as part of the rehabilitation process and then to deny that same offender the right to practice that occupation because of licensing regulations. In fact, some state civil disabilities following a criminal conviction—especially those which are unreasonable and dysfunctional—may actually be unconstitutional.

The well-known case of *Griggs v. Duke Power Company* (1971),[65] decided by the U.S. Supreme Court, may be used in the future by other courts to eliminate some of these artificial barriers to the employment of ex-offenders.

In *Griggs,* thirteen blacks sued the Duke Power Company under Title VII of the Civil Rights Act (1964) which forbids employers from discriminating on the basis of race, color, religion, sex, or national origin. The company required all new employees (for most jobs) to have a high school education and to pass two intelligence tests. Neither test was intended to measure an applicant's ability to learn a particular job. The new requirements operated to disqualify blacks at a substantially higher rate than white applicants, and the jobs in question had been filled only by white employees as a part of the company's long-standing practice of giving preference to whites.

The district court dismissed the suit and the court of appeals affirmed in part, holding that the diploma and test requirements were proper absent a showing of purposeful discrimination.

On certiorari, the U.S. Supreme Court reversed. A unanimous Court held that, while the use of testing or measuring procedures for employment are permissible, such requirements must *bear a demonstrable relationship to job performance.* As noted by Chief Justice Burger, writing for the *Griggs* Court:

> . . . the Act does not command that any person be hired simply because he was formerly the subject of discrimination, or because he is a member of a minority group. Discriminatory preference for any group, minority or majority, is precisely and only what Congress has proscribed. What is required by Congress is the removal of artificial, arbitrary, and unnecessary barriers to employment when the barriers operate invidiously to discriminate on the basis of racial or other impermissible classification.[66]

One might ask whether all or most of the current employment disabilities following a criminal conviction *bear a demonstrable relationship to job performance* under the *Griggs* rationale. Of course it is easy to distinguish employment practices legally, but that decision could invite future lawsuits as authority to make rational some of our irrational regulations and practices governing employment barriers against ex-offenders.

Civil Death

Today, thirteen states provide by statute that an offender sentenced to life imprisonment or death is deemed "civilly dead."[67] Such a status may dissolve a marriage or leave children subject to adoption (as though the offender were dead).[68] In addition, civil death may abrogate the right to contract, make a will, and inherit or transfer property; it may also impose other limits as noted above. Parole operates to remove the status of civil death in most jurisdictions.

Restoration of Civil Rights

The civil disabilities incurred automatically following a criminal conviction may be either permanent or effective only during the period of imprisonment.[69] In all jurisdictions, there are provisions for restoring one's civil rights. The oldest form of relief is the *pardon.*[70] Only the state of Rhode Island does not have a pardoning procedure; there, the legislature alone has the power to restore an offender's civil rights. In the other forty-nine states, the power to pardon belongs to the governor, the pardoning board, or both.[71] However, executive clemency (e.g., pardon) is rarely used.[72]

In general, a pardon is reserved for those cases in which an individual is probably innocent or where the judicial process has produced an unfair result.[73] Parenthetically, in light of a 1915 Supreme Court decision which held that a pardon is an implied expression of guilt, one might inquire as to the rationale for the pardon given to (and accepted by) former President Nixon.[74]

In about one-fourth of the states, an offender's civil rights are automatically restored via statute upon the successful completion of probation, parole, or a sentence.[75]

In some jurisdictions, the civil rights lost following a criminal conviction are restored at the discretion of the parole board or the court in which sentence was imposed.[76]

Twelve states provide that an offender's criminal record shall be expunged (erased and sealed) or annulled upon the successful completion of probation, parole, or sentence.[77] But most restoration procedures are ineffective, since many offenders lack the knowledge or ability to pursue them.[78]

In summary, the civil rights lost following a criminal conviction vary from jurisdiction to jurisdiction. Some require conviction of a felony; some specify "infamous crimes"; and others include crimes of "moral turpitude." It is obvious that many of the civil disabilities incurred are only remotely connected to the punishable criminal behavior and often result in needless additional "punishment" which is likely to undermine the rehabilitation efforts of the correctional authorities and the process of reintegrating the offender into the community.[79]

In light of the above, the American Law Institute's *Model Penal Code* has made the following proposal:

> No person shall suffer any legal disqualification or disability because of his conviction of a crime or his sentence on such conviction, unless the disqualification or disability involves the deprivation of a right or privilege which is: (*a*) necessarily incident to execution of the sentence of the Court; or (*b*) provided by the Constitution or the Code; or (*c*) provided by a statute other than the Code, when the conviction is of a crime defined by such statute; or (*d*) provided by the judgment, order, or regulation of a court, agency, or official exercising a jurisdiction conferred by law, or by statute defining such jurisdiction, when the commission of the crime or the conviction of the sentence is reasonably related to the competency of the individual to exercise the right or privilege of which he is deprived.[80]

Next we will examine the problems of jurisdiction and remedies available to redress inmates' complaints.

15.04 JURISDICTION AND REMEDIES AVAILABLE TO REDRESS INMATES' COMPLAINTS

Federal or state judicial remedies are available to vindicate prisoners' claims in all jurisdictions. However, most of the prisoners' rights cases have come from the federal courts.[81] This is because of the many obstacles and barriers to prisoners' suits brought in state courts in the past.

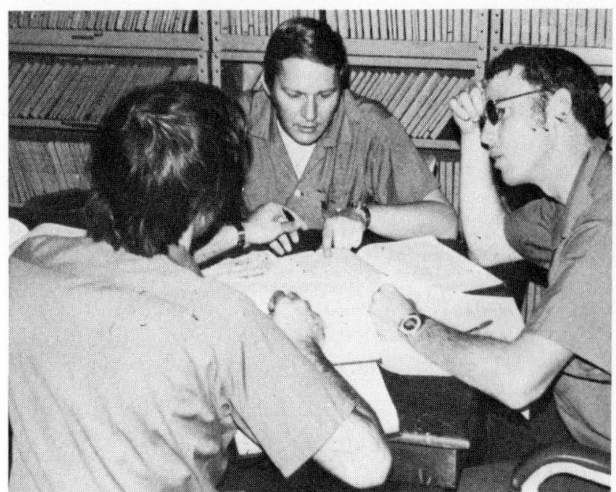

A session of "Writ Writers" club is held at the Florida State prison.

Historically, the *doctrine of sovereign immunity* posed a serious impediment to inmates' suits against correctional authorities. According to this doctrine, private citizens (e.g., inmates) may not sue a governmental agency without its consent. The underlying reasons in support of this doctrine are that (1) "the King [government] can do no wrong," (2) public funds should not be used to redress private injuries, and (3) government officials need to be free from the threat of a lawsuit in order to function most efficiently.[82] Thus, in those states where sovereign immunity is recognized, the state correctional system is immune from a private suit filed by an inmate. However, a suit may be filed, even in those jurisdictions recognizing the doctrine, against state officials in their individual capacity if they have violated the constitutional rights of inmates. Many states have totally or partially abolished the doctrine of sovereign immunity; its viability depends on the law in each state.[83]

Another barrier, in the past, to inmates' complaints filed in state courts was the "hands-off" doctrine noted earlier. Typical of such judicial restraint was the Supreme Court's pronouncement in 1948 that "[L]awful incarceration brings about the necessary withdrawal or limitation of many privileges and rights."[84] As we have indicated, the courts felt obliged to defer to the expertise of prison officials on matters involving internal correctional affairs. Today this passive judicial restraint has been replaced with an increasing eagerness on the part of the courts to redress legitimate inmate complaints. As noted by the Sixth Circuit Court of Appeals, "[a] prisoner retains all the rights of an ordinary citizen except those expressly, or by necessary implication, taken from him by law."[85]

Although state remedies are today available to redress legitimate inmate complaints (e.g., state habeas corpus, criminal prosecutions against correctional authorities who mistreat inmates, contempt of court, etc.), most inmate complaints have been filed in the federal courts for a variety of reasons.[86]

Federal Jurisdiction and Remedies for Inmates' Complaints

Federal remedies, in order to review state prison practices, are available under two principal methods: federal habeas corpus petitions (See Chapter 12) and suits filed under the 1964 Civil Rights Act (42 U.S.C. § 1983, the so-called § 1983 suits). Although release from custody is usually sought under a habeas corpus petition, this remedy can also be used to challenge most in-prison practices.[87] Most inmates' suits challenging prison conditions and practices are filed under § 1983 of the Civil Rights Act. The reasons for this will become apparent later. The applicable federal civil rights statutes provide the following:

> 42 U.S.C.A. § 1343
>
> The district courts shall have *original jurisdiction* of any civil action authorized by law to be commenced by any person:
>
> (3) To redress the deprivation, under color of any state law, statute, ordinance, regulation, custom or usage, of any right, privilege or immunity secured by the Constitution of the United States or by any Act of Congress providing for equal rights of citizens or of all persons within the jurisdiction of the United States;
>
> 42 U.S.C.A. § 1983
>
> Every person who, under color of any statute, ordinance, regulation, custom, or usage, of any State or Territory, subjects or causes to be subjected, any citizen of the United States or other person within the jurisdiction thereof to the deprivation of any rights, privileges, or immunities secured by the Constitution and laws, shall be liable to the party injured in an action at law, suit in equity, or other proper proceeding for redress.

Thus an inmate must allege two claims under a § 1983 suit: (1) that the defendants (state or local officials) acted "under color of state law" and (2) that the defendants deprived the inmate of a constitutional (or federal) right.

The major advantages of a § 1983 suit over a habeas corpus petition are twofold: (1) a § 1983 suit does *not* require an exhaustion of available state remedies before the federal district courts have jurisdiction (as is required for state prisoners filing a federal habeas corpus petition)[88] and (2) an award of monetary damages is possible in order to redress a denial of constitutional rights.[89] Apparently three classes of monetary damages are available to bring redress to an inmate whose constitutional rights have been violated: (1) *actual damages,* compensation for an inmate's out-of-pocket expenses and mental suffering; (2) *nominal damages,* which vindicate an inmate's rights if no actual damages were sustained; and (3) *punitive damages,* which would apply when the wrongful acts were intentional and malicious.[90]

The major disadvantage (from the viewpoint of inmates of a § 1983 suit is that such an action cannot be used to secure a release from imprisonment (the sole federal remedy is a writ of habeas corpus).[91] Thus, federal habeas corpus (which requires an exhaustion of available state remedies for state prisoners) can be used to secure release from imprisonment or to challenge prison practices. On the other hand, a § 1983 suit (which does not require an exhaustion of state remedies) can be utilized only to redress prison practices or regulations; release from confinement is not available under § 1983. In addition, § 1983 is *not* available to federal prisoners, since federal correctional authorities do *not* act *under color of state law.* However, the Supreme Court, in 1971, judicially created a federal cause of action when a federal agent, acting under color of federal law, violates a person's constitutional rights.[92] Specifically, the Court held that money damages may be obtained upon a showing of a Fourth Amendment violation by federal officials.[93] Presumably, all constitutional violations by federal officials acting in their official capacity are now actionable in the federal courts.

In addition to monetary damages, there are other available remedies in the federal courts under a § 1983 suit filed by a state inmate. The Federal Declaratory Judgment Act allows a federal court to declare the legal rights, responsibilities, and liabilities of two or more adverse parties prior to the commission of some act which might result in actionable liabilities. The Declaratory Judgment Act provides, *inter alia:*

> In a case of actual controversy within its jurisdiction . . . any court of the United States, upon the filing of an appropriate pleading, may declare the rights and other legal relations of any interested party seeking such declaration. . . . [94]

Under the act, a federal court may grant "necessary or proper relief."[95] Such relief may include an *injunction,* a judicial order directing some party to do a specific thing or refrain from doing it (e.g., ordering inmate removed from solitary confinement). But where an injunction is sought against the enforcement of a state statute which is alleged to be unconstitutional (e.g., statute requiring the segregation of prisoners by race), federal law requires that a three-judge court must be convened to hear that case;[96] a decision by a three-judge federal court permits a *direct appeal* to the U.S. Supreme Court, thereby bypassing the court of appeals.[97] Finally, *criminal prosecutions* of correctional authorities are permissible under the Civil Rights Act as well as under the normal *contempt power* of federal courts[98] (the applicable federal statutes are presented the appendix at the end of this chapter).

We have omitted discussion of other procedures such as venue requirements, class actions, the writ of mandamus, the Federal Tort Claims Act, etc., since this is best left to more advanced courses.

In summary, inmates seeking redress of legitimate complaints usually have a choice of resorting to either the federal or state courts; the available remedies depend upon which forum the plaintiff has chosen. Next we will examine some of the recent case law which has developed in the area of prisoners' rights.

15.05 RECENT PRONOUNCEMENTS BY FEDERAL COURTS ON PRISONERS' RIGHTS

In this section we will examine some of the recent litigation on prisoners' rights in the federal courts, with an emphasis on First Amendment rights, prison disciplinary hearings, Eighth Amendment rights, and probation and parole revocation hearings. Particular attention will be given to the relatively few Supreme Court pronouncements in this area of the law.

Inmates and the First Amendment

The First Amendment to the United States Constitution provides that:

> Congress shall make no law respecting an establishment of religion or prohibiting the free exercise thereof; or abridging the freedom of speech,

> or of the press; or the right of the people peaceably to assemble, and to petition the Government for a redress of grievances.

Thus, the First Amendment contains five separate guarantees: (1) freedom of religion, (2) freedom of speech, (3) freedom of the press, (4) the right to peaceful assembly, and (5) the right to petition the government. If the First Amendment is read literally, it would seem to prohibit prison officials from restricting many of the activities of inmates. However, this is not the case. The full scope of the First Amendment is not enjoyed by inmates. But, as noted recently by a federal court, there can be no doubt that the First Amendment "reaches inside prison walls."[99] The courts have attempted to strike a balance between First Amendment rights and legitimate prison practices which, in some instances, may necessitate some restrictions on these fundamental rights. We begin with a discussion of two Supreme Court pronouncements on prisoners' access to the courts. Without access to the courts, even legitimate inmate claims cannot be redressed.

In 1941 the Supreme Court held, in *Ex parte Hull,*[100] that prison officials may not deny inmates access to the courts. Specifically, the Court held that "[T]he state and its officers may not abridge or impair petitioner's right to apply to a federal court for a writ of habeas corpus."[101] In *Ex parte Hull,* prison officials refused to allow the petitioner, an inmate, to mail a writ of habeas corpus and a letter to a federal court.

More recently, in *Johnson v. Avery* (1969),[102] the Supreme Court struck down a Tennessee prison regulation that prohibited inmates from assisting one another in the preparation of writs and other legal matters. As noted by the Court in *Avery:*

> Since the basic purpose of the writ is to enable those unlawfully incarcerated to obtain their freedom, it is fundamental that access of prisoners to the courts for the purpose of presenting their complaints may not be denied or obstructed.[103]

It is one thing to have access to the courts, but it may be quite something else to "win" a suit on its merits. Accordingly, most federal courts that have had to decide issues involving the First Amendment rights of prisoners have articulated a two-step analysis. In order for a state to restrict an inmate's First Amendment freedoms, the state has the burden of showing (1) that the prison regulation is necessary under a "balancing of interests" test and (2) that the limitation on the right is the *least* restrictive alternative available.[104]

A variety of suits by inmates alleging a denial of First Amendment rights have been filed in the federal courts. They have included issues of (1) visitation,[105] (2) personal appearance,[106] (3) censorship of mail,[107] (4) receipt of publications,[108] (5) prisoners' manuscripts,[109] (6) freedom of expression within a prison,[110] (7) freedom of religion within prison,[111] and (8) freedom of the press within prison.[112]

In most instances, the federal courts have struck down prison regulations which are not shown to serve a legitimate governmental purpose and which have a "chilling effect" on First Amendment rights.[113] However, these decisions do not mean that First Amendment rights in prison are absolute. Rather, arbitrary prison regulations which do not further legitimate correctional goals (e.g., rehabilitation, prison security) have not withstood judicial scrutiny.

Supreme Court pronouncements on the First Amendment rights of prisoners have been relatively few, although recently the Court seems to be more willing to examine this particularly troublesome area.

In *Cooper v. Pate* (1964),[114] the Supreme Court held that a § 1983 claim filed by a Black Muslim inmate presented a cause of action upon which relief could be granted. The claim alleged that, because of his religious beliefs, the plaintiff was denied the right to purchase certain religious publications. In *Cruz v. Beto* (1972),[115] the Supreme Court held that a § 1983 claim filed by a Buddhist prisoner was actionable on the merits of the case. In this instance, the plaintiff alleged that he was placed in solitary confinement on a bread-and-water diet for 2 weeks because he shared his Buddhist religious materials with other prisoners. In *Arciniega v. Freeman* (1971),[116] a federal prisoner was released on parole on condition that he not "associate" with ex-convicts. When he obtained employment in a restaurant-nightclub that employed other ex-convicts, his parole was revoked. The Supreme Court reversed and held that "incidental contacts" between ex-convicts during the course of work on a legitimate job for a common employer do not violate a parole restriction forbidding association with other convicts.

More recently, in *Pell v. Procunier* (1974)[117] and *Saxbe v. Washington Post* (1974),[118] the Supreme Court examined restrictions on press interviews of inmates in prison. In each case certain reporters and journalists sought to interview specifically designated inmates. However, a state regulation in the first case and a policy statement by the Federal Bureau of Prisons in the second case prohibited face-to-face interviews between journalists and individually designated inmates. The reporters and inmates challenged these restrictions as violative of the First Amendment's freedom of speech and press. The Supreme Court disagreed. As to the allegation that such regulations abridged the inmates' freedom of speech, the *Pell* Court held that:

> . . . in light of the alternative channels of communication that are open to prison inmates, we cannot say . . . that this restriction on one manner in which prisoners can communicate with persons outside of prison is unconstitutional. So long as this restriction operates in a neutral fashion . . . it falls within the "appropriate rules and regulations" to which "prisoners necessarily are subject," . . . and does not abridge any First Amendment freedom retained by prison inmates.[119]

With regard to the journalists' argument that such regulations violate the guarantee of freedom of the press, the Court stated that:

> . . . newsmen have no constitutional right of access to prisons or their inmates beyond that afforded the general public. [T]he First and Fourteenth Amendments bar government from interfering in any way with a free press. The Constitution does not, however, require government to accord the press special access to information not shared by members of the press generally.[120]

The Court went on to note that the press is regularly excluded from grand jury proceedings, Supreme Court conferences, and other meetings, and that journalists have no constitutional right of access to crime scenes, disasters, or places where the general public is excluded.[121] Thus, restrictions on the right to interview individually designated inmates does not violate the First Amendment freedom of the press.

In *Procunier v. Martinez* (1974),[122] the Supreme Court examined the issue of prisoner-mail censorship regulations. There, state inmates in California filed a class-action suit challenging the California Department of Corrections' regulations pertaining to inmate correspondence. The regulations prohibited inmate correspondence that "unduly complained," "magnified grievances," or "expressed inflammatory political, racial, religious or other views or beliefs." In addition, the regulations provided that inmates could not "send or receive letters that pertain to criminal activity; are lewd, obscene, or defamatory; contain foreign matter or are otherwise inappropriate."[123] Both incoming and outgoing inmate mail was screened by prison employees. In the event that personal mail was deemed objectionable by prison employees, they could (1) refuse to mail or deliver the letter; (2) submit a disciplinary report on the inmate involved; or (3) place a copy of the letter in the inmate's file, where it might be a factor in determining the inmate's future work and housing assignments as well as his or her parole eligibility.

The three-judge district court held that the prisoner-mail censorship regulations were in violation of the First Amendment and that they were void for vagueness.

On direct appeal, the Supreme Court affirmed. In an opinion by Justice Powell, the Court held that censorship of prisoner mail could be justified only if (1) the regulation or practice furthers an important or substantial governmental interest which is unrelated to the suppression of expression, (2) the mail censorship furthers one or more of the substantial governmental interests of *security, order,* or *rehabilitation;* and (3) the restrictions on First Amendment rights are not greater than is necessary or essential to the protection of the particular governmental interest involved.[124]

The Court went on to state that any mail censorship regulations must be accompanied by minimum procedural safeguards, and it approved of the district court requirements that (1) inmates be notified if letters written by them or addressed to them are rejected; (2) the author of a rejected letter be given a reasonable opportunity to protest that decision; and (3) complaints be referred to a prison official other than the employee who originally disapproved the correspondence.[125] As noted by the Court:

> [T]hese regulations fairly invited prison officials and employees to enjoy their own personal prejudices and opinions as standards for prison mail censorship. Not surprisingly, some prison officials used the extraordinary latitude for discretion authorized by the regulations to suppress unwelcome criticism.[126]

Although the Supreme Court has refused to consider the scope of an inmate's right to free speech in prison, the *Martinez* decision suggests that the "hands-off" doctrine is outdated and that its death knell has been sounded by the federal courts. As noted by the Supreme Court:

> . . . a policy of judicial restraint cannot encompass any failure to take cognizance of valid constitutional claims whether arising in a federal or state institution. When a prison regulation or practice offends a fundamental constitutional guarantee, federal courts will discharge their duty to protect constitutional rights.[127]

Recently, the Supreme Court has made several pronouncements on prison disciplinary and revocation procedures in light of the Due Process Clause of the Fourteenth Amendment.

Prison Discipline and Due Process

A central issue which has been drawing the increasing attention of the federal courts is this: What process is due before an inmate may be punished for violating prison regulations or may be returned to prison for violating conditions of parole or probation?

The Supreme Court has examined what process is due inmates within a prison context. Specifically, the Court has reviewed the due process requirements for probation revocation hearings,[128] parole revocation hearings,[129] and in-prison disciplinary hearings.[130]

In *Mempha v. Rhay* (1967),[131] the Supreme Court held that a right to counsel attaches at a combined *probation-revocation sentencing and hearing.* Although the *Mempha* Court did not specify what other due process procedures are required at such a hearing, it did indicate that a probation-revocation hearing is a stage of the criminal process and, by implication, that other due process rights might be required.

In *Morrissey v. Brewer* (1972),[132] the Supreme Court held that although a parole revocation is not a part of the criminal process and the full panoply of rights is not due a defendant at such a hearing, some minimum due process standards are required. Specifically, the *Morrissey*

Court held that minimum due process in parole-revocation hearings includes (1) written notice of the alleged violations, (2) disclosure to parolees of the evidence against them, (3) opportunity for parolees to be heard in person and to present their own witnesses and documentary evidence, (4) the right to confront and cross-examine witnesses, (5) a "neutral and detached" hearing body (e.g., parole board), and (6) a written statement of the facts and the reasons for revoking parole. The Court expressly left open the question whether the right to counsel is required at a parole-revocation hearing.

In *Gagnon v. Scarpelli* (1973),[133] the Court held that the minimum due process standards under Morrissey are required in *probation-revocation hearings* where a sentence has previously been imposed. Specifically, the Court held that a defendant is entitled to both (1) a *preliminary hearing* to determine whether there is probable cause that the defendant violated the conditions of probation and (2) a *final hearing* as to whether probation should be revoked. The Court went on to state that there is no per se constitutional right to counsel at such hearings but that the body conducting the hearing should determine on a case-by-case basis whether an indigent probationer or parolee needs the assistance of counsel.

With the above decisions as a background, the Supreme Court recently pronounced what due process standards are required at an *in-prison disciplinary hearing.*

In *Wolff v. McDonnell* (1974),[134] the defendant filed a § 1983 suit challenging several of the practices, rules, and regulations of the Nebraska Penal and Correctional Complex. Specifically the suit alleged, *inter alia,* that prison disciplinary proceedings did not comport with the Due Process Clause. After decisions by the district court and the court of appeals, the Supreme Court granted certiorari.

First, the Supreme Court held that prison disciplinary proceedings are not a part of a criminal prosecution. Therefore the full panoply of rights due a defendant is not applicable. But, since an inmate can lose good-time credits for serious infractions, minimum requirements of procedural due process must be observed. Second, the Court held that the *Morrissey-Scarpelli* procedures need not in all respects be followed in prison disciplinary hearings. Third, the Court held that the following due-process procedures are required at a prison disciplinary hearing: (1) advance written notice of the charges must be given to the inmate no less than 24 hours before his or her appearance before the hearing body; (2) a written statement by the hearing body as to the evidence relied on and the reasons for the disciplinary action must be given to the inmate; (3) the inmate may call witnesses and present documentary evidence in his or her defense if doing so will not jeopardize prison safety or correctional goals.

The Court further held that an inmate has no constitutional right to confront and cross-examine witnesses at a prison disciplinary hearing, this being discretionary with prison officials. Finally, the Court held that inmates have no right to retained or appointed counsel at such proceedings, although substitute counsel should be provided in some cases (e.g., when an illiterate inmate receives the aid of a fellow inmate). As noted by the Court in *Wolff:*

> The insertion of counsel into the disciplinary process would inevitably give the proceedings a more adversary cast and tend to reduce their utility as a means to further correctional goals. There would also be delay and practical problems in providing counsel in sufficient numbers at the time and place where hearings are to be held. At this stage of the development of these procedures we are not prepared to hold that inmates have a right to either retained or appointed counsel in disciplinary proceedings.[135]

Prison disciplinary actions and their outcomes can have serious repercussions on inmates. Punishment can include the loss of good time;[136] solitary confinement;[137] a denial of certain privileges[138] (e.g., Saturday night movie; a denial of access to work-release programs, educational-release programs, or more desirable jobs;[139] and transfers to other institutions.[140] Moreover, such punishments may jeopardize an inmate's chances for parole.[141]

The Supreme Court's pronouncements (cited above) seem to suggest that the closer one gets to prison, the less procedural due process is required. If the rehabilitation of criminals is truly one of the major goals of the correctional process, as the Supreme Court has often stated, then its decisions seem to be an odd way of promoting that ideal.

There is a growing body of case law dealing with the "cruel and unusual" provision of the Eighth Amendment and prisoner litigation.

"Cruel and Unusual Punishment," Institutions, and Inmates

The Eighth Amendment prohibition against cruel and unusual punishment has been the source of prisoner litigation involving prison conditions,[142] medical treatment,[143] the right to rehabilitation,[144] and disciplinary punishment.[145]

Recently, the U.S. Supreme Court ruled that medical malpractice by prison officials on an inmate does not per se give rise to a cause of action under a § 1983 claim, even though prison officials have an obligation to provide reasonable medical care to its inmates; only a showing of "deliberate indifference to serious medical needs" by prison officials is sufficient to bring the Eighth Amendment into play. Most of the recent case law in this regard, however, have come from the lower federal courts, and the decisions have not been uniform.[146]

Prison Conditions In the well-known case of *Holt v. Sarver* (1970),[147] the U.S. Court of Appeals held that confinement in the Arkansas Penitentiary System was cruel and unusual punishment in violation of the Eighth Amendment. This decision marked the first time that an entire prison system was held to be unconstitutional. The *Holt* Court found that the overall prison conditions were shocking and intolerable. The opinion emphasized such factors as (1) the trusty system, which placed unfettered power in the hands of certain inmates rather than paid correctional officers; (2) inadequate supervision in the dormitories, leaving the inmates subject to homosexual attacks; (3) the ghettolike conditions of the isolation cells, which were overcrowded, filthy, and unsanitary (e.g., infested with rats); (4) the absence of rehabilitation services and facilities; (5) inadequate medical and dental facilities; (6) poor sanitary conditions generally; and (7) inadequate clothing for inmates. The Court ordered the prison authorities to devise a plan for alleviating the conditions and explicitly stated that it would close down the entire prison system if necessary.

Similarly, other federal courts have held that shocking jail conditions may also violate the Eighth Amendment.[148] However, the results have not been uniform because of a lack of Supreme Court guidance on institutional conditions. For example, a district court in Alabama found conditions similar to those found in Arkansas to be "unpleasant" but not unconstitutional.[149]

It is likely that barbaric prison conditions will continue to draw the attention of the federal courts through prisoners' suits, and a state's fiscal inability to comply with a court order mandating drastic and expensive change will not be acceptable. As noted by Justice Blackmun while serving on the Court of Appeals for the Eighth Circuit, "Human conditions and constitutional requirements are not, in this day, to be measured or limited by dollar considerations."[150]

Medical Treatment in Correctional Institutions Complaints from inmates that they have been denied or received inadequate medical care are becoming increasingly frequent in the courts,[151] and most courts have held that correctional officials owe their inmates a duty of ordinary and reasonable medical care.[152] The overall adequacy of a medical-care program is one factor in a decision as to whether the conditions of an institution are unconstitutional.[153] However, most courts have not been receptive to complaints from individual inmates that they were denied proper medical treatment. The courts are reluctant to "second guess a licensed physician as to the propriety of a particular course of medical treatment afforded a prisoner-patient in his care."[154] Accordingly, the principle of an inmate's right to medical treatment on constitutional grounds has not been accepted by most courts.[155] As noted by one federal court:

> The power of this court is to measure the adequacy of the petitioner's medical treatment within the framework only of the Constitution of the United States. It is not for this court to say that better or more regular examinations could or could not have been made. If the treatment or lack of treatment of a prisoner is such that it amounts to indifference or intentional mistreatment, it violates the prisoner's constitutional guarantees.[156]

Another federal court has held that medical personnel may be liable for (1) improper nonmedical treatment of inmates, (2) an unjustifiable refusal to provide medical care, or (3) obviously inadequate medical care.[157]

In general, the federal courts have been unwilling to allow the Federal Civil Rights Act be utilized as a federal forum for alleged medical malpractice suits. Other, more traditional remedies—such as torts, injunctions, declaratory relief, and, for federal prisoners, the Federal Tort Claims Act as well as habeas corpus and its collateral remedies—are available to redress state inmates' claims of inadequate medical treatment.[158]

Judicial scrutiny of the medical treatment of inmates in light of the Eighth Amendment may be broadening in scope. One federal district court found the medical-care program in the Alabama Penal System to be cruel and unconstitutional.[159] And Professor Sheldon Krantz had suggested that some courts may be ready to hold that there is a constitutional right to treatment for inmate-alcoholics, drug addicts, and homosexuals.[160]

An issue related to the medical treatment problem is the right of an inmate to receive rehabilitative treatment.

The Right of Inmates to Receive Rehabilitative Services The question of whether there is or is not a constitutional right to treatment, rehabilitation, and "cure" for inmates has been drawing increasing attention in the literature and in court decisions. Some authorities have argued that rehabilitative services and programs in prison are constitutionally required;[161] others argue against this view.[162] However, the Supreme Court has never explicitly held that an inmate has a constitutional right to be rehabilitated—although the Court has emphasized in a number of decisions the importance of the rehabilitative process.

Some federal courts have held that mental institutions have an affirmative duty to provide some program of treatment at least to patients committed involuntarily. In *Rouse v. Cameron* (1967),[163] the defendant was found not guilty by reason of insanity for the misdemeanor offense of carrying a dangerous weapon. He was involuntarily committed to a mental institution. Five years later, the defendant, on a federal habeas corpus petition, sought release on the ground that he had not received any psychiatric treatment—although a 1964 Washington, D.C., statute stated that such patients were entitled to medical care as well as psychiatric care and treatment.[164]

On appeal, the Circuit Court of Appeals of the District of Columbia reversed and remanded. In an opinion by Justice Bazelon, the court held that such patients have a statutory right to receive *adequate treatment* and that, in the absence of *compelling reasons* by the institution for such denial, release of the patient might be an appropriate remedy. Judge Bazelon also noted that failure to provide such treatment might violate the inmate's constitutional rights.

In *Wyatt v. Stickney* (1972),[165] a federal district court in Alabama held that, even in the absence of a statutory right to treatment, a state has an affirmative constitutional duty to provide *meaningful* services and treatment for patients in mental institutions, otherwise they must be released.

Other federal courts have begun to follow the *Rouse, Wyatt* rationale at least with regard to the treatment of the mentally ill.[166] But as noted by Singer, it is only a short step from those decisions to a holding that adult prisoners also have a right to receive adequate rehabilitative services in prison.[167]

Assuming, even if only for the sake of argument, that offenders may have a constitutional right to treatment and rehabilitation, other legal, ethical, and moral questions will have to be answered. For example, does an offender have a right to be "cured"? Does an offender have a right to refuse treatment without fear of punishment?

What are the legal and ethical constraints on techniques of treatment? For example, certain treatment methods have been severely criticized as being cruel and unusual (e.g., sterilization, experimental psychosurgery, the use of certain psychotropic drugs, etc.).

Although the legal and ethical standards on rehabilitation, treatment techniques, and the right to treatment are presently unclear and subject to much lively debate, these issues are likely to arouse considerable attention in future prisoner litigation.

Other prisoner litigation issues, not explored in this chapter, have been the subject of court decisions. For example, the rights of *pretrial detainees* (those defendants awaiting trial in jail who were unable to make bail) have received increasing attention from the federal courts.[168] In addition, the scope of the Fourth and Fifth Amendment privilege against self-incrimination as applied to inmates, probationers, and parolees is beginning to become the source of prisoner litigation. A full discussion of these issues is not possible in this text; the student should explore this emerging body of law in a more advanced course.

SUMMARY

In this chapter we indicated that until quite recently, the prevailing attitude of the judiciary toward prisoners' suits was one of judicial restraint—the so-called "hands-off" doctrine. Because of this attitude, correctional authorities were left to their discretion in administering the regulations, rules, and policies of their institutions and there was no undue interference from the courts. Over time, however, and especially since the adoption of the 1964 Civil Rights Act, the federal courts have been willing to review legitimate inmates' complaints. So much so that the "hands-off" doctrine is no longer viable and prisoners' suits have been steadily increasing.

State inmates are given direct access to the federal courts by 42 U.S.C. § 1983 to redress legitimate constitutional or federal claims against those correctional authorities who act under color of state law. Remedies under a § 1983 suit include (1) monetary damages, (2) injunctions, and (3) declaratory relief. Although a § 1983 claim is not available to federal prisoners, the Supreme Court judicially created a remedy for the redress of constitutional violations against federal inmates.

Certain civil disabilities may attend a criminal conviction. There may be a loss of the rights to vote and to sue or be sued, the right to contract or enforce a contract, the right to make a will or inherit property, and the right to obtain licenses for certain occupations. These civil disabilities are, for the most part, a question of individual state law and are usually limited to convictions for felonies, crimes of "moral turpitude," or "infamous crimes." Most jurisdictions provide methods for restoring the loss of civil rights.

Prisoners' lawsuits have dealt with a variety of constitutional issues including the First Amendment rights to speech, press, religion, and assembly. Other sources of prisoner litigation include probation and parole revocation hearings, in-prison disciplinary hearings, and certain Eighth Amendment claims involving prison conditions and treatment programs, both medical and rehabilitative.

Only recently has the Supreme Court begun to examine certain inmates' claims under § 1983 actions. Although it is clear that all one's constitutional rights are not left at the prison door, the relative lack of Supreme Court pronouncements in this area has caused a divergence of views by the lower federal courts.

APPENDIX:
OTHER RELATED FEDERAL STATUTES APPLICABLE TO PRISONERS' SUITS

18 U.S.C.A. § 241

If two or more persons conspire to injure, oppress, threaten, or intimidate any citizen in the free exercise or enjoyment of any right or privilege secured to him by the Constitution or laws of the United States, or because of his having so exercised the same. . . .

They shall be fined not more than $10,000 or imprisoned not more than ten years, or both; and if death results, they shall be subject to imprisonment for any term of years or for life.

18 U.S.C.A. § 242

Whoever, under color of any law, statute, ordinance, regulation, or custom, willfully subjects any inhabitant of any State, Territory, or District to the deprivation of any rights, privileges, or immunities secured or protected by the Constitution or laws of the United States, or to different punishments, pains, or penalties, on account of such inhabitant being an alien, or by reason of his color, or race, than are prescribed for the punishment of citizens, shall be fined not more than $1,000 or imprisoned not more than one year, or both; and if death results shall be subject to imprisonment for any term of years or for life.

TORT

Federal Tort Claims Act
28 U.S.C.A. § 1346(b), 1674

[C]laims against the United States . . . for injury or loss of property, or personal injury or death caused by the negligent or wrongful act or omission of any employee of the Government while acting within the scope of his office or employment, under circumstances where the United States, if a private person, would be liable to the claimant in accordance with the law of the place where the act or omission occurred . . . [and that] the United States shall be liable . . . in the same manner and to the same extent as a private individual under like circumstances. . . .

18 U.S.C.A. § 4042

The Bureau of Prisons, under the direction of the Attorney General, shall—

(1) have charge of the management and regulation of all Federal penal and correctional institutions;

(2) provide suitable quarters and provide for the safekeeping, care, and subsistence of all persons charged with or convicted of offenses against the United States, or held as witnesses or otherwise;

(3) provide for the protection, instruction, and discipline of all persons charged with or convicted of offenses against the United States. . . .

References

CHAPTER 1

1 *Mother Goose,* Grosset & Dunlap, New York, 1968.

2 R. Scott, "A Proposed Framework for Analyzing Deviance as a Property of Social Order," in R. Scott and J. Douglas (eds.): *Theoretical Perspectives on Deviance,* Basic Books, New York, 1972, pp. 9–35.

3 Richard Quinney, *The Social Reality of Crime,* Little, Brown, Boston, 1970.

4 H. Packer, *The Limits of the Criminal Sanction,* Stanford University Press, Stanford, Calif., 1968, pp. 154–173.

5 While most crimes in the United States are also punishable in the communist countries, the First Amendment freedoms so fundamental to our democracy (speech, press, religion, assembly) are less protected in the socialist countries.

6 *Connally v. General Construction Co.,* 269 U.S. 611 (1972).

7 W. LaFave and A. Scott, *Criminal Law,* West, St. Paul, Minn., 1972, pp. 83–89.

8 *Papachristou v. City of Jacksonville,* 405 U.S. 611 (1972).

9 *Gooding v. Wilson,* 405 U.S. 581 (1972).

10 *Smith v. Goguen,* 415 U.S. 566 (1974).

11 *Coates v. City Of Cincinnati,* 402 U.S. 611 (1972).

12 *Lewis v. City Of New Orleans,* 415 U.S. 130 (1974).

13 4 *Blackstone Commentaries* 5.

14 1 Bishop, *New Criminal Law* 32 (8th ed.) 1892.

15 Clark and Marshall, *A Treatise on the Law of Crimes,* 7th ed., Callaghan, Chicago, 1967, p. 92.

16 R. Perkins, *Perkins on Criminal Law,* 2d ed., Foundation Press, Mineola, N.Y., 1969, p. 9.

17 La. R.S. 14: 7 (1967).

18 R. Perkins, op. cit., p. 23.

19 *People v. Rehman,* 253 Ca. App. 2d 119,150,61 Cal. Rpt. 65,85 (1967). This is, however, the minority view. Most commentators and courts refer to the common law as all the English statutory and case law prior to 1607. See LaFave and Scott, op. cit., pp. 57–69.

20 The original nine common-law felonies were murder, manslaughter, mayhem, robbery, burglary, arson, rape, larceny, and sodomy.

21 3 Stephen, *A History of the Criminal Law of England* pp. 359–360 (1883).

22 Oliver W. Holmes, *The Common Law,* Little, Brown, Boston, 1881.

23 *Commonwealth v. Mochan,* 177 Pa. Super. 454, 110A.2d 788 (1955).

24 LaFave and Scott, op. cit., pp. 5–7.

25 *Robinson v. Calif.,* 370 U.S. 660 (1962).

26 Mr. Justice Holmes, dissenting in *Hyde v. U.S.,* 225 U.S. 347,388 (1912).

27 *The Poulterer's Case,* 77 Eng. Rep. 813 (1611).

28 For the leading case on ex post facto laws in the United States, see *Calder v. Bull,* 3 U.S. 386 (1798), lising such laws as: "1st. Every law that makes an action done before the passing of the law, and which was innocent when done, criminal; and punishes such action. 2d. Every law that aggravates a crime, or makes it greater than it was, when committed. 3d. Every law that changes the punishment, and inflicts a greater punishment, than the law annexed to the crime, when committed. 4th. Every law that alters the legal rules of evidence, and receives less, or different testimony, than the law required at the time of the commission of the offense, in order to convict the offender." at 390.

29 Both the Fifth (federal) and Fourteenth (states) Amendments require due process when life, liberty, or property are at issue.

30 *People v. Pulley,* 225 Ca. App.2d 366,37 Cal. Rptr. 376 (1964).

31 *People v. Griggs,* 17 Ca. 2d 621, 110 P. 2d 1031 (1941) holding that delirium tremens is a form of insanity while "drunken madness" is not.

32 Devlin, "The Enforcement of Morals," in S. Kadish and M. Paulsen (eds.), *Criminal Law and Its Processes,* Little, Brown, Boston, 1969, pp. 10–15.

33 S. Kadish, *The Crisis of Overcriminalization,* 374 *Annals* 157 (1967), pp. 159–162.

34 LaFave and Scott, op. cit., pp. 571–582.

35 William L. Prosser, *Torts,* 4th ed., West, St. Paul, Minn., 1971.

36 *In Re Winship,* 397 U.S. 358 (1970).

37 Perkins, op. cit., pp. 9–23.

38 LaFave and Scott, op. cit., p. 28.

39 25 Edw. III, C.2.

40 LaFave and Scott, op. cit., p. 26.

41 Ibid.

42 18 U.S.C.A. § 1 (3).

43 Perkins, op. cit., p. 23.

44 R. Gerber and McAnany (eds.), *Contemporary*

Punishment: Views, Explanations, And Justifications, University of Notre Dame Press, Notre Dame, Ind., 1972.

45 D. Glaser, *The Effectiveness of a Prison and Parole System,* Bobbs-Merrill, Indianapolis, 1966.

46 Ibid.

CHAPTER 2

1 G. Geis, "Statistics Concerning Race and Crime," *Crime and Delinquency,* vol. II, pp. 142–150, 1965.

2 Federal Bureau of Investigation, *Uniform Crime Reports,* Washington, D.C., 1975.

3 Personal communication from Dr. Francis C. Nance, Professor of Surgery and Physiology, Louisiana State University Medical Center, New Orleans, Louisiana. Students were referred to an excellent article by Dr. Nance and Dr. Isidore Cohn, Jr., "Surgical Judgment in the Management and Prospective Analysis Based on a Study of 600 Stabbed Patients," *Annals of Surgery,* vol. 170, pp. 569–580, October 1969.

4 J. Carver, Executive Director, Massachusetts Council on Crime and Correction (3 Joy Street, Boston, Mass.), article summarized in *Criminal Justice Newsletter,* vol. 5, pp, 4–5. (November 4, 1974.)

5 Personal communication from a New Orleans Police Department undercover agent.

6 "Bank Robber 'Young Dumb,' " *The Times-Picayune,* New Orleans, La., June 18, 1975, p. 5B.

7 This section summarizes data presented by Rita J. Simon in *The Contemporary Woman and Crime,* National Institute of Mental Health Monograph, 1975.

8 Professor Oscar Newman is quoted in "Policy Development Seminar on Architecture, Design and Criminal Justice," *Proceedings of the LEAA,* June 15–17, 1975, p. 52.

9 "Lee Remick: From Baton Twirler," *Parade,* January 11, 1976, pp. 4–5.

10 P. Ennis, "Crime, Victims, and the Police," *Trans-action,* vol. 4, pp. 36–44, 1967.

11 *Crime and Delinquency,* vol. 21, p. 189, April 1975.

12 J. Price, "A Test of the Accuracy of Crime Statistics," *Social Problems,* vol. 14, pp. 214–222, 1966.

13 J. Hoover, "The Faith of Free Men," *Vital Speeches of the Day,* vol. 32, pp. 71–74, 1965.

CHAPTER 3

1 Gerald F. Uelmen and Victor G. Haddox, *Drug Abuse and the Law,* West, St. Paul, Minn., 1974, p. 1.

2 Ibid., p. 7.

3 Department of Justice, *Uniform Crime Reports,* Washington, D. C., 1975.

4 *Criminal Justice Newsletter,* January 5, 1976, vol. 7, p. 6.

5 Don Martindale, *The Nature and Types of Sociological Theory,* Riverside, Cambridge, Mass., 1960, p. 340.

6 Robert Coles, Joseph H. Brenner, and Dermot Meagher, *Drugs and Youth: Medical, Psychiatric and Legal Facts,* Liveright, New York, 1970.

7 Uelmen and Haddox, op. cit., p. 20.

8 *Criminal Justice Newsletter,* op. cit.

9 Richard R. Lingeman, *Drugs from A to Z: A Dictionary,* McGraw-Hill, New York, 1969, p. 142.

10 Edward M. Brecher, *Licit and Illicit Drugs,* Consumers Union, Mount Vernon, N.Y., 1972, p. 395.

11 Interview with professor of social work, Mississippi State University, 1975.

12 Uelmen and Haddox, op. cit., p. 94.

13 Brecher, op. cit., p. 460.

14 Ibid., p. 402.

15 Ibid.

16 Lingeman, op. cit., p. 144.

17 Ronald L. Akers, *Deviant Behavior,* Wadsworth, Belmont, Calif., 1973. p. 99.

18 Gallup poll results published in the New Orleans *Times Picayune,* July 7, 1972. Informal surveys of college students by the present authors have found as many as 70 percent of a class having tried marijuana "at least once."

19 Brecher, op. cit., p. 413.

20 Ibid., p. 415.

21 Lingeman, op. cit., p. 144.

22 *UCR,* 1965 and 1974.

23 "News and Notes," *Crime and Delinquency,* vol. 21, p. 397, October 1975.

24 Brecher, op. cit., p. 278.

25 Lingeman, op. cit., p. 5.

26 Ibid.

27 Brecher, op. cit., p. 281.
28 Lingeman, op. cit., p. 165.
29 Brecher, op. cit., p. 287.
30 Personal observation, The Pirate's Den, New Orleans, La., January 1976.
31 Lingeman, op. cit., p. 15.
32 Tennessee Williams, "Memoirs," in *Book Digest Magazine,* February 1975, p. 25. Seconal is a short-acting, fast-onset barbituate hypnotic and sedative; in drug argot, the capsules are nicknamed "reds." It would be a gross error to infer that gifted writing is the result of drugs. Mr. Williams is a talented and exact wordsmith who has paid his dues to discipline.
33 Lingeman, op. cit., p. 99.
34 Brecher, op. cit., p. 3.
35 Brecher, op. cit., p. 49.
36 "Catch-22" designates an unpleasant situation from which you can escape only by meeting certain conditions; but if you meet those conditions, you can't escape. The expression was popularized by Joseph Heller's novel of the same name.
37 Uelmen and Haddox, op. cit., p. 37.
38 Little is known of Draconian laws (Athens, ca. 621 B.C.) except that they were so harsh that one observer remarked the code had been written not in ink but in blood. Walter T. Wallbank and Alstair M. Taylor, *Civilization Past and Present,* 3d ed., Scott, Foresman, Chicago, 1954, p. 131.
39 This section is summarized from *Drug Enforcement: Drugs of Abuse,* special issue. Drug Enforcement Administration, United States Department of Justice, Spring 1975.
40 Ibid., p. 5.
41 For a state-by-state review of the penalties for marijuana and other drug offenses, see Coles, Brenner, and Meagher, op. cit., pp. 205–247. The student is cautioned that this review was published in 1970 and will be somewhat dated.
42 Alexander Bassin, "Daytop Village," *Addictions,* Summer 1970, p. 42.
43 Lewis Yablonsky, *The Tunnel Back: Syanon,* Macmillan, New York, 1965.
44 Brecher, op. cit., p. 79.
45 Frances R. Gearing and Morton D. Schweitzer, "An Epidemiologic Evaluation of Long-Term Methadone Maintenance Treatment for Heroine Addiction," *American Journal of Epidemiology,* vol. 100, pp. 101–113, August 1974.
46 This estimate represents a consensus among researchers of alcoholism, but the student should be aware that some challenge this on the basis of the nonuniform definition of alcoholism applied.
47 *UCR,* 1975.
48 M. Keller, "The Definition of Alcoholism and the Estimation of Its Prevalence," in D. Pittman and C. Snyder (eds.), *Society, Culture, and Drinking Patterns,* Wiley, New York, 1962, pp. 310–329.
49 The concept of the "gamma" type alcoholic is presented in E. Jellinek, *The Disease Concept of Alcoholism,* Hillhouse, New Haven, Conn., 1960.
50 Alfred Freedman, Harold Kaplan, and Benjamin Saddock, *Modern Synopsis of Psychiatry,* Williams & Wilkins, Baltimore, 1972, p. 397.
51 M. Bailey, P. Haberman, and H. Alksne, "The Epidemiology of Alcoholism in an Urban Residential Area," *Quarterly Journal of Studies on Alcohol,* vol. 26 pp. 19–40, March 1965.
52 Survey and Reports Section, Biometry Branch, Office of Program Planning and Evaluation, National Institute of Mental Health, Statistical Note 31.
53 *U.S. News and World Report,* October 29, 1973, p. 46.
54 D. Cahalan, I. Cissin, and H. Crossley, *American Drinking Practices,* New Brunswick, N.J., 1969.
55 J. Roebuck and R. Kessler, *The Etiology of Alcoholism,* Charles C Thomas, Springfield, Ill., 1973.
56 Ibid.
57 Ibid.
58 S. Ross, "Should We Jail Alcoholics?" *Parade,* Feb. 14, 1965, p. 5.
59 Will Durant, *Our Oriental Heritage,* Simon and Schuster, New York, 1954, p. 45.
60 Ibid., p. 245.
61 Ibid., p. 444.
62 Ibid., p. 790.
63 Ibid., p. 862.
64 Will Durant, *The Life of Greece,* Simon and Schuster, New York, 1954, p. 116.
65 Will Durant, *Caesar and Christ,* Simon and Schuster, New York, 1954, p. 267.
66 Will Durant, *The Age of Faith,* Simon and Schuster, New York, 1954, p. 76.
67 Kingsley Davis, "Sexual Behavior," in Robert K. Merton and Robert Nisbet (eds), *Contemporary Social Problems,* 3d ed., Harcourt Brace, Jovano-

vich, New York, 1971, pp. 313–360. Many virtuous wives, of course, dispense their sexual favors in an attitude of complete emotional indifference.

68 Seth Mydans, "American Attitudes on Prostitution May be Changing," *Morning Advocate,* Baton Rouge, La., February 15, 1976, p. 4J.

69 ibid.

70 Ibid.

71 This discussion on the objections to prostitution is built upon the reading of Professor Kaplan's stimulating published lecture on the topic: John Kaplan, "Criminal Justice: Introductory Cases and Materials," *Teacher's Manual,* Lecture XXVI, pp. 431–448.

72 Durant, *The Age of Faith,* op. cit., p. 348.

73 Ross, op. cit., p. 166.

74 Durant, *Caesar and Christ,* op. cit., p. 823.

75 Durant, *The Age of Faith,* op. cit., p. 347.

76 Durant, *Caesar and Christ,* op. cit., p. 823.

77 Will Durant, *The Age of Louis XIV,* Simon and Schuster, New York, 1954, p. 17.

CHAPTER 4

1 Martin A. Gosch and Richard Hammer, *The Last Testament of Lucky Luciano,* Little, Brown, Boston, 1975, p. 35.

2 Edwin H. Sutherland, *White Collar Crime,* Holt, New York, 1945, pp. 174–175.

3 Clarence M. Kelly, "Organized Crime—A Battle, Report," address before the Inland Daily Press Association, Denver, Colo., March 4, 1974, p. 12.

4 Ibid., p. 2.

5 President's Commission on Law Enforcement and the Administration of Justice, *Task Force Report: Organized Crime,* Washington, D.C., 1967, pp. 14–15. (Hereafter referred to as *Task Force Report.*)

6 Orson Wells, *War of the Worlds,* a radio program broadcast on October 31, 1938, that led to abnormal amounts of hysterical behavior in the New York City area. See Walter C. Rohrer (ed.), *The Fabulous Century*: 1930–1940, Time Inc., New York, 1969, pp. 35–37.

7 *Task Force Report,* op. cit., p. 1.

8 Ibid., pp. 19–24.

9 See Chamber of Commerce, *Desk Book on Organized Crime,* Washington, D.C., Chamber of Commerce of the United States, Washington, D.C., 1969, p. 3; Law Enforcement Assistance Administration, *Role of State Organized Crime Prevention Councils,* Washington, D.C., 1968, p. 15; Marshall B. Clinard and Richard Quinney, *Criminal Behavior Systems,* Holt, New York, 1973, p. 224; Donald R. Cressey and David A. Ward (eds.), *Delinquency, Crime and Social Process,* Harper and Row, New York, 1969, p. 848.

10 Frederic D. Homer, *Guns and Garlic,* Purdue University Studies, West Lafayette, Ind., 1974.

11 Ibid., pp. 7–9.

12 Office of the Counsel to the Governor of New York, *Combating Organized Crime: A Report of the Oyster Bay, New York Conferences on Organized Crime,* Office of the Governor, Albany, N.Y., 1965, p. 19. Hereafter referred to as *Oyster Bay Conference.*

13 Gordon Hawkins, "God and the Mafia," *The Public Interest,* vol. 14, pp. 32–46, 1969.

14 "The Demise of a Don," *Time,* June 30, 1975, p. 26.

15 *Task Force Report,* op. cit.,

16 Homer, op. cit., p. 7. See also Donald Cressey, "Methodological Problems in the Study of Organized Crime as a Social Problem," *The Annals,* vol. 374, pp. 101–112, 1967.

17 Dwight C. Smith, Jr., *The Mafia Mystique,* Basic Books, New York, 1975, pp. 70–71.

18 *Task Force Report,* op. cit., p. 1.

19 Richard Quinney, *Criminology,* Little, Brown, Boston, 1975, p. 137.

20 *Task Force Report,* op. cit.

21 Ibid., p. 9.

22 Richard Quinney, *Critique of the Legal Order,* Little, Brown, Boston, 1974, p. 66.

23 Homer, op. cit., p. 10.

24 *Oyster Bay Conference,* op. cit.

25 It is significant to note the discrepancy between the tone of the Oyster Bay Conference minutes and the report that the conference made to the public. The former offers a promise of objectivity; and the latter is more consistent with the *Task Force Report* that followed. See Smith, op. cit., pp. 244–251.

26 Smith, op. cit., p. 246.

27 Hank Messick, *Lansky,* Putnam, New York, 1971, p. 7.

28 Smith, op. cit., p. 251.

29 This definition was arrived at through a synthesis of concepts and related terms found in the minutes of the Oyster Bay Conference (cited in Smith, ibid., 247) and Homer, op. cit., pp. 12–20.

30 Organized Crime Control Act of 1970, Public Law 92-452;   1955 (c).

31 Homer, op. cit., pp. 12–13.

32 Smith, op. cit., p. 38.

33 Francis A. J. Ianni, *Family Business,* Russell Sage Foundation, New York, 1972, p. 2.

34 Smith, op. cit., pp. 40–45.

35 Gay Talese, *Honor Thy Father,* World Publishing, New York, 1971, pp. 189–190.

36 Ed Reid, *The Grim Reapers,* Regnery, Chicago, 1969, p. 4.

37 Ianni, op. cit., p. 15.

38 Danilo Dolci, *Report from Palermo,* Bartholomew House, New York, 1961, pp. xv–xvii.

39 Gosch and Hammer, op. cit., p. 298.

40 Luigi Barzini, *The Italians,* Atheneum, New York, 1964, p. 194.

41 Ianni, op. cit., p. 31.

42 Ibid., p. 25.

43 Barzini, op. cit., 264.

44 For further information on the Camorra, see Arthur Train, *Courts, Criminals and the Camera,* Chapman and Hall, London, 1912.

45 Smith, op. cit., pp. 55–61.

46 Ianni, op. cit., p. 43.

47 Smith, op. cit., p. 33.

48 Ianni, op. cit., pp. 54–55.

49 Gus Tyler, "The Crime Corporation," in Abraham S. Blumberg (ed.), *Current Perspectives on Criminal Behavior,* Knopf, New York, 1974, p. 197.

50 While knowledgeable gourmets may disagree, the general consensus is that chop suey—at least in its familiar form—is an American hybrid rather than an authentic Chinese food.

51 Ianni, op. cit., p. 48.

52 Ibid., p. 50.

53 Humbert S. Nelli, "Italians and Crime in Chicago: The Formative Years, 1890–1920," *AJS,* vol. 74, p. 374, 1969.

54 Ibid., p. 375.

55 Ibid., p. 377.

56 Ibid., p. 378.

57 John Kobler, *Capone,* Fawcett, Greenwich, Conn., 1972, p. 84.

58 Nelli, op. cit., p. 387.

59 Ianni, op. cit., p. 54.

60 Ibid., p. 56.

61 Kobler, op. cit., p. 83.

62 Gosch and Hammer, op. cit., p. 32.

63 Thomas Plate and the editors of New York Magazine, *The Mafia at War,* New York Magazine Corporation, New York, 1972, p. 28.

64 Gosch and Hammer, op. cit., p. 143.

65 Smith, op. cit., p. 65.

66 See W. N. Leonard and N. G. Weber "Automakers and Dealers: A Study of Criminogenic Market Forces," *Law in Society,* vol. 4, pp. 407–424, 1970. Herein, a criminogenic market structure is defined as one in which occupational crime is a direct consequency of a legally established market situation.

67 Nelli, op. cit., pp. 376–377.

68 Smith, op. cit., p. 84.

69 Gosch and Hammer, op. cit., p. 146.

70 Smith, op. cit.

71 Leonard Katz, *Uncle Frank,* Pocket Books, New York, 1975, pp. 199–200.

72 Smith, op. cit., p. 138.

73 Katz, op. cit., p. 208.

74 Alfred R. Lindesmith, *The Addict and the Law,* Indiana University Press, Bloomington, Ind., 1965.

75 Smith, op. cit., p. 222.

76 *Task Force Report,* op. cit., p. 6.

77 Bell, op. cit., pp. 127–150.

78 See Gordon Hawkins, "Organized Crime: Is There a Summit?" in Leon Radzinowicz and Marvin E. Wolfgang (eds.), *The Criminal in Society,* Basic Books, New York, 1971, pp. 235–240.

79 Vincent Teresa, *My Life in the Mafia,* Doubleday, New York, 1973.

80 *Task Force Report,* op. cit., p. 9.

81 Ianni, op. cit., p. 110.

82 Bell, op. cit., p. 139.

83 Hawkins, op. cit., pp. 374–387.

84 Gosch and Hammer, op. cit., pp. 144–146.

85 Henry A. Zeiger, *Sam the Plumber,* Signet Books, New York, 1970, p. 86–87.

86 See Peter Maas, *Serpico,* Viking, New York, 1973.

87 Oliver Wendell Holmes, "Mechanism in

Thought and Morals," *A Collection of Essays,* Riverside Press, Cambridge, Mass., 1891, pp. 283–284.

88 See Troy Duster, *The Legislation of Morality,* Free Press, New York, 1970; Donald Dickson, "Bureaucracy and Morality: An Organization Perspective on a Moral Crusade," *Social Problems,* vol. 16, pp. 143–156, 1968; James Graham, "Amphetamine Politics on Capitol Hill," *Transaction,* vol. 9, pp. 14–24, 1972; Alfred R. Lindesmith, "Dope Fiend Mythology," *Journal of Criminal Law, Criminology and Police Science,* vol. 31, pp. 199–208, 1940.

89 Newsday, *The Heroin Trail,* New American Library, New York, 1974.

90 Howard Lewis and Martha Lewis, *The Medical Offenders,* Simon and Schuster, New York, 1970, pp. 143–151 and 229–238; Charles Winick, "Physician Narcotic Addicts," in Howard Becker (ed.), *The Other Side,* Free Press, New York, 1964, pp. 261–279.

91 James A. Inciardi, *Careers in Crime,* Rand McNally, Chicago, 1975, pp. 122–123.

92 Francis A. J. Ianni, *Black Mafia,* Simon and Schuster, New York, 1974.

93 *Task Force Report,* op. cit., p. 3.

94 Thomas C. Schelling, "Economic Analysis and Organized Crime," in *Task Force Report,* op. cit., pp. 114–126.

95 "Senators Blow Lid Off Interest," *The Atlanta Constitution,* January 14, 1976.

96 Francis A. J. Ianni and Elizabeth Reuss-Ianni, "The Godfather is Going Out of Business," *Psychology Today,* vol. 9, 1975, pp. 86–92.

97 Sutherland, op. cit., p. 90.

98 Don Martindale, *The Nature and Types of Sociology Theory,* Houghton Mifflin, Boston, 1960, p. 251.

99 Sutherland, op. cit., p. 9.

100 Herbert Edelhertz, *The Nature, Impact and Prosecution of White Collar Crime,* U.S. Government Printing Office, Washington, D.C., 1970, pp. 3–4.

101 See Sutherland, op. cit., chap. 13.

102 Talese, op. cit., p. 478.

103 Richard Austin Smith, "The Incredible Electrical Conspiracy," in Cressey and Ward, op. cit., p. 884.

104 Ibid., p. 886.

105 Ibid., p. 911.

106 Philip Shaw, "The Privileges of Monopoly Capitalism: Market Power in the Ethical Drug Industry" *The Review of Radical Political Economics* vol. 2, p. 6, Summer 1910.

107 Ibid., p. 13.

108 Ibid., p. 9.

109 Sutherland, op. cit., p. 110.

110 Ibid., p. 105.

111 Shaw, op. cit., p.

112 Ibid,, p. 15.

113 Ralph Nader, *Unsafe at Any Speed,* Grossman, New York, 1965.

114 Robert F. Buckhorn, *Nader: The People's Lawyer,* Prentice-Hall, Englewood Cliffs, N.J., 1972, pp. 1–34.

115 Ralph Nader, "GM and the Auto Industry: The Threat of Corporate Collectivism," in Jerome H. Skolnick and Elliott Currie (eds.), *Crisis in American Institutions,* Little, Brown, Boston, 1970, pp. 137–141.

116 Harvey A. Farberman, "A Criminogenic Market Structure: The Automobile Industry," *The Sociological Quartery,* vol. 16, p. 455, 1975.

117 Ibid., p. 456.

118 A "short sale" is the practice of having a customer make out a check for less than the selling price (to "help" avoid a higher sales tax) and covering the difference in the actual price with cash. The unrecorded cash allows the dealer to skim from the top and use the money for kickbacks to franchised dealers. Ibid., p. 442.

119 "The Embattled Businessman," *Newsweek,* February 16, 1976, pp. 55–60.

120 Donald J. Newman, "Public Attitudes Toward a Form of White Collar Crime," *Social Problems,* vol. 4, pp. 228–232.

121 See p. 79 of this text.

122 Homer, op. cit., p. 9.

123 Gus Tyler, op. cit., p. 195.

124 William J. Helmer, "Rat-A-Tat-Tat!" *Playboy,* January 1974, p. 234.

125 David M. Gordon, "Class and the Economics of Crime," *The Review of Radical Political Economics,* vol. 3, p. 11, Summer, 1971.

126 Smith, op. cit., pp. 327–328.

127 Jeff Gerth, "The Americanization of 1984," in Richard Quinney (ed.), *Criminal Justice in America,* Little, Brown, Boston, 1974, p. 214.

128 "Security System for Organized Crime Intelligence Capability," document prepared by NYSIIS and released through the Law Enforcement Assistance Administration, 1974.

129 Gerth, op. cit., p. 221.

130 Arthur Niederhoffer, "Criminal Justice by Dossier: Law Enforcement, Labeling, and Liberty," in Abraham S. Blumberg (ed.), *Current Perspectives on Criminal Behavior,* Knopf, New York, 1974, pp. 64–65.

131 "Organized Crime Statutes Enacted Since 1961," summary statement requested of, and released by, the FBI, December 23, 1975.

132 Richard Quinney, *Critique of the Legal Order,* Little, Brown, Boston, 1974, p. 108.

133 *LEAA Newsletter,* vol. 3, p. 1, 1973.

134 Smith, op. cit., p. 335.

CHAPTER 5

1 Personal interview with a patrolman of the New Orleans Police Department, January 1976.

2 Will Durant, *Our Oriental Heritage,* Simon and Schuster, New York, 1954, p. 25.

3 Marvin Harris, *Culture, Man and Nature,* Crowell, New York, 1971, pp. 371–373.

4 This section on the development of the London police was prepared by Ms. Nancy Wingate, Adjunct Instructor, Tulane University. Virtually every article or book dealing with Scotland Yard's early days refers to this incident. One source is *Hue and Cry: The Story of Henry and John Fielding and Their Bow Street Runners,* by Patrick Prringle (William Morrow, New York, undated). Pringle is actually more concerned with the period predating Scotland Yard. Other books dealing with the subject are Douglas G. Browne, *The Rise of Scotland Yard: A History of the Metropolitan Police* (George G. Harrop & Co., London, 1956), rather dull; Belton Cobb, *The First Detectives* (Faber & Faber, London, 1957), vivid portraits of specific cases and contemporary attitudes; George Dilnot, *The Story of Scotland Yard,* revised Centenary edition (Geoffrey Bles, London, 1929), an ordinary biography; Dilnot, *New Scotland Yard* (Thomas Nelson & Sons, London, 1938), a reworking of the material in *The Story . . .*; Laurence Thompson, *The Story of Scotland Yard* (Random House, New York, undated), a simplified book designed for children, but quite readable; Sir Basil Thomson, *The Story of Scotland Yard* (Literary Guild, New York, 1936), another ex-commissioner's dramatic highlighting of specific cases from Sir John Fielding's time to his own.

5 Patrick Pringle, *Hue and Cry: The Story of Henry and John Fielding and Their Bow Street Runners,* Morrow, New York, undated, p. 15.

6 Douglas Hay, "Property, Authority and the Criminal Law," in *Albion's Fatal Tree: Crime and Society in Eighteenth Century England* (Pantheon, New York, 1975), p. 18. Hay cites evidence that although the number of capital offenses and convictions increased, the number of executions carried out did not keep pace with them. Hay advances the theory that the class which both made the laws and carried them out was reluctant to act on its own strictures.

7 A highly readable fictionalized account of this period is John Creasey's *The Masters of Bow Street,* Simon & Schuster, New York, 1974.

8 Pringle, op. cit., p. 12.

9 Jurgen Thorwald, *The Century of the Detective,* Harcourt, Brace & World, New York, 1965, p. 38. This contains only a very short passage on the growth of Scotland Yard and is most useful for information on the great advances in forensic medicine, ballistics, and toxicology.

10 Pringle, op. cit., pp. 12–13.

11 Cf. Philip John Stead, *The Police of Paris,* Staples Press, London, 1957, which begins with the days of Vidocq, the celebrated ex-convinct who became the first chief of the Sûreté; or Francois Vidocq, *Memoirs of Vidocq, Principal Agent of the French Police,* H.G. Bohn, London, 1859.

12 Interview with Donald Rumbelow, Curator of the Black Museum of the City of London Police at Wood Street and author of *The Complete Jack the Ripper* (New York Graphic Society, Boston, 1975), July 3, 1976.

13 Police Commissioner Edmund Henderson, quoted in Thorwald, op. cit., p. 41.

14 For modern-day police history, see Anthony Martiensen, *Crime and the Police,* Martin Secker & Warburg, London, 1953; and Sir Harold Scott, Scotland Yard, Random House, 1954. Scott was Commissioner of the metropolitan police from 1945 to 1953. There are numerous other memoirs by detectives, constables, and superintendents, but despite fascinating individual cases, these seem very much alike after the third or fourth book. Two of the best are Sir Percy Sillitoe, *Cloak Without Dagger,* Pan Books, London, 1955, the reminiscences of a chief constable who later headed M.I. 5, and Sir Sydney Smith, *Mostly Murder,* George G. Harrap, London, 1959, the autobiography of a medicolegal expert who worked in Egypt, India, and Scotland. Of interest also is Belton Cobb's *Murdered on Duty: A Chronicle of the Killing of Policemen,* William H. Allen, London, 1961, which covers approximately one hundred such cases from 1829 to 1960, pointing up the changing attitudes of the public.

15 President's Commission on Law Enforcement and the Administration of Justice, *Task Force Report: The Police,* Washington, D.C., 1967, pp. 3–7.

16 Harold J. Vetter and Clifford E. Simonsen, *Criminal Justice in America: The System, The Process, The People,* Saunders, Philadelphia, 1976, pp. 98–99.

17 Wilson's trilogy is discussed in Herbert L. Packer, *The Police and the Community,* 22 *Stanford L. Rev.* 1314–1317 (1969).

18 December 3, 1976, New Orleans, La.

19 Edwin Newman, *Strictly Speaking,* Warner Books, New York, 1975, p. 86.

20 Abernathy quoted in Jean Jefferies, "The Black Genocide Myth," *National Review,* February 16, 1973, 206–207.

21 Ibid.

22 "For Better Police Protection," *Ebony,* (June 1974), pp. 140–141.

23 Ibid., p. 140.

24 Ibid.

25 George M. Foster, *Traditional Cultures and the Impact of Technological Change,* Harper and Row, New York, 1962, p. 127.

26 *Encyclopedia Britannica,* William Benton Publisher, Chicago, 1973, vol. 14, pp. 662–677.

27 Deborah Johnson and Robert J. Gregory, *Police-Community Relations in the United States: A Review of Recent Literature and Projects,* 62 CRIM. L.C. & P. S. 94–103 (1971).

28 *UCR,* 1975, p. 231.

29 "Cops and Couples," *Newsweek,* July 8, 1974, pp. 79–84.

30 *Encyclopedia Britannica,* op. cit.

31 Personal interview, Dr. Ralph James, Zebulon, N.C., April 1, 1976.

32 Albert J. Reiss, Jr., "Police Brutality—Answers to Key Questions," *Trans-Action,* July–August, 1969, pp. 10–19.

33 George Bliss, "Bad Apples on the Beat," *Nation,* February 9, 1974, pp. 171–174.

34 Reiss, op. cit.

35 Jeff Radford, "The Brazilian Death Squads," *Nation,* July 30, 1973, pp. 71–73.

36 Richard Ichord, Lawsuits that Handcuff Our Lawmen," *Nation's Business,* November 1972, p. 27.

37 Robert W. Balch, *The Police Personality: Fact or Fiction?* 63 J. CRIM. L. C. & P. S. 106–119 (1972).

38 Robert C. Trojanowicz, *The Policeman's Occupational Personality,* 62 J. CRIM. L. C. & P. S. 551–559 (1971).

39 Jerome H. Skolnick, *Justice Without Trial,* Wiley, New York, 1966. It is probably also true that blacks who often come into contact with the police develop a "stereotyping perceptual shorthand," e.g., "Bluecoats equal danger."

40 M. Banton, *The Policeman in the Community,* Tavistock, London, 1964.

41 Don Martindale, *The Nature and Types of Sociological Theory,* Houghton Mifflin, Boston, 1960.

42 George L. Kirkham, "From Professor to Policeman," *Reader's Digest,* December 1974, pp. 247–248.

43 Ibid., p. 248.

44 Michael F. Heiman, *The Police Suicide,* 3 J. P. S. & AD. 267–273 (1975).

45 "Spotting the Problem Policeman," *Science Digest,* April 1973, pp. 29–30.

46 Letty Cottin Pogrebin, "The Working Woman," *Ladies Home Journal,* September 1973, p. 36.

47 "No Longer Men or Women—Just Police Officers," *U.S. News and World Report,* August 19, 1974, pp. 45–46.

48 Pogrebin, op. cit.

49 Lewis J. Sherman, *An Evaluation of Policewomen on Patrol in a Suburban Police Department,* J. P. S. & AD. 434–438 (1975).

50 Ibid., p. 436.

51 *U.S. News and World Report,* op. cit. One Miami policewoman used a woman's ultimate weapon to bring in a muscular male shoplifter. She burst into tears and cried, "If I don't bring you in, I'll lose my job." "The Woman in Blue," *Time,* May

1, 1972, p. 60.
52 David Knox and Jack Wright, "Two Careers in One Marriage?" *Modern Bride,* April–May 1976, p. 14.
53 Sherman, op. cit.
54 Corinne Ina Brown, *Understanding Other Cultures,* Prentice-Hall, Englewood Cliffs, N.J., 1963, pp. 19–20.
55 "Police Still Have Doubts About Women on Patrol," *Criminal Justice Newsletter,* October 25, 1976, pp. 2–3.
56 Ibid.
57 Irwin Ross, "What Right of Privacy?" *Reader's Digest,* November 1974, pp. 41–50.
58 "Arrest Record," *New Republic,* July 27, 1974, p. 7. Records do not indicate a case disposition when the case has not yet been adjudicated or when the reporting police department fails to supply the FBI with follow-up data. Laws covering these records are Title 28 Sec 534 of U.S. Code and Public Law 92-544 (86 Stat 1115).
59 *Encyclopedia Britannica,* op. cit., p. 672.
60 Leland Stowe, "How K-9s Catch Crooks," *Reader's Digest,* November 1974, pp. 172–175.
61 "The Dumdum debate," *Newsweek,* September 9, 1974, p. 53.
62 Ibid.
63 "The Hunt for Nonlethal Guns," *Business Week,* July 19, 1972, pp. 34–36.
64 *Encyclopedia Britannica,* op. cit., p. 671.
65 Andre A. Moenssens, Ray Edward Moses, and Fred Inbau, *Scientific Evidence in Criminal Cases,* Foundation Press, New York, 1973. The police and other law enforcement agencies also use fingerprints, voice prints, and narcoanalysis. These and other techniques of crime detection are discussed in this fine work.
66 Ibid.
67 Jack Wright, New Orleans Police Academy Graduation, February 1976.

CHAPTER 6

1 President's Commission on Law Enforcement and the Administration of Justice, *Task Force Report,* "The Courts," U.S. Government Printing Office, 1967, p. 37.
2 Ibid.
3 Phillip E. Johnson, *The Elements of Criminal Due Process,* 1975, p. 57.
4 Ibid.
5 *McGinnis v. Royster,* 410 U.S. 263 (1973).
6 See, for example, *San Antonio School District v. Rodriguez,* 411 U.S. 1 (1973), and *Boddie v. Connecticut,* 401 U.S. 371 (1971).
7 President's Commission, op. cit., pp. 37–38.
8 Ronald Golfarb, *Ransom: A Critique of the American Bail System,* 1965.
9 *Stack v. Boyle,* 342 U.S. 1 (1951).
10 See, for example, 18 U.S.C.A. § 3146 (1966).
11 Daniel J. Freed and Patricia M. Wald, *Bail in the United States: 1964.*
12 Foote, "The Coming Constitutional Crisis in Bail," 113 U.P.A. L. REV. 959, 1125 (1965); Note, "Bail: An Ancient Practice Reexamined," 70 YALE L. J. 966 (1961).
13 *Bellamy v. Judges and Justices Authorized to Sit in the New York City Criminal Court and the New York State Supreme Court in New York County,* 41 App. Div.2d 196, 342 N.Y.S. 2d 137 (1973).
14 Ibid.
15 *Bandy v. United States,* 81 S. Ct. 197 (1960) (opinion of Mr. Justice Douglas).
16 John Kaplan and Jon R. Waltz, *The Trial of Jack Ruby,* 1965.
17 Ibid.
18 Freed and Wald, op. cit., p. 18.
19 A. Beeley, *The Bail System in Chicago,* 1927.
20 Ibid., p. 33.
21 Ibid., p. 157.
22 Ibid., p. 158.
23 Ibid., p. 166.
24 Note, "Compelling Appearance in Court: Administration of Bail in Philadelphia," 102 U. PA. L. REV. 1031 (1954).
25 Ibid., p. 1048.
26 Ibid.
27 Ibid., pp. 1049–1050.
28 Ibid.
29 Ibid., p. 1048.
30 Note, "A Study of the Administration of Bail in New York City," 106 U. PA. L. REV. 693 (1954).
31 Ibid., p. 711.
32 Ibid., p. 727.
33 Charles E. Ares, Anne Rankin, and Herbert Sturz, "The Manhattan Bail Project: An Interim Report of the Use of Pre-trial Parole," 38 N.Y.U.L. REV. 67 (1963).

34 Ibid., pp. 70–74.
35 Ibid., p. 86.
36 Ibid., p. 82.
37 Anne Rankin, "The Effect of Pretrial Detention," 39 N.Y.U.L. REV. 641 (1964).
38 Ibid., pp. 641–642.
39 Freed and Wald, op. cit.
40 Wisotsky, "Use of a Master Bond Schedule: Equal Justice Under Law," 23 U. MIAMI L. REV. 808 (1970).
41 18 U.S.C. § 3148 (1966).
42 Phillip E. Johnson, op. cit., p. 57.
43 See, for example, Federal Bail Reform Act 18 U.S.C. § 3150 (1966).
44 *The New York Times,* September 28, 1972.
45 *Task Force Report,* op. cit., p. 38.
46 "Preventive Detention: An Empirical Analysis," HARVARD CIV. RIGHTS-CIV. LIB. L. REV. VI (1971), No. 2, p. 294.
47 Ibid.
48 *Task Force Report,* op. cit., p. 39.
49 Ibid., pp. 40–41.
50 Comment, "Pretrial Release Under California Penal Code Section 853.6: An Examination of Citation Release," 60 CALIF. L. REV. 1339 (1972).
51 Berger, "Police Field Citations in New Haven, 1972 WISC. L. REV. 382 (1972).
52 Comment, "An Analysis of the Citation System in Evanston, Illinois: Its Value, Constitutionality and Viability," 65 J. CHEM. L. & C. 75 (1974).
53 Ibid., p. 79.
54 Ibid., p. 78.
55 Ibid., p. 79.
56 Ibid.
57 Ibid.
58 Ibid., pp. 83–84.
59 Ibid., p. 84.
60 Ibid.
61 Ibid., p. 86.
62 Boyle, "Bail Under the Judicial Article," 17 DEPAUL L. REV. 267 (1968).
63 Ibid., p. 272.
64 § 110-2. Illinois Revised Statutes (1963).
65 D.C. Code (1973) 23-1322-1331.
66 John N. Mitchell, "Bail Reform and the Constitutionality of Pretrial Detention," 55 VA. L. REV. 1223 (1969).
67 Lawrence H. Tribe, "An Ounce of Detention: Preventive Justice in the World of John Mitchell," 56 VA. L. REV. 371 (1970).
68 Nan C. Bases and William F. McDonald, *Preventive Detention in the District of Columbia: The First Ten Months,* 1972.
69 Gilbov, J. *The Dilemma of Seeking Bail . . .,* 67 J. CRIM. & CRIM. LAW 259 (1977).
70 342 U.S. 1 (1951).
71 Ibid., p. 5.
72 342 U.S. 1, 8 (Jackson, J., concurring).
73 *Bandy v. United States,* 81 S. Ct. 197 (1960).
74 Ibid., p. 198.
75 404 U.S. 357.
76 Ibid., p. 360.

CHAPTER 7

1 Robert D. Sharp, "Grand Juries: An Investigative Force," *Trial,* January–February, 1973, p. 10.
2 Richard P. Alexander and Sheldon Portman, *Grand Jury Indictment versus Information—An Equal Protection–Due Process Issue,* 25 HASTINGS L. REV. 997, 998 (1974).
3 1 Holdsworth, A HISTORY OF THE ENGLISH LAW 313 (3d ed. 1922); 1 Pollock and Maitland, THE HISTORY OF ENGLISH LAW 143 (1902); Kuh, *The Grand Jury "Presentment." Foul Blow or Fair Play,* 55 COLUM. L. REV. (1963); 1 J. Stephen, A HISTORY OF THE CRIMINAL LAW OF ENGLAND 294 (1883).
4 1 Holdsworth, op. cit., p. 77.
5 Richard L. Braun, *The Grand Jury—Spirit of the Community? 15 ARIZONA L. REV. 893, 895 (1973).*
6 1 Holdsworth, op. cit., p. 313.
7 Notes, *American Grand Jury: Investigatory and Indictment Powers,* 22 CLEV. STATE L. REV. (139–240) (1973).
8 Alexander and Portman, op. cit., p. 999.
9 *American Grand Jury . . .,* op. cit., p. 999.
10 1 Holdsworth, op. cit., p. 325.
11 William J. Campbell, *Eliminate the Grand Jury,* 64 J. CRIM. L. & C. 174, 175 (1973).
12 Note, *Indictment Sufficiency,* 70 COLUMB. L. REV. 876, 881 (1970).
13 Leroy D. Clark, *The Grand Jury: The Use and Abuse of Political Power,* 1975, p. 13.
14 Ibid.
15 *Wood v. Georgia,* 370 U.S. 375, 390 (1962).
16 Campbell, op. cit., p. 177.
17 Comment, *The Grand Jury: Powers, Procedures,*

and Problems, 9 COLUM. L. REV. 681, 685 (1973).
18 Ibid., p. 686.
19 Ibid.
20 Note, *The Grand Jury as an Investigatory Body*, 74 HARV. L. REV. 590, 594 (1962).
21 *Ex parte Bain*, 121 U.S. 1, 10–11 (1887).
22 *The Grand Jury: Powers . . .*, op. cit., p. 688.
23 Ibid.
24 Peter Weisman and Andrew D. Postal, *The First Amendment as a Restraint on the Grand Jury Process*, 10 AM. CRIM. L. REV. 671 (1972).
25 *The Grand Jury: Powers . . .*, op. cit., p. 689.
26 Ibid.
27 *Kastigar v. United States*, 406 U.S. 441, 443–444 (1972).
28 U.S. Constitution, Fifth Amendment.
29 *Kastigar v. United States*, 406 U.S. 441, 448–462 (1972).
30 *Dionisio v. United States*, 410 U.S. 1, 5–7 (1973). *Mara v. United States*, 410 U.S. 19, 22 (1973).
31 *United States v. Calandra*, 414 U.S. 338 (1974).
32 *Costello v. United States*, 350 U.S. 359 (1956).
33 *In re Groban*, 352 U.S. 330 (1957) (*dictum*).
34 *The Grand Jury: Powers . . .*, op. cit., p. 689.
35 Ibid.
36 Ibid.
37 *Hale v. Henkel*, 201 U.S. 43, 76–77 (1906).
38 *Petition of Borden Co.*, 75 F. Supp. 857 (N D Ill. 1948).
39 Braun, op. cit., p. 900.
40 Ibid.
41 Comment, *Grand Jury Proceedings: The Prosecutor, the Trial Judge, and Undue Influence*, 39 U. CHI. L. REV. 761, 765 (1972).
42 See generally Note, *The Grand Jury as an Investigatory Body*, 74 HARV. L. REV. 590 (1961).
43 William J. Campbell, DELAYS IN CRIMINAL CASES, 55 F.R.D. 229 (1972).
44 Comment, *The Grand Jury: Powers, Procedures and Problems*, 9 COLUM. J. L. & SOC. PROB. 681 (1973).
45 *Grand Jury Proceedings . . .*, op. cit., p. 765.
46 Robert A. Carp, *The Harris County Grand Jury—A Case Study*, 12 HOUSTON L. REV. 90 (1974).
47 Ibid., p. 101.
48 Ibid.
49 *Grand Jury Proceedings . . .*, op. cit., p. 769.
50 Ibid., p. 770.
51 *The Grand Jury: Powers . . .*, op. cit., p. 706.
52 *Grand Jury Proceedings . . .*, op. cit., p. 767.
53 Note, *Discretionary Power in the Judiciary to Organize a Special Investigatory Grand Jury*, 111 U. PA. L. REV. 954, 960–967 (1963).
54 Comment, *Grand Jury Proceedings: The Prosecutor, the Trial Judge, and Undue Influence*, 39 U. CHI. L. REV. 761, 768 (1972).
55 Ibid.
56 Ibid.
57 R. Younger, *The Peoples Panel: The Grand Jury in the United States* (1963).
58 *Dennis v. United States*, 384 U.S. 855 (1966).
59 *Harris v. United States*, 382 U.S. 162 (1965); See also Rule 42, *Federal Rules of Criminal Procedure.*
60 See, for example, Rule 6(d), *Federal Rules of Criminal Procedure.*
61 *The Grand Jury: Powers . . .*, op. cit., p. 704.
62 Ibid.
63 *Costello v. United States*, 350 U.S. 359, 363 (1959).
64 Spain, The Grand Jury, Past and Present: A Survey, 2 AM. CRIM. L. Q. 119, 126–142 (1964).
65 Rule 6(a), *Federal Rules of Criminal Procedure.*
66 Ibid., Rule 6(f).
67 Ibid., Rule 6(e).
68 *The Jenks Act*, 18 U.S.C. § 3500 (1970).
69 Comment, *Grand Jury Selection: Voter Registration Lists as a Cross Section of the Community*, 52 OREGON L. REV. 482, 484 (1973).
70 Robert A. Carp, *The Harris County Grand Jury—A Case Study*, HOUSTON L. REV. 90, 93(1974).
71 Ibid., pp. 93–94.
72 Ibid., p. 94.
73 Ibid., p. 96.
74 Ibid., p. 94.
75 *Alexander v. Louisiana*, 405 U.S. 625 (1972).
76 *Grand Jury Selection . . .*, op. cit., p. 491.
77 Ibid., p. 485.
78 Comment, *Grand Jury Selection: Voter Registration Lists as a Cross Section of the Community*, 52 OREGON L. REV. 482, 497–498 (1973).
79 28 U.S.C. § 1863 (b) (2) (1970).
80 Comment, *Indictment Sufficiency*, 10 COLUM. L. REV. 876, 882 (1970); F.R.C.P. 7(a).
81 *Hurtado v. California*, 110 U.S. 516 (1884).
82 Yale Kamisar, Wayne R. LaFave, and Jerold H.

Israel, *Modern Criminal Procedure,* 4th ed., 1974, p. 865.

83 Ibid.

84 *Federal Rules of Criminal Procedure,* Rule 7(b).

85 Richard P. Alexander and Sheldon Portman, *Grand Jury Indictment versus Prosecution by Information—An Equal Protection–Due Process Issue,* 25 HASTINGS L. REV. 997, 999 (1974).

86 1 J. Stephen, A HISTORY OF THE CRIMINAL LAW OF ENGLAND 294 (1883).

87 1 W. Holdsworth, A HISTORY OF ENGLISH LAW 238 (3d ed. 1922).

88 *Indictment Insufficiency,* op. cit., p. 882.

89 Ibid.

90 Dean W. Morse, *A Survey of the Grand Jury System,* 10 OREGON L. REV. 101, 119–120 (1931).

91 Comment, *Indictment Sufficiency,* 70 COLUM. L. REV. 876, 882 (1970).

92 Ibid.

93 *Stirone v. United States,* 361 U.S. 212 (1960).

94 *Indictment Insufficiency,* op. cit., p. 880, no. 33.

95 Ibid., p. 883.

96 *Contemporary Studies Project: Perspectives on the Administration of Criminal Justice in Iowa,* 57 IOWA L. REV. 598, 629–630 (1972).

97 *Bureau of Criminal Statistics, Crime and Delinquency in California,* 90 (1968).

98 Kamisar et al., op. cit., p. 868.

99 Note, *Grand Jury Reports not Amounting to Presentments,* 18 WAYNE STATE L. REV. 1645, 1645 (1972).

100 5 W. Blackston, COMMENTARIES 301 (Tucker ed. 1803).

101 *Federal Rules Criminal Procedure,* Rule 7(b).

102 Ibid., Rule 7(a).

103 *The Grand Jury: Powers . . .,* op. cit., p. 686.

104 Comment, *The California Grand Jury—Two Current Problems,* 52 CALIF. L. REV. 116, 118 (1964).

105 Amsterdam, Segal, and Miller, *Trial Manual for the Defense of Criminal Cases,* 2d ed., 1971, § 2 156.

106 See, for example, Rule 5, *Federal Rules of Criminal Procedure.*

107 *Thies v. State,* 178 Wisconsin 98, 103, 189 N.W. 539, 541 (1922).

108 *Lem Woon v. Oregon,* 229 U.S. 586 (1913).

109 *Gerstein v. Pugh, U.S., 420 U.S. 103 (1975).*

110 F. Lee Bailey and Henry B. Rothblatt, *Successful Techniques for Criminal Trials,* 1971, 18.

111 Ibid., § 14.

112 *Federal Rules of Criminal Procedure,* Rule 5(c).

113 Bailey and Rothblatt, op. cit., § 17.

114 Kamisar et al., op. cit., p. 958.

115 *Coleman v. Alabama,* 399 U.S. 1 (1970).

116 *Gerstein v. Pugh,* op. cit.

117 Bailey and Rothblatt, op. cit., § 17.

118 Comment, *Grand Jury Indictment versus Prosecution by Information—An Equal Protection–Due Process Issue,* 25 HASING L. REV. 997 (1974).

119 Robert D. Sharp, "Grand Juries: An Investigative Force," *Trial,* vol. 10, January–February 1973.

120 Comment, *Grand Jury Proceedings: The Prosecutor, the Trial Judge, and Undue Influence,* 39 U. CHI. L. REV. 761 (1972).

121 *Wood v. Georgia,* 370 U.S. 375, 390 (1962).

122 *United States v. Cox,* 342 F. 2d 167, 186 fn. 1 (5th Cir. 1965).

123 Leonard B. Boudin, *The Federal Grand Jury,* 61 GEO. L. J. 1 (1972).

124 Sharp, op. cit., p. 27.

125 8 J. Moore, FEDERAL PRACTICE § 6.02, at 6–7, 9, 10 (2d ed. 1973).

126 *Grand Jury Proceedings . . .,* op. cit., p. 761.

127 Leroy D. Clark, *The Grand Jury: The Use and Abuse of Political Power,* 1975.

128 *United States v. Mara,* 410 U.S. 19, 23 (1973) (Douglas, J., dissenting).

129 William J. Campbell, *Eliminate the Grand Jury,* 64 J. CRIM. L. & C. 174, 175 (1973).

130 Richard L. Braun, *The Grand Jury: Spirit of the Community?* 15 ARIZONA L. REV. 893, 894 (1973).

131 Dean W. Morse, *A Survey of the Grand Jury System,* 10 OREGON L. REV. 101 (1973).

132 Ibid., p. 295.

133 Ibid., p. 141.

134 Ibid., p. 151.

135 Ibid., 134.

136 Ibid., p. 363.

137 Ibid., p. 99.

138 Commentary, *An Examination of the Grand Jury in New York,* 2 COLUM. J. L. & SOC. PROB. 88, 98–99, (1972).

139 Cited in Notes, *American Grand Jury: Investigatory and Indictment Powers,* 22 CLEVELAND STATE L. REV. 136, 144 (1963).

140 *Federal Rules of Criminal Procedure,* Rule 7(e).

141 Ibid.
142 *Pittsburgh Plate Glass v. United States,* 360 U.S. 395, 405 (1949) (Brennan, J., dissenting).
143 Leonard B. Boudin, *The Federal Grand Jury,* 61 GEO. L. J. 1, 30 (1972).
144 *United States v. Procter & Gamble Co., v. United States,* 356 U.S. 677 (1958), and *Pittsburgh Plate Glass v. United States,* 360 U.S. 359 (1970).
145 18 U.S.C. § 3500 (1970).
146 See, for example, California Penal Code § 938.1 (West 1970).
147 Cited in Notes, *American Grand Jury . . .,* op. cit., p. 149.
148 Boudin, op. cit.
149 Peter Weisman and Andrew D. Postal, *The Grand Jury: The First Amendment as a Restraint of the Grand Jury Process,* 10 AM. CRIM. L. REV. 671 (1972).
150 Boudin, op. cit., p. 4.
151 See, for example, *Schneck v. United States,* 249 U.S. 47 (1919).
152 See, for example, *Dombrowski v. Pfister,* 380 U. S. 479, 487 (1965).
153 Boudin, op. cit., p. 4.
154 Comment, *Federal Grand Jury Investigations of Political Dissidents,* 7 HARV. CIV. RIGHTS-CIV. LIB. L. REV. 432 (1972).
155 Leroy D. Clark, *The Grand Jury: Use and Abuse of Political Power,* 1975.
156 Ibid.
157 *In Re Caldwell,* 311 F. Supp. 358 (N D California 1970).
158 Ibid., p. 362.
159 *Caldwell v. United States,* 434 F.2d 1081 (CA9 1970).
160 *Branzburg v. Hayes* and *In Re Pappas,* 408 U.S. 665 (1972).
161 408 U.S. 665, 688.
162 Ibid., p. 685.
163 Ibid., p. 690.
164 Ibid., p. 692.
165 Ibid., p. 710 (Powell, J., concurring).
166 Ibid., p. 725.
167 Weisman and Postal, op. cit., p. 696.
168 *Hale v. Henkel,* 201 U.S. 43, 71 (1906).
169 Baudin, op. cit., p. 9.
170 18 U.S.C. § § 2510–2520 (1970).
171 Ibid., § 2515.
172 *Gelbard v. United States,*
173 *United States v. Mara,* 410 U.S. 19 (1973).
174 Ibid., p. 20.
175 *United States v. Dionisio,* 410 U.S. 1 (1973).
176 414 U.S. 338 (1974).
177 Ibid., p. 354.
178 Ibid., p. 350.
179 Ibid., p. 356.
180 *Kastigar v. United States,* 406 U.S. 441, (1972).
181 18 U.S.C. § 6002 (1970).
182 *Kastigar v. United States,* 406 U.S. 441, 460 (1972).
183 18 U.S.C. § 2514 (repealed).
184 *Kastigar v. United States,* 406 U.S. 441, and *Zicarelli v. New Jersey State Commission of Investigation,* 406 U.S. 472.
185 Harold P. Fahringer, "Lawyer for the Witness," *Trial,* January–February, 1973, p. 14.
186 *United States v. Mandujano* in PREVIEW OF UNITED STATES SUPREME COURT CASES, October 1975 Term, no. 15, December 11, 1975.
187 *The Grand Jury . . .,* op. cit., p. 715.
188 *Federal Rules of Criminal Procedure,* Rule 6(d).
189 *The Grand Jury . . .,* op. cit., p. 720.
190 Ibid., p. 721.
191 *In re Evans,* 452 F.2d 1239 (D.C. Cir. 1971) (dissenting).
192 Ibid., p. 1253.
193 Leonard B. Boudin, *The Federal Grand Jury,* 61 GEO. L. J. 1, 16 (1972).
194 Comment, *The Grand Jury Witness' Privilege Against Self-Incrimination,* 62 NW. U. L. REV. 207, 219, 228–232 (1971).
195 *In re Groban,* 352 U.S. 330 (1957).
196 Ibid., p. 333.
197 Baudin, op. cit., p. 17.
198 Ibid.
199 See, for example, Richard P. Alexander and Sheldon Portman, *Grand Jury Indictment versus Prosecution by Information—An Equal Protection–Due Process Issue,* 25 HASTINGS L. REV. 997 (1974).
200 T. Plucknett, A CONCISE HISTORY OF THE COMMON LAW, note 1 at 112 (5 ed. 1956).

CHAPTER 8

1 Two excellent texts on the administration of justice are Frank W. Miller et al., *Criminal Justice Administration and Related Processes,* Foundation

Press, Mineola, N.Y., 1971, and Frank J. Remington et al., *Criminal Justice Administration: Materials and Cases,* Bobbs-Merrill, Indianapolis, 1969.

2 Y. Kamisar, W. R. LaFave, and J. H. Israel, *Modern Criminal Procedure,* West, St. Paul, 1974, pp. 1–4.

3 *Crime in the United States: Uniform Crime Reports,* U.S. Government Printing Office, 1973, p. 121, Table 24.

4 Kamisar, LaFave, and Israel, op. cit., p. 1.

5 Robert Jackson, *The Federal Prosecutor,* 31 J. CRIM. L. C. & P. S. (1940).

6 *President's Commission on Law Enforcement and Administration of Justice: The Courts,* U.S. Government Printing Office, 1967, p. 73.

7 Tumey v. Ohio, 273 U.S. 510 (1927); *Ward v. Village of Monroeville,* 409 U.S. 57 (1972).

8 Paul M. Bator et al., "Note on the Business of the District Courts," in *Hart and Wechsler's The Federal Courts and The Federal System,* Foundation Press, Mineola, N.Y., 1973, pp. 49–55.

9 Bator, op. cit.

10 "Standards Relating to the Prosecution Function and the Defense Function," in *American Bar Association Standards for the Administration of Criminal Justice,* Chicago, 1970, pp. 17–20.

11 F. Lee Bailey, *The Defense Never Rests,* New American Library, New York, 1972, p. 16.

12 Ibid., p. 285.

13 Ibid.

14 F. Lee Bailey, *For The Defense,* Atheneum, New York, 1975, pp. 238–331.

15 Howard R. Sacks, *Defending the Unpopular Client,* New York Council on Legal Education for Professional Responsibility, New York, 1961, pp. 5–10.

16 Warren E. Burger, quoted in the *American Bar Association Journal,* February 1974, pp. 173–174.

17 See, for example, *Powell v. Alabama,* 287 U.S. 45 (1932); *Gideon v. Wainwright,* 372 U.S. 335 (1963); *Argersinger v. Hamlin,* 407 U.S. 25 (1972); *Coleman v. Alabama* 339 U.S. 1 (1970); *White v. Maryland,* 373 U.S. 59 (1963); *Miranda v. Arizona,* 384 U.S. 436 (1966). The list is not inclusive.

18 Leonard Savitz, *Dilemmas in Criminology,* McGraw-Hill, New York, 1967, p. 91.

19 Ibid.

20 3 Cranch 137. 94 S. Ct. 3090.

21 The vote of the Court was 8 to 0 because Mr. Justice Rehnquist excused himself, apparently because of his prior service with the Justice Department. Previously he had written a policy statement regarding the scope of executive privilege.

22 *Dred Scott v. Sanford,* 60 U.S. (19 How.) 393, 15 L. Ed. 691, holding that the descendants of Africans who were imported into this country, and sold as slaves, were not intended to be included under the word "citizen" in the United States Constitution.

23 *Fletcher v. Peck,* 10 U.S. 87, 3 L. Ed. 162 (1810).

24 *Martin v. Hunter's Lessee,* 14 U.S. 562, 4, L. Ed. 97 (1816); *Cohens v. Va.,* 19 U.S. 82 5, L. Ed. 257 (1821).

25 Remarks before the American Bar Association, August 6, 1973.

26 Op. cit.

27 Other inferior courts have been established by the Congress, for example, the U.S. Tax Court, Court of Customs and Patent Appeals, Court of Claims, etc. For the most part these courts are unimportant in the study of criminal justice.

28 *Ex parte McCardle,* 74 U.S. 506, 19 L. Ed. 264 (1869).

29 For example, the Congress abolished the so-called McNabb-Mallory rule in the Omnibus Crime Control and Safe Streets Act (1968). The Court has not to date decided the constitutionality of that section of the act.

30 Charles A. Wright, *Law of Federal Courts,* West, St. Paul, 1970, p. 500.

31 Ibid.

32 The Supreme Court, 1973 term, 88 HARVARD L. REV. 277–278 (1974).

33 29 U.S.C.A. 1254 (3).

34 28 U.S.C. 631–639.

35 94 S. Ct. 2842.

36 418 U.S. 416.

37 *President's Task Force: Corrections* (1967) p. 1.

38 Ibid.

39 Ibid.

40 Galvin and Karacki, *Manpower and Training in Correctional Institutions* report of Joint Commission on Correctional Manpower and Training, 15 (1969).

41 The statistics in this section are largely taken from Kamisar, LaFave, and Israel, op. cit., p. 134.

42 Roland Perkins, *Elements of Police Sciences,*

1972, pp. 223 and 227.
43 *McNabb v. U.S.,* 318 U.S. 332 (1943), and *Mallory v. U.S.,* 354 U.S. 449 (1957).
44 18 U.S.C.A. 3501 (1968).
45 399 U.S. 1.
46 380 U.S. 400.
47 See *Lem Woon v. Oregon,* 229 U.S. 586 (1930).
48 408 U.S. 204.
49 402 U.S. 389.
50 350 U.S. 359.
51 *Wood v. Georgia,* 370 U.S. 375, 390 (1962), and Wayne Morse, *A Survey of the Grand Jury Systems,* 10 OREGON L. REV. 101 (1931).
52 110 U.S. 516.
53 372 U.S. 353.
54 417 U.S. 15.

CHAPTER 9

1 *Barron v. Baltimore,* 32 U.S. 243 (1833). *Barron* specifically held that the Fifth Amendment prohibition against the taking of private property without just compensation was not applicable to the states. The specific holding of *Barron* was later overruled in *Chicago, B. & Q. R. Co. v. City of Chicago,* 166 U.S. 266 (1897).
2 *Hurtado v. California,* 110 U.S. 516 (1884). The *Hurtado* position has subsequently been reaffirmed. See, for example, *Gaines v. Washington,* 277 U.S. 81 (1928).
3 For an excellent summary of the nationalization of the Bill of Rights, see Jerald H. Israel and Wayne R. LaFave, *Criminal Procedure: Constitutional Limitations,* 2d ed., West, St. Paul, 1975, pp. 4–23.
4 *Palko v. Connecticut,* 302 U.S. 319 (1937), opinion by Mr. Justice Cardozo.
5 Ibid. At his first trial, Palko was convicted of second-degree murder. Pursuant to a Connecticut statute, the state appealed his conviction to the Connecticut Supreme Court. That court found that reversible error had occurred at the first trial and remanded the case for a new trial. At the second trial, over Palko's objections on double-jeopardy grounds, he was reconvicted, this time for first-degree murder. He was given the death penalty.

Palko was overruled more than thirty years in *Barron v. Maryland,* 395 U.S. 784 (1969), where the Supreme Court held that the Fifth Amendment provision prohibiting double jeopardy is applicable to the states. At first trial, Benton was convicted of burglary and found not guilty of larceny. Subsequently, his conviction was refersed and remanded by the Maryland Court of Appeals. Upon retrial (for both offenses) and over his objections, Benton was convicted of both larceny and burglary. Even the earlier view of "fundamental fairness" would seem to have prohibited Benton's retrial on the larceny charge. See dissenting opinion of Mr. Justice Harlan in *Benton,* p. 801.
6 *Adamson v. California,* 322 U.S. 46 (1947), reaffirming *Twining v. New Jersey,* 211 U.S. 78 (1908). *Twining* had rejected the application to the states of the Fifth Amendment privilege against self-incrimination. Subsequently, *Malloy v. Hogan,* 378 U.S. 1 (1964), overruled *Twinning; Adamson* was specifically overruled by *Griffin v. California,* 380 U.S. 609 (1965), where the Court held that "the Fifth Amendment . . . forbids either comment by the prosecution on the accused's silence or instructions by the court that such silence is evidence of guilt." Opinion by Mr. Justice Douglas, p. 615.
7 Ibid., Mr. Justice Black dissenting. See also Mr. Justice Frankfurter's concurring opinion in *Adamson* where he rejected the idea of "total incorporation" and referred to an "eccentric" justice, apparently in reference to Mr. Justice Black. In addition, see Mr. Justice Brennan's concurring opinion in *Rochin v. California,* 342 U.S. 165 (1952).
8 Ibid. Justices Murphy and Rutledge dissenting. See also Mr. Justice Douglas's opinion in *Griswald v. Connecticut,* 381 U.S. 479 (1965), where he stated that a constitutional right of privacy is found in the First, Third, Fourth, Fifth, and Ninth Amendments (suggesting a "total incorporation plus" view).
9 *Cohen v. Hurley,* 366 U.S. 117, 158 (1961).
10 *Ker v. California,* 374 U.S. 23 (1963), holding, inter alia, that the reasonableness of a state search is governed by federal constitutional standards. State courts must follow standards on Fourth Amendment problems set by the federal courts. Also, on review of a state court judgment, the U.S. Supreme Court will respect the Fourth Amendment state court findings to

the extent that they comply with federal constitutional standards.

11 *Duncan v. Louisiana,* 391 U.S. 145 (1968), holding that the Sixth Amendment right to a trial by jury is applicable to the states for "serious offenses." Duncan had been convicted of simple battery, which carried a possible 2-year jail sentence (although defined as a misdemeanor in Louisiana). Under Louisiana law at that time, only defendants charged with a felony involving possible punishment at hard labor were entitled to a trial by jury. In *Baldwin v. New York,* 399 U.S. 66 (1970), the Court held that a right to a trial by jury is required where the possible sentence can exceed 6 months' imprisonment. (See Chapter 10, "The Criminal Trial.")

12 *Mempha v. Rhay,* 389 U.S. 128, 134 (1967), holding that the right to counsel is a "critical stage" at a probation revocation hearing where no prison sentence had been imposed at sentencing.

13 *Douglas v. California,* 372 U.S. 353 (1963) and *Ross v. Moffitt,* 417 U.S. 15 (1974). Both cases were apparently decided, in part, on the basis of Fourteenth Amendment equal protection grounds.

14 *Griffin v. Illinois,* 351 U.S. 12, 19 (1956). The *Griffin* rule has been extended to include a right of indigent defendants to receive (at state expense) transcripts for misdemeanor convictions. *Mayer v. Chicago,* 404 U.S. 189 (1971). See also, *Burns v. Ohio,* 360 U.S. 252 (1959); *Smith v. Bennett,* 365 U.S. 708 (1961); *Long v. District Court of Iowa,* 385 U.S. 192 (1966); *Gardner v. California,* 393 U.S. 367 (1969); *Roberts v. LaValee,* 389 U.S. 40 (1967); *Williams v. Illinois,* 399 U.S. 235 (1970); *Tate v. Short,* 402 U.S. 395 (1971); *Britt v. North Carolina,* 404 U.S. 226 (1972).

15 *Douglas v. California,* op. cit.

16 *Gideon v. Wainwright,* 372 U.S. 335 (1963), overruling *Betts v. Brady,* op. cit.

17 *Powell v. Alabama,* 287 U.S. 45 (1932).

18 *Johnson v. Zerbst,* 304 U.S. 458 (1938).

19 *Betts v. Brady,* 316 U.S. 455 (1942).

20 *Chewning v. Cunningham,* 368 U.S. 443 (1962), in which the Court struck down a 10-year sentence imposed when the defendant was not represented by counsel.

21 *Townsend v. Burke,* 334 U.S. 736 (1948).

22 *Moore v. Michigan,* 335 U.S. 155 (1957).

23 *Hamilton v. Alabama,* 368 U.S. 52 (1961).

24 *White v. Maryland,* 373 U.S. 59 (1963).

25 372 U.S. 335.

26 Ibid., p. 337.

27 Ibid., p. 344.

28 384 U.S. 436 (1966).

29 *United States v. Wade,* 388 U.S. 218 (1967) and *Gilbert v. California,* 388 U.S. 163 (1967).

30 *Kirby v. Illinois,* 406 U.S. 682 (1972).

31 *Mempha v. Rhay,* op. cit.

32 *Gagon v. Scarpelli,* 411 U.S. 778 (1973).

33 Ibid., p. 791.

34 *Morrissey v. Brewer,* 408 U.S. 471 (1972).

35 *Coleman v. Alabama,* 399 U.S. 1 (1970).

36 Ibid., p. 11. See also *Gilbert v. California,* op. cit. p. 272.

37 *Chapman v. California,* 386 U.S. 610 (1967).

38 *Fahy v. Connecticut,* 375 U.S. 85, 86 (1963).

39 See, for example, *Burgett v. Texas,* 389 U.S. 109 (1967) and *Loper v. Beto,* 31 L Ed 2d 374 (1972).

40 407 U.S. 25 (1972).

41 387 U.S. 1 (1970).

42 Ibid., p. 40.

43 *Ross v. Moffitt,* op. cit.

44 *Wolff v. McDonnell,* 418 U.S. 539 (1974).

45 *Faretta v. California,* 422 U.S. 806 (1975).

46 Ibid., p. 581.

47 Ibid., p. 581, N. 46.

48 *In re Groban,* 352 U.S. 330 (1957).

49 *Davis v. Mississippi,* 394 U.S. 721 (1969).

50 *Gilbert v. California,* op. cit.

51 *Schmerber v. California,* 384 U.S. 218 (1966).

52 *United States v. Dionisio,* 410 U.S. 1 (1973).

53 *United States v. Ash,* 413 U.S. 300 (1973).

54 A. Amsterdam, *Perspectives on the Fourth Amendment, 58 MINN. L. REV. 349, presented as the Oliver Wendel Holmes Lecture Series at the University of Minnesota School of Law on January 22–24, 1974 (hereinafter cited as Amsterdam).*

55 Ibid., p. 353.

56 *Marcus v. Property Search Warrant,* 367 U.S. 717, 729 (1961) (Brennan, J.).

57 The exclusionary rule, applicable to the federal courts, *Weeks v. United States,* 232 U.S. 383 (1914), and the states, *Mapp v. Ohio,* 367 U.S. 643 (1961), has been described as putting "teeth" into the Fourth Amendment. See LaFave, *Improving Police Performance Through the Exclusionary Rule,* 30 MO. L. REV. 391 (1965),

Oaks, *Studying the Exclusionary Rule in Searches and Seizures,* 37 U. CHICAGO L. REV. 665 (1970), and Spiotto, *The Search and Seizure Problem—Two Approaches: The Canadian Tort Remedy and the U.S. Exclusionary Rule,* 1 J. POLICE SCI. & AD. 36 (1973).

58 Fourth Amendment (United States Constitution).

59 *Rabinowitz v. United States,* 339 U.S. 56, 66 (1950).

60 What was reasonable at one time has been held to be unreasonable at another.

61 389 U.S. 347 (1967).

62 In *Katz,* the Court seemed to lay down a less fluid rule suggesting that warrantless searches are automatically unreasonable absent "exigent circumstances" which justify the government intrusion. The *Katz* Court suggested that these exceptions are few and well-delineated. Analysis reveals that the Court may have overstated that position, and recent cases suggest that the Burger Court may be willing to expand the perimeters of these exceptions. See, for example, *United States v. Robinson, Guftason v. Florida, United States v. Edwards, Cardwell v. Lewis, United States v. Matlock, United States v. Calandra, Cady v. Dombrowski,* and *Adams v. Williams,* op. cit.

63 *Katz v. United States,* op. cit., p. 357.

64 *United States v. Jeffers,* 342 U.S. 48, 51 (1951), cited in *Collidge v. New Hampshire,* op. cit., 455.

65 See generally W. Ringel, *Searches and Seizures, Arrests and Confessions* (1972).

66 *Chimel v. California,* 395 U.S. 752 (1969).

67 *Schneckloth v. Bustamonte,* 412 U.S. 218 (1973).

68 *Warden v. Hayden,* 387 U.S. 294 (1967).

69 *Carroll v. United States,* 267 U.S. 132 (1925).

70 *Almeida-Sanchez v. United States,* 413 U.S. 266 (1973).

71 *Terry v. Ohio,* 392 U.S. 1 (1968).

72 On *Lee v. United States,* 343 U.S. 747 (1952), reaffirmed in *United States v. White,* 401 U.S. 745 (1971) (plurality). See also *Lopez v. United States,* 373 U.S. 427 (1963); *Osborn v. United States,* 385 U.S. 323 (1966); *Lewis v. United States,* 385 U.S. 206 (1966); and *Hoffa v. United States,* 385 U.S. 293 (1966).

73 *Abel v. United States,* 362 U.S. 217 (1960).

74 *Burdeau v. McDowell,* 256 U.S. 465 (1921).

75 *United States v. Biswell,* 406 U.S. 311 (1972). See also *Colonnade Catering Corp. v. United States,* 397 U.S. 72 (1970), forbidding forcible entries of inspection of liquor dealers' premises without statutory authorization.

76 *Harris v. United States,* 390 U.S. 234 (1968). Also *Hester v. United States,* 265 U.S. 57 (1924) holding that "open fields" are not within the protection of the Fourth Amendment even during a trespass by officers without a warrant.

77 *Almeida-Sanchez v. United States,* op. cit., pp. 272–273. The Court reaffirmed the principle in *Carroll v. United States,* op. cit., note 39, saying that "Travelers may not be stopped in crossing an international boundary because of national self-protection reasonably requiring one entering the country to identify himself as entitled to come in, and his belongings as effects which may be lawfully brought in," p. 154. See *United States v. Byrd,* 483 F. 2d 1284 (1974) (per curiam).

78 Note, *The United States Courts of Appeals: 1973–1974 Term Criminal Law Procedure,* 63 GEORGETOWN L. J. 381 (1974).

79 *Henderson v. United States,* 390 F. 2d 805 (9th Cir. 1967), holding that a vaginal search at a border even with the assistance of a medical doctor is unreasonable without a "clear indication" that the subject may be concealing contraband. See also *United States v. Holtz,* 479 F. 2d 89, 92 (9th Cir. 1973); and Notes, 87 HARVARD L. REV. 196 (1973).

80 *Almeida-Sanchez v. United States,* op. cit.

81 The Supreme Court has decided to date only four cases involving the issue of "stop and frisk." *Terry v. Ohio,* op. cit.; *Sibron v. New York*; *Peters v. New York,* 392 U.S. 41 (1968); and *Adams v. Williams,* 407 U.S. 143 (1972).

82 *Terry v. Ohio,* Ibid., pp. 16–19.

83 Ibid., p. 27.

84 Ibid., pp. 30–31.

85 *Biswell,* and *Colonnade,* op. cit.

86 *Colonnade,* op. cit., p. 77.

87 *Biswell,* op. cit., p. 315.

88 *Colonnade,* op. cit., p. 75.

89 *Coolidge v. New Hampshire,* op. cit.

90 *Draper v. United States,* 358 U.S. 307, 313 (1959).

91 *Bivens v. Six Unknown Named Agents,* 358 U.S.

388 (1971).

92 Ibid., p. 417.

93 232 U.S. 383 (1914).

94 Ibid., p. 393.

95 *People v. DeFore,* 242 N.Y. 13, 150 N.E. 585 (1926).

96 Ibid., p. 21.

97 388 U.S. 25 (1949).

98 Ibid., p. 27.

99 Today, an aggrieved person may sue a defendant who violates his or her constitutional rights under the Civil Rights Act (42 U.S.C. § 1983).

100 *People v. Cahan,* 44 Cal 2d 434, 455, 282 P. 2d 905, 911 (1955).

101 *Rea v. United States,* 350 U.S. 214 (1956).

102 *Elkins v. United States,* 364 U.S. 206 (1960).

103 367 U.S. 643 (1961).

104 Ibid., p. 657.

105 Leonard W. Levy, *Against the Law: the Nixon Court and Criminal Justice,* Harper & Row, New York, 1974.

106 *Bivens,* op. cit., pp. 415 and 430.

107 *United States v. Calandra,* 414 U.S. 338 (1974).

108 *Griffin v. California,* op. cit.

109 *The Bill of Rights: A Source Book for Teachers,* "The History and Scope of the Privilege," California State Department of Education, 1967, pp. 79–81.

110 *Murphy v. Waterfront Commission,* 378 U.S. 52 (1964).

111 *Malloy v. Hogan,* 378 U.S. 1 (1964).

112 *Boyd v. United States,* 116 U.S. 616 (1886).

113 Ibid., p. 630.

114 *Hoffman v. United States,* 341 U.S. 479, 486 (1951); McCormick, *Evidence,* 2d ed., West, St. Paul, 1972, § 123.

115 *Twining v. New Jersey,* op. cit.

116 297 U.S. 278 (1936).

117 See, for example, *Haynes v. Washington,* 373 U.S. 503 (1963).

118 See, for example, *Crooker v. California,* 357 U.S. 433 (1958); *Cicenia v. LaGay,* 357 U.S. 504 (1958); *Spano v. New York,* 360 U.S. 315 (1959); *Blackburn v. Alabama,* 361 U.S. 199 (1960); and *Rogers v. Richmond,* 365 U.S. 534 (1961).

119 Also *Mallory v. United States,* 354 U.S. 449 (1957), and *McNabb v. United States,* 318 U.S. 332 (1943).

120 384 U.S. 436 (1966). Also see *Escobedo v. Illinois,* 378 U.S. 478 (1964).

121 *Malloy v. Hogan,* op. cit.

122 *Miranda,* op. cit., p. 479.

123 Ibid., p. 467.

124 Ibid., p. 477.

125 *Walder v. United States,* 347 U.S. 62 (1954).

126 *Harris v. New York,* 401 U.S. 222 (1972).

127 Frank Carrington, *Speaking for the Police,* J. CRIM. L. C. & P. S. 244 (1970); Donald R. Cressey, *Crime and Criminal Justice,* Quadrangle Books, Chicago, 1971, pp. 3–17; James Vorenberg, *Is the Court Handcuffing the Cops?* The New York Times Magazine, May 1, 1969; Daniel Gutman, *The Criminal Gets the Breaks, The New York Times Magazine,* November 29, 1964.

In a speech before the United States Senate, Senator John McClellan of Arkansas indicated that since 1960 the Supreme Court reversed 63 of 112 federal criminal convictions and 113 of 144 state criminal convictions. He states: "I simply cannot believe that our federal circuit judges are so incapable and lacking in qualifications or that our state supreme courts are so incompetent and prone to error as to warrant such an overwhelming record of reversals by the Supreme Court." (S. CONG. REG., 91st Cong., 1st Sess., Vol. 115, No. 136, PS9565, Aug. 11, 1969).

A Gallup Poll of 1,471 adults indicated that 75 percent of the respondents believed that the courts did not deal harshly enough with criminals. ("Public Wants Harder Line to Win War on Crime," *The Denver Post,* Feb. 16, 1969).

Another Gallup Poll indicated that only 31 percent of the 1,515 adults surveyed rated the decisions of the Supreme Court as "excellent or good." ("Public Esteem for High Court Has Fallen in Past Six Years," *The Denver Post,* June 15, 1969).

128 *Interrogation in New Haven: The Impact of Miranda,* 76 YALE L. J. 1519 (1969); Seeburger and Wettick, *Miranda in Pittsburgh: A Statistical Study,* 29 U. PITT. L. REV. 1 (1967), p. 594.

129 Medalie, Leitz, and Alexander, *Custodial Police Interrogation in our Nation's Capitol: The Attempt to Impliment Miranda,* 66 MICHIGAN L. REV. 1347 (1968).

130 *Michigan v. Tucker,* 417 U.S. 433 (1974).

131 *Schmerber v. California,* op cit.
132 Ibid., p. 761.
133 *United States v. Wade,* op. cit.
134 Ibid., p. 223.
135 *United States v. Dionisio,* op. cit.
136 *United States v. Mara,* 410 U.S. 19 (1973), and *Gilbert v. California,* op. cit.
137 *Davis v. Mississippi,* op. cit.
138 *United States v. Ash,* op. cit.
139 *California v. Byers,* 402 U.S. 424 (1971).
140 *Couch v. United States,* 409 U.S. 322 (1973).
141 *Stovall v. Denno,* 388 U.S. 293 (1967).
142 Ibid., p. 302.
143 *Simmons v. United States,* 390 U.S. 377 (1968).
144 Ibid., p. 384.
145 Ibid., p. 386.
146 *Neil v. Biggers,* 409 U.S. 188 (1972).
147 Ibid., p. 198.
148 Ibid., p. 199.
149 *United States v. Wade,* op. cit.

CHAPTER 10

1 Chief Justice Warren Burger, "Address at American Bar Association Annual Convention," *The New York Times,* August 11, 1970, p. 24, col. 4.
2 *In re Oliver,* 333 U.S. 257 (1948).
3 The distinction between *mala in se* and *mala prohibita* crimes is often utilized by courts in determining the degree of an offense, especially in manslaughter and battery cases. It is sometimes held that if one's conduct is *mala in se* (e.g., speeding 50 m.p.h. over the limit) and an unintentional death or injury results, one may be guilty of manslaughter or battery. But, conduct that is *mala prohibita* (e.g., speeding 5 m.p.h. over the limit) and causes the same death or injury is less likely to result in a manslaughter or battery conviction. Wayne R. LaFave and Austin W. Scott, *Criminal Law,* West, St. Paul, 1972, pp. 29–31.
4 Patton v. U.S., 281 U.S. 276 (1930).
5 391 U.S. 145 (1968).
6 Ibid., p. 157.
7 Ibid., p. 162.
8 *Baldwin v. N.Y.,* 399 U.S. 66 (1970).
9 Ibid., p. 90.
10 LaFave and Scott, op. cit., p. 39, citing J. Sanforn, in *In re Nevitt,* 117 F. 488, 458 (8th Cir. 1902).
11 *Shillitani v. U.S.,* 384 U.S. 364 (1966).
12 *Cheff v. Schnackenberg,* 384 U.S. 373 (1966).
13 *Bloom v. Illinois,* 391 U.S. 194 (1968).
14 Frank v. U.S., 395 U.S. 147 (1969).
15 *Illinois v. Allen,* 397 U.S. 337 (1970).
16 Ibid., p. 339.
17 Ibid., p. 340.
18 Ibid.
19 *Mayberry v. Pennsylvania,* 400 U.S. 455 (1972).
20 Ibid., p. 466.
21 Ibid.
22 *Codispoti v. Pennsylvania,* 418 U.S. 506 (1974).
23 *Taylor v. Hayes,* 418 U.S. 488 (1974).
24 *Maness v. Meyers,* 419 U.S. 449 (1975).
25 *Williams v. Florida,* 399 U.S. 78 (1970).
26 Ibid., p. 100.
27 *Johnson v. Louisiana,* 406 U.S. 404 (1972).
28 Ibid., p. 362.
29 *Apodaca v. Oregon,* 406 U.S. 404, 410 (1972).
30 Ibid., p. 410.
31 397 U.S. 358.
32 Ibid., p. 364.
33 See also *In re Burrus et al.,* 403 U.S. 528 (1971).
34 J. Hogarth, *Sentencing as a Human Process,* University of Toronto Press, Toronto, 1971; also H. Kalven, Jr., and H. Zeisel, *The American Jury,* Little, Brown, Boston, 1966.
35 *A.B.A. Standards, Trial by Jury,* 1968, pp. 30–34.
36 Rule 23(a), *Federal Rules of Criminal Procedure.*
37 *Singer v. United States,* 380 U.S. 24 (1965).
38 Ibid., p. 34.
39 *Adams v. U.S. ex rel. McCann,* 317 U.S. 269 (1943).
40 *Annot.,* 46 A.L.R. 2d 919 (1956).
41 F. Lee Bailey and Henry B. Rothblatt, *Successful Techniques for Criminal Trials,* Lawyers Cooperative Publishing Co., Rochester, N.Y., 1971, p. 122.
42 Kairys, *Jury Selection: The Law, A Mathematical Method of Analysis, and a Case Study,* 10 AM. CRIM. L. REV. 771 (1972).
43 Note, 52 VA. L. REV. 1069, 1072 (1966).
44 *Rawlins v. Georgia,* 201 U.S. 638 (1906).
45 *Frazier v. U.S.,* 335 U.S. 497 (1948).
46 Glasser v. U.S., 315 U.S. 60 (1942); and Federal Jury Selection Service Act, 1968.
47 *Swaim v. Alabama,* 380 U.S. 202 (1965).

48 *Bush v. Kentucky,* 107 U.S. 110 (1883).
49 *Strauder v. West Virginia,* 100 U.S. 303 (1880).
50 Peters v. Kiff, 407 U.S. 493 (1972).
51 *Carter v. Jury Comm. of Greene Co.,* 396 U.S. 320 (1970).
52 *Whitus v. Georgia,* 386 U.S. 545 (1967).
53 *Alexander v. Louisiana,* 405 U.S. 625 (1970).
54 *Turner v. Fouche,* 396 U.S. 346 (1970).
55 Bailey and Rothblatt, op. cit., p. 78.
56 Tone, *Voir Dire, New Supreme Court Rule 24-1; How It Works,* 47 ILL. BAR J. 140, 142 (1958).
57 See Fred E. Inbau, et al., *Criminal Procedure,* Foundation Press, Mineola, N.Y., 1974, pp. 926–930; and 52 VA. L. REV. 1069, 1072 (1966).
58 Melvin M. Belli, *Ready for the Plaintiff,* Bobbs-Merrill, Indianapolis, 1956.
59 Bailey and Rothblatt, op. cit., p. 78.
60 *New York Times Co. v. U.S.,* 403 U.S. 713, 723 (1971).
61 *Irvin v. Dodd,* 366 U.S. 717 (1961).
62 Ibid., pp. 722–723.
63 384 U.S. 333 (1966).
64 Ibid., p. 363.
65 Ibid.
66 *Marshall v. U.S.,* 360 U.S. 310 (1959).
67 *Rideau v. Louisiana,* 373 U.S. 723 (1963).
68 *Moore v. Dempsy,* 261 U.S. 86 (1923).
69 *Tumey v. Ohio,* 273 U.S. 510 (1927); and *Ward v. Village of Monroeville,* 409 U.S. 57 (1972).
70 *Turner v. Louisiana,* 397 U.S. 466 (1965).
71 *Parker v. Gladden,* 385 U.S. 363 (1966).
72 *Groppi v. Wisconsin,* 400 U.S. 505 (1971).
73 *Estes v. Texas,* 381 U.S. 532 (1965).
74 *Leonard v. U.S.,* 277 F. 2d 843 (9th Cir.), 1960.
75 *Gladden v. Frazier,* 399 F. 2d 777 (9th Cir.), *affirmed* (1969), 394 U.S. 731; also *Frazier v. Cupp,* 394 U.S. 731 (1969), *affirmed sub. nom.*
76 *Berger v. U.S.,* 295 U.S. 78 (1935).
77 Rule 52(b), *Federal Rules of Criminal Procedure.*
78 *Leonard v. U.S.,* op. cit.
79 93 ALR 2d 951.
80 Bailey and Rothblatt, op. cit., p. 112, and chap. 4 *Opening Statement to the Jury,* pp. 113–126.
81 Ibid.
82 Ibid.
83 Ibid.
84 *Benton v. Maryland,* 395 U.S. 784 (1969).
85 *A.B.A. Standards,* 5.5 (7.4).
86 *Coffin v. U.S.,* 156 U.S. 432 (1895).
87 *In re Winship,* op cit.
88 *Davis v. U.S.,* 160 U.S. 469, 488 (1895).
89 *In re Winship,* op. cit., p. 363.
90 *Commonwealth v. Webster,* 59 Mass. 205 (1850).
91 Ibid.
92 *Lego v. Twomey,* 404 U.S. 477 (1972).
93 For a full discussion of the law of evidence, see J. Wigmore, *Evidence,* 3d ed., 1940 (ten volumes); Edward W. Cleary, *McCormick on Evidence,* 2d ed., 1972; Spencer A. Gard, *Jones on Evidence,* 1972; Charles E. Torcia, *Wharton's Criminal Evidence,* 1972; Phillip F. Herrick, *Underhill's Criminal Evidence,* 1956; *Rules of Evidence for U.S. Courts and Magistrates,* H.R. 5463, signed by President Ford, January 3, 1975.
94 *Malloy v. Hogan,* 378 U.S. 1 (1964).
95 *Murphy v. Waterfront Comm.,* 378 U.S. 52 (1964).
96 *Griffin v. California,* 380 U.S. 609 (1965).
97 See, for example, LaFave and Scott, op. cit., and Roland M. Perkins, *Perkins on Criminal Law,* Foundation Press, Mineola, N.Y., 1969.
98 Cleary, op. cit., p. 4.
99 Ibid.
100 Note, 40 N. D. L. REV. 164 (1964).
101 Ibid.
102 Henry B. Vess, *Walking a Tightrope: A Survey of Limitations on the Prosecutor's Closing Argument,* 64 J. CRIM. L. & C. 22 (1973).
103 John Kaplan, *Criminal Justice: Introductory Cases and Materials,* Foundation Press, Mineola, N.Y., 1973, p. 15.
104 Fred E. Inbau et al., op. cit., p. 1287.
105 F. Lee Bailey and Henry B. Rothblatt, op. cit., pp. 229–313.
106 Ibid., p. 302.
107 Vess, op. cit., p. 23.
108 *People v. Vasquez,* 291 N.E. 2d 5 (1972).
109 Vess, op. cit., footnote 18.
110 *Chapman v. California,* 386 U.S. 18 (1967).
111 *Cool v. U.S.,* 409 U.S. 100 (1972).
112 *Skidmore v. Baltimore and Ohio R. Co.,* 167 F. 2d 54, 65 (2d Cir.), 1948.
113 Mason Ladd and R. Carlson, *Cases and Materials on Evidence,* Callaghan and Co., Chicago, 1972, p. 101; See also rule 105, *Rules of Evidence for U.S. Courts and Magistrates,* op. cit.
114 The most definitive study to date on the jury is Kalven and Zeisel, op. cit.

115 *Hyde v. U.S.,* 225 U.S. 347 (1912); *McDonald v. Pleas,* 238 U.S. 264 (1896).
116 *Allen v. U.S.,* 164 U.S. 492 (1896).
117 *U.S. v. Fioravanti,* 412 F. 2d 407 (3rd Cir.), (1969); and *U.S. v. Thomas,* 449 F. 2d 1177 (U. S. App. D.C.), 1971.
118 *A.B.A. Standards,* 5.4; see also Note, 53 VA. L. REV. 123 (1967).
119 Yale Kamisar et al., *Modern Criminal Procedure,* West, St. Paul, 1974, p. 1358.
120 *A.B.A. Standards* 5.5 (tentative draft, 1969).

CHAPTER 11

1 *Dickey v. Florida,* 398 U.S. 30 (1970).
2 *Washington v. Texas,* 388 U.S. 214 (1967).
3 *Smith v. Illinois,* 390 U.S. 129 (1968).
4 *Drope v. Missouri,* 420 U.S. 162 (1975).
5 386 U.S. 213 (1967).
6 Ibid., p. 222.
7 393 U.S. 379 (1969).
8 *Dickey v. Florida,* 398 U.S. 30 (1970).
9 Ibid., p. 37.
10 404 U.S. 307 (1971).
11 Ibid., p. 310.
12 Ibid., p. 321.
13 Ibid., p. 324.
14 Ibid.
15 407 U.S. 514 (1972).
16 Ibid., p. 532.
17 Ibid., p. 533.
18 406 U.S. 715 (1972).
19 412 U.S. 434 (1973).
20 Ibid., p. 435.
21 Ibid., p. 439.
22 18 U.S.C. § 208, PL 93-619.
23 18 U.S.C. § 3162(a)(1).
24 388 U.S. 14 (1967).
25 Ibid., pp. 16–17.
26 Ibid., p. 19.
27 409 U.S. 95 (1972).
28 Ibid., p. 99.
29 410 U.S. 284 (1973).
30 Ibid., p. 294.
31 409 U.S. 100 (1972).
32 397 U.S. 358 (1970).
33 409 U.S. 100, 103–104.
34 *California v. Green,* 399 U.S. 149, 157 (1970).
35 380 U.S. 400 (1965).
36 Ibid., p. 404.
37 391 U.S. 123 (1968).
38 *California v. Green,* op. cit.
39 *Taylor v. United States,* 414 U.S. 17 (1974).
40 *Illinois v. Allen,* 397 U.S. 337 (1970).
41 *Barber v. Page,* 390 U.S. 719 (1968).
42 Ibid.
43 *Mancusi v. Stubbs,* 408 U.S. 204 (1972).
44 *Dutton v. Evans,* 400 U.S. 74 (1970).
45 Ibid.
46 *Smith v. Illinois,* 390 U.S. 129 (1968).
47 *Davis v. Alaska,* 415 U.S. 308 (1974).
48 *Schneble v. Florida,* 405 U.S. 427 (1972).
49 *In re Gault,* 387 U.S. 1 (1967).
50 *Hannah v. Larche,* 363 U.S. 420 (1960).
51 *Chambers v. Mississippi,* 410 U.S. 284 (1973).
52 *Gagnon v. Scarpelli,* 411 U.S. 778 (1973).
53 *Morrissey v. Brewer,* 408 U.S. 471 (1972).
54 *Wolf v. McDonnell,* 418 U.S. 539 (1974).
55 *Williams v. New York,* 337 U.S. 241 (1949).
56 Abraham S. Goldstein, *The Insanity Defense,* 1967, p. 3.
57 Patricia M. Wald, *Alcohol, Drugs, and Criminal Responsibility,* 63 GEO. L. J. 69 (1974).
58 Nicholas N. Kittrie, *The Right to Be Different,* 1971, p. 52.
59 Ibid., p. 51.
60 *The Washington Post,* July 13, 1959, p. A13.
61 Comment, *Civil Insanity in The Law of Alabama,* 18 ALA. L. REV. 340–342 (1966).
62 Heathcote W. Wales, *The Rise, the Fall, and the Resurrection of the Medical Model,* 63 GEO. L. J. 88 (1974).
63 Wayne R. LaFave and Austin W. Scott, *Criminal Law,* 1972, p. 268.
64 Ibid., pp. 267–268.
65 H. Wales, op. cit., pp. 87–105.
66 *M'Naghten's Case,* 8 Eng. Rep. 718 (1843).
67 Ibid., p. 722.
68 Goldstein, op. cit., chap. 11.
69 LaFave and Scott, op. cit., pp. 280–283.
70 Seymour L. Halleck, *Psychiatry and the Dilemmas of Crime,* 1967, pp. 205–228; and Wechsher, *The Criteria of Criminal Responsibility,* 22 U. CHI. L. REV. 367 (1955).
71 *Regina v. Oxford,* 175 Eng. Rep. 941, 950 (1940).
72 *Regina v. Burton,* 176 Engl. Rep. 354, 357 (1863).
73 *Commonwealth v. Rogers,* 48 Mass. 500 (1844).
74 *Parsons v. State,* 81 Ala. 577, 2 So. 854 (1887).

75 Ibid., pp. 596–597; 2 So., pp. 866–867.
76 *Royal Commission on Capital Punishment,* 1949–1953, Report 110 (1953).
77 Goldstein, op. cit., 70–75.
78 Wechsler, op. cit., note 70, p. 375.
79 *Parsons v. State,* 81 Ala. 577, 593, 2 So. 854, 864 (1887).
80 49 N.H. 399 (1869).
81 50 N.H. 369, 398 (1871).
82 214 F. 2d 862 (1954).
83 Ibid., pp. 874–875.
84 Ibid., 874.
85 Ibid., p. 875.
86 See, for example, Roche, *Criminality and Mental Illness—Two Faces of the Same Coin,* 22 U. CHI. L. REV. 320 (1955), and Guttmacher, *The Psychiatrist as an Expert Witness,* 22 U. CHI. L. REV. 325 (1955).
87 See, for example, Wechsler, op. cit., note 78.
88 William J. Brennan, *Chief Judge Bazelon's Constributions to the Law,* 6 GEO. L. J. 3 (1974).
89 *Stewart v. United States,* 214 F. 2d 879 (1954).
90 Wales, op. cit., p. 93, note 62.
91 *McDonald v. United States,* 312 F. 2d 847, 851 (1962).
92 471 F. 2d 969 (1972).
93 *Model Penal Code, § 4.01 (Final Draft, 1962).*
94 *Model Penal Code,* § 4.01 (Tent. Draft No. 4, 1955).
95 Kuh, *The Insanity Defense—An Effort to Combine Law and Reason,* 110 U. PA. L. REV. 771, 797–799 (1962).
96 Goldstein, op. cit., p. 87, note 56.
97 LaFave and Scott, op. cit., p. 294, note 63.
98 *Dusky v. United States,* 362 U.S. 402 (1960).
99 LaFave and Scott, op. cit., p. 297, note 56.
100 *Bishop v. United States,* 350 U.S. 961 (1956).
101 *Pate v. Robinson,* 383 U.S. 375 (1966).
102 Note, *The United States Courts of Appeals: 1972–1973 Term,* 62 GEO. L. J. 401, 629 (1973).
103 *Jackson v. Indiana,* 406 U.S. 715, 733 (1972).
104 LaFave and Scott, op. cit., p. 301.
105 420 U.S. 162.
106 43 L. Ed. 2d 103, 109 (1975).
107 Ibid., p. 113.
108 Ibid., p. 119.
109 Patricia M. Wald, *Alcohol, Drugs, and Criminal Responsibility,* 63 GEO. L. J. 69 (1974).
110 Presidents' Commission on Law Enforcement and Administration of Justice, *Task Force Report: Drunkenness,* Washington, D.C., 1967, p. 1.
111 *Presidents' Commission on Crime in the District of Columbia Report,* Washington, D.C., 1966, p. 474.
112 361 F. 2d 50 (1966).
113 Ibid., p. 53.
114 356 F. 2d 761, 765 (4th Cir. 1966).
115 392 U.S. 514 (1968).
116 Alcoholic Rehabilitation Act of 1967, D.C. Code Ann., § 24, pp. 521–535.
117 Jerome H. Jaffe, "Drug Addiction and Drug Abuse," in L. Goodman and A. Gilman, *The Pharmacological Basis of Therapeutics,* 4th ed., Macmillan, New York, 1970, pp. 276 and 284.
118 370 U.S. 660 (1962).
119 Ibid., p. 666.
120 Wald, op. cit., pp. 74–82, note 109.
121 486 F 2d. 1139 (D.C. Cir.).
122 Ibid., pp. 1231–1234.
123 414 U.S. 980 (1973), denying certiorari to *Moore v. United States,* 486 F. 2d 1139 (1972).
124 White, Stewart, Douglas, and Brennan, J. J., Burger, C. J., and Blackmun, Powell, Rehnquist, and Marshall, J. J., joined the Court post-*Robinson.*
125 See generally Roland Perkins, *Perkins on Criminal Law,* 1969, pp. 878–883, and LaFave and Scott, op. cit., pp. 325–332.
126 LaFave and Scott, op. cit., pp. 326–327.
127 Ibid., p. 327.
128 Ibid., p. 330.
129 Note, 43 CORNELL L. Q. 283, 286 (1957).
130 LaFave and Scott, op. cit., p. 331.
131 Goldstein, op. cit., p. 199, note 56.
132 LaFave and Scott, op. cit., p. 332.
133 *Model Penal Code § 4.02 (1962).*

CHAPTER 12

1 President's Commission on Law Enforcement and Administration of Justice, *Task Force Report: The Courts,* Washington, D.C., 1967, p. 9.
2 James E. Bond, *Plea Bargaining and Guilty Pleas,* 1975, pp. 15–20.
3 Note, *Plea Bargaining—Justice Off the Record,* 9 WASHBURN L.J. 430, 432 (1970).
4 Bond, op. cit., p. 12.
5 See, for example, *People v. Bonheim,* 307 Ill. 316,

138 N.E. 627 (1923).
6 Bond, op. cit., p. 3.
7 *Kercheval v. United States,* 274 U.S. 220, 223 (1927).
8 Comment, *The Influence of the Defendant's Plea on Judicial Determination of Sentence,* 66 YALE L. J. 204 (1956).
9 *Lefkowitz v. Newsome, U.S. (1975).*
10 Ibid.
11 *Boykin v. Alabama,* 395 U.S. 238, 243 (1969) (opinion by Justice Douglas).
12 Note, *Guilty Plea Bargaining: Compromises by Prosecutors to Secure Guilty Pleas,* 112 U. PA. L. REV. 865 (1964).
13 Bond, op. cit., pp. 16–18.
14 Ibid., pp. 18–19.
15 Note, *Boykin v. Newsome,* op. cit.
16 Ibid. and Bond, op. cit., pp. 19–21.
17 Davis, *Sentence for Sale: A New Look at Plea Bargaining in England and America,* CRIM. L. REV. 150, 218 (1971).
18 Commentary, *A.B.A. Standards—Pleas of Guilty,* 1968, § 1.8(a) and Bond, op. cit., p. 41.
19 Comment, *The Influence of the Defendant's Plea . . .,*" op. cit.
20 Bond, op. cit., pp. 19 and 20.
21 W. White, *A Proposal for Reform of the Plea Bargaining Process,* 119 U. PA. L. REV. 439 (1971).
22 Ibid.
23 Bond, op. cit., p. 225.
24 Ibid., p. 33.
25 *McCarthy v. United States,* 394 U.S. 459, 465 (1969) (opinion by Justice Warren).
26 Ibid.
27 395 U.S. 238 (1969).
28 Ibid., p. 243.
29 Ibid., pp. 241–243.
30 See, for example, *Carnley v. Cochran,* 369 U.S. 506, 516 (1962).
31 397 U.S. 742 (1970).
32 397 U.S. 742, 749.
33 Ibid., p. 750.
34 *United States v. Jackson,* 390 U.S. 570 (1968).
35 397 U.S. 759 (1970).
36 378 U.S. 368 (1964).
37 397 U.S. 759, 774.
38 Ibid., p. 768.
39 Ibid., p. 771.
40 397 U.S. 790 (1970).
41 397 U.S. 790, 797–798 (1970).
42 400 U.S. 25 (1970).
43 Ibid., p. 31.
44 Ibid., p. 37.
45 Ibid., p. 38, note 11.
46 *Pennsylvania v. Claudy,* 350 U.S. 116 (1956).
47 *Tollett v. Henderson,* 411 U.S. 258 (1973).
48 *Dukes v. Warden,* 406 U.S. 250 (1972).
49 *Santobello v. New York,* 404 U.S. 257 (1971).
50 *Lefkowitz v. Newsome,* U. S. (1975).
51 *Lynch v. Overholser,* 369 U.S. 705 (1962).
52 *Santobello v. New York,* 404 U.S. 257, 260 (1971).
53 Ibid., p. 261.
54 R. Quinney, *Criminology: Analysis and Critique of Crime in America,* 1975, p. 209.
55 Standard 3.1, "Abolition of Plea Negotiation," National Advisory Commission on Criminal Justice Standards and Goals: Courts, Washington, D.C., 1973, p. 46.
56 M. Frankel, *Criminal Sentences: Law Without Order,* 1972, p. vii.
57 R. Singer and W. Statsky, *Rights of the Imprisoned,* 1974, p. 271.
58 *Williams v. New York,* 337 U.S. 241 (1949).
59 Ibid.
60 R. Quinney, *Criminology: Analysis and Critique of Crime in America,* 1975, p. 220.
61 T. Thornberry, *Race, Socioeconomic Status and Sentencing in the Juvenile Justice System,* 64 J. CRIM. L. & C. 90 (1973).
62 Ibid., pp. 219–222.
63 See L. Orland and H. Tyler (eds.), *Justice in Sentencing,* 1974.
64 Standard 5.1, National Advisory Commission on Criminal Justice Standards and Goals, *Courts,* Washington, D.C., 1973.
65 In 1958, the Congress authorized the convening of sentencing institututes in the federal system. 28 U.S.C. § 334(c).
66 Frankel, op. cit., p. 74.
67 Ibid., p. x.
68 Orland and Tyler, op. cit., p. 46.
69 R. Goldfarb and L. Singer, *After Conviction: A Review of the American Correctional System,* 1973, p. 11.
70 Orland and Tyler, op. cit., p. 46.
71 Paul W. Tappan, *Crime, Justice and Correction,* 1960, p. 430–435.

72 Saul Rubin, *The Law of Criminal Correction,* 1973, p. 157; and Singer and Statsky, op. cit., p. 271–495.
73 Singer and Statsky, op. cit., pp. 277–278.
74 Goldfarb and Singer, op. cit., pp. 167–169.
75 Ibid., p. 168.
76 S. Rubin, op. cit., p. 258.
77 Ibid., p. 159.
78 Goldfarb and Singer, op. cit., p. 178.
79 Rule 32, *Federal Rules of Criminal Procedure,* op. cit.
80 *Chaffin v. Stynchcombe,* 412 U.S. 17, 21 n. 7 (1973).
81 Ibid. See also *McGautha v. California,* 402 U.S. 183, 196–208 (1971).
82 Goldfarb and Singer, op. cit., p. 209.
83 Ibid., pp. 234–240.
84 Davis, *A Study of Adult Probation Violation Rates by Means of the Cohort Approach,* 55 J. CRIM. L. C. & P. S. 70 (1964).
85 40 Mo. R.S. & 559. 140 (1939).
86 Barrett, *The Role of Fines in the Administration of Criminal Justice in Massachusetts,* 48 MASS. L. Q. 435, 1974.
87 *Williams v. Illinois,* 399 U.S. 235, 240 (1970).
88 *Griffin v. Illinois,* 351 U.S. 12, 19 (1956) (opinion by Justice Black).
89 *Williams v. Illinois,* 399 U.S. 235 (1970).
90 Ibid., p. 243.
91 401 U.S. 395 (1971).
92 Ibid., p. 399.
93 California Penal Code, § 1205 (1970) (misdemeanors), and New York Code Criminal Procedure, § 470d (1) (b) (Supp. 1970).
94 President's Commission on Law Enforcement and Administration of Justice, *Task Force Report: The Courts,* Washington, D.C., 1967, p. 18.
95 Goldfarb and Singer, op. cit., p. 131.
96 Ibid., p. 178.
97 Herbert L. Packer, *The Limits of the Criminal Sanction* 1968, pp. 48–53.
98 Orland and Tyler, op. cit.
99 Packer, op. cit., p. 49.
100 Ibid.
101 C. Eichmann, *Impact of the Gideon Decision upon Crime and Sentencing in Florida: A Study of Recidivision and Socio-Cultural Change,* 1966.
102 Frankel, op. cit., pp. 76–77.
103 American Bar Association Project on Standards for Criminal Justice, *Standards Relating to Appellate Review of Sentences,* 1968, pp. 1–2.
104 See, for example, opinion of Justice Marshall in *Furman v. Georgia,* 408 U.S. 238, 364 (1972) (concurring).
105 *The New York Times,* November 26, 1972, p. E3.
106 The pros and cons of capital punishment have been summarized in Hugo A. Bedau, *The Death Penalty in America,* rev. ed., 1967, pp. 120–231.
107 Ibid., p. 120.
108 Other biblical passages included "Whoever sheds the blood of man, by man shall his blood be shed; for God made man in his own image" (Gen. 9:4–6, RSV); "Whoever strikes a man so that he dies shall be put to death. . . . If a man willfully attacks another to kill him treacherously, you shall take him from my altar that he may die" (Exod. 21:12, 14, RSV); "If any one kills a person, the murderer shall be put to death on the evidence of witnesses. . . ." (Num. 35:30–34, RSV).
109 Bedau, op. cit., pp. 122–123.
110 *Robinson v. California,* 370 U.S. 660 (1962).
111 See, for example, *Weemer v. United States,* 217 U.S. 349 (1910).
112 *Furman v. Georgia,* 408 U.S. 238 (1972).
113 *Trop v. Dulles,* 356 U.S. 86 (1958).
114 *Trop v. Dulles,* op. cit., p. 101 (opinion by Justice Warren).
115 *Wilkerson v. Utah,* 99 U.S. 130 (1878).
116 Ibid.
117 *Trop v. Dulles,* op. cit.
118 *Furman v. Georgia, op. cit.*
119 *Robinson v. California,* op. cit.
120 *Powell v. Texas,* 392 U.S. 514 (1968).
121 *In re Kemmler,* 136 U.S. 436 (1890).
122 *Louisiana ex rel. Francis v. Resweber,* 329 U.S. 459 (1947).
123 *Wilkerson v. Utah,* op. cit.
124 *Uphaus v. Wyman,* 360 U.S. 72 (1959).
125 *McDonald v. Massachusetts,* 180 U.S. 311 (1901).
126 *Trop v. Dulles,* op. cit.
127 *Pervear v. Massachusetts,* 5 Wall 475 (1867).
128 *Wilkerson v. Utah,* op. cit.
129 *Howard v. Fleming,* 191 U.S. 126 (1903).
130 Ibid.
131 408 U.S. 23, 239–240.
132 Note, *Discretion and the Constitutionality of the New Death Penalty Statutes,* 87 HARV. L. REV.

1690, 1691 (1974).
133 *Gregg v. Georgia,* 428 U.S. 153 (1976); *Profitt v. Florida,* U.S. (1976); *Jurek v. Texas,* 428 U.S. 262 (1976).
134 *Woodson v. North Carolina,* 428 U.S. 280 (1976); *Roberts v. Louisiana,* 428 U.S. 325 (1976).
135 *Ball v. United States,* 140 U.S. 118 (1891).
136 *Green v. United States,* 365 U.S. 301 (1961).
137 *Hill v. United States,* 368 U.S. 424 (1962).

CHAPTER 13

1 E. Sutherland and D. Cressey, *Principles of Criminology,* 7th ed., Lippincott, Philadelphia, 1970.
2 V. Evjen, "The Federal Probation System: The Struggle to Achieve It and Its First 25 Years," *Federal Probation* vol. 39, pp. 3–15, June 1975.
3 Sutherland and Cressey, op. cit.
4 President's Commission on Law Enforcement and the Administration of Justice, *Task Force Report: Corrections,* Washington, D.C., 1967.
5 Evjen, op. cit.
6 Ibid., p. 3.
7 Sutherland and Cressey, op. cit.
8 Hartshorne, "The 1958 Federal 'Split-Sentence' Law," *Federal Probation,* vol. 23, June 1959.
9 D. Peterson and D. Friday, *Early Release From Incarceration: Race as a Factor in the Use of 'Shock Probation,'* 66 J. CRIM. L. & C. 79–87 (1975).
10 H. Allen and C. Simonsen, *Corrections in America: An Introduction,* Glencoe Press, Beverly Hills, Calif., 1975, p. 131.
11 J. Arcaya, "The Multiple Realities Inherent in Probation Counseling," *Federal Probation,* vol. 37, pp. 58–63, December 1973.
12 J. Stratton, "Correctional Workers: Counseling Con Men?" *Federal Probation,* vol. 37, pp. 14–17, September 1973.
13 E. Czajkoski, "Exposing the Quasi-Judicial Role of the Probation Officer," *Federal Probation,* vol. 37, pp. 9–13, September 1973.
14 R. Carter and L. Wilkins, *Some Factors in Sentencing Policy,* 58 J. CRIM. L. C. & P. S. 503–514 (1967).
15 Czajkoski, op. cit., p. 9.
16 R. Carter and L. Wilkins, *Probation and Parole,* Wiley, New York, 1970.
17 E. Dicerbo, "When Should Probation Be Revoked?" *Federal Probation,* vol. 30, pp. 11–17, 1967.
18 K. Lenihan, "The Financial Condition of Released Prisoners," *Crime and Delinquency,* vol. 21, pp. 266–281, July 1975.
19 Florida Probation and Parole Commission, *18th Annual Report,* 1968.
20 Ibid.
21 Louisiana Department of Corrections, *1972–73 Fiscal Year Statistical Report,* Baton Rouge.
22 R. England, *What Is Responsible for Satisfactory Probation and Post-Probation Outcome?* 47 J. CRIM. L. C. & P. S. 667–676 (1957).
23 G. Davis, *A Study of Adult Probation Violation Rates by Means of the Cohort Approach,* 55 J. CRIM. L. C. & P. S. 70–85 (1964).
24 R. Vasoli, "Some Reflections on Measuring Probation Outcome," *Federal Probation, vol. 31, pp. 24–32, 1972.*
25 S. Bates, "When Is Probation Not Probation?" *Federal Probation,* vol. 24, pp. 13–20, 1960.
26 Lenihan, op. cit.
27 Ibid.
28 C. Newman, *Sourcebook on Probation, Parole and Pardons,* Charles C Thomas, Springfield, Ill., 1968.
29 D. Dressler, *Practice and Theory of Probation and Parole,* Columbia University Press, New York, 1959.
30 V. Hugo, *Les Miserables.*
31 R. Wright, *Wanted—A Clear Understanding of Parole,* 1 JAIL ASSOC. J. 8–12 (1939).
32 E. Cass, "De-bunking the Parole Experts," *The Prison World,* vol. 3, pp. 4–6, 1941.
33 Federal Bureau of Investigation, *Uniform Crime Reports: 1970,* Washington, D.C., 1970.
34 Thomas, op. cit.
35 D. Gottredson, P. Hoffman, M. Sigler, and L. Wilkins, "Making Paroling Policy Explicit" *Crime and Delinquency,* vol. 21, pp. 34–44, January 1975.
36 D. Jackson, "A Day at the Parole Board," *Life,* vol. 70, pp. 54–64, 1970).
37 H. Griswold, M. Misenheimer, A Powers, and E. Tromanhauser, *An Eye for an Eye,* Holt, New York, 1970.
38 J. Bennet, op. cit.
39 Gotterdson et al., op. cit.
40 M. Schoonmaker and J. Brooks, "Women in Probation and Parole, 1974," *Crime and Delinquency,* vol. 21, pp. 109–115, April 1975.

41 Allen and Simonsen, op. cit.
42 K. Daniel, "Parolees Controlled by Electricity," *Midnight,* vol. 16, pp. 4–5, 1969.
43 J. Berecochea, A. Himelson, and D. Miller, *The Risk of Failure During the Early Parole Period: A Methodological Note,* 63 J. CRIM. L. C. & P. S. 93–97 (1972).
44 B. Tyler, "A Parolee Tells Her Story," *Federal Probation,* vol. 32, pp. 54–56, 1968.
45 D. Glaser, *The Effectiveness of a Prison and Parole System,* Bobbs-Merrill, Indianapolis, 1966.
46 Tyler, op. cit.
47 A. Scott, *The Pardoning Power,* 284 ANNALS 95–100 (1952).
48 R. Cozart, "Pardons: Their Place in Correctional Procedure," *American Journal of Corrections,* vol. 20, pp. 12–15, 1958.
49 "Effect of Nixon Pardon," *Crime and Delinquency,* vol. 21, p. 185, April 1975.
50 Scott, op. cit.

CHAPTER 14

1 Norval Morris, *The Future of Imprisonment,* University of Chicago Press, Chicago, 1974.
2 Jessica Mitford, *Kind and Usual Punishment,* Knopf, New York, 1973.
3 Morris, op. cit.
4 James Q. Wilson, "Lock 'Em Up and Other Thoughts on Crime," *The New York Times Magazine,* March 9, 1975. Robert Martinson, "The Effectiveness of Correctional Treatment: A Survey of Treatment Evaluation Studies," *Criminal Justice Newsletter,* Oct. 21, 1974, and Nov. 18, 1974.
5 Elmer H. Johnson, *Crime, Correction, and Society,* 3d ed., Dorsey, Homewood, Ill., 1974, p. 397.
6 Ibid., p. 398.
7 Harry E. Allen and Clifford E. Simonsen, *Corrections in America: An Introduction,* Glencoe Press, Beverly Hills, Calif., 1975.
8 Wayne Morse (ed.), "State Prisons in America, 1787–1937," The Attorney General's Survey of Release Procedures (1940) in George G. Killinger and Paul F. Cromwell, Jr. (eds.), *Penology,* West, St. Paul, 1973.
9 Allen and Simonsen, op. cit., p. 50.
10 Morse, op. cit., p. 47.
11 Donald Clemmer, *The Prison Community,* New York, 1966.
12 Norval Morris and Gordon Hawkins, "Rehabilitation: Rhetoric and Reality," *Federal Probation,* December 1970, pp. 9–17.
13 John Godwin, *Alcatraz,* Doubleday, New York, 1963.
14 "Prisoners in State amd Federal Institutions on December 31, 1971, 1972, and 1973," *National Prisoner Statistics Bulletin,* May 1975. 5 LEAA NEWSLETTER 5 (1976).
15 Vernon Fox, *Introduction to Corrections,* Prentice-Hall, Englewood Cliffs, N.J., 1972, p. 151.
16 Gresham M. Sykes, *The Society of Captives,* Atheneum, New York, 1966.
17 Personal interview with Hayden Dees, Associate Warden for Custody, Louisiana State Penitentiary, Angola, August, 1968.
18 John Irwin, *The Felon,* Prentice-Hall, Engelwood Cliffs, N.J., 1970, pp. 67–85.
19 Edwin H. Sutherland and Donald R. Cressey, *Principles of Criminology,* Lippincott, New York, 1966, p. 608.
20 Daniel Glaser, *The Effectiveness of a Prison and Parole System,* Bobbs-Merrill, New York, 1966.
21 Ibid., also see James M. Watts, *Adult Correctional Institutions in Louisiana: A Summary Report,* Institute of Human Relations, Loyola University, New Orleans, La.
22 *Rutherford v. Hutto,* 377 F. Supp. 268 (E. D. Ark. 1974).
23 Harold J. Vetter and Jack Wright, Jr., *Introduction to Criminology,* Charles C Thomas, Springfield, Ill., 1974, p. 510.
24 Jack H. Griswold, Art Powers Misenheimer, and Ed Tromanhauser, *An Eye For An Eye,* Pocket Books, New York, 1971, p. 77.
25 Glaser, op. cit., p. 182.
26 Ibid., p. 187.
27 U.S. Department of Justice, *Federal Bureau of Prisons 1974,*
28 Glaser, op. cit., p. 91.
29 Clemmer, op. cit., p. 234.
30 Griswold, Misenheimer, and Tromanhauser, op. cit., P. 24.
31 Clemmer, op. cit., p. 234.
32 Portraits of Christ on the cross often depict Him as being very slim.
33 Glaser, op. cit., p. 90.
34 This count is declining, as the penitentiary is under a court order to reduce overcrowding.

35 The authors recognize that although penitentiaries have, at different historical periods, been intended to serve as places of repentance and/or rehabilitation, not much of either has taken place.
36 Religious leaders themselves are no strangers to confinement. According to tradition, St. Peter was confined in the Mamertime Prison at Rome. John the Baptist was beheaded in prison at the request of a dancing girl (Mark 6:27). Indeed, Jesus admonished His followers that one of the criteria for entrance into His Heavenly Kingdom was to have visited persons in prison (Matt. 25:36). Despite this incentive, Clemmer reports that about one-third of the prisoners in his study have almost no visits and receive almost no mail. Clemmer, op. cit., p. 41.
37 First National Conference of Jesuit Prison Chaplans, Loyola University, New Orleans, La., Jan. 8–11, 1975.
38 Richard P. Vogelman, "Prison Restrictions—Prisoner Rights," 59 J. CRIM. L. C. & P. S. 386–396 (1968).
39 Morris, op. cit.
40 Lawrence S. Root, "Work Release Legislation," *Federal Probation,* vol. 36, March 1972, pp. 38–43.
41 Ibid.
42 Johnson, op. cit., p. 529.
43 Root, op. cit., p. 42.
44 Lawrence S. Root, "State Work Release Programs: An Analysis of Operational Policies," *Federal Probation,* vol. 37, December 1973, pp. 52–58.
45 Ronald L. Goldfarb and Linda R. Singer, *After Conviction: A Review of the American Correctional System,* Simon and Schuster, New York, 1973.
46 Root, op. cit., p. 56.
47 Jessica Mitford, *Kind and Usual Punishment,* Knopf, New York, 1973, p. 209.
48 Goldfarb and Singer, op. cit., p. 544.
49 Ibid.
50 Root, op. cit.
51 Goldfarb and Singer, op. cit., p. 537.
52 Mitford, op. cit.

CHAPTER 15

1 Saul Rubin, *The Law of Criminal Corrections,* 2d ed., 1973.
2 Note, *Beyond the Ken of the Courts: A Critique of Judicial Refusal to Review the Complaints of Convicts,* 72 YALE L. J. 506 (1963).
3 Note, Constitutional Rights of Prisoners: The Developing Law, 110 U. PA. L. REV. 985 (1962).
4 *Ruffin v. Commonwealth,* 62 Va. 790, 796 (1871).
5 R. Singer and W. Statsky, *Rights of the Imprisoned,* 1974, p. 581.
6 See, for example, S. Krantz, *The Law of Corrections and Prisoners' Rights,* 1973.
7 D. Rothman, *The Discovery of the Asylum,* 1971.
8 Krantz, op. cit.
9 See, for example, *Johnson v. Avery,* 393 U.S. 483 (1969); *Mempa v. Rhay,* 389 U.S. 128 (1967); *Procunier v. Martinez,* 416 U.S. 396 (1974); *Wolff v. McDonnell,* 418 U.S. 539 (1974). The list is not exhaustive.
10 The statistics cited in section 15.02 are taken from the following sources: President's Commission on Law Enforcement and Administration of Justice, *Task Force Report: Corrections,* Washington, D.C., 1967; M. Hermann and M. Haft, eds., *Prisoners' Rights Sourcebook: Theory, Litigation and Practice,* 1973; S. Krantz, *The Law of Corrections and Prisoner's Rights,* 1973; Singer and Statsky, op. cit.; Rubin, op. cit.; and R. Goldfarb and L. Singer, *After Conviction,* 1973.
11 F. Adher, *Sisters in Crime,* 1975.
12 Special Project, *The Collateral Consequences of Criminal Convictions,* 23 VAND. L. REV. 929 (1970).
13 J. Tepper and H. Feinstein, "Attacking Barriers to Employment: The Former Offender's Dilemma," in Hermann and Haft, op. cit.
14 The President's Commission on Law Enforcement and the Administration of Justice: Corrections, "Collateral Consequences of a Criminal Conviction," *Task Force Report: Corrections,* op. cit., pp. 88–92.
15 *The Collateral Consequences of Criminal Convictions,* op. cit.
16 See, for example, Rubin, op. cit., p. 698.
17 *Task Force Report: Corrections,* op. cit., pp. 89–90.
18 Ibid., p. 89.
19 *Richardson v. Ramirez,* 418 U.S. 24, 79.
20 Ibid., p. 81.

21 *Task Force Report: Corrections,* op. cit., p. 89.
22 Ibid., p. 90.
23 418 U.S. 24.
24 Ibid., p. 43.
25 *The Collateral Consequences of Criminal Convictions,* op. cit., pp. 1051–1059.
26 National Advisory Commission on Criminal Justice Standards and Goals, *Corrections,* Washington, D.C., 1973, p. 592.
27 *Task Force Report: Corrections,* op. cit., p. 90.
28 National Advisory Commission on Criminal Justice Standards and Goals, op. cit.
29 *Model Penal Code* § 306, 3(2).
30 *The Collateral Consequences of Criminal Convictions,* op. cit., pp. 987–1001.
31 *Task Force Report: Corrections,* op. cit., p. 90.
32 Ibid.
33 Neil P. Cohen and Dean H. Rivkin, *Civil Disabilities: The Forgotten Punishment,* 35 FED. PROB. Q. 19 (1971).
34 *Task Force Report: Corrections,* op. cit., p. 90.
35 Cohen and Rivkin, op. cit.
36 National Advisory Commission on Criminal Justice Standards and Goals, op. cit., p. 592.
37 *The Collateral Consequences of Criminal Convictions,* op. cit., pp. 1030–1035.
38 Ibid.
39 Ibid.
40 Ibid.
41 Ibid.
42 *Task Force Report: Corrections,* op. cit., p. 90.
43 Cohen and Rivkin, op. cit.
44 Ibid.
45 Ibid.
46 National Advisory Commission on Criminal Justice Standards and Goals, op. cit., Standard 16, 17 (2).
47 *Task Force Report: Corrections,* op. cit., p. 89.
48 *The Collateral Consequences of Criminal Convictions,* op. cit., p. 1037.
49 Cohen and Rivkin, op. cit.
50 Ibid.
51 Ibid.
52 P. Lewis and H. Allen, *Remedies Governing Inmates' Claims Arising from Injuries: A Denial or a Master-Servant Relationship,* 23 CHITTY'S L. J. 1, 12–17 (1975).
53 Ibid.
54 Cohen and Rivkin, op. cit.
55 Lewis and Allen, op. cit.
56 Tepper and Feinstein in Hermann and Haft, op. cit.
57 Ibid., and Rubin, op. cit.
58 A. Trebach, "No. 1 Domestic Priority: New Careers," *City,* October–November 1970, p. 18.
59 *Task Force Report: Corrections,* op. cit., pp. 32–33.
60 Address by Attorney General John Mitchell, "New Doors, Not Old Walls," National Conference on Corrections, Williamsburg, Va., on December 6, 1971. The speech was delivered prior to Mr. Mitchell's convictions arising out of the Watergate trials.
61 Tepper and Feinstein in Hermann and Haft, op. cit.
62 D. Glasser *The Effectiveness of a Prison and Parole System,* 1964, p. 329.
63 *Task Force Report: Corrections,* op. cit., p. 32.
64 Glasser, op. cit., p. 214.
65 401 U.S. 424.
66 Ibid., p. 431.
67 Rubin, op. cit., p. 704.
68 Ibid.
69 Ibid., pp. 698–699.
70 Singer and Statsky, op. cit., p. 1127.
71 Ibid.
72 Rubin, op. cit., p. 721.
73 Singer and Statsky, op. cit., p. 1127.
74 *Burdick v. United States,* 236 U.S. 79.
75 Singer and Statsky, op. cit., pp. 1127–1128.
76 Rubin, op. cit., p. 724.
77 Singer and Statsky, op. cit., p. 23.
78 *Task Force Report: Corrections,* op. cit., p. 92.
79 Cohen and Rivkin, op. cit., p. 23.
80 *Model Penal Code,* § 306.1(1).
81 William B. Turner, "Federal Jurisdiction and Practice in Prisoner Cases," in Hermann and Haft, op. cit., p. 243.
82 John W. Palmer, in Hermann and Haft, op. cit., p. 135.
83 William L. Prosser, *Law of Torts,* 4th ed., 1971, pp. 984–987.
84 *Price v. Johnson,* 334 U.S. 266, 285 (1948).
85 *Coffin v. Reichard,* 143 F. 2d 443, 445 (6th Cir. 1944).
86 Palmer, op. cit., pp. 133–149.
87 Turner, op. cit., p. 244.
88 *Wilwarding v. Swenson,* 404 U.S. 249 (1971).

89 Palmer, op. cit., p. 141.
90 Ibid. See Also *Wilson v. Prasse,* 325 F. Supp. 9 (W. D. Pa. 1971).
91 *Preiser v. Rodriquez,* 411 U.S. 475 (1973).
92 *Bivens v. Six Unknown Named Agents of Federal Bureau of Narcotics,* 403 U.S. 388 (1971).
93 Ibid., pp. 395 and 397.
94 28 U.S.C. § 2201 (1970).
95 28 U.S.C. § 2202 (1970).
96 28 U.S.C. § 2281 (1970).
97 28 U.S.C. § 1253 (1970).
98 Palmer, op. cit., pp. 144–145.
99 *Sobell v. Reed,* 327 F. Supp. 1294 (S. D. N.Y. 1971).
100 312 U.S. 546 (1941).
101 Ibid., p. 549.
102 393 U.S. 483.
103 Ibid., p. 485.
104 Barry M. Fox, "The First Amendment Rights of Prisoners," 63 J. CRIM. L. C. & P. S. 162 (1972).
105 *Rowland v. Wolff,* 336 F. Supp. 257 (D. Neb. 1971).
106 *Blake v. Pryse,* 315 F. Supp. 625 (D. Minn. 1970), affirmed 444 F. 2d 218 (8th Cir. 1971).
107 *Procunier v. Martinez,* 416 U.S. 396 (1974).
108 *Fortune Society v. McGinnis,* 319 F. Supp. 901 (S.D. N.Y. 1970); *Sostre v. Otis,* 330 F. Supp. 941 (S.D. N.Y. 1971).
109 *Berrigan v. Norton,* 451 F. 2d 790 (2d Cir. 1971).
110 *Roberts v. Pepersack,* 256 F. Supp. 415 (D. Md. 1966); *Kritsky v. McGinnis,* 313 F. Supp. 1247 (N.D.N.Y. 1970).
111 *Sostre v. McGinnis,* 334 F. 2d 906 (2d Cir. 1964); *Theriault v. Carlson,* 339 F. Supp. 375 (N.D. Ga. 1972).
112 *Pell v. Procunier,* 417 U.S. 817 (1974); *Saxbe v. Washington Post Co.,* 417 U.S. 843 (1974).
113 Fox, op. cit.
114 378 U.S. 546 (1964).
115 405 U.S. 319 (1972).
116 404 U.S. 4 (1971).
117 417 U.S. 817 (1974).
118 417 U.S. 843 (1974).
119 *Pell v. Procunier,* 417 U.S. 817, 827–828.
120 Ibid., p. 834.
121 Ibid.
122 416 U.S. 396 (1974).
123 Ibid., pp. 399–400.
124 Ibid., pp. 413–414.
125 Ibid., p. 418.
126 Ibid., p. 415.
127 Ibid., p. 405.
128 *Mempha v. Rhay,* 389 U.S. 128 (1967); and *Gagnon v. Scarpelli,* 411 U.S. 788 (1973).
129 *Morrissey v. Brewer,* 408 U.S. 471 (1972).
130 *Wolff v. McDonnell,* 418 U.S. 539 (1974).
131 389 U.S. 128.
132 408 U.S. 471.
133 411 U.S. 778.
134 418 U.S. 539.
135 Ibid., p. 570.
136 *Sostre v. Rockefeller,* 312 F. Supp. 863 (S.D. N. Y. 1970).
137 *Wright v. McMann,* 387 F. 2d 519 (2d Cir. 1967).
138 *United States ex rel. Neal v. Wolfe,* 346 F. Supp. 569 (E. D. Pa. 1972).
139 Michael Millemann, "Due Process Behind Walls," Hermann and Haft, op. cit., pp. 80–81.
140 *Urbano v. McCorkle,* 334 F. Supp. 161 (D. N.J. 1971).
141 *Meyers v. Alldredge,* 348 F. Supp. 807, 824 (M. D. Pa. 1972).
142 *Holt v. Sarver,* 309 F. Supp. 362 (E. D. Ark. 1970), affirmed 442 F. 2d 304 (8th Cir. 1971).
143 *Mayfield v. Craven,* 299 F. Supp. 111 (E.D. Calif. 1969), affirmed 443 F. 2d 873 (9th Cir. 1970).
144 *Rouse v. Cameron,* 128 U.S. App. D.C. 283, 387F. 2d 241 (1967).
145 *Knuckles v. Prasse,* 302 F. Supp. 1036 (E.D. Pa. 1969).
146 Sheldon Krantz, *The Law of Corrections and Prisoners' Rights,* 1973, p. 517.
147 309 F. Supp. 362 (E.D. Ark. 1970), affirmed 442 F. 2d 304 (8th Cir. 1971).
148 *Brenneman v. Madigan,* 343 F. Supp. 128 (N.D. Cal. 1972); *Jones v. Wittenberg,* 323 F. Supp. 93 (N.D. Ohio 1971; *Commonwealth ex. rel. Sprowal v. Hendrick,* 438 pg. 435, 265 A. 2d 348 (1970).
149 *Lake v. Lee,* 329 F. Supp. 196 (S.D. Ala. 1971).
150 *Jackson v. Bishop,* 404 F. 2d 571, 580 (8th Cir. 1968).
151 Marvin Zalman, *Prisoners' Rights to Medical Care,* 63 J. CRIM. L. C. & P. S. 185 (1972).
152 Ibid.
153 William B. Turner, "Challenging Conditions in Prisons Which Violate the Eighth Amendment," Hermann and Haft, op. cit., p. 116.
154 *Mayfield v. Craven,* 299 F. Supp. 111 (E.D. Calif.

1969), affirmed 443 F. 2d 873 (9th Cir. 1970).

155 Krantz, op. cit., p. 591.

156 *Sawyer v. Sigler,* 320 F. Supp. 690, 696 (D. Neb. 1970), affirmed 445 F. 2d 818 (8th Cir. 1971).

157 *Mayfield v. Craven,* op. cit.

158 Zalman, op. cit., pp. 187–191.

159 *Newman v. State,* 349 F. Supp. 278 (M.D. Ala. 1972).

160 Krantz, op. cit., p. 591.

161 National Advisory Commission on Criminal Justice Standards and Goals, *Rehabilitation,* op. cit., standard 2.9.

162 American Friends Service Committee, *Struggle for Justice,* 1971.

163 125 U.S. App. D.C. 366, 373 F. 2d 451.

164 D.C. Code § 21-562 (Supp. V, 1966), 1964 Hospitalization of the Mentally Ill Act.

165 344 F. Supp. 373 (M.D. Ala. 1972).

166 Richard Singer, "The Coming Right to Rehabilitation," in Hermann and Haft, op. cit., pp. 189–198.

167 Ibid., p. 195.

168 See, for example, Krantz, op. cit., pp. 218–234.

Index